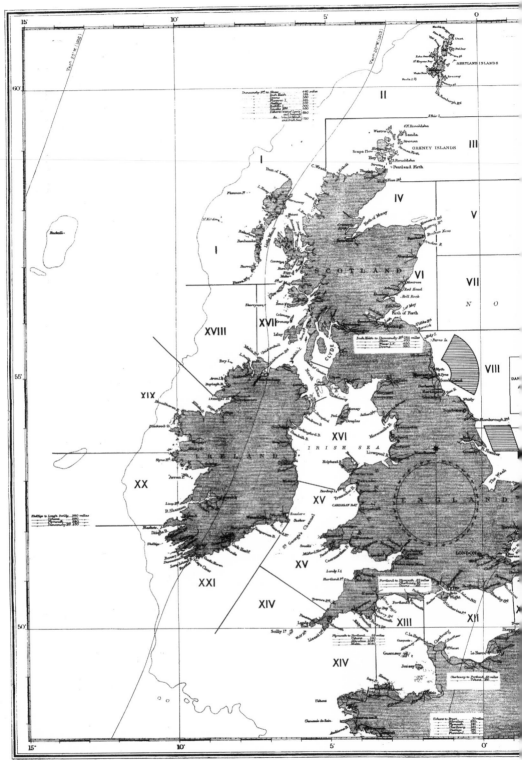

Prepared in the Historical Section of the Committee of Imperial Defence from a chart supplied by the Hydrographic Department of the Admiralty.

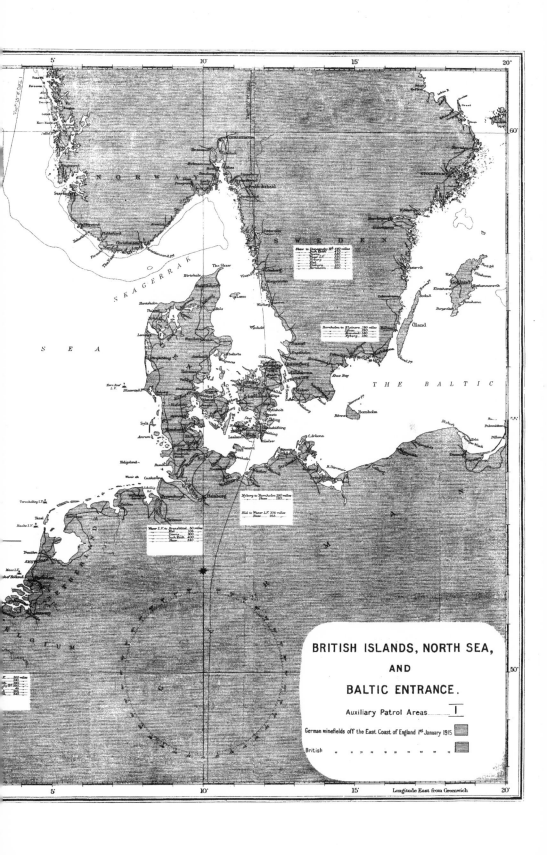

BRITISH ISLANDS, NORTH SEA,

AND

BALTIC ENTRANCE.

Auxiliary Patrol Areas_____ I

German minefields off the East Coast of England 1ˢᵗ January 1915

British

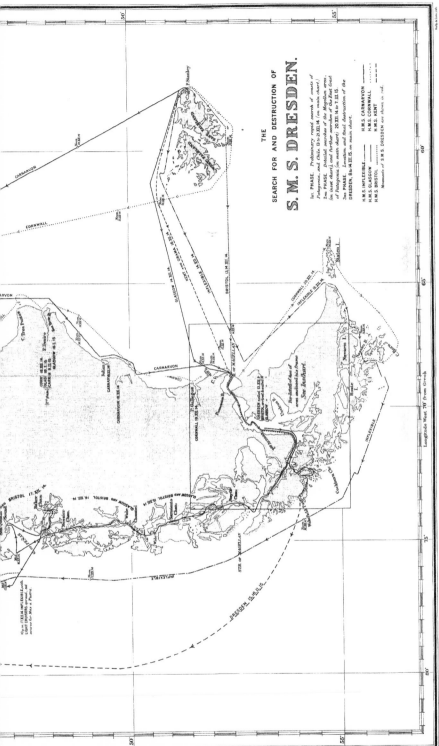

THE

SEARCH FOR AND DESTRUCTION OF

S.M.S. DRESDEN.

1st PHASE. *Preliminary rapid search of coasts of Patagonia, and Chile. 13 to 21.XII.14 (on main chart.)*
2nd PHASE. *Detailed searches of the Magellan area. (on inset chart,) and further searches of the East Coast of Patagonia (on main chart) 20.XII.14 to 7.III.15.*
3rd PHASE. *Location, and final destruction of the DRESDEN, 8 to 14.III.15, on main chart.*

H.M.S. INFLEXIBLE	H.M.S. CARNARVON
H.M.S. GLASGOW	H.M.S. CORNWALL
H.M.S. BRISTOL	H.M.S. KENT

Movements of S.M.S. DRESDEN are shown in red.

Longitude West 70° from Greenwich

Prepared in the Historical Section of the Committee of Imperial Defence.

NAVAL OPERATIONS

The Lords Commissioners of the Admiralty have given the Author access to official documents in the preparation of this work, but they are in no way responsible for his reading or presentation of the facts as stated.

NAVAL OPERATIONS

History of the Great War
Based on Official Documents

VOL. II

by

SIR JULIAN S. CORBETT

The Naval & Military Press Ltd

Published by
The Naval & Military Press Ltd
5 Riverside, Brambleside, Bellbrook
Industrial Estate, Uckfield, East Sussex,
TN22 1QQ England
Tel: +44 (0) 1825 749494
Fax: +44 (0) 1825 765701

PREFACE

THE present volume is mainly concerned with the Dardanelles operations from their inception as a naval diversion to their development into a combined eccentric offensive and their failure as a *coup de main*.

The narrative, though related from the naval point of view, is necessarily concerned with military movements, but they have been dealt with only in so far as seemed essential for elucidating what the navy did in endeavouring to facilitate the task of the sister service. The account of the shore operations must, therefore, in no way be regarded as an adequate or complete exposition of the fine work done by the army in face of the difficulties of every kind under which it had to be carried out. A special and detailed account of this aspect of the campaign is in preparation as a separate section of the Official History.

The purely naval operations treated include the raid on the Yorkshire coast and the Dogger Bank action. With regard to these chapters it seemes necessary to emphasise once more that the Admiralty are in no way responsible for the presentation of the narrative or for the opinions expressed. The part of the Admiralty has been to place at the disposal of the author the whole of the documents in their possession relating to the war, and subsequently to examine the proofs with a view to pointing out errors of statement which may have arisen from a misreading of the existing documentary evidence. A prevalent idea that anything in the nature of censorship by the Admiralty has been exercised is purely erroneous.

Authorities.—Besides the classes of documents mentioned in the preface to the first volume, many others have become available with the lapse of time, both from our own and enemy sources. The principal of these are :—

1. The Report of the Dardanelles Commission with the statements prepared for its information and the evidence taken before it.

2. The "Mitchell Report," being the report of a special naval and military committee, sent out to Constantinople after the armistice, under Commodore F. H. Mitchell, to

investigate the course of the operations and the defences in the Dardanelles.

3. Books written by high officers concerned with particular operations, the chief of which are :—

> *Gallipoli Diary*, General Sir Ian Hamilton.
> *Fünf Jahre Türkei*, General Liman von Sanders.
> *Germany's High Sea Fleet in the World War*, Admiral Scheer.
> *My Memoirs*, Grand-Admiral von Tirpitz.
> *Aus Aufzeichnungen und Briefen*, Admiral Hugo von Pohl.

The German Official Naval History, *Der Krieg zur See, 1914–1918* (Baltic Sea, Vol. I.), has also been consulted. Other books of less importance are mentioned in footnotes when special use has been made of them.

The publication of these works since the history began to be written has proved of great assistance in correcting false impressions and supplying gaps in our own information. Their value increases in Vol. III., which will include the opening of the Salonica operations, the Dardanelles from the Suvla landing to the evacuation, the Mesopotamia campaign to the capitulation of Kut al Amara, the commencement of the German extended submarine campaign and the battle of Jutland.

J. S. C.

July, 1921.

NOTE TO SECOND EDITION

RATHER more than eight years have elapsed since Sir Julian Corbett sent this book to press. During this interval a great deal of historical material has been published in England, Germany and indeed in all the countries engaged in the war. In particular the German Official Naval History and General Aspinall-Oglander's researches into the Gallipoli campaign have established a number of facts which would have influenced the author's narrative of events and comment upon it.

In so far as I have been able, I have made such alterations of comment and of fact as the author himself would have made, had he lived.

E. Y. DANIEL.
Lieutenant-Colonel, R.M.
Secretary, Historical Section, Committee of Imperial Defence.

September, 1929.

CONTENTS

PLANS

CHAPTER I

REDISTRIBUTION OF THE HOME FLEETS AND OPERATIONS ON
THE BELGIAN COAST—NOVEMBER 20 TO DECEMBER 16, 1914

WITH the destruction of Admiral von Spee's squadron
at the Falklands the war in its naval aspects entered a new
phase. The first stage in the essential work of the fleet
was, in fact, accomplished. The object of that stage was,
as always, to establish a general command of the sea, and
now that the enemy had no organised squadrons outside his
own home waters we could regard the work—judged at
least by traditional standards—as practically done. On the
great southern and western trade routes, however, there
was little immediate relaxation of the strain on the navy.
The watch on the German liners in American ports and
at the Canaries had still to be maintained, and this menace,
coupled with the escape of the *Dresden* from the battle and
the still unsolved mystery of the *Karlsruhe*, compelled us
to keep a considerable force of cruisers in the Atlantic and
on the South American Station.[1] But the end of these
isolated ships could not be far distant, nor their power of
disturbance serious. In those seas there was nothing else at
large except two armed merchant cruisers, the *Prinz Eitel
Friedrich* and the *Kronprinz Wilhelm*, while Eastern waters
had been made absolutely safe by the destruction of the
Emden and the blockade of the *Königsberg* in the Rufiji
River.[2]

In Home waters there was a different tale to tell. There
the conditions were making it more evident every day that
the command could no longer be measured by the old
standards. If command of the sea meant the power to
move fleets, troops and trade freely where we would, then
our command was not undisputed, and indeed it seemed
to be growing gradually more precarious, as the mining

[1] On January 1, 1915, there were still forty-one ships of war in the
Atlantic, only six of which were under orders for home.

[2] The Russian prize *Cormoran*, which we last saw making for the
Western Carolines (Vol. I., p. 303) remained there for two months, and
then, failing to find coal and provisions, on December 14, she put in at the
United States island of Guam in the Mariana group, where she was at once
interned.

activities of the enemy extended to our western coasts and their submarines with increasing power and range spread further and further afield. By the time we had freed the ocean highways there was scarcely an area in the Narrow Seas where movement could be considered safe. We found ourselves, in fact, faced with a new struggle of which we had no experience, and from now onwards the crucial question was whether the old sea genius would prove still vigorous enough to devise some means of overcoming the new forms of attack, or whether it would have to recognise that its day was done.

With sure instinct it was to the old well-spring of our sea power we went to renew our youth for the anxious contest. The fleet would no longer suffice, but behind it were still the deep-sea fishermen and the great seafaring population to whom nothing afloat came amiss. We have seen already how they had been called on to form an organisation which later on was known officially as the Auxiliary Patrol, but as yet the call was only beginning. Over 150 trawlers and drifters had already been taken up, besides yachts and other small vessels, and as far as possible they were being fitted with guns and explosive sweeps.[1] As the men threw themselves into the work their increasing skill and enterprise proved the utility of the new force, and the cry for more became insatiable. Already during November the Commander-in-Chief had been promised for Scapa four units, each consisting of a yacht and twelve trawlers; Vice-Admiral Sir David Beatty at Cromarty was to have three yachts and eighteen trawlers, and these only for securing free movement for the Grand Fleet in the vicinity of its bases. Everywhere else, in the Straits of Dover, the English Channel, the Irish Sea, and especially in northern waters, the demand was scarcely less. In all tradition it had been a constant duty of the Grand Fleet to protect our fishing fleets; now it was the fishing fleets that must protect the Grand Fleet.

Still the dominating fact of the naval position, it may even be said the key fact of the whole war, was that, in spite of the secret and sudden danger by which it was encompassed, the Grand Fleet held on to its controlling position. Except for teasing it from time to time with submarines, the Germans had made no attempt to disturb it. Notwithstanding every provocation the High Seas Fleet showed a

[1] These sweeps were lines towed astern. At the end of the line or wire were explosive charges which could be detonated electrically when a submerged submarine was located.

convinced unwillingness to try conclusions in a general action. The command of the Baltic was vital to the German position, and it is doubtful whether their main fleet could at this period have been devoted to any better object. The soundness of this strategical idea can only have become more indisputable as our overwhelming concentration became more pronounced with the addition of powerful new battleships, new light cruisers and others that were flocking home from distant seas where their work was done. Neither our operations on the Belgian coast nor the temptation of our lines of communication across the Channel had availed to stir the German Staff from the attitude they had taken up.[1] They had not even ventured to hold out a hand to Admiral von Spee, as he perhaps, and certainly Germans in America, had expected. As against the enemy's main fleet, then, we could claim, and actually enjoyed, a command outside the Baltic as complete as ever it was in the old days of the blockades of Brest and the occupation of the Western position. Indeed in one respect it was more complete, for whereas in certain normally recurrent conditions of weather the Brest fleet could always get away into the Atlantic, our northern position rendered it impossible for the High Seas Fleet to escape without hazarding an action with a force strong enough in favourable conditions to annihilate it.

In these circumstances the keen desire for the return of the three battle cruisers which had been detached to deal with Admiral von Spee needs explanation. Now that the outer seas had been cleared the paramount need was to obtain a closer hold on the North Sea, with a view to the possibility of ultimately pressing our offensive into the enemy's waters. Such operations would involve coastal attack and inshore work, and required a special class of vessel. The necessary programme had been inaugurated when Lord Fisher returned to the Admiralty, and was being pressed on with energy. The ships designed were mainly of the monitor type, made as far as possible unsinkable by mine or torpedo, and certain very fast ships of battle cruiser size lightly protected, but with very heavy gun-power. But until the programme was well forward nothing could be done, and in the meanwhile the enemy might be expected to use

---

[1] It appears from the Diary of Admiral von Pohl, who was then Chief of the Staff, that this attitude had been imposed upon him. He relates that on October 2 the Emperor again explicitly reserved to himself absolute control over the fleet, and directed that Admiral von Ingenohl, who commanded it, was to confine offensive action to submarines and destroyers, though occasional sorties of heavy cruisers might be attempted. (Von Pohl: *Aus Aufzeichnungen und Briefen während derKriegszeit.*)

the opportunity for operating in the North Sea in a way which would require the utmost activity and vigilance from our own fleet.

Seeing how deeply the German idea of war was imbued with the offensive spirit, it was not to be believed that the inactivity of their fleet could continue. The view that they would never undertake operations which might render them powerless to keep us out of the Baltic seems at this time to have had little weight with our own High Command. The more general conviction was that the apathy with which the Germans had suffered us to crush their Pacific squadron and wipe out their trade was only to be explained by an intention to husband their fleet for some sudden blow when the long winter nights would give them the best chance of evasion and surprise. Now that their failures in France had forced them to recognise that the war would not be the short and brilliant affair they had expected, they were already having to give anxious attention to the question of food supply, and however prudently inclined the High Command of the navy might be, its hand might at any time be forced into some desperate attempt to diminish the stringency of the blockade, or to deter us from sending further troops to France.

It was at the end of October that these considerations began to raise a doubt as to whether the distribution of the Home fleets was the best that could be made, and whether the principle of extreme concentration on which it was based was not the child of pure theory rather than of sound doctrine founded on the practical experience of past naval warfare. During November, when the Grand Fleet was back at Scapa from its temporary withdrawal to the westward, the whole question was gone into with the help of the veteran flag officers who during their period of active command had acquired most completely the confidence of the service. The general result was in favour of further dispersal; Sir Arthur Wilson, the highest authority amongst them, after full consideration of all that could be said in favour of close concentration by its best advocates, pronounced emphatically against its continuance. "The dream of most naval officers," he wrote, " seems to be a great sea fight in which, by some means or other, we are to be enabled to collect all our forces together and crush the Germans at one blow. This, however, is only a dream. What we have to do is to dispose our forces so as to prevent the Germans from doing us more injury than we can possibly help and never to miss a good opportunity of injuring them. It is, above all, important to dispose the fleet so that the greatest possible number of troops may be spared for the front, and this makes some dispersion of the fleet absolutely necessary." Taking this broad view of the situation, which included military as well as naval considerations, he was specially opposed to the Harwich Force being regarded as an adjunct of the Grand Fleet to be sent to join the Commander-in-Chief when a battle was imminent. " First," he continued, " because there would be no possible chance of their arriving on the scene till many hours after the action was over; and secondly, because the object of the German main fleet in courting an engagement would probably be to enable a landing to be effected on the coast."

That the Germans might be intending to hazard some such desperate enterprise was certainly an eventuality which could not be neglected, seeing how the situation in France had been developing.

The long-drawn battles of Ypres were coming to an end, and the costly effort of the Germans to break through to Calais had failed.   The German offensive was ending in a series of local actions, the prelude to the long period of trench warfare; day after day there was "no change to report"; and the defeat of the enemy's purpose was proving to be as complete as his effort had been powerful and persistent.   Though it was clear the German plan for solving the formidable problem which the battle of the Marne had set them was now abandoned, too much had been staked upon it for them to be likely to sit down under the rebuff.   The intention had obviously been to break down our commanding naval position by getting a foothold on the Straits of Dover, and it was only natural to suppose that they would seek the same end by other means. The most likely plan, since they had not ventured an attempt to break into the Channel and disturb the lines of communication by which we nourished our army in France, was to give us a strong inducement to keep our troops at home. In these circumstances long experience taught us to anticipate an attempt to invade, or at least the threat of a formidable military raid on our coasts.   Special precautions, indeed, had been under consideration since the end of September, and these began to be put in action very soon after the battle cruisers were detached from the Grand Fleet to deal with the German Pacific Squadron.   At all likely places of descent arrangements were made for meeting the first shock of any raiding force that might elude the vigilance of the Grand Fleet.   The local naval defence was strengthened

by additional guardships which were now available. Loch
Ewe, where the *Illustrious* had been stationed, was no longer
required as a Grand Fleet base, and Stornoway had been
found to be a more convenient base for the auxiliary patrol
of the Hebrides area. The *Illustrious* was therefore moved
down to the Tyne, which, though an imperfectly defended
repair base, had hitherto had no regular guardship. The
Humber, as being the nearest secondary base to Wilhelmshaven, was better provided for. There was the headquarters
of Rear-Admiral G. A. Ballard, the Admiral of Patrols, with
his flag in the *St. George*. The *Victorious* and *Mars* were also
with him, and he was now to be reinforced by the *Majestic*
and *Jupiter*. Lower down in the Wash the three original
monitors were stationed, and at all the principal ports along
the east coast were distributed the old light cruisers, sloops
and gunboats which had been commissioned for bombarding
the Belgian coast in support of the army. In addition to
these precautions preparations were being made for instantly
blocking the ports and disabling their wharf gear in case of
need, while at certain of those which were undefended, such
as Blyth, South Shields and Sunderland, observation mines
were laid. But it was by no means on such measures of
passive defence that reliance was placed. The old way had
ever been to do all that was possible to meet the invading
force at sea, and to this end, as a result of the deliberations
already referred to, the time-honoured practice reasserted
itself in a redistribution of the Grand Fleet.

What was required was obviously a closer hold on the
North Sea than had hitherto prevailed, but no such hold
could be obtained so long as the Grand Fleet was kept completely concentrated in the far north. It was on that basis
our distribution had hitherto rested. It served admirably
so long as we could rest content with interrupting the enemy's
communications north-about and trusting to the pressure
so exercised to force his fleet to action. But that hope had
now grown cold, and if, as seemed more likely, he meant
to adopt the old French device of a direct attack on our
coasts, a mere concentration on the great trade highway in
the north would no longer serve.

The objections to opening out the original distribution
were, of course, far from negligible. For an inferior naval
Power the threat of military attack was a stock method of
loosening the concentration of a fleet with a view to making
an opportunity for bringing part of it to action under conditions of advantage. And now, if ever, seemed the enemy's
chance of playing the well-known game. At home both from

a military and a naval point of view we were passing through a stage of weakness. Of the regular army there was nothing in the country except the troops arriving from India and the more distant colonial garrisons which were being formed into the XXVIIth, XXVIIIth and XXIXth Divisions; the Territorial Force had not completed the six months' training which was supposed to be necessary for its efficiency in the field; many of its best units had gone abroad, and the new armies were still in leading-strings. The Grand Fleet, moreover, was at its lowest ebb. The *Audacious* was gone, and although her place was more than supplied by two new " Iron Dukes," *Benbow* and *Emperor of India*, it was not till November 20 that they were ready to go to Queenstown to carry out their gunnery. Neither ship for some time could be really fit to lie in the line, and the new battle cruiser *Tiger*, which had recently joined the fleet, was scarcely less raw.[1]

In addition to these drawbacks the base at Scapa was still insecure, though by this time it was less exposed. Something at least had been done to reduce the number of channels by which the Flow could be entered. By using twelve blockships Rear-Admiral F. S. Miller, in spite of the strong tidal streams, had succeeded in closing three of them, leaving besides the main southern entrance only one on the west side and two on the east. For the rest, anti-submarine defences of a type which had been successfully tried at Cromarty were being prepared, but had not yet arrived. Until they were in position, the Grand Fleet had to rely for security on the destroyers and Auxiliary Patrol vessels that had been attached to it for this special purpose. There were twelve destroyers that had been so lent, and every week the call for their return to their normal patrol functions in the south was becoming more urgent. The growing activity of the enemy's submarines in the Channel called for increased protection for the transports that were continually crossing to France.[2] On November 21 a new plan for barring the Straits of Dover had been instituted. The whole zone was divided into eight areas, each of which was to be patrolled continuously by a British destroyer, while French submarines

	Tons.	Designed speed.	Guns.
[1] *Benbow* ⎱ *Emperor of India* ⎰	25,000	21	10–13·5''; 12–6''; 2–3'' Anti-aircraft
Tiger	28,500	30	8–13·5''; 12–6''; 2–3'' Anti-aircraft.

[2] During November nearly 70,000 troops and over 16,000 horses went over, occupying, with stores an average of about twelve transports a day.

were to be always ready, when the alarm was g!ven, to occupy the lines from Gris Nez to the Varne and from Calais to the Goodwins. But besides this cover the transports required escort, and nothing but destroyers could provide it adequately. A large number were therefore wanted, more indeed than we could possibly find, and in spite of the assistance the French were giving with their flotillas, less important ships had frequently to go over without escort, and a large convoy from India which arrived in the middle of the month, instead of coming to Southampton, was diverted to Devonport.[1] The insecurity of the Channel had just been emphasised by the loss of the *Niger*. On November 11 this old torpedo-gunboat was torpedoed and sunk off Deal,[2] and on the following day Admiral Sir John Jellicoe was instructed to return the twelve detached destroyers as soon as the Scapa defences were secure.

A further effect of the enemy's activity was that the cruisers of the Western Patrol were ordered not to risk submarine attack by boarding merchant vessels. They were to make it their main duty to look out for suspicious ships rather than, as hitherto, to stop the passage of contraband. The situation in the Northern Patrol area was also bad. The six old " Edgars " of the 10th Cruiser Squadron had proved to be so completely worn out, that the wonder was they had been able to do their work at all. Yet, thanks to the devotion of officers and men, they had maintained the blockade with splendid efficiency, and Rear-Admiral D. R. S. de Chair had lately received from the Commander-in-Chief a letter expressing his high appreciation of the manner in which the ships of the squadron had kept the sea, in spite of their age and the difficulty of keeping their machinery in order. Now, so bad was their condition, that orders had been issued to pay them off, and as yet only a few of the armed merchant cruisers which were to take their place on the Northern Patrol were ready. But this defect would soon be remedied. For since it had been found unnecessary to form a new squadron for the West Coast of Africa to deal with Admiral von Spee, the *Warrior*, *Black Prince*, *Duke of Edinburgh* and *Donegal* were on their way to join Admiral Jellicoe's flag, and so were the *Leviathan* from dockyard hands and the *Hampshire* released from the East Indies after the destruction of the

---

[1] The convoy consisted of six ships carrying ten battalions of infantry and eleven batteries R.F.A., besides one transport with three batteries of heavy artillery, which was the only one allowed to proceed up Channel.

[2] She was sunk by *U 12*, a boat which was destroyed by the *Ariel* later on. See *post*, p. 280.

Emden, while the *Cumberland* was soon to follow from the Cameroons. To make up for the loss of the battle cruisers Admiral Jellicoe would therefore have in the near future three ships of the 1st Cruiser Squadron, with the *Leviathan* as the fourth ship, while the 6th Cruiser Squadron, of which he hitherto had only had the *Drake* and other stray units, would be completed with the *Donegal, Cumberland* and *Hampshire.*

When therefore we consider that the first of the " Queen Elizabeths " was nearly ready for sea, and that it could not be long before the Germans discovered the absence of the three battle cruisers, it was obvious they might well conceive they would never again have so good a chance of striking a damaging blow at our fleet. The risk of loosening its concentration at such a moment was therefore undeniable, but the new Board had shown already that when time-honoured principles were at stake it was ready to accept risks. It was one of those principles that where invasion or a raid is within reasonable probability, every possible step must be taken to ensure that it shall be met at sea, or at least when it reaches the coast. So the risk was taken now.

As a station to secure the end in view Scapa was too distant, and so was Cromarty, where Admiral Beatty was already stationed with his battle cruisers and the light cruisers. Yet for effectively securing the command of the north-about passage both bases had to be maintained. In order to meet the new situation it was therefore necessary to establish a third base further south. Rosyth, with all its drawbacks, was the only possible place, and as its first anti-submarine defences were on the point of being completed, it was now practicable to use it for a considerable force. Admiral Jellicoe, in view of his reduced battle strength, had asked to have returned to him the 3rd Battle Squadron, which it will be remembered had been called down to the Channel in the early days of November. But this request could not be granted in its entirety. Owing to the increasing menace of submarines in the Channel, and as the best means of abating it, the Admiralty had decided to attack the bases from which they were acting. For this hazardous operation they had already earmarked the five " Duncans," which, with the *Revenge,* were to be formed into a new special service squadron, designated the 6th Battle Squadron, under command of Rear-Admiral Stuart Nicholson. The eight " King Edwards," however, could be spared. Vice-Admiral E. E. Bradford, therefore, was ordered to take them north again, and

on November 13 seven of them left Portland to rejoin the
Grand Fleet. But Scapa was not to be their base. On the
previous day (November 12) the new plan for meeting any
attempt of the Germans to land troops upon our coasts had
been completed. Its base idea was that whether the enemy's
expeditionary force appeared north or south of Flamborough
Head, we should be in a position to strike immediately at its
covering force, in order either to break through and attack the
transports and their escort, or enable the flotillas to deal with
them. For the northern area this duty was assigned to
Admiral Bradford, and in order that he might perform it
he was to be permanently stationed at Rosyth, and there
he was to be joined by Rear-Admiral W. C. Pakenham with
the 3rd Cruiser Squadron (*Antrim, Argyll, Devonshire, Roxburgh*) and half a flotilla of destroyers.

In the southern area the idea of the plan was more difficult to realise effectively. Here there was little available,
nothing indeed but the comparatively old and slow 5th
Battle Squadron and the still older " Duncans." Moreover, the only possible base was Sheerness, a port which
did not admit of egress at all states of the tide or of
indispensable fleet exercises. This was a specially serious
drawback, because under the original War Orders the Channel
Fleet was regarded as a reserve, and men were being continually drafted from it, so that it always contained a large
proportion of untrained ratings. The inadequacy of the
force was further emphasised by the fact that there was
no cruiser squadron or flotilla available to act with it. Still
the position had to be occupied, and there was nothing else.
On November 14, therefore, Admiral Burney left Portland with
the 5th Battle Squadron for Sheerness and the " Duncans "
for Dover.[1] Vice-Admiral Sir Cecil Burney's orders were
that at the first intimation of a hostile expedition he was
instantly to attack it, regardless of its strength, and call
up the 6th Battle Squadron to his flag. In this way it
was thought fairly certain that with the assistance of the
Harwich and Nore flotillas he could prevent any landing
in force, while ample provision was made with submarines
and minelayers to render the enemy's retreat disastrous.
Fresh orders were issued to Admiral Ballard by which

---

[1] The 5th Battle Squadron at this time comprised *Lord Nelson*, flag of
Admiral Burney, *Agamemnon* and seven " Formidables," of which two were
in dockyard hands, and two light cruisers.

To get over the difficulties of Sheerness it was intended to form a protected anchorage in the Wallet, off the Essex coast, where the Gunfleet shoals
made a submarine attack very difficult, but the plan was abandoned.

he was to regard the primary function of the East Coast patrol flotillas as being a first line of defence against military raids. This had been their function under the first distribution, but owing to the German activity in minelaying it had gradually been eaten into. Instead of being concentrated at certain selected ports, the patrol destroyers had been more and more devoted to intercepting the enemy's minelayers. As often as not they acted singly, and had thus become too widely scattered for immediate and effective action against a raid. Early in November the risk that was involved came prominently under notice by the Gorleston raid, and after a conference at the Admiralty it was decided to restore the original disposition as designed by Rear-Admiral J. M. de Robeck in April 1914. Admiral Ballard was therefore informed that he was to reconcentrate the destroyers in divisions as laid down in the War Orders, and leave the prevention of minelaying to the trawlers of the Auxiliary Patrol.[1]

As the month wore on our intelligence seemed to confirm both the wisdom of the decision and the risk it involved.[2] There were increasing indications of unusual activity in German naval ports. First on November 20 came warning of a submarine attack about to be made in strength on one or more of the Grand Fleet bases. But this caused little concern, since the chances were they would find the bases empty. As usual the signs of German restlessness were to be met by a full-strength sweep to the Bight, this time in conjunction with an air raid on the Cuxhaven Zeppelin sheds as an additional means of goading the enemy to action. So much on the alert, however, did he appear to be that the air raid was countermanded, but from the 22nd to the 25th all squadrons of the Grand Fleet, together with the Harwich Force, made the sweep up to the Bight. As usual, nothing was seen, and all units returned to their newly-allotted stations.

But the period of the operation was not entirely barren.

---

[1] In accordance with these orders Admiral Ballard's two flotillas, the 7th and 9th, were each organised in four divisions, one division of each flotilla to be always in reserve cleaning boilers. Of the active divisions, two of the 7th Flotilla were kept at Yarmouth ready for immediate action night and day, and one in the Humber. In the Humber also was one division of the 9th Flotilla; another division lay in the Tyne and the third patrolled between Flamborough Head and Hartlepool.

[2] Captain W. R. Hall was now Director of Naval Intelligence. From commanding the *Queen Mary* he had been appointed in place of Rear-Admiral H. F. Oliver, that officer having become Chief of the War Staff when Admiral Sturdee was given his memorable command afloat.

On November 20 a message came from General Joffre saying that since we had ceased operating on the Belgian coast, the enemy's guns east of Nieuport had been getting very troublesome. General Foch was, in fact, being subjected to a violent bombardment which he had no means of reducing, and the French Commander-in-Chief begged that the Admiralty would resume more active co-operation with him. Though, as will be seen directly, we had an operation of our own on foot in that quarter, the request was immediately complied with, and Rear-Admiral The Hon. H. L. A. Hood went over to Dunkirk with such ships as were immediately available. His force consisted of the *Revenge*, the *Bustard* and six destroyers, and at our suggestion four French destroyers and a torpedo-gunboat were placed at his disposal, and having done what was required, he was ordered on the 22nd to send the *Revenge* back to Dover.

Simultaneously our own operation had taken place. Owing to the increasing annoyance of submarines in the Channel, the occasion of the Grand Fleet sweep had been seized to inaugurate the new offensive policy against the enemy's submarine bases. The port that caused us the most uneasiness was Zeebrugge. Here the Germans were known to be establishing a submarine base for disturbing the army's lines of communication across the Channel. When the port was evacuated, the reasons for leaving it intact were indisputable. The risk was frankly accepted, but now the consequences were beginning to be felt.[1] The increasing annoyance had already given birth to several projects for closing it with blockships, as the Japanese had so strenuously attempted to do with Port Arthur. Their failure, however, the reasons of which were perhaps not fully known, caused the design to be pronounced impracticable in the face of modern fortress artillery. Long afterwards, when improved technical devices had changed the conditions of the problem, one of the most daring exploits in the annals of our navy was to disprove the finality of this opinion, but for the present it stood, and operations against the port were confined to a bombardment.

On November 21, as the Grand Fleet was about to start its great sweep, Admiral Nicholson was directed to proceed off Zeebrugge with two of the "Duncans," *Russell* and *Exmouth*. He was to be joined by eight destroyers, as many Lowestoft minesweeping trawlers and two airships for directing his fire. On November 23 the operation was carried out. Owing to the low speed of the trawlers and the continual difficulty they had with sweeps parting on the

[1] See Vol. I., p. 215.

shoals the approach was very slow, and finally Admiral Nicholson had only one pair in action. As for the two airships, they failed to appear at all. Still he held on, and by 2.30 the two ships opened fire on the canal lock at a range of 12,500 yards. Running on till the range was 11,000 yards, Admiral Nicholson altered four points to port, so as to bring all guns to bear, and then distributed his fire between the railway station and the harbour and its forts. On this course he reached the Wielingen lightship, with the range down to 6,000 yards. Then he turned sixteen points and repeated the run on the opposite course, till 3.40 when, after just over an hour's bombardment, action ceased. Owing to the absence of the airships it was impossible to tell what damage had been done. About 400 rounds had been fired, and one large conflagration and several smaller ones could be seen. If later reports from Holland could be believed, the success had been considerable. It was said that all the stores, buildings and cranes of the port had been destroyed, and that the sections of six submarines which were about to be put together were reduced to a tangle of twisted iron. The place, in fact, so it was said, had been made for the time impossible as a submarine base. We now know that the only serious damage done was to the electric power station for the locks, and Zeebrugge continued to be a source of anxiety to our cross-Channel transport lines.

Of the increasing enterprise of the enemy's submarines there could be no doubt. The day the attack on Zeebrugge took place, a small British steamer called the *Malachite*, from Liverpool to Havre, was stopped by submarine *U 21* close off the latter port and within sight of the patrol boat. After the crew had abandoned the ship, the submarine fired into her for nearly half an hour without interruption, nor was any attempt made from the shore to salve the *Malachite*, though she remained afloat for at least twenty-four hours. For the next few days, however, the submarine was diligently hunted by French destroyers. Several times she was seen, and on one occasion fired three torpedoes at one of her pursuers without effect. Still she held her ground, and on November 26, off Cape d'Antifer, just north of Havre, caught a collier, the *Primo*, bound for Rouen. This she treated in the same way as the *Malachite*, again without interference, and with no effort to salve after the enemy left her.

The actual loss was small, but what the incident signified was of the deepest gravity. The long-expected attack on the army's communications had begun, and it was obvious that existing measures were inadequate to deal with it.   Though the French had eighteen destroyers at Cherbourg, their end of the line seemed almost unprotected.   Our own arrangements for escort were as yet incomplete.   Twelve armed trawlers with three leaders [1] from Great Yarmouth were under orders for the duty, but would not begin operations till November 26.   The sailing of all transports had to be stopped, and five about to leave Southampton had to wait till six destroyers came round from Harwich to escort them.   This duty done the destroyers were to sweep back along the British coast in search of submarines and floating mines, of which a large number were being reported in the area.   On November 26, the day the *Primo* was sunk, another division was detached from Harwich to sweep from Dover to the Needles, and the French were asked to do the same on their own coast. Dover was then drawn upon for six more destroyers for regular escort work, and by the time they arrived a division of " Beagles," one of the two that had been recalled from the Mediterranean to form a new flotilla for the North Sea, reached Devonport.   They were at once assigned to Portsmouth for escort work, and it was then possible to use the Yarmouth trawlers to form a permanent patrol between Winchelsea and Poole which would cover the Dieppe route as well as that to Havre.   In this way the new situation was rapidly met and henceforth no important ship was allowed to cross without escort, and sailings were timed so that vessels should arrive at the French coast after dark.   These measures were also supplemented by a new device.   Since the submarine had been using gun-fire on the ships she stopped, there seemed a good chance of entrapping her.   Instructions were therefore given for a decoy vessel, the *Victoria*, to be fitted out and armed with two concealed 12-pounder guns.

To all its other cares the navy had thus a new one added. At a time when, owing to the apprehension of an attack on our coasts, every destroyer was wanted in the North Sea, the army communications became a source of real anxiety, and from now onward an ever-increasing strain upon our flotilla strength.   Yet for the moment it was not there that the enemy's main submarine effort was being made.   On the day of the Zeebrugge bombardment, while the Grand Fleet was in position off the Bight, the expected attack on its base appears to have taken place.   A submarine was observed by the trawler *Dorothy Grey* a mile or so south-west of Hoxa.   So close was she that the trawler made a smart attempt to ram. It appears that the submarine was hit, but, in any case, she

---

[1] The " leaders " of the trawler patrols were simply larger trawlers provided for the commissioned officers commanding the several patrol units.

was forced to dive so hurriedly that she struck her nose on the rocks off Muckle Skerry, and was so badly injured that she had to come up and surrender to the destroyer *Garry*. She proved to be *U 18*, and amongst the many distinctions which the trawlers earned, to the *Dorothy Grey* fell the honour of being the first Auxiliary Patrol vessel to bring about the loss of a German submarine. At 8.30 next morning a trawler reported a submarine off Duncansby Head steering west-south-west. A couple of hours later the *Dryad*, a mine-sweeping gunboat attached to the Northern Patrol, sighted and chased one of a large type forty miles east by south of the same point, which dived and got away. Early in the afternoon another was seen off Hoy, proceeding from Torness towards Stroma, that is, across the Pentland Firth.

The activity continued on November 25 as the fleet was making its way back. The officer in command of the Aberdeen minesweeper group chased and lost a submarine off that port, and the minesweeping gunboat *Shipjack* failed to catch another, *U 16*, near the Pentlands. How many there were it was impossible then to say, but there were enough to indicate a concerted attack on the Scapa area,[1] and to increase the anxiety for the still unprotected anchor-age. To add to the trouble, a succession of gales interfered with the placing of the improvised boom obstructions which had been prepared on the spot, and November came to an end without any assurance that the Cromarty type defence would soon be ready.

A certain sense of insecurity therefore continued in some measure to cramp Admiral Jellicoe's freedom of action, and at the time it was intensified by a terrible catastrophe which occurred in the Channel Fleet at Sheerness. The 5th Battle Squadron, in pursuance of the new disposition, had arrived there on November 15, and on the 26th the *Bulwark* (Captain G. L. Sclater) was taking in ammunition when she suddenly blew up with an appalling explosion. When the smoke cleared she had entirely disappeared, and of her complement of 750 only twelve lives were saved. The suddenness and com-pleteness of the disaster seemed unaccountable. For some time foul play was strongly suspected, and did little to lighten the moral effect of the blow, and it was not till the middle of December that a court of inquiry established that the explosion was due to accidental ignition of ammunition.

The anxious period of stormy weather and long, dark nights, so favourable for any desperate enterprise the enemy might be contemplating, had now fairly set in, and with it

[1] There were five in all : *U 8, U 16, U 17, U 18, U 22.*

came fresh indications of the menace in view of which the new distribution of the fleet had been established. On December 1 our Minister at Copenhagen sent home for what it was worth a specially detailed report of a numerous landing flotilla and a score or more of large liners being prepared and concentrated at Kiel. The original source was not very trustworthy, and even if the information were true, the nature of the preparations and the probabilities of the situation suggested the Russian ice-free coasts in the vicinity of Libau rather than our own as the objective. After General Hindenburg's victory at Tannenberg had put an end to the Russian invasion of East Prussia, the German advance had been brought to a standstill near the frontier, and the Higher Direction at Berlin had been forced to turn their attention to assisting the Austrians to stem the invasion of Galicia. Their hope of pushing their counter-attack into the Baltic Provinces was not, however, abandoned, and as the Russians were in strong positions in difficult country nothing was more likely than that the Germans were preparing to turn the position by an operation from the sea. The command of the Baltic was now, in fact, essential not only to German defence, but also to the success of their main offensive. The attempt, however, was not likely to be made till the spring, while on the other hand the long winter nights were specially favourable for a combined expedition across the North Sea against our own shores. In any case the possibility could not be ignored, particularly as the propaganda which had been so active during the years preceding the war in connection with the movement for introducing compulsory service had done nothing to diminish our national sensitiveness to threats of invasion. Moreover, it was quite probable that within a week or two Vice-Admiral Sir Doveton Sturdee would have struck his blow, and it would then no longer be possible to conceal the weakening of Admiral Jellicoe's battle cruiser force. There was therefore every reason why his fleet should be brought up to the highest possible pitch of strength, reach and mobility, and for this purpose the prompt return of the battle cruisers was essential. Still, the Admiralty had measured the risk, and having done all that was possible to make up to Admiral Jellicoe for what he had lost, they stood by it.

By this time he had his 1st Cruiser Squadron complete and the 6th nearly so. He had also been told that the *Yarmouth* and *Gloucester* were coming to join him from the East Indies. It was an addition that would bring his light cruisers up to eight, and further to ease his task the armed merchant cruisers for the Northern Patrol were beginning to arrive. But no inroad was suffered upon the great plan for dealing with Admiral von Spee.

While the Admiralty thus held doggedly to the work of clearing the seas of all outlying enemy ships, in spite of the risks it involved, the impression that the High Seas Fleet was waking from its long slumber continued. As day by day went by with no visible sign, vigilance only increased. For the first week of December Admiral Jellicoe had planned another sweep down the North Sea. It was to be carried out from the 7th to the 10th by the battle and light cruisers, with the 1st Battle and 1st Cruiser Squadrons in support, but as after the recent violent weather mines were certain to have broken adrift in all directions, the Admiralty did not consider a mere reconnaissance worth the risk, and the movement was cancelled.

The Admiral accordingly devoted his attention to the protection of his base. There was need enough for it, for on December 3 a submarine had almost succeeded in penetrating the upper eastern entrance of the Flow. She was immediately detected by the *Garry*, the destroyer on guard. There was a very heavy sea running, and in such narrow waters ramming was impossible, but the *Garry* engaged her twice and the submarine fired a torpedo. It did not take effect, but the enemy got away to sea, and on reaching the 10-fathom line dived apparently uninjured before the *Garry* could get on to her.[1] Further precautions were obviously necessary, and the Commander-in-Chief submitted proposals for rendering his base proof against submarines. But this was not the only anxiety. It had been found that, useful as the minesweeping trawlers were, their speed was too low to allow them to work far enough afield to give him elbow-room. To overcome the difficulty the Admiralty made a further draft on the mercantile marine by taking up eight fast railway packets and commissioning them as " Fleet Minesweepers," till specially constructed vessels came forward.[2]

To meet the increasing submarine menace the Admiralty were engaged in reorganising the whole system of patrols. For some time the increasing numbers of anti-submarine craft had outgrown the original organisation, and the conflicting calls for further protection which kept coming in from all quarters could only be met by a comprehensive

---

[1] There is no mention of this in the German Official History.

[2] They were the *Reindeer*, *Roebuck*, *Lynn* and *Gazelle* of the Great Western Railway; *Folkestone* and *Hythe* of the South-Eastern and Chatham Railway; and *Clacton* and *Newmarket* of the Great Eastern Railway.

system which would embrace the whole of our coasts. On December 8 the post of " Captain Supervising Modified Sweeps " was abolished, and in its place was set up a " Submarine Attack Committee," with Captain L. A. B. Donaldson at its head. Its function was to develop and organise the various methods of attack, which at this time were ramming, gunfire, explosive sweeps and indicator nets, the latter as yet in an early experimental stage.[1] At the same time a scheme was being worked out for apportioning all the Home waters into twenty-three Patrol areas, each with its base close to the local Naval Centre, so as to ensure the rapid transmission of intelligence gained by the patrols. The duties of the Patrol would be not only to act against submarines, but also to prevent minelaying and spying. The actual sweeping of mines remained a separate organisation. To provide what was necessary it was calculated that seventy-four yachts and 462 trawlers and drifters would be required, besides motor boats for inshore work wherever suitable waters were found.[2] The system was formally inaugurated on December 20, but

[1] Indicator nets were made of thin, strong wire and sustained by kapok, small buoys, or glass balls. By means of special clips each net was detachable from the whole " fleet " of nets, as soon as a submarine collided with it. The net would then envelop the submarine, and simultaneously would indicate the submarine's presence by means of a buoy moving along the surface of the sea.

[2] The Patrol areas under this organisation, which about August 1915 began to be styled the " Auxiliary Patrol," were as under :—

	Area.	Base.
I.	Hebrides and the Minch.	Loch Ewe and Stornoway.
II.	Shetlands.	} Longhope
III.	Orkneys.	
IV.	Moray Firth.	Cromarty.
V.	Off Rattray Head.	Peterhead.
VI.	Forth to Rattray Head.	Rosyth.
VII.	Seaward of the Forth.	Granton.
VIII.	Tyne.	Tyne.
IX.	Humber.	Grimsby.
X.	Off East Anglian coast.	Yarmouth and Harwich.
XI.	Dover Straits.	Dover.
XII.	East Channel.	Portsmouth.
XIII.	Mid-Channel.	Portland.
XIV.	Western Approach.	Devonport.
XV.	St. George's and Bristol Ch.	Milford (sub-base Rosslare).
XVI.	Irish Channel.	Liverpool, Kingstown, Belfast.
XVII.	North Coast of Ireland.	Lough Larne.
XVIII.	N.W. Coast Ireland.	Lough Swilly.
XIX.	West Coast Ireland.	Blacksod Bay.
XX.	West Coast Ireland.	Galway Bay.
XXI.	S. and S.W. Coast Ireland.	Queenstown, Berehaven.

There were, besides, the two special areas of the Clyde and the Nore. The main areas formed a continuous belt round the coast. (See Plan No. 1.)

although the necessary craft were being taken up in large numbers and armed under high pressure, it was some time before enough were available to supply every area with its allotted contingent.

Elaborate as was the defensive system, the Admiralty were not content to rely upon it. They were pushing forward with all speed the building programme, by means of which they hoped to open the second phase of the war by a vigorous offensive against the enemy's North Sea ports. The recent attack on Zeebrugge had been the firstfruits of the plan, and the need of persisting in such minor offensive operations as were possible was emphasised by the continued activity of the enemy's submarines. There was reason to believe that Zeebrugge was still being used. When, therefore, on December 9, there came through Colonel Bridges at the Belgian Head-quarters a suggestion for a combined attack on the port, the idea was quickly taken up. The suggestion was to use the " Duncans " from Dover, but they were no longer there. On November 3 the boom had carried away in a gale. The port would no longer afford protection for a squadron against submarines, and after five days exposure to attack they were ordered away to Portland. The three monitors, however, were called down from the Wash and the *Majestic* and *Mars* from the Humber, and Admiral Hood, as well as Admiral Nicholson, commanding the " Duncan " Squadron, were sum-moned to the Admiralty to concert plans. Some horse boats were also ordered to be armed with 4·7″ guns for service in inland waters, and a score of drifters to be fitted with 3-pounders and shields. But on the 11th the operations were postponed. All ships, however, were to stand-by at Dover and Dunkirk, except the *Mars*, which was ordered on to Portland.

Before this order came to hand Admiral Hood, in response to an invitation from the military authorities at Dunkirk, had landed there to visit the Army Headquarters. On his arrival it would seem he found the idea of a combined attack on Zeebrugge had not materialised, and that all General Foch was contemplating was operations of a purely subsidiary character. To risk ships in the boisterous weather that prevailed merely to assist minor military operations was quite a different thing from risking them to eliminate finally a dangerous submarine base. Admiral Hood was therefore told on December 14, while he was still at Dun-kirk, that he was not to hazard the ships if the weather continued to be bad. Still he was loth to abandon the operations entirely. The *Majestic* and *Revenge* had already left Dover for Dunkirk, and next day, December 15, they proceeded with two or three of the gun vessels to try to find the obnoxious guns. Little good, however, could be done. They were almost impossible to locate, and the *Majestic* was recalled by the Admiralty to Dover, as they did not wish any battleship except the old *Revenge* to engage in the operation. The *Revenge* stayed on and bombarded again on the 16th, but on both days she had a bad hit from apparently 8″ shell, and the second damaged her so much below the water-line that she had to retire to be docked. Then, as in Admiral Hood's opinion the monitors could not do the work without support, further operations were stopped. It was a moment, indeed, when there could be no thought of detaching other battleships for minor coastal work, for what appeared to be the long-expected counter-offensive of the German fleet had suddenly developed, and everything had to be subordinated to meet it.

CHAPTER II

BY December 10 news of the Battle of the Falklands had revealed the weakening of the Grand Fleet. Now if ever was the enemy's moment to strike, and by the 14th reports that an attack of some kind was in preparation so far confirmed our expectation that it was decided to put the fleet in motion to meet it. It appeared to be a cruiser raid that was in the wind, with or without transports, but where it would try to strike, and from what point it would start, was uncertain. Under these conditions long experience had shown there was only one effective form of counteraction. So long as the objective was unrevealed it was hopeless to try to intercept the attack without a wholly vicious distribution of the fleet. But without any undue prejudice to a sound concentration it was possible to make certain that the enemy should have no time to land any serious force without interruption—or if a mere naval raid was intended, to ensure that, subject to the chances of the sea, he should never get back.

On these lines the Admiralty made their dispositions. In the southern area, while the 5th Battle Squadron was kept at the shortest notice for sea, Commodore R. Y. Tyrwhitt, who now had with his two flotillas at Harwich two more of the new "Arethusa" class—*Aurora* and *Undaunted*—as well as the *Fearless*, was directed to endeavour to get touch with the enemy off our coasts as soon as they were reported, and to shadow them. The northern area would be dealt with by the Grand Fleet. The Commander-in-Chief was to send out Admiral Beatty from Cromarty with the four remaining battle cruisers and two divisions of the 4th Flotilla which were attached to them, and Commodore W. E. Goodenough was to join him at sea from Scapa with the 1st Light Cruiser Squadron. From Scapa one battle squadron, preferably the 2nd, which was the fastest and most powerful, was to act in support, and together they should make for some point at which they were most likely to intercept the enemy as he returned, at whatever point he struck.

Admiral Ballard, who as Admiral of Patrols had charge of the floating coast defence, had also orders to be specially on the alert. He himself was in the Humber, with his flag in the depot ship *St. George*. Here also were the *Victorious, Illustrious,* and the old light cruiser *Sirius,* with the *Skirmisher* leading two divisions of the 7th Flotilla (eight torpedo-boats), and two divisions of the 9th ("River" class destroyers), and four submarines. The other two divisions of the 7th Flotilla were based at Yarmouth. In the Tyne were the *Jupiter* and *Brilliant* and six submarines of the 6th Flotilla. At Hartlepool, besides one submarine, there was the 3rd Division of the 9th Flotilla, with the cruisers *Patrol* and *Forward,* the 4th Division being on patrol off Whitby. To the northward in the Forth was the 8th Flotilla, with its leader the *Sentinel*. The Wash, where the monitors had been stationed, was being taken over by the sloop *Rinaldo* from the Tees, as they were under orders for Dunkirk.[1]

How close to the truth was our appreciation of the German intentions we did not then know. Ever since the Heligoland action the High Seas Fleet had been fretting at the inaction which was then imposed upon it by the Kaiser and his military advisers. Recently, as Admiral von Ingenohl, the Commander-in-Chief, had watched its spirit deteriorating, he had begged to be allowed greater latitude. The reply was a rebuff. It was explained to him that it was essential, in view of the general outlook, to keep the fleet in being, in order to preserve the command of the Baltic and to release the coast defence troops for the active army. "The fleet," so the Naval Staff minute concluded, "must therefore be held back and avoid action which might lead to heavy losses. This does not, however, prevent favourable opportunities being used to damage the enemy. Employment of the fleet outside the Bight, which the enemy tries to bring about by his movements in the Skagerrak, is not mentioned in the orders for operations as being one of such favourable opportunities. There is nothing to be said against an attempt of the big cruisers in the North Sea to damage the enemy."[2]

This intimation seems to have been taken by Admiral von Ingenohl as a hint to attempt something with his battle

---

[1] Of the other East Coast guardships, *Mars* had joined the "Duncans" at Portland and the *Majestic* Admiral Hood at Dover.

[2] Admiral Scheer, *Germany's High Sea Fleet in the World War*, English Ed., p. 60. The remark about our movements in the Skagerrak will be noted as showing how little the Naval Staff believed the fiction, which was so industriously spread for popular consumption, that the Grand Fleet was skulking in port to avoid action.

cruisers, and he quickly devised a plan for a raid on our coast which would serve to restore the spirit of the fleet, and might possibly tempt a detachment of the Grand Fleet within his reach. For this reason, therefore, he decided to stretch his limited instructions to the extent of supporting the raid with his three battle squadrons.

It was early in the morning of December 15 that the raiding force, under the command of Admiral Hipper, left the Jade. It comprised his four battle cruisers, *Seydlitz, Moltke, Von der Tann,* the newly completed *Derfflinger* and the heavy cruiser *Blücher,* which formed the "1st Scouting Division," and to these were also attached the "2nd Scouting Division," composed of the light cruisers *Strassburg, Stralsund, Grandenz* and *Kolberg,* the latter carrying a hundred mines, and the 1st and 9th Destroyer Flotillas. This force steamed N.N.W. at 15 knots, and at 5 p.m., on reaching the 56th parallel, altered course to the south-westward for the English coast. In support were the 1st, 2nd and 3rd Battle Squadrons, which met at 8 p.m. at a rendezvous 20 miles to the northward of Heligoland, whence they steered W.N.W. for the Dogger Bank. The cruisers *Prinz Heinrich, Roon* and *Hamburg,* with a flotilla, formed a screen ahead of them; the flanks were covered by five light cruisers and two flotillas; and the light cruiser *Stettin,* with two flotillas, covered the rear. The function of the battleship force was to cover the retirement of the raiding cruisers, after they had struck their blow.

By the time the German forces were in motion our own dispositions for meeting the expected movement were already taking shape. The squadrons detailed were already under steam, and had received orders to proceed to their intercepting position. The choice of it, a matter of no less difficulty than importance, had been left to Admiral Jellicoe. Seeing that some 300 miles of coast had to be considered, the first question was to determine the most likely objective for a raid. The obvious points were those which were most vulnerable, furthest from a naval centre, and best calculated to yield good results to a raiding force. On this principle of selection the Humber and the Tyne naturally suggested themselves. The Germans, moreover, had considerably simplified the problem by the extensive mining they had carried out in the North Sea. The chief of the danger areas lay off the East Anglian coast, where we had reinforced the German minefield as a defensive measure against raids. This was known to us as the Southwold minefield. Further north, off the Yorkshire coast, were the areas which the Germans had mined just before the Heligoland Bight action.[1] Neither we nor they themselves apparently knew precisely where the mines were. Those who had done the work appear to have reported to the German Staff that the mines had been laid in groups, one twenty to thirty miles off the Humber and the other five or six miles off the Tyne, but, in fact, we had found this minefield some thirty miles out to sea.[2] In these circumstances the Admiralty had declared two danger areas, one extending from the Farn Islands to the Tees, and the other from Flamborough Head to the Humber, with a passage between them about twenty-five miles broad off Scarborough and Whitby. Notices to mariners defining these danger areas had been issued, and one set of them at least had probably been captured by the enemy in the British s.s. *Glitra* towards the end of October. The Germans, being perhaps uncertain as to the exact position of their northern minefields, and also as to whether we had not extended them as we had done the others, possibly used the captured information in designing the plan of operations which they had in hand. It was not, however, entirely the basis on which our counteraction rested. So many floating mines had recently been reported to the eastward, that Admiral Jellicoe had marked as a danger area on his own chart all the waters between the old mined area and a line running roughly parallel to the trend of coast from the latitude of the Forth to that of Flamborough Head at a mean distance of about eighty miles. Of this Vice-Admiral Sir George Warrender, whose battle squadron was to act with Admiral Beatty, was informed before leaving Scapa, with instructions that no capital ships were to operate within the danger zone. Upon this basis and that of the gap between the areas originally marked the rendezvous for our squadrons was fixed. It was a point about twenty-five miles south-east of the south-west patch of the Dogger, on the direct line between Heligoland and Flamborough Head, and about equidistant from the tracks to the Tyne and to the Humber. It was actually 180 miles from Heligoland and 110 from Flam-

[1] See Vol. I., p. 160. Von Pohl states the mines were laid on the night of August 25–26 by the minelayers *Albatross* and *Nautilus*, under escort of two light cruisers and two half flotillas. They reported having laid the mines *in* the Tyne and Humber (*Diary*, August 26, 1914).

[2] The declaration made by the Germans under the terms of the Armistice shows this minefield close off the Tyne. A similar error occurs in the Southwold field, which was begun by the *Königin Luise* on the first day of the war. The declaration shows it in the fairway to the Thames east of the Galloper, whereas in a few hours it was found some twenty miles further north.

borough Head, and moreover was about fifty miles to the south-eastward of the rendezvous which Admiral von Ingenohl had appointed.

The selection of the supporting battle squadron was a simple matter, for the 2nd Squadron, which the Admiralty preferred, happened to have the guard that day and was ready.[1] With the light cruisers there was more difficulty. The *Liverpool* was under refit, and the *Lowestoft*, which had been out with the 1st Cruiser Squadron, had just come in to coal, so that Commodore Goodenough had only four ships available, *Southampton*, *Birmingham*, *Nottingham* and *Falmouth*, but the *Blanche* was added to his command.[2] To make matters worse, the squadron, in coming out, encountered such heavy seas in the Pentlands that both the *Boadicea* and the *Blanche* were disabled and had to return. It was due to the foresight of the Commander-in-Chief that this loss of cruiser strength was not more severely felt. Realising, early, the need of a strong cruiser force for the work in hand, he had added the 3rd Cruiser Squadron at Rosyth to the force originally ordered by the Admiralty; and this squadron under Admiral Pakenham had joined up with the 2nd Battle Squadron during the afternoon of the 15th.[3] Admiral Jellicoe had, moreover, suggested that Commodore Tyrwhitt should be ordered to the Dogger Bank rendezvous, as the heavy weather might make it impossible for Admiral Beatty's destroyers to keep up with him, and he now urged it again, as the light cruisers attached to the Harwich flotillas were also required, but no immediate change was made in this part of the Admiralty plan. Accordingly Commodore Tyrwhitt proceeded off Yarmouth, and arriving there at 6.30 a.m. on December 16, kept his flotillas under way in the shelter of the banks to await orders.

Meanwhile all the other squadrons, under the command of Admiral Warrender, had joined up, and were approaching the rendezvous, which they were timed to reach at 7.30, that is, just before dawn.[4] The order which he adopted for the night was for the battle cruisers to be five miles ahead of him, with the light cruisers five miles on their starboard beam and the 3rd Cruiser Squadron similarly disposed to port of

---

[1] Second Battle Squadron : *King George V* (flag of Admiral Warrender), *Ajax, Centurion, Orion*(flag of Rear-Admiral Sir Robert Arbuthnot), *Monarch, Conqueror,* and *Boadicea* (attached light cruiser).

[2] The *Blanche* was the attached light cruiser of the 3rd Battle Squadron at Rosyth, but she was not now with them.

[3] Third Cruiser Squadron : *Antrim, Devonshire, Argyll, Roxburgh.*

[4] The rendezvous was in Lat. 54°10′ N., Long. 3°00′ E.

them. Admiral Beatty's destroyers, of which there were only seven, he kept ten miles to port of the battle squadron, with orders to close at daylight and act as a screen for the battleships.[1] As they were proceeding thus at 5.15 a.m. the *Lynx* (Commander R. St. P. Parry), which was leading the flotilla line, and had just reached a point about twenty miles north-east of the German rendezvous, was aware of a destroyer on the port bow. She was challenged, and, on her replying wrongly, fire was opened on her at an estimated range of 500 yards. As she moved away in a northerly direction the *Lynx* led the flotilla 16 points round to port and gave chase. Before long the leading boats could see her again dimly and they had been firing for some minutes when the rear of the line became aware of other destroyers to port, and they too had begun to fire, when the *Lynx*, who had been hit several times, suddenly led some 14 points to port.[2] As the enemy to port had by this time disappeared all the boats as they followed the *Lynx's* turn engaged the original enemy till she made off to the eastward and was lost in the darkness. But she had left her mark. The *Ambuscade* next astern of the *Lynx* had been holed forward, and at about 5.50 was compelled to leave the line with five feet of water on her mess-deck.[3]

The *Lynx* now altered course to S. 8° W., and led down to resume station on the battle squadron, with which she hoped to fall in at daylight; but, three minutes later (5.53), a cruiser was sighted before the port beam of the *Hardy* and *Shark* at a distance of about 600 to 700 yards. She switched on recognition lights, and the *Hardy* at once opened fire on her, followed by the *Shark*. The enemy then got her searchlights on them and replied with a heavy fire on both boats, forcing the *Hardy* to haul out a little to starboard. The boats astern of her followed, while the *Unity* and *Lynx* ahead, not being under fire, held straight on. The result was that they lost touch with the rest of the division, for the *Hardy* quickly led the rear boats back to a course parallel to that of the enemy and continued the action. By 6.0, however, the *Hardy* was so severely damaged that her captain, Lieutenant-Commander L. G. E. Crabbe, had to turn out of the line and take

---

[1] The destroyers were :—

> 1st Division : *Lynx, Ambuscade, Unity, Hardy.*
> 2nd Division : *Shark, Acasta, Spitfire.*

[2] The *Lynx* in her report states that her helm jammed at about this time, and that, although she turned, she was able to resume her original course. It seems probable that her turn to the southward was made deliberately, after the accident to her steering gear had been put right.

[3] It has been assumed that the *Ambuscade* left the line after the *Lynx's* turn to the southward; but it is possible that she hauled out before.

station astern. His steering gear was disabled, but fortunately he had installed a special fitting in case of emergency, and he was able to turn. Still he was in great difficulty; both engine-room telegraphs and all communications had been cut, and he had to con the ship from the engine-room hatchway.

After he had turned about 10 points to port, the cruiser, now on his starboard beam, again switched on searchlights and re-opened fire. The *Hardy* replied at less than 500 yards, and the gunner, who had orders to fire a torpedo when he saw a chance, seized his opportunity. Every one who saw the shot believed it got home. There was certainly an up-heaval of water alongside the enemy, her lights went out, she ceased fire and disappeared to the southward. So by her own exertions the *Hardy* saved herself from destruction, and the *Shark* (Commander Loftus W. Jones), who with the rear division had followed the *Hardy's* lead, quickly came to her assistance. As soon as he ascertained her plight he decided to stand by with all his division. But the *Hardy* was still undefeated, and was soon ready to proceed, steering with her engines. At 6.20 she took station astern of the *Spitfire*, which was rear ship, and course was shaped to regain station on the battle squadron. Somewhere ahead of them were the *Lynx* and *Unity*, holding on with the same intention. When a little after 6.0 the firing astern of them ceased, they could hear the crippled *Ambuscade* calling for a vessel to be told off to stand by her, and the *Lynx* had ordered the *Unity* to go to her assistance. The *Unity*, however, soon reported that she was cut off from the *Ambuscade* by a cruiser, and the *Lynx* could now (6.15) see three enemy cruisers on her starboard quarter. These ships challenged, and the *Lynx* replied with something like the signal which she had seen the first German destroyer make. Fortunately, it seemed to satisfy the new-comers, for they made off and disappeared to the eastward.

As for the *Lynx*, finding at daylight there was none of our squadron in sight, and that her injuries were too serious for her to carry on alone, she turned to the north-westward to proceed to Leith for repairs, with the *Unity* standing by.[1] The *Shark* division, however, was able to keep its formation, and held on at 25 knots, with the *Hardy* as rear ship, to resume station on the battle squadron.

To the flotilla officers it was now fairly clear that what they had run into was a screen of light cruisers and destroyers working to the north-westward, and that behind it was probably

---

[1] After seeing the *Lynx* out of danger the *Unity* was ordered to look for the *Ambuscade*, whom she found and brought safely into Leith.

a more serious force. Their appreciation was accurate. It is now known that the light cruiser which our destroyers had engaged was the *Hamburg*, one of the cruisers attached to the advanced screen of the enemy's battle fleet.[1] The torpedo which the *Hardy* fired at the *Hamburg* seems to have missed, while on her part the *Hamburg* incorrectly reported she had sunk a destroyer. In any case the bold attack by our destroyers had its effect. The presence of some of our flotilla units had been reported to Admiral von Ingenohl as early as 4.20 a.m., when a German destroyer in an advanced position sighted some of the destroyers which must have been those covering Admiral Warrender's port flank. The result was that when, about an hour and a quarter later, news of the destroyer engagement was received in the German flagship, the Admiral's apprehension of a torpedo attack increased. It still wanted two and a half hours to daylight, and mindful of his orders not to risk losses, he made a general signal for all squadrons to turn south-east. Even so he could not rest. A few minutes later he heard from the *Hamburg* of her encounter with our flotilla and then, finding that he had passed considerably beyond the arc from Terschelling to Horn Reef which defined the limit of the Bight, the courage with which he had hitherto strained his instructions gave way, and at 6.10, knowing nothing of the presence of our squadrons, he fairly turned tail and made for home, leaving his raiding force in the air.

Of all this we knew nothing till long afterwards. At the moment none of our cruisers even knew clearly what was happening to the flotilla. Since 5.30 the *Lion* had been feeling German wireless and seeing gun-flashes away to the north-eastward, but it was not till ten minutes later that a signal was received from the *Lynx* to say that she was chasing the first German destroyer. Admiral Beatty, therefore, carried on for the rendezvous, nor was it till nearly 7.0 that he heard the *Ambuscade* was in need of assistance. Still no change of course was made, nor, presumably to avoid using wireless, was any warning sent to the coast stations.

By this time the appreciation of the flotilla officers was being confirmed. At 6.50 the *Shark* division was again in touch with the enemy, and this time it was game that could not be ignored. The four destroyers were then coming down S. 30° E., and had just sighted smoke about three miles south-east on the port bow. They at once altered to close it, and by 7.0 could make out five destroyers, which they proceeded to chase to the eastward at 30 knots, with the *Hardy* gamely

---

[1] *Hamburg* (1902–3), 3,200 tons, trial speed 22 knots, guns 10–4·1".

keeping her station in spite of her injuries. When within 4,000 yards they opened fire. It was still an hour to daylight, and nothing could be seen beyond the faint outline of the destroyers. But in a few minutes they were surprised to see that close ahead of the ships they were chasing was a large cruiser which looked like the *Roon*.[1] She was steering an easterly course (N. 75° E.), and without a moment's hesitation the *Shark* led away eastwards to keep her in sight on the starboard bow. Though she was at first within 5,000 yards the cruiser did not open fire, possibly because she was unwilling to attract attention. So Commander Jones held boldly on, doing his best to get a signal through to Admiral Warrender.

It was not till nearly 7.30 that his message was received. By that time all four squadrons had reached the rendezvous, expecting to find there Commodore Tyrwhitt and his destroyers. Daylight was breaking serenely with a cloud-flecked blue sky and a calm sea. The visibility was all that a fine winter's morning could give, but he was nowhere to be seen. In fact he was still a hundred miles away, waiting for orders inside the banks off Yarmouth. It was therefore necessary to act without him, and as soon as the *Shark's* signal was received Admiral Warrender turned his squadron 8 points to port and began to zigzag to the eastward. At the same time Admiral Beatty, who had just sighted the battle squadron, but had not received the signal, turned back 16 points to the northward; this move was also in accordance with the pre-arranged plan; and he made it with the more confidence in that it brought his course into the direction from which for the last two hours signals had been coming in from the *Lynx* division that they were engaged with enemy destroyers and cruisers. So they held on for about half an hour, when, shortly before 8.0, Admiral Warrender signalled to his colleague, " Are you going after the *Roon ?* " Admiral Beatty replied that he had heard nothing about her, but in a few minutes he got the *Shark's* message and turned to the eastward at increased speed to cut off the enemy's big cruiser. Of this he informed Admiral Warrender (8.20), telling him he was proceeding with the battle and light cruisers, which latter were spread to the north of him, and leaving the 3rd Cruiser Squadron to keep with the battleships. With this Admiral Warrender concurred and said that he would conform, adding that he meant to retire north at 2.30, and that Admiral Beatty was not to go too far on his

[1] The *Roon* was of the *Yorck* type—9350 tons; 21·2 knots; 4–8·2", 8–5·9".

proposed course. Admiral Warrender then turned to the southward to get touch with the 3rd Cruiser Squadron, while Admiral Beatty, with his battle and light cruisers, carried on to the east-north-east at high speed to try to intercept the enemy, little thinking that he was chasing the whole German battle fleet.

In the meantime the situation of the shadowing destroyers had entirely changed. The weather conditions were no longer favourable, and, although it was still calm, there was a baffling mist which caused the visibility to vary continually between one mile and four.[1] About 7.40 it was so low that the destroyers had to close the chase still more in order to keep her in sight. Ten minutes later it cleared again, and they saw not only the *Roon*, but three light cruisers to the eastward which failed to answer the *Shark's* challenge.[2] The tables were now completely turned. The strange light cruisers at once began to chase them off the *Roon*, and it was no longer possible to shadow her. The only thing to do was to entice the enemy into the area of our own squadrons, and with this object the *Shark* led away to the north at 30 knots, turning gradually to port till they were going north-west, with the chasing cruisers on their starboard quarter. The pace soon proved too much for the crippled *Shark*, and at 8.15 the division slowed down to 25 knots. The *Shark* then signalled to the Admiral that they were being chased by three light cruisers, but long before the signal was received the enemy, as though fearing a snare, had given up the chase and turned back eastward towards the *Roon*. The destroyers held on, till by 8.35 they had lost sight of the enemy and were heading southward direct for the original rendezvous. A quarter of an hour later they became aware of our own light cruisers on their port bow making to the eastward, and they held away to join them. It was some time, however, before our cruisers, intent on their search for the *Roon*, were aware of them in the bad light, and it was twenty minutes before they were certain what to make of them.

In the meantime a new situation had arisen. Something —as yet it was not clear what—seemed to be happening on the Yorkshire coast. Just when the destroyers began to get sight of Commodore Goodenough's light cruisers, Admiral Warrender on his south-easterly course had got touch with the 3rd Cruiser Squadron, and at the same moment the wireless rooms of both Admirals took in a disturbing intercept. Over

---

[1] It would appear as though the weather conditions had been fairly good to the east of Long. 3° E., and very bad to the west of it. See Scheer, p. 72.

[2] They were probably those sighted previously by the *Lynx* and *Unity*.

150 miles away to the westward the *Patrol*, leader of the Hartlepool flotilla, was telling the Tyne guardship, *Jupiter*, that she was engaged with two enemy battle cruisers, and Admiral Warrender at once turned and made away north-westwards for the gap between the minefields—the shortest way to the threatened coast. Scarcely had he turned when at 8.55 an urgent message came in from the Admiralty, saying that, at 8.20, Scarborough was being shelled. A few minutes earlier Admiral Beatty had also intercepted the same report, but, serious as it was, he hesitated to abandon the chase of the *Roon*. It was only an intercept, and he knew some of the enemy were near him, for he had just received the *Shark's* signal of 8.15 that her division was being chased. Being as yet unaware that these destroyers had sighted his light cruisers, he seemed almost in touch with an enemy, and, feeling it his duty to go to the rescue, at 8.54 he turned to the northward. Scarcely had he done so when he also received the Admiralty message. With all doubt thus removed, he immediately turned west, so that, a few minutes after 9.0, all four squadrons were making at high speed for the new scene of action, and, on this course, the destroyers soon joined up.

The long-expected raid had, in fact, taken shape. A few minutes before 8.0 three ships, which were taken to be two battle cruisers and a light cruiser, suddenly appeared out of the mist off Scarborough. One of them with three funnels at once turned east-south-eastwards, and apparently made in the direction of Flamborough Head to lay a minefield as a protection against interference from the Humber and Harwich flotillas. In any case the existence of a new mine-field in this area was disclosed by the loss of three small steamers shortly afterwards.[1] The two larger ships, which were actually the battle cruisers *Derfflinger* and *Von der Tann*, turned south-eastward parallel to the coast, and at 8.0 opened fire on the coastguard station and some empty yeomanry barracks behind it.[2] There could be no doubt they did not believe the place was defended, for continuing to the southward they at once closed to within a mile of the shore, shelling the ruined castle and the Grand Hotel.[3] Pass-

---

[1] See *post*, p. 47. We now know from Admiral Scheer that minelaying in the coastwise track was one of the objects of the raid, and that the mines were laid by the light cruiser *Kolberg*.

[2] *Derfflinger*, 26,180 tons; 26·5 knots; 8–12″, 12–5·9.″ *Von der Tann*, 19,100 tons; 26 knots; 8–11″, 10–5·9.″

[3] According to Admiral Scheer the Germans had information there was a battery defending the place, but as it did not fire, he alleges they thought it had been evacuated.

ing the whole front without ceasing to fire, they then opened
a heavy bombardment on Falsgrave, a suburb of the town at
which there was a wireless station, but no damage was done
except to the neighbourhood and to the open country beyond.
Off the White Nab they turned north again and once more
began to distribute their broadsides indiscriminately all
over the town. Having thus indulged in their inexcusable
breach of the declared laws of maritime warfare for half an
hour, they disappeared in the mist to the north-east.[1]

This, however, was only half the raiding force. On nearing
the coast it had divided, and while part headed for Scarborough, the flagship *Seydlitz*, with the *Moltke* and *Blücher*,
turned more to the northward for Hartlepool. Here they
had more excuse, for it was a defended port with three 6″
guns, two on the headland north of the bay, known as The
Heugh, and one on the other side of the headland near the

---

[1] The bombardment was in direct breach of Convention No. 9 of the
Second Hague Conference. Chapter I provides as follows :—

I.—The bombardment by naval forces of undefended ports, towns,
villages, dwellings or buildings is forbidden.
A place may not be bombarded solely on the ground that automatic
submarine contact mines are anchored off the harbour.
II.—Military works, military or naval establishments, depôts of arms or
war material, workshops or plant which could be utilised for the needs of the
hostile fleet or army, and ships of war in the harbour, are not, however,
included in this prohibition. The commander of a naval force may destroy
them with artillery, after a summons followed by a reasonable interval of
time, if all other means are impossible, and when the local authorities have
not themselves destroyed them within the time fixed.
The commander incurs no responsibility for any unavoidable damage
which may be caused by a bombardment under such circumstances.
If for military reasons immediate action is necessary and no delay can
be allowed to the enemy, it is nevertheless understood that the prohibition
to bombard the undefended town holds good, as in the case given in the
first paragraph, and that the commander shall take all due measures in order
that the town may suffer as little harm as possible.
III.—After due notice has been given, the bombardment of undefended
ports, towns, villages, dwellings, or buildings may be commenced, if the local
authorities, on a formal summons being made to them, decline to comply
with requisitions for provisions or supplies necessary for the immediate use
of the naval force before the place in question.
Such requisitions shall be proportional to the resources of the place.
They shall only be demanded in the name of the commander of the said
naval force, and they shall, as far as possible, be paid for in ready money;
if not, receipts shall be given.
IV.—The bombardment of undefended ports, towns, villages, dwellings, or
buildings, on account of failure to pay money contributions, is forbidden.

Scarborough was clearly an undefended port within the meaning of the
Convention. For if a port may not be bombarded because automatic mines
defend it, *a fortiori* it cannot be bombarded because cavalry are encamped
in its vicinity.

lighthouse commanding the bay.[1] It was also a flotilla station, and the Germans were not able to reach it entirely undetected. For some time past, as we have seen, the East Coast patrol flotillas had had special warning to be on the alert at daybreak, but as Hartlepool is only a tidal harbour there was some difficulty in carrying out the order. It will be recalled that Captain Alan C. Bruce, who was Senior Naval Officer in the port, had under his command his own ship, the *Patrol*, and another patrol leader, the *Forward*, with a division of the 9th Flotilla (*Doon, Waveney, Test* and *Moy*), and submarine *C 9*. At 5.30 the destroyers had put to sea, but as they reported a heavy swell outside, which in the low state of the tide would make the bar dangerous, the light cruisers and submarine remained in the harbour ready to proceed at full speed. At eight o'clock, that is, just as the Scarborough bombardment began, and the two British Admirals were committed to the chase eastward in search of the *Roon*, the destroyers, who were patrolling five or six miles north-east of Hartlepool, became aware of three ships to the south-eastward standing direct inshore. Though it was nearly daylight the mist was too thick to make out what they were, and the destroyers, who were then heading southerly, increased speed to investigate. Five minutes later the strangers opened fire, and they were seen to be two battle cruisers, *Seydlitz* and *Moltke*, and a heavy cruiser, which was the *Blücher*.[2] As the destroyers were well out of torpedo range, and the salvoes began to straddle them almost at once, a daylight attack seemed impossible. They therefore turned away, scattered and made off to the north-eastward. By skilful manœuvring they were all able to baffle the enemy's gunlayers, but three of them were hit by fragments of large shells that burst on contact with water, before in about a quarter of an hour they ran out of sight into the mist. In the meantime, the *Seydlitz* and *Moltke*, when about 4,000 yards from the shore, had turned to the northward, and steaming slowly up the coast began to engage the Heugh battery, while the *Blücher*, stopping opposite the harbour, fired at the gun near the lighthouse. As the batteries were on the alert they immediately replied.

In the harbour Captain Bruce, the moment he got the alarm, had begun to work the *Patrol* out of the basin under fire, for shells were already falling about the docks, which were in the line of fire of the enemy ships. Possibly, therefore,

---

[1] See Plan p. 34.
[2] *Seydlitz*, 24,600 tons; 26·7 knots; 10–11″, 12–5·9″.
  Moltke, 22,640 tons; 27 knots; 10–11″, 12–5·9″.
  Blücher, 15,500 tons; 25 knots; 12–8·2″, 8–5·9″.

they were only overs, but by the time he opened the fairway he found it and the entrance alive with bursting shell. The two battle cruisers were passing successively beyond the arc of fire of the Heugh battery, and when its guns could no longer bear, the enemy lengthened his range and began firing salvoes at the docks and harbour entrance. The result was that the *Forward* was greatly delayed in getting out, and the *Patrol* found herself faced with a barrage fire between her and the sea. Whether it was so intended by the enemy in order to prevent the submarine getting out is uncertain; but there it was, and without a moment's hesitation Captain Bruce put on full speed to make a dash for it, while close on his heels came Lieutenant C. L. Y. Dering in submarine *C 9*. For a time neither was hit, but as soon as the *Patrol* was far enough out to bring the *Blücher* into sight she was struck twice by heavy shell. In another minute or so the two battle cruisers could see her and the submarine, and both began to fire on them. As the salvoes straddled *C 9* at once, she was forced to dive, though it was nearly low water and there were only three fathoms on the bar. She bumped, but managed to scrape over. The *Patrol* had already taken the ground hard and seemed doomed.

But the Germans were not having it all their own way. Although, owing to the bad visibility and the clouds of dust thrown up by the enemy's shells as they hit the houses in rear of the battery, laying was very difficult, the Heugh battery was hitting the *Moltke*, and the lighthouse gun had been making such good practice on the *Blücher* that she had moved northwards out of its arc of fire. But this only brought her within the bearing of the Heugh battery, which since the two battle cruisers had moved to the northward had nothing to do. Only too glad to find a new target, it at once opened on her with spirit and accuracy. Shell after shell burst on her superstructure, till she was forced to turn away to the eastward. The two battle cruisers at once ceased fire, turned back to the rescue and re-opened on the Heugh battery to cover the *Blücher's* retreat. But not for long. After a few rounds, which again failed to find the battery, they too, about 8.50, turned away after their damaged consort. It was too late for the submarine to attack, nor could the *Forward*, who was just out of harbour, and was ordered to follow them, succeed in regaining touch. By 9.0 they had completely disappeared in the mist to the eastward— just as our four squadrons to seaward were heading westward to meet them.

The military damage they had done was small. None of

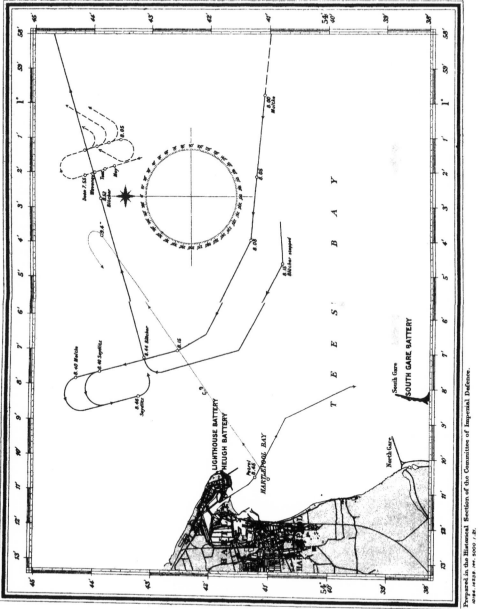

TEES BAY

LIGHTHOUSE BATTERY
HEUGH BATTERY
HARTLEPOOL BAY
SOUTH GARE BATTERY

South Gare
North Gare

the guns was struck, though the Durham Garrison Artillery, who had worked them, and the 18th Durham Light Infantry, who manned the defences, lost nine killed and twelve wounded. Thanks moreover to their promptness and good shooting the navy suffered as little. Neither the *Forward* nor the submarine was touched, but had it not been for the fine work of the batteries the *Patrol* when she took the ground could scarcely have escaped destruction. As it was, though badly holed and too deep in the water to recross the bar, she was able to reach the Tees in safety.[1]

On the other hand, the civil damage was serious. The casualties amongst the townsfolk and seamen in the harbour were no less than 86 killed and 424 wounded. Structural damage, especially in the central business part of the town, was extensive. In all seven churches, ten public buildings, five hotels and some 300 houses were more or less injured. In the docks and shipyards three ships were hit and the buildings and marine engine works damaged.

Nor did the mischief end here, for the raid was not yet over. After the southern group of the enemy had done their work at Scarborough, they steamed north to rejoin the Hartle-pool group. A few minutes after 9.0 the *Derfflinger* and *Von der Tann* appeared off Whitby from the southward and fired about fifty rounds at the signal station and town. This place also was entirely without defence, but in ten minutes they made off in an obvious hurry, for they left unmolested two tramp steamers that were passing southward at the time. As we have seen, it was about half an hour before these ships ceased fire, and just when the Hartlepool group was disappearing into the mist to rejoin them, that the British squadrons headed at high speed for Scarborough, and it looked as if nothing short of a miracle could prevent the enemy running into their arms through the unmined channel. The opposing battle cruisers can only have been about 150 miles apart, and in a little over three hours they should come into contact.

Meanwhile, Admiral Jellicoe, after making an exhaustive study of all mines reported, was coming to the conclusion that there was a clear gap in his declared danger area between latitudes 54° 40′ and 54° 20′ N., that is, opposite Whitby. He judged it to be about twenty miles broad and to extend from his danger line to Long. 0° 20′ E., that is, to a mean distance of twenty miles from the land. As soon as he heard that the enemy were on the coast, he felt fairly sure that they

---

[1] Her losses were four killed and seven wounded. The *Doon* lost three killed and six wounded. The other ships had no casualties.

would make off through this corridor; there was, however, a possibility they might keep up the coast inside the mine-fields and get back round the north of them. He therefore ordered Admiral Bradford to take the 3rd Battle Squadron from Rosyth to a rendezvous fifty miles east of the Firth of Forth.

Commodore Tyrwhitt had also got the alarm, and at 8.40 started for Scarborough with his four light cruisers and both his flotillas. His intention was to go out through the Hais-borough Gat; but, as soon as he was clear of the shoals, he found the sea so steep and short that, with the wind blow-ing strong to a gale from nearly ahead, he felt compelled to order the destroyers back to Yarmouth, and proceed with his four light cruisers alone.

Meanwhile, Admirals Warrender and Beatty, having continued their converging course, had come together again, and shortly after 9.30 were both proceeding to the west-ward, but neither Admiral as yet knew anything of the Hartle-pool bombardment. The battle cruisers were ahead and the light cruisers still spread to the north of them, for Admiral Beatty was still unaware that the enemy's light cruisers had long given up the chase of the destroyers, and his main concern for the moment was that they should not get sight of him. Commodore Goodenough, therefore, had orders to drive them off if they appeared.

This was the position when a signal was intercepted telling that Hartlepool was being bombarded as well as Scarborough, and, the message said, by three Dreadnoughts. It was clear, therefore, that large operations were taking place on the coast, and the enemy were apparently moving northward. The two British Admirals could no longer be in any doubt that the *Roon* and the light cruisers to the northward should be let alone. The problem with which they were confronted was to devise, immediately, a plan for intercepting the enemy off our coasts. They knew that he must then be considerably more than 100 miles away, and that he had, in consequence, ample opportunities of evasion. But, at the moment, a solution came from the Commander-in-Chief. At 10.10 a signal from him was received informing them of the corridor which seemed to exist in the danger area, and intimating that the enemy would probably retire through it.[1] It was evident, then, that the best intercepting position must now be where the corridor

---

[1] The signal was worded as follows: " *From* C.-in-C. H.F.   *To* S.O. 2nd B.S.; S.O. 1st B.C.S.   Gap in minefield between parallel Lat. 54° 40′ and 54° 20′, and as far as 20′ E. Long.   Enemy will in all probability come out there."

debouched on the danger line.   The difficulty was that their
course to it was not quite clear.   Right off the mouth of
the gap lay the south-west patch of the Dogger Bank,
and much of it in such a sea as was running was unsafe,
at least for the battle cruisers, and both wind and sea were
increasing.   It had to be passed either to the north or south,
and if they went one way the enemy might well escape the
other.   Admiral Beatty had already informed Admiral Warrender that he would have to haul more to the north in order
to clear the patch, as the enemy seemed to be moving up
the coast.   After receiving this message, Admiral Warrender
altered course for the south of the patch, but on the vague and
apparently contradictory information they had intercepted
there was still some doubt if this was the best course to
pursue.   Some of the messages gave a different picture of
what the enemy was doing.   To Admiral Warrender it
appeared that his Dreadnoughts must be off Scarborough,
and his light cruisers at Hartlepool; and he was still
discussing with his colleague the surest means of getting
contact when, about 10.55, they got direct information
from the Admiralty as to what the real facts were.   The
message informed them that the enemy had retired from
the coast and were probably making for Heligoland, and
that they were to keep outside the minefields and try to
cut them off.   On this it was clear that each Admiral was
doing the right thing on a wrong inference.   Admiral
Beatty therefore carried on for the north of the patch,
with his light cruisers spread before his starboard beam,
while Admiral Warrender continued his course for the south
of it and ordered his cruisers to spread to the south of him.
He also called up Commodore Tyrwhitt to meet him in the
southern entrance to the gap (Lat. 54° 20′, Long. 1° 30′ E.),
and with the 3rd Battle Squadron blocking the line of escape
northward it seemed almost impossible for the enemy to get
away unfought.

Indeed, before long it began to look as if the disposition
had succeeded.   By 11.0 Admiral Beatty was clear of the
north edge of the patch, and, slowing down to let his cruiser
screen get well ahead of him on a broad front, he altered direct
for the gap; but the bad conditions of weather off the
coast were making themselves felt, and, by this time, the
wind and sea had increased considerably.   Although the
visibility was rapidly falling, he became aware, in half an
hour's time, that the left wing of his light cruisers was
engaged on his port bow.   The wing ship was the *Southampton*, in which Commodore Goodenough was flying

his broad pennant. At 11.25, being between three and four miles ahead of the *Lion,* he had sighted an enemy cruiser and seven or eight destroyers crossing his course to the southward about three miles away. By this time the visibility was very bad; a strong wind, moreover, was blowing in his teeth, and spray and seas were drenching the forecastle. Under such conditions it was practically hopeless to fight an enemy dead to windward. The Commodore therefore turned to starboard to improve the position; and seeing the enemy continued to the southward, he turned to the same course and opened fire with the chase well on his weather bow. As he did so he signalled (11.30) to his squadron to close, and to Admiral Beatty that he was engaged with a light cruiser and destroyers. The *Birmingham* had already turned to join the chase, and the *Nottingham* and *Falmouth* did so as soon as they received the Commodore's signal. After the chase had continued for nearly a quarter of an hour, with no result, owing to the difficulty of the weather, the Commodore at 11.44 again signalled to Admiral Beatty that he was engaged, adding that the enemy were running south. This information was taken in by the *Lion* three minutes later, and in another three minutes the *Lion* was signalling by searchlight " Light cruisers —resume your position for look-out. Take station ahead five miles." This, however, it would seem, did not express Admiral Beatty's intention. The signal was directed to the *Nottingham,* and was intended for her and the right wing cruiser *Falmouth* only. He was convinced that the best chance of bringing the enemy's battle cruisers to action lay in preventing the German light forces from detecting his presence. It was with this purpose in view that he decided to retain two ships of his screen, knowing that Commodore Goodenough would not require their support, owing to the presence of the 3rd Cruiser Squadron further south.

The *Nottingham,* however, as the signal was addressed to the light cruisers, passed it on in the ordinary course, and the result was that Commodore Goodenough, having just signalled that he was engaged with the enemy, felt there was no course but to obey. This he did the more reluctantly, for he had just sighted two more enemy cruisers to the southwest. Still his main function had been discharged, for he had driven the enemy's look-outs away from the front of the battle cruisers, and the newly-sighted vessels were well away, and apparently making direct for the position which Admiral Warrender's cruisers were to take up. As he turned, however, he sighted yet another light cruiser, which he took to be the

Prinz Adalbert,[1] bearing south by east, and this about noon he signalled to the Admiral. Still the recall was not negatived, and he accordingly held on to resume his look-out station. In fact he was almost in visual touch with the flagship. Since 11.54 the battle cruisers had been steering down towards him, for in order to avoid a fleet of trawlers, for fear they might be enemy minelayers, Admiral Beatty had turned to the southward. At 12.5 he resumed his westerly course, and about ten minutes later the *Southampton* was sighted. Admiral Beatty did not yet appreciate that the enemy were lost, but a rapid interchange of signals explained the position. The supposed *Prinz Adalbert* had been dropped in the mist, and the Commodore could only reply to his queries "No enemy in sight." And then, and not till then, did he know that the recall had been intended for the *Nottingham* and *Falmouth* only.

The whole episode was another stroke of extraordinary luck for the enemy. The ships which had been encountered were part of the light forces attached to the German battle cruisers. The intention was that they should take part in the bombardment; but at 6.0 a.m., when they reached the zone of bad weather, they reported that, owing to the steep, short seas, it was impossible to carry on, and Admiral Hipper had ordered them all, with the exception of the *Kolberg*, to rejoin the main fleet. In this way it happened that they were far ahead of the battle cruisers when the retirement began, and thus it was that, owing to the poor sea-going qualities of his light cruisers, and to no foresight of his own, Admiral Hipper got news almost immediately that there was something in his path to be avoided; and this timely warning, combined with the low visibility, gave him the one and only chance of making good his escape. But our dispositions were still in favour of bringing him to action, and touch was almost immediately recovered. For just as the *Southampton* was resuming her look-out station ahead of the *Lion*, Admiral Warrender had got up to within fifteen miles of his intercepting station. His intention on reaching it—that is, at 12.30—was to shift his cruiser line from the south to the north-westward of him and to establish a patrol with his whole force off the south entrance of the gap. He had just given the order when, at 12.15, he was suddenly aware of some cruisers and destroyers on his starboard bow. They were proceeding on the opposite course to himself at high speed. How many or what they were it was impossible to tell. They could merely be seen from time to time as they ran out of one rain squall and disappeared into another,

---

[1] Probably the *Stralsund*, which he had first sighted.

but they must have been the same with which our light cruisers had just lost contact. Evidently as soon as Commodore Goodenough, after receiving the recall signal, had left them, they had turned to the eastward, in which direction they were now making off. The chance of catching them was now very small, for Admiral Warrender's cruisers were still spread to the south of him and away from the enemy. All he could do was to turn his battleships north-eastward to try to cut off the newly-sighted vessels, and to order his cruisers to follow his movements and get ahead of him.

The news of what was happening quickly reached Admiral Beatty, who was then some twelve miles to the northward on the other side of the patch. More firmly convinced than ever that he must soon run into anything the enemy had behind the screen he had disturbed, he was still pressing to the westward for the middle of the gap, when, at 12.25, he received from Admiral Warrender a signal that " enemy cruisers and destroyers were in sight," and then another that he had turned north-easterly to engage them. Admiral Beatty at once (12.30) turned back 16 points to port and ran east to make sure of getting to seaward of the enemy's battle cruisers. Meanwhile the comparatively slow cruisers of the 3rd Squadron had been straining every nerve to get ahead of the battle squadron, and trying, in response to an order from the Admiral, to cover it by attacking the enemy's destroyers. But all their efforts were in vain. Seeing themselves chased the enemy turned away to port to escape across the patch. Though the Admiral pursued at his utmost speed the glimpses of them grew more fitful, and in twenty-five minutes, before his cruisers could get into position or the battleships fire a gun, the enemy were completely lost in the thickening mist.

What was now to be done? In ten minutes Admiral Warrender had seen enough of the enemy to make sure there were no battle cruisers among them, and this he then signalled to Admiral Beatty. The ships that had carried out the bombardment were therefore probably still to the westward, and in that direction Admiral Warrender at once turned (12.40). For twenty minutes he held this course and then altered to the south in order to resume his original station for barring the southern outlet from the gap. On hearing that this was his intention Admiral Beatty had little doubt as to the correlative movement he should make. Since the German light cruisers must have seen the battle squadron to the south, the battle cruisers would almost certainly try to get away to the north of the patch. At 1.15, therefore, when on his easterly course he had got back to the shoal, he led to the northward, keeping his light cruisers spread to the westward.   He fully shared Admiral Warrender's view that the German battle cruisers must still be in that direction, and by this time further light had been obtained by two signals which Admiral Ballard had made.

At the first alarm he had put to sea in the *Skirmisher* with the Humber flotilla, but finding the torpedo-boats which composed it could not face the sea that was running, he had sent them in again and come north alone.   He was now off Flamborough Head, and his first signal (received at 12.40) was that there was no enemy between him and the Humber.   Then came a second to say that all the German ships had steered east from the neighbourhood of Whitby and Filey Bay at about 9.0 a.m., and had not since reappeared. This signal Admiral Beatty received at 1.18, and ten minutes later he informed Commodore Goodenough that he intended to continue north at 15 knots until he was clear of the patch, and then turn to the westward again, and as the enemy, in his opinion, must still be to the westward, he wished the light cruisers to extend further from him in that direction.   Judging from the time the enemy had left the coast, they should be very near him, and keeping on as he was, he felt fairly certain he must soon find himself cutting across their course.   He was, therefore, still going north when at 1.43 he took in a signal from the shore saying that the enemy battle cruisers had been located an hour and a half previously about a dozen miles short of the outlet of the gap, and that they were then steering east by south at about 23 knots. The situation thus indicated was difficult to understand. The course mentioned seemed to be necessarily an error, for it led right over the patch, and this was a risk Admiral Beatty considered the enemy would not venture to take. The probability, therefore, was that they were making to escape to southward—and this seemed to him almost a certainty, since his cruisers had not met with them to the northward.   Still there was doubt, and the golden rule in an operation of this kind, when a retreating enemy was to be intercepted, is to make sure of keeping between him and his base.   It was on this principle that he had turned back when at 12.30 he learnt that Admiral Warrender had sighted the enemy to the westward of him.   On this principle he again decided to act, and at 1.55 he turned eastward and began working round the outside of the patch, till in half an hour he was going S. 60° E. at 25 knots on a course which converged with the line between the southern outlet and Heligoland Bight.

Meanwhile Admiral Warrender had reached the southern

limit of the gap without meeting anything. It was clear, therefore, the enemy had no mind to escape that way, and at 1.24 he turned north. In this movement he was confirmed when, twenty minutes later, he received the shore message giving the position and course of the German battle cruisers at 12.15. Had they continued that course he must have sighted them, and as he had not done so he concluded they had turned to the northward, and he held on as he was. Both Admirals were keenly expecting further information. But time went by and nothing came, nor was it till 3.20 that they had any further light. Then a message from shore was taken in saying that at 12.45 the enemy had turned north when they were close to the southern outlet, just as Admiral Warrender had assured himself the battle cruisers were not with the ships he had sighted making away across the patch. Admiral Beatty, still with a faint hope of cutting across the enemy's homeward course, turned to the northward. But all was of no avail. Neither he nor his colleague could find a trace of what they were so eagerly seeking, and by the luck of the weather had so narrowly missed.

How the German battle cruisers got away is now fairly certain. From various sources it appears that they must have been about fifty miles to the westward when Commodore Goodenough got into touch with their returning light cruisers, which, quite by accident, acted as a far advanced screen. When he forced them southwards, the German battle cruisers must have inclined away to starboard towards the southern outlet in the corridor, for, at 12.45 they were located close to it. But, finding that Admiral Warrender was blocking the way, they appear to have turned north, half an hour or so before Admiral Beatty did the same. They must, therefore, have got away ahead of him. Indeed between 2.30 and 3.30 they were seen by two British trawlers some twenty-five miles to the north of the patch, steering eastward at high speed. About 3.0 Admiral Warrender must have been over twenty miles south of them, heading to cross their wake, while Admiral Beatty was forty-five miles to the south-eastward of them on a diverging course.

Till 3.30 the search was continued, the battle squadron steering north and the battle and light cruisers continuing their sweep to seaward. By that time Admiral Warrender was well past the northern limit of the gap, and as it was now only too evident that the enemy must have stolen away in the mist, he signalled (3.47) to Admiral Beatty to discontinue the search and rejoin him to the northward next day.

The meaning of this was that at about 1.50 it had become

known to the Admiralty that at 12.30 the High Seas Fleet was out, some seventy or eighty miles north-west of Heligoland. It was to this point its retirement had brought it, but to the Admiralty it seemed it was putting to sea. A concentration of the whole Grand Fleet, including the Harwich Force, had therefore been ordered, in the hope of bringing them to action next morning. Admiral Jellicoe was already at sea; shortly after noon he had left Scapa with his two remaining battle squadrons for a rendezvous which he had fixed midway between Aberdeen and the Skagerrak, where, as soon as he knew that the raiders had got away, he ordered his whole fleet to meet him at daybreak. The concentration duly took place as arranged, and he then moved south-east feeling for the High Seas Fleet, but before he had proceeded fifty miles towards the Bight he was informed by the Admiralty of wireless indications which made it fairly certain that the High Seas Fleet had gone back to harbour, and after spending a couple of hours in tactical exercises with the whole fleet he turned to the northward for Scapa and dispersed the squadrons to their stations.

So ended this remarkable incident. In all the war there is perhaps no action which gives deeper cause for reflection on the conduct of operations at sea. On our own side the disappointment was profound. Two of the most efficient and powerful British squadrons, with an adequate force of scouting vessels, knowing approximately what to expect, and operating in an area strictly limited by the possibilities of the situation, had failed to bring to action an enemy who was operating in close conformity with our appreciation and with whose advanced screen contact had been established. Our own general dispositions for intercepting the raiders were as admirable as ripe judgment could achieve. If any exception can be taken to them it is that too much reliance was placed upon the negative evidence as to the quiescence of the High Seas Fleet. We had reason to expect the raid would be made by cruisers only, and the possibility of its being supported in force was not adequately provided for. Admiral Jellicoe was not therefore moved down in support of our counter-dispositions, but this in no way affects the merit of his own disposal of our intercepting force.

It can now be seen that that was perfectly correct, and that what caused it to fail was primarily the movement which Admiral Beatty made to the eastward at 12.30 p.m. But this movement was equally inspired by the soundest principles of war. Seeing how impenetrable a cloud the weather had cast over the scene of action at the critical moment, and

how uncertain was the situation of Admiral Warrender, the
was nothing to do—by all tradition—but to make sure
keeping between the enemy and his home base.   It was,
fact, upon that well-tried principle that the whole dispositi
had been based.   But for the fear of missing the retiri
raiders in the mist he would certainly have pressed on in
the gap, and could then scarcely have failed to bring them
decisive action.   It was a chance of the sea beyond hum
calculation.

On the German side—though much was made in pub
of the bombardments—the chagrin was even greater,
least amongst the more ardent spirits in the navy.   " (
December 16," wrote Admiral von Tirpitz about three wee
later, " Ingenohl had the fate of Germany in the palm
his hand.   I boil with inward emotion whenever I think
it."   Similarly Admiral Scheer, " Our premature turning
the east-south-east course had robbed us of the opportunity
meeting certain divisions of the enemy according to the p
arranged plan which is now seen to have been correct.   .
all events the restrictions enforced on the Commander-i
Chief of the fleet brought about the failure of the bold a
promising plan. . . . At 7.0 a.m. the two main fleets we
only about fifty miles apart.[1]   It is extremely probable th
if we had continued in our original direction the courses
the two fleets would have crossed within sight of each oth
during the morning."

It must be admitted that there was at least a chan
of the Germans so dealing with two detached squadro
as to bring the Grand Fleet and the High Seas Fleet to
least something like equality.   It is to be observed, howeve
that it was not Admiral von Ingenohl's orders that caus
him to turn back when he did, but the fear of destroy
attack in the dark.   Orders or no orders, this reason wou
presumably have made him turn back till daylight.   Abo
four hours would thus have been lost, but even so he mig
have gained contact early in the afternoon, when the Rosy
battle squadron would have been about 150 miles to t
northward, and the rest of the Grand Fleet only just leavi
Scapa.   On the other hand, the British squadrons had
considerable advantage of speed which might well ha
enabled them to close on the Rosyth squadron had th
chosen to do so.[2]

[1] That is : 6.0 a.m. Greenwich Mean Time.
[2] Our 2nd Battle Squadron had a seagoing full speed of 19 knots.
Admiral von Ingenohl's fleet only his four " Kaisers " had as much—
other sixteen ships were several knots slower.

The situation is therefore too full of vague possibilities and indeterminate factors to allow of a final judgment, and each man must decide for himself whether or not Admiral von Ingenohl, but for his orders, had this day the fate of Germany in his hands.

The information which the Admiralty had sent to Admiral Jellicoe and closed his operations was true. The German battle squadrons had got back to port untouched, but the raiding force had a narrow escape. Till the very last they were in danger. When the operations began Commodore R. J. B. Keyes, on Admiralty orders, was forming a line of submarines off Terschelling.[1] About daylight on the 16th they were in position, and there they remained till about 10.30 a.m., when the Commodore intercepted a faint signal that the enemy were off Scarborough. It was at once obvious that his position was useless for intercepting them on their return, and the Commodore, being out of wireless distance, sent away the *Firedrake* to get touch with Yarmouth and ask the Admiralty for instructions. Meanwhile he proceeded to collect his submarines in readiness to act as soon as new orders arrived. At 3.35 p.m. they reached him, and, as he anticipated, their purport was that he was to take his submarines into the Bight and lie in wait for the retiring enemy. As the submarines were submerged he had great difficulty in finding them, and by 5.0 p.m. he had collected no more than four, *E 10, 11, 15* and the *Archimède*. These he sent into the Bight with orders to form a line from north-west to south-west of Heligoland and himself continued to search for the rest till the weather became too bad to give any hope of success, when he went off to the North Hinder lightship to intercept them as they would be returning.

The result of his dispositions was that shortly after 7.0 a.m. on December 17, Lieutenant-Commander M. E. Nasmith in *E 11*, which had the southernmost station in the line off the Weser, became aware of a number of destroyers searching at high speed in all directions. An hour later he could see to the north-eastward two ships coming down from inside Heligoland. They can only have been the leading ships of Admiral Hipper's squadron which he was bringing into the Jade. He at once made for them, and though they were at very wide intervals and zigzagging independently, he succeeded in getting within 400 yards of the leading ship and firing a torpedo. Unhappily, owing apparently to the boat rolling heavily in the

---

[1] He was in the destroyer *Lurcher* and also had the *Firedrake*. The submarines with him were *E 2, 7, 8, 10, 11, 12, 15* and the French *Archimède.*

short steep sea that was running, the torpedo ran too deep and missed. Attention was at once turned to the third ship of the squadron, but just as *E 11* got within 500 yards of her she turned in course of zigzagging dead for her. A very rapid dive was imperative to avoid being rammed. It was successfully accomplished, but unhappily the extensive flooding that it entailed disturbed the trim, and on coming up to a proper depth for renewing the attack she broke the surface and was seen. In a moment the German squadron had scattered. Increasing speed they raced round the unlucky boat beyond her danger area, and in spite of a daring effort to cut off the last ship they all disappeared into the rivers untouched. As the Germans had come down inside Heligoland, none of the other submarines saw anything, and though the three British boats remained out another day they had to return empty-handed. So it was that the luck of the weather clung to us, and in spite of Commodore Keyes's prompt action there was nothing to relieve the impression which the unpunished raid necessarily created.

It was over two centuries since anything like it had occurred upon our shores, and not since De Ruyter's raid on Sheerness had a foreign enemy killed British troops on English soil. Still it must be said that the country bore the blow with exemplary fortitude. With the nation at large the prevailing note was one of stern resentment at the shameless breach of the laws of civilised warfare. An open seaside resort had been ruthlessly shelled, a crowded seaport with slender defence had been bombarded without the notice which the Hague Convention prescribed, and the effect was rather to intensify the popular conviction that a people capable of such barbarity could not be permitted to escape chastisement. If, as was supposed at the time, the main idea of the enemy was to intimidate, the actual result was to harden the war spirit.

Materially, the most disturbing result of the raid was the minefield which the German light cruiser had laid. Whether or not the enemy's chief object in laying it was to entrap ships acting against them and to cover the retirement of the raiding force, what they actually achieved was a serious interference with our coastwise traffic and an increased pressure on our hard-worked North Sea minesweepers. Hitherto these flotillas had only had to keep clear a swept channel from the Downs to Flamborough Head—that is, inside the minefields which the Germans had laid off the Eastern counties and the Humber, and which we had purposely left intact. Now the channel had to be continued northwards past Scarborough, and until it was swept all navigation between the Tyne and Flamborough Head had to be stopped. The minefield was particularly difficult to locate. It was only known by the loss of passing coasters, and the work of clearing a channel past it is typical of the unceasing drudgery by which the devoted minesweepers contributed so much and so obscurely to the war.

In order to ascertain how the mines lay, it was necessary to work in all states of the tide, with a consequent increase of danger from those near the surface. Three days after the raid (December 19), the three minesweeping gunboats, *Skipjack*, *Gossamer* and *Jason*, in charge of Commander L. G. Preston of the *Skipjack*, began sweeping from Flamborough Head, but nothing was found till they were off Scarborough, when two mines were caught in the sweep of the *Skipjack* and *Gossamer*. Having found them they made for the harbour. The trawlers were then at work south-east of the bay, and when the *Skipjack* came up with them, one (*Orianda*) was blown up close alongside her and two others were damaged by mines. The *Skipjack* was obviously in extreme danger, but with prompt resource Commander Preston anchored where he was and proceeded to destroy mines all round him as the trawlers brought them to the surface.[1]

Under Commander R. H. Walters, R.N., the sweeping was carried on till the end of the year. To assist him in the difficult work, he was given the *Halcyon* and eight drifters from Lowestoft—in all he had fourteen trawlers and twelve drifters. He reported the whole water to be thickly mined, and day after day the dangerous work went on, varied only by the still more hazardous duty of rescue. On December 20, Admiral C. J. Barlow, who was then serving as a Commander, R.N.R., in command of the armed yacht *Valiant*, and was on his way to Cromarty, had the propellers and rudder of his vessel blown off. Two trawlers were ordered to his assistance, and, though it was low water, they fearlessly went straight through the minefield to the rescue and brought him safely into Scarborough.[2] The same day the patrol trawler *Garmo* was sunk off the town with the loss of an officer and five men. By Christmas eve the swept channel was complete as far as

[1] For his courageous and well-judged action Commander Preston was commended and afterwards promoted, and a General Order was issued recommending his action as an example to be followed in similar circumstances.

[2] Admiral Barlow was only one of a score of retired flag officers who in the early part of the war volunteered their services, and in a never-to-be-forgotten spirit accepted commissions as Captains or Commanders R.N.R. for service with the auxiliary forces. Generally they served in command of armed yachts and in charge of trawler units, or were appointed Senior Naval Officers at patrol bases.

Scarborough, but there was still more to do.   On Christmas morning the minesweeping trawler *Night Hawk* was blown up off Whitby and foundered with a loss of six men.   Further south two merchant steamers were struck, one the Norwegian s.s. *Gallier*, and in assisting her the drifter and trawler skippers gave a fine example of their devotion.   In spite of heavy weather two drifters, the *Hilda and Ernest* and the *Eager*, stood by her till she sank, and the trawler *Solon*, though it was dark and low water and the injured vessel showed no lights, proceeded to search for her in the minefield.   From now onward the channel was declared safe in daylight, and some fifty steamers that had accumulated in the Humber were allowed to proceed.   By the end of the year the work of buoying the extended channel began, but till well into January losses of trawlers and vessels continued.   When the buoying was complete there still remained for the mine-sweepers and patrols the unceasing work in all weathers of keeping free the East Coast channel, which was now 500 miles long.   Further south, and particularly about the Straits of Dover, where the heavy winter weather and strong tides were always setting both our own and the German mines adrift, the work was particularly arduous.   The Irish mine-field, moreover, which the *Berlin* had laid off Tory Island, was still unswept.   Week by week, as the weather permitted, the trawlers worked at it, many mines were destroyed, yet on December 19 the liner *Tritonia* was sunk within a few miles of the spot where the loss of the *Manchester Commerce* first revealed the existence of the danger.

It is difficult to gain a full impression of all the toil and danger, the skill and devotion which went to make up what minesweeping flotillas were giving to the common cause. Their part was but the sober background against which the more conspicuous exploits of the navy are thrown into relief, yet, if we would grasp what the sea service gave, we must never forget how that background was being worked in patiently, incessantly, stroke by stroke, in fair weather and in foul, with the old tasks never complete and new ones constantly being set.   Nor must we fail to remember that all this grim fishing was over and above the hunt for submarines, for which, as we have seen, a special and vast organisation was just coming into operation as fast as the innumerable trawlers and drifters could be fitted with guns and gear. We have been taught to be proud of how in days gone by the sea spirit of the nation answered the call at the hour of danger, but never in all our long story had there been such an answer as this.

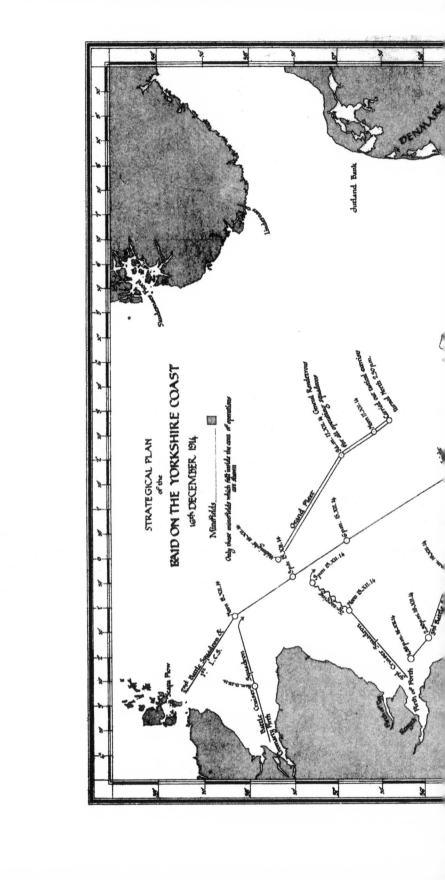

STRATEGICAL PLAN
of the
RAID ON THE YORKSHIRE COAST
16th DECEMBER 1914

Minefields ▄▄▄▄▄

Only those minefields which lay inside the area of operations
are shewn

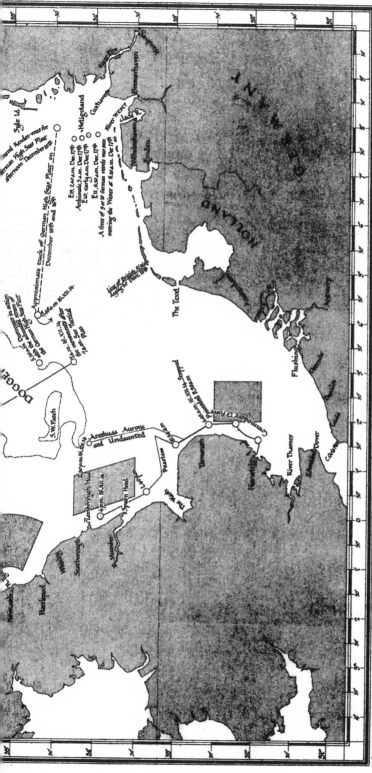

General Rendez-vous for German High-Seas Fleet afternoon December 15th

track of German High-Seas Fleet on December 15th and 16th

E8. 7.40 a.m. Dec.16th
Arethusa, 5 a.m. Dec.16th
E10. early a.m.Dec.16th
E11. 6.30 a.m. Dec.16th

A force of 3 or 19 German vessels was seen entering the Weser at 8 a.m. on Dec 16th

River WESER
Jade R.

Wilhelmshaven

Cuxhaven

Heligoland

Sylt Id.

G E R M A N Y

HOLLAND

The Texel

Line of British Fleet Light Cruisers on Dec 16th

Flushing

River Scheldt

River Thames

Harwich

Dover

Ostend

Calais

Beachy Head

DOGGER

S.W.Patch

Arethusa Aurora and Undaunted

Scarborough

Flamborough Head

Spurn Head

The Wash

Prepared in the Historical Section of the Committee of Imperial Defence.

Malby & Sons, Lith.

CHAPTER III

HOME WATERS, DECEMBER 18 TO JANUARY 13—FURTHER PRE-
CAUTIONS AGAINST INVASION—LOSS OF THE *FORMIDABLE*
—REVISION OF THE WAR PLAN—BELGIUM AND THE
DARDANELLES

ALTHOUGH the long-expected activity of the enemy at
sea had taken the form of a purely naval, and not a combined
operation, the intelligence which continued to come in made
it impossible to relax the measures taken to stop an attempt
to land troops on our coasts. Seeing how narrowly the
enemy's squadron had escaped destruction in the northern
area, there was an increased probability that any further
attempt to invade would be made in the southern area.

Here the arrangements that it had been possible to make
looked more unsatisfactory than ever. They were based
on the old idea that an inferior fleet by bold offensive action
might render a superior one incapable of further mischief
even if it were itself annihilated. But on December 9 had
been received the news of the Falklands victory, confirming
the lesson of Coronel that our time-honoured belief was no
longer tenable. It was pointed out how the two actions left
little doubt that under modern conditions the normal result
of an action between two unequal squadrons would be that
the one with inferior speed and gun-power would be destroyed
by the one that was faster and more powerfully armed, without
being able to inflict upon the enemy any material damage.
It was further urged that the destruction of a squadron
detailed for stopping an invading force would have a very
serious effect on the spirit of the nation. Nor could it be
denied that since the orders of November 12 the southern
areas had been substantially weakened by the loss of the
Bulwark and the necessity of sending the 6th Battle Squadron
back to Portland when the Dover anti-submarine defences
were carried away. It was suggested, therefore, that the
only means of securing the situation was to bring a squadron
of battle cruisers, with a proportion of light cruisers and
destroyers, down to Sheerness.

This, however, was regarded as too great an inroad on the
concentration of the Grand Fleet; but something was done

to bring the battle cruisers more closely into the anti-invasion system. On December 20 Admiral Beatty was ordered to move down from Cromarty and join the 3rd Battle Squadron and 3rd Cruiser Squadron at Rosyth. His squadron was still incomplete.[1] The *Indomitable* had not finished refitting after her return from the Mediterranean, and the *Princess Royal* was only just leaving the West Indies. The moment it was known that Admiral von Spee's squadron had been destroyed she had been recalled, and she accordingly left Jamaica on December 11, the day before Admiral Sturdee was first warned that his two battle cruisers of the 2nd Squadron were wanted at home as soon as convenient, but she was not allowed to proceed without interruption. The ghost of the dead *Karlsruhe* still haunted the West Indian seas : she had just been reported to be lurking about her old lair in the Bahamas; and so anxious were the Admiralty to complete the clearing of the oceans, that the *Princess Royal* was ordered to join the local cruisers in hunting her down. The search, which lasted a week and was of course without tangible result, necessitated a return to Jamaica for coal, and finally it was not till December 19 that she left Kingston for Scapa Flow. By the New Year, however, the squadron would be complete, and the Admiral would also have a squadron of the fastest light cruisers attached to his flag.

This could now be done without depriving Admiral Jellicoe of that class of ship, for as new ships were now ready and others were coming home, it was possible to form two light cruiser squadrons, of which the second, under the command of Rear-Admiral T. D. W. Napier, would remain with the Commander-in-Chief's flag.[2] The other cruiser squadrons which continued to be based at Scapa could moreover be used entirely as fleet cruisers—that is, without any preoccupation with the watch on the north-about trade routes. Of this duty the Grand Fleet was completely relieved by the development of the new 10th Cruiser Squadron, under the command of Admiral de Chair, with his flag in the *Alsatian*. This blockading force, which was designed to consist of twenty-four armed liners, had already twelve ships on patrol, and eight more were about to join. It was thus possible to organise them in four divisions and distribute them in such a way that it was very difficult for a ship to get through undetected. They worked in four areas, which, though modified from time

---

[1] *Lion* (flag), *Tiger, Princess Royal, Queen Mary, New Zealand, Indomitable.*
[2] 2nd Light Cruiser Squadron—*Falmouth* (flag), *Liverpool, Gloucester, Yarmouth* and *Dartmouth,* but for the present the last ship was detached to the Pernambuco area in search of the *Karlsruhe.*

to time, were generally as follows :   Area A was north of the
Faeroes; Area B north of the Shetlands; Area C west of the
line between the Faeroes and Sule Skerry (north-east of Cape
Wrath); and Area D west of the Hebrides.   The arrangement
worked well.   Ships began to be intercepted in large numbers,
and during the first week in January, when all four areas
were fully occupied, no less than twenty were sent into
Lerwick.

Though the shifting of Admiral Beatty's base to Rosyth
meant a further loosening of the main concentration, it was not
intended to affect Admiral Jellicoe's supreme control.   He was
to be in complete charge as before.   At the first sign of
another raid he would put to sea and assume the general
direction, but as Whitehall was the centre of intelligence
the Admiralty would directly instruct Admiral Beatty what
should be the rendezvous.   For the same reason they also
reserved to themselves the initial control of Commodore
Tyrwhitt and his flotillas, as well as Commodore Keyes's
"oversea" submarines, but as soon as these came in touch
with Admiral Jellicoe the direction would pass to him.

The various squadrons had scarcely assumed their new
stations before the scheme was tested.   For Christmas day
another air raid on the Cuxhaven Zeppelin sheds had been
planned.   The attempt was to be made with nine seaplanes,
carried in the *Engadine, Riviera* and *Empress*, with the Harwich
destroyers and submarines and their attached cruisers
Arethusa, Undaunted and Fearless in support.   As before,
it was hoped that the enterprise might provoke a fleet action,
and the whole Grand Fleet was concentrated in the middle of
the North Sea.   The idea was for all the machines to drop
their bombs on the Cuxhaven sheds, if they could find them,
and if not to attack any ships or military works they could
locate.   In returning they were to endeavour to report what
ships were at Kiel and at Wilhelmshaven, or in the Schillig
roads.

It was a perfect Christmas morning, still and sunny, when
the force arrived in position, and though only seven of the
machines could start, there was every prospect of success.
But as soon as they passed the coastline they encountered
a dense frost fog which made it impossible to locate anything.
Still some of them dropped their bombs, and apparently with
effect, though the damage done was variously reported.   A
cruiser was also attacked on the return, but whether she was
hit or not could not be seen.   The airship sheds for which the
seaplanes had been searching were not at Cuxhaven, but
six miles to the south-westward of it.   One of the 'planes

had circled over them, but the pilot failed to recognise them, and the bombs he dropped fell among some trees. In the Schillig roads were four battle cruisers, besides other cruisers and some destroyers. One of the *Riviera* section (No. 136, Flight-Commander C. F. Kilner) could see them well when he cleared the fog, but though he was fired upon by the battle cruisers, a hit seemed scarcely possible and no attempt to bomb them was made.

The return was full of adventure. Though no ships came out, Zeppelins and seaplanes were about, trying to attack our supporting force. They had no success; the airships were easily eluded by our cruisers; the seaplanes, though their bombs were well aimed, hit nothing, and were driven off by gunfire. Our aircraft, however, had no such easy work. Owing to their prolonged search in the fog their oil was barely sufficient, and only the two that had reconnoitred Schillig roads succeeded in getting back to their carriers. The others had to drop short in the sea. One was rescued by Commodore Keyes in the *Lurcher* and three others close off Norderney by Lieutenant-Commander Nasmith in sub-marine *E 11*, who here was to found the reputation he completed in the Sea of Marmara. He had just taken off the pilot from one and got her in tow when two more alighted beside him. At the same time a Zeppelin was seen coming up fast. It was a critical moment. But he immediately cast off the first one, after removing her bombing sights, and then went off to rescue the newcomers. By the time he got them on board the Zeppelin was very close, and there was only just time to dive when two bombs fell harmlessly over the top of him. *D 6*, which was coming up to help, had also been forced to dive by the Zeppelin, but she came to the surface again, and did not leave the spot till she was satisfied that all three seaplanes were sunk. Flight-Commander F. E. T. Hewlett, in the seventh seaplane (No. 135), after an action with a Zeppelin, came down into the sea and was taken in tow by a Dutch trawler. Being unable to find any of our ships, he destroyed his machine, and was eventually taken in to Ymuiden, whence he was finally released as a shipwrecked mariner.

Though from the luck of the weather the main object of the raid had not been attained, the experience was as valuable as it was encouraging. From 4 a.m. till noon Commodore Tyrwhitt's supporting force had occupied the enemy's waters and no ship had put to sea to interfere with him. Their attempts to drive him off were confined to the air, and it had been shown how little ships in the open sea had to fear from aircraft—the Zeppelins had been avoided with ease, and the

German seaplanes, in spite of their activity, had not secured a single hit. Moreover the operation, so far as it was a test of the new disposition of the Grand Fleet, was equally satisfactory. The concentration had worked smoothly, but its end was marked by a misfortune which entirely outweighed any possible success we may have obtained in the course of the air raid.

On December 27, as the battle fleet made its way back to Scapa it began to blow hard from the southward. As they approached the base to enter as usual in the dark a whole gale was raging in the Pentlands with a heavy sea of the worst type, and the result was that as they were going into the narrow entrance the *Conqueror* collided with the *Monarch*, her next ahead. Both ships suffered severely. The stern of the *Monarch* was stove in and the stempiece of the *Conqueror* fractured and her forepart badly damaged. The first examination showed that neither ship could be fit for service again without extensive repairs in dock, and before long it was found that a special salvage plant must be sent up before the *Conqueror* could even be patched up enough to enable her to leave Scapa. Thus two Dreadnoughts besides the lost *Audacious* were out of action for a considerable time and the 2nd Battle Squadron was reduced to five units. Still even this blow did not shake the determination of the Admiralty to keep their hold on the North Sea, and in spite of the serious diminution in strength the new disposition was maintained.

The drawing down of the Grand Fleet was only part of it. In the southern area the striking force had been strengthened by definitely attaching to the Channel Fleet the 6th Battle Squadron and moving it back to Dover in spite of the insecurity of that port. The Channel Fleet now therefore consisted of two " Lord Nelsons " and seven " Formidables " of the 5th Battle Squadron, with five " Duncans," and the *Revenge* of the 6th. The command was also changed. The day after the Scarborough raid Vice-Admiral Sir Lewis Bayly, who had been commanding the 1st Battle Squadron in the Grand Fleet, was called down to take the dangerous position, and Admiral Burney went north to fill the command his successor had vacated.

When Admiral Bayly hoisted his flag he found that the 6th Battle Squadron had gone back to Portland for firing exercises. Nevertheless he begged to be allowed to undertake certain offensive operations with the 5th Squadron against the enemy's coast in retaliation for Scarborough. This proposal, however, was negatived, since at the moment destroyers and fleet sweepers sufficient for his protection could not be spared. But

he was consoled with the information that one of the most
important functions of the Channel Fleet would probably
be the bombardment of the enemy's shore defences in a
combined operation with the military.

The fact was, that quite apart from the prospect of an
enemy attack on our East Coast or the Thames Estuary,
there was another sufficient reason for increasing the
strength of the southern force. The point where the
two opposed armies touched the coast still offered the
most promising chance of breaking the threatened deadlock; for here it was that the fleet could be brought in to
turn the balance against the Germans. So far as could then
be seen it was conceivable that the whole course of the war
might turn on whether or not the Germans could prevent
us from bringing our coastal squadron into action at the decisive moment. This the Admiralty were fully prepared to do,
although, in view of the larger offensive operations that
were under consideration, they were as unwilling as ever to
risk ships in making diversions for minor military attacks.
If a real offensive were intended with the object of turning
the German flank, or even recovering Ostend and Zeebrugge,
they were prepared to throw all that was needed into the
scale, but so large an operation was not as yet the intention
of General Foch. On December 19, however, he informed
our liaison officer he meant to advance his heavy guns
and would be glad of help from the sea. Admiral Hood,
who still had the Dover command, intimated that he
was ready. Though the 6th Battle Squadron was away
at Portland, the *Majestic*, which was under orders to join
them, was still at Dover, and he said he could act next day
with her and the monitors; but nothing came of it. A week
later there was another request for two or three days' bombardment. Again Admiral Hood said he was ready, but
again nothing was done.

The reason was that a much more serious project was in
the wind. Sir John French, reckoning on the additional
strength to be provided by the three new Regular divisions,
was elaborating a plan for devoting the whole British
and Belgian armies in one homogeneous force to a great
effort to turn the German right by a push up the Flemish
coast. There was much to recommend it. Not only was
there the sentimental reason that it was to protect Belgium
that we had gone to war, but it was there, and there only, that
we could develop to the full our peculiar war strength. There
our sea and land force could be concentrated in a single
effort, there navy and army could work tactically hand in

hand and our surplus naval strength could be brought in
directly to redress our comparative military weakness. To
the Admiralty the idea was naturally welcome, for it was in
line with the great plan of offensive which was now their
main preoccupation. If successful it would not only turn the
enemy's flank, but it would also go far to solve the submarine
problem by depriving the enemy of his best-placed bases.
It amounted, in fact, to a development of the plan they had
begun to attempt single-handed, and for which they had
revived the 6th Battle Squadron. It was, moreover, in
keeping with their best tradition. Whenever it had been
found impossible for the British fleet to seek out and destroy
that of the enemy, the primary alternative had always been
to seek out and destroy the enemy's bases in concert with
the army. Lorient, Rochefort, Brest, Ostend, Flushing,
Antwerp, the Texel, Toulon, Copenhagen and St. Malo had
all been objectives of this type, besides other ports in the
East and West Indies. Here, then, was a chance of reviving
the old manner, and it could be undertaken without prejudice
to the higher function of dominating the enemy's main fleet.
Our surplus of suitable vessels, and especially of obsolescent
battleships, was ample—so ample indeed that the effort of the
army could be supported in great strength—even perhaps in
decisive strength; and grave as would be the risk to the ships
employed, this was what the Admiralty intended to do. They
were no longer content with the 6th Battle Squadron, they
would have all available "Majestics" as well. Most of these
fine old vessels were still being used as guardships, but for
a Board so thoroughly inspired as it was with the spirit
of offence they were too good for passive defence, and the
intention, as we have seen, was to withdraw all of them as
soon as the cruisers of the old 10th Cruiser Squadron could
be refitted to take their place.

So well did the British combined plan seem to fit the
situation that General Joffre gave it his full approval. Both
he and the British Commander-in-Chief were anxious to strike
before the new German formations that were in training
could take the field. General Joffre's idea was to concentrate
his army on two points where the German communications
were most exposed, and for this he wished his colleague to
release the French units which were still holding part of the
line to the northward of the British. An amalgamation of
the British and Belgian armies therefore entirely suited his
plan, and at a conference at Chantilly on December 27 the
matter was settled. But when it was submitted to the King
of the Belgians he was unable to agree. If the Field-Marshal

decided to make the attempt on Ostend he was ready to co-operate to his full strength, but he could not consent to the proposed unity of command.

Whether the operation would now be possible was very doubtful, and no decision had been come to when a sudden shock of disaster brought home with compelling force the need of doing what the Field-Marshal had in mind. Since the new system of patrolling the Straits against submarines had got to work, and light and navigation marks had been extinguished or altered, there had been a comparatively quiet time in the Channel. At this period indeed our anti-submarine system seemed fully effective. Drafts and stores were incessantly streaming across to France, an unending procession of merchant vessels was moving in mid-channel to the Downs, and there unmolested the flotilla of boarding vessels was engaged in the never-ending task of seeing that no contraband passed onwards for Germany. For many days not a single submarine had been reported; yet it was not to be believed that the attack on the army's communications would not be renewed, and every precaution was being taken. Since the first week in December transports had been ordered to sail singly, each with a destroyer for escort, and all had gone well. On the 19th the system was to be severely tested. On that day the XXVIIth Division was to begin to cross, and it was the first occasion since the submarine attack that a large unit had to be taken over. It was a specially anxious task, for the whole passage could not be completed in the dark—the state of the tide making it impossible to enter Havre till some time after daybreak. Admiral Favereau was asked to have all his available destroyers off the port to meet the transports, and Admiral The Hon. Sir Hedworth Meux was ordered to send over some of his Auxiliary Patrol from Portsmouth. Though the new system of areas was not yet started, he had received three units, all furnished with guns and modified sweeps and the unit leaders with wireless. Besides he had his eight "Beagle" class destroyers, so that the transports could sail in groups of eight. In this way it was managed without accident.

The success of the operation, remarkable as it was, did little to relax precautions against the reappearance of submarines in the Channel. How impossible it was to regard the danger as negligible, even in waters that seemed undisturbed, was now to be demonstrated. At Portland the 6th Battle Squadron had just completed its firing exercises; the 5th Battle Squadron, in Admiral Bayly's opinion, needed similar practice, and as Sheerness was unsuitable the 6th Battle Squadron was called up to take its place, and on the 26th he received permission to go to Portland, with the usual caution to arrange his passage with due regard to the possibility of submarine attack *en route*. The practice for squadrons moving through the Straits was to time their sailing so as to pass the narrows in the night, or, if a daylight passage was unavoidable, not to move without destroyer protection. On December 28, Admiral Bayly informed the Admiralty that he wished to sail at 10.0 a.m. on the 30th, and they thereupon arranged for Commodore Tyrwhitt to send six destroyers to the Nore to accompany the squadron as far as Folkestone. The Admiral sailed according to programme and at Folkestone the destroyers escorting the squadron turned back. From that point it was unguarded. It had no flotilla or cruiser squadron, nothing indeed but its two attached light cruisers, *Topaze* and *Diamond*, and it was therefore peculiarly exposed to torpedo attack. Nevertheless the Admiralty had directed that in making the passage every opportunity was to be taken of carrying out exercises and firing. Accordingly when at daybreak next morning Admiral Bayly reached the vicinity of Portland, instead of taking the squadron in, he began exercising tactics. The exercises, which were conducted within twenty-five miles from the Bill, lasted the greater part of the day. At their conclusion, so free did the Channel appear to be from submarines, the Admiral decided to remain at sea, and steamed direct for the south of the Isle of Wight, intending to continue the exercises next day.

By a Fleet Order it was laid down that where submarine attack was possible an alteration of course should be made just after dark. To comply with the order, although no submarine had been reported in the Channel during the whole of the month, Admiral Bayly made a 16-point alteration of course at 7.0 p.m., when he was abreast of the Needles, and so went back to the westward almost in his wake, with his two attached cruisers astern. The night, though cloudy, was remarkably clear, with a visibility of about two miles. There was moreover a stiff breeze from the southward, with a sea rough enough to make the detection of a submarine very difficult. Still, so little was danger apprehended, that the Admiral led on upon a straight course in line ahead at no more than ten knots, with the ships closed up and the *Formidable* (Captain A. N. Loxley) as rear ship. At 3.0 a.m., fifteen miles short of Start Point, they were to turn again sixteen points, and all went well till 2.30, when, as the squadron was passing through a number of fishing craft, the *Formidable* was seen by the cruisers to turn out of the line. The *Topaze* (Commander

W. J. B. Law) at once hurried up to her, to find she had a list to starboard and was already lowering her boats.

About 2.20 she had been struck by a torpedo abreast of the foremost funnel on the starboard side. The immediate effect was to cut off all steam and to give her a list of 20°, and she was brought up hard into the wind to get her head to the rising sea. With the increasing violence of the weather what light there had been was disappearing, and in complete darkness the launch and pinnace were got out. The two barges were also got out full of men, but one of them capsized, and then, about three-quarters of an hour after the first explosion, another torpedo hit the battleship abreast of the after funnel on the port side. The effect was to bring her on to an even keel, and as there was great difficulty in getting out the boom boats without steam, the hands were set to work bringing up all woodwork and breaking up the after shelter deck for saving life.

By this time the *Topaze* was circling round the *Formidable* and was ordered to close. Seeing boats on the water she tried to get hold of them, but the heavy sea made the work difficult and hazardous. Still she had succeeded in rescuing forty-three men out of the barge when Captain Loxley ordered her to go off to close a brilliantly-lighted liner that was passing and direct her to stand by. Commander L. L. Dundas in the *Diamond* immediately took her place, but though he passed the order to the liner and she acknowledged it, she continued her course. Rockets and lights from the *Formidable* made no better impression on her, and the *Topaze* went back to the stricken ship. Her bows were now awash, but Captain Loxley hailed the cruiser to say there was a submarine on his port bow, and with fine devotion ordered her to clear away out of danger and go after another steamer that was appearing. The weather was growing rapidly worse. Sea and wind were rising and it was intensely dark. Still the ship held her own on an even keel till, about 4.45, nearly two hours and a half after she had been first hit, she suddenly gave a lurch to starboard and began to heel over rapidly and settle by the bows. Captain Loxley then gave the word for every one to take to the water, and all that could started slipping down the sides. But before all were clear she turned over and plunged down head foremost. For a minute or two she stayed with her screws out of water and her rudder swinging disconsolately from side to side as though she had struck the bottom, and then she entirely disappeared. What had happened was that *U 24* (Lieutenant-Commander Schneider), one of the submarines which had recently begun operating from Flanders

upon our southern coast, had been dogging the squadron all
the previous afternoon and at last found herself in position
to attack as the squadron returned on its tracks.[1]

The work of rescue was naturally extremely difficult. The
officers, all but two of whom were in the water, came off
best, as they had safety waistcoats, but the collars the seamen
were wearing proved of little use in the sea that was running.
Of Captain Loxley nothing more was seen. Survivors saw
him standing with his terrier on the bridge till the last,
giving his orders as coolly as though the ship were lying
in harbour, cheering and steadying the men, praising the
officers for each smart piece of work, and his reward was to
see perfect discipline and alacrity maintained to the end. No
effort was spared at every risk to save life. In spite of the
darkness, the heavy sea, and the danger of another submarine attack, the *Diamond* succeeded in saving thirty-seven
officers and men. The launch, too, got clear in charge of
the boatswain with about a dozen hands, and was soon
crowded with men he picked up. With only eight oars
she drifted away and with the utmost difficulty was kept
afloat through the night, nor was it till noon next day that
she was found by any ship. Then near Berry Head the
Brixham trawler *Provident*, who herself had been lying-to in
the gale waiting to make the harbour, came up, and after
three abortive attempts to pass her a line the skipper,
Captain W. Pillar, in defiance of the full gale that was now
blowing, gybed his vessel and brought her close alongside the
sinking boat. His crew numbered only four hands all told, but
he was thus able to pass the launch a warp, and by a clever
movement got her under his own lee. By this brilliant and
fearless piece of seamanship all the men, to the number of
seventy-one, were taken off, and the launch sank almost
immediately.[2] As for the other boats, a cutter was found
bottom upwards on Abbotsbury beach, and another boat
with forty-six men drifted ashore near Lyme Regis, but
out of the *Formidable's* complement of 780 there were
drowned or died of exposure 35 officers and 512 men.

What made the loss of so fine a ship and so many good
lives the more regrettable was that it appeared to have been
due to taking risks for no good purpose. The Admiral was
called upon to give an explanation, and after considering his
reply the Admiralty agreed that although there had been a

[1] Gayer, *Die Deutschen U-Boote in ihrer Kriegführung*, 1914–1918,
Vol. I., p. 21.

[2] For this fine piece of service the *Provident* was awarded a gratuity of
£550, and each member of the crew received the silver medal for gallantry
in saving life at sea.

lack of precision in the orders issued by the War Staff, and that the failure to provide flotilla protection was to be deprecated, yet the neglect of what they regarded as ordinary precautions against submarine attack which had been so unaccountably displayed could not be overlooked, even in so valuable and intrepid an officer as Admiral Bayly. In vain he pleaded that the exercises he had been ordered to carry out without destroyer protection involved higher risk than any he had run. The plea was not accepted. He was therefore ordered to strike his flag and Vice-Admiral The Hon. Sir Alexander Bethell was appointed in his place.[1]

Although in this particular instance the disaster was attributed to the neglect of ordinary precautions, it was clear that, unless something drastic was done to check the activity of the enemy's submarines, they must continue seriously to hamper the necessary movements of the fleet. This impression was increased in force by the fact that a similar though less tragic event had just occurred in the Adriatic. On Christmas day the French Admiralty announced that the *Jean Bart*, one of their new Dreadnoughts, had been torpedoed by an Austrian submarine in the Straits of Otranto. She was coming down from a rendezvous in the Adriatic at the head of the line when the submarine fired two torpedoes at her in rapid succession. The first passed astern, the other hit her forward, but though the damage was severe it was not enough to sink her, and she managed to reach port. The effect of the incident was that the French decided to withdraw their battleships to Malta and Bizerta till a defended anchorage could be prepared at Corfu, and to leave the blockade to the cruisers and destroyers, and active operations to the submarines which were acting from a base in Plateali Bay.[2]

The line which the British Admiralty took was more aggressive. Their case was different from that of the French. Our disaster had occurred in our own waters and on our army's line of communication, and there they had no mind

---

[1] Admiral Bayly took over the Presidency of the Royal Naval College, Greenwich, and six months later, when the submarine trouble became acute, was recalled to active command and appointed to the Coast of Ireland Station, with its limits considerably extended. His able and energetic conduct of the command received special recognition from the Admiralty.

[2] La Bruyère, *Deux Années de Guerre Navale*, p. 43. The French submarines had been showing considerable enterprise. In November the *Cugnot* had entered Cattaro Bay and attempted to attack the old battleship *Rudolph* in Castelnuovo, but she was caught in nets and hunted by destroyers, and barely escaped. In December the *Curie* had penetrated Pola itself, where the Dreadnoughts *Tegetthoff* and *Viribus Unitis* were lying, but she was hopelessly netted and had to surrender. Her loss was acknowledged on December 25. *Ibid.*, pp. 44-6.

to submit to the domination of the enemy, whatever means he might employ. In order to watch Zeebrugge they transferred two of the " C " class submarines from Dover to the command of Commodore Keyes; one of these, *C 34*, had already made two reconnaissances of the port and arrived safely at Harwich; but the other, *C 31*, which left Dover on January 4 for the Belgian coast was never heard of again. Apart from this, the Admiralty's main action was at once to press for a revival of the idea of a combined attack on the enemy's submarine bases. A week earlier it had practically been decided on by the British and French Commanders-in-Chief at the conference at Chantilly. But at this time the Allies were very far from unity of command, and, as we have seen, the project had fallen through owing to the opposition of the Belgians. But with this it was now impossible for the Admiralty to rest content, and as soon as ever the loss of the *Formidable* was known, they communicated the news to Sir John French as fresh and cogent evidence of the difficulties that were being imposed upon them by the development of Zeebrugge as a submarine station, and inquired definitely whether he saw his way to capture that place, as well as Ostend, in conjunction with the fleet.

He replied with a memorandum to the War Office, in which he said that the effect of the Admiralty's application was to raise in an acute form the very question which he had been earnestly studying for some weeks, and for which he at present saw but one solution that would fit the general situation. What that situation was he set out quite frankly, without an attempt to disguise the difficulties of realising the idea upon which he was as ardently bent as the Admiralty. Its dominating feature was that, in the view of the French High Command, a moment had arrived when the existing deadlock might be broken. According to his own and General Joffre's information the Germans would be in inferior force to the Allies on the Western Front for some months—that is, till their new formations were ready to take their place in the line. It, therefore, seemed to him most important that the Allies should strike at the earliest possible moment with all their available strength. It was to this end that General Joffre was massing as many troops as he could lay his hand on in order to strike simultaneously at Reims and Arras. In order to free the units which he had to the north of the British army he had approved the Field-Marshal's idea of amalgamating the Belgian and British armies, and although that plan had fallen through, he was still pressing for the release of the French troops in Flanders. The Field-Marshal explained that it would be impossible for him to do this and also to carry out the operation which the Admiralty desired unless he received large reinforcements. Over and above the XXVIIIth, XXIXth and Canadian Divisions, which were already ear-marked for him, he would require at least fifty battalions of Territorials or the New Army.

The difficulty in coming to a decision on the point was very great. The main question which the Government had under consideration at the moment was in what theatre the new armies could be best employed—that is, whether they should be used in France or on some alternative line of operation which promised to give a decisive result more quickly. The issue was extremely complicated, for while Sir John French's memorandum in answer to the Admiralty seemed to indicate concentration on the Western Front, an appreciation which he sent at the same time to Lord Kitchener threw grave doubt on its utility. In this paper he frankly stated that no decisive result was to be looked for in the west. It was not that he admitted the impossibility of breaking through—that, he said, was only a question of men and munitions—yet he was of opinion that even if the Germans could be driven back to the Rhine it would not mean a decision of the war. It was only in the east—the Russian Front—that ultimate victory could be attained. On the other hand, if the French suffered a crushing defeat the consequences would be disastrous. For this reason he was convinced that not a man must be moved from France. This view in effect ruled out operations in any other theatre. Apart from the fact that he did not believe that any of the alternative plans under consideration could lead to a decisive result, he had no hesitation in saying that none of them could be attempted without first line troops. In conclusion, therefore, he expressed a strong conviction that the whole of our army should be employed in France, notwithstanding his confession that no decision could be expected on the Western Front.

It was excusable if Ministers were not convinced and were unwilling to commit themselves to such an *impasse*, which seemed to declare the bankruptcy of all our old traditions. Remembering the latest precedent, that of the Peninsular war, where our main army, with the navy at its back, had been used with so much effect away from the central theatre, they could not so easily reject the possibility of employing it on some independent line of operation where our command of the sea would give us the same advantage over Germany that it gave Wellington over Napoleon. But no such line

of operation was clearly in view.   So long as Denmark and
Holland remained neutral, northern Europe was out of the
question.   Operations against Austria from the Adriatic,
even should Italy come in, seemed barred by the submarine.
A third alternative was an advance from Salonica in concert
with the Serbians and Greeks.   Here was the closest analogy
to the Peninsula, but the long and difficult line of communication it would involve was held to render it impracticable
under modern conditions of warfare.   There remained
Turkey, but at this time military opinion seems to have
been almost unanimously in accord with Sir John French
that no success in that quarter could lead to a decisive result.
As yet, moreover, when the reality of Germany's aims in
the Near East was not fully appreciated, it was believed that
her forcing Turkey to take up arms had no direct relation
to the object of the war, but was designed as a diversion to
induce us to dissipate our force.   Consequently to operate
against Turkey would be to play the German game.   At
first sight, therefore, particularly in view of the paramount
need of securing a real command of Home waters, it looked as
though, hopeless as it was, the Field-Marshal's plan of concentrating our effort against Zeebrugge and Ostend was the
best available.

   But, in fact, the matter was not so clear.   For it so happened
that while Sir John French was drafting his appreciation
other considerations were beginning to obscure the situation.
The shadow of the first naval failure in the Mediterranean,
which had been deepening ever since the *Goeben* had escaped
into the Dardanelles, was already reaching the Flemish
coast.   It began to fall the day after the *Formidable* was
lost, and it was first perceived in a telegram received early on
January 2 from Sir George Buchanan, our Ambassador in
Petrograd.   As the Turks ever since they entered the war
had been left undisturbed in the Mediterranean, they had been
able to devote their resources, under German direction, not
only to the preparation of an invasion of Egypt, but also to
organising an enveloping movement in the Caucasus, which
was causing the Russian General in command grave anxiety.
He was crying urgently for reinforcement, but the
Grand Duke could spare nothing from the main theatre.
Though he had just succeeded in checking the invasion of
Poland before Warsaw, the German advance had gone far
enough to stop his own invasion of Galicia, and unless he
could deal a staggering blow in Poland the promising penetration of Austria could not be resumed.   He was bent therefore
on concentrating everything he could at Warsaw, and the

General in the Caucasus was informed that he must hold on
as best he could.   But at the same time, as a means of
relieving the pressure, the Grand Duke sent a message to Lord
Kitchener to know whether it would be possible for him to
arrange for a diversion against the Turks elsewhere.

We had little faith in the effect of such a measure, but
as the result of a conversation with the First Lord, Lord
Kitchener replied next day through the Foreign Office
that a demonstration of the kind suggested would be taken
in hand.   As no troops were then available he at once consulted the Admiralty as to the possibility of making a naval
demonstration at the Dardanelles.   Lord Fisher was more
than doubtful.   In his opinion the bombardment in November
had shown that no possible purpose could be served by
repeating it with the squadron which Admiral Carden had
on the spot.   For effective action a much larger and
differently constituted force would certainly be needed.
Still he strongly held the view that as an alternative theatre
Turkey was the best in the field, if a sufficient military
force was available to co-operate with the fleet, and he put
forward a scheme for operating on that line with the assistance of the Balkan States.   But as his plan involved the
diversion of a substantial force from France it was barred
by Sir John French's view that no troops could be moved
away without General Joffre's consent, and that that consent
would never be given.   The only course that remained was
to increase the Dardanelles squadron by such of our older
battleships as were available and to provide it with a sufficient
force of minesweepers and other auxiliaries, which it would
require if it was to act alone.   The idea was that thus reinforced it might be able to force the Straits and reach Constantinople.   It would certainly involve a considerable expenditure
of ships, and with the fate of the *Formidable* and the disablement of the *Monarch* and *Conqueror* fresh in mind it was
strongly felt by the First Sea Lord that the greatest caution
must be exercised in hazarding the loss of our naval superiority
by minor operations.

Still in this case the operation was of such vital importance
to the common cause that it could not be discarded without
the fullest consideration, and it was decided to send a telegram
to Vice-Admiral S. H. Carden to ask his opinion whether at the
cost of serious loss the Dardanelles could be forced by ships
alone.   He replied that in his opinion the Straits could not be
" rushed," but might be forced by extended operations with
a large number of ships.   He was then (January 6) directed
to send home particulars of the operation he contemplated

and the force he would require. Simultaneously at the request
of the First Lord, Admiral Sir Henry Jackson prepared a
memorandum on the practicability of forcing the Straits
without military co-operation. In this it was strongly
emphasised that however successful the fleet might be by
its own efforts, it could not hope to obtain any effective
result unless there was a large military force available to
occupy Constantinople. In his plan, which was very similar
to Carden's, the Russian Black Sea Fleet was to co-operate
by keeping a watch on the mouth of the Bosporus, to prevent
the escape of the enemy into the Black Sea.

Seeing how deeply we were already involved in France, the
readiness with which we took up the Russian invitation
appears almost quixotic. But looking back upon it against
the background of our past war history, we seem to see in
what prompted our action at this time a first indistinct
warning that the old influences, which had never permitted
us to concentrate in the main European theatre of a great
war, were about to reassert themselves. Whether rightly
or wrongly, they had always gained the upper hand over pure
military doctrine. It would look as though they were inherent
in the preoccupations of a world-wide maritime Empire and
must always cause its action to differ from that of more
compact Continental Powers. Probably at this juncture the
stirring of the old instinct was rather felt than consciously
realised. At all events it was held that to commit so large
a part of our force as Sir John French demanded to the
Continent was premature, and the reply which the Field-
Marshal received was precisely in line with the attitude the
elder Pitt always adopted towards Frederick the Great.
Our obligation to France would be fulfilled. So long as she
was liable to successful invasion the place for our troops
would be shoulder to shoulder with hers. As it was likely
that the situation would shortly develop into one of stalemate,
and a successful offensive in the main theatre would be
impossible for the Allies until they had greatly increased
their supply of men and munitions, it was necessary to
consider whether we could not seek decisive results elsewhere.
In these circumstances, then, Sir John French's new plan for
combined operations against Zeebrugge and Ostend could not
be sanctioned. The Admiralty, although anxious to see the
submarine bases destroyed, had declared that the possession
of those ports by the enemy was not vital to our naval position,
and on no other consideration were the Government willing
to sanction a plan of operations which, apart from the inevitable cost in men, would mean the extension of our line to the

Dutch frontier, and in all probability involve developments on so great a scale that our whole military force would be committed irrevocably to the Western Front.

This conclusion was reached on January 8, and the question of an alternative theatre continued to be studied. Sufficient progress had already been made to admit of a general agreement that it was only in the Mediterranean that a new line of operation was to be found. A direct attack on Austria by way of Trieste or some other point in the Adriatic was one possibility, but apart from the difficulty of finding an adequate base on the enemy's coast it was out of the question until Italy came in. There was also the Salonica line, but that was impracticable without Greece, and Greece had already intimated that she could do nothing until the neutrality of Bulgaria was assured. There remained Turkey. As the result of a special study of this theatre by the General Staff, Lord Kitchener reached the conclusion that the Dardanelles was the most suitable objective. He believed that 150,000 men would suffice, though on this point further study would be required. He also inclined to a minor attack on Alexandretta with from 30,000 to 50,000 men. This force, he considered, would soon be available from Egypt. For there on November 19 it had been decided to land the Australian and New Zealand troops for the completion of their training, and by December 15 the disembarkation was complete.

Though it was resolved, in view of the paramount obligation of defending France, that nothing could be done till the result of the next German attack was known, the proposal was regarded as having much to commend it. For, as Lord Kitchener pointed out, the Dardanelles was the spot where the naval and military arms could act in closest co-operation, and there too we could hope to achieve the largest political, economic and financial results. The importance of the results was indeed so great that the wonder is, not that the scheme attracted, but that it was not at once adopted with higher conviction and complete singleness of purpose. But so long as the French High Command held the sanguine view that a repetition of the Allied successes on the Marne was possible during the next campaign, and so long as French soil was under the heel of the invader, Paris could not see with the same eyes as London. Though our own Government were ready to hold their hands till the resisting power of the Allied line was proved by the next attack, which every indication declared to be imminent, they were profoundly sceptical of anything being possible beyond maintaining the position intact. Sir John French's appreciation had only confirmed the prevailing view. It was that, seeing how the rhythm of the art of war seemed to be bringing the defensive into dominance, there was little chance of being able to break the German hold till a very great preponderance of strength had been gathered, and for this they could see nothing but to develop the unlimited man power of Russia. She had at her call untold hosts of men, and she only needed arms, munitions and financial support to provide all that was required. Once she was fully armed, and not till then, a great concentric attack by all the Allies might avail to overcome the advantages which the Central Powers enjoyed in their interior position. But till the Dardanelles was open the work of arming the giant could not be done. In effect the Germans, by cheating the Turks into the war, had obtained an intolerable position on the main lateral line of communication between the Western Powers and Russia, and until the obstruction was removed a real combined effort such as was needed to crush so great a military Power as Germany was impossible.

This consideration alone might have seemed to justify the new departure even from the view of pure military strategy. But there was much more behind; for the political results that success would bring were almost invaluable. They promised, indeed, to complete the investment of the Central Powers with a ring of enemies and to cut them off— as Napoleon had been cut off by our naval and combined operations in the Mediterranean—from spreading the war effectively beyond the confines of Europe. At one stroke we could remove all danger to Egypt, secure the Balkan States, win the wavering respect of the Arabs and put an end to the hesitation of Italy.

The actual situation in the Balkans was specially calling for drastic treatment. Though in the middle of December the Serbians had driven the last Austrian from their territory and had reoccupied Belgrade, it was just now becoming apparent that Germany was insisting that Austria should make an end of her victim, so that a road might be driven through to Turkey. So entirely isolated was our unhappy little Ally that except for driblets through neutral territory we could give her no assistance. Nor was there any hope of saving her and the vital interests of the Allies in the Near East unless the other Balkan States could be persuaded to combine against Germany. Diplomacy—especially with such an opportunist as Ferdinand of Bulgaria holding the keys— could do little. What was required was some resounding feat of arms that would shatter the legend of German infallibility, and nowhere was such consummation within reach except at the Dardanelles.

Diplomatically, then, the case for developing our military power in the Eastern Mediterranean was overwhelming, and far outweighed all that could be said for the Flanders plan. From a military point of view it was scarcely less justifiable; for it was not, as it appeared to some, an eccentric operation, but an operation to clear lateral communications that were vital to securing a complete decision in the main theatre. Its financial and economic promise was equally great. With the Dardanelles open Russian corn could flow again through the Mediterranean to relieve the already menacing question of food supply for the Western Powers, and to re-establish Russian finance. Owing to the shutting down of her exports, foreign exchange was running dangerously against her, and materially increasing the difficulty of supplying her needs. Beyond this again was the general question of shipping. The enormous drain which the war was making on available tonnage was fast becoming a serious anxiety, and in the Russian Black Sea ports were locked up no fewer than 129 steamships, Allied, neutral and interned enemy, with an aggregate of nearly 350,000 tons gross, all of which would be released for service when the Dardanelles was opened.

It was on these grounds, then, that Lord Kitchener commended his selection of an alternative objective. The case for it was obviously very strong. It followed, moreover, the traditional lines of the system of warfare upon which—whether or not ideally the best—the British Empire had been built up. Still, in spite of all that could be said, military opinion in France remained unshaken. The Germans were on French soil, and at the French Headquarters, as well as at our own, the Staff clung to their conviction that during the next month or so, before the strength of the enemy was fully developed, there was a chance of dislodging them that might mean disaster if it were missed. So strongly was this view held that the whole question was re-examined on January 13 in consultation with Sir John French. There was nothing new to urge. He made no secret of the fact that neither he nor General Joffre looked for a decisive result except from the east, but he still pressed to be allowed to operate against Zeebrugge in co-operation with the fleet. Lord Kitchener was ready to reinforce him by the middle of February with two Territorial divisions, and with these he believed he could push through to the Dutch frontier and hold the extended line the advance would involve. Though it would be an isolated movement, which could not be claimed as leading up to a decision, it was, in his opinion, the only place where we could take the offensive for the present. Although this proposal did nothing to remove the weighty objections to further committals on the Western Front, the influence of the purely military school of thought was so strong that in the end it was agreed that the necessary preparations should go forward and that a final decision should be postponed till February.

Meanwhile the study of possible action in the Mediterranean was proceeding, and as an immediate contribution to it the Admiralty put forward a plan of operations for the Dardanelles which had been received two days earlier from Admiral Carden. It was his reply to the instructions to furnish a detailed explanation of those extended operations by which the men on the spot considered the Straits might be forced. The War Staff had considered it and it had been passed by them as a feasible operation. An alternative project, which was felt to merit examination as likely to give more direct and immediate political results, was an attack on Cattaro. The conclusion was that while the preparations for the Zeebrugge scheme went forward the Admiralty should also study the question of Cattaro, and also prepare for a naval expedition in February to bombard and take the Gallipoli peninsula, with Constantinople as its objective. Finally the Government definitely laid down that if in the spring a deadlock occurred in the west the new armies would be used elsewhere, and a committee was appointed to study this aspect of the question and prepare for the eventuality.

CHAPTER IV

THE effect of the decision so far as it had gone was that the Mediterranean began to regain the prominence which it had never been for long denied in any great war. Since Admiral Carden's short bombardment of the entrance of the Dardanelles when, early in November, Turkey had first been driven helplessly into the war, it had attracted little attention. In the Adriatic the French had found it impossible to do anything effective in the face of the Austrian submarines, and their powerful fleet, still based at Malta, had to be content with maintaining a strict blockade of its outlet, and providing cruisers to escort our convoys between Malta and Egypt. But in the Black Sea there had been more activity. There Admiral Ebergard, who commanded the Russian squadron, had on November 6, in the course of a cruise, mined the entrance to the Bosporus, bombarded Zungaldak, the port of the Heraklea colliery district, and sunk four Turkish transports carrying troops or stores. A week later the Russian Admiral was out again, and on November 17 bombarded Trebizond, the supply port of the Turkish army operating in the Caucasus. At the moment there were five Turkish transports making for the port under escort of the *Hamidieh* and *Medjidieh*, and Admiral Souchon, fearing these might be cut off, put to sea with the *Goeben* and *Breslau* to give them protection. The low coal endurance of the Russian squadron had by that time compelled them to return to their base. At about noon on November 18 they were some twenty miles to the south of the Crimean coast when the *Almaz* in the van reported the *Goeben* and *Breslau* ahead. The weather, which had been very thick in the morning, had cleared, but it was still misty, and a brief action began at a range of under four miles. It lasted less than a quarter of an hour, for the high speed of the German vessels enabled them to get out of reach. The Russian flagship *Evstafi*, on whom the *Goeben* had concentrated her fire, was hit four times, and the casualties in this ship amounted to five officers and fifty men killed and wounded; the other vessels were not touched. The damage and losses sustained by the enemy were not known, but reports from spies gave the impression that the *Goeben* suffered severely.[1] On the strength of this information the Admiralty, in their anxiety to add the Mediterranean battle cruisers to the Grand Fleet, proposed to hand over the blockade of the Dardanelles to the French. The Minister of Marine insisted, however, that one battle cruiser should be left until it could be ascertained that the damages to the *Goeben* were really serious, and the ultimate result of this interchange of views was an arrangement that the *Indefatigable, Dublin* and three British submarines should remain, the other British ships being replaced by French destroyers and old battleships, the command to be eventually taken over by a French Admiral. By the end of November, Admiral Carden had been joined by six French destroyers, three French submarines and the French battleships *Gaulois* (flag of Rear-Admiral Guépratte) *Vérité, St. Louis* and *Charlemagne;* and with this force he was entirely absorbed in maintaining his watch on the approaches to the Dardanelles, and doing his best to prevent contraband reaching the Turks by Smyrna and the Bulgarian port of Dedeagatch.

So great was the demand for destroyers at home to meet the submarine menace that he was only allowed to keep the six he had on his urgent representation that the six boats the French had sent were of too old a type to deal with the modern Turkish ones. The *Goeben* moreover was soon active again. From December 7 to 10 she had been out in the Black Sea with the *Hamidieh* escorting troops and transports, and had bombarded Batum for a short time. At the same time the *Breslau* had been detected apparently laying mines off Sevastopol, but had been met by bombing aeroplanes. In the Dardanelles was another cruiser, the *Messudieh,* guarding the minefield below the Narrows. Without more cruisers it was therefore impossible to maintain a blockade of Smyrna and Dedeagatch, and at the same time guard the flying base which had been established for the flotilla at Port Sigri, in Mityleni. The French, however, came to the rescue by sending up two ships, the cruiser *Amiral Charner* and the seaplane carrier *Foudre,* which, having left her seaplanes in Egypt, had been doing escort duty on the Port Said–Malta line. They were still on their way when a brilliant piece of service was performed, which did something to

---

[1] The *Goeben* was hit by a heavy shell, but was not seriously damaged. She remained at sea for two days longer.

relieve the Admiral's anxiety and much to brighten the monotony of the eventless vigil.

For some time the three British submarines (*B 9*, *10* and *11*) and the three French, had been itching for a new experience. There were known to be five lines of mines across the fairway inside the Straits, but Captain C. P. R. Coode, the resourceful commander of the destroyer flotilla, and Lieutenant-Commander G. H. Pownall, who commanded the submarines under him, believed that by fitting a submarine with certain guards the obstacle could be passed. Amongst both the French and the British submarine commanders there was keen competition to be made the subject of the experiment. Eventually the choice fell on Lieutenant N. D. Holbrook, of *B 11*, which had recently had her batteries renewed and had already been two miles up the Straits in chase of two Turkish gunboats. On December 13, having been duly fitted with guards, she went in to torpedo anything she could get at. In spite of the strong adverse current Lieutenant Holbrook succeeded in taking his boat clear under the five rows of mines, and, sighting a large two-funnelled vessel painted grey with the Turkish ensign flying, he closed her to 800 yards, fired a torpedo and immediately dived. As the submarine dipped he heard the explosion, and putting up his periscope saw that the vessel was settling by the stern. He had now to make the return journey, but to the danger of the minefield a fresh peril was added; the lenses of the compass had become so badly fogged, that steering by it was no longer possible. He was not even sure where he was, but taking into consideration the time since he had passed Cape Helles, and the fact that the boat appeared to be entirely surrounded by land, he calculated that he must be in Sari Sighlar Bay. Several times he bumped the bottom as he ran along submerged at full speed, but the risk of ripping open the submarine had to be taken, and it was not till half an hour had passed and he judged that the mines must now be behind him that he put up his periscope again. There was now a clear horizon on his port beam, and for this he steered, taking peeps from time to time to correct his course since the compass was still unserviceable. Our watching destroyers noticed a torpedo-boat apparently searching for him; but after he had dived twice under a minefield and navigated the Dardanelles submerged without a compass, so ordinary a hazard seems to have escaped his notice. It was not till he returned to the base, having been nine hours under water, that he learned that the vessel he had torpedoed was the cruiser *Messudieh*. Such an exploit was quite without precedent. The Admiralty at once telegraphed their highest appreciation of the resource and daring displayed. Lieutenant Holbrook received the V.C., Lieutenant S. T. Winn, his second in command, a D.S.O., and every member of the crew a D.S.C. or D.S.M. according to rank.[1]

Encouraged by this success Admiral Carden asked for one of the latest class of submarines. He was sure that if fitted like *B 11* she could go right up to the Golden Horn. But as the Scarborough raid had just taken place and the High Seas Fleet showed signs of awakening none could be spared, and the blockade settled down again to its dull routine. Though there were constant rumours of a coming destroyer attack in retaliation for the loss of the *Messudieh*, the indications were that at the Dardanelles the enemy's only thought was defence.

In the Egyptian area there was greater liveliness. It was here the Turks were preparing their offensive, and the signs that an attack on the canal in large force was pending were unmistakable. It was on December 1 that Vice-Admiral R. H. Peirse, in pursuance of the Admiralty order to shift his headquarters from Bombay to the canal, re-hoisted his flag in the *Swiftsure* at Suez, and took over the new station which had been added to his own East Indies command in view of the expected invasion of Egypt. The immediate trouble, however, was at the lower end of the Red Sea. There the Turks had re-occupied Sheikh Syed, and were repairing the forts which the *Duke of Edinburgh* and a detachment of her Indian convoy had destroyed in November; and it became a serious question whether another combined attack should not be made upon the re-occupied fort, from which heavy guns would command Perim. The Admiralty were ready to provide the *Ocean*, which, after the capture of Kurnah, had been recalled from the Persian Gulf for the defence of Egypt. But in view of the situation in Mesopotamia the Government of India were strongly impressed with the importance of giving the Arabs no cause of offence. We had issued a proclamation declaring a policy of non-interference, and action

[1] The Turks state that the *Messudieh* was placed in this exposed position by the Germans contrary to Turkish opinion. They also say she was hit before she saw the submarine or could open fire, and that she turned over and sank in ten minutes. Many men were imprisoned in her, but most of them were extricated, when plant and divers arrived from Constantinople and holes could be cut in her bottom. In all 49 officers and 587 men were saved. The casualties were 10 officers and 27 men killed. She sank in shoal water and most of her guns were afterwards salved and added to the minefield and intermediate defences.

on the coast was regarded as highly impolitic unless they showed an openly hostile attitude. Finally therefore, beyond occupying the Farisan Islands and restoring the light-houses which the Turks had abandoned, it was agreed to do nothing more than maintain a patrol in the southern part of the Red Sea and keep a careful watch on the proceedings at Sheikh Syed.

On the coast of Syria, however, Admiral Peirse was given a free hand. When he arrived in Egypt the threatened invasion seemed to be hanging fire. The Arabs that had appeared across the Sinaitic frontier had retired, and though a concentration of troops had been located by French sea-planes at Beersheba, the main army of invasion seemed still to be in training at Damascus. Thanks to the long hesitation of the Turks in declaring war, the defences of the canal were nearly complete. Besides the Australian and New Zealand Divisions, which had been in training in Egypt since the be-ginning of December, the Indian troops which the *Swiftsure* had brought on had been landed at Suez and distributed along the canal. To shorten the line of defence its banks had been cut close to Port Said and the country to the eastward inundated as far south as Kantara. At Ismailia was the French coast defence ship *Requin*, while the *Minerva* and *Doris* were watching our right and left flanks at Akaba and El Arish respectively. Air reconnaissances found no sign of movement at either place, and the lull seemed to give a tempting opportunity for harrying the Turkish communica-tions along the Syrian coast.[1]

The opening came on December 11, when Admiral Peirse received instructions, if he had ships available, to watch the Syrian ports, particularly Alexandretta, Beirut and Haifa, with a view to stopping supplies for the Hejaz railway. He had two light cruisers immediately available, the *Doris* (Captain F. Larken) and the *Askold*, which the Russian Admiralty had recently placed at his disposal. This ship he sent forward to reconnoitre the coast as high as Alexandretta, and on her way she smartly cut a German ship out of Haifa. The *Doris* was to follow as soon as she had seen another air reconnaissance carried out in the Beer-sheba area. As no considerable force was found there Captain Larken at once went north, and proceeded to interpret the Admiralty instructions in a liberal manner. He began by bombarding a small earthwork near Askalon and landing a demolition party. They were fired on from the hills till a few shells dispersed the enemy. Similar reconnaissances at Haifa and Jaffa revealed no signs of a

[1] See Plan p. 118.

concentration. Further north, four miles south of Sidon, a party was landed to cut the coastal telegraph and telephone lines to Damascus. For over two miles the wire was removed and the posts cut down without opposition, and the *Doris* then carried on for Alexandretta, the *Askold* having returned to Port Said.[1]

At Alexandretta a large concentration of Turkish troops was reported, and much activity on the railway, which for some miles northward of the town ran close to highwater mark.[2] Arriving after nightfall on December 18, Captain Larken landed a party two and a half miles north of Bab-i-Yunus (Jonah's Pillar, the old " Syrian Gates "), in spite of the heavy weather that prevailed. In silence they loosened a couple of rails, cut the telegraph, and successfully eluding the patrols regained the ship in safety unobserved. An hour later a train came down from the northward and was derailed. A second which appeared in the morning was shelled, but an attempt to cut off its retreat by destroying a bridge behind it failed, as its ferro-concrete construction resisted the effect of the shells.

In the afternoon of the following day, in accordance with the Ninth Hague Convention (1907), an ultimatum was sent in demanding the surrender of all engines and military stores under penalty of bombardment, and during the night searchlights were kept on the town to prevent the engines being removed. The Turkish reply was that one or more of the British subjects they had in detention would be executed for every Ottoman killed by the threatened bombardment. As this reply came ostensibly from Jemal Pasha, the Commander-in-Chief in Syria, Captain Larken informed him that if any such outrage was perpetrated it would be made one of the terms of peace that he and his staff should be handed over to the British Government for punishment. A few hours' grace was given for a further answer, and the delay was used by the *Doris* to land a party just north of Payas, at the mouth of the Deli Chai, near Durt Yol, where they drove in the patrol and destroyed the railway bridge over the river. The railway station was then wrecked, the telegraph cut and the Armenian Staff brought off at their own earnest entreaty. In return for this service they afforded valuable information with regard to troop movements. Having thus stopped all railway traffic between Adana and Alexandretta, at 9 a.m. on December 22, when the period of grace expired, the *Doris* returned to find the ultimatum accepted.

During the night, under cover of a heavy rainstorm, the military stores had been secretly removed, but two

[1] See Plan p. 382.   [2] See Plan p. 80.

locomotives remained, and these the Kaimakam was ready to destroy provided he could have the loan of some dynamite. Captain Larken, regretting that he had none, offered gun-cotton, and a destruction party under the torpedo-lieutenant of the *Doris* went ashore with it. Then a new difficulty arose. Turkish dignity could not submit to our torpedo-men having anything to do with the destruction. As it was equally impossible to trust them to use the explosive for the purpose intended, there was a deadlock. It was only broken by an intimation that gun-cotton in unfamiliar hands was apt to give unintended results. The Kaimakam then so far changed his attitude as to allow our men to lay the charges, but he still protested he could not permit any one but a Turkish officer to fire them. Hours were spent over the technical difficulty, but eventually it was overcome, with the assistance of the American Vice-Consul, by formally rating the torpedo-lieutenant as a Turkish naval officer for the rest of the day. Further delays ensued from the in-tractability of the engine drivers, and it was not till dark that the comedy was ended by a party of Turkish cavalry rounding up both locomotives and bringing them to the place of execution, when they were duly blown up under the beam of the *Doris's* searchlight.

Having completed his work at Alexandretta Captain Larken stood across the gulf to Ayas Bay, where he had heard of a likely prize. There he found the Deutsche-Levante liner *Odessa*, a new ship of 3,475 tons, but she had been abandoned by her crew and sunk in $2\frac{1}{2}$ fathoms. After driving off a field battery that tried to interrupt the pro-ceedings, an attempt was made to float her, but it was found to be impossible, and she was blown up and burned on Christmas eve. Thence the *Doris* moved to Mersina to see what could be done, but finding the place fully on the alert, she retired to Port Said. Further south the *Askold* had been active again since December 22. On Christmas day she visited Ruad Island and landed a reconnoitring party south of Tripoli. The party was fired on, but nowhere did she observe any serious movement of troops. She also returned to Port Said, but the French cruiser *d'Entrecasteaux* came to Larnaca to carry on with the coastal operations.[1]

In Egypt all was still quiet. On December 19 the Regent had been proclaimed Sultan under British protection, and the severance of connection with Turkey had been well

[1] The *Amiral Charner* seems also to have been in the vicinity. She had arrived at Port Sigri on December 19 in order to take up the Smyrna patrol, but Admiral Carden ordered her to Alexandretta to operate with the *Doris*.

received.   Nor were the good effects of the measure confined
to the country itself.   According to our information this
step, combined with the bold action of the *Doris* at Alexandretta, had produced a marked moral effect in Syria.   Still
there were difficulties about continuing the operations.   The
American Ambassador at Constantinople reported that the
Doris's proceedings at Payas and Alexandretta had led to the
imprisonment of all British subjects in the Damascus district,
and they were threatened with death if Alexandretta or any
undefended port were bombarded.   In view of the Turkish
bombardment of undefended places in the Crimea before
declaration of war the threat was impudent enough, and the
Foreign Office confined itself to instructing our High Com-
missioner at Cairo that, while anxious that British and French
non-combatants should not be exposed to imminent danger,
it was desired to avoid hampering operations unnecessarily
or appearing to yield to Turkish menaces.   There were
certain features in the situation that made the continuance
of coastal operations desirable.   We had intelligence of much
Turkish energy in southern Syria, of the road from Hebron
to Beersheba being completed preparatory to laying a railway, of much railway material at Haifa, of stores of grain
and forage at Gaza; but at the same time there were no
signs of a speedy advance, and, for the present, operations
on the Syrian coast were confined to patrolling against
contraband.

On the Akaba side things were equally quiet.   Turkish
cavalry patrols were occasionally seen by the seaplanes,
and on December 29 the *Minerva* shelled working-parties of
infantry in the hills, but a landing-party which reconnoitred
the road into the interior saw nothing.   This end of the
canal line was now greatly strengthened by the presence of
the *Ocean*, from the Persian Gulf.   Captain A. Hayes-Sadler
had brought her into Suez on December 29, and was directed
to remain there as Senior Naval Officer till further orders.
All local indications pointed to there being no imminent cause
for anxiety, and this impression was confirmed by our Military
Attaché at Sofia.   His report was that Jemal Pasha, the
new commander of the Syrian army, had informed his
Government that it would be impossible to send an expedition against the canal for three months.   There seemed,
therefore, no immediate necessity for risking the safety of
British and French subjects by drastic coastal operations,
and for a time they were discontinued.

But in the first days of the New Year the outlook entirely
changed.   Intelligence gathered in Egypt left no doubt

that the invasion was to be hurried on. The unpopularity of the war was breeding discontent and desertion at Damascus, and the Germans seem to have come to the conclusion that if the blow were not struck quickly it would not be struck at all. The apparent inertia was simply due to the need of establishing food and water supplies well forward, and it was expected that enough had been done to warrant an advance very soon. The force of the invading army was estimated at 20,000 men, besides Arabs, and it seemed probable that one Turkish corps would move down by the coast routes to protect the exposed sea flank of the main advance.

In view of this information, which Admiral Peirse sent home on January 3, he was anxious to resume activity on the Syrian coast, and the *Doris*, which, after another air reconnaissance over Beersheba, had gone north again to look into Mersina, began a systematic harrying of the coast route. On January 5 she tried to land a party to destroy the Mersina railway bridge, but they were detected. Captain Larken, therefore, recalled them, and had to be content with wrecking the bridge by shell-fire. On the following day a double landing-party was put ashore at Jonah's Pillar, where on her previous visit the *Doris* had destroyed the bridge. Here the telegraph and railway lines were cut, and the timber which had been collected to repair the bridge was used as fuel for a fire to twist the rails. All was done in the face of sharp opposition from the railway patrols, and next day (the 7th) a party which had landed to blow up a road bridge further south was beaten back to the boats with the loss of one killed and one wounded. Still the bridge was afterwards dealt with by the ships' guns.

At the same time the Russians were equally active on the Anatolian coast off Sinope. On January 4 a cruiser with a division of destroyers sank a Turkish transport which was being escorted by the *Hamidieh*. Two days later the Russian fleet encountered the *Breslau* and *Hamidieh*, also on escort duty, but they escaped after a few shots had been exchanged. The Russians then proceeded to harry the coastwise traffic, and during the 7th–8th destroyed over fifty vessels at Sinope, Trebizond, Platana and Surmene, and finished by bombarding Khopi. Similar operations were kept up incessantly upon the sea communication of the Turkish army of the Caucasus. On January 19–20 eleven schooners and fifteen feluccas with supplies were sunk between Batum and Trebizond. The Germans could do little to stop the havoc. On January 27 the *Breslau* and *Hamidieh*, which had been continuously engaged in escort and patrol duty along the coast, had again to fly from a squadron of Russian cruisers. The *Goeben* never appeared, and a rumour spread that she had been seriously damaged in a minefield at the entrance of the Bosporus on January 2.[1]

On the Mediterranean side the severity of the blockade tended to increase, and the French were now invited to take a hand. Admiral Boué de Lapeyrère was only too anxious to assist, though some slight difficulty arose in adjusting the respective spheres of action. Since the French had already consented to both the Dardanelles and Egyptian areas being removed out of their general command of the Mediterranean, it was very desirable not to encroach upon it further. But as Admiral Peirse was responsible for the defence of Egypt, the logical arrangement was that he should have in his sphere the whole coast road from Mersina to El Arish, and particularly Alexandretta. Upon this nodal point of the Turkish Imperial communications he wished to maintain an unbroken watch, not only to keep an eye on the movements of Turkish troops southward, but also with a view to future operations. A combined attack on the place was, as we have seen, one of the alternatives for action against Turkey which Lord Kitchener was suggesting. By very weighty opinion it was even regarded as a more suitable objective than the Dardanelles. From this point both the Bagdad and the Hejaz railways were open to attack, so that a lodgment there would go far to secure our position both in Mesopotamia and Egypt, and it could be done with much less force than the Dardanelles required. Even by those who favoured the more ambitious design it was not rejected. For it was felt that if the Dardanelles defences proved too strong to be reduced, the operation could be broken off and given the colour of a feint by an immediate transfer of our attack to Alexandretta.

Admiral Peirse's view of his responsibilities was at once accepted by his French colleague, who agreed to confine himself to the patrol between Mersina and Smyrna. So the *Doris* remained at Alexandretta, while the *Askold* patrolled to the south of her, and two ships of the canal defence force, our own *Proserpine* and the French *Requin*, were told off to support and relieve them when necessary.[2] On

---

[1] She had, in fact, struck two mines in the Black Sea on December 26, and, though with difficulty she was repaired, her speed was reduced.

[2] These two ships did one spell of patrol duty in the first half of January, but at the end of the month, when the *Philomel* and *d'Entrecasteaux* joined, they returned to the canal stations.

January 11 the *Doris* reported that she had so damaged the cliffs near Alexandretta that no wheeled traffic seemed able to reach the town from the northward, and on the 16th the *Askold* damaged a railway bridge near Tripoli. For the rest the work was confined to blockade and reconnaissance, but till the end of the month nothing was seen to move on the coast road. Yet it was certain that a forward movement was being made, and it would look as though the operations had caused the enemy to abandon any idea they may have had of using it.

In Egypt all preparations for defence, both naval and military, had been completed, and the country remained quiet. At the Dardanelles there was, of course, no movement of any kind, but preparations for a naval attack had gone so far that on January 15 Admiral Carden had been informed the force he required would be completed that month; till then there was nothing to do but to keep up the appearance of profound inaction.

Such, then, was the situation in the Eastern Mediterranean as January drew to an end, and the time was at hand when a final decision had to be made in regard to the Dardanelles and Zeebrugge. In the meantime events on the Western Front had begun to fix the most indeterminate factors of the problem. In the middle of the month General Joffre had developed a strong attack in the Soissons area which, though at first successful, was ultimately defeated with severe loss, and he had now decided that in order to carry out his offensive plans he must increase his mobile reserves. For this purpose he was definitely withdrawing from the line between our own army and the sea about 100,000 men, on whose presence in Flanders Field-Marshal French had relied for carrying out his push up the coast. It was clear, therefore, that a combined operation against Zeebrugge was out of the question unless reinforcements were sent him from home in such numbers as would throw out of gear the whole organisation of the new armies and irrevocably commit them to the French theatre.

Even from a defensive point of view, the situation on the Western Front was still not free from anxiety, though the latest events went far to increase confidence in the power of the Allied line to hold. On January 25 the Germans tested the strength of the British front by a heavy attack on both sides of the La Bassée Canal. To the north of it the line held, but on the south bank they gained ground, and it was not until after much sharp fighting lasting well into February that the position was restored. Elsewhere,

ALEXANDRETTA

Scale of Miles

GULF OF ALEXANDRETTA

BAY OF AYAS

ALEXANDRETTA (ISKANDERUN)

Ras el Khanzir

Reproduced from G.S.G.S. Map Nº 1522 by permission of the Geographical Section, General War Office.

at several points of the long line held by the French, there were similar outbursts of local fighting towards the end of the month, but in general the resistance which the Allied line displayed did much to clear the outlook, and from the North Sea the news was equally encouraging.

CHAPTER V

SINCE Christmas time, when the test of the new distribution in the North Sea had terminated in the unfortunate collision between the *Monarch* and *Conqueror*, reports of restlessness in the German naval ports had never ceased, and there was every reason to believe that the comparative impunity with which they had raided the Yorkshire coast in December would tempt the enemy to repeat the venture there or elsewhere.[2] From time to time the Grand Fleet had warning to stand-by for sea at two hours' notice, and occasional reconnaissances were made to the Bight by the Harwich Force, but up till the middle of the month nothing happened.

Considering that it was possible for the Germans to strike at their selected moment and, if they chose to leave the Baltic bare, to strike with their full force, the situation was not without anxiety. With the loss of the *Formidable*, the disablement of the *Conqueror*, and ships away docking, Admiral Jellicoe could only count on eighteen "Dreadnoughts" and eight "King Edwards" against the seventeen German "Dreadnoughts" and twenty-two other older battleships. The *Queen Mary* had just sailed for Portsmouth to be docked, the *Invincible* was at Gibraltar, and the *Inflexible* in the Mediterranean, so that Admiral Beatty had only five battle cruisers against the enemy's four. In view of recent accidents the margin was not great, though ship for ship ours were the more powerful, and about this time there was again some thought of sending the Channel Fleet to the north, that is, the 5th Battle Squadron ("Lord Nelsons" and "Implacables"), of which Admiral Bethell was once more in command, with Rear-Admiral C. F. Thursby as second flag. The three Dreadnought battle squadrons were based at Scapa with the 1st and 6th Cruiser Squadrons and the 2nd Light Cruiser Squadron. The 2nd Cruiser Squadron was at Cromarty. At Rosyth were the battle cruisers, the 3rd Battle Squadron, the 3rd Cruiser Squadron and the 1st Light Cruisers. At Harwich Commodore Tyrwhitt had the light cruisers *Arethusa*, *Aurora*,

---

[1] See Plan No. 3 (*Moltke* and *Derfflinger* to be transposed), and Plan, p. 102.
[2] The *Monarch* rejoined the Grand Fleet on January 20.

Fearless and *Undaunted* and the 1st and 3rd Destroyer Flotillas. Here also was the "oversea" submarine flotilla under Commodore Keyes.[1]

Such was the distribution in the North Sea when, on January 15, more circumstantial reports began to come in. The battle cruisers *Seydlitz* and *Derfflinger* were known to have left the Jade, and our agents reported such feverish activity at Kiel and Wilhelmshaven that an attack seemed imminent. Our battle cruisers, which had been about to go to the north for gunnery practice, were accordingly directed not to leave the base, and on the 17th Admiral Beatty was ordered to proceed with his battle and light cruisers west of Heligoland Bight to support a reconnaissance in force by the Harwich destroyer and submarine flotillas. It was duly carried out on the morning of January 19, but nothing was seen, and one of our submarines, *E 10*, which left Yarmouth for a patrol station north-west of Heligoland, never returned. Nor in the next few days was there any further sign of activity, except that during the night of January 19–20 a new form of coastal attack was made. During the past month two Zeppelin reconnaissances had taken place towards the East Coast, but on this occasion for the first time they penetrated inland. Three naval airships made the attempt, but only two (*L 3* and *L 4*) reached our shores, and they dropped bombs on King's Lynn, Yarmouth and Sheringham. Two men and two women were killed and seventeen men, women and children injured. The material damage amounted to a few thousand pounds. The object of the exploit was obscure. By the crabbed psychology of the Germans a terrorising effect seems to have been looked for. Such influence as it had was in the reverse direction, stimulating effort and hardening purpose.

Signs of more serious offensive measures were dying away, and at sea things seemed to quiet down so much that the Commander-in-Chief proposed to bring the *Iron Duke* down to Cromarty for docking and himself to take a rest ashore, of which, after his six months' strenuous and anxious work, he was in sore need. At the same time special arrangements were made to keep watch by means of submarine patrols on each side of Heligoland and off the Ems, and orders were issued to Harwich for another reconnaissance on the 23rd. But neither arrangement was put into effect, for that morning intelligence came in which set in motion the whole machinery for controlling the North Sea.

What exactly was in the wind was a matter of inference

[1] See Appendix A.

Great activity was reported in the Bight, and another coastal raid seemed probable. The Germans afterwards gave out that their intention was less ambitious. According to an official announcement the operation was provoked by our recent raid into the Bight, and had for its object to clear the Dogger Bank of our fishing vessels and its patrol, which they had persuaded themselves were there mainly for observation and espionage.[1] The connection is not obvious, and we must assume that if the fishing trawlers were really the objective the operation must have been designed to clear the way for some more formidable operation. The force consisted of the battle cruisers *Seydlitz* (flag), *Moltke*, *Derfflinger* and *Blücher*, under Admiral Hipper. The light cruisers *Graudenz* and *Stralsund* formed a screen ahead, and the *Rostock* and *Kolberg* on either flank. Each light cruiser was accompanied by a destroyer half-flotilla. The *Von der Tann* could not take part, as she had been placed in dock-yard hands that morning.[2] Although the precise object of the coming operation was not known to the Admiralty, they were practically certain that a sortie was to take place on the evening of the 23rd. Their inference from the intelligence at their disposal was that they had to deal with a reconnaissance in force as far at least as the Dogger Bank, and that the force engaged would be four battle cruisers, six light cruisers and twenty-two destroyers. Information to this effect was sent out shortly after noon to the Commander-in-Chief at Scapa, to Admiral Beatty and Admiral Bradford (Commanding the 3rd Battle Squadron) at Rosyth, and to Commodore Tyrwhitt at Har-wich, with orders which put in active operation the pre-arranged plan for meeting the long-expected attack.

Accordingly on the night of Saturday, January 23, as the German force was getting under way from its anchorage at Wilhelmshaven, Commodore Keyes, with the *Firedrake*, *Lurcher* and four submarines, was feeling his way out of Harwich in a dense fog, bound for Heligoland and the Ems. Commodore Tyrwhitt, with the *Arethusa*, *Aurora* and *Undaunted* and every destroyer ready for sea,

---

[1] "Das Kreuzergefecht bei der Doggerbank am 24 Januar, nach amtlichen Quellen": von Kapitan zur See D. von Kühlwetter, *Weser Zeitung*, June 19, 1915.

[2] *Derfflinger* had 8–12″, *Seydlitz* and *Moltke* 10–11″ and all three 12–5·9″; *Blücher* 12–8·2″ and 8–5·9.″ Against this the *Lion*, *Tiger* and *Princess Royal* had 8–13·5″ and the *New Zealand* and *Indomitable* 8–12.″ (See also foot-notes (²), pp. 31 and 33.)

The German light cruisers had 12–4·1″ against 8 or 9–6″ of our "Town" class.

followed, making for a rendezvous which the Admiralty had fixed on the north-east part of the Dogger Bank, clear of certain areas to the westward, which on fishermen's reports were suspected of having been mined. At the same time and for the same point Admiral Beatty was coming down with his five battle cruisers. The course he was taking was about south-east, in order to pass through the gap between the Dogger Bank and a suspected area of floating mines to the north of it. His light cruisers, under Commodore Goodenough in the *Southampton*, steamed straight out to sea, with orders to turn southward for the rendezvous when north of the Dogger.[1] Between these two courses Admiral Bradford was taking the 3rd Battle Squadron and 3rd Cruiser Squadron to a rendezvous thirty miles north of the Dogger. Admiral Jellicoe, who had not yet started for Cromarty, was clear of Scapa by 9.0 p.m., and was proceeding, with the Dreadnought fleet, and his three Cruiser squadrons (1st, 2nd and 6th), disposed abreast fifteen miles on either hand and ahead of him, to a rendezvous midway between the Aberdeen coast and Jutland. Further ahead was his light cruiser squadron, under Admiral Napier, who was to reach the rendezvous at 8.0 a.m.—that is, an hour and a half before him—and then spread southwards. His flotilla was also to be there at the same time. His intention was to pass through the rendezvous at 9.30 a.m. on the 24th, and then carry on south-south-east, and on this course the 4th Flotilla from Invergordon was to join him an hour later. These movements, it will be seen, practically covered the whole East Coast, with the exception of the approaches to Aberdeen, between the tracks of the battleships and the battle cruisers. The trap was perfected by a strict order that no wireless was to be used till the enemy was sighted, except for messages of the first importance.

So all night, stealthily and in silence, the various sections of the Grand Fleet sped to the appointed stations. The whole movement worked to time like a clock, except that, owing to the fog at starting, the Harwich flotillas were a little late. Up in the north it was very still, with a gentle breeze from the north-east and a quiet sea, and, as the hours slipped by, excitement grew, for now and again German wireless could be heard that seemed to indicate something serious was in the wind. But nothing further could be done, and the well-ordered combination went on unchecked.

By 7.0—with the first shimmer of dawn—Admiral Beatty

[1] 1st Light Cruiser Squadron: *Southampton, Birmingham, Nottingham, Lowestoft.*

was passing through his rendezvous with his four light cruisers, who had joined about half an hour earlier, running on a parallel course five miles on his port beam. Within ten minutes Commodore Tyrwhitt was sighted ahead in the *Arethusa*, with seven of the new " M " class destroyers in company, led by Captain The Hon. H. Meade.[1] The *Aurora* (Captain W. S. Nicholson) and *Undaunted* (Captain F. G. St. John), with the rest of the destroyers, having been delayed by the fog at starting, were about thirteen miles astern.[2]

After passing through the rendezvous, Admiral Beatty proceeded due south in the order *Lion* (Captain A. E. M. Chatfield), *Tiger* (Captain H. B. Pelly), *Princess Royal* (Captain O. de B. Brock), *New Zealand* (Captain L. Halsey), with Rear-Admiral Sir Archibald Moore's flag, and *Indomitable* (Captain F. W. Kennedy). He was on this course when he came in sight of the *Arethusa*, and being thus assured there was no enemy to the southward, he signalled his light cruisers, which had been opening out their distance from him, to spread for look-out duties at extreme signalling distance in a line of bearing north-east by north from the flagship. This was at 7.15, but while the signal was being made the *Southampton* could see gun flashes in the grey of the coming dawn ahead of her. To the *Lion* they were also visible on the port bow, that is, to the south-eastward, and hope beat high when, a few minutes later, the long-prayed-for signal came in from the *Aurora* that she was engaged with the enemy's fleet. The last signal to the light cruisers to spread was promptly negatived, with an order to " chase S. 10 E. (mag.); " and at 7.35 the Admiral held away at 22 knots

---

[1]

Meteor	*Mentor*
Milne	*Mastiff*
Minos	*Morris*

The *Miranda*, Commander Barry Domvile, having reached Harwich from Sheerness too late to follow the *Arethusa*, came on with *Undaunted*.

[2] FIRST FLOTILLA.

Flotilla Cruiser : *Aurora.*

1st Division	3rd Division	4th Division	5th Division
Acheron	*Ferret*	*Hornet*	*Goshawk*
Attack	*Forester*	*Tigress*	*Phœnix*
Hydra	*Defender*	*Sandfly*	*Lapwing*
Ariel	*Druid*	*Jackal*	

THIRD FLOTILLA.

Flotilla Cruiser : *Undaunted.*

1st Division	2nd Division	3rd Division	4th Division
Lookout	*Laurel*	*Laforey*	*Legion*
Lysander	*Liberty*	*Lawford*	*Lark*
Landrail	*Laertes*	*Lydiard*	
	Lucifer	*Louis*	

south-south-east (mag.) for the point where the flashes of the guns had been seen.

It could not yet be told whether the force of the enemy was what we expected; but from the course on which it was sighted he appeared to be making to pass north of his Dogger Bank minefield on a course which cut across that on which Admiral Beatty had come out. To this extent the intelligence on which the Admiralty had formed their appreciation was confirmed. The *Arethusa*, being well up to time, must have passed ahead of the raiding force without sighting them, but the *Aurora*, being half an hour astern, had fallen in with them. Shortly after 7.0, as she led her destroyers northward, she had made out a three-funnelled cruiser and four destroyers on her starboard beam. Dawn was only just breaking, and thinking she was probably the *Arethusa*, Captain Nicholson closed a little and gave the challenge. She was, in fact, the *Kolberg*, and at 7.15 she opened fire at over 8,000 yards with salvoes. At first they were fairly accurate, and the *Aurora* was hit slightly three times, but as she replied and began to hit in her turn the enemy's fire became ragged. In about ten minutes a shell was seen to explode under the enemy's forebridge, and she turned away to the eastward. The *Aurora* then continued to make for the rendezvous in company with the *Undaunted*, who had not been able to get near enough to share the action. Further enemy forces now appeared in the distance on their starboard quarter, and our two light cruisers with their flotillas turned to the north-eastward to keep contact. On this course they were soon in touch (7.30) with the *Southampton*, and through her the *Aurora* reported the presence of enemy forces to S.E. and E.S.E. of her. A few minutes later the *Southampton* sighted the battle cruisers and a group of light cruisers. They then seemed to be heading north-west, but, according to the German account, having already spread for their sweep of the Dogger, the whole force reconcentrated at the first alarm from the *Kolberg*, and then headed for home at high speed.[1]

Since Admiral Beatty, on the *Aurora's* report, had altered to S.S.E. (mag.) in chase, he had been working gradually up to full speed and turning slightly to the eastward. The effect was, that in a few minutes (7.50) he himself could see the enemy's battle cruisers on his port bow fourteen miles away.

---

[1] The *Aurora* actually reported that the enemy's light cruisers were to the E.S.E., and their battle cruisers to the S.E. of her; but this cannot be reconciled with the *Southampton's* report made a few minutes later or with the German accounts of the battle. It is probable that *Aurora* was mistaken in thinking that the vessels to the S.E. of her were battle cruisers,

Commodore Goodenough, who was keeping touch, had just reported there were four of them, and in a few minutes the whole force was seen to be steaming homewards on a south-easterly course.[1] Though the visibility was high, the dim light and the volumes of smoke which the enemy were emitting as they stoked up to escape made their movements and numbers uncertain.   At a signal from the flagship, Commodore Tyrwhitt sent his "M" class destroyers ahead to report their strength, and himself followed in support, while Admiral Beatty kept on in a general south-easterly direction and continued to increase speed.

The "M" class destroyers, led by Captain Meade in the *Meteor*, raced on till they had closed to 9,000 yards.   The enemy then (8.15) altered course to engage them, and the rear ship, opening fire, forced them to turn away.   But after half a dozen rounds the Germans resumed their flight, and Captain Meade carried on again till he was near enough to report definitely their strength and course.   For the past hour the flotilla cruisers had also been sending in reports, so that by about 8.45 it was clear that the enemy consisted of four battle cruisers, at least four light cruisers, and a whole flotilla of destroyers.

By this time Admiral Jellicoe had received full information of what was going on.   With his three battle squadrons and the 1st, 2nd and 6th Cruiser Squadrons disposed fifteen miles ahead and on either beam, and four divisions of the 4th Flotilla ahead of all, he had reached, shortly before 8.0 a.m., a point about 150 miles north-north-west of where the fighting had begun.   He had been steering a south-easterly course, but now altered more to starboard, to intercept the enemy if they broke away north.   The 2nd Light Cruiser Squadron he had sent on to the southward to join Admiral Bradford, who, with the 3rd Battle and 3rd Cruiser Squadrons, had reached his rendezvous north of the Dogger.   To complete the net Admiral Jellicoe now sent him an urgent order to proceed at his utmost speed to the eastward towards a point where he would be in a position to cut the enemy off if they should make to the north-westward.   These dispositions exactly supplemented those of Admiral Beatty.

His intention was to engage the enemy on their lee quarter, and this position he had not quite gained, when, at 8.15, he settled down to the chase on a parallel course.   It was a stern chase and must inevitably be a long one, but as knot by knot

[1] The tracks and relative positions of the various units of the enemy before 7.50 are very doubtful, and up to this point no attempt has been made to plot them on the chart.

the battle cruisers worked up speed it became clear they were gaining. The response of the engine-room was magnificent. By 8.30 they were doing 26 knots, and the Admiral called for 27. Yet the *Indomitable*, whose mean trial speed was only just over 25, was keeping up, and the flagship, in admiration, signalled "Well steamed, *Indomitable*." The work of the *New Zealand*, which, though on her trial she had done 26, was designed for 25, was scarcely less splendid. But every man in the engine-rooms knew it was the chance of a lifetime, and all that men could do they did.

The situation was now growing clearer. The *Meteor* was able to signal the enemy's strength, and having got up to within 9,000 yards of them, was being fired on by the *Blücher*. Accordingly, Admiral Beatty, who was getting into extreme range of the enemy, recalled the Commodore and the "M" class destroyers, and directed them to take station ahead of the line. The rest of the destroyers were about two miles astern, and Commodore Goodenough's light cruisers were in a good position for observing on the enemy's port quarter. Admiral Hipper was leading the German battle cruisers in the *Seydlitz*, with the *Moltke* second, *Derfflinger* third, and *Blücher* last; two light cruisers were ahead, and the other two with all the destroyers were on the engaged side.

At 8.30 Admiral Beatty informed the Commander-in-Chief of the exact situation. On receiving the message Admiral Jellicoe held on as he was, and ordered Admiral Bradford, with the 3rd Battle Squadron, to steer for Heligoland in support of our cruisers and flotillas.

For Admiral Beatty the action had now settled down to a plain, stern chase. Speed was the dominating factor, and at 8.52 he signalled for 29 knots, well knowing that his two rear ships must begin to fall astern; but much had to be risked to get a hold on the rear of the flying enemy. The range was then judged to be down to 20,000 yards, and the *Lion* tried a shot. It fell short; a second at extreme elevation was over, and making the signal to engage, Admiral Beatty began a slow and deliberate fire on the rear ship. The firing was quickly taken up by the *Tiger* and *Princess Royal ;* and, a quarter of an hour after the engagement began, the *Lion* seemed to be hitting the *Blücher*. The range was still well over eight miles; but our leading battle cruisers, which had now worked up to their utmost speed, were gaining fast. At 9.14, as our fire was becoming effective, the enemy returned it. The *Lion* now shifted to the *Derfflinger*, leaving the *Tiger* and the *Princess Royal* to deal with the *Blücher*. As our ships began hitting almost at once, Admiral Beatty altered slightly to starboard to bring the after turrets into bearing, and all three commenced regular salvoes. Both the enemy's rear ships began to suffer. Prisoners stated that the third salvo fired at the *Blücher* hit her well down on the water-line and materially reduced her speed. The fourth did enormous damage, both to ship and crew, almost carrying away the after super-structure, and disabling two turrets aft and between 200 and 300 men. Several of the *Lion's* salvoes were reported to have hit her new target, and from prisoners it was learned that she received a large amount of damage aft. Now, however, three of the enemy's ships were concentrating on the *Lion*, and at 9.28 she felt her first hit. The shell took her on the water-line and penetrated her bunkers. The damage was soon made good with hammocks and mess stools, but it was clearly time to break the enemy's fire concentration. Already the *New Zealand* had begun to engage the *Blücher* ; so that at 9.35 the Admiral, seeing he had gained enough on the enemy, made the signal to engage opposite numbers. He himself took on the *Seydlitz*, who was leading, and had just opened fire with her 11″ guns, but as the range was still up to 17,500 yards the shots fell short; but, on the other hand, the *Lion* must have found the target at once. According to Admiral Scheer the *Seydlitz* was so badly hit astern, in the early stages of the battle, that she could not use her heavy guns aft for the rest of the action. " The first shell that hit her had a terrible effect. It pierced right through the upper deck in the ship's stern and through the barbette-armour of the rear turret, where it exploded. All parts of the stern, the officers' quarters, mess, etc., that were near where the explosion took place were totally wrecked. In the reloading chamber, where the shell penetrated, part of the charge in readiness for loading was set on fire. The flames rose high up into the turret and down into the ammunition chamber, and from thence through a connecting door usually kept shut, through which the men from the ammunition chamber tried to escape into the fore turret. The flames thus made their way through to the other ammunition chamber, and from thence up to the second turret, and from this cause the entire gun crews of both turrets perished very quickly. The flames rose above the turrets as high as a house."

Meanwhile the *Princess Royal*, in accordance with the signal, had shifted to the third ship, the *Derfflinger* but the *Tiger* unfortunately misinterpreted Admiral Beatty's meaning. At 9.41, when Captain Pelly took in the signal, he was already engaging the leading ship. As the British force was five to four, and he thought the *Indomitable* was by this time in action with the fourth ship of the enemy's line, he believed, that, by engaging the leading ship, he was acting in accordance with the General Fleet Instructions, which laid special emphasis on the tactical importance of disabling the enemy's van. To some extent the principle was a legacy from the sailing era, when disablement of the van necessarily threw a close-hauled fleet into confusion. Though of less decisive importance with ships of free movement, the principle was still cherished, but latterly, as the increasing power of guns and torpedo tended to long-range actions, and fire control became the dominant factor, it had been overshadowed by other considerations. It had become vital that the enemy's fire control should not be undisturbed, and consequently the master principle was that no ship should be left unfired upon.

This principle was not being observed. In spite of her fine effort the *Indomitable* had not yet got within range, the *New Zealand* was engaging the *Blücher* and the *Princess Royal* the *Derfflinger*, so that the *Moltke* was not being fired at. The Germans were clinging to the principle of concentrating on the van, and their three leading ships were all engaging the *Lion*. The result was that the *New Zealand* and *Princess Royal*, being undisturbed, were making excellent practice on their opposite numbers. But, on the other hand, the *Moltke*, the middle ship of the three that were on the *Lion*, was also undisturbed. To make matters worse, in the gloom of the dull morning, interference from the enemy's smoke, as it drifted down the range, became so bad that the *Tiger* soon lost sight of the leading ships, and the *Southampton* signalled that her salvoes were all going over.

At this time, moreover, there was distraction from destroyers. Two of the enemy's ships, besides the *Blücher*, were observed to be on fire, and to us it appeared that the German flotillas were meditating an attack, in order to check the chase. For the past quarter of an hour Admiral Beatty had been expecting an effort of this kind, but Commodore Tyrwhitt, in order not to foul the range with his smoke, had been gradually dropping back with the flotillas to a position broad on the battle cruisers' port quarter, and at 9.20 the Admiral had again ordered him to get ahead at utmost speed. But so fast were the battle cruisers going, that, do what they could, the flotillas had scarcely gained on them, when Admiral Beatty signalled a general warning to the squadron, and turned away two points (9.40). The battle cruisers had, in fact, to rely on their own powers of defence. Commodore Tyrwhitt, for all his efforts, had been unable to work his flotilla up to the head of the line, and, in desperation he ordered his " M " class destroyers to go on ahead at their utmost speed. Captain Meade, in spite of the odds, led away with alacrity in the *Meteor*, yet so great was the pace of the battle cruisers that even the *Meteor*, with her three fastest sisters, *Miranda*, *Mentor* and *Milne*, could only creep forward by inches. The anticipated attack did not take place, and for the next half hour the artillery duel continued with great intensity.   It was at about this time that the *Seydlitz* was struck by the shell which put her after guns out of action, and our concentration of fire was certainly telling on the two last ships of the enemy's line, both of which were reported to be on fire.   The *Seydlitz* which was leading was blazing amidships.

Our own flagship also began to suffer.   At 9.54 a heavy shell struck the roof of " A " turret, smashed it in and disabled one of the guns.   A few minutes later (10.1) an 11-inch shell from the *Seydlitz* pierced the *Lion's* armour. The engineer's workshop was flooded; the water spread to the open switch-board compartment, short-circuited two of the dynamos, disabled the after fire control and secondary armament circuits, and the ship began to take a list to port; but her speed, which had just been reduced to 24 knots to allow the squadron to close up, appears to have been maintained, and the battle continued at a range which increased considerably after our turn away at 9.40.[1]

Shortly after 10.0 the action assumed a new aspect, but what occurred is difficult to determine, for from now the movements of each Admiral became obscure to the other. Away on the port beam of the battle cruisers, Commodore Goodenough, who all this time had been maintaining his observing position on the enemy's port quarter, came under so heavy a fire from the *Blücher*, that he had to turn his squadron right away and open out the range, before he could resume his course.   To him it seemed that the *Blücher* had sheered away from our battle cruisers, and so come within range of the light cruiser squadron; but to Admiral Hipper it appeared that our light cruisers were closing him, and he ordered his battle cruisers to engage with their port armament and drive them off.

---

[1] It would seem there was some reason to believe that the 10.1 hit narrowly missed having still more serious consequences.   After piercing the ship's armour without exploding it passed through the top of the 4-inch magazine trunk and then broke in two.   Had it by some chance burst at this precise moment an explosion in the magazine would probably have followed, which must have badly crippled the ship's fighting power, but the chance of course was fairly remote.

Our own battle cruisers were no less uncertain of the enemy's movements. Their destroyers were setting up a dense screen of smoke, so that it was no longer possible even to spot the fall of our shells, and the impression on Admiral Beatty's mind was that another attempt from their flotilla was imminent, and that the heavy ships were sheering to the northward to get out of range.

But none of the German authorities, who have described the battle, make any mention of such a manœuvre; and it is unlikely that Admiral Hipper should have committed his squadron to a move calculated to reduce its lead on our ships at the very moment when he was making every effort to get away. It is probable, therefore, that the *Blücher*, which by now had suffered severely, yawed away to the northward at about 10.0, and that the remainder of the German squadron roughly maintained its course and speed, except for an occasional zigzag to throw out the range.

At 10.18, when Admiral Beatty, by successive turns towards the enemy, had brought the range down to about 17,500 yards, two more shells struck his flagship simultaneously. So great was the shock that at the moment it was thought a torpedo had got home. In any case it was bad enough. One shell hit the armour below the water-line, drove several plates through the timber backing and flooded the foremost port bunkers. The other pierced the armour on the water-line forward, burst in the torpedo body room, and in a few minutes all the adjacent compartments were flooded up to the main deck. It was too hot to last. The enemy's fire was accurate and very rapid; the salvoes fell well together; their leading ships had got her range so well that splashes from their " shorts " were drenching the conning-tower and turret hoods like green seas, and Admiral Beatty was forced to begin zigzagging. All that our battle cruisers had left in them was now needed if they were to come to a decision. By this time it was fairly certain that under cover of the smoke screen the enemy's rearmost ships had hauled out on the port quarter of their leader. At 10.22, therefore, Admiral Beatty, in spite of the damage to his flagship, responded with a signal for his squadron to take up a line of bearing N.N.W. (mag.) from him, and to proceed at utmost speed. He was desperately anxious to close the range for decisive action, but he could do no more than this, for the enemy's flotilla at once altered to starboard, and it seemed as though they meant to parry any attempt of ours to get to port by forcing us to cross their wake if we persisted in it. This was a risk that could not be taken for fear of minelaying, and there was nothing for it but to rely on speed to overlap the flying enemy, and so either force them to the northward towards Admiral Jellicoe or compel them to accept close action. The day was still young, they were over a hundred miles from Heligoland, our battle fleet was on its way down, barely 150 miles to the northward, and all the ships, except the *Derfflinger*, showed signs of suffering. There could, indeed, be little doubt of a crushing victory if only our speed would hold.

The *Blücher*, at least, was clearly doomed. She was still burning; and, while making a desperate effort to return our fire, she seemed getting out of control and was dropping astern, but was able to follow her consorts. The remaining enemy ships were evidently bent on getting back to their base, and to this end they were wisely staking everything on disabling the British flagship. Two of them, if not all three, were still concentrating on her, and not without effect. Between 10.35 and 10.50 shell after shell hit her. Again the armour was pierced and more bunkers flooded. A shell burst in "A" turret lobby and caused a fire. It was quickly extinguished, and still the only thought was to get to decisive range, and that nothing should check the rush the Admiral made a signal, which, like the old "general chase," made tactics subservient to the one thing needed. It was to close the enemy as rapidly as they could without throwing guns out of bearing. At the moment (10.48) the *Blücher*, out of control, began a wide circle to port, a movement which quickly brought her within range of our own light cruisers, who engaged her. Her movement was at once detected by the Admiral, and he signalled to his rear ship, the *Indomitable*, which had just come into action, to "engage the enemy breaking away to the northward."

To all appearance the prospect of a crushing victory, worthy to rank with the two famous chases of Anson, was in Admiral Beatty's grasp, when suddenly the whole outlook was changed. Shortly before 11.0 the *Lion* was shaken from stem to stern by a hit that drove in the armour on the water-line abreast of one of the boiler-rooms, and did so much damage to the feed tank and in the engine-room that the port engine had to be stopped. No. 1 dynamo was also thrown off by a short circuit, so that both light and power failed, and the list to port increased to 10 degrees. So the flying enemy attained his end. The *Lion* could now do no more than 15 knots, and though as full of fight as ever, she had to fall out of her station and see her consorts race past her.

Since the flagship was leading the result was all that the advocates of concentration on the van could wish. The Admiral lost control, but he did not transfer the command to Admiral Moore. In fact, a period ensued at the crisis of the action when neither Admiral was in a position to direct the movements of the fleet, and inevitable confusion of aim occurred. Just before the *Lion* was forced to fall out of the line, and while the Admiral was still in control, submarines were reported on her starboard bow.[1] To avoid them the Admiral signalled for eight points together to port (10.54). The movement was not without danger. On the new course the squadron must pass across the track of the enemy's destroyers and be exposed to the peril of mines. The Admiral quickly saw, however, that the turn as ordered was unnecessarily wide. It made the course north by east, almost at right angles to that of the enemy, and would mean losing a lot of ground before the chase could be resumed. All that was needed was that the squadron should not pass over the spot where the rear of the destroyers line had been at the moment when the turn was made; if that was cleared, the mine danger was cleared. Accordingly at 11.2 two minutes after the eight-point signal had been hauled down, he hoisted " Course N.E." The new course, while it converged with that of the enemy, was enough to avoid the danger point, and at the same time would cut the *Blücher* off from the rest of the German squadron, and, as he hoped and expected, force them to turn back to her support. If, however, they decided to leave her to her fate, his intention was to turn again to a parallel course as soon as he was clear of the track of the enemy's destroyers.

German authorities claim that at about this moment Admiral Hipper did in fact make an effort to save the *Blücher* by ordering his flotillas to attack, and by turning his squadron to the southward. If by this last movement he

[1] Gayer, (Vol. I., pp. 22–3), states: " During the afternoon of the 23rd *U 19*, *U 21*, *U 32* and *U 33* had been made ready to proceed on that day to the rendezvous of our battle cruisers. They might, therefore, have been used decisively on the 24th. . . . Regardless of these considerations, *U 21* left harbour during the afternoon of the 23rd for the Irish Sea; *U 19* and *U 33* were kept ready in the Ems, and *U 32* was out on patrol fifteen miles to the north of Borkum. . . . On the morning of January 24, the submarine captain on duty in the Ems, when he received the signal from Admiral Hipper that enemy forces had been sighted, sent out the three submarines then in readiness to support our own squadron, which was then returning to the Heligoland Bight in action with a superior force. But it was too late." On these facts it is clear that none of these submarines could have been on the spot where they were reported or have taken any part in the action.

hoped to lead our battle cruisers from his stricken ship, the
sharp turn which we made in an opposite direction at eleven
o'clock must have disconcerted him. He had, as it were,
offered a gambit which his opponent had declined. It is
quite clear, however, that his attempt to extricate the *Blücher*
was abandoned almost at once; for neither the destroyer
attack nor the turn to the southward was so much as noticed
in our squadron. It may well be that the German Admiral,
when he saw our eight-point turn at right angles to his own
course, believed he would be able to gain enough ground on
his pursuers to save his squadron. It must at least have
seemed to open up a new prospect of escape which should
be exploited to its utmost possibility, and he therefore
resumed his course for home, leaving the *Blücher* to her
fate. If our estimate of the damage suffered by his
remaining ships is accurate, it was the best thing that he
could do.

On our side, Admiral Moore took charge of the squadron
in circumstances of exceptional difficulty. By Admiral
Beatty's orders the squadron had just been turned at right
angles to the enemy's course to avoid a reported submarine.
The range was therefore opening out very fast, and, if we
are to understand rightly what followed, it must be borne
in mind that Admiral Moore had not sighted a submarine
and was unaware of the reason that had caused the Vice-
Admiral to order an abrupt turn across the rear of the
flying enemy. Nor was it possible for Admiral Beatty
to explain. The *Lion* was fast dropping astern and she
could no longer act as guide to the squadron. Her wireless
was out of action, she had only two signal halyards
left, and Admiral Beatty felt that all he could do to
make his intentions clear before abandoning control of
the action was to hoist two short signals. The first was,
" Attack the enemy's rear," and the second that which
Nelson had used as his last word at Trafalgar, " Keep closer
to the enemy." Unhappily the signals were very difficult
to read. As the wind was, the flags blew end on to the
other three battle cruisers, and the first of the two signals
seems to have been hoisted before the compass signal " Course
N.E." had been hauled down. The result was that the
Rear-Admiral concluded that his Chief was ordering the
squadron to " attack the enemy's rear bearing N.E.," that
being the meaning of the flag groups as they were seen from
the *New Zealand,* as well as from the *Tiger* and *Indomitable,*
who both logged the signal in the same terms. The misunderstanding would, in all probability, have been cleared

up by the Vice-Admiral's final signal, "Keep closer to the enemy"; but none of the battle cruisers took it in. The *Blücher*, which bore about N.E. from the *New Zealand*, was therefore taken to be the objective indicated, both by the eight-point turn made at 11.0, which had actually broken off the action and by the signals subsequently received. The *Tiger* and *Princess Royal* at once ceased firing on the *Moltke* and *Derfflinger*, and edged off to starboard to circle round the *Blücher*. True, she was still fighting gamely. In spite of her condition she had been straddling our light cruisers so accurately that Commodore Goodenough had been forced to turn away. But he was again engaging her and, what is more, Captain Meade, seeing it was hopeless to reach the enemy's flotilla, was concentrating his four " M " class destroyers to make an attack on her, so that escape was no longer possible for the forlorn ship.

Thus the German battle cruiser squadron, half beaten as it was, was left alone. The luck which had snatched the Germans from our grasp in the Scarborough raid stood by them, and, for the second time, gave them a means of escape.

Admiral Moore had no difficulty in performing the duty that he thought had been assigned to him, for the *Blücher's* final destruction was now certain. It could be seen that Commodore Goodenough's ships were hitting her effectively at 14,000 yards, and she could only fire with two of her turrets. A Zeppelin which came over and tried to intervene was driven off. The *Arethusa* was also coming up, and so were the " M " class destroyers, and at 11.20 the *Meteor* was near enough to fire a torpedo; but, as she was manœuvring for position, she was hit forward by a heavy shell, which burst in the foremost boiler-room and put her out of action. The other three destroyers took their turn and hits were claimed. The *Arethusa* had just come into action with her foremost 6″ gun, and, holding on till the range was down to 2,500 yards, starboarded her helm and engaged with torpedo. Two were fired and both, it was claimed, took effect, one under the fore-turret and one in the engine-room, with the result that all her lights were extinguished. The *Blücher*, too, fired torpedoes at the *Arethusa*, and possibly also at the battle cruisers as they crossed astern of her, but the distance was too great, and they circled round her, pouring in salvoes till she was a mere mass of smoke and flame. Then, at last, deserted, completely out of control and without power of resistance, she gave up the unequal struggle.

For three hours, during which she had been the focus of

an overwhelming concentration of fire, she had never ceased to reply. Twice our light cruisers had approached to com- plete her destruction, and twice she had forced them to draw off. As an example of discipline, courage and fighting spirit her last hours have seldom been surpassed.

At 11.45 Commodore Tyrwhitt signalled that she appeared to have struck. Admiral Moore then ceased fire, and turned his attention to the ships that had abandoned her. In circling round her he had come to about his original course, and could at once resume the chase. But the three flying battle cruisers were now well out of range—over twelve miles away—and still apparently doing their full 25 knots. Was it possible to overtake them? It must be two hours, he calculated, before he could get into effective range again, and by that time, since he made his position a little over eighty miles from Heligoland, they would be close to the island. It would be practically impossible to push things home to a decision, particularly as the squadron had intercepted a signal to Commodore Keyes, who was disposing his sub- marines on their intercepting positions, that the High Seas Fleet was coming out. There was also the *Lion* to consider. Not a word could be got from her, and in grave fear for her safety Admiral Moore decided to retire in her direction, and leave the light cruisers to rescue the *Blücher's* survivors.

As he held away back to the north-westward, Commodore Tyrwhitt closed the burning ship in the *Arethusa*. " She was," he says, " in a pitiable condition—all her upper works wrecked, and fires could be seen raging between decks through enormous shot holes in her sides." She had a heavy list to port, and on her upper deck and net shelves were clustered some 300 men, who raised a cheer as the *Arethusa* drew near to the rescue. She had got within a hundred yards when, at 12.10, the *Blücher* suddenly capsized, and after floating a few minutes bottom upwards disappeared. All boats were immediately lowered, and with the help of the destroyers 260 survivors were picked up. More might have been done, but a seaplane came up and began to bomb the rescuers. It was quickly driven off by gunfire, and did no harm, except to kill some of the *Blücher's* men who were still struggling in the water. It must be assumed that the German airmen mistook her for a British ship, and in their eagerness to damage her, failed to take in the real situation. The survivors could only be left to their fate, particularly as a Zeppelin was coming up, bent, apparently, on repeating the sorry attack, and Commodore Tyrwhitt had to call off his destroyers and boats.

Of all this Admiral Beatty knew nothing. So far as he could tell the chase was still being pressed as he had intended, and he was doing his utmost to rejoin it.   In about a quarter of an hour after the *Lion* fell out of the line, having ascertained that immediate repairs were impossible, he determined to shift his flag and endeavour to resume command. At his call the destroyer *Attack* was smartly brought alongside while the *Lion* was still under way, and by 11.50 he was away in her to rejoin the squadron at her utmost speed. But the effort was in vain. When at noon he came in sight of them they were coming back towards him.

At a loss to know what it meant, he held on till he was abreast of the *Princess Royal*, and then, going alongside, transferred his flag to her. His hope was that at least one of the three flying ships had been sunk, and even before he heard they had all been suffered to carry on homewards in their damaged condition, he signalled to turn back 16 points after them. Further inquiry and reflection, however, convinced him that no more could be done. It was now too late, the crucial half-hour had been missed, and he came reluctantly to the conclusion that there was nothing left to do but re-form the squadron and go back to the *Lion* to cover her retirement.

When he picked her up she was heading homewards, still steaming with her remaining engine at about 12 knots, but her position was not a little precarious. Enemy submarines had been sighted by the squadron shortly before they closed her, and so tempting a target was likely to need all the destroyer protection that could be afforded. On the other hand, the flotillas, having heard the report of the High Seas Fleet being out, were anxious to sweep back at dark and make an attack upon it in force. At 2.30 Admiral Beatty proposed to the Commander-in-Chief that he should keep one flotilla to screen the *Lion* and send the rest back towards Heligoland to try to catch the German fleet after dark. About the same time, however, the *Lion's* starboard engine began to give trouble—her speed dropped to 8 knots, and it looked as if she would soon not be able to steam at all. By 3.30, before Admiral Beatty received an answer about the destroyer attack, it was clear she could not carry on alone, and he had to order the *Indomitable* to take her in tow. Shortly afterwards, and before he knew the state of affairs, Admiral Jellicoe sent word that he was detaching the 4th Flotilla to provide a screen, and that Commodore Tyrwhitt might sweep towards Heligoland with his own two flotillas to cover the withdrawal of the injured ship. But the movement was never carried out. With the *Lion* in tow the danger of torpedo attack was greater than ever, and all available protection would be needed. By the time Admiral Jellicoe's message was received the two sections of the Grand Fleet, which since the abandonment of the chase had been rapidly approaching one another, were in visual contact, and having fully realised the situation, the Commander-in-Chief ordered that the whole of the flotillas should be devoted to screening the two exposed ships.

Nor was even this considered sufficient. They were also to be protected to the eastward by a cruiser screen. At 2.15 p.m. Admiral Jellicoe had ordered the 2nd Light Cruisers, which he had sent down to act with the 3rd Battle Squadron, to carry on to Admiral Beatty, and both light cruiser squadrons now formed in line ahead ten miles on the Heligoland side, and the whole force proceeded to the northward, till at 4.30, when the two Admirals were in sight of one another, the Commander-in-Chief turned back for Scapa. An hour later the *Lion* was in tow. The night was now falling—at any moment the German destroyers might appear—but not till he knew all was going well did Admiral Beatty move northward out of the danger area with his three remaining battle cruisers, and leave his wounded flagship with her escort to make her way direct to Rosyth.

It was an anxious night. Shortly after Admiral Beatty parted company the *Lion's* engines broke down altogether, and the *Indomitable* could make but little more than 7 knots. It was scarcely to be believed that the enemy would not attempt a destroyer attack, and in the night a change of course was made, so as to avoid the direct route north of the Tyne minefield. Hour after hour went by with no sign of the enemy, and the fear that he might be postponing an attack until daylight increased the anxiety when morning broke. It found the *Lion* well within the area of the enemy's submarine activities and over a hundred miles from her base. It was an ideal spot for submarines to lie in wait. With break of day the flotillas reformed as a submarine screen, but still no enemy showed himself. All that day they toiled on, increasing speed as some of the *Lion's* flooded compartments were pumped out, and so at last, by a fine display of seamanship, she was brought into safety, and before dawn on January 26 was anchored in the Forth.

So ended the second timorous attempt of the Germans to prove their allegation that the old spirit of the British navy was dead. Their cue was to boast that their enemy was skulking in port with no power to assert a domination of the

North Sea. They had their answer, but it was not such an answer as our own men could have wished. The old spirit was too vigorously alive to be content with such a victory. Still, much had been done, and the solid outcome was that for many a long day the Germans did not venture again to make good their idle claim. Several months elapsed before the German Government issued a detailed account of the action, and this long silence, combined with the inaccuracies of the report, when published, told plainly enough how severe had been the moral shock of the encounter. The assertion that our forces consisted of "thirteen large ships and seven small cruisers" is certainly difficult to explain. Admiral Scheer has accurately described the composition of our squadron in his narrative of the battle, and we are forced to conclude that documents accessible to him were either withheld from the official reporter, or handed over in a garbled condition. The report also alleges that, excepting the *Blücher*, the German ships were hardly hit at all, and this statement must have been read with great surprise on board the three surviving cruisers. Their claim to have inflicted heavy losses on us, though untrue, was probably more honest. The enemy had twice seen Commodore Goodenough's squadron come within range and turn away as though badly hit; they had twice brought our destroyers under a heavy fire; they had observed their shells exploding upon the *Lion*, and had watched her turn away out of the line with a heavy list, whilst, as she did so, our squadron made a movement, which, to them, must have looked as though we had given up the fight. In addition to all this the commander of the German destroyer *V 5*, which took part in the attack at the close of the action, was confident that he had torpedoed one of our battle cruisers; and he was corroborated by the German airship, which did so much execution amongst the helpless survivors of the *Blücher*. Her report was that only four of our large ships withdrew from the battle.[1]

These things combined very likely induced the German authorities to believe, quite honestly, that we had suffered more than we chose to admit. In reality we had nothing to conceal, for our losses, with the exception of damage to the *Lion*, were negligible. The *Meteor* was towed safely into the Humber by the *Liberty*, with four dead and two wounded, and no other destroyer was touched. In the *Lion*, the casualties were eleven men wounded; in the *Tiger*, Captain C. G. Taylor the Squadron Engineer Officer and nine men were killed, and

[1] See Scheer, pp. 83–4.

three officers and five men wounded. The other three battle cruisers were not once hit. According to the German official account, of the *Blücher's* crew of 1026, the killed or drowned numbered 792 and the wounded 45; the remaining 189 were taken prisoners. The *Seydlitz* lost 159 killed and 33 wounded, due to the effect of one disastrous hit. The only other casualites were 3 killed and 2 wounded in the *Kolberg*. The *Seydlitz* was again ready for sea on April 1, and the *Derfflinger*, which was also seriously damaged, on February 17.[1]

[1] *Der Krieg zur See 1914–18. Nordsee*, Vol. III, pp. 237, 241.

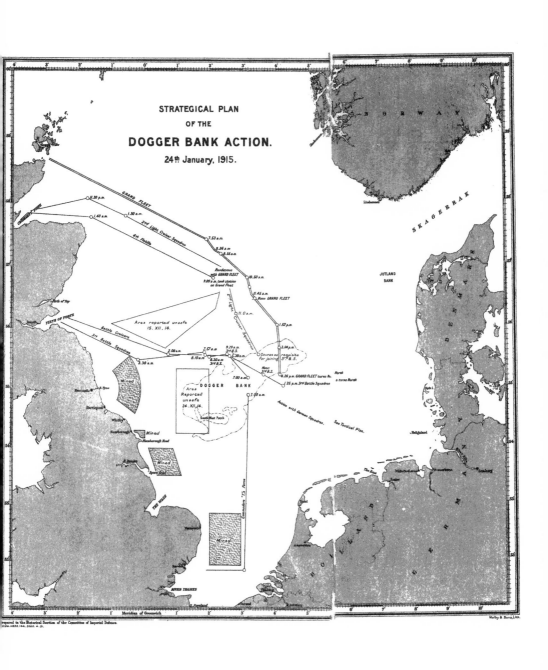

STRATEGICAL PLAN

OF THE

DOGGER BANK ACTION.

24th January, 1915.

Prepared in the Historical Section of the Committee of Imperial Defence.

Malby & Sons, Lith.

CHAPTER VI

ABANDONMENT OF THE OFFENSIVE IN BELGIUM AND FINAL
DECISION TO ATTACK THE DARDANELLES—JANUARY 28

THE effect of the action on the general situation was to
demonstrate the efficacy of the new distribution for improving
our hold on the North Sea, and materially to reduce the
chances of the enemy being tempted to hazard a military
raid upon our coasts. The need of maintaining large numbers
of troops for Home Defence was sensibly less, and, as we
have seen, in the days immediately following the action,
anxiety for the security of our position in Flanders was
equally relieved by the results of the fighting then in
progress.

It was on January 28, four days after the action, that the
final decision to attack the Dardanelles was taken by the
Government. Although Admiral Carden had been informed
that his plan was accepted, the matter was still far from
settled. The committee which had been appointed to consider
the question of alternative objectives for the new armies, had
not yet come to any conclusion, but it would seem that the
course of events had been tending to move opinion towards
direct action in the Balkans by way of Salonica. On
January 23 negotiations were opened with Greece, offering
her certain territorial concessions if she would take the field
to assist Serbia. On the 27th her reply was received. She
was ready and willing to act if Bulgaria would co-operate,
but if Bulgaria would go no further than benevolent neutrality,
then the assistance of Roumania would be necessary. If
Bulgaria's neutrality could not be assured, then Greece would
require, in addition to Roumania's active co-operation, the
support of such a contingent from the Entente Powers as
would ensure her against possible fluctuations in the attitude
of her shifty neighbour. For this purpose, M. Venizelos
explained, two army corps, either British or French, would
suffice.

Under these conditions it was evident nothing could be
done from Salonica for the present, with the result that
opinion was solidifying in favour of an attack on the Dardanelles. It seemed at least the quickest way of fixing

the attitude of Bulgaria, and though the naval attack on the Dardanelles had not been definitely sanctioned, the preparatory work which the Admiralty had been directed to undertake had made such rapid progress that the necessary ships were already on their way out. The project, moreover, had been communicated to our Allies and had received their approval. Russia was particularly eager in favour of the project as a means of relieving the pressure on her army in the Caucasus. In the first week of January it had heavily defeated the Turks at Ardahan, and having practically annihilated their Vth Corps at Sarakamuish, had broken up Enver Pasha's ambitious plan of envelopment with which it had been threatened, but the effort had exhausted the Russian impetus, and it had not been possible to pursue the victory to Erzerum.

At the moment, however, the Turks thought the place was in imminent danger. The shattered army which had retired there was clamouring for reinforcement, and at Constantinople the alarm was so great that there was a strong movement for abandoning the Egyptian expedition. This, of course, the Germans violently opposed, but so strained were their relations with the Turks at this time, in consequence of the disaster in the Caucasus, that a massacre was feared and they were sending their families away. From Greece it was reported that Egypt had actually been given up, in spite of German pressure, but this was not so. Reinforcements for the Caucasus were found from the Constantinople district, and the panic passed as it was found that the Russian pursuit had stopped far short of Erzerum. There the Turks had securely established themselves and were reorganising their army. There, too, the reinforcements were beginning to reach them, and anxiety passed to the other side. At Petrograd it was now feared that unless something was done to stop the flow the position of the Russian army would soon become as critical as ever. Not a man could they spare from the Eastern Front. In that quarter their hands were more than full. The defence of Warsaw, and the fighting in Galicia and Poland were taxing their strength to the last ounce. They were once more looking eagerly to the situation in the Mediterranean, and to the Grand Duke the Dardanelles project seemed to promise just the kind of diversion that he required. The French also so far recognised its possibilities that when, after the preliminary decision of January 13, the First Lord informed them of the project Monsieur Augagneur, the Minister of Marine, had come over to discuss it. He himself was of opinion, so well did he think of it, that the French fleet should take part in the enterprise, but nothing had yet been definitely settled.

Still there was serious opposition, and it came from the best British naval opinion, with the First Sea Lord at its head. There was no question of his not realising the importance of drastic action in the Eastern Mediterranean. Indeed, we have seen how, early in January, when the question of an alternative theatre first came up, he pronounced in favour of Turkey, and how the scheme he then formulated for a large combined operation had to be rejected as impracticable. Naval opinion, of course, never doubted the unwisdom of engaging in such an undertaking except in combination with a military force, but if a military force was not to be obtained, it was not their way to sit down and protest they could do nothing when action of some kind was so crying a necessity. So long, therefore, as it was a mere question of a demonstration to relieve the pressure on the Russian Caucasus Front, the First Sea Lord had not a word to say against the fleet trying to do its best alone. He even suggested adding the *Agamemnon* and *Lord Nelson* to the older battleships that had been assigned to Admiral Carden, and as late as January 12 he proposed that the *Queen Elizabeth*, which was under orders to do her gunnery at Gibraltar, might just as well spend the ammunition on the Dardanelles forts. But when the enterprise began to take on the aspect of a serious attempt to force the Straits, and reduce Constantinople, without military co-operation, he began to contemplate it each day with graver apprehension. The enterprise would certainly entail the use of a large force and the loss of many ships. So much, indeed, would have to be staked for success, that it would gravely prejudice, and even render impossible, the plans he was elaborating to secure a perfect control of Home waters and the Baltic.[1] So firmly convinced did he become of the viciousness of the navy getting prematurely involved in so extensive an oversea enterprise while the Home control was imperfect, that on January 25 he placed a memorandum before the Prime Minister setting forth his views. The principle on which his objections were based, the principle, that is, of command of Home waters being the condition precedent of all large oversea operations, was fully in accord with our naval tradition. So well established was it that no exception had ever been recognised except overwhelming political necessity. Assuming, however, that a naval attack on the Dardanelles was technically feasible, there had seldom been a case when

[1] See *post*, p. 410.

political necessity more fully covered the exception. The First Lord therefore was able to meet his colleague's objections with another memorandum, in which he compared the relative naval strength of Great Britain and Germany, and showed that our superiority was sufficient to allow us to undertake a subsidiary operation, without prejudicing our command of the North Sea. It was submitted to the Prime Minister on the 27th, and thus it will be seen that when the War Council met next morning the Board of Admiralty was not in a position to give it a firm opinion on the all-important question.[1]

It is to be doubted, however, whether it was a case which could be decided on naval authority at all. A purely naval attack on a strongly fortified base was admittedly a departure from established doctrine which involved manifest risk. Once, and once only, had such an attempt succeeded, and that was when Rooke, with the fleet alone, had seized Gibraltar by a *coup de main*. But the famous rock fortress was then but in its infancy, and scarcely comparable, as an objective, with the Dardanelles. On the other hand, owing to new technical developments, the chances of a fleet against a fortified naval position could not be measured by the most accomplished experts with any degree of certainty. All that was clear was the political necessity for action and the decisive advantages that success would bring. It was pre-eminently therefore a matter for Ministers to decide. When expert opinion differed it was they, and they alone, who must judge the extent of the risk involved, and they, and they alone, who must judge whether the probable advantages of success justified the acceptance of the risk.

The main question, it must be borne in mind, was to settle, in accordance with the earlier resolution, whether the time had not come to select an alternative offensive theatre, for the employment of the new armies, in case of a deadlock in France. That such a deadlock would soon have to be recognised scarcely admitted of doubt. It was already evident that for a considerable time at least it would be out of the power of either side to make any decisive impression on the other, and since General Joffre had withdrawn over 100,000 men from the Flanders area, it was obvious that Sir John French's plan for an advance on Zeebrugge was out of the question. No immediate decision was taken, and it appears to have been understood that the special committee that was considering alternative objectives would make a final report in the afternoon.

[1] *Dardanelles Commission Report*, I., pp. 25–7.

As there was little doubt of what it would be, the Council when it met in the morning of January 28 had to face the fact that the point had been reached, when, for the present, we had in view no plan for offensive action except the proposed attack on the Dardanelles. At the previous meeting the plan of operations elaborated between Admiral Carden and the War Staff had been fully explained and a decision to carry it out had been taken, and, since that date, the Admiralty had pushed forward their preparations. But, in view of the First Sea Lord's memorandum, Mr. Churchill felt it his duty to raise the question afresh. After stating with what enthusiasm the Grand Duke had welcomed the project, how the French also favoured it and had promised co-operation, and how far the preparations had gone for opening the enterprise in the middle of February, he once more explained the plan which Admiral Carden believed to be feasible and asked for an opinion as to whether the Council considered the enterprise was of sufficient importance to justify the undoubted risks it involved. The First Sea Lord at once protested. He had understood, he said, that the question was not to be raised that day. Early in the morning they had both met in the Prime Minister's room to place their divergent views before him. After a full hearing the Prime Minister had decided that those of the First Lord had the greater weight, and he now ruled that the matter had gone too far to be left any longer in abeyance. Lord Fisher then left the table with the intention of handing his resignation to the Prime Minister's private secretary. Lord Kitchener also rose and took the First Sea Lord aside before he left the room. After pointing out to him that he was the only one present who disapproved of the operation, he induced him to forgo his intention of resigning and to return to his seat. Lord Kitchener then expressed the opinion that the naval attack was vitally important. If successful it would be equivalent to winning a campaign with the new armies, and it had the great merit that it could be broken off at any time if progress became unsatisfactory. The other Ministers concurred in the decisive political effects success would produce, and the final word seems to have been left to the Admiralty, to say whether, in view of the opinions expressed as to the great political advantages of success, they would proceed to face the risks.[1]

Nothing definite was said about the troops, though the First Lord appears to have made no secret of his conviction that the attack could not be made decisive unless a military

[1] *Dardanelles Commission Report*, I., pp. 26–7, 53.

force was present to secure the ground as the fleet advanced. It was by no means clear whether in any case we had troops to spare, and this all-important question was one which the committee on alternative objectives was directed to investigate. Its urgency at the moment was the desire to send assistance to Serbia, and this, rather than operations at the Dardanelles, was the line on which the discussion proceeded. As to the advantage of giving immediate support to Serbia there was general agreement, and further, that Salonica was the best place of disembarkation for the purpose, but the difficulty was to find the troops. All available units at home had been promised to Sir John French. They were the XXIXth, the Canadian and two Territorial divisions. But seeing that the promise, except as regards the Canadian division, was made to enable him to operate his plan against Zeebrugge, which was no longer feasible, there was no reason at the moment why we should commit ourselves further to the French theatre. It was therefore agreed to request the Government to decide whether Sir John French should not be definitely informed that his coastal advance was not to be undertaken, and that the reinforcements he had asked for to carry it out would not be sent.

Accordingly the War Council met again in the evening. In the course of the discussion on the committee's report it became obvious that the weight of military opinion was so much averse to diverting any troops to the Mediterranean at the present juncture that the idea for the time being was dropped. The Admiralty, however, were authorised to construct twelve more monitors for use on the Danube in view of possible future developments.[1]

The idea of a naval attack on Zeebrugge was also abandoned. Unless some pressing need arose the Admiralty had come to the decision to confine operations to aerial attack until the heavy monitors which were under construction were ready.[2] The older battleships were required elsewhere, for the Admiralty, as the First Lord now announced, had decided to take the risk of attempting to force a passage

[1] *Dardanelles Commission Report*, I., p. 30.
[2] There were fourteen of them due for delivery between the beginning of April and the end of July. Their armament was as under :—

Monitors.		Guns.
2	with	2–15″
4	with	2–14″
8	with	2–12″

The last eight were to be armed by removing the turrets out of four of the "Majestics."

single-handed, and they expected the first shot would be fired in a fortnight.

Thus the previous decision to attempt a naval attack on the Dardanelles was confirmed, but, although the risk of failure and the decisive importance of success were fully recognised, yet up to this point there seems to have been no clear conviction that if troops could be found for an alternative theatre they should be given the same objective as the fleet. Something, however, was done to form a general reserve. As a result of the abandonment of the Zeebrugge project it was decided that nothing but the Canadian division should go forward to France. The rest of the troops were either to remain at home, ready to proceed to France if required, or to go at once, on condition that they might be withdrawn in a month. To make the position quite clear Mr. Churchill was asked to go out and explain matters to the Field-Marshal. At the same time he was to impress upon him the importance which the Government attached to a diversion—for so they still called it—in the Near East, and to consult with him as to putting their ideas before the French Government with a view to securing their concurrence and co-operation.

The outcome of the conference was that Sir John French strongly deprecated reopening the arrangement he had made with General Joffre under the belief that he was to have four more divisions from England. While General Joffre agreed to take over the front of two corps on the British right, Sir John French had agreed to take over the Ypres salient, an arrangement which would give him the control of the Allied line from Armentières to the Franco-Belgian coast zone. With the four divisions he had been led to expect he felt he could do this with safety, but not with less. If, however, the Government were bent on what he, too, regarded as a diversion in the Near East, he believed that from the middle of March he would be able to keep two divisions at their disposal. It was understood, therefore, that by March 15, but not before, two divisions would be available for withdrawal from France.

CHAPTER VII

A NOTEWORTHY feature of the deliberations of January 28 is the little concern expressed in regard to Egypt. There is no sign that its defence in any way affected the decision to attack the Dardanelles, and yet it was known that the long-expected attempt on the most sensitive point in our Imperial communications was in the act of materialising. It was known that an unusual rainfall in Sinai had facilitated the advance of the Turks, and that they were already approaching the canal. But it caused Lord Kitchener no uneasiness. Indeed his hope was that the enemy would continue to come on, for, as we had a strong naval force on the spot, it would be in our power to strike at their communications from the sea at Gaza. He obviously saw in their adventure a chance of inflicting on them a telling disaster, but it does not appear that any instructions to this effect were sent out either to the naval or the military commanders. Possibly the blow fell even more quickly than he expected, for while he was making his announcement our outposts beyond the canal were actually being attacked by the advance parties of the enemy.

Though the operation had apparently been forced upon the Turks prematurely and without adequate preparation, everything except the counter-stroke from Gaza was ready to meet it. By the navy the protection of this vital and vulnerable section of the great eastern highway had always been accepted as one of its inalienable functions, and when the hour struck it was there in force to give the garrison what it most needed—a mobile heavy artillery. Every ship that had been selected for this essential function, including the *Ocean*, was on the spot, and the whole defence system of the canal had been reported as satisfactory.

Since the middle of November the canal defences had been under Major-General Alexander Wilson, with Brigadier-General A. H. Bingley as Chief Staff Officer, his headquarters being at Ismailia. By the instructions of General Sir J. G. Maxwell, Commander-in-Chief in Egypt, the line had been organised in three sections : No. 1 from Port Tewfik, at the Red Sea entrance, to Geneifa, at the southern end of the Great

[1] See Plan p. 118.

Bitter Lake, with headquarters at Suez; No. 2 from Deversoir, at the head of the Great Bitter Lake, to El Ferdan, twelve miles north of Lake Timsah, with headquarters at Ismailia; and No. 3, the northern section, from El Ferdan to Port Said, with headquarters at Kantara, where the Mediterranean coast-road crosses the canal. The three sections thus corresponded to the three main lines of approach : the Suez section to the southern route through Nekhl from Akaba; the Ismailia section to the central or Maghara route; and the Kantara to the coast route through Katia from El Arish.

The difficulty of all these approaches rendered the position naturally strong, and without hesitation the canal had been accepted as the right line of defence for Egypt. The total length of the canal is about a hundred miles, but twenty-four of these consisted of lakes impassable for troops.[1] The remaining seventy-six miles of front to be defended had been further reduced to about fifty by the inundation which had been produced in the Plain of Tina. In all sections a number of posts had been prepared on the east bank as bridge-heads, to cover the most important ferries, and to provide facilities for counter-attack. Between them, on the west bank, at short intervals, were entrenched posts—all connected by the railway, which ran the whole length of the line, and for the patrol of which an armoured train was stationed at Kantara. The canal itself was patrolled by the six torpedo-boats which had been specially sent from Malta, and a flotilla of armed tugs and launches, provided by the Canal Company, and manned by ratings from the Royal Navy.[2]

The troops allotted for holding the defences consisted almost entirely of the Xth and XIth Indian Divisions, with a brigade of mountain artillery. The mounted troops were an Imperial Service cavalry brigade, and the Bikanir Camel Corps. No part of the Egyptian army was used except some machine gun sections of the Camel Corps, some mountain artillery and a section of Engineers. The East Lancashire Territorial division provided six batteries of field artillery. For heavy artillery reliance had to be placed on the navy. The ships under Admiral Peirse's command in the canal area were the two battleships *Swiftsure* (flag)

---

[1] The distances in this chapter are expressed in land miles.

[2] These craft were armed with a 12-pounder or a 3-pounder and one Maxim, and had steel protection for the wheel and boilers. As parent ships there was a canal hopper in each section, and they were fitted with a searchlight on a platform high enough to clear the banks.

at Port Said and the *Ocean* at Suez, and the French coast defence ship *Requin*, for whom a special berth had been dredged in Lake Timsah east of the canal channel.   Besides these heavy ships there were the cruisers *Minerva* and *D'Entrecasteaux*, the sloop *Clio*, the armed merchant cruiser *Himalaya* and the Royal Indian Marine ship *Hardinge*.   Though the canal provided excellent lateral communication, its advantage was a good deal discounted by the fact that in many places the sand dunes on the east bank were too high for the shell of the heavy guns to clear.   This was specially the case from El Ferdan to Lake Timsah, also with all the centre section from Timsah to Deversoir, and finally the four miles between the southern end of the Bitter Lake and Shallufa.   This difficulty also necessitated special arrangements for indirect fire wherever the gunlayers could not see over the banks, and their work was further hampered by the almost continuous mirage in the desert.   A minor direct fire, however, was obtained by mounting light quick-firing guns and Maxims on the tops.   The patrol boats could, of course, in no case fire over the banks, but they had power to enfilade any trenches the enemy might try to establish on the banks themselves.

With these naval and military elements of defence it had been decided to adhere to the original plan and await the attack on the line of the canal.   There were no advanced posts of any importance, but behind the line were the equivalent in numbers of three divisions of the British and Oversea forces (East Lancashire Territorials, Australian and New Zealand), with seven squadrons of Yeomanry (Hertfordshire, Duke of Lancaster's, and Westminster Dragoons).   The bulk of these troops were stationed in the delta, but complete railway arrangements had been made for moving them up as required.

This was the position when, about the middle of January, it became clear that an attack was imminent.   On January 18 a French seaplane located from 8,000 to 10,000 men at Beersheba; on the 22nd advanced troops showed themselves at Moiya Harab, twenty miles from the Little Bitter Lake, and our mounted troops had contact with hostile patrols at Bir el Dueidar, thirteen miles from Kantara.   Other troops were reported at Ain Sudr, thirty-five miles from Suez, so that all three sections of the defence seemed threatened. During the next two or three days the hostile advance guards increased to the strength of 2,000 or 3,000 men each, some 5,000 of them being at Moiya Harab and the adjacent Wadi um Mukhsheib, opposite the Bitter Lakes, where the southern and centre sections joined.   Those facing the northern section advanced so far as to engage our covering troops near Kantara, but they retired in the afternoon.

Upon this the ships entered the canal to take up their assigned stations, and the troops in the various posts and trenches were reinforced.   In the northern section the *Swiftsure* took station just north of Kantara, and the *Clio* at the Ballah ferry to the south of it.   In the southern section the *Ocean* went up to El Shatt, where the Nekhl road crosses the canal before entering Suez, while the *Himalaya* went up to Shallufa, and the *Minerva* into the southern end of the Little Bitter Lake.   In the middle section the *D'Entrecasteaux* joined the *Requin* in Lake Timsah, moving down, subsequently, to Deversoir, at the head of the Great Bitter Lake, where she was to have the *Hardinge* to the northward of her, just south of Lake Timsah.   At the same time the northern section was reinforced from the General Reserve at Ismailia by two battalions from the XIth Division, who occupied the trenches on the west bank between the Bench-mark post and Ballah ferry.   The New Zealand Infantry Brigade was also brought up from Cairo, two battalions (Otago and Wellington) reinforcing the El Kubri Post north of Suez, while the brigade headquarters, with the Auckland and Canterbury Battalions, detrained at Ismailia to fill up the reserve.

All these dispositions were complete on January 27, and during that day it was clear the enemy was being rapidly reinforced.   Five miles east of Kantara he had established himself in a position astride the El Arish road, and at 3.0 a.m. the Baluchistan and El Kubri posts, immediately north of Suez, were attacked, both attacks being repelled without loss.   At 2.45 in the morning of the 28th the outpost at Kantara was attacked, but here again the enemy was easily driven off.   By daylight he was seen to have retired to Point 70 on the Kantara–El Arish road, but from there he was quickly dislodged by five rounds of lyddite from the *Swiftsure*. The only result of these demonstrations on the two flanks was that General Wilson reinforced the centre by sending another battalion from the reserve to Serapeum.

During the next three days the enemy continued to close on the canal, and it soon became clear that their main concentration was in the Gebel Habeita, where the Maghara and Moiya Harab roads converge, opposite the Deversoir–Serapeum–Tussum section of the canal, between Lake Timsah and the Bitter Lakes.   Still the day traffic in the canal was not stopped, and on January 31 the second Australian and

New Zealand convoy of twenty ships passed through for
Alexandria.[1]

From statements made by Turkish prisoners it afterwards
appeared that the troops which had been brought across the
desert belonged to the IIIrd, IVth, VIth and VIIIth Turkish
Army Corps, under Jemal Pasha, numbering probably 20,000.
They had for certain nine field batteries, as well as one or more
6″ guns. Their plan, it seems, was to attack all along the line
simultaneously—at Kantara, El Ferdan, Ismailia, Shallufa
and Suez, but the main effort to cross was to be at Tussum.
By February 2 it was clearly approaching development. On
that afternoon our advanced troops from Ismailia ferry
encountered the enemy, and there was a desultory action
till 3.30 p.m., when it was broken off, and the enemy began
entrenching two and a half miles south-east of our defences.

Still General Wilson awaited the attack in his lines and
no move was made, except to reinforce posts which seemed
to be strongly threatened. He had not to wait long, for in
the early hours of February 3 the storm broke, such as it was.
In the northern section there was nothing but a weak attack
near Kantara on two piquets of the 89th Punjabis. It
was stopped without difficulty, and at daylight thirty-six
unwounded prisoners were found in our entanglements, and
twenty dead on the field. The enemy were falling back, and
as soon as it was light enough their retreat was punished and
accelerated by the *Swiftsure*, who kept up a long-range fire
whenever she got a target till 1.0 p.m. Otherwise the northern
section remained undisturbed. A similar holding attack
took place in the southern section at El Kubri, where the
New Zealand battalions, flanked by the *Ocean* and *Himalaya*,
made short work of it.

The main effort, as was expected, was in the centre. It
began shortly after 3.0 a.m. with a plucky and determined
attempt to cross the canal at Tussum by means of boats.
These craft were made of galvanised steel, 24 feet long, 5 feet
beam, 2 feet 9 inches depth, each capable of holding thirty
men, and they had been hauled over the desert on wheels.
In the section threatened we had three posts on the east bank
of the canal, at Tussum, Serapeum and Deversoir, each held
by half a battalion (92nd Punjabis, 62nd Punjabis, and
2/10th Gurkha Rifles respectively). On the west bank,
between Lake Timsah and the Bitter Lakes, there were twelve
posts, each held by two platoons, and each responsible for
about 600 yards of front. In the centre, at Serapeum, was

[1] 4th Australian Brigade, 2nd Australian Light Horse Brigade, New
Zealand Mounted Rifles, Infantry and Howitzer battery.

a local reserve of three double-companies.[1] The bulk of the force consisted of the three above-named battalions and the 2nd Queen Victoria's Own Rajputs, but there were also two platoons of the New Zealand Canterbury Battalion, the 19th Lancashire T.F. Battery R.F.A. (four guns), the 5th Battery, Egyptian Artillery (four mountain guns and two Maxims), with two platoons of the 128th Pioneers as escort. For naval support there was the *Requin* in Lake Timsah and the *Hardinge* at the lower end of it, gared up in the siding (K 84), with the armed tug *Mansourah* patrolling between them. To the southward was the *D'Entrecasteaux* at Deversoir, with torpedo-boat *043* patrolling.

At the point just south of Tussum where the attempt was made the banks are fifty feet high, so that nothing was detected till the enemy was launching the first boat and sliding others down the slope. It was then 3.25 a.m., dark, with little moon, but the post of the 62nd Punjabis, who held this part of the line, saw them in the dim moonlight and opened fire. They were quickly joined by the 5th Egyptian Battery, which was established on the top of the western bank hard by. With case and shrapnel at 150 yards, and rifle fire, reinforced by a double company of the 62nd and six platoons of the 2nd Rajputs, the attempt was soon stopped. The boats were abandoned one after the other and left to their fate. In the darkness, however, three of them succeeded in crossing. One boatload landed opposite " Mile 48·3," half-way between Tussum and Serapeum, but it was immediately charged by Major O. St. J. Skeen, with a party of the 62nd, and annihilated. Two more boatloads which got ashore close to Tussum at " Mile 47·6 " were attacked by Captain Morgan of the same regiment; some twenty of the enemy escaped (to be captured later by the Rajputs), but the rest were killed or captured, and the attempt to cross was all over by 5.30 a.m.

But the main attack had not yet begun. By daylight it was found that an enemy force had closed on Tussum and occupied some of our advanced trenches which were only used in the daytime. A desultory attack then began, but it was never pushed within 1,200 yards of our line. In front of Serapeum as yet there was little doing, while down at Deversoir it was so quiet that at 8.40 a.m. Brigadier-General

---

[1] In the Indian army organisation at this date, an infantry battalion consisted of four double-companies of 200 men each, subdivided into companies and half-companies. Later, in 1915, the Indian army adopted the British army organisation, in which the battalion consists of four companies of 227 men each, subdivided into four platoons of 55 men each.

S. Geoghegan, commanding the 22nd Brigade, moved out a detachment of four double-companies from the Rajputs and Gurkhas to clear the east bank. As this counter-attack proceeded numbers of the enemy fled from the broken ground where they had made their attempt to cross, but it was soon discovered that from their camp at Kataiib el Kheil the Turks were deploying about two brigades and six guns on a line two miles north-east of Serapeum, as though to attack that post. Our troops at once delivered a counter-attack, and occupying a ridge half a mile north-east of Serapeum, held the enemy there till 2.0 p.m., when they retired eastward and our men fell back on their posts.

In this affair the ships could take little part owing to the height of the banks, but at Brigadier-General Geoghegan's request, Lieutenant-Commander G. B. Palmes, who was then at Deversoir in torpedo-boat *043*, went up to destroy the abandoned pontoons. This was soon done by gunfire, and then, together with the armed tug *Mansourah*, which had also been ordered to the spot, he devoted his fire to assisting the counter-attack. The *Hardinge*, Commander T. J. Linberry, three miles south of Tussum, was doing the same, but about 7.0 a.m. the enemy found her range with 4″ and heavier guns which she could not locate or reach. She therefore gave all her attention to infantry in the open. By 8.15 she had located and silenced a field battery, but about ten minutes later she had both funnels damaged by high explosive, and was otherwise so badly hit that she was obliged to slip and move out of the channel into Lake Timsah for fear of being sunk in the fairway. The big guns then found the *Requin*, which had been firing at the enemy's field guns as directed from the army posts. Before she was touched, however, she was lucky enough to see a whiff of the big guns' smoke, and by 9.0 a.m. she had silenced them with her forward 10·8″ gun. Later in the day the Admiral, in the *Swiftsure*, came down to take the *Hardinge's* place, and ordered the *Ocean* up to Deversoir. Serapeum was also strongly reinforced from the General Reserve at Ismailia, but at that time the half-hearted attack had spent itself, and beyond some casual sniping all was quiet.

Next morning (February 4) a considerable part of the enemy were found to be still entrenched on the east bank, and Major-General A. Wallace, commanding the XIth Division, who had taken over the command of the central section when the main attack was developed there, sent out two double-companies of the 92nd Punjabis to clear them away. The *Mansourah* and torpedo-boat *043* assisted, and after they had well enfiladed the trenches the troops charged. The

Turks at once put up a white flag, but when our men advanced fire was reopened. Our men had to fall back and General Wallace sent up a double-company from each of the 27th and 62nd Punjabis and 128th Pioneers to reinforce them. A charge was then made and the enemy surrendered. Their loss was fifty-nine killed and as many wounded, with 190 prisoners and three Maxims. Amongst the killed was a German major. Simultaneously in the process of clearing up to the northward a further capture was made. From the ferry post at Ismailia, General Watson had moved out with the Cavalry brigade, two battalions, and a mountain battery, and coming across a convoy of ninety camels, with an escort of twenty-five men, captured the whole force. It was a loss which, according to prisoners, went far to disconcert all the enemy's further plans.

In any case there was little more they were able to do. By this time the *Ocean* had moved to the south of Lake Timsah in preparation for a renewal of the attack, but in fact it was all over. The lesson had been a severe one, and the enemy were found to be retiring through Katia, and to their camp at Gebel Habeita. On the 5th there was a deployment at this point for a renewed attack, but it never got forward. Some prisoners said the failure to advance was due to dissension, others that they would not face the naval guns, which were still firing, as targets offered, at 12,000 yards and over. On the 7th the airmen found Gebel Habeita had been abandoned, the enemy having fallen back to El Rigum, Gebel um Mukhsheib and Moiya Harab. It was soon clear, in fact, that the attempt, whatever its object, had been abandoned. If intended as a serious attack it was certainly made with inadequate force and inadequate preparation, and was never within measurable distance of success. The only wonder is that it was not punished more severely than it was. There was no real pursuit, nor even a serious attempt to harass the retreat. Yet the Turkish loss must have reached quite 2,000, besides a large number drowned in the canal. Our men buried 238 dead, and the prisoners wounded and unwounded numbered 716; over and above these a prisoner told of 200 buried before Kantara, but what the losses were in the main attack could not be known. Our own casualties all told were only 32 killed and 131 wounded.

During the next few days the enemy continued to fall back on El Arish and Bir el Jifjaffa, and by February 11 the immediate danger was so far over that the canal was reopened for night traffic. Next day the *Triumph*, which had arrived from Hongkong on the 7th, was allowed to proceed on her way to join Admiral Carden's flag at the Dardanelles. Otherwise Admiral Peirse's squadron remained as it was, except for the arrival of the *Bacchante* and *Euryalus* from the Western Channel Patrol. They had been ordered out at the end of January when, owing to the danger of submarines, the Admiralty came to the conclusion that the patrol work should be left to the armed boarding service and that a strong cruiser squadron at the mouth of the Channel was no longer required. The two heavy cruisers were therefore available for Egypt, where the menace of invasion could not be regarded as over.

For the Turks the repulse was undoubtedly a serious defeat, but it fell short of a decisive disaster such as Lord Kitchener presumably had in view when he conceived the idea of striking in behind them from the sea at Gaza. It seemed on the face of it an admirable opportunity for effective use of the freedom of strategical movement which the sea gave us. Even, however, if the difficulty of transport could have been overcome, and the available troops had been sufficiently well trained, a landing near Gaza could have had very little effect, unless the force was prepared to march inland for twenty-seven miles and capture Beersheba, whence the main body of the enemy had advanced.

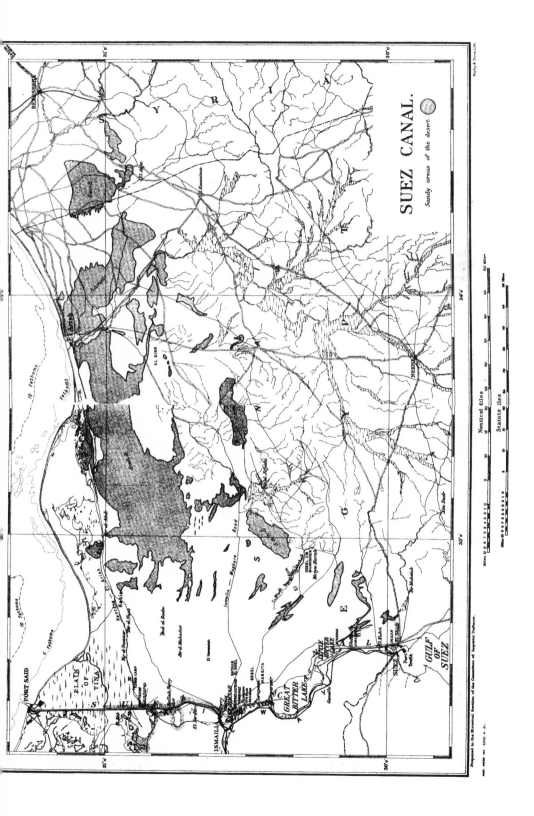

SUEZ CANAL.

Sandy areas of the desert.

Nautical files

Statute files

Prepared in the Historical Section, of the Committee of Imperial Defence.

Malby & Sons, Lith.

CHAPTER VIII

SALONICA AND THE DARDANELLES—MODIFICATION OF THE PLAN—FIRST ALLOCATION OF TROOPS—FEBRUARY 9–16—SITUATION IN HOME WATERS—NEUTRAL OBJECTION TO THE "BLOCKADE" AND GERMAN THREAT OF RETALIATION

THOUGH the collapse of the attack on the canal did something to clear the air, the Turks had escaped without any such punishment as Lord Kitchener had had in mind, and the need for more resounding success in the Near East was more pressing than ever. Egypt itself could not yet be considered safe, for it was not to be believed that after so much sounding of trumpets nothing more was to come of the threat to cut the main artery of the Empire. Our information was that the Germans were urging a new attempt at the end of the month, but it was said the Turks were too anxious about the Caucasus and Mesopotamia to be pushed into a repetition of the adventure, and were sullenly opposing their taskmaster's plan. Considerable bodies of troops, however, were found to be still in occupation of our frontier posts at Katia, Bir el Abd and Nekhl. There was also a small force investing Tor Harbour, at the bottom of the Gulf of Suez, and as this place was favourably situated for mining operations on the transport line it was decided to dislodge it.[1] For this purpose a small expedition, consisting of half a battalion of the 2/7th Gurkha Rifles under Lieutenant-Colonel C. L. Haldane, left Suez in the *Minerva* on February 11, to join the *Dufferin*, which had been lying off Tor for the past fortnight. That evening in less than three hours they had all landed silently at the pier, and at once moved out into the desert with 150 men of the 2nd Battalion of the Egyptian Army, which formed the garrison of the place. By daylight the enemy's camp was found and surprised. In a few hours it was surrounded and captured, and by noon we had over 100 prisoners. Of the rest of the force about 60 were killed. Only a few stragglers got away, while our own loss was one Gurkha killed and one wounded, and by 5.30 p.m., after being nearly twenty hours under arms, the whole force was on board again.

On the Syrian coast the watch on the Gulf of Alexandretta

---

[1] See Plan p. 382.

was being well maintained. On February 6 the *Philomel*, Captain P. H. Hall Thompson, took over the patrol from the *Doris*, and remained for nine days. A landing party was sent ashore to investigate the reason for the large number of pack animals that were seen entering and leaving the town by night. They were attacked after they had advanced for some distance, and were compelled to retire with loss.

The episode showed that the Turks were more on the alert than had been expected, and Captain Hall Thompson replied by patrolling as close in-shore as he could, and opening fire on the entrenchments that he saw being constructed in the approaches to the town. A further exchange of notes took place with the local governor, who repeated the previous threat of reprisals against British subjects which he had made in December when the *Doris* was operating.[1] Eventually, however, no reprisals took place. Hostages were actually detailed for execution, but the following month we learned that they had been allowed to return to Aleppo, where they were living in comparative freedom.

On the 16th the *Bacchante* took over the patrol, and found that activity ashore was increasing. The Turks were evidently expecting an attempt on the place. To them, as to a large section of British opinion, such an attack seemed the most obvious way of relieving the pressure on both Egypt and Mesopotamia. In Egypt the question of sending an expedition to Alexandretta had been studied, and though the idea was now in abeyance the Turks were feverishly fortifying its approaches. Infantry and artillery were being brought down from Aleppo, and a considerable force of troops with heavy guns was concentrating at the head of the gulf, where the railway was most exposed to interruption from the sea.

All this looked as though the Turks were thinking more of defence than attack, and though the situation required watching, there was at least no immediate anxiety for Egypt. The unexpected size of the force which had crossed the desert raised, however, doubts at headquarters whether the canal itself was the best line of defence, in view of the interference with traffic which another such attack would certainly cause.

But a far more disturbing element in the Allied position was the condition of the Russian Front. There during the first week in February the outlook had changed ominously for the worse. The Germans were continuing their offensive, begun in January, against Warsaw, and counter-attacks had also been launched on the Russian extreme flanks in East Prussia

[1] See *ante*, p. 75.

and the Bukovina; and though the Grand Duke successfully resisted the German attempt to reach Warsaw, he was pinned down on that section of the front, and was therefore unable to reinforce his flanks, both of which were pushed back with heavy losses.   This sudden change of fortune was chiefly due to superior German strategy, but amongst the contributory causes was the fact that Russia had nearly exhausted her supply of munitions, and so small was her capacity for renewing it, that until the Dardanelles could be opened there was little hope of her being able to resume the offensive.

The reactions of our Ally's retirement were peculiarly inopportune in view of the growing appreciation of the vital importance of the Near East.   Ferdinand of Bulgaria had accepted a loan from Germany—on what terms it was not difficult to guess.   As Russia fell back in the Bukovina Roumania saw herself being left in the air, and, though she had secured a loan from the British Government, the negotiations which M. Venizelos had initiated at Bucharest for joint action by the Balkan States to save Serbia from the impending Austrian attack had entirely broken down.   Our Dardanelles venture, however effective it might be in relieving the pressure on Russia in the Caucasus, was obviously too indirect a stroke to prevent the invasion of Serbia from the north, nor could it even be hoped that it would avail to alter the determination of either Greece or Roumania— particularly as the enterprise was then conceived.

For Lord Kitchener it was essentially a diversionary operation, which could be discontinued at any moment, and it was this view of it that appears to have appealed to the French.   By this time they had given the project their definite approval.   They had promised to supply four battleships and a flotilla of minesweepers, and had agreed that the whole Allied force should be under the British Admiral.   The French Minister of Marine had declared that he could see no flaw in the plan of operations : it seemed to him to be conceived with prudence and caution, since, as he specially remarked, it permitted of the operations being broken off at any stage without loss of prestige if insurmountable difficulties were encountered.   There can be no doubt that this was at the time the consideration which more than any other had appeared to limit the danger to a justifiable risk, and had been the chief factor which had turned the scale for accepting it.

This being so, it was clear, in view of the critical situation in the Balkans, that the Allies must have another string to their bow.   Though military authority continued to speak of France as the decisive theatre, Ministers were coming to feel instinctively that at least in the existing phase of the war the decisive theatre was rather to be looked for in the Balkans. In other words, a preliminary decision in that theatre seemed essential if the Allies were ever to be able to bring to bear a sufficient preponderance of force to secure a final decision on the Western or any other front. To them, in fact, it was not clear that the area in which the enemy was strongest was necessarily the decisive theatre, or that a decision must in all circumstances be sought at the point where his power of resistance was highest. There could, of course, be no doubt that, if we could destroy the German armies in the west, a decision would follow, but what Ministers did gravely doubt, in view of the deadlock that had set in, was whether in existing conditions of relative resources there was any prospect of being able to drive the enemy back even to his own frontier before the Allies themselves were exhausted.

So strong was this feeling that even in France the pure military doctrine was not accepted without question, and on February 6 Monsieur Delcassé, who was then Foreign Minister, came over to discuss the possibility of an alternative objective, with a view to saving the situation in the Balkans. Since Roumania, held fast as she was between Bulgaria and the victorious Austro-German army, could not move, and Serbia could not see her way to make the territorial concessions which Bulgaria was demanding as the price of her assistance, direct military action by the Allied Powers could alone avert the catastrophe which threatened vastly to increase the war strength of the Central Powers, and render the prospect of a decision in the main theatre more remote than ever.

In any case the immediate necessity was to do something to save Serbia. Greece alone was in a position to act at once, and without definite assurance of support from the Allies she could not be expected to commit herself. Naturally, then, the idea of sending troops to Salonica gathered new force. The suggestion was that Russia, France and Britain should each furnish one division, but if Russia had no troops to spare the demonstration would have to be Franco-British. It would, of course, amount to little more than a demonstration till greater force was available. Still it was hoped that in Greece it would suffice as evidence that the Western Powers were in a position to guarantee her against a flank attack from Bulgaria if she took action in accordance with her defensive treaty with Serbia. The reception

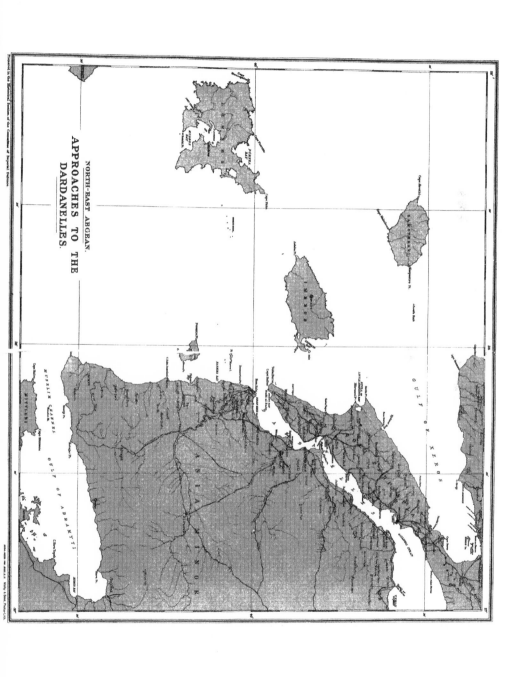

NORTH-EAST AEGEAN.

APPROACHES TO THE
DARDANELLES.

GULF OF XEROS

GULF OF ADRAMYTI

of belligerent troops in her territory would, of course, place her in an equivocal position such as she might not be willing to accept, but M. Venizelos had just shown that an equivocal position for which any plausible solution could be found was not enough to move him from his benevolent attitude to the foster-parents of his country.

As Admiral Carden and his Staff worked out their plans for the Dardanelles it was evident that a good advanced base would be necessary, and none was so good as Mudros in Lemnos. The island was in the possession of Greece, and she had been approached as to whether she could permit its use. Without breach of neutrality this was a difficult matter, but M. Venizelos found a way. Though the island had been in Greek occupation since the last Balkan war, Turkey had never recognised it as having ceased to be Turkish. The Greek garrison, therefore, had only to withdraw and the Allies could treat it as enemy territory, and this M. Venizelos proceeded to arrange, with a significant intimation that the batteries would be left all standing for the British to look after.

On February 9, when the new proposal for action at Salonica came up for consideration, Russia had informed us that a contingent of 1000 Cossacks was the most she could spare, but so urgent was the need of doing something quickly, it was agreed that in any case we should send a division at once if the French would do the same. It was further agreed that first line troops were indispensable, and Lord Kitchener proposed to send the XXIXth Division, which had just been formed from the seasoned troops of our more distant Imperial garrisons. In its place Sir John French could have a Territorial division, which would serve well enough now that his offensive movement up the coast was abandoned. To this he made no serious objection, and it was finally decided to urge Greece once more to honour her obligations to Serbia, and to promise her, if she marched, two, and perhaps three, Allied divisions to protect her communications against Bulgaria.

Although, owing to the attitude which Greece felt forced to maintain, this resolution had no effect of the nature contemplated, its reaction on the Dardanelles enterprise was profound. The discussion had revealed the possibility of finding troops for the Mediterranean, and ever since the enterprise had been sanctioned, opinion had become more and more impressed with the unwisdom of attempting it without a military force of at least sufficient strength to secure at each stage what the fleet might win. In the leading

case of Admiral Duckworth's abortive attempt on Constantinople in 1807 the failure had been due, not to inability to
pass the Straits, but to inability to hold them behind him
after he got through. The desire to avoid a repetition of
this error was very strong, and the new proposal gained
special weight as a possible means of doing so. The troops
would at least be on the spot if the navy found—as was
only to be expected—that they could not do without them,
and in this way the needed success might be won even if,
in the event of Greece and Roumania persisting in their
refusal to co-operate with Serbia, nothing could be done
directly from Salonica.

On the same day (February 9) the Government learnt of
M. Venizelos' promise to evacuate Lemnos, and on receiving
the undertaking the Admiralty at once ordered two battalions
of Marines to proceed there. It was clearly understood
that they were only intended to land after the entrance
forts were silenced, in order to destroy the torpedo tubes
which were believed to be part of the entrance defences.
They could, in fact, be regarded as little more than a
demolition force, but Lord Kitchener gave his assurance
that if troops were required at a later stage they would be
forthcoming.

Thus was taken the first step to translate into definite
action the policy of the general conclusions previously
reached, that if the situation in France settled down to a
deadlock, all British troops not necessary to maintain it
should be devoted to a more promising objective. Primarily
the idea of sending troops to the Eastern Mediterranean was
to save Serbia, and in the second place to provide the fleet
at the Dardanelles with a landing-force.

The Marines had sailed on February 6, under Colonel C. N.
Trotman as Brigadier-General in Command, and, having
received Lord Kitchener's promise of eventual military
assistance, the Admiralty could only see a prospect of lost
chances if the troops did not follow them immediately. A
memorandum, drawn up on February 15 by Admiral Sir Henry
Jackson, may be taken to express the Admiralty's final
opinion on the question of military assistance to the fleet;
it concludes with the following sentence: "The naval
bombardment is not recommended as a sound operation
unless a strong military force is ready to assist it, or, at least,
to follow it up immediately the forts are silenced."

This paper was forwarded to Admiral Carden on the same
day "for his guidance," but his orders—received two days
earlier—had been drawn up on the basis of a purely naval

operation. The two Marine battalions attached to the
expedition were " to serve as the garrison for the base, or
for any small landing operation of a temporary nature."

There was no time to lose, for it was now the middle of
February, and the 15th was the day on which it had been
hoped the first shots would be fired. It was also the day
on which the *Queen Elizabeth* was due to join Admiral Carden's
flag. But it was not to be. Persistent gales throughout
January had thrown everything back. Though pressed at
least to open operations on that day, Admiral Carden objected
that in order to make real progress and to husband ammunition—which here, as everywhere, was then a source of serious
anxiety—it was essential that the work should be continuous. Without his minesweepers and seaplanes it was
useless to begin; and they could not be ready before the 19th.

But though the later date had to be accepted, the 15th
was marked by an event even more important to the development of the enterprise than the opening of the attack. France
had agreed to furnish a division for Salonica, the proposal
had been made to Greece, and on this day her reply was
received. It was to the effect that without the co-operation
of Roumania M. Venizelos absolutely declined to entertain
the idea of Greek intervention. To approach Roumania again
was at the moment obviously useless. On the East Prussian
Front the Russians had just been driven over the frontier
after the disaster to their Tenth Army in the Masurian Lake
district; in Galicia they were still being pressed back, and
were rapidly retiring from the small section of the Bukovina
which was not already in Austrian hands. It was therefore
impossible for Roumania to move a finger, and we were
thus thrown back upon the Dardanelles as the only possible
alternative objective, and the only possible means of inducing
the hesitating Balkan States to move to the rescue of
Serbia.

Without a moment's delay action was now taken, and
on February 16 the whole question was reviewed in the
light of the latest information. It was now known from
Russian sources that Marshal von der Goltz had inspected
the Dardanelles in the middle of January, and, coming
to the same conclusion as our Admirals on the spot, had
pronounced that in the existing condition of their defences
the Straits could be forced by the fleet. But as Bulgaria
had by that time been bought, it was possible for the Turks
to increase their strength by bringing up guns from Adrianople and the Chatalja lines. Further evidence that the
enemy were expecting an attack was furnished by a

report that at the neck of the Gallipoli peninsula, where the shore sloped down to Xeros Bay from the Bulair lines, every practicable beach had been mined. For tactical reasons, therefore, no less than political, there was not a moment to lose. Still there could be no thought of advancing the date of the naval attack, for on February 12 came news that the *Queen Elizabeth*, while doing her gunnery at Gibraltar, had stripped the blades of one of her turbines and, being thus unable to steam at more than half speed, could not possibly arrive under a week.

On the other hand, in the west the military outlook had improved. The Germans had abandoned all attempts to break through to the Channel, and their offensive effort was clearly being concentrated on the Eastern Front. Egypt, moreover, seemed absolutely safe. Indeed our information was that the bulk of the Turkish army was being drawn to the Caucasus to assist the general offensive reaction against Russia, or to Bagdad to stop our further progress from the Persian Gulf. In the Constantinople and Dardanelles districts it was reported there were very few divisions left, and most of these were being replaced by a hastily-raised reserve corps. It looked, then, as if a comparatively small body of troops could give all the weight that the naval attack required behind it, and it was equally clear that with Egypt no longer in danger we had a further force immediately available from its garrison.

In addition to these new considerations there was another that went to the root of our whole war plan. Since the beginning of the year there had been obtained a clearer perception of Germany's main object in bringing about the war. At first we could see nothing but an intention of realising the Pan-German aspirations so far as to get possession of Belgium and a freer access to the ocean by seizing the French Channel ports. But since the Germans had found the complete attainment of this object beyond their strength, they seemed to be turning to another goal. The idea of a great central European Federation under Prussian hegemony, and its connection with the idea of a Pan-German Empire that was to stretch from Hamburg to the Persian Gulf, had never been taken quite seriously by responsible British statesmen. But now that Prussia was so obviously taking control of Austria and was so clearly bent on forcing her way through Serbia to the Dardanelles, what had hitherto been regarded as little more than a fantastic speculation of imaginative political writers began to take the firm outlines of a reasoned policy of expansion.

That she had long been dazzled with the idea that some day Turkey might become for her another India was well known, but hitherto the difficulties in her way had looked insurmountable. Now it suddenly became manifest that with Austria and Turkey already bound to her chariot wheels, and the Balkan States hopelessly divided and helpless, the hour had come when the long-sought road might be opened. Everything that had been obscure—from the retirement of the *Goeben* into the Bosporus to the recent abandonment of the attempt to reach the Channel coast—seemed at once to fall into its place in a far-reaching war plan, and many things which had hitherto looked like acts of impotence began to crystallise into a settled purpose of almost inconceivable ambition. Our Government, at least, began to feel that all other German efforts were to be sacrificed or made to subserve to the vassalage of Turkey and the unmeasured consequences that would come of it. In the west the character of the war was apparently changing from the characteristic form in which it had been conceived and begun. In the conception of the German High Command it was becoming degraded to a lower category. Having failed to attain their end by their favourite method of crushing the armed force of the enemy, they were going to hold what they had got, seize what remained to be seized, and then defy the Allies to break their hold.

In adopting such an attitude the hope of a belligerent is to induce his enemy to exhaust himself in efforts to break it down. The enemy, if he is alive to the situation, will naturally seek to attack elsewhere on some line where his adversary is less well prepared to meet him and where he may hope to forestall him in attaining his further objects. In these circumstances the Dardanelles became more strongly accentuated as the best alternative objective for everything that was available and not required in Flanders, and the War Council took a further step on the new road. But it would seem that the new orientation of the war was not yet apprehended with sufficient conviction for a wholehearted new departure to be taken. It was settled that the XXIXth Division was to proceed to Lemnos as soon as possible—it was hoped in about ten days; arrangements were to be made for the despatch of a force from Egypt; all small craft required for a landing flotilla were to be sent out, and the Admiralty were authorised to build a special squadron of transports and lighters for the conveyance of 50,000 men to be landed as any point where they might be required.

The last provision related to projected operations in the Baltic at a later date; there was as yet no definite committal to military action in the Levant. The troops were only to move from Egypt if required, and none of them were as yet pledged to the fleet. The naval attack was not yet transformed into a true combined operation, for it was expressly provided that the whole military force was merely to be held available to support the naval operations in case of need.

There was still no frank adoption of a new theatre for our offensive. It was as yet no more than a recognition of the view, to which the Admiralty were now turning, that whatever the success of the fleet, the fruits could not be secured without a military force. For the higher effort, for which we can now see the situation was calling, the time was not deemed to be ripe. True, in some quarters it was held that not only at home, but also abroad, there were other troops that might well have been spared, but to such a suggestion neither our own Headquarters in France nor the French High Command could listen for a moment. In view of the disquieting reverses which the Russians were suffering on the Eastern Front there was a growing possibility of the Germans reacting suddenly to the west. Their interior position afforded them so much facility for thus quickly changing their front of attack that the risk of sacrificing our strategical reserve could not be accepted. In any case our engagements to the French were such that the XXIXth Division could not be diverted without the full accord of their High Command. General Joffre was of opinion that at any moment the Germans might turn from the defeated Russians and develop an offensive in the Verdun– St. Mihiel area—and if they did he would want every man, and particularly every seasoned man, that he had been led to expect. An intimation to this effect was actually received from him through the French Ambassador, and it could not be ignored.

Although in the naval view the Russian reverses were an additional reason for pressing hard and at once at the Dardanelles, the military opinion was too unanimous and too plausible to be resisted. No doubt it was to some extent coloured by a constitutional dislike of seeing troops diverted from what current military doctrine taught soldiers to regard as the only decisive theatre. But even so, it was an article of military faith which Ministers could scarcely override. Indeed, seeing how deeply France was concerned, there was no one in a position to measure or accept the risk with the same kind of detachment as, in an analogous case at sea, Lord Fisher had been able to do, when for a definite strategical end he took the responsibility of detaching three battle cruisers from the Grand Fleet.

The decision to attack the Dardanelles before an adequate military force was provided to act with the fleet was, in fact, a compromise between two ideas. On the one hand was that of a pure diversion to be made by the fleet, on the other that of using our command of the sea to strike at the point where the combination of the Central Powers was still incomplete. The last was undoubtedly, in the eyes of the Government as a whole, the best method in which we could use our unengaged force for bringing the war to a speedy and successful conclusion. The apprehension of our own and the French Headquarters as to what might happen on the Western Front was as little shared by them as had been the preceding sanguine expectation. Having before them more constantly and clearly the whole view of the war, they believed more firmly than ever that no decision could be reached except by a vast concentric attack on the position of the Central Powers. To bring this about, it was now more essential than ever to nourish the wasting strength of Russia, and more urgent than ever to complete the ring where it stood broken by the Balkan *impasse*. There, it still seemed to them, was the point against which we should throw everything we had available after providing for the fundamental defensive basis in France. But it must be remembered that the conception which appealed to Ministers did not appeal to either the naval or the military High Command. Both had become absorbed in the problems which had confronted them at the outset of the war, before its real meaning was apparent, and both believed they could solve the new problems, without any preliminary clearing of the board, by direct operations aimed at the destruction of the enemy's armed forces by sea and land at their highest points of concentration.

So it was that the vast preparations which Lord Fisher had set on foot when he became First Sea Lord for pushing our naval offensive into German waters, were still being pressed simultaneously with those for developing a new departure in the Mediterranean. Indeed, from a naval point of view, the reasons for speedily crushing the German navy, even by a direct attack, so soon as the necessary material was completed, were as weighty as ever. It cannot be too strongly or too often emphasised—if we are to feel the situation as it really was—that in every plan which the Admiralty had to consider there was always upon them the dead weight of having to protect the army's lines of supply and the home ends of our trade terminals. Not only did that cramping pressure never relax, but every week it grew more severe. Against surface craft the Home fleets made the position as secure as the disposition of convenient Grand Fleet bases permitted. To some extent the difficulties had been met by the redistribution which had been made at the end of 1914, but the situation still left much to be desired, and at this time a plan was under consideration for carrying the redistribution to its logical conclusion by basing the Grand Fleet on the Forth and the Humber, instead of at Scapa and Rosyth. It was a question by no means easy to decide. The Commander-in-Chief deprecated so radical a change. Although on paper the more southerly ports were obviously better situated for getting contact with the enemy's fleet in the North Sea, yet he pointed out that while Scapa was convenient in every way, the other two were so confined, so liable to fog and so hampered by tidal conditions and the neighbourhood of the enemy's minefields, that in practice little time could be gained, and in adverse circumstances much might be lost. So strong was the case he made out for keeping things as they were that by the first week in March it had been decided to retain Scapa as the main base, and forthwith to commence work to render the fleet as secure and comfortable as possible.

Still, although the essence of the original plan was retained, a change, or rather a development, was introduced which, by giving the fleet a greater reach and resilience, went a long way to minimise the objections to the northern bases. Since the outer seas had been cleared of the enemy a number of cruisers, including the *Australia*, had been set free for duties nearer home, and besides this accretion of strength, the new light cruisers of the " Arethusa " and " Calliope " classes were coming forward rapidly for service.[1] It was therefore found possible to reorganise the Grand Fleet so as to provide it with a powerful and self-contained striking force capable of acting in any part of the North Sea with promptitude and effect, while the bulk of the fleet held its dominating position at Scapa. The idea began to take shape soon after the Dogger Bank action. That affair and the two previous sorties of the Germans pointed to the conclusion that

---

[1] The " Arethusa " class belonged to the 1912–13 programme and the " Calliope " to that of 1913–14. There were eight of each, all with a designed speed of 28·5 knots, and with an armament of two 6″ and eight 4″. Of the " Arethusas " six were in commission and of the " Calliopes " two.

any offensive movements beyond minor attacks were likely to be confined to battle cruiser raids.[1] Such raids were, therefore, the immediate concern of the Grand Fleet, and to provide against them Admiral Jellicoe's force was organised into two fleets. Under his immediate command was the battle fleet, consisting of the first four battle squadrons, the three Dreadnought squadrons being usually based at Scapa, and the "King Edward's" at Rosyth. This fleet had for its cruiser force the 1st, 2nd, 3rd and 7th Cruiser Squadrons, whose normal duty was to reinforce and cover the "blockading" work of the 10th Cruiser Squadron. Under Admiral Beatty, with the *Lion* as fleet flagship, was the Battle Cruiser Fleet. Now that the *Australia* and the three ships detached against Admiral von Spee were free to join it, its establishment would be ten units—that is, when the *Lion* had made good the damage received in the Dogger Bank action, and the *Invincible* and *Indefatigable* had completed their refit, and the *Inflexible* could be released from watching the *Goeben* at the Dardanelles. The organisation was in three squadrons, with a light cruiser squadron attached to each of them. Thus, with the *Fearless* and the 1st Destroyer Flotilla moved up to Rosyth from Harwich, the Grand Fleet would have a fast and homogeneous force capable, like the old "Flying Squadrons," of independent action, and, being based on the Forth, it would be in a position to seize every opportunity of forcing the High Seas Fleet to action if it ventured out, and of striking quickly at any lesser force that might attempt to dispute our hold on the North Sea.[2]

With this reorganisation, which, although as yet incomplete, came into force on February 21, and the increasing efficiency of our directional wireless, there was little to fear from a repetition of the recent raids. But there still remained the under-water menace. As yet all that it had been found possible to provide against the submarine attack was far from effective. As soon as the destruction of Admiral von Spee's squadron had completed our general command of the sea according to old standards, submarine interference had

---

[1] We now know that orders to this effect had actually been issued. Scheer, pp. 67–8.

[2] For details of this organisation see Appendix C. The *Australia*, *Invincible* and *Indefatigable* reached Rosyth successively between February 17 and 24; the *Lion* in April, and the *Inflexible* not till June. An extensive redistribution of cruisers on Foreign Stations was also being arranged, especially for the Atlantic, where the German liners had still to be closely watched. In the course of it the 6th Cruiser Squadron was removed from the Grand Fleet and suppressed, the *Drake* was paid off for refit, the *Leviathan* allotted to the North American Station and the *Cumberland* to the coast of Spain.

begun to show itself as a new danger which could not be measured.   Naval authorities of the highest distinction had foretold before the war that the Germans would not scruple to use the new weapon against merchant ships both belligerent and neutral, but the more general belief was that they were too sound strategists to risk raising fresh enemies against them by so flagrant a violation of the ancient customs of the sea.   Though this saner view seems certainly to have been weightily held in Germany, it was now becoming apparent that under the provocation of our blockade it had had to give way to the more reckless policy.

No extreme step was taken at once.   It is true that during October and November there had been cases of a relapse from the recognised practice of dealing with enemy merchantmen.   Unarmed vessels had been sunk instead of being captured, regardless of peril to non-combatants, but the cases were sporadic, and as they indicated no settled system, they had little or no effect upon the general outlook.[1]   For two months no further attack took place, and it looked as though the sounder views of German statesmen had succeeded in getting submarines confined to the legitimate military function of seeking by all means to reduce the strength of our fleet, and to hamper the oversea communications of our army.   On the other hand, there were signs that this policy had not been maintained without resistance, and that the more truculent sections of German opinion were fighting against it.   Possibly the forbearance was from the first only temporary, while their submarine flotilla was being increased and furnished with a larger type of vessel of sufficient sea-endurance for the work.   This appears to have been the idea of Grand Admiral von Tirpitz, Minister of Marine, and in November, with a view to sounding opinion in the United States, he granted an interview to an American journalist in which he foreshadowed a regular submarine campaign against Allied commerce in the near future.[2]   This idea was warmly taken up in the German

[1] October 20 *Glitra* captured and sunk by *U 17* off Stavanger in Norway. October 26 *Amiral Ganteaume*, Calais to Havre with Belgian refugees, torpedoed without warning.   She succeeded in reaching port, but thirty lives were lost.   November 23 *Malachite*, from Liverpool to Havre, sunk off Havre by *U 21*.   November 26 *Primo*, Tyne to Rouen, sunk off Cape d'Antifer, also by *U 21*.
Article 112 of the German Naval Prize Regulations provided that "an enemy ship may be destroyed if it seems inexpedient or unsafe to bring her in, but before destruction all persons on board are to be placed in safety with their goods and chattels if possible. . . ."[1]

[2] See Von Tirpitz, *My Memoirs*, Vol. II., p. 392.   The interview was not made public till the end of December.   See *The Times*, December 24, 1914.

Press, and in influential papers a systematic and reckless war of retaliation against British commerce was openly advocated.

The excuse offered was, of course, retaliation for the measures we had taken to prevent food and contraband from reaching them either through their own or adjacent neutral ports. In order to do this we had certainly extended the rule of ultimate destination to its utmost limits, by applying it to food and other kinds of conditional contraband. Still, neither in America nor in our own country was it believed that Germany would venture on so dangerous a remedy as to tread underfoot the fundamental restrictions of commerce warfare which from time immemorial had been held sacred by all maritime nations. So deeply, indeed, were we ourselves impressed with the unwisdom of contentious extensions of belligerent rights, that in our anxiety to avoid giving offence to neutrals we were still seriously crippling the power of our fleet to exercise full pressure upon the enemy. The recent Orders in Council by which we had gradually extended our list of contraband, had all been the subject of negotiations with America before they were issued. In deference to her wishes we had even gone so far as to exclude cotton altogether from our list of goods liable to detention, and the general result was that notwithstanding a growing tone of acrimony in the Press of the two countries the relations between the Governments continued to be those of cordial sympathy with each other's difficulties. Naturally, therefore, it was almost incredible that Germany would recklessly defy the goodwill which we ourselves were sacrificing so much to cherish, and no special measures were taken to meet what looked like an empty threat.

None, indeed, seemed necessary beyond those already on foot. The large number of destroyers and other anti-submarine craft which were on order for the Baltic project were being pushed forward to the utmost possibilities of the eager staff of the dockyards. Moreover, the new organisation of the Auxiliary Patrol was fast maturing, and the more important areas were being filled up with their assigned complement, as yachts, trawlers and drifters were got forward for service. After the Grand Fleet bases, priority was given to the Portsmouth area (No. XII), where Admiral Meux was responsible for the main army line of communication from Southampton to Havre, and by the end of January he had a very strong protective force. In what was known as the "Portsmouth Extended Defence," which covered the Southampton terminal area, he had six old destroyers, seventeen torpedo-boats and twenty net drifters available for general patrol work, as well as seventeen trawlers with guns and modified sweeps and sixty-three net drifters working from Poole.   Besides these were eleven minesweepers, and for escort duty his eight " Beagle " class destroyers.   The Dover area (No. XI), which was scarcely less important as barring the approach to the cross-Channel lines of communication from the new submarine bases at Zeebrugge and Ostend, was also provided for.[1]   The measures taken for the security of our cross-channel communications were most opportune, as an important reinforcement—the XXVIIIth Division—was due to sail for France on the 15th.   It was a highly anxious operation, the first of the kind since the submarines had become active in the Channel, and though the passage of such a unit did not materially increase the average number of vessels daily crossing with drafts and supplies, it was naturally, if known to the enemy, likely to attract a special effort on their part.   With four more destroyers from Harwich for escort, the transports began to sail on the appointed day.   No sooner was the first group over than submarines were reported lurking near the line. For a day the transports were stopped, but on the 17th the movement was continued, and by the 18th it was completed without accident.   As there could now be no doubt the Germans were doing their best to obstruct the flow of troops to France, it was a fine feat, which bore gratifying testimony to the success of the system that had been adopted.   Nor did the transport of the XXVIIIth Division represent by any means all that was done.   Drafts and details numbering about 8,000 a week were also being put across, besides horses and stores.   In the four weeks ending January 31 nearly 50,000 men and over 5,000 horses were transported, and this meant 234 separate voyages.   This was from Southampton alone, without counting the regular flow of transports from Newhaven and Avonmouth, the escort of outward and homeward bound military convoys and the protection of battleships coming and going in the Channel for docking or after completion.

So far, then, as the Channel was concerned, the situation, anxious and exacting as it was, seemed well in hand, but before the month was out the Admiralty had to provide for a new and very disturbing development of the submarine

---

[1] By February 18, when the German submarine " blockade " became operative, the Dover patrol comprised the 5th Destroyer Flotilla, the 4th Submarine Flotilla, two Auxiliary Patrol units (3 yachts, 12 trawlers), 20 armed drifters, 63 net drifters and 8 mine-sweeping trawlers—in all 140 vessels.

attack.   On January 28 a drifter on patrol between Wicklow Head and Bardsey Island, on the Welsh coast, reported two submarines with an oil tank steamer in company, which she had been unable to attack owing to her engines breaking down.   Next day these same or similar vessels were said to have been seen off Liverpool.   Neither of these reports was confirmed, but in the afternoon of the 29th a large submarine certainly appeared off the Walney Island battery which defended Messrs. Vickers' works at Barrow.   For half an hour she lay on the surface apparently reconnoitring, but it was not till she opened fire that the battery commander— although previously warned that an attack was expected— could make up his mind that she was an enemy.   It was then too late for his guns to tell, and the submarine escaped.[1] There were also reports of others off Milford Haven, and though these were doubtful it was clear that the enemy's submarine effort was spreading to our west coast.   Commodore Tyrwhitt was at once ordered to detach to Pembroke a division of the Harwich destroyers, and the Vice-Admiral Commanding the 1st Battle Squadron, who, in the temporary absence of the Commander-in-Chief, was in charge at Scapa, was to send one or two of his divisions to work down as far as Holyhead.   The Morecambe Bay lightship was removed, and Admiral Jellicoe was warned not to send ships to Liverpool till further orders.   Liverpool, it must be remembered, was not only important as a commercial port; it was also one of the bases of the 10th Cruiser Squadron, that is, the Northern Patrol, on which the blockade of Germany depended. It had just been brought up to its full strength of twenty armed liners, less the *Viknor*, which about the middle of the month had been lost with all hands, apparently by a mine, somewhere off Tory Island.

While the Admiralty were thus taking measures for the safety of the Irish seas there was a new outburst of piracy in the English Channel.   On January 30 two steamships, one from Buenos Aires and one from New Zealand, were

---

[1] It was subsequently ascertained from prisoners who had served in her that ғhe was *U 21*, Lieutenant-Commander Hersing, one of the most adventurous and successful of the German submarine commanders.   In the first days of the war he had left Germany for a cruise between Stavanger and the Forth. During his next cruise, on September 2, 1914, he is believed to have entered the Forth and passed under the bridge when the *Invincible*, but few other ships, was lying there.   Being detected and fired on by the inner batteries and hunted by picket boats, he had to retire without accomplishing anything. Three days later, however, he torpedoed the *Pathfinder* (see Vol. I., p. 163), and on November 23 he inaugurated the attack on merchantmen by sinking the *Malachite* and *Primo* in the Channel.

torpedoed off Havre. The General Steam Navigation Company's *Oriole*, plying between London and Havre, was also lost with all hands, and worse still, on February 1, the hospital ship *Asturias* was attacked without warning in the same waters. Fortunately the torpedo missed; but the attempt aroused a storm of indignation, and by that time there was further evidence that the views of the more ruthless German school were gaining ground. The same day that the ships were sunk off Havre, two coasting vessels and an Admiralty collier were destroyed close off the Liverpool bar. The submarine which did the work was identified as *U 21*, the same that had appeared off Barrow.[1] In reply to the Admiralty the officer in charge of the area protested that his patrol vessels were too slow to deal with such fast craft. They therefore directed Commodore Tyrwhitt to send eight more destroyers with a light cruiser, under Captain (D.), to hunt for the intruders. A division of the 2nd Flotilla from the Grand Fleet was also on its way, and orders were given that no ships of the Northern Patrol were to leave Liverpool until the destroyers arrived, and that it was to use Loch Ewe as its coaling base till further orders. Two Cunard liners, homeward bound, were also diverted to Queenstown.

The general dislocation was thus serious, not only to trade, but to the general disposition in Home waters. The Commander-in-Chief was sending down yet another division of destroyers, and thus about a score of them were absorbed in hunting out the newly-infested areas. The drastic action which the Admiralty so promptly took was not without risk. From now onwards, indeed, they had to grapple with what was perhaps the most serious strategical effect of the enemy's submarine activity. Instead of the main destroyer flotillas being able to devote themselves to offensive action with the Grand Fleet and the control of the North Sea, which was their proper function, they were tending by constant detachment to become in a large measure an anti-submarine force for the whole of Home waters. The effect was immediately felt. An offensive operation in the North Sea had been planned from Harwich for January 31, but owing to the call from Irish waters it had to be cancelled, and eight more of the twenty destroyers, which Commodore Tyrwhitt had left, were detached instead to cover the minelayers engaged in completing the new anti-submarine minefield east of Dover.

---

[1] It was believed at the time that another was with her, but subsequently it appeared that *U 21* was alone. The ships destroyed were *Ben Cruachan*, *Linda Blanche* and *Kilcan*.

Bad as the outlook was for maintaining our initiative in the North Sea, the next few days cast a still deeper shadow, which, though not entirely unexpected, was scarcely credible till it became a reality. Hitherto nearly all the submarine attacks that had been made were at various points in the army's line of communication, and this view of the sudden recrudescence was, to some extent, corroborated by an official notice issued in Germany on February 2, warning neutrals of the risks they would run from submarines operating against the transport of troops and war material in the Channel and North Sea. As a consequence the route by which the Canadian division was to proceed to France was altered from Southampton–Havre to Avonmouth–St. Nazaire. Otherwise shipping was hardly affected, and military authorities were forbidden to stop the sailing of ships from ports under their control, and insurance rates suffered no change.

This view, however, was quickly blown upon. Public opinion was still suffering from the shock of the outrage upon the *Asturias* when, on February 4, a notice which left no doubt as to which school of opinion was gaining ground in Germany was issued from the Admiralty at Berlin. Regardless of all established doctrine that set a limit on restrictions of the free use of the sea, it declared the waters round the British Isles, including the whole of the Channel, a " war zone," in which all enemy ships would be destroyed and neutrals would navigate at their peril. Neutrals making for north European ports were to be left a free passage round the Shetlands and down the Netherlands coast, and Germany would not hold herself responsible for the consequences if any other route was taken. The intention was obviously to give the declaration effect by the use of mines and submarines. It was, in fact, a peculiarly ruthless attempt to revive the high-handed methods of Napoleon, and the United States, as we fully expected, at once protested.

The excuse given by the German Government was twofold. In the first place, the British Admiralty had recently advised merchantmen to protect themselves against the piratical form of attack that was threatened, by the time-honoured device of flying neutral colours, and as the *Lusitania* shortly afterwards came into Liverpool under the American flag the plea was received with some sympathy in the United States. The other excuse turned on an unsettled question of contraband. Since the early days of the war, on a report that the German Government had assumed control of food-stuffs, we had claimed to treat them as absolute contraband subject to the doctrine of ultimate destination, and to stop them if consigned in excessive quantities to Dutch or Danish ports. Though no such control was actually assumed by Germany till January 25, we had continued to interfere with the traffic. Our contention now was that a new control order, which extended to grain and flour, justified what we were doing in regard to those commodities. The Germans not only took the opposite view, but claimed that our action entitled them to take extreme counter-measures. This was a claim the United States could not admit. They were, however, content for the time to give notice that they would hold the German Government strictly accountable for the loss of American ships and lives, and the declaration of the war zone stood. It was to come into operation on and after February 18, so that at the moment when the Admiralty saw themselves about to be committed to a distant operation of which the limits could not be foretold, they also had to face the fact that the weight of protecting Home waters was settling more heavily than ever upon their shoulders. Thus it will be seen that the discussions in which the Dardanelles project had been maturing were carried on to a jarring and sinister accompaniment which made it extremely difficult for Ministers to judge with confidence between the conflicting views of their expert advisers. Nor can we rightly appraise the adverse attitude of Lord Fisher and those who shared his views unless it is borne in mind how deeply the new developments in Home waters emphasized the merits of his plan for attacking the enemy on his own coasts—a plan which he foresaw would never be realised if we became entangled on unsound lines in the Mediterranean.

On the military side the reason for shrinking from the new enterprise was due less to anxiety for defence than to desire for attack. Although, as we have seen, neither the French nor the British Headquarters looked for decisive results in the Western theatre, they did hope in due time to bring such pressure to bear on that front as would enable the Russians to force a decision in the Eastern theatre. In the light of later knowledge we can see how hopeless was that expectation so long as the Balkan gap in the Allied line remained open. But it was not so clear then, and certainly not clear enough to justify Ministers in overriding the General Staff. Further, it must be remembered that the plan, which involved remaining on the defensive when we had baffled the enemy's crucial stroke, would have involved a perhaps insupportable burden of endurance on France, and without her concurrence we could not in loyalty have

gone our own traditional way.   Even if the new armies
had been ready to replace the troops which we should have
wanted to withdraw from France it would have been hard
enough to get our Ally's assent.   But they were not ready,
and, on the other hand, something had to be done at once.
Quite apart from giving up the Balkan gap without a struggle
there were Serbia and the Russian army in the Caucasus to
consider, and in these circumstances a compromise between
a purely naval operation and a true combined expedition
was practically inevitable.

CHAPTER IX

THE DARDANELLES—OPENING OF THE NAVAL ATTACK
AND THE QUESTION OF MILITARY SUPPORT

DURING all the difficult discussions concerning military assistance at the Dardanelles Admiral Carden had been pushing on the preparations for a naval attack without interruption, except for the adverse weather. It was still very bad. During all January, except on three days, it had blown a gale from the south-west. February brought no change except gales from the north-east. Since January 15 no active operation had been undertaken. On that day a French submarine, the *Saphir*, although strict orders had been issued that no submarine was to go in without special instructions, attempted to repeat the exploit of our own *B 11*, but she was less fortunate. Inside the Straits she ran aground and was lost.

The magnitude of the force detailed for the operation and the extent of the necessary preparations were, of course, quite beyond the capacity of one Admiral, and Admiral Carden was given two other flag officers, both of whom were destined to play the leading parts in the enterprise. The first was Rear-Admiral Rosslyn E. Wemyss. Having had, while in command of the combined Western Patrol, exceptional experience and success in working with the French, he seemed peculiarly qualified in all respects to take charge of the Allied naval and military base. As soon therefore as it was decided we were to use Mudros, he was instructed to hand over the patrol to his senior captain [1] and proceed there as Senior Naval Officer in accordance with the arrangement come to with the Greek Government. The second was Rear-Admiral de Robeck, who, since the beginning of the war, had been displaying so much mastery of his business in command of the Coast of Spain Station. On January 22 he was directed to shift his flag at Gibraltar to the *Vengeance*, which had been doing duty as supporting battleship on the Cape Verde Station and was now under orders for the Dardanelles,

[1] Captain C. B. Hutton of the *Diana*.

and to proceed in her to join Admiral Carden as second-in-command.[1] Admiral Carden was also given a Chief of Staff. The officer selected was Commodore Keyes, whose duties as Commodore (S) were taken over by Captain Sydney S. Hall. The appointment, however, now became mainly administrative, in accordance with the original intention, and the active command of the submarines of the Harwich striking force was definitely assigned to Captain A. K. Waistell as Captain (S).

The arrival of Admiral de Robeck about the beginning of February enabled Admiral Carden to hand over the blockade to him. Admiral Carden's flag was now flying in the *Inflexible*, with the scars of the Falkland action still upon her. After a short refit at Gibraltar she had arrived on January 24 to relieve the *Indefatigable*, who proceeded to Malta for her long-deferred dockyard overhaul. On February 7, Admiral Carden followed in the *Racoon*, intending to make Malta his headquarters for the final stages of the preparations, and during the week he was absent Admiral de Robeck was left in charge of the squadron at the Dardanelles.

It was not, however, intended that either battle cruiser should remain in the Mediterranean. Owing to the activity the Germans had been displaying in the North Sea, both of them were required to complete the new distribution, particularly in view of the fact that the work of repairing the *Conqueror* after her collision with the *Monarch* was likely to take much longer than had been expected, and that the call of the Dardanelles had reduced the Channel Fleet to half its normal strength. The *Bulwark* and *Formidable* were no more, the *Agamemnon* and *Irresistible* had already sailed, and as soon as the accident to the *Queen Elizabeth* was known, the *Lord Nelson* had been ordered out to take her place. In order to complete a 2nd Battle Cruiser Squadron which had been instituted with two ships only, before the Dogger Bank action, the *Indefatigable* was to go home after her overhaul and the *Inflexible* was to follow as soon as the *Agamemnon* arrived to relieve her. When, however, Admiral Carden learned that the result of the *Queen Elizabeth's* accident was greatly to reduce her speed he could not be easy with this arrangement. For the *Goeben*, after a long quiescence, was reported to be active again, and to have recovered from the damages of the Russian mines. With only 15 knots to her credit the *Queen Elizabeth* could not be relied on for bringing her to action, and on

---

[1] He was succeeded on the Coast of Spain Station by Admiral Sir Archibald Moore.

Admiral Carden representing this, he was allowed to keep the *Inflexible*.

His other ships were fast gathering to his flag, some from home, and some from the distant commerce protection stations from which the Falklands action and the destruction of the *Emden* had set them free.   In the Ægean Sea or at Malta were already the *Albion* from the Cape, the *Triumph* from China, the *Vengeance* from the Cape Verde Station and the *Canopus* from South America.   In Egypt the *Ocean* from the Persian Gulf and the *Swiftsure*, which the *Euryalus* was coming out to relieve as Admiral Peirse's flagship, were standing by for the word to join.   For the rest of the battleships Home waters were drawn upon.   The *Cornwallis* from the 6th Battle Squadron had already arrived; the *Majestic* and *Prince George*, which recently had been doing duty mainly as guardships, were well on their way.   In addition to these, the 5th Battle Squadron, which now constituted the Channel Fleet, was still more heavily drawn upon.   Except the *Venerable*, which was detailed for service on the Belgian coast, nearly all Admiral Bethell's squadron was devoted to the Dardanelles.   The *Irresistible* sailed with the *Majestic* on February 1, the *Agamemnon* on the 9th, and the *Lord Nelson* to replace the *Queen Elizabeth* on the 15th.   This left at Portland only the *Queen, Implacable, Prince of Wales* and *London*, with the attached cruisers *Diamond* and *Topaze*, which were held in reserve.   The French were contributing four old battleships, *Suffren, Bouvet, Gaulois* and *Charlemagne*, under Admiral Guépratte, which brought the Allied fleet to a total of sixteen capital ships.

The question of command presented some difficulty.   By the Convention of August 6, 1914, France was to have the general direction of operations in the Mediterranean, but after the intervention of Turkey our Dardanelles and Egyptian Commands had removed the greater part of the Levant from the French sphere.   No precise limits had been settled, but Admiral Peirse's ships had been patrolling the whole of the Syrian coast.   The French were now willing that the coming operations at the Dardanelles should be under the British Admiral, but they wished to take over the coast of Syria as far south as Jaffa.[1]   On these lines the matter was amicably adjusted.   We explained that we had no desire to infringe on the original convention, but pointed out that it was made in view of war with Germany and Austria, and before any question of the Eastern Mediterranean had arisen. The intervention of Turkey had materially altered the conditions, but we were quite ready to meet them on the lines

---

[1] See Plan p. 382.

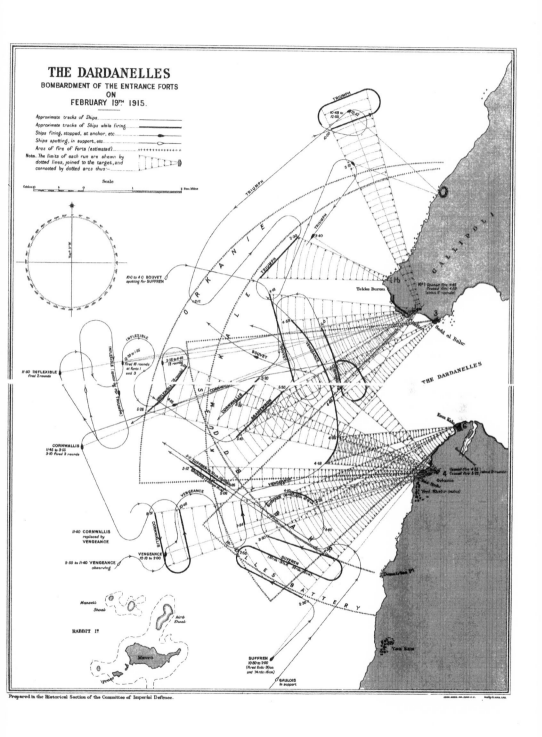

THE DARDANELLES

BOMBARDMENT OF THE ENTRANCE FORTS
ON
FEBRUARY 19TH 1915.

Approximate tracks of Ships.
Approximate tracks of Ships while firing.
Ships firing, stopped, at anchor, etc.
Ships spotting, in support, etc.
Arcs of fire of Forts (estimated).
Note. The limits of each run are shewn by dotted lines, joined to the target, and connected by dotted arcs thus:-

Scale

desired. The Syrian coast should revert to them, and Admiral Peirse should act in conjunction with, or under the French Admiral on that station. Further we agreed, as the project of landing at Alexandretta was again under consideration, that nothing should be done there except concurrently and in full co-operation.

The arrangement gave the French all they desired, and at the same time considerably eased the situation at the Dardanelles. They proceeded to form a third squadron for the Syrian coast, under Admiral Dartige du Fournet, consisting of the battleships *St. Louis*, *Jauréguiberry*, the cruiser *D'Entrecasteaux* and the coast defence ship *Henri IV*. By this means the Egyptian cruisers were liberated and the Admiralty were able to place some of them at Admiral Carden's disposal. When the operations began, however, he had, besides the *Dublin* and *Dartmouth*, only the *Amethyst*, which had just been commissioned for the 6th Battle Squadron, and the *Sapphire*, which had come out from home as flotilla cruiser. His destroyers numbered sixteen ("Beagle" and "River" class) and his submarines five, besides two the French had. He had also the *Blenheim* as parent ship for the destroyers, the *Ark Royal* with six seaplanes, and the gunboat *Hussar*, watching the cable at Syra. His force was completed by three groups of mine-sweeping trawlers—two from Lowestoft and one from Grimsby—numbering twenty-one vessels in all, but only seven had arrived. The French were to provide fourteen more, and they also promised six destroyers and their seaplane carrier *Foudre*.

February 19 still held as the day the attack was to commence. The choice was full of omen, for it was the anniversary of the day on which Admiral Duckworth had rushed the Straits in 1807. In the present case, the operation was certain to be of a very different nature, and at Malta, Admiral Carden had worked out all details of his plan. It was based on seven main phases :—

1. Reduction of the defences at the entrance to the Straits, in Bashika Bay and on the north coast of Gallipoli.
2. Sweeping the minefields and reducing the defences up to the Narrows.
3. Reduction of the Narrows.
4. Sweeping the principal minefield (which was off Kephez).
5. Silencing the forts above the Narrows.
6. Passing the fleet into the Sea of Marmara.
7. Operations in the Sea of Marmara and patrolling the Dardanelles.

In dealing with the forts, the general principle was to be an attack in three stages: first, a long-range bombardment (direct or indirect) out of range or bearing of the enemy's guns;[1] secondly, a bombardment at medium ranges, using secondary armament and direct fire, and thirdly, the final reduction of the forts by an overwhelming fire at decisive ranges of from 3,000 to 4,000 yards. Special importance was attached to ships not being hit in the initial stages, and if they came under unexpected fire they were to withdraw and resume the long-range bombardment.

For the first phase six ships were selected, the *Suffren* (flag of Admiral Guépratte), *Bouvet*, *Inflexible* (flag of Admiral Carden), *Triumph*, *Cornwallis* and *Albion*, with the *Gaulois* as supporting ship for the *Suffren*, and *Amethyst* for *Albion*. The *Vengeance* (flag of Admiral de Robeck) was to observe the fire for her division.[2]

By the operation orders the *Suffren* was to bombard the main fort on the Asiatic side of the entrance. This was Kum Kale (known to us as Fort No. 6), a modern work, constructed to supersede the old castle which still stood, with its high walls and rounded flanking towers. The new work, which was close on the water's edge immediately in front of the old castle, consisted of two circular bastions with a low curtain between them, and its main armament was nine guns from 6″ to 11″. A mile down the coast, near Cape Yeni Shehr, was its supporting battery Orkanie (Fort No. 4), a modern work 125 feet above sea level, armed with two 9·4″ guns. The *Suffren* was to begin her attack from a station off Yeni Keui village, where she would be out of the arc of fire of both forts. From this point she would bombard Kum Kale by indirect fire over Cape Yeni Shehr at from 9,000 to 10,000 yards, and the *Bouvet* was to spot for her from a point about five miles to the westward of Cape Helles, while the *Gaulois* patrolled off Bashika Bay to prevent the flagship being molested by field guns on the quarter.

The main defence on the European side, Sedd el Bahr, was assigned to the *Inflexible*. Like Kum Kale it was a low-lying work which in comparatively modern times had been constructed of earth within the enceinte of the original

---

[1] Effective range of Turkish 22 to 35 calibre guns was to be taken, for L/22 10,000 yards, for L/35 12,000 yards.

[2] The organisation at this time was in three divisions, as under :—

1st Division.	2nd Division.	3rd Division.
Inflexible	*Vengeance*	*Suffren*
Agamemnon	*Albion*	*Bouvet*
Queen Elizabeth	*Cornwallis*	*Charlemagne*
	Irresistible	*Gaulois*
	Triumph	

stone castle, facing south-east to south-west, with a main armament of six heavy guns from 9·4″ to 11″. It, too, had its supporting fort at Cape Helles, practically identical with Orkanie, and about 100 feet above sea level. It was known as Helles (No. 1), and was to be engaged by the *Triumph* from a position 8,000 yards to the north-north-westward, where she would be masked from its fire by Tekke Burnu. She would therefore have to use indirect fire over the headland. The *Inflexible* was to spot for her from her bombarding position to the west of Sedd el Bahr. Its opposite number, Orkanie, on the Asiatic side, since its guns bore on the British manœuvre area, was also taken over by the British, and was to be dealt with by the *Cornwallis* from an area west-south-west of Cape Yeni Shehr, where she could use direct fire without coming into the fire arc of Kum Kale.

On the European side the *Albion*, the *Amethyst* and seven British minesweepers were detailed to sweep from one mile north to three miles south of Gaba Tepe, so as to clear that area for the *Queen Elizabeth* who, in the third phase, was to bombard the Narrows forts over the peninsula. The *Albion* was also to destroy any defences found in the vicinity.[1]

The general idea and purpose of the operation the Admiral explained in a fleet signal on February 18. He had just arrived from Malta, and found that the air reconnaissances had fully confirmed the information as to the armament of the forts on which his plan was based. There was nothing therefore to prevent the attack beginning to time, for although the *Queen Elizabeth* and *Agamemnon* had not yet joined, they were not required for the opening, and both were due to arrive from Malta during the day.

It was at 9.51 on the morning of February 19 that the first shot heralded the opening of the unparalleled operations which were destined to attain such vast proportions, to consume so much heroism, resource and tragic effort, and to end with so glorious a failure. It was fired by the *Cornwallis* at Orkanie (No. 4); the *Triumph* followed in ten minutes on Helles (No. 1), with her 10″ guns at 7,700 yards, and by 10.32 the *Suffren*, who had anchored between Yeni Keui and Rabbit Islands, was engaging Kum Kale.[2] There was no reply from any of the forts, and in order to improve the shooting the Admiral ordered the other ships to anchor. But the *Cornwallis*, owing to a defective capstan, could not anchor in deep water, and consequently at eleven o'clock the *Vengeance* was

---

[1] For details of the standing defences, see Plan No. 4.

[2] All times given are East European, *i. e.*, two hours in advance of Greenwich Mean Time.

ordered to take her place, while shortly afterwards the *Cornwallis* was directed to carry out the duty of spotting ship for the *Triumph* and *Inflexible* if required.   The flagship anchored at 11.50, about seven miles to the westward of Cape Helles lighthouse, and tried two rounds at Helles fort at 15,400 yards, but as both fell short she weighed and went 2,500 yards nearer in.   At 12.20 she opened fire again at Helles. Though fire was kept slow and deliberate, spotting at these long ranges proved very difficult.   The *Triumph* fired only fourteen rounds from 10.0 to 12.15, when, as she could not hit Helles, she was shortly afterwards ordered to cease fire and transfer her attention to a party of men who were showing signs of activity in a new fieldwork two miles north of Tekke Burnu.

The *Inflexible* herself continued to engage Fort Helles, and, so far as could be seen, with so much success that at 1.0 she transferred to Sedd el Bahr, and the *Gaulois* reported that her sixth shot got home.   The *Suffren*, who had anchored 11,800 yards from Kum Kale with the *Bouvet* spotting for her, was firing entirely by indirect laying over Cape Yeni Shehr, mainly with her secondary armament, and seemed also to be making excellent practice.   The *Vengeance*, who had taken the *Cornwallis's* place and was engaging Orkanie by direct fire, appeared to be doing equally good work; but at noon, according to the report of a seaplane, all the guns in Sedd el Bahr, Orkanie and Kum Kale were intact. Still, so good had been the shooting since the ships anchored, that the Admiral considered the effect of the long-range bombardment had been severe enough for the ships to close nearer, and at 2.0 he made the signal for the second stage of the operation to begin.

By the operation orders it involved " Bombardment at closer ranges, overwhelming of forts at close range, and sweeping channel towards the entrance of Straits."   In this stage the ships were to keep moving.   The *Suffren* was to steer to the N.W., from Yeni Keui village till she opened up Kum Kale, when at 7,000 yards she would engage it with direct fire from her secondary armament, making repeated short runs at decreasing distances, but she was not to pass north of the line S. 84° W. from Orkanie, so as not to come under fire from its guns till she had silenced her original objective.   She would then take on Orkanie by direct fire at 5,000 yards.   In this work the *Vengeance* would assist her, while the *Bouvet* would join the *Inflexible* in dealing with the European forts on a similar plan, the destruction to be completed at close range.   The *Bouvet*, however, was not to begin till a field gun battery above the landing-place at Tekke Burnu (known as No. 1 B) was silenced if it showed signs of activity. This was to be done by the *Triumph* after Orkanie and Kum Kale had been destroyed; she was to open fire at 5,000 yards, and make a series of short runs, her limit of manœuvre to the southward being a line drawn west from Cape Helles.

About 3.0 the *Inflexible* anchored 11,000 yards from Sedd el Bahr, and to ascertain if it was still alive fired five more rounds. There was no response, and the inshore squadron continued to move in. By 3.50 the *Suffren* had made three runs as directed, still maintaining a deliberate fire on Kum Kale. As there also no reply was made, Admiral Guépratte asked leave to go in to decisive range. This he did, and at 4.10 opened a more rapid fire. In twenty minutes the southern face of the fort was in ruins, all three guns on that face had disappeared, and the whole place was blackened with melinite. By this time Admiral de Robeck in the *Vengeance* was also plunging shells into the ruins of the fort. He and the *Cornwallis* had been ordered to move in for the final effort just as the *Suffren* began her rapid fire, and after engaging Sedd el Bahr and Kum Kale they were now using their secondary armament on Orkanie and Helles respectively. Out of the clouds of dust and smoke that enveloped the forts came no sign of life; they seemed completely overwhelmed, and at 4.40 Admiral Carden, in order to verify their condition, signalled to the *Suffren* to close them and to the *Vengeance* " Cease fire and examine forts." Unfortunately the two signals seem to have been confused by the *Suffren*, for she read the order " Cease fire and close the *Inflexible*." At the moment she was in excellent position to destroy the Orkanie battery, the armament of which she could see was still intact. She was about to attack it, but regarding the order as a peremptory recall she began to haul off. As she gathered way Admiral de Robeck, in response to the order to examine the forts, was coming up at good speed straight for the centre of the entrance, when suddenly both Helles and Orkanie opened a hot fire on him as though they had not been touched.

It was a complete surprise, that gave ominous presage of the difficulties that lay ahead, but he was equal to the occasion. To the admiration of the French, instead of retiring to open out the range he at once turned and engaged the Helles fort. " The daring attack of the *Vengeance*," wrote Admiral Guépratte in his report, " in flinging herself against the forts when their fire was in no way reduced was one of the finest episodes of the day." The French were as ready with support as with admiration. The *Bouvet* even tried salvoes over the *Vengeance* and *Cornwallis,* while the *Suffren,* as she made away to the north-west to close the Admiral, re-opened on Helles fort, and the *Gaulois* came up and fired salvoes at about 9,000 yards into Orkanie. Kum Kale fortunately was quite silent, and Sedd el Bahr could only manage a few desultory shots, but the fire of Orkanie was particularly well nourished, and the *Vengeance* was soon in the thick of it. She was not hit, but four shots fell close enough to damage her spars and rigging. The *Cornwallis* also came in for a share, but not so severely. They were not long without support, for as soon as the forts began to show that they still had fight in them the Admiral had weighed to come to the rescue, and by 5.15 the *Inflexible* was engaging Orkanie, with the result—so good was her practice—that the Turkish fire quickly became wild. Nor was this all, for the *Agamemnon,* which, with the *Queen Elizabeth,* had just joined the Fleet, had come up in the nick of time, and she, too, was ordered in to support the *Cornwallis.* She was not in action, however, more than twenty minutes, for at 5.20 the Admiral, judging it now too late to do more that evening, made the " General Recall." Admiral de Robeck, undeterred by his exposed position, felt quite equal to completing the business, and begged to be allowed to carry on. No ship had yet been hit, but in the opinion of Admiral Carden the request could not be approved. The light to landward was getting bad, while the ships were clearly silhouetted against the western sky, and in his instructions he had insisted on the moral importance of avoiding injury to the ships in the initial stage. Besides, there was the serious question of the shortage of ammunition, which was destined to cramp the operations all through. To fire it away with a fading light into the clouds of smoke and dust that obscured the targets could scarcely give returns which would justify the drain on the precious store. The guns of the old ships, moreover, were nearing the end of their efficient life, and against the remote chance of decisive results, there was the very real risk of torpedo attack if the ships were not got away before dark. At 5.30 therefore " Cease firing " was signalled. By that time Helles appeared to be silenced, but Orkanie was still firing when the squadron withdrew.

At 7.0 the *Albion* with *Amethyst* and the minesweepers rejoined from the western side of the peninsula, and reported that no mines or guns had been found and that the area had been swept. Starting from a point N. 52° W. 5⅓ miles from Cape Helles, an approach had been cleared to within 5,000 yards of Gaba Tepe. Eight 6″ shells were spent to draw the enemy's fire, but even when the channel was being buoyed in the presence of a large number of troops, no opposition was offered. The *Triumph* during her reconnaissance of the coast beyond Cape Helles had the same experience. Nothing was seen except some trenches and field works near Tekke Burnu, on which she fired, causing considerable damage.

On the whole the first day's experience was promising for the success of the enterprise. It seemed clear that an hour's more good light would have entirely finished the entrance forts, yet in one important particular the results were disappointing. Eventual success depended mainly on the superiority of the fleet in long-range armament, and the unexpected activity of Forts Helles and Orkanie at the close of the day had shown, in the Admiral's opinion, that the effect of long-range bombardment on modern earthworks was slight. They appeared to have been hit by a number of well-placed 12″ common shell, but when the critical moment came all the heavy guns which these forts contained were in action. It began to be clear, in fact, that nothing short of a direct hit would knock out a gun, and that the necessary accuracy for a direct hit—particularly when ammunition had to be husbanded—could not be obtained by indirect fire, and was scarcely to be hoped for by direct fire unless the ships were anchored.[1]

Nevertheless, although the first phase of the operation had not been quite completed to time, the attack had been sufficiently successful to stiffen the confidence of those at home who believed the fleet could accomplish what it had undertaken. It seemed likely to take longer than had been estimated, and under existing arrangements the troops would be well in time to make good the initial steps. The Admiralty on the previous day had ordered the Deal and Portsmouth battalions of Marines to follow the other two. They had also ready the ten battalions of the Royal Naval Division, which was then in training camp at Blandford, and were preparing orders for them to proceed to Lemnos on the 27th. The War Office, however, had not given effect to the proposals of the last War Council. In fact, the arrangements then contemplated had been modified.

While the bombardment was going on (February 19 there began a series of meetings of the War Council at which an endeavour was made to settle the thorny question of

[1] The enemy's casualties seem to have been very slight. The Turks report one officer and a few men killed on the European side and one officer and two men at Orkanie.

military action at the Dardanelles. The problem was by no means simple, and its complexity had just been increased by a new difficulty. Owing to the continued bad news from the Eastern Front, Lord Kitchener did not feel justified in letting the XXIXth Division go. The Russians had just lost Czernowitz and had had to evacuate the whole of the Bukovina, while in East Prussia the Germans were still pushing them back. The prisoners claimed amounted to 100,000; the Russians were known to be very short of rifles, and they had lost vast numbers during the various retreats. Whatever the ultimate result of their setback, their armies, it was feared, had been reduced to impotence, at least for some considerable time, and in military opinion the Germans would soon be in a position to transfer troops to the west, and would endeavour to do so before April, when the first of our new armies would be ready. It was necessary therefore to keep a good division in reserve. Already the French had been informed, in reply to an inquiry from them as to whether we wanted their division sent to Lemnos, as Salonica was barred, that our division was not going. This did not mean that no military assistance was to be given, but that a sufficient force would be provided without the Old Army division. As the Turks had completely retired from the Egyptian frontier the whole of the Australasian Expeditionary Force could go. This would mean 39,000 men or, without the cavalry, 30,000, and these troops could be on the spot more quickly than any from home, while if the cavalry remained, Egypt would still be left with a garrison of 44,000 men.

This sudden and unexpected development was very disturbing, particularly to the Admiralty. From their point of view the new arrangement was open to a serious objection. All experience taught—and in previous discussions the point had been specially insisted on—that for such an operation as was before them a stiffening of first line troops was essential. The Royal Naval Division, though much improved in training and equipment since their Antwerp adventure, were not first line troops, nor were, as yet, the Australasians. It was further argued that in France the situation had clearly reached a deadlock, the condition on which it had been agreed another objective should be undertaken, and as for the plight of the Russians, it was only another reason for striking hard and quickly at the Dardanelles. This view was in general accordance with that of the civilian Ministers. Being less absorbed with the exigencies of the actual position in France, they were able, perhaps, to take a wider view and appreciate more justly the political deflections of the broader strategical situation. To them it seemed fairly clear that the Germans were now committed to their Near Eastern objectives, and that any force they could spare from the Russian Front would be used against Serbia in order to break a way through the Balkans. On this appreciation the only effective parry, since Salonica was for the present off the board, was a counter-blow at the Dardanelles. They believed the necessary force was available, for with the XXIXth Division, the Royal Naval Division, the Australasians and the Marines, added to the 15,000 men whom the French had at disposal, and possibly 10,000 from Russia, we should have close on 100,000 men. The Admiralty had also to point out another flaw in the contention of the military authorities. Their argument that time would be saved by taking troops from Egypt ignored the question of transports. Most of the shipping required would have to be sent out from home, and could not reach Alexandria in under three weeks. Still Lord Kitchener did not feel he could give way. The weight of his responsibility for the security of the Western Front was too heavy. In military opinion the Germans, during their recent unsuccessful attack, had not displayed anything like the force or energy of which they were capable, and it was believed that if they attacked again and really meant to break through we should have a much more formidable task to stop them. The furthest then that Lord Kitchener could go for the present was to undertake that in case of emergency the XXIXth Division should go, but not yet. No action therefore was taken, but the Admiralty undertook to prepare transports and send them to Alexandria.

The process of concentrating the troops in the Ægean went on accordingly. On February 20 Lord Kitchener instructed General Maxwell to prepare two divisions of Australians and New Zealanders for service at the Dardanelles, under command of General Birdwood, commanding the Australasian Expeditionary Force. The Admiralty continued the work of collecting the necessary transports both for them and the Royal Naval Division. On February 16, in pursuance of the War Council's resolution of that day, they had also ordered transports to be got ready for the XXIXth Division, and the Transport Department put forward a scheme by which it could have been embarked on the 22nd at Avonmouth. Nothing but preliminary steps, however, could be taken till after the meeting of the 19th. Next day the Transport Department was ordered to carry on, but on the 21st Lord Kitchener sent over his Military Secretary to say the division was not to go, and that no action was to be taken in preparing transport. Shortly afterwards the First Sea Lord gave a similar order to the Director of Transports, and the arrangements for transporting the XXIXth Division were countermanded. It was not until a week later that the First Lord became aware of the step taken. He at once protested not only against the irregularity of the order, but also against what appeared to be a departure from the promise that the division was to be ready to go if required, and directed the Transport Department to carry out their original orders.

The gravity of this hitch was increased by the slow progress of affairs at the Dardanelles. Admiral Carden had, of course, intended to go in again early on February 20, to complete the destruction of the entrance forts, and then push on with the second phase of his plan. But once more the luck of the weather turned against us. In the night it came on to blow again, and the morning broke so stormily that operations of any kind were out of the question. Next day it was no better. On the 22nd the weather abated a little, and the Admiral could telegraph that he hoped to begin again the following morning. But the 23rd was as bad as ever, and so, day after day, the fleet had to lie chafing at its anchorage, while the Turks had breathing time to recover from the effect of the first blow.

The result of the exasperating delay seems to have been to convince Admiral Carden of the necessity of having military assistance at hand as soon as possible. For this contingency Lord Kitchener had provided on the lines of his own plan. On February 20, in instructing General Maxwell to prepare the Australasian troops for the Dardanelles, he had told him that the transports would reach Alexandria about March 9, but that he was to communicate at once with Admiral Carden, who might require a force earlier. Further, General Maxwell was not to wait for the transports from home, but was to take up what shipping he could locally, and send some troops to Lemnos immediately. In the matter of transports, the Admiralty had already taken action. For this same day they sent out specific orders for some half-dozen ships which were in the vicinity to be concentrated at Alexandria ready to embark troops by February 27, and directed that for the short voyage contemplated 50 per cent. more troops than normal could be carried. Steps were also taken to collect locally a landing flotilla sufficient to disembark 10,000 men.

General Maxwell lost no time in getting into communication with Admiral Carden, and the result was that the Admiral expressed his desire to see the end of the Gallipoli peninsula occupied as soon as he had finished the destruction of the entrance forts. His idea was that 10,000 troops might be landed at once to hold the line of the Soghanli Dere, and onward across the Chana plain to the coast where the width of the peninsula is little more than five miles from sea to sea. Had the Admiral's plan been feasible, it would have ensured him against the reoccupation of the forts on the Gallipoli side, would have enabled him to deal with the torpedo tubes, and also given him control of the dominating position of Achi Baba or Three Tree Hill.

The proposed operation was clearly beyond what the War Office contemplated. In their opinion, the occupation of the tail of the peninsula was not an operation necessary to secure the first main object—which was the destruction of the batteries. But meanwhile, General Maxwell had suggested sending off one brigade of Australian infantry at once to join the Marines at Lemnos, and in the afternoon of February 23, a few hours before he knew what Admiral Carden wanted to do, he sanctioned the movement. General Birdwood also was ordered to proceed to the Dardanelles with instructions to confer with the Admiral, and ascertain whether he considered that troops would be necessary for the capture of the forts, and if so, how many he wanted, and in what manner he proposed to employ them.

Clearly the matter could no longer rest where it had been left on February 19, and the day after it was known what was passing between Egypt and the fleet another meeting of the War Council was held (February 24), at which an earnest effort was made to reconcile the conflicting views of the Admiralty and the War Office. The discussion turned inevitably on the XXIXth Division.[1] It may appear strange, seeing how many divisions were engaged on the Western Front, that so much importance should be attached to the allocation of a single one. The explanation is, that its destination had almost insensibly become a symbol which marked in objective form the conflicting views of the two schools of strategical thought. Whether or not it would suffice to turn the scale at the Dardanelles, it could scarcely be contended that one division, however good, could make the difference between success and failure in the defence of the Western Front; but its allocation to the Ægean would mean a long step further to an admission that the Dardanelles venture was passing definitely from the category of a diversion and a side issue to that of an alternative theatre of offensive operation. Already

[1] *Dardanelles Commission Report*, I., p. 32.

it had moved by imperceptible degrees very far in that direction. It will be observed that the original idea of breaking off at any moment, on which Lord Kitchener and the French had originally approved the venture, had disappeared. Possibly this was due mainly to the breakdown of the Salonica alternative, which left success at the Dardanelles as the only possible means of bringing in the Balkan States to complete the investment of the Central Powers. The decision to send troops implied that we intended to get through, even if the navy failed to do the work alone. If the XXIXth Division went it would mean that success was recognised as so vital to the common cause as to justify taking a considerable risk on the Western Front and abandoning there for some indefinite time the hope of an offensive return. The XXIXth Division was, in fact, the bone of contention between the school which believed in attacking the enemy where he was comparatively weak, and where great material and moral results might be obtained with comparatively small force, and the school which believed in throwing every available man into the main theatre, where the enemy was strongest and where alone a *coup de grâce* could be given to his armed force. For this school France was the " decisive " theatre; for the other it was not, at least not for practical purposes at the moment, since, as already explained, they did not see how a final decision was attainable anywhere until a true combined effort of all the Allies had been rendered possible by a preliminary decision in the minor theatre.

Though it does not appear that these opposing views were clearly formulated at the Meeting, they plainly underlay the discussion that ensued.[1] What the Admiralty wanted was a force, not merely to enable them to make good the passage of the Straits when the forts were crushed, but one large enough to seize their ultimate objective, which was Constantinople. It was held that a force of 100,000 men, with the fleet at its back, would suffice, and such a force was in sight. On February 22 the French Government had issued orders for the formation of a *Corps Expeditionnaire d'Orient*, which was to include one infantry division, and be ready by March 1. This force, with the XXIXth Division and a Territorial division added to the troops already promised, besides a division the Russians were ready to furnish, would provide the required total. So large a force appeared to contemplate a combined attack, but this intention the Admiralty distinctly repudiated. The troops were not to be used for the reduction of the forts unless the fleet nearly

---

[1] *Dardanelles Commission Report*, I., p. 32.

succeeded. But it was possible that in the final stage it might be held up by a well-defended minefield, and in that case troops would be wanted. Still Lord Kitchener could not give way. If the navy could do what it expected he saw no reason for so many troops; but he did make a frank admission which definitely altered the character of the enterprise from its original conception. It was that the enterprise must not fail. His profound knowledge of the East assured him that a defeat in the Levant would have the most serious consequences, and we were already too far committed to permit of going back. If therefore the navy could not do the work alone the army must see it through. It was a large concession to make, particularly in view of the increasing delicacy of reconciling our own ideas of a war plan with those of the French High Command, but, unhappily, it amounted to no more than a compromise between the two schools of thought.

So delicate and complex, indeed, were both the military and political considerations involved, that no definite decision was reached that day. All that was settled was a confirmation of Lord Kitchener's instructions to General Birdwood to confer with Admiral Carden on the possibilities of the situation. As soon as the Admiral's proposal for seizing the tail of the peninsula came forward, it was referred to the War Office, and they quickly replied that in their opinion its occupation " was not necessary for the reduction of the forts." Now the reduction of the forts was primarily, at least, a question of naval gunnery, depending in a great measure on accurate observation. Without an observing position ashore, on one side or other of the entrance to the Straits, accuracy was very difficult to attain; yet the decision appears to have been accepted by the Admiralty without comment. The Admiral, at any rate, was at once informed of the conclusion the military authorities had come to, and he was given clearly to understand that the operation committed to him was to force the Dardanelles without military assistance. In the present stage landings must be confined to demolition parties of Marines, but later on, if he was successful, an ample military force would be available to reap the fruits. For this purpose the Royal Naval Division, two Australasian divisions and one French, in all 56,000 men, were to be moved within striking distance, and possibly the XXIXth Division would come out from home. He was also informed that 10,000 men were to be held ready for immediate action, part in Egypt and part in Lemnos. It was not intended for the present that they should be used to assist naval operations, but General Birdwood was coming at once in the *Swiftsure* to confer with him on the whole situation, and if he was of opinion that the army could help him he was at liberty to submit suggestions.   The same evening (24th) the War Office sent out similar instructions for General Birdwood, based on the proposition that a military expedition was deprecated as unsound till the navy had forced the passage, the idea being, of course, that until this was done the Turks would be perfectly free to reinforce the Gallipoli peninsula.   His special duty was to report whether the results of the operations up to date indicated the need of a large landing force, but he was not to commit himself to an extended enterprise.

So the matter stood till two days later.   On February 26 the War Council resumed the discussion of the crucial question of the XXIXth Division.   In the meantime the news from Russia was worse.   Lord Kitchener made no secret of his anxiety.   The Germans had crossed the Niemen at one point, and the railway line between Petrograd and Warsaw was threatened.   The latest reliable information, moreover, showed that the Russian armies were in a serious position owing to a falling supply of rifles and munitions.   Although therefore the Admiralty again pressed for the XXIXth Division, Lord Kitchener was still unable to consent.   In view of the probability of the Germans being able to transfer troops from the Russian Front, he felt more than ever that he could not take the responsibility of risking the Western Front being broken, and in any case there was not sufficient ammunition for the large force that was asked for.   The upshot was that the XXIXth and a Territorial division were to be kept in reserve at home.   If the Russian situation cleared they could probably go, and as it was now manifest that the naval work would take longer than had been estimated, they could still arrive in time.   And so the matter rested, with a definite understanding that there was to be no going back. At best it was still a compromise between the two schools, but seeing how short we then were of men and munitions, and how the integrity of the Western Front was the bed-rock on which all our efforts depended, it was a long step on the road to an alternative theatre.

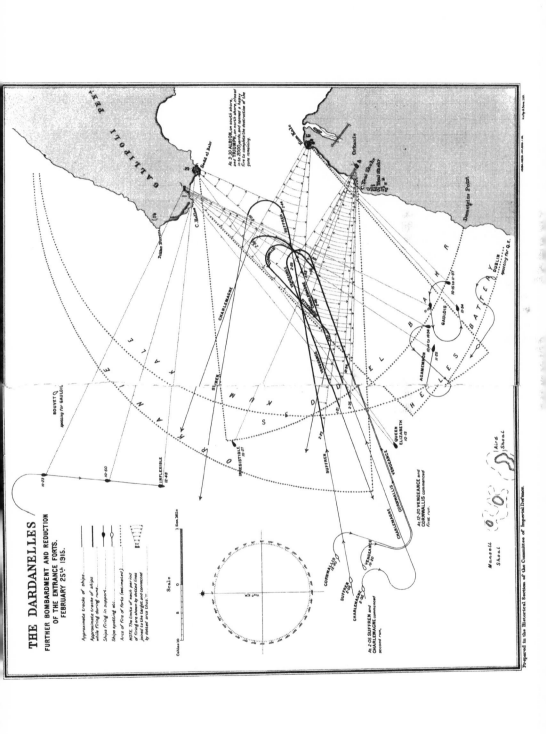

THE DARDANELLES

FURTHER BOMBARDMENT AND REDUCTION
OF THE ENTRANCE FORTS,
FEBRUARY 25th 1915.

Approximate tracks of ships

Approximate tracks of ships
while firing during runs.

Ships firing in support.

Ships spotting etc.

Area of fire of forts (estimated)

NOTE. The limits of each period
of firing are shown by dotted lines
joined to the target and commenced
by dotted area thus :—

Scale

Cables 10   5   0   3 Sea. Mile

GALLIPOLI PEN.

DARDANELLES

KUM   KALE

HELLES

BATTERY

As 3.30 ALBION on south shore,
and TRIUMPH on north shore, closed
in to 2000 yards, and turned a heavy
Fire to complete the destruction of the
guns remaining

BOUVET   spotting for GAULOIS

INFLEXIBLE
10·48

IRRESISTIBLE
10·27

SUFFREN

VENGEANCE

QUEEN
ELIZABETH
10·15

As 12·20 VENGEANCE and
CORNWALLIS commenced
first run.

CHARLEMAGNE

CORNWALLIS

CHARLEMAGNE

CORNWALLIS

SUFFREN
2·05

VENGEANCE
2·20

As 2·05 SUFFREN and
CHARLEMAGNE commenced
second run.

GAULOIS

AGAMEMNON

DUBLIN
spotting for Q.E.

Morell
Shoal

Aird
Shoal

Dardanos Point

Prepared in the Historical Section of the Committee of Imperial Defence.

CHAPTER X

By the time these conclusions were reached, it was known that the attack on the entrance forts had been resumed. By February 24 the weather had so far improved that Admiral Carden saw his way to completing the first day's work. The previous day General Trotman had arrived with the Plymouth and Chatham battalions of Marines, and it was agreed to use them ashore to cover the fleet demolition parties. In all battleships these parties were told off with instructions to destroy guns first and magazines if time permitted. But on the 25th, though the weather had moderated sufficiently to allow a renewal of the bombardment, no landing was ordered, and the Marines remained in the transports at Mudros. It was also impossible to use the seaplanes—a misfortune which seriously affected the success of the work.

The object of the day's operations was to complete the second part of the first phase—that is, the destruction of the outer forts at close range and sweeping as far as the entrance. The new orders were an amplification of those originally issued. The general plan was that four ships, working in pairs, were to make a run up to the jaws of the Straits and back, and engage Helles and Orkanie with their secondary armament until the range was down to 3,000 yards. Since the first day's work had taught how little hope there was of silencing a battery permanently by merely dropping shells into it, the instructions for the attacking ships were to aim " to destroy each individual gun by a direct hit." The first run was to be made by Admiral de Robeck with the *Vengeance* and *Cornwallis*, and the second by Admiral Guépratte with the *Suffren* and *Charlemagne*. In support the *Agamemnon*, *Queen Elizabeth*, *Irresistible* and *Gaulois* would anchor, and, firing deliberately at long range into Forts 1, 3, 4 and 6—that is, all the forts on both sides from Helles to Orkanie—would endeavour to prevent the guns being manned, the *Agamemnon* and *Irresistible* being assigned the special duty of checking the enemy's fire while the forts were being closely engaged.

In pursuance of these orders, the *Queen Elizabeth* anchored 11,600 yards south-west from Helles lighthouse and engaged Sedd el Bahr. To spot for her, the *Dublin* took station a mile west-south-west from Demetrios Point. The Admiral, in the *Inflexible*, took station to the northward of the *Queen Elizabeth* about 11,500 yards north-west from Helles. The *Agamemnon* anchored between the *Queen Elizabeth* and the shore, about two and a half miles west-south-west of Cape Yeni Shehr. There at 10.17, about half an hour after she had taken up her berth, Helles opened on her, and she was soon engaging it at a range of 10,000 yards.

It was only too evident that this fort was far from having been destroyed on the first day. Both of its 9·4″ guns were working, and their fire was being controlled with great skill. In a quarter of an hour it was straddling the *Agamemnon ;* she was immediately ordered to weigh, but in ten minutes she was hit seven times with armour-piercing shell. Most of it broke up without bursting, but before she got way on her she had three men killed and five seriously wounded, with a hole six feet above the water-line, and her hydraulic engine and main derrick damaged.[1] Still there was nothing that could not be put right. As soon as she was ordered to move the Admiral signalled to the *Queen Elizabeth* to take on Helles in her place, and in the interval the fort turned its attention to the *Dublin* off Demetrios Point. Though she was already being annoyed by a field gun ashore, she held her spotting station and returned the fire till the Admiral, seeing the fort guns were straddling her, signalled her to extend her distance from the enemy, and the flagship herself took up the spotting for the *Queen Elizabeth*. It was some little time before she got the range. She was a raw ship, and though she fired deliberately, it was not till nearly noon that with her sixteenth and seventeenth shots she got direct hits, one of which dismounted a 9·4″ gun. By that time the *Agamemnon* was in action again, and between them they had put both guns of the battery out of action and so wrecked the barracks which stood in rear of it that the garrison could be seen streaming out of them down the hill.

All this time the *Gaulois* had been engaging Kum Kale (No. 6). She was anchored off the Asiatic shore, between

---

[1] The first shot broke the head casting of the derrick, a fragment of which shattered the leg of Acting Chief Yeoman of Signals, A. A. Bishop. Nevertheless he continued to pass signals in the fore top.

the *Agamemnon* and Demetrios Point, nearly two miles north of the *Dublin's* original position, with the *Bouvet* about four miles north-west of Helles spotting for her as before. The *Irresistible*, with the *Agamemnon* as her observing ship, was firing on Orkanie. Beginning at 10.27, she had the range by 10.55, and thenceforward, by slow and deliberate fire, kept the battery silent. With the *Gaulois* things did not go so smoothly, for by 10.45, when the *Agamemnon* and *Dublin* had moved out of reach of the Helles battery, it shifted its fire to the French ship. She was quickly straddled and in as bad a position as the *Agamemnon* had been, but she at once opened rapid fire with every gun that would bear, and so entirely smothered the battery that she was able to slip and move further out uninjured. Shortly after 11.0, when she had brought the range to about 10,000 yards, she began again to engage her obnoxious disturber, leaving Kum Kale alone. This she kept up till about 11.30, when the *Queen Elizabeth* began to drop her 15″ shells into Helles; then the *Gaulois* returned to her proper target, Kum Kale, with telling effect.

By noon not one of the forts was firing, and at 12.15 the Admiral made the signal for the *Vengeance* and *Cornwallis* to prepare for the first run in. From a position close to the *Queen Elizabeth* Admiral de Robeck, in the *Vengeance*, led in, with the *Cornwallis* five cables astern. The course was straight for the entrance, and just before one o'clock they began to fire on Orkanie and Helles and certain other points in the vicinity of Kum Kale and Sedd el Bahr, as Admiral de Robeck directed. In ten minutes, having advanced to within 4,000 yards of Kum Kale, the *Vengeance* circled to port 16 points, the *Cornwallis* carrying on for three minutes and, according to orders, making a wider circle to cover the Admiral's turn. Sedd el Bahr fired only four badly-aimed rounds in return, and one gun from Kum Kale, another near Helles, one from Orkanie and some field guns also fired on the *Cornwallis*. By 1.22, when the run was completed, both ships had secured hits on Helles and Orkanie. The covering ships then checked fire, and Admiral de Robeck was able to report that Helles had one gun pointing in the air, the other invisible, and that the battery was no longer manned; at Sedd el Bahr three guns were visible on the west front; at Orkanie both guns were still laid horizontal, but the battery was not manned.

Communicating this information to Admiral Guépratte, Admiral Carden signalled him to begin the second run and concentrate on Sedd el Bahr, Orkanie and Kum Kale, but especialiy Orkanie. The two French ships made their run a little to the north of the first, and, according to the plan, it was carried in closer. It began at 2.10 at 12 knots, and by 2.28 the *Suffren* was firing on Orkanie at about 9,000 yards. This was kept up for a quarter of an hour : there was no reply, but the *Agamemnon* reported that most of the shots were too far to the right. At 2.40 Admiral Guépratte shifted to Kum Kale, keeping his course and making excellent practice till the range was down to 3,000 yards. He then began his turn to port and engaged Sedd el Bahr for six minutes. The *Charlemagne* turned short of her leader, and, making a flatter curve, was able to keep up her fire on Kum Kale longer. The only reply was a single shot from Kum Kale.

There could be little doubt the batteries were now practically silenced, and just after 3.0 the Admiral signalled for the minesweeping trawlers and their escorting destroyers to close the entrance, and for their covering ships, the *Albion* and *Triumph*, to close the forts, *Albion* on the south shore and *Triumph* on the north, and, keeping way on, to destroy the few guns that might still be intact. Going in to 2,000 yards, they opened a heavy fire with their secondary armament, and while they were thus engaged a gun from Orkanie fired on the *Albion*. She, with the *Agamemnon* and *Irresistible*, at once attacked it, and it fired no more. Helles and Kum Kale also fired one round each, while Sedd el Bahr was reported to have every gun dismounted. Except for some desultory firing from field guns, which could not be located and did not hit, these were the last shots, and at 4.0 the trawlers received orders to commence sweeping under cover of the *Vengeance, Albion* and *Triumph*. The rest of the fleet went back to the Tenedos anchorage for the night.

So just a week from the start the first phase of the operations was well in hand, and, though the weather had so seriously delayed it, the outlook was considered promising. " An excellent day," wrote Admiral Guépratte, " allowing us to augur well for the success of the campaign, as I have announced this evening to the Government of the Republic." [1]

Enough at least had been done for the second phase of the operations to be commenced. It was to begin with an attack on the group of batteries below the Narrows known as

---

[1] From Turkish information, obtained after the Armistice, it appears that by this day's bombardment all the guns in Kum Kale and Sedd el Bahr were put out of action and in the latter fort one of the old towers fell in on a battery. At Orkanie one gun was smashed and the other put out of action, and at Helles both guns were disabled.

the Dardanos group, and designed as a special defence for the minefields.[1] Fort Dardanos itself (No. 8), the principal one, stood on the Asiatic side, 300 feet or more above sea level, hard by the ruins of the ancient city which gave the Straits their name. According to our information, it contained two long 5·9″ guns, but three more had been added after the guns had been recovered from the wreck of the guardship *Messudieh*, which we had torpedoed in Sari Sighlar Bay. About two miles to the south of it another battery, known to us as White Cliff, and to the Turks as Djevad Pasha (No. 8E), had recently been constructed, but had not yet received its armament. Of this work we knew nothing and almost as little of the five subordinate batteries of the group, all of which had been completed since the first bombardment, and were armed with light naval quick-firing and Hotchkiss guns and field guns, in all thirty-two. On the European side opposite Dardanos was another new battery, known as Messudieh (No. 7), which had also been armed with three of its namesake's 5·9″ guns, and had its group of seven minor batteries armed with thirty-three field and light naval guns, making the total number guarding the outer group of minefields sixty-five. The general plan of the attack was for one battleship to move up each side of the Straits with minesweepers preceding them and others clearing behind them. "These ships," ran the operation order, "will destroy the land defences on both sides as high up as Kephez Point, mutually supporting each other. They will carry howitzers for use against enemy field guns, and must not approach within range of the forts at the Narrows. Seaplanes will assist them."

For over a century no ship had entered the Dardanelles from the Ægean side without the acquiescence of the Porte. The entrance of Admiral Duckworth in 1807 and that of Admiral Hornby in 1878 had both been unopposed; there was, in fact, no precedent for hostile ships passing in in defiance of the virgin defences since they were first constructed in 1659.

The ships selected for the honour of breaking the inviolate tradition were the *Albion* and the *Triumph*, but with them was joined the famous old *Majestic*, for she had arrived from home the day before, with a howitzer mounted on each of her turrets. Still they were not actually the first to go in. The distinction of being the first to pass between the forts fell to a humbler class of vessel, which had already done so much to mark the new era in naval warfare. During the night the group of trawlers which, with an escort of destroyers,

[1] See Plan No. 4.

had started sweeping when the ships drew off, had penetrated four miles up the Straits. They reported all clear : no mines had been found, and at 8.0 the three battleships followed in their wake.

Their first duty was to complete the ruin of Sedd el Bahr and Kum Kale from inside. The *Albion* was also to shell the observation post and torpedo station below the disused De Tott's battery, and the *Majestic* to destroy the bridge over the Mendere River by which the road from Chanak reached Kum Kale. All this was done with their 6″ guns without eliciting a reply, and between 10.0 and 11.0 both ships started to push on to the limit of the swept area, preceded by the trawlers and their escorting destroyers. The *Albion* took the north shore, and shortly before noon, when she was within 12,000 yards of Fort Dardanos, she began engaging it with her 12″ guns. The *Majestic*, on the opposite side, soon joined in at extreme range, and also fired at a field battery she had located on the In Tepe mound, at the western edge of the Achilleum heights. It made no reply, but others fired occasionally, and the two ships moved on, trying to locate them and using deliberate fire on Fort Dardanos. It remained silent, and the ships held on, while the destroyers searched the north shore for field batteries and sank the Turkish ranging buoys. So far the work had been done with impunity, but about 3.0 the trouble of the concealed batteries became more insistent. Both ships came under fire from howitzers and field guns which they were quite unable to locate. They seemed to be somewhere on the hill south-west of Eren Keui village, but the airmen failed to find them. This time the range was so short that they became very troublesome. It was, in fact, our first experience of a difficulty which, though not entirely unexpected, was destined to develop a serious power of interference and to prove one of the most formidable obstacles to success. The defence scheme had been prepared since the first bombardment in November. Nothing beyond the regular batteries and the few field guns allotted to them had then existed, but by the end of the year twenty mobile 6″ howitzers had been concealed about Eren Keui and twelve more on the European side amongst the broken hills about Fort Messudieh (No. 7). During January and February four more were added, as well as twenty-four mortars (8″ and 6″), so that about this time there were in these areas over fifty heavy pieces, besides a number of smaller mortars and howitzers. The function of this extensive mobile armament was quite distinct from the protection of the minefields. Its main duty, besides harassing ships in the Straits, was to set up a barrage fire on defined areas, so as to force ships to keep on the move in the position from which they could best bombard the inner defences. In this they proved immediately effective, and both the *Albion* and *Majestic* soon found that only by constantly shifting their ground could they avoid serious damage. As it was, the *Majestic* had received a hit below the water-line which caused a leak when, at 4.0, Admiral de Robeck signalled the recall.

He himself had been busy outside all the morning searching the Asiatic coast for concealed guns. He was so far successful as to detect and disperse a field battery at Achilles' Tomb, a mound near Yeni Shehr, while his cruiser, the *Dublin*, lower down the coast, was searching the vicinity of Yeni Keui, where parties of the enemy could be seen retiring from Kum Kale as the *Majestic* bombarded from the inside. When, however, the bombarding division moved on up the Straits after 12.0 he closed the entrance, and there, on the beach near Kum Kale, was discovered another field battery, obviously abandoned, though the guns were still intact. It was an ideal chance for a demolition party. The weather was favourable for a landing and everything was quiet. But, as there had been no intention to land that day, the Plymouth battalion of Marines, from which the first covering companies were to come, was twelve miles away at the Tenedos anchorage. Still the opportunity was too tempting to be lightly forgone, and Admiral de Robeck signalled to the flagship for permission. It was given, subject to an adequate landing force being provided to cover the demolition parties. That presented little difficulty. So deserted was the vicinity that the marines from the ships would suffice not only for carrying out his original intention on the Asiatic side, but for something further. As everything seemed quiet Admiral de Robeck had decided to land demolition parties on both shores and by no means to confine the work on the Asiatic side to the deserted field battery. By 2.0 the orders were given. For the European side the demolition party was furnished by the *Irresistible*, and that for Kum Kale by the *Vengeance*, and both ships, together with the *Cornwallis*, *Dublin*, *Racoon* and *Basilisk* were to take up positions to cover the operation from the sea. The *Vengeance* party, which had the more extended programme, was the first to land. It consisted of fifty marines under Major G. M. Heriot, and a demolition party under Lieutenant-Commander E. G. Robinson, R.N. Its instructions were not only to deal with Kum Kale, but to push on as far as Orkanie and destroy the guns in the battery and also two anti-aircraft guns that had been located hard by at Achilles' Tomb. They were also to endeavour to complete the destruction of the bridge over the Mendere River. It was an ambitious programme, but to cover the more hazardous part the *Dublin* took station close in to Yeni Shehr, while the *Vengeance* lay off the cemetery behind Kum Kale and the *Basilisk* stood by inside off the mouth of the river.

The landing took place at 2.30 at the pier, just east of the ruined fort, undisturbed. Advancing at once through the village, the party reached the cemetery beyond, without meeting any opposition. Here, however, they came under fire, and it looked as though an attack was about to be launched on them from Yeni Shehr. Still they pushed on, till the fire grew so hot that they were held up in a hollow beyond the cemetery. The worst of it seemed to be coming from some windmills on a ridge between them and Yeni Shehr. This was soon settled by the *Dublin*, who was so close in that by firing lyddite she had the mills in ruins in three minutes. Still the marines could not advance. Their flanking party, which had been thrown out on the left towards the Mendere River, had been ambushed, with the loss of a sergeant killed and two men wounded, and the result was that the main body was now under a cross fire from the direction of the river and also from the north part of the cemetery in their rear. To reach Orkanie under these conditions seemed hardly possible, but Lieutenant-Commander Robinson believed he could at least get as far as Achilles' Tomb, and got leave to try. Leading his party out, he reached a point half-way to the mound without loss, and then, not knowing whether Orkanie was occupied, and being unwilling to expose his men, he decided to proceed alone with a charge of gun-cotton. His reward was to find the anti-aircraft position deserted, and after destroying one of the guns he made his way back for another charge. But by this time the *Dublin* had subdued the fire from Yeni Shehr, so he took his party with him, for he had also found that the Orkanie battery was as deserted as the mound. He was thus able to destroy both the second anti-aircraft gun and the mounting of the only remaining gun in the battery. For this well-judged and intrepid piece of work in addition to his previous record in mine-sweeping Lieutenant-Commander Robinson was awarded the Victoria Cross. The Mendere bridge remained, but no more was

possible. Major Heriot had signalled to the *Vengeance* that
the enemy was in force, and Admiral de Robeck replied
with the recall. Though they met with some opposition on
the way back, especially from snipers in the cemetery, they
reached the boats without further loss, bringing with them
the two wounded men of the flanking party.

On the European side the *Irresistible's* men had much
the same experience. On landing at Sedd el Bahr the
covering party of forty-five marines, under Captain H. B. N.
Panton, took post near the windmills east of the village,
with a picket thrown out in the old castle on the heights
above, while the demolition party of thirty petty officers
and men got to work in four sections. The marines' picket
was at once attacked in superior force and compelled to retire,
but the *Irresistible* quickly stopped the enemy's further
advance with 6″ common shell. Four of the six heavy guns
which the fort contained were found to be undamaged, but
all were quickly destroyed by filling them up with gun-
cotton and pebble powder from the Turkish magazine.
Thus the main fort was settled. There were no casualties
beyond a few slight wounds from the debris of four guns that
were burst at once, and as there was still no show of opposition, signal was made to proceed to Fort Helles. But as
they advanced it became clear that the enemy had gathered
in too much force for this part of the programme to be carried
out. They did, however, succeed in destroying two 12-pounder
field guns near the fort, and then the whole landing party was
withdrawn.

As an impromptu it was on the whole a promising beginning, but much remained to be done. The forts had still
to be demolished, there had been no time to deal with the
guns in Kum Kale nor with the abandoned field battery
by the Mendere River, and the bridge, though a good deal
damaged by the *Majestic* and *Basilisk*, was far from being
destroyed. It was Admiral Carden's intention, therefore, to
resume the operations next day, and Admiral de Robeck was
ordered to continue the bombardment of the forts to prevent their reoccupation. At nightfall the trawlers, covered
as before by destroyers, went on with the sweeping, and
Admiral Carden prepared to move up with the transport
carrying Marines of the Royal Naval Division. But again
the luck of the weather turned. The morning (February 27)
broke with a heavy gale, and rain reduced visibility so low
that little or no progress could be made inside the Straits,
and the intended landing in force had to be postponed.
Later in the day, however, the *Irresistible* was able to put

ashore at Sedd el Bahr a demolition party, under Lieutenant F. H. Sandford, with a Marine covering force of two officers and seventy-eight men. The object was to destroy a battery of six modern 6″ Krupp B. L. mortars. The covering party was attacked, as before, from the old castle, and the mortars had to be dealt with under fire, Lieutenant Sandford himself preparing the last two, which stood in the open, with the enemy at 500 yards. Still the four inside the battery were blown to pieces, and the other two had their breech ends blown off. Then under cover of the *Irresistible's* 6″ and 12-pounder guns firing on the village and windmills, the whole party was re-embarked without casualty.[1]

The 28th was more stormy than ever. A heavy north-easterly gale blew all day with such force that not only the landing, but all operations inside the Straits had to be negatived. So the month came to an end, with no further progress made. March showed little improvement. It came in proverbially like a lion. The hills were covered with snow, another gale was blowing, and, though all arrangements had been made for extensive landing operations on both shores, with a proper covering force of marines, they had to be cancelled. But Admiral de Robeck was instructed, if possible, to send three of his battleships inside to reduce the guns that commanded the swept area and silence the field guns, and to watch the abandoned forts with his fourth ship. As usual, Admiral de Robeck saw no objection, and responded by sending in all four ships and watching the forts himself in the *Irresistible*, to which ship he had transferred his flag, as the *Vengeance* had had to go to Mudros to attend to her boilers.

The Commander-in-Chief's instructions he interpreted as authorising a further attack on the intermediate batteries, and accordingly he directed the *Albion* and *Triumph* to go up and engage Fort Dardanos and also reconnoitre the new battery two miles below it at White Cliff, while the *Ocean* and *Majestic* looked after the mobile guns. All the morning the *Ocean* had been searching the old castle and its vicinity in rear of Sedd el Bahr, from which so much trouble had been caused to the landing parties. Towards noon, when the *Majestic* came in and joined her, both ships moved on, and were quickly under fire from two field batteries in the Achilleum area. These they dispersed in a few minutes, and were steaming on towards Eren Keui when the howitzers about the village opened on them. Admiral de Robeck,

---

[1] For his services on these two days and his mine-sweeping work Lieutenant Sandford was awarded the D.S.O.

who had anchored off Sedd el Bahr, at once weighed and went in to their assistance as high as Eski Kale, which lies some two miles below Eren Keui. From this point at about 12.30 the three ships began to develop so effective a fire on the obnoxious area that it soon became quiet, and at 1.0 the Admiral could signal for the *Ocean* and *Triumph* to begin their run. But at this moment some of the concealed guns on the European side which the *Ocean* had been trying to locate for some time developed so galling a fire that the signal was cancelled, in order to give time for the new interference to be dealt with. At 1.15 they were quieter, and the order to proceed was repeated, while the Admiral withdrew with the *Ocean* for further work he had in mind at the entrance.

Meanwhile the *Albion* and *Triumph* were proceeding slowly up the Straits, with their two destroyers ahead of them, to engage Dardanos, but when they reached the edge of the swept area and were in position to open fire it was found that the destroyers, who were examining a mine they had just located, were in the way. The ships consequently had to slow down till the range was clear, and while they waited, the European guns opened again. This time so accurate was their fire that the ships had to begin circling to avoid it. Effective fire on Dardanos under these conditions was hopeless, and both ships turned their attention to the European side and also to Eren Keui, which was still firing occasionally. Their fire soon told; the *Triumph* marked two direct hits on the European redoubts, and by 2.25 a further attempt on Dardanos was thought possible. The *Ocean*, therefore, led round to starboard away from the European shore, but immediately the Eren Keui guns were upon them with a fire so furious and well directed that there was nothing for it but to continue circling and endeavour to subdue it. So widely distributed and well concealed were the guns that little could be done with them, and, though the *Majestic* moved up till she could use her howitzers, shells came thick from both shores. Under the cross fire the ships were constantly being hit, though not seriously. By keeping continuously on the move and circling, they could baffle the enemy's gunlayers, but it was only a waste of ammunition to attempt Dardanos in these circumstances. Consequently after completing two circles the ships were recalled for more promising work.

At the entrance they found that Admiral de Robeck, after his wont, had seized a favourable moment to snatch some success from a day of failure. As the afternoon wore on the weather had improved so much that he judged a landing at Kum Kale was possible. Seeing there was no sign of movement in any of the entrance forts, he therefore determined to try what could be done to complete the demolition that had been left unfinished the previous day, and the *Triumph* was to help to cover the attempt. Again Lieutenant Sandford landed with his demolition party and a covering force of fifty marines. Proceeding straight to the fort, he found that, in spite of the bombardment, seven of the nine guns it contained were entirely untouched and only one of them unserviceable. They were all destroyed in the same way as before; [1] and then he made off for the field guns to the westward. There were six of them, 12-pounders, all of which were demolished and their breech blocks carried away as trophies. The party then returned to the boats, destroying four Nordenfeldt guns and a motor searchlight on the way, and re-embarked without a single casualty.

It was a good finish, but the experience of the day was far from satisfactory. Though casualties had been negligible and damage slight, the ships had been hit many times. The Turkish barrage, indeed, as was intended, had proved effective in keeping the ships moving, and it was clear that until it could be mastered systematic bombardment inside the Straits was not possible. In an appreciation of the day's work which Captain M. S. FitzMaurice of the *Triumph* sent in the same evening he submitted that, from the experience gained, there was little hope of dealing with the widely-dispersed and well-concealed guns from the sea. " It would appear," he said, " that the best way of reducing the guns on the Asiatic side would be by the employment of guns or howitzers on shore from the European side. The enemy guns protecting Eren Keui Bay, being mostly of movable armament, present the maximum of difficulties from a ship fire-control point of view." This unforeseen difficulty, moreover, was likely to increase, for the seaplanes reported many new gun emplacements ready for occupation, and that the armament of certain of the batteries had been increased. It was, in fact, becoming evident that one of two courses would have to be taken. The choice lay between abandoning the attempt to break through, or using troops at once to clear the shores. For abandonment no moment was more favourable, since operations might have now stopped without too much loss of prestige, on the ground that, with the destruction of the

---

[1] The guns actually destroyed in Kum Kalé were two 11″, two 10″, two 9·4″, one 8″ and two 5·9″. One long naval 5·9″ had been added recently.

outer forts, enough had been done to facilitate a close blockade. But this solution, prominent as it had been when the decision to attempt the enterprise was first taken, had dropped out of consideration, and on this day (March 1) General Paris, with five battalions of the Royal Naval Division and two battalions of Marines left Avonmouth for Lemnos.[1]

That a considerable force of troops would be wanted, and wanted quickly, was becoming every day more plain to those on the spot, and during the night the need was strongly emphasised. For it could not now be concealed that annoyance to the ships was the least part of the trouble the guns of the intermediate area were going to cause. During the night the trawlers carried on the sweeping towards Kephez Point, under protection of the 2nd Division of destroyers (*Basilisk*, *Grasshopper*, *Racoon* and *Mosquito*), supported by the *Amethyst*. But shortly before 11.0, being then 3,000 yards from the Point and just short of the first of the minefields between Kephez Bay and the Soghanli Dere, they came under the beam of a searchlight at the mouth of the stream. All the minefield protection guns on both sides opened on them, and they had to slip their sweeps, while the destroyers dashed ahead of them, making all the smoke they could and firing at the gun-flashes and searchlight to cover their retirement. For forty minutes the action was kept up, till at last the *Amethyst* and the destroyers between them, aided by the *Jed* of the 1st Division, quenched the searchlight, and the trawlers, though shells burst thickly amongst them, got away undamaged. Though they failed to reach the minefield, their conduct had excited every one's admiration, and in the morning Admiral Carden made the following general signal: "Minesweepers are doing fine work. Their perseverance and steadiness are excellent. Much depends on them."

Indeed almost everything depended on them, but how with their low speed they were to do their work in the strong current till means were found of mastering the minefield defence was far from clear. To make matters worse, the morning (March 2) was as tempestuous as ever, and once more the landing operations had to be postponed. One new development, however, was possible. Now that Admiral Carden had with his flag the whole of the ships allotted to the enterprise, he was able to extend

---

[1] Royal Naval Division, 1st Brigade (Nelson and Drake), 2nd Brigade (Hood, Anson, Howe). Marines, Portsmouth and Deal battalions.

his operations.[1] On February 25, Admiral Carden had informed the Admiralty that if only 10,000 troops were coming he intended to base them on Mudros, and make occasional feints in the Gulf of Xeros without actually landing, and for a demonstration of a similar nature Admiral Guépratte's division had been told off. His instructions were to bombard the Bulair lines, to destroy the Kavak Bridge, which at the head of the Gulf carries the main road from Adrianople to Gallipoli, and to reconnoitre all possible landing-places on that side.[2] For the rest nothing could be done but to make another attempt on the intermediate area. This time the operations were carried out by the 4th Sub-Division under Captain Heathcoat Grant of the *Canopus*, glad enough, after her experiences as a battery at the Falklands, to become an active ship again. The plan of the runs was changed. It had been found that close in along the European shore the water was dead for the guns and howitzers on that side up to 7,000 yards from Fort Dardanos, and, moreover, that a ship hugging the shore could not be reached from Eren

---

[1] The battleships now numbered eighteen, and the organisation he was using, known as "The Third," was as under :—

DIVISION I

1st Sub-Division

Queen Elizabeth (Capt. G. P. W. Hope).
Inflexible (flag) (Capt. R. F. Phillimore).

2nd Sub-Division

Agamemnon (Capt. H. A. S. Fyler).
Lord Nelson (Capt. J. W. L. McClintock).

DIVISION II

Vengeance, Div. Flagship (Capt. Bertram H. Smith).

3rd Sub-Division.

Ocean (Capt. A. Hayes-Sadler)..
Irresistible (Capt. D. L. Dent).
Majestic (Capt. H. F. G. Talbot).

4th Sub-Division

Canopus (Capt. Heathcoat S. Grant).
Cornwallis (Capt. A. P. Davidson).
Swiftsure (Capt. C. Maxwell-Lefroy).

5th Sub-Division

Albion (Capt. A. W. Heneage).
Triumph (Capt. M. S. FitzMaurice).
Prince George (Capt. A. V. Campbell).

DIVISION III

Suffren (flag), Admiral Guépratte).
Bouvet (Capt. Rageot de la Touche).
Gaulois (Capt. Biard).
Charlemagne (Capt. Lagrésille).

There were also four light cruisers :—
Dublin (Capt. John D. Kelly).
Sapphire (Capt. P. W. E. Hill).
Minerva (Capt. P. H. Warleigh).
Amethyst (Commander G. J. Todd).

[2] See Plan p. 123.

Keui. This line the *Canopus* was to take, supported by the *Swiftsure*. The *Cornwallis* was to devote herself to subduing minor batteries, beginning with In Tepe, with its four 6″ howitzers just inside the entrance, and having disposed of it, to carry on and engage Eren Keui at 7,000 yards.

Entering the Dardanelles about 1.30, the *Canopus* and *Swiftsure* kept along the north shore till they were at the limit of the dead water nearly due west of Dardanos. There they stopped within 1,000 yards of the shore, and at 2.20 began a deliberate fire on the battery across the Straits at a range of 7,500 yards. Almost immediately what was thought to be an observation mine exploded just ahead of the *Canopus*,[1] but it did no harm, nor for a time was there any interference, except from a small field-gun battery close by, which could not be accurately located. Dardanos did not reply, and for nearly two hours the ships kept up their deliberate fire, disturbed only by a howitzer battery above Messudieh, whenever their movements took them out of the dead water. But at 4.15 Dardanos suddenly opened in earnest, and so accurate was the fire that the ships were straddled at once, and the *Canopus* had a shell on her quarter-deck which wrecked the ward-room; another carried away her main topmast, and a third went through her after funnel and riddled two of her boats. Captain Grant, in accordance with instructions, immediately ordered the range to be opened out, and fell back to a position further out in the Straits, where he could make things more difficult for the Turkish gunlayers. This movement, however, brought him within the fire area of Eren Keui. The *Cornwallis*, having quickly disposed of In Tepe, was now engaging the barrage batteries in that quarter, but without much effect, and the other two found themselves under a heavy and accurate fire, not only from Dardanos, which was still straddling them, but also from the howitzers on both sides. By keeping in motion, however, and turning at different points they avoided any direct hits, while at the same time they were able to develop so accurate a fire on Dardanos that by 4.40 it was silent, and they could see that one gun had been knocked over. The *Swiftsure* was then ordered to help the *Cornwallis* with Eren Keui, while the *Canopus* put a few more shells into Dardanos. It was still silent, and the Eren Keui area was soon so quiet that the *Cornwallis* joined her consorts and put two more shells into the fort. Then, as there was no reply, the ships were withdrawn, having suffered

[1] The Turks state that no observation or electric contact mines were used during the war.

some minor damage, but no casualties beyond one man slightly wounded.

Of the actual damage done to the enemy little was known, for the weather was still too bad for the seaplanes. Of the guns at Dardanos only one was seen to be dismounted,[1] and, as with the entrance forts, although the effect of the fire seemed to render the working of the guns impossible, it certainly failed to destroy them. As for the mobile and concealed guns and howitzers on both shores, they proved quite as formidable as on the previous day. While they had done a good deal of minor damage to the ships, they seemed to have suffered little themselves. The minefield defence, moreover, was still intact, and when that night the destroyers and minesweepers attempted once more to attack the Kephez field, the fire that greeted them was so severe that no progress could be made.

In the Gulf of Xeros Admiral Guépratte had carried out his mission with good results. While the *Suffren* engaged Fort Sultan, and the *Gaulois* Fort Napoleon on the Bulair neck and set the barracks on fire, the *Bouvet* attacked the Kavak bridge, but though badly damaged it was not destroyed. The minesweepers which accompanied the division found no mines, and two landing-places were reported, one at the Kara Dere,[2] between Gaba Tepe and Suvla Bay, and the other about seven miles from the Bulair lines.

The following day (March 3) it was intended to repeat the attack on the intermediate area with the 5th Sub-Division (*Albion, Triumph* and *Prince George*). It was further intended to land a strong party at Sedd el Bahr to complete the demolition of the work on that side. But when the morning broke the weather was so thick and stormy that both operations had to be countermanded, and Admiral de Robeck had to content himself with making what preparations he could for the landing when the weather should permit. The point of disembarkation was to be Camber Beach, just inside Sedd el Bahr, at the western extremity of Morto Bay, and it was now decided to examine and buoy its approaches. The point had hitherto been avoided, as it was encumbered with a reef. Morto Bay itself, from which the works at the back of Sedd el Bahr could be reached by ship fire, was swept by a group of French trawlers which had just arrived. No mines were found, and as soon as the work was completed they were ordered up the Straits under the protection of our destroyers,

---

[1] The Turkish official reports state that no gun was injured.
[2] Marked on Plan No. 4 as Kara Georgi Leitunlik Dere.

and covered by the *Albion* and *Triumph* occasionally firing
at Eren Keui.   During the afternoon the surveying party
left the *Irresistible* in boats, and the *Triumph* was recalled to
cover it from off De Tott's, while the *Prince George* and the
Albion supported the minesweepers.   Eren Keui, at which
the *Prince George* fired a few rounds, kept silent, but she came
under an accurate fire from In Tepe, and only subdued it
after a smart engagement.

After completing their work the reconnoitring party discovered on the beach, well concealed in the arches under the
fort, a battery of six 15-pounder field guns of modern type.
They were all destroyed, and then the party entered the fort,
only to find that all the ammunition had been removed.
There had been no opposition, thanks apparently to the
effective fire of the *Triumph* on parties of the enemy she was
able to detect above Morto Bay.   The party then returned
to the ship without a casualty.

Meanwhile the visibility had become so good that the
Prince George was ordered to carry on under the European
shore and engage Dardanos.   Four runs were made against it
without eliciting a reply, but during the fourth, which was
made further out than before, she came under well-directed
fire from the European side, not only from howitzers, but
also from Messudieh (No. 7) firing accurate salvos of three.
Being unable to locate it she turned back into dead water
again and then was recalled.   All the ships then retired outside, leaving the destroyers *Wolverine, Scorpion, Renard* and
Grampus to escort the trawlers for another attempt on the
Kephez minefield during the night.

It was now just a fortnight since the operations had
begun.   Thanks to the activity of Admiral de Robeck's
landing parties Phase I was nearly completed.   The actual
destruction of the forts alone remained.   Still little progress
had been made with Phase II.   So far as it had gone nothing
certain had come of it, except a clear recognition of the difficulties that lay ahead.   The abandonment of so many guns
by the Turks, and their readiness to cease working those that
were in their possession, both in the forts and on the hills,
showed how great a demoralisation the ships had caused;
but, on the other hand, the inability of the seaplanes to
observe and report during bombardment proved that the
work would be of indefinite duration if proceeded with
by ships alone.   More obviously than ever troops were
required, not only to make good what the fleet had won,
but also to give it the eyes it needed.   This was the experience of the Japanese, who alone had any practical knowledge

of ships engaging forts under modern conditions. For this reason the Admiral had been specially instructed to avail himself of the experience of Captain FitzMaurice of the *Triumph,* who had come straight from taking part in the operations against Tsingtau. While on guard in Morto Bay during the last day's work he had had a good opportunity of observing what was happening, and the effect had been to deepen the impression he had formed already. In the appreciation he now sent in he arrived at the conclusion that " no real progress could be made without the assistance of land forces to supplement and make good the work done by the fleet." He went even further, and submitted a suggestion as to where the most effective supplementary work could be done, and that was on Achi Baba. This hill, destined to become so famous, was the commanding feature of the end of the Gallipoli peninsula. It had naturally not escaped Admiral Carden's attention. In the telegram of the 25th, in which he had suggested using the troops in the first instance for feints in the Gulf of Xeros, he had added that if it became necessary to prevent serious interference with the fleet by concealed guns, a force could be landed at Sedd el Bahr to occupy the tail of the peninsula up to the Soghanli Dere line, which included Achi Baba, but as the maintenance of such a force would depend upon the weather, he did not intend to attempt the operation unless it was essential. He did not, however, specially emphasise its value from the point of view of gunnery. Captain FitzMaurice, on the other hand, who had seen at Tsingtau how ineffective the naval bombardment had been till an observing station was established on the dominating height known as Prince Henry Hill (Prinz Heinrich Berg), left no doubt about it. " It is considered," he wrote, " that if Achi Baba could be occupied and entrenched a most invaluable spotting position could be established, which could enable a far more accurate fire to be delivered from the fleet. And, if shore guns are available, they could be effectively directed on those situated on and around Eren Keui."

Though attention had been called to the tactical importance of Prince Henry Hill in the reports of our Naval Attaché with the Japanese fleet, and to the hopelessness of ships silencing modern forts except by direct hits on the guns, which a good observing station could alone secure, little or no attention had been directed to the point in the instructions which Admiral Carden received.[1] In the last and

---

[1] In a staff memorandum on the best means of overcoming the difficulties of the operation, Sir Henry Jackson, on February 15, had advised the

closest analogy to the Gallipoli operations, which was the Japanese capture of the Port Arthur peninsula, the lesson had been even more strongly brought out than at Tsingtau. As is well known, the fate of Port Arthur turned on the capture of 203-Metre Hill. From the first Admiral Togo had pointed out that this indispensable observing station was the decisive primary objective for the army, but the army, ignoring the exigencies of naval gunners, tried every other means before its chiefs were convinced. Yet in our service the cardinal lesson appears to have been missed. The experience of the Japanese was taken as showing the great difficulty of destroying modern forts by ship fire, but the only means of overcoming the difficulty was ignored.

That at this stage of the Dardanelles operations the available troops could have landed without serious opposition and seized Achi Baba seems to be agreed, but whether it could have been held without a stiffening of first line troops is more doubtful. Besides the two Marine battalions of the Royal Naval Division on the spot, there was nothing within reach except the 3rd Australian Brigade, which had left Alexandria on March 2 and was approaching Lemnos. All were raw and imperfectly trained, and possibly even with the powerful support the ships could give from both flanks they could not have maintained themselves long enough for reinforcements to arrive. Still the proposal to seize the tail of the peninsula was rejected because in the opinion of the War Office the occupation of the southern end of the peninsula up to the line proposed was not " an obligatory operation for the first main object," which was the destruction of the permanent batteries by the fleet. Those naval officers who could speak from experience thought otherwise, but unfortunately the lessons of Port Arthur and Tsingtau were ignored by the high authorities of both services, and the decision appears to have been taken without due regard to the proved indispensability of such a spotting position if a modern fleet is to develop its full power against forts. Owing to our imperfect machinery for bringing together the naval and military staffs for intimate study of combined problems, such failures in council were inevitable. Although by this time it was apparent that observation of ship fire and location of concealed batteries would be the crux of the situation, in Lord Kitchener's

---

early seizure of spotting stations ashore. This memorandum was sent to Admiral Carden " for information," but he was not to consider himself bound by it. It is now known that Achi Baba did not afford a view of the Narrows forts, the limit of vision from its summit being Kephez Bay.

instructions to General Birdwood there was no suggestion of using the troops to overcome the difficulty. General Birdwood was simply told to ascertain whether a landing force would be required to take the forts in reverse. At the same time he was warned that as the Turks had 40,000 men in the peninsula it was not a sound military operation to land 10,000 men in face of them till the passage was forced by the fleet, in which case the peninsula would probably be evacuated. Lord Kitchener did, however, authorise him, if it could be done without compromising the troops, to employ part of his force " to secure hold of forts or positions already won and dominated by ship fire."

Under the latter authority General Birdwood would probably have felt justified in suggesting the occupation of Achi Baba had its cardinal importance been clearly brought to his notice. As it was, in the appreciation which he sent from the Dardanelles the previous day (March 3) after the conference with Admiral Carden, the point was entirely missed. During the recent operations General Birdwood had had an opportunity of making a reconnaissance up the Straits, and he, too, had come to the conclusion that troops were needed at once. He had seen enough to realise that the concealed barrage guns were the real trouble, and his opinion was that the fleet must choose between ignoring the damage those guns could inflict and waiting till the army could co-operate for their destruction. Which of the two alternatives should be chosen, he assumed would depend on the urgency of the case. It was clear to him that it could be no question of mere minor operations, and his intention was to bring up the whole of his infantry, to the number of 30,000 men. They could not be ready till the 18th, but as soon as they arrived, he proposed—and in this he said Admiral Carden concurred—to land a strong force at Cape Helles under cover of a demonstration at Bulair. It would then work its way north as far as the line Gaba Tepe–Kilid Bahr, that is, the heights just short of the Narrows, a point from which the main forts on the European side could be taken in reverse and the minor concealed batteries on both shores dealt with. Here clearly the idea was that from which the War Office were shrinking. It was a plan to assist the navy in taking the forts by direct combined operations, and not a plan to give the navy what they required to destroy them themselves.

As to whether Achi Baba could have been permanently held if it had been seized, the precise position was this. According to our more recent information the Turks were

believed to have in the peninsula some 30,000 or possibly
40,000 men; those we had immediately available, with the
two battalions of Marines and the Australians, were about
12,000, but so long as we threatened a landing at Bulair, as
was subsequently shown, it would have been difficult for the
Turks to have brought their whole disposable force against
our own, and our own could be supported by powerful ship
fire.[1] After some delay the Turks could have been strongly
reinforced from the Bosporus, where troops were believed
to be ready in transports, but the possibilities of deployment
at the tail of the peninsula were limited.[2] On the other hand,
we had the means of strongly reinforcing our hold within a
measurable time. Besides the rest of the Australasian Corps
in Egypt, the remainder of the Royal Naval Division were
coming down the coast of Portugal, and the French had just
telegraphed that the division they had originally destined
for Salonica was to go to Mityleni, if the Greeks consented,
and if not to some other convenient base. It would seem,
therefore, that there was at this stage a possibility of Achi
Baba, if not the Soghanli Dere line, being seized and made
good. General Birdwood, at least, believed it could be done.
In his evidence before the Commission, after explaining why
he rejected the plausible idea of a landing at Bulair or Suvla
Bay, he said, "I felt that if I landed on the toe of the
peninsula I should be sure of holding my own, with the help
of the navy, and my flanks quite secure. I did not care what
force could be brought against me, because I felt that in any
case I should be safe. In those days the problem was very
different to what it was later on. I felt quite confident I
could land there and in three days get Achi Baba." The
seizure of Achi Baba as an observing station was then at
least a possibility which warranted a mature consideration
as to whether it was not an easier and more effective way of
co-operating with the fleet than an attempt to take the
forts in reverse. But there is no evidence that it was seriously considered. History is filled with cases in which

---

[1] The Turkish official reports of the utterly demoralising effects of our
ship fire on their troops until they got used to it tend to show that this, for
some time, would have been a decisive factor.

[2] According to the Turkish official statement the troops available for
defence of the Dardanelles against landing attacks consisted in February of
the IXth Division, of which one regiment had its headquarters at Bulair,
one at Gaba Tepe and one at Maidos, with detachments at Helles and Kum
Kale. After February 19 another division, the XIXth, became available.
It was allotted to the Gallipoli peninsula, and the IXth Division moved
across to the Asiatic side. It was not till the end of March that a third
division, the VIIth, became available as a reserve.

councils of war were unable to reach a sound and quick conclusion simply from failure to state with perfect lucidity and precision what the problem was they had to solve. This would seem to be another case in point. The real problem was how to enable the fleet to master the forts, not how the forts could be taken in reverse by a land force. General Birdwood, following his instructions, now left for Alexandria to complete arrangements for bringing up his corps.[1]

So matters stood on March 3, with no immediate prospect of a move; but no sooner was his back turned than the weather changed and a landing became possible. He had left at Admiral Carden's disposal the 3rd Australian Brigade, but it was only just approaching Mudros and was not immediately available. Even if it had been, it probably would not have been used, for what the Admiral did was only to put in action the existing arrangements for demolition parties which had been held up so long.

In making his report on the evening of the 3rd, Admiral de Robeck said he intended to get to work next day on Messudieh (No. 7), which for the first time apparently had been showing activity. Since he believed that Dardanos was out of action, for a time at least, he considered the inner forts could now be bombarded at long range from the dead water on the north shore, but he did not think this advisable till Dardanos and Messudieh were both completely silenced; but this programme was not put into effect, for, contrary to all expectations, it was found possible to carry out the landing of the Marines to complete the first phase of the operations by making sure of Forts Helles and Orkanie.

The morning of March 4 broke in perfect serenity, and for the first time for a week the landing orders were not cancelled. The force of Marines originally detailed was not increased. It comprised only two companies, one for each shore, and each with four machine-guns. The covering ships were in two divisions. For the north side Captain Hayes-Sadler, fresh from his experience in Mesopotamia, was in charge, with his own ship, the *Ocean*, off Sedd el Bahr, the *Lord Nelson* off Helles and the *Majestic* inside off Morto Bay. Admiral de Robeck took the south side, with the *Irresistible* off Kum Kale, the *Cornwallis* inside off the Mendere River and the *Agamemnon* and *Dublin* outside off Yeni Shehr. As a further precaution on this side the *Canopus* was to make a demonstration along the Ægean coast from

[1] The real importance of Achi Baba lay in the fact that it was the chief artillery command post of the Turks and their main observing station in the south.

Yukyeri Bay as high as the north end of Bashika Bay, the object being to hold the enemy troops in that vicinity and prevent their reinforcing the Kum Kale area. As a general support for the main operations Admiral Carden came up in the *Inflexible*, but the direction of the day's work remained in the hands of the second-in-command.

The Marines' transport, *Braemar Castle*, had been moved up to Imbros, and early in the morning the two companies were brought in by destroyers, and on reaching the entrance they were joined by the boats of the squadron bringing the demolition and beach parties from the ships, while General Trotman directed operations, with his headquarters in the destroyer *Wolverine*.

The southern force was the first to land, under Lieutenant-Colonel G. E. Matthews, commanding the Plymouth battalion. About 9.0 the scouts and an advanced guard of a half company, with a demolition and beach party from the *Lord Nelson* under Lieutenant-Commander W. L. Dodgson,[1] shoved off and made for the Kum Kale pier, while the *Cornwallis* from off the Mendere River shelled the fort and the village in rear of it, shifting to the bridge as the boats advanced. From the first it was clear that, owing to the long delay caused by the weather, the advantage of surprise had been lost, and that the Turks were prepared to show considerable opposition. From the *Cornwallis* numbers of troops could be seen entering the cemetery from the direction of the bridge and passing on to Yeni Shehr, upon which the *Agamemnon* also began to fire, and between the two ships the enemy seemed to suffer severely. Guns and howitzers were also located, but throughout the day the work of covering the advance proved very difficult, since the ships had no clear information of the line the troops on this side intended to take.

The general idea was to enter the fort and push on through the village, so as to make the ground good from Kum Kale to the south of Yeni Shehr village, and this they were to hold for three hours, while the demolition parties were at work and a reconnaissance was made to select ground for an aerodrome. As the tow carrying the Marines approached the shore, it was received with a shower of shrapnel, which forced the boats to cast off and take to their oars to scatter. Still the actual landing, as usual, was made without opposition, but no sooner were the men out of the boats than it was obvious the village had been reoccupied.

---

[1] Covering party 120; Demolition party eighteen men and five marines; Beach party one lieutenant, one surgeon and eight men.

Snipers opened a well-directed fire from the houses and wind-mills in the vicinity, guns from somewhere joined in with shrapnel, and so hot was the reception that the whole party had to take shelter under the walls of the fort, leaving the machine-guns and demolition gear on the pier. It was now the turn of the ships. The *Irresistible* took the windmills and quickly reduced them to ruins. The *Scorpion* closed in to the mouth of the Mendere River, found the battery that was firing shrapnel near In Tepe, silenced it and then attended to the village snipers. As the enemy retired it could be seen that a number of Germans were with them, but the Turks could not be got to face the ships' fire. As they gave way the demolition party was able to recover its gear and explo-sives, but the machine-guns remained on the pier. The beach master called for volunteers to recover them, and a boat's crew from the *Agamemnon's* second cutter was quickly formed, under its coxwain, Leading Seaman Ludgate. Under a galling fire they rowed to the pier, and Ludgate, with one able seaman and two marines, by crawling along it, was able to take off the maxims and restore them to their crews without any casualty.[1]

Meanwhile the shore party had been pushing on round the fort into the village, but it was still found impossible to get beyond the first houses, and there was nothing to do but wait for the supports, while the *Irresistible* and *Cornwallis* bombarded it. There was consequently some delay in getting the other half company ashore, and it was not till 11.30 that they came up. Even then so galling was the fire from the houses that it took them an hour and a half to reach the open ground beyond the village. Here they were again stopped by a report from the rear guard holding their line of retirement that they were being fired on, and that the enemy were working round to enfilade our lines. This movement was quickly stopped by ship fire, and at 2.45 Colonel Matthews felt he could make a push for Orkanie. An advanced guard and the naval demolition party were sent forward, but only to find themselves held up near Achilles' fountain by a heavy rifle fire that came from the Orkanie battery and some trenches on the slope of Yeni Shehr Hill. Still the demolition party attempted to advance in face of it, but were forced at last to take cover on the beach.

---

[1] Colonel Matthews' account is: " The fire did not slacken, and it became necessary to bring the guns off the pier, and this was well done under heavy fire by Lieutenant F. C. Law, Sergeant E. J. Williams, Corporal Cook (severely wounded), Privates C. A. Sims and J. A. Threlfall "—all Plymouth battalion.

It was now pretty clear that no further advance could be made with so small a force. Indeed in an hour's time the fire had increased so much that it seemed impossible even to hold the ground they had gained. Colonel Matthews, therefore, called up the reserve to cover a retirement, and signalled a request for destroyers to close and enfilade the Yeni Shehr trenches. The *Amethyst* at once went in with the *Basilisk* and *Scorpion*, as well as *Renard*, *Wolverine* and *Grampus*, who had just taken the northern landing party back to the *Braemar Castle*. The *Agamemnon* and *Dublin*, which were off Yeni Shehr, were able to lend a hand, and the *Cornwallis* was busy shelling a howitzer battery on the ridge with her 12" and the barracks near Orkanie with her 6". Under this weight of shell the fire, both from the fort and the Yeni Shehr trenches, was soon subdued, and about 5.0 Colonel Matthews was able to begin his retreat. But no sooner did he move than a heavy rifle fire opened from the cemetery. On account of our own men the ships could not touch it, and again he had to call up his reserve. Even so the withdrawal was not done without loss, for in spite of the fire of the Marines' machine-guns, which had been mounted on the walls of the fort, snipers became active again in the village, and many casualties occurred before the shelter of the fort was reached.

It was not till 6.45, when it was quite dark, that the withdrawal was effected, and even then a small party of two officers and five men—two of them wounded—had been cut off on the beach. These, however, were pluckily rescued by an armed whaler from the *Scorpion*. Not content with this, the boat returned and for two hours searched the beach for stragglers and wounded from Kum Kale to Yeni Shehr, but without finding any one. In all Colonel Matthews had to report seventeen non-commissioned officers and men killed, twenty-four wounded and three missing, and that the operation had entirely failed in its object.

The northern force had no better success. Here the company of the Plymouth battalion was under Major H. D. Palmer, R.M.L.I., with demolition, survey and beach parties from the *Inflexible* and *Ocean*, under Lieutenant-Commander Frederic Giffard. Major Palmer's instructions were to hold the line from Morto Bay to the fountain north of Tekke Burnu for three hours in order to cover the work of the demolition and survey parties. Here, profiting by experience, the landing was better prepared by the *Ocean* shelling Sedd el Bahr and the neighbouring houses while the *Majestic*, from off Morto Bay, dealt with the old castle above, and some trenches which the seaplanes had located in rear of it. At 9.30 the disembarkation began at the Camber, and patrols at once went forward up the steep and narrow path leading up the cliff to Sedd el Bahr. It debouched upon an open space between the fort and the village; on reaching the top, they found that this space was being swept with fire from a large building athwart the far end. Further advance being impossible, an attempt was made to turn the obstacle by passing through the breaches in the shattered fort, while another party endeavoured to reach the village by scaling the cliff. But everywhere the fire was too hot. The whole party therefore took cover, and signal was made for the ships and destroyers to reopen fire. This quickly told. The enfilading building was smashed, the snipers were driven from the houses, and under the *Majestic's* fire the main body of the enemy fell back from the old castle into the battery behind. Sedd el Bahr fort was then made good, and a footing obtained in the village, but it was still found impossible to debouch into the open. The enemy were stealing back into the old castle trenches again, and field guns were sweeping the front of the village from somewhere to the right. This was the position at noon when, in response to a signal from the *Ocean* to report progress, Major Palmer said he could not advance further without 200 more men. Captain Hayes-Sadler at once prepared to send them, but by this time General Trotman had joined Admiral de Robeck in the *Irresistible*, and as, "in view of the conditions obtaining," he did not consider it advisable to risk more men, the reinforcement was negatived. It was not till 1.40 that the *Majestic*, with the *Ocean's* help, was able to turn the enemy out of the old castle again. But she herself did not escape, for five minutes later she was hit by a shell from In Tepe on the starboard side of the quarter-deck. As things stood, it was now considered too late to complete the work that day, and at 2.10 the General ordered the party to withdraw. To cover the retirement the ships reopened on the village, and by 3.30 the whole force was back in the destroyers that had brought them in. All that had been done was to smash two Nordenfeldt guns, and the casualties were three men killed and one wounded.

It was a most regrettable setback, the more to be deplored because the main object of the operation had already been obtained. Fort Helles had been put completely out of action by the *Queen Elizabeth* during the bombardment of February 25, and Orkanie had been rendered equally harmless by the *Irresistible* and Lieutenant-Commander Robinson's demolition party. At the time, however, this was uncertain, and it was necessary to clear up the situation before the next phase of the operations could be begun in earnest. What seemed a favourable moment had therefore been seized, but, as the experience of the day proved, the time had gone for using so small a force. It was precisely the same that had been fixed when the landing was first projected, but the delay had told. The Germans had had time to whip the Turks into facing the ships, and they had met with a distinct success, which lent itself to being worked up to an inspiriting victory. The moral effect could not fail to be serious, and it was becoming more evident that without a strong force of troops there was little likelihood of the fleet being able to do even the preliminary work of forcing the Straits.

CHAPTER XI

IT is noteworthy that while the officers on the spot were
beginning to realise the full measure of the enterprise in
hand, everywhere else the initial operations were taken to
promise success. In the Balkans a distinct change of attitude
was perceptible. M. Venizelos was trying to induce the
King of Greece—at first with some hope of success—to offer
the Allies the assistance of his fleet and one division of
infantry for the Dardanelles. Even Bulgaria began to trim
her sails for a shift of wind; her relations with Roumania
grew smoother, and for a time there was a glimmer of hope
that the Balkan Confederation might be re-born. It was
on March 4, moreover, that Italy made her first approaches
for joining the Allies, and though the progress at the Dardanelles was not with her the deciding factor, it was certainly
a weight in the right scale. To Russia our operations
were especially welcome. On February 28 she had been
invited to co-operate with her Black Sea fleet when the
right moment came, and also with any troops she could spare.
A Russian naval officer had already joined Admiral Carden
in order to arrange communication with Admiral Ebergard
at Sevastopol, and on March 3 an official reply came in to
say not only that the necessary orders had been given to
the fleet, but that a whole army corps was being prepared
for embarkation at Odessa and Batum as soon as the
Dardanelles was forced and that it would be ready in a
fortnight or three weeks.

The fact was that from a distance the outlook was so
hopeful that the Allies at this time were as much concerned
with the lion's skin as with the means of killing the lion.
When the Dardanelles next came up in the War Council—
that is, on March 3—the discussion was mainly occupied with
considering the plan of campaign to be followed in concert
with Russia after the Straits had been forced, when a new
line of operation against the Central Powers would be open
by way of the Danube. Instructions next day were sent to
Admiral Carden for his guidance when he got through into
the Sea of Marmara, and our three original monitors, *Severn*,

Humber and *Mersey,* were ordered to prepare to go out for work in the Danube.

The general view that obtained at home was conveyed by Lord Kitchener in a despatch to General Birdwood on March 4. The idea that the fleet was to do the work of breaking through still held the field, and it was assumed that Admiral Carden expected to be in the Sea of Marmara by the 20th. By that time it would be possible to have concentrated at Lemnos a force of over 60,000 men, composed of the Australasian Corps, a French division and the Royal Naval Division, but no more troops were to leave Egypt till the 12th, the date at which it was anticipated it would be fairly clear how long it would take the fleet to get through without military co-operation on a large scale. Till it was certain that such assistance would be required, it was not intended to use troops in the Gallipoli peninsula at all, and if they should prove to be necessary for its capture, probably a reinforcement would have to be sent out for which the operations might have to wait. In the meantime small detachments from the Australian brigade at Lemnos could be supplied for minor operations as the Admiral required them. The real objective of the troops was Constantinople, and if by March 18 the fleet had successfully silenced the forts the transports were to follow it through the Straits to the point fixed for the operations against the capital to begin. If reinforcements came from home they were to do the same, and as the Turks would almost certainly evacuate the peninsula if the fleet got through, nothing would be required there except a force sufficient to hold the Bulair lines. Finally, to leave no doubt as to what was intended it was clearly laid down that the concentration of troops off the Dardanelles was not so much for operations in the Gallipoli peninsula as for subsequent work in the neighbourhood of Constantinople in co-operation with the Russian army corps from the Black Sea. This telegram confirmed and amplified the instructions sent by the Admiralty to Admiral Carden on February 24.

The weak points of the arrangement, as General Birdwood again pointed out in his reply, were that there was little chance of the fleet being able to get through alone, and that, even if it did, the transports would be exposed to severe loss from the concealed guns, which, as was now certain, the ships could not be counted on to destroy. For this reason, after his visit to the fleet, he had been in favour of a landing at Sedd el Bahr, and for an advance hand in hand with the ships, and with this idea he returned to Egypt on March 5, the day after Lord Kitchener's instructions were received. In the face of them General Birdwood's plan was inadmissible. The fleet was to endeavour to force its way into the Sea of Marmara unaided, and the army was to be landed at the most convenient point for an advance on Constantinople. So, with all its obvious defects, the original plan held. The fleet was left to do the best it could alone, and the troops on the spot remained in inactivity, serving no purpose by their presence beyond that of giving the Germans a further pretext for spurring the Turks to energetic work on the defence of the peninsula.

So for the next fortnight the operations were purely naval. So far from any endeavour to seize an observing station, not even the arrested work of demolition was renewed. From now onward attention was entirely concentrated on the work which would finally determine how far it was possible for the fleet to go without assistance. On March 5 the bombardment of the inner defences was to begin, and for the first time the *Queen Elizabeth* was to fill the leading part, and prove whether she could do to them what the German heavy howitzers had done to the forts of Antwerp and Namur.

The inner and main defences, which were now to be the immediate objective, consisted of five main forts, closely grouped on either side of the actual Narrows.[1] All were low-lying, on a system which had become discredited, but most of them had been remodelled and to some extent re-armed in the past ten years. In the Kilid Bahr group, on the European side, were three. Of these the nearest was Fort Rumili Medjidieh (No. 13), armed with two old 11″ and four modern 9·4″ guns. Facing down the Straits and imperfectly traversed it was liable to enfilade from the west and south-west. Next to it, but higher up the hillside, came Fort Hamidieh II (No. 16), a more modern work, armed with two modern 14″ guns. It also faced down the Straits and was liable to enfilade from the westward. Immediately beyond it was the principal fort, Namazieh (No. 17), adjoining the ancient castle of Kilid Bahr. It was a large, wedge-shaped work, with its salient upon a projecting point of the coast, and was armed with sixteen guns (exclusive of howitzers), most of them of old type. On the southern face, looking down the Straits, were five 9·4″, all but two of old type. At the salient were three old 8·2″, and the rest of the guns—that is, six more old 9·4″, and two heavier guns (10″ and 11″)—were on the eastern face looking across the channel.

The most formidable battery of all was on the other side,

---

[1] See Plan No. 4.

in the Chanak group. This was Hamidieh I (No. 19), a solid, well-traversed work close on the beach and facing directly down the Straits, with two modern 14″ guns ranging to 17,000 yards and seven 9·4″ ranging to 15,000. It was, moreover, well furnished with new range-finders and equipment, and was manned, the Turks say, entirely by Germans. About 1,000 yards to the north of it, on the point opposite Namazieh and adjoining Chanak town, was Chemenlik (No. 20),[1] a conspicuous earthwork clearly marked by the old keep of Chemenlik castle, which remained enclosed within its ramparts. It had but one modern 9·4″ and an older 8·2″ upon its southern front, and looking across the Straits it had two 14″, one of which was of long range, with an arc of fire from south-west to north-west. Besides these main batteries both groups had in or near them howitzers, field guns and Nordenfeldts.

The orders for attacking these central defences, the character of which was fairly well known to us, had been worked out in detail during the delay which the persistent bad weather had enforced, and in the process the lack of an observing station ashore had declared itself with new distinctness. Indeed, it was on this defect that the operation orders were based. The idea was for the *Queen Elizabeth* to anchor on the west side of the peninsula in a berth previously swept for her two and a half miles south-west of Gaba Tepe. From there she would bring a conspicuous summit of Haji Monorlo Dagh in line with the principal works of the Kilid Bahr or European group. A cairn on the top would serve for laying over the peninsula, and this method she was to use unless forced to shift her berth or until she was directed to change her target to the Chanak or Asiatic group. As the distance would be about seven and a quarter miles, good spotting was essential. Seaplanes were to be used, but they were not too efficient, and the chief reliance had to be placed on ships within the Straits. But here was a serious difficulty. Owing to the failure of the attempts to dominate the guns and howitzers of the intermediate area, no spotting ship could anchor. They would have to keep moving, and it was consequently necessary to tell off no less than three battleships for the work. The ships selected, *Cornwallis*, *Irresistible* and *Canopus*, were to run up in succession at twelve minutes' interval to within five miles of Kephez Point—that is, about as far as Eren Keui—then turn across the Straits and back, keeping ready to fire on Messudieh, Dardanos, and White Cliff should they show activity. The spotting would thus be

---

[1] Also called Sultanieh or Hamidieh III.

done at a distance of from seven to eight miles. During the operation the *Agamemnon* was to watch the entrance, and the *Dartmouth* the Bulair lines, in order to report movements of troops, while the *Prince George* was to keep under way close to the *Queen Elizabeth*, to protect her from any stray guns in the vicinity.

Even if all went well, long-distance firing under these conditions was none too promising. As it was, the necessity of getting the demolition parties of the previous day and the rescued marines back to their ships caused much delay in starting. It was not till noon that the *Queen Elizabeth* was able to fire her first shot at Rumili Medjidieh (No. 13), the most advanced of the Kilid Bahr group. Even then the seaplanes were not available. The first to go up had engine trouble at 3,000 feet and nose-dived into the sea a complete wreck; the pilot of the second received a bullet wound and had to return, so that the spotting had to be done entirely by the ships. As the firing was across the line of observation, range could be fairly well controlled, but direction was mere guess work. To   [1] to the difficulties all the ships were exposed the whole tim to fire from shore guns, which they had the greatest difficulty in locating.[1] None of the spotting ships was touched, but the *Queen Elizabeth*, in spite of all the *Prince George* and the Admiral himself in the *Inflexible* could do to protect her, was hit seventeen times by mobile guns which the sweeping operations appear to have attracted. She was not seriously damaged; the fire was no more than annoyance. What was worse was that, owing to the late start, three or four hours of good visibility had been lost, and the usual afternoon mirage began to confuse the spotting ships before the work was half done. Still, after eighteen rounds at Rumili the *Queen Elizabeth* seemed to drop her next ten shots into the fort, and she was directed to shift to Namazieh (No. 17). In doing so she must have hit Hamidieh II (No. 16), which lay between the two, for its magazine was seen to blow up. But every minute the mirage was getting worse. The third seaplane now went up, but by this time the light was so bad that further firing was useless. The pilot had only made one report when the *Queen Elizabeth* was ordered to cease fire.

What the effect had been it was impossible to tell. It was thought that Rumili and Hamidieh were probably done for, and though the howitzers and field guns had been active, the intermediate forts were not observed to open fire. All, however, that could be known for certain was that the system

---

[1] The Turkish battleship *Barbarousse* also replied with indirect fire.

of spotting by a succession of ships on the move with a constant change of spotting officers would never do. A single ship must be used, in spite of the certainty of her having continually to shift out of the field of the enemy's fire. For the present it was the best that could be done, but Admiral Carden had now seen enough to convince him that without good aerial observation firing was little better than waste of ammunition. The seaplanes were clearly not equal to the work. They could not rise high enough to clear the rifle-fire, and he now reported that if he was to do any good with indirect firing he must have aeroplanes. Possibly, however, better results could be obtained if he were permitted to send the *Queen Elizabeth* to a carefully-selected position inside the Straits. This had been forbidden by the Admiralty's instructions to Admiral Carden, but he had already applied for a modification of the order that she was not to be hazarded inside, and in the early hours of March 5 the risk was approved, on condition that all precautions were taken, and that there was to be no undue expenditure of ammunition or wearing of her 15″ guns.

The following day, however, a further trial of the indirect method was made with a single ship spotting. The *Albion* was chosen, with orders to take a position in the comparatively dead water on the European side, where Admiral de Robeck would cover her with the *Majestic*, *Prince George* and *Vengeance*, in which ship his flag was again flying. Admiral Guépratte was to go in with the *Suffren* in order to watch the proceedings, with a view to the French division taking the duty next day. The *Triumph* and *Swiftsure* took no part, having, as will be seen, been detached for special duty; but the two remaining battleships available, *Ocean* and *Agamemnon*, were to cover the *Queen Elizabeth*, while the *Lord Nelson* watched the outer forts, and the spotting division kept an eye on Dardanos and Messudieh.

The idea was to see what could be done with the lesser Chanak Fort, Chemenlik (No. 20), on the Asiatic side. As the white houses of the little town sloped down to the inner wall of the fort, it looked as if the fall of the shot could be easily marked. It was hoped, at least, that the ships inside would do enough to permit a renewal that night of the attack on the Kephez minefield. But the results were even less favourable than those of the previous day. Operations began late, visibility was not good, and the spotting met with every kind of interruption. As the ships passed in they were fired on by a field battery which had been brought down to Kum Kale in the night, as well as by other guns on a ridge to the eastward of it.   Leaving these to the *Lord Nelson*, the spotting division went on, but only to run into a rapidly-developing howitzer fire from Eren Keui and elsewhere.   In vain did the *Albion* try to find dead ground on the European side; that, too, was now commanded, and though Messudieh and White Cliff were silent, Dardanos was firing again. Under such conditions accurate spotting would be impossible, and at 10.0 Admiral de Robeck formed all four ships in line and engaged Dardanos and Eren Keui till they were quiet. The *Suffren* now came in, and, not content with merely looking on, the French Admiral took station astern of the line.

But the *Queen Elizabeth* was not yet able to fire.   The moment she anchored in her old berth heavy shells from hidden howitzers began to fall so close that she had to shift 1,000 yards out.   Here by 12.30, at the extreme range of her three-quarter charges, she was able to begin.   But the inside squadron was in difficulties and the *Albion's* spotting corrections were very long in reaching her.   Messudieh had also begun firing, but White Cliff seemed still to be unarmed. Messudieh got a hit on the *Majestic*, but Dardanos, which had continued firing till noon, was put out of action shortly afterwards.   Meanwhile the *Albion* had found a quiet spot on the north shore where she could for a time mark the fall of the shot in peace, but howitzers on the same side, apparently brought up for the purpose, presently found her. Not a trace of them could be detected, and as their shells sent up volumes of water all round her, spotting was almost impossible.   The consequence was, that in an hour and a quarter the *Queen Elizabeth* got off only five rounds. During this time another howitzer battery had got her range, and once more she had to shift—this time she moved 3,000 yards to the westward, bringing the range to over 20,000 yards.   Here at 3.30 she began again with full charges.   Two rounds were fired, but as the light was now too bad for either of them to be spotted Admiral de Robeck signalled her to cease fire for the day.   There were still, however, a few hours of daylight, and unwilling to waste them, he himself decided to continue his runs inside. Rumili fort, which the *Queen Elizabeth* had first engaged the previous day, had been firing now and then with two of her 9·4″, and he wanted to see if he could finish it.   With all his ships he closed it to within 12,000 or 13,000 yards, and though they came under a fairly heavy fire, especially at the turns, and suffered a few hits, there were no casualties.   Till the light actually failed he kept on, but the day was too far spent to see what damage was done.

Still he had done all that was possible to prepare the way for the trawlers' night attack on the Kephez minefield. As he retired the *Amethyst* brought them in with their destroyer escort, while the *Ocean* and *Majestic* followed in support. Towards midnight the trawlers advanced, but only, as before, to come under searchlight beams and a heavy fire from the mine defence guns. Nevertheless, with their usual tenacity the skippers held on while the ships and destroyers blazed away at the searchlight. Once or twice it seemed to be knocked out, but still its beams shone forth again and followed the trawlers, till at last the fire grew so hot that they had to retire with nothing done.

It was a thoroughly unsatisfactory day's work. The hopelessness of an indirect long-range bombardment with such wholly inadequate means of spotting was its plain lesson, and Admiral de Robeck urged that the *Queen Elizabeth* should go inside. Admiral Carden, however, though no less eager, was unwilling to consent to this extreme measure till he had tried another plan which he had arranged with the French Admiral. During Admiral Guépratte's reconnaissance he had been able to locate several of the troublesome howitzer batteries, and the idea was that the two sister ships, *Agamemnon* and *Lord Nelson*, should make another attack on the Narrows under cover of the French division. The first objective was to be Rumili (No. 13), in order to complete the previous day's work, and the second the formidable Hamidieh I (No. 19), opposite to it, which, lying close down to the shore as it did against its background of trees, was very difficult to make out and had not yet been engaged.

The French division went in first; shortly after noon the two British ships passed them, keeping a mile from the north shore, and about 12.30, when Rumili could be clearly seen beyond the point off Soghanli Dere, they engaged it with their forward guns at 14,000 yards. Continuing thus till the range was down to 12,000 the *Agamemnon* led across the Straits and brought her broadside to bear. As yet, though she had had one harmless hit on her armour from a 6″ shell, there had been no reply from the forts. But as she made across the Straits she quickly ran into a hail of projectiles from the Kephez, Messudieh, White Cliff and Eren Keui batteries, as well as from concealed guns, all of which the French division hotly engaged. Then at 12.45, when she was about mid-channel, Rumili opened with well-concentrated salvoes of four 9·4″ guns, as though it had never been touched. Five minutes later the Germans in Hamidieh I began for the first time. Both ships were now steaming eastward in the midst of a rain of shell and firing broadsides from their 12″ and 9·2″ turrets. Twice they were straddled by salvoes from the forts, the shells missed them by inches and their decks were deluged by the huge columns of water which the enemy's heavy shell threw up. Speed was increased to 14 knots, and as they neared the Asiatic shore the fire slackened. Then they turned westward to complete their triangular run, but as soon as they were in mid-channel again it was as bad as ever. At 1.0 what seemed to be a 14″ shell, falling almost perpendicularly, took the *Agamemnon* on her quarter-deck, blew out a huge hole, wrecked the ward-room and gun-room below, and drove splinters of the deck plating through the maintop 100 feet above. Though she still went on it was almost too hot to last, but five minutes later the *Lord Nelson* got a lucky hit on Rumili which caused a violent explosion. She then took on Hamidieh I. In spite of its difficult location she soon got on to it, and developing rapid fire as she turned across for the second run, set it on fire. About 1.50 a magazine blew up and the fort temporarily ceased fire.

During the run the *Agamemnon* was hit twice again by heavy shell, and in spite of all the French division could do, both ships were still worried by the scattered guns. The *Lord Nelson* was now back on Rumili, but as the ships went west again the Germans reopened, and she had to return to them. By 2.0, however, the fire of both forts was obviously slackening, and during the third run the *Agamemnon*, firing salvoes of four 12″ and five 9·2″, believed she had dismounted two guns in Rumili. In any case the scattered guns were as bad as ever. Both ships were hit by them several times, their rigging and upper works a good deal cut about, and splinters which entered the conning-tower of the *Lord Nelson* wounded Captain McClintock in the head, as well as two others of the occupants. Still the run went on, another explosion occurred close to Rumili, and by 2.30 both the forts were again silent. One or two guns then began to fire from the vicinity of Namazieh, but they were soon stopped, and at 3.10, when everything but the scattered guns had been quiet for twenty minutes, Captain Fyler, according to instructions, asked leave of Admiral Guépratte to retire.

So the British ships, with their special work apparently done, went out, leaving Eren Keui and the rest to the French division. It had been a hard day. Besides damage from field guns and howitzers, the *Agamemnon* had been hit eight times by hea᾽ shell, and the *Lord Nelson* seven times. The *Agamemnon* ！ ᾽d also fouled a small floating mine which had apparently become detached from the Turkish anti-submarine defences, but it did her no harm. The casualties were few, nothing, in fact, but scratches and slight wounds, saying much for the efficiency of the armour. Indeed, the only telling hit upon the armour was a shot below the *Lord Nelson's* water-line, which caused two of her bunkers to fill. Much of the immunity was due to the French division, which kept up an incessant fire on the innumerable howitzers and field guns on both sides of the Straits and materially reduced the annoyance.

As usual, the day concluded with an attack on the Kephez minefield. This night it was attempted by the French mine-sweepers, attended by seven of our destroyers, whose special duty it was to deal with the searchlights at the mouth of the Soghanli Dere, but on this occasion they were not burning. Little progress, however, appears to have been made, owing, it would seem, to the trawlers' lack of engine-power to work against the current.

The work in the Dardanelles was not the whole of the day's proceedings. Off Bulair, the *Dublin* had taken over the watch from the *Dartmouth,* to find that a battery she could not locate had been established there. She was hit four times, but not seriously. Not being able to find the guns, she turned her attention to the Bulair forts, where she could detect movement, and reported that she had destroyed the barracks in Fort Napoleon. More notable was the development at the other end of the Straits. There the Black Sea fleet had become active. While the Franco-British squadron was at work in the Dardanelles, the Russian Admiral was bombarding the coal ports of Zungaldak, Koslu and Kilimli. The object was to destroy the structures and plant of the ports in order to prevent shipments, and it seems to have been well attained. Fires and explosions were seen ashore, the batteries were silenced, and eight steamers and a large sailing ship destroyed.

On the Dardanelles side the result of the day's experience was to leave no doubt that if the work of the fleet was to be done within reasonable time more drastic measures must be adopted. It was obvious that the periodical silence of the forts meant, not that they had been put out of action, but that the gunners took shelter ready to return to the guns as occasion offered. Heavier shell was required to wreck the forts, and Admiral Carden, putting aside all hesitation about using the *Queen Elizabeth* inside, ordered her to conduct a direct bombardment next day (March 8). Every care was taken to protect her from annoyance. Her manœuvre area was to be in mid-channel, and beginning opposite Eren Keui, she was to engage Rumili. As soon as that fort was done for, she would finish Hamidieh I on the Asiatic side, and then deal with the other two European batteries, Hamidieh II and Namazieh, and end with the Chemenlik fort (Sultanieh). Four battleships (*Vengeance, Canopus, Cornwallis* and *Irresistible*) were to cover her from the barrage guns, one on either beam and one on either quarter. Their special objective was the scattered howitzers, and the two advanced ships were specially ordered not to become engaged with the forts. They were, however, to be ready to close them if it became necessary to force them to man their guns, but as soon as the forts began to fire they were to withdraw. The most serious obstacle to the success of the plan was the shortage of ammunition. It was becoming a source of real anxiety, and particular orders had to be given to confine the day's work to deliberate fire. Still hope ran high. The instructions to be ready for closing, no less than the fact that all five of the principal forts in the Narrows were indicated as objectives, show that much was expected from the risk that was to be taken, and Admiral Carden himself took charge, with his flag in the *Queen Elizabeth*.

But again there was a tale of disappointment; once more the weather played false. The visibility was so bad that the targets could hardly be made out, spotting from the ships was impossible, and the clouds were so low that the seaplanes could not mark the fall of a single shot. In three runs the *Queen Elizabeth* got off no more than eleven rounds—all at Rumili—and only one seemed to be a hit. The forts made no reply, but the howitzer and field batteries were as active as ever, and in the bad light more difficult than ever to locate. Till 3.30 the Admiral persevered, and then, as the light was growing worse, the ships were withdrawn with nothing done.[1]

So for a time, with deep disappointment, the attack on the Narrows came to an end. Three weeks had now gone by—three out of the four which Admiral Carden had originally

---

[1] According to reliable Turkish reports the effect of the bombardments carried out from February 26 to March 8, was as follows :—

February 26 to March 4: the batteries engaged sustained no damage beyond a few casualties to the personnel.

March 5: Rumili fort was struck eleven times but no gun was put out of action. Namazieh was hit six times. This indirect bombardment had a great moral effect on the guns' crews.

March 6: the Kilid Bahr forts were hit five times.

March 7 and 8: no damage of military importance and no casualties. The batteries only ceased fire to keep their ammunition for lower ranges, or when compelled to clear the guns from grit and debris thrown up by exploded shells. They could have continued in action had they so desired.

estimated the whole operation would take—and the second phase seemed no nearer completion. To proceed under existing conditions was useless, for, as the Admiral pointed out in a summary of the operations which he now sent home, efficient air reconnaissance was essential to further progress. Until the concealed guns and howitzers on either side could be better located, all ships inside in the daytime were in serious danger from plunging fire, and though hitherto it had not been very accurate, it was getting better every day. Till something was done to supply the cardinal defect he did not propose to continue the attack. But this was not the only consideration. Quite apart from the difficulty of spotting, experience had shown that long-range fire alone could never render the forts innocuous. Ships must close to decisive range to finish them, and closing was impossible while the enemy's mines were intact. Accordingly, while waiting till he had the means of making a bombardment on a large scale effective, he intended to devote himself to clearing the minefields which barred the approach—working the trawlers by night with two battleships in support, and at the same time having two others on guard at either side of the entrance to prevent the enemy collecting there or bringing up guns. He also proposed to bombard the Bulair lines with a similar object.

Here, then, was another juncture at which, had the original conception been followed, the operations might have been dropped—or, since that idea had long been abandoned, an attempt might have been made to secure an observing station, if indeed it was still possible. The French division, which was at Bizerta, was announced to sail in two convoys on March 10 and 13, the Royal Naval Division was due to arrive at Lemnos on the 12th, and all the Australasians could be there within a week. If the seizure of the end of the Gallipoli peninsula was not a practicable operation with the force available, two other objectives, which had been often mentioned as alternatives to the Dardanelles, were still open. It is the conspicuous advantage of amphibious warfare that such changes of plan are possible. But they are by no means easy to arrange with an allied force—even when strategical considerations alone are involved; and when, as in this instance, there is a tangle of political interests that has to be previously unravelled by negotiation, the difficulties tend to become insuperable.

The alternatives were Alexandretta, which at this time was again being urged with high authority at home as complementary to the Persian Gulf adventure, and, in the second place, Smyrna, where we had already been operating. This was, in fact, the scene of the special service on which, as we have seen, the *Triumph* and *Swiftsure* had been detached the day the *Queen Elizabeth* began her attack on the Narrows.

The operations were entrusted to Admiral Peirse, who on March 2 received instructions to come up from Egypt in the *Euryalus* and meet the two battleships at a rendezvous off the Smyrna Gulf. He was also to have a group of mine-sweepers and the seaplane carrier *Anne Rickmers*, while the Allies would be represented by the Russian light cruiser *Askold*, which had been operating with the French Syrian squadron. There was no idea of an occupation—indeed, a landing was strictly forbidden. But rumours of submarine interference with the Dardanelles operations were already rife, and the intention was to prevent the gulf from being used as a submarine base. The more clear it became that the operations would be prolonged and would demand the assistance of troops, the more insistent became the need of forestalling the submarine menace. Submarines had frequently been reported as being sent in sections from Germany to the Bosporus, but though such rumours were little regarded, there was a real and present danger of their coming from the Adriatic. There the French fleet had been requested to keep a special watch, but that was not enough, and Admiral Peirse's instructions were to bombard and destroy the Smyrna forts, so as to permit of its being blockaded and leave it open to attack.

The principal defences, according to our intelligence reports, which were not very recent, were situated on the south side of the channel giving access to the inner part of the gulf. They were Fort Yeni Kale or Hamidieh, with seven 9·4″ short guns, and, a little to seaward of it, on Paleo Tabia Point, amongst the olive groves, Moun-i-Zaffer, a battery of four 6″ guns with an extreme range of 12,000 yards.[1] Between them were an inner and an outer minefield, protected by searchlights and by light and machine-guns. Reaching the rendezvous about dawn on March 5, Admiral Peirse went in at once to attack Fort Yeni Kale, and in the early afternoon the three ships bombarded it deliberately for an hour at 14,000 yards, and an hour at 10,000. The weather conditions were perfect, and the *Euryalus* was able to make very accurate shooting with her 9·2″ guns. Thirty-two hits were observed, and two heavy explosions occurred, apparently in magazines.[2] Owing to the range

---

[1] See Plan p. 210.
[2] But not the main one. It was very conspicuous and was hit many times, but the Turks say none of the shells penetrated.

being too great Yeni Kale was silent, nor was a single shot
fired in reply from the other batteries and gun positions, and
it was consequently impossible to locate any of them.   About
4.0 the Admiral withdrew, intending next day to get up his
minesweepers and go in to complete the work at short range.
But this was not done with impunity.   When next morning
(March 6) the minesweepers, under cover of the ship fire,
were sent in to work a passage through the minefield, the
batteries which defended it were suddenly unmasked.   There
were apparently two of them, one was the 6″ battery at
Paleo Tabia Point, and the other Badenilik, a work armed
with five 4·7″ guns and well placed 150 feet up on a spur
of the hills a mile to the westward.   Still further to seaward,
opposite the Narrows at Pelican Point, was a field-gun battery,
near Chiflik guard house, besides other guns to the eastward
that could not be located.   So hot and accurate was the
Turkish fire that sweeping was seen to be out of the question
till the covering guns were silenced.   The trawlers were
therefore withdrawn, and the ships proceeded to engage the
newly-found batteries at from 7,000 to 8,000 yards.   They
replied vigorously, but Fort Yeni Kale fired only one round,
and appeared to be out of action from the previous day's
punishment, though, in fact, only one gun had been knocked
out.   Both the *Triumph* and *Euryalus*, as well as the minesweepers, were hit, but, after an hour's work on the other
two batteries, they ceased fire, and our casualties were only
two officers wounded (one of whom died) and six ratings.
In the afternoon therefore another attempt was made on
the minefield.   As the position was still uncertain, only one
pair of trawlers was used, the ships closing in again to 8,000
yards from Paleo Tabia to cover them.   The Admiral's
caution proved to be well justified, for though the fort
remained silent, the fire of the unlocated guns on the hill
was so accurate that nothing could be done, and again the
attempt had to be abandoned.

The operations were not at once resumed, for as Admiral
Peirse retired for the night, information reached him from the
Admiralty that our object might possibly be achieved by
negotiation.   The powerful Vali of Smyrna, who had always
been well disposed to French and British subjects, was known
to have openly deplored the part Turkey had taken, and
there was reason to believe that in order to save the port and
vilayet from the horrors of war he might be disposed on terms
to agree to their practical neutrality.   At home, the somewhat sanguine view that then prevailed about the progress
of the operations in the Dardanelles induced a belief that

the danger to the capital might determine the Vali to lend a willing ear, and Admiral Peirse was instructed, after destroying the forts, to endeavour to get into communication with him. The idea was that on our undertaking not to operate against the town or vilayet, he might agree to surrender to us the small craft we required for operations elsewhere, and consent to our clearing a passage through the minefields and leave us the general control of the gulf.

The necessary steps were at once taken to get in touch with him, and on the following day (the 7th) the Admiral proceeded to attempt the final destruction of the forts. The three ships again closed Paleo Tabia and shelled it and the other batteries that had been located. But there were still others that were firing, and owing to the uncertain light and the undulating nature of the country they were hard to find. Bad weather and engine trouble rendered the seaplanes useless, but eventually a battery of small howitzers was located on an isolated hill 200 feet high, and some more field-gun emplacements down by the shore. Owing, however, to the position of the minefields, only one of these works, which was at Chiflik, could be approached close enough for decisive work, but this one the *Triumph* destroyed during the afternoon.

There were still, however, too many concealed guns untouched for sweeping to be attempted except under cover of night, and even so there was little chance of success till the searchlights were destroyed. After dark the *Triumph* tried her hand, but though she prevented them from burning more than a few seconds at a time, she failed to touch them, and the Admiral decided that before making a serious attempt with the trawlers he must have another day at the defences. To this work the 8th was devoted. The three ships began on Yeni Kale at 7,000 yards, but as there was no reply the Admiral went off in his flagship to investigate Vourlah, a small roadstead in the outer part of the gulf. The *Askold*, which had joined on the 6th, had reported having been fired on from this place, and he wished to see what he could make of it. In his absence the two battleships engaged Paleo Tabia. It also was silent and good practice was made. Before long the *Triumph* got a direct hit on one of the guns. The result was startling. Immediately after the gun toppled over all three of the heavy batteries opened as if never a shot had been fired at them. As the ships were only 8,000 yards away the surprise should have had serious results. Fortunately the nerves of men who have been pent for many hours in bomb-proof shelters are seldom at their best, and the gunnery was bad; the ships stood their ground and returned the fire, and although the *Triumph* was hit there were no casualties, and in half an hour all the forts had ceased fire.

It was not pleasant news for the Admiral on his return, especially as he had been unable to find anything at Vourlah. In his report to the Admiralty that evening he summed up the situation by informing them that after four days' operations the only certain results were the destruction of one heavy gun and four field guns. The experience, in fact, was exactly the same as at the Dardanelles. It was clear that till the fire of the ships became really effective the Turks simply kept their men under cover and there was no way of stopping the game till the ships could close in to decisive range and completely smash the guns and works. Till the minefields were cleared this could not be done, and during the night a determined attempt was made on them. It was pushed in with much boldness, and as the battleships were again able to keep the searchlights to occasional fitful flashes the trawlers succeeded in clearing a channel up to within 3,000 yards of Yeni Kale, but it was only done at the cost of one of them, No. 285 (*Okino*), which struck a mine and sank. The skipper and four men were saved, but the rest of the crew were reported missing.

Operations were now suspended; for next day (March 9) a reply was expected from the Vali. The two battleships therefore closed the forts flying a flag of truce and the signal to communicate, but shortly after noon one of the batteries fired on the *Triumph*, and the ships were recalled. Till 3.0 p.m. they awaited the reply, and then, after a seaplane reconnaissance, the two ships began deliberate fire on the offending fort. In half an hour, however, a boat came out from Vourlah under a flag of truce with an envoy from the Vali, and they desisted. The envoy explained the regrettable incident as a misunderstanding on the part of the officer of the battery, and an amicable conversation ensued. Admiral Peirse offered to undertake not to attack the town or harm it in any way if the forts and batteries were surrendered for demolition and a passage cleared through the minefield, so as to give free access to the port. The reception of the proposal was conciliatory; a truce was arranged till 10.0 a.m. on the 11th, and the envoy took his departure with every indication of friendliness.

So promising, indeed, was the opening that there was good prospect of success. The only doubt was whether the Vali would be able to overcome the opposition of the military authorities. The feeling of the soldiers was clear enough from their heavy guns having fired on our flag of truce, and if they prevailed the Admiral now knew there was little likelihood of the negotiations being carried much further. He had, moreover, been warned by the Admiralty that he might have to convert his operations into a demonstration, and that he must be prepared to send back the battleships to the Dardanelles at any moment. The hour was, in fact, at hand when the power of the fleet to force the Narrows must be put to the final test, and Admiral Carden had been authorised to recall the *Swiftsure* and *Triumph* the moment he was ready to begin.

CHAPTER XII

THE DARDANELLES—FURTHER DEVELOPMENT OF THE PLAN — DECISION TO USE THE XXIXTH DIVISION — ORDERS TO ATTACK THE NARROWS—END OF THE SMYRNA OPERATIONS—MARCH 10 TO 17

MARCH 10 was the date by which Lord Kitchener expected to be able to decide whether the XXIXth Division was to be employed at the Dardanelles or not: whether, that is, by allocating first line troops to the Eastern Mediterranean theatre, it was to be given the status of a recognised alternative line of operation, or whether it was to remain, as originally intended, a mere area of diversion. By that time he believed the general military situation would be sufficiently clear to judge whether the division could be spared from France. This was the view he held on March 3, and during the following week events had marched so rapidly that by the end of it he was able to come to a final decision. At the War Office it was recognised that on the Western Front we had not as yet sufficient force or sufficient reserves of ammunition to make a break-through possible. On the other hand, our line had now been reinforced. The Canadian division was just taking its place in the trenches; the North Midland division—the first of the Territorial divisions to take the field as a complete unit—was in the general reserve, and a number of independent Territorial battalions had gone out, sufficient to allow one to be attached to each existing brigade. It was therefore considered that our line was sufficiently strong to resist any pressure it was in the power of the Germans to bring to bear upon it for some time.

Our Headquarters in France, however, were not content with this attitude. There a more sanguine view obtained, and for March 10 Sir John French had planned a serious attempt to break through at Neuve Chapelle, where a success seemed to promise decisive advantages. In any case an offensive movement was highly desirable, whether for the sake of preventing further troops being withdrawn to break down the Russian resistance on the Eastern Front, or for enheartening our own troops after their long period of defensive warfare against superior forces. There was, however, a real expectation that a well-planned attack would effect a break-through, and in order to turn it to the fullest account it was necessary to occupy the attention of the German reserves. To this end the French and Belgians were to demonstrate about Nieuport and the Yser, and, in order to give weight to the diversion, the navy was asked to co-operate. The *Venerable* and *Excellent*, with the usual attendance of destroyers and minesweepers, were sent over with instructions to bombard the batteries near Westende on March 11. The attack on Neuve Chapelle was made on the 10th, and was so far successful that the village was stormed and held. Next morning the naval bombardment began. Though met by a heavy return fire the ships were not touched, but in the view neither of the Admiral nor the Admiralty was the expenditure of ammunition justified by any tangible effect at Neuve Chapelle. German reserves were brought down from the north, and though Sir John French had all ready to push the cavalry through the gap that had been made, no such opportunity presented itself. The wings had been held up, and though the effort was continued both ashore and afloat till the 13th, no further progress could be made. The fact had to be faced that troops and ammunition supply were insufficient to bring about a decision.

The effect of the battle was, in fact, to confirm the War Council in the attitude they had already reached, for the day it began a decision had been taken. What precisely was the consideration which finally induced Lord Kitchener to cast the lot in favour of the Dardanelles is not clear. Possibly, as in Sir John French's case, the Russian recovery had its weight. The alacrity with which the Russians had taken up the idea of co-operation in the new departure, and their promise of an army corps, certainly gave better hope of far-reaching results. It seemed to make possible an Allied concentration in the alternative theatre which might well avail to paralyse Turkey and open the vital communications between Russia and the Western Powers, and so permit the development of a formidable offensive against Austria. Even if such a movement failed in its immediate object, it would certainly, so long as it lasted, keep Bulgaria off Serbia, and it could only be defeated by the Germans withdrawing troops from the Western Front. It seemed clear, therefore, if only as a means of breaking the deadlock in France, the prospect justified the employment of the best troops we could possibly spare. Less than ever could the enterprise be rightly regarded as an eccentric operation : the future of Turkey and the control of the Straits were declaring themselves with ever-increasing clearness to be cardinal points of the struggle, as vital as the integrity of Belgium, and they were taking their place as a main member in the rib-work of the war.

Accordingly, when on March 10 the War Council met to consider the question, Lord Kitchener announced that he had decided that the XXIXth Division might go, and that the force which the Allies would be able to use against Constantinople would amount, if the Russian corps was up to full strength, to little less than 130,000 men, with nearly 300 guns.[1] The force it was likely to meet was believed to be about 60,000 in the Dardanelles area and perhaps 120,000 in or near Constantinople. It was not therefore more than the Allied army should be able to tackle with such powerful naval co-operation as was expected from the Russian side. The instructions that Admiral Ebergard received, which were communicated to London, were that so long as the Allied fleet was operating in the Dardanelles the Black Sea fleet would confine itself to purely naval demonstration, but as soon as Admiral Carden appeared before the Princes Islands, which defended the approach to Constantinople, the Russians would undertake a serious attack on the Bosporus forts. The troops were not to be landed till the Turkish fleet was destroyed and the two Allied fleets had joined hands, but it was specially provided that these orders were not to stand in the way of Admiral Ebergard's acting on any suggestion his British colleague might wish to convey to him.

Up to this point, then, the objective, both of the Anglo-French and the Russian troops, was Constantinople, and there was still no intention of forcing the Dardanelles by a combined operation, although in a minute which Admiral Jackson submitted the following day he pointed out that unless the Gallipoli peninsula was occupied, the fleet, even

---

[1] *Dardanelles Commission Report*, I., p. 33 and II., p. 9. The estimated details of the force were :—

	Men.	Guns.
Royal Naval Division	11,000	6
Australasian Infantry	30,600	64
Australasian Mounted	3,500	12
XXIXth Division	18,000	56
French Division	18,000	40
Russian Corps	47,600	120
	128,700	298

Besides these troops it was intended to send General Peyton's Yeomanry Division to Egypt as a reserve.

if it succeeded in reaching the Straits, could not keep them open for the passage of troops. The decision, in fact, involved no real change of war policy; it was merely the ratification of what had been adopted in principle three weeks before; but from the point of view of our Imperial policy it meant a radical departure.

During the whole of the nineteenth century the conviction that Russia could not be permitted to control Constantinople had been axiomatic, and scarcely less so with France than with ourselves. It was in defence of this view of the balance of power that our last European war had been fought in alliance with France, and at Berlin it had been consecrated by the last of the great Congresses. But with the dawn of the new century the creed was losing its hold. Naval opinion, on which it had mainly rested, began to perceive that the old grounds of their objection were passing away, and already in 1903 the Committee of Imperial Defence, after a thorough study of the question, had placed on record that the exclusion of Russia from the Straits was not for Great Britain a primary naval or military interest. Nothing therefore stood in the way of a complete accord with her, and there were at the moment special political reasons for making the accord as complete as possible. Partly as a result of her premature effort to relieve the pressure on France, Russia had been suffering severely all along the line, so severely indeed that Germany, as our Foreign Office well knew, was already engaged in an insidious scheme for inducing her to make a separate peace and abandon her Allies. Nothing therefore could so well meet the exigencies of the hour as a frank abandonment of our old obstructive policy. On these grounds therefore, with the full assent of the leaders of the Opposition, it was agreed that Russia should be at liberty to assume the control she had so long desired. The sole condition was that she would prosecute the war to a victorious conclusion, so that the French and British Governments would on their part be able to acquire the correlative compensations both in the Ottoman Empire and elsewhere.

The resolution in no way lessened the need of doing everything that was possible with the fleet, and to enable this to be done it was decided to allow the Admiral a freer hand. To this end on the following day he was given fresh instructions, pointing out that the time seemed to have come for taking extreme risks. The original restriction to " cautious and deliberate methods " was superseded, and he was told that the success so far obtained was enough to justify loss both of ships and men to complete the forcing of the Narrows.

Could it be done it would have consequences of a decisive character upon the war, and it was suggested to him that, choosing favourable weather, he should make an attempt to overwhelm the forts with every gun he could bring to bear. Under cover of the fire he might land demolition parties and do all he could to clear the minefields.   Possibly such an operation might have to be repeated, but as it was now clear that at a certain point of the operations he would have to press for a decision with his whole force, they desired to know whether in his opinion that point had not now been reached.

Such an expression of opinion from the Admiralty, however carefully worded so as not to bring undue pressure upon the man on the spot, could have for a loyal officer but one interpretation.   Even as it stood it could only be read as an intimation that more strenuous methods were expected.   But, as it happened, it was further emphasised.   Soon after it was despatched the Admiralty received from Admiral Carden a report of fresh disappointments.   Ever since the failure of the long-range bombardment on the 8th, he had been devoting his attention to solving the problem which had proved so unexpectedly to be the crux of the whole enterprise.   It was no longer a question of whether ships could destroy forts, but of how they could get close enough to do it in the face of minefields protected by mobile guns.   Till that difficulty could be overcome further bombardment seemed little better than waste of precious ammunition and wear and tear to irreplaceable guns.   To this work he had been devoting every night, confining the days to preparing the ground at various points for the coming of the troops.   He began on the 9th with steps to prevent the reoccupation of the Kum Kale area, sending in the *Albion, Prince George* and *Irresistible* to destroy the remains of the Mendere bridge and all boats they could find.   A number were dealt with in the river by the destroyer *Grampus*, and two more wide gaps made in the bridge by the *Irresistible*, while the *Prince George* destroyed some field guns she located near Sedd el Bahr. The night attack on the Kephez minefield, however, had no success.   It was made under escort of the destroyer *Mosquito* by three trawlers and two picket boats, but they were at once found by the searchlights, and came under so heavy a fire that nothing could be done.

Daylight operations were now centred in the Gulf of Xeros.   Their main object appears to have been a thorough reconnaissance of the Bulair lines and their approaches, combined with an investigation of the possibilities of landing on that side.   The *Dublin* was still watching the lines, and early on the 10th the *Cornwallis* and *Irresistible*, with the seaplane carrier *Ark Royal*, went up to join her. The morning, however, proved too bad for an air reconnaissance, but the *Cornwallis* bombarded the village of Bulair which had lately been included in the lines, while the *Dublin* shelled and apparently demolished the barracks in Fort Sultan, but having nothing larger than 6″ guns, and being severely restricted in expenditure of ammunition, she could make little or no impression on the fort itself. In the afternoon a seaplane was able to get up, and her report was that the Kavak bridge on the Adrianople road, in spite of the previous attempts to destroy it, was still intact. Nothing further was done, and the *Cornwallis* returned to Tenedos, leaving the rest of the work for Admiral Guépratte, who was to take over the command next day. He arrived with the *Suffren* and *Gaulois*, and after detaching the *Irresistible* to bombard the little village port of Bakla in rear of the lines, and the coast forts north and south of it, he carried on with the reconnaissance. No attempt to destroy the Kavak bridge is mentioned, and it was not till the afternoon that the weather permitted a seaplane to go up. Her report was that neither Fort Sultan nor Fort Napoleon appeared to be much damaged, and that the lines had been strengthened and extended with a view apparently to prevent their being turned or taken in reverse from the sea. Four lines of traversed trenches had been dug from Bulair village down to the Kavak River, and an entrenched camp with two large redoubts had been constructed east of the village. Next day (the 12th) the clouds were so low that all air reconnaissance was impossible. The *Ark Royal* returned to Tenedos, and Admiral Guépratte, embarking in the destroyer *Usk*, devoted himself to reconnoitring the north coast of the gulf from Cape Bustan to the Pasha River.

Meanwhile two more attempts had been made to get at the Kephez minefield—on a larger scale and a new plan. On the night of the 10th the force detailed was seven trawlers of the 3rd Group, and two picket boats, with four destroyers for escort and the *Canopus* and *Amethyst* in support. Previous failures had shown that the trawlers had not sufficient engine power to sweep against the strong current that always sets down the Straits, and it had therefore been decided to try getting above the first minefield before beginning. This by good luck they were able to do, for at the critical period the searchlights were extinguished for twenty minutes. Thus they managed to steal up unperceived and get out the sweeps. The first pair of trawlers at once caught two mines, both of which exploded, and one of them unfortunately so close to trawler No. 339 (*Manx Hero*) that it sank her. But that was only the beginning of trouble. At the sound of the explosions the searchlights were immediately switched on and the trawlers were quickly in a rain of shell. In vain the ships tried to extinguish the lights; they still burnt defiantly; the fire increased; two trawlers were hit by 6″ shell, and there was nothing to do but for all to retire as best they could under cover of the destroyers.

Next night the same plan was tried again with the 1st group of trawlers, but the results were more discouraging than ever. As before, the trawlers stole up in line ahead, but now the searchlights were on the alert, and as soon as the leading boat came into the beams and the shells began to fall she turned 16 points and began to run back. Her example infected all the rest, and nothing the *Amethyst* could do would induce them to face the fire again. The behaviour of the skippers was as surprising as it was depressing. Hitherto the conduct of the crews had been so cool and intrepid that everything was expected of them. But it was now clear that though they had no fear whatever of mines, they had not the discipline required for the unaccustomed experience of working steadily under shell-fire; or, as Admiral de Robeck reported, " In some cases the crews appear to have no objection to being blown up by mines, though they do not seem to like working under gun-fire, which is a new element in their calling." Other measures, then, had to be adopted if the indispensable work was to be carried through, and the Admiral decided to call for volunteers from the fleet to command and man the trawlers. The response was naturally overwhelming, but the new system could not be tested that night. It was the turn of the French. They tried, as before, against the current, but found they could scarcely make headway, and after several of them had been hit they, too, retired empty-handed.

A summary of these operations was the first news which reached the Admiralty from Admiral Carden after the telegram urging more drastic action had been sent to him. The impression it conveyed was that he had been brought to a standstill, and a second message was sent him urging vigorous action still more plainly. His plan of calling for volunteers for the sweeping was approved, and he was told he was not expected to do the work without loss, and that the operations must be pressed on by day and night. The information of the Admiralty was that the German officers were sending in desponding reports of shortage of ammunition,

and that a submarine was coming out. Now therefore was
the time to strike, before the enemy could receive fresh
supplies of ammunition or submarines interfere. To make
good the losses he must sustain, the last two ships of the
Channel Fleet, *Queen* and *Implacable*, had been ordered to
join him, under Rear-Admiral Thursby. He was also informed that General Sir Ian Hamilton, who had been
appointed to command the troops, would be with him on the
16th. To get over the difficulty of observing, Commander
Samson, who had been so active at Dunkirk, was coming
out with eighteen aeroplanes by way of Marseilles, where the
Phaeton from Gibraltar had been ordered to meet them, and
the *Ark Royal* was immediately to clear and level an aerodrome for their use. The French had also been asked to
help, and they ordered six of the air squadron they had sent
to Egypt to hurry to Mudros.

So far as the second telegram can be regarded as putting
further pressure on the Admiral it was not needed. Before
it came to his hands he had already sent his reply to the
first message. The pith of it was that he fully agreed that
the time had come for vigorous sustained action. So confident, moreover, was he of what such action could accomplish that he submitted that military operations on a large
scale should commence at once, so as to secure his communications from the moment he entered the Sea of Marmara.
His intention was, he said, to make a final attempt on the
minefield that night (March 14). If it failed he would have
to destroy the guns that defended it, and before the ships
could do this they would have to silence the guns in the
Narrows forts. This done he would proceed to work at the
minefields day and night. It would take time and involve
great expenditure of ammunition, as the guns would need
silencing repeatedly.

As he wrote, the first attempt with the reorganised
trawlers had been made on the minefields, and it was carried
out in a spirit that left nothing to be desired. Two powerful
searchlights were illuminating the approach, and as soon as
the boats entered the lighted area they came under fire from
Dardanos and Messudieh forts, as well as Rumili, and
possibly also Yildiz (No. 9), an old advanced battery of the
Kilid Bahr group with six short 6″ high up on the edge of
the plateau. Thus supported, the light guns of the minefield
defence were as galling as ever. But there was no stopping
the new crews. On they went through the storm of shell
till the point was reached where the downward sweep was to
begin. By that time they had suffered heavily. In two of

the trawlers all the working crew were killed or wounded, and in the others so much damage had been done to gear and winches that only two of them could get out their sweep. Still they carried on as best they could and with some little effect. A number of mines were destroyed, and the picket-boats that were of the party did excellent service in blowing up cables with explosive sweeps. Finally they got through without the loss of a single vessel, though four trawlers and one of the picket boats were put out of action. The casualties were more serious. They amounted to twenty-seven killed and forty-three wounded, but nearly the whole of them were in the *Amethyst*, who at the critical moment, near Kephez Point, boldly exposed herself to draw the fire from the sweepers. Two shells which exploded in the stokers' bath-room and on the mess-deck alone caused sixty casualties. As the Admiral reported, it was a very gallant enterprise, admirably conducted by all concerned, but in his opinion it proved that the defence of the minefields was so well organised that effective sweeping by night was impossible, and there was nothing for it but to proceed with his whole force by daylight on the lines he had already indicated in his reply to the Admiralty.

He was still confident he could get through, and his message concluded with a request for fleet-sweepers to accompany the fleet when it entered the Sea of Marmara. In this spirit he replied to the Admiralty's second telegram, explaining what he meant to do, and dwelling again on the need of more powerful sweepers. Of those he had, nearly a third were sunk or out of action, and as a makeshift he was fitting light sweeps to destroyers. The Admiralty responded at once by ordering thirty of the fastest trawlers from Lowestoft to go out at once. The Malta torpedo-boats that had been patrolling the Suez Canal were also directed to Mudros, and the French were urged to provide any 15-knot boats they could lay hands on.

On the same day also (March 15) they ordered Admiral Peirse to send back to Mudros the two battleships with which he had been operating at Smyrna. By this time it was clear nothing further could be done there by negotiation. The day after the truce was agreed, his seaplane carrier, *Anne Rickmers*, had been disabled, as was then supposed by a torpedo or a mine towed across her bows by a small steam-boat. We now know that this was the work of the *Demir Hissar*, an adventurous old torpedo-boat of under 100 tons, under the command of Lieutenant-Commander von Fircks, with a Turkish and German crew. During the night of

March 7–8, when Admiral Peirse was operating in the Smyrna Gulf, she had stolen out of the Dardanelles, and passing round Imbros, had lain hid in the Ægean all day. It does not appear, however, that Admiral Peirse's squadron was her objective, for in the evening she made for our Tenedos anchorage, but encountering a patrol, she was forced to run for the Smyrna Gulf. The following night (the 9th) she claims to have attacked two enemy ships which she saw lying inside the gulf off Chustan Island (Long Island). The *Triumph* was coaling there at the time from a newly-arrived collier, but both shots missed and the attack was not noticed. After this failure the *Demir Hissar* ran out of the gulf and lay hid in Khios Strait. Next night, having got up her reserve torpedo, she went in again, and at 2 a.m. made her successful shot at the *Anne Rickmers*, the outermost ship of the squadron. Having no torpedo left and being short of coal, she stole into Smyrna harbour where she had a warm welcome from the officials and the civil population.

These facts were, of course, unknown to the British Admiral at the time, and taking what he saw as evidence that the Vali had no power to carry through the proposed arrangement in face of the military authorities, he decided to return to Mityleni and await instructions. He was able to report that the object was practically achieved, for after the successful minesweeping on the nights of the 8th and 9th the Turks had sunk two steamers in the channel off Fort Yeni Kale, and so practically had blocked the port. As he retired, however, the Vali's envoy again appeared to explain that the attack on the *Anne Rickmers* had not been made in breach of the truce, but by an irresponsible torpedo-boat that had been hiding amongst the Vourlah Islands. The negotiations were therefore continued by an officer of the General Staff whom General Birdwood had sent round to assist. An interview with the Vali convinced him that the military element was too strong for any arrangement to be possible, and as three more steamers had been sunk in the channel so as to block it completely, Smyrna could no longer be used as a submarine base. Nothing therefore was to be gained by further operations unless backed by a large military force. In this view Admiral Peirse concurred, and on March 15 he received orders to return to Egypt.

Thus by March 16 Admiral Carden had with his flag the whole force with which the great attack on the Narrows was to be made on the lines the Admiralty had suggested, and in which he concurred. With regard to his suggestion that military operations on a large scale should begin at once,

SMYRNA.

Note:- *Heights on land are given in feet.*

SMYRNA HARBOUR

GULF OF SMYRNA

GULF OF GUL-BAGHCHI

BAY OF ERITRA

Prepared in the Historical Section of the Committee of Imperial Defence.

he was told he must concert measures with General Hamilton
when he arrived, and meanwhile they had asked the War
Office to send the rest of the Australasian force to Mudros at
once.   The Royal Naval Division had now joined, and the
French division, after concentrating at Bizerta, had been
coming in by groups since March 11, and the last of them was
due at Mudros on the 17th.   This, with the Anzacs, would give
some 60,000 men on the spot by the 18th.   The troops would
thus be well in time, as the Admiralty understood the sweeping
operations would probably take several days.   To make
matters quite clear they informed the Admiral that his plan,
as they conceived it, was in the first place to clear a passage
through the minefields so as to enable the forts to be engaged
eventually at close range, the work of sweeping to be covered
by the battle fleet, which would engage the forts and
the mobile guns.   He would then attack the forts in the
Narrows at close range, and when they were destroyed would
pass on to deal with those beyond.   They further understood
that no premature attempt to rush the passage was to be
made, and at any rate, before such desperate measures were
resorted to, they expected him to consult them as to whether
a combined operation for the capture of the Kilid Bahr
plateau would not be a less costly method.

The Admiral replied that they had expressed his intention
exactly, and that he proposed to begin on March 17 if the
weather was favourable, that is, in two days' time.   In the
meanwhile he was busy clearing mines from the area in which
the ships were to manœuvre.   It was a necessary precaution,
for the last attack on the minefield had broken it up and
the seaplanes had been able to report that a number of mines
had been dragged into shallow water.   As their position
could be clearly indicated by the airmen, such good progress
was made that it was expected to begin the grand attack
on the day fixed.   But now a sudden and unlooked-for
hitch occurred.   For some time Admiral Carden's health
had been giving cause for anxiety, and on the 16th a Medical
Board pronounced it imperative that he should relinquish
the command and go on leave.   There was nothing for it
but to obey.   It must always be a serious loss to an enterprise, particularly to one so original in conception, that the
mind that designed it should not be able to see it through
to completion.   Unfortunate as his breakdown was, it did
not mean a complete rupture of continuity.   Admiral de
Robeck, who was next in command of the fleet, had had
immediate charge of most of the direct operations, and had
been intimately associated with his chief in preparing the

plan for the grand attack. The only difficulty in passing
the command to him was that Admiral Wemyss was his
senior, but this was easily overcome. Admiral Wemyss, who
was already absorbed in the intricate work of establishing
a base at Mudros, felt that with the Allied troops arriving
he was more than ever required for the work for which he
had been specially selected. It was proving to be a task
of the most arduous and exacting nature. He had been
sent out without a staff to establish a base for the fleet
and a small auxiliary force of troops in what was *de facto*
a neutral island, with a motley Levantine population of
dubious character and sympathies, for whose behaviour
he was responsible as Acting Governor. He had, in fact, to
create a base out of nothing and with wholly inadequate
assistance; and when it is considered that, in addition to
the delicate administrative and police duties, the work had
to be done and its infinite difficulties overcome without
offence to neutral or allied susceptibilities, it will be obvious
that even for the comparatively small and simple force
originally contemplated it required tact, resource, and
organising ability of a high order. Now that it was a question
of a base for a large Allied army, as well as an Allied fleet,
and to the former difficulties were to be added all the com-
plexities of a large combined operation, the labour promised
to be beyond the power of any one coming fresh to the task.
With all the existing threads in his hands, Admiral Wemyss
might hope to succeed when a new-comer could scarcely
escape failure. He was therefore of opinion he ought to stay
where he was, and in intimating this he expressed his perfect
readiness to serve under Admiral de Robeck. So the change
was smoothly effected. Admiral de Robeck was given acting
rank as Vice-Admiral, and Admiral Wemyss, as second-in-
command, continued under his orders the excellent work he
was doing at the base. But in appointing the new officer
to the command the Admiralty were careful not to bind him
to a plan of operations for which he was not primarily
responsible. He was asked whether, on his separate and
independent judgment, the proposed attack was sound, and
urged not to hesitate to say if he could not approve it. He
replied at once that he fully intended to carry on, and that,
weather permitting, the operations approved by his pre-
decessor and by the Admiralty, would be commenced next
day (18th).

CHAPTER XIII

THE DARDANELLES—FAILURE OF THE ATTACK ON THE NARROWS
AND THE CHANGE OF PLAN—MARCH 18–24

By the operation orders, which had been completed before Admiral Carden had to resign the command, the fleet had been reorganised in three divisions. In the first were the four modern ships, under Admiral de Robeck's immediate command, with his flag in the *Queen Elizabeth;* in the second were eight of the older British battleships, under Captain Hayes-Sadler of the *Ocean,* for whom the rank of Commodore had been asked; and in the third were the four French battleships and two British, under Admiral Guépratte.[1]

The " General Idea " was to silence the defences of the Narrows and of the minefields simultaneously. The destruction of the forts at 8,000 yards was not expected, but it was hoped to dominate them sufficiently to prevent their interfering with sweeping operations. The scheme of attack was based on two lines. In the first (known as Line A) were the four ships of the First Division.[2] Taking station in line-

---

[1] This was designated the "Fourth Organisation." Its detail was as under :—

FIRST DIVISION

1st Sub-Division	2nd Sub-Division
Queen Elizabeth	*Agamemnon*
Inflexible	*Lord Nelson*

SECOND DIVISION

3rd Sub-Division	4th Sub-Division	5th Sub-Division
Ocean	*Swiftsure*	*Canopus*
Irresistible	*Majestic*	*Cornwallis*
Albion		
Vengeance		

THIRD DIVISION

6th Sub-Division	7th Sub-Division
Suffren	*Triumph*
Bouvet	*Prince George*
Gaulois	
Charlemagne	

[2] See Plan p. 230.

abreast, 14,000 yards from the Narrows (that is, about opposite Eren Keui, and at the extreme range of the Narrows forts), they would engage the principal forts on both banks (that is, Nos. 16, 17, 13, 19 and 20) and carry out the long-range bombardment. The second line (known as Line B) was for closer action, and the honour of forming it in the first instance was accorded to Admiral Guépratte's division. The four French battleships were to take station astern of the First Division on the 16,000 yard line, while the two British battleships attached to them, *Triumph* and *Prince George*, would advance to the 15,000 yard line to act as covering force against the barrage guns. Taking station on either quarter of the First Division, they would first deal with the Messudieh battery (No. 7) and Yildiz (No. 9), and on the Asiatic side with Dardanos and the White Cliff battery, which had by this time received part of its intended armament.[1] If unable to silence them they were to be assisted by the wing ships of the French division, and afterwards to devote themselves to the concealed howitzers. As soon as the First Division began to dominate the main forts, the four French ships would pass through the intervals and engage the same targets, gradually advancing to the limit of the swept area, that is, 8,000 yards from Rumili. As they progressed the First Division would follow in support up to the 12,000 yard line, and when they had reached the limit of their advance the *Inflexible* would engage Fort Anadolu Medjidieh (No. 24), the main work beyond the Narrows, and if necessary close to decisive range.[2]

The opposition, at any rate to begin with, was likely to be severe. Through the airmen and other sources it was now ascertained that the six main forts to be attacked contained forty-two guns of 8″ and over, of which six were 14″, besides the guns in the intermediate batteries and an increased number of mobile howitzers and field guns on both banks. It was possible therefore that the enemy's fire might prove too powerful for the second line to advance as arranged. An alternative method of attack was therefore provided, under which Admiral Guépratte's division was to keep circling round the first line, and attack in a series of runs at gradually

---

[1] Three 5·9″ guns on the higher level of the battery at its left end, with a maximum range of 8,000 yards. Its official designation was Djevad Pasha.

[2] No. 24 was a low-level work of old type armed with fourteen short-range Krupp guns—three 11″, four 10·2″, two 9·4″, two 8·2″, three 5·9″. Being very conspicuous and open to enfilade from the south, it was regarded by the Turks as of little importance, and most of the guns were afterwards removed to strengthen the barrage, but it had, of course, to be destroyed before the passage could be freely used for transports, etc.

decreasing ranges till the forts were sufficiently dominated for the first method to be resumed. In any case the final close work was not to be put upon the French division. After four hours it was to be relieved by Captain Hayes-Sadler with his 3rd and 4th Sub-Divisions, the two ships of his 5th Sub-Division being reserved for supporting the minesweepers during the night. As for the guns not in the forts, those defending the minefield were to be dealt with by the centre ships of the second line, while the dispersed howitzers and field guns were to be the business of the wing ships of both lines. By these arrangements it was hoped that sweeping could begin two hours after the bombardment commenced. The trawlers were then to be ready to clear a passage 900 yards broad past Kephez Point into Sari Sighlar Bay, and as the work proceeded the advanced line would move on into the bay and endeavour to complete the destruction of the forts at decisive range. Finally, by way of diversion, and as a means of distracting the attention of the mobile guns on the European side, the Royal Naval Division, with seven transports, was to make a demonstration of landing on the western side of the peninsula. There also the *Dartmouth* would endeavour to silence any batteries that might be firing at the ships inside the Straits, and the *Dublin* would operate similarly in Bashika Bay and watch Yeni Shehr.

Observation of fire was left entirely to the airmen, and the *Ark Royal* was to arrange for one seaplane to go up every hour. To provide against the danger of floating mines an armed picket boat was to attend each battleship, ready to sink any that might be seen.

Such was the well-thought-out plan by which the great question of the fleet's capacity to achieve the work assigned to it was at last to be put to the test. In the afternoon of March 16 the whole scheme had been communicated and explained to all Commanding Officers at a conference on board the *Queen Elizabeth*, over which Admiral de Robeck presided, and which Admiral Guépratte attended, and on the evening of the 17th, as the weather promised well, the operation orders were issued to the fleet. Nor did the morning of the 18th belie the promise. Dawn came up with a warm southerly breeze and a cloudless sky in all the jewelled serenity for which the Ægean is famous at its best. At an early hour the British minesweepers could report that during the night they had seen all clear between the White Cliff and Kephez Bay, that is, to within 8,000 yards of the Narrows forts, while the French had made good as far as the White Cliff. Nothing therefore stood in the way of the great effort being made.   As the sun rose the haze over the land cleared, the southerly wind died away and at 8.15 the signal to carry on was flying from the flagship.

Shortly before 10.0 the fleet was approaching the entrance, and at 10.30 the *Agamemnon* began to lead the First Division into the Straits, with destroyers sweeping ahead and the *Prince George* and *Triumph* on either beam.   Within half an hour they came under howitzer fire from the back of Kum Kale.   The ships returned it, but the annoyance continued to increase as they advanced to their firing position.   In another half-hour they had reached it, and as they proceeded to take up their assigned positions and opened fire (about 11.30) vessels could be seen moving in the Narrows off Chanak. There were one large merchant ship, two small tugs and a destroyer, but little notice was taken of them at the time, for as soon as the ships opened fire they made off hastily up the Straits and disappeared.   Attention was now absorbed with the scattered guns and howitzers, which seemed more numerous and better directed than ever, but in spite of the galling fire, the first half-hour of the bombardment gave good promise of success.   The *Queen Elizabeth*, which was the wing ship on the European side, took for her first target the formidable Hamidieh I on the opposite shore, but, owing probably to the great range, its German garrison seems to have given no reply. Next to her was the *Agamemnon* on Rumili, the fort she had previously punished.   Then came the *Lord Nelson* on the other main European fort, Namazieh, while the *Inflexible*, on the starboard wing, took the small battery between them, Hamidieh II.   Ten minutes after the flagship opened all the first line ships were in action, and seemed soon to be making good practice.   From the forts there was little or no reply, but the barrage fire increased in volume and intensity.   Hits, however, continued to be reported in spite of it, and about noon the *Queen Elizabeth*, who had just shifted to Chemenlik (No. 20), now a fine target against the sunlit houses of Chanak, saw a tremendous double explosion in that fort. At the same time the *Triumph* was putting shell after shell into Dardanos, the most formidable of the intermediate batteries, and using her secondary armament against the barrage guns.   For some minutes longer the deliberate long-range fire continued, but with what precise effect it was difficult to see, for the light southerly breeze had freshened and was rolling the smoke straight down the range.   Still it was clear that Chemenlik must have suffered badly by the explosion; the other forts had also sustained obvious damage, and by 12.6 enough seemed to have been done for Admiral de Robeck to signal the French division to pass through the British line and begin closer work.

All this time the concealed guns and howitzers had been getting more and more troublesome. As yet, however, none of the ships had been badly hit, but the *Agamemnon* and *Inflexible* in Line A soon began to suffer. Ten minutes after the bombardment began, a battery of four 6″ howitzers somewhere south of Eren Keui concentrated upon the former, and at 12.45 got her range. In the next twenty-five minutes she was hit twelve times, five times on the armour without injury and seven times above it. So much structural damage was done that Captain Fyler turned 32 points to throw out the range and then resumed his original position.

The *Inflexible* was also in serious trouble. Being the outermost ship of Line A on the Asiatic side, she had been receiving the main attention of the Eren Keui howitzers. At 12.20, as the French division was passing through the line, she was hit on the forebridge and had her wireless put out of action. Within the next ten minutes she was hit three times more and her picket boat was sunk alongside her. The first hit had set fire to her forebridge and it was burning fiercely. Twice again she was hit, but since the French were now closing the forts and required all the support Line A could give Captain Phillimore stuck to his target, Hamidieh II. The Admiral, however, seeing his plight, signalled him to shift his berth. About the same time it was seen that the flames had spread to the fore top. It was full of wounded, and in order to save them from being burnt alive Captain Phillimore, having silenced his battery, decided to fall out of the line.

This he could do with less scruple, for the French had ceased to advance. On receiving the signal Admiral Guépratte had steamed up the Asiatic coast with the *Suffren* and *Bouvet,* while the *Gaulois* and *Charlemagne* conformed on the opposite side, so as to leave an open field of fire for the British line in the middle of the Straits. Even before they reached their firing position they were received with a heavy fire both from the Narrows forts and the barrage. Still, with great gallantry, Admiral Guépratte led them in to 10,000 yards, concentrating on the forts with his heavy guns and making apparently good practice. For a time the struggle for mastery was very severe. It was evident that although the intermediate batteries were now silent, the Narrows forts had been far from dominated by the morning's bombardment. A seaplane which had passed up the Straits reported that Dardanos and Chemenlik were no longer manned, but that the other principal targets were all firing. The bombardment of the eight battleships engaged now began to tell. By 1.45 the enemy's fire had so far slackened that Admiral de Robeck considered the time had come for calling up the minesweepers to clear a passage for closing to decisive range. To cover the operation he also ordered Captain Hayes-Sadler's division, which had not yet been engaged and was quite fresh, to relieve the French line, which had naturally been suffering. At the range to which they had closed—about 9,000 yards—the fire of the forts was fully effective. The ships had been hit again and again, and the *Gaulois* had just been so badly holed forward that Admiral Guépratte called to the *Dublin* to come inside and stand by her.

Still up to this time things had gone as well as could be expected, and there was good promise of the new scheme of attack proving a success. But before the relief had been carried out a startling incident suddenly gave the fortunes of the day an ugly turn. It was nearly two o'clock when the *Suffren* was coming out at high speed on the Asiatic side, with the *Bouvet* following. Admiral Guépratte's method of attack was for the ships of each pair to take alternately the most exposed position, and when the recall was made the *Bouvet* was engaging Namazieh. Early in the action she had suffered a good deal of damage, mainly from Messudieh (No. 7). Two of her casemates had been put out of action, and her bridge and steering compartment were on fire before she effectually silenced the battery. On the other shore were the *Charlemagne* and *Gaulois*, the *Gaulois*, who had gamely declined the *Dublin's* offer of a tow, coming along as best she could with a list to starboard and down by the bows, and clearly unfit for further action. The French flagship had just passed through the British line, and the *Bouvet* was about to do so, when a huge column of reddish black smoke shot up from under her. Whether it was a shell or a mine could not be seen. It was followed almost immediately by another, higher and more dense, which seemed to tell a magazine had gone. As the smoke cleared she was seen to have taken a heavy list, and then in two minutes she turned turtle and went down. A rush to the spot was made by the nearest destroyers and the picket boats that were attending the British ships. The *Agamemnon* and the French ships also closed to the rescue, but so sudden and complete was the disaster that out of her whole complement only 48 officers and men could be saved. As many more had been left at Tenedos in charge of her boats, and of the rest over 600 must have perished.

Such was the tragic spectacle which greeted Captain Hayes-Sadler as he led his ships up to take the place of the retiring French. Sudden and terrible as was the disaster, it did nothing to check the British advance. Captain Hayes-Sadler, in the *Ocean*, was on the right of the line, that is, on the Asiatic side, the *Vengeance* (Captain Bertram Smith) on the left. Between them were the *Albion* (Captain Heneage) and the *Irresistible* (Captain Dent). In support were the *Swiftsure* (Captain Maxwell-Lefroy) and the *Majestic* (Captain Talbot) who were coming up to relieve the *Prince George* and *Triumph*. At 2.39, when the range was 12,000 yards, they opened fire, and gradually closed to 10,600, using their secondary armament against guns that were firing on the boats rescuing the *Bouvet's* crew and at the mouth of the Soghanli Dere, for one of the torpedo tubes was reported to be there, and, as some thought, might have caused the *Bouvet* disaster. The reply from the forts was not formidable. The only one that was firing briskly was the German-manned Hamidieh I (No. 19), which, though the nearest of the Chanak group, had proved the most baffling target.

Though the *Vengeance*, whose target it was, kept dropping shells right into it, the seaplane, which was observing, reported that most of them fell into the centre of the fort and did no damage. Chemenlik, the fort behind it, was still not manned, and two of its guns were pointing at a sharp angle upwards. On the European side the *Irresistible* engaged Namazieh, which for the moment made no reply; the *Ocean* had five hits out of her first seven shots on Hamidieh II, and shortly after 3.0 the *Vengeance* set a large fire burning at the back of Rumili. A few minutes later Hamidieh II ceased fire. From that time it was silent, and the *Ocean* shifted to Rumili, which was still firing. It is difficult to state with certainty what effect our bombardment was producing. Several commanding officers speak of forts which had been reduced to silence, but the Admiral asserts that at a quarter past three all forts were firing rapidly but inaccurately. It is quite clear, however, that Hamidieh I was undamaged. It was as active as when she first opened fire, and was concentrating salvoes of four on the *Irresistible*, in spite of Line A, which was keeping up the bombardment from the 14,000 yard line. At 3.14 there was a heavy explosion alongside her, and then the *Queen Elizabeth* began to treat the obnoxious fort with salvoes in reply. A quarter of an hour later (3.32) it could be seen that the *Irresistible* had taken a slight list, and as the enemy's fire did not slacken the Admiral signalled the advanced line to open out the range.

Though the forts ceased firing from time to time, it was evident they were not really out of action, and obviously the projected attack on the minefield could not yet take place.[1] But danger had already been found. On reaching Line A the trawlers had got out their sweeps and were proceeding up stream when they exploded three mines. For a time it seemed that the ships, though far short of Kephez, were themselves in the midst of mines, some of which at least were believed to be of the floating Léon type.[2] Between 3.30 and 4.0 the ships had from time to time to go astern to avoid them, the sweepers exploded one close to where the *Bouvet* went down and apparently brought two others, horned carbonite mines, to the surface, which the *Ocean*, *Agamemnon* and picket boats tried in vain to destroy. A floating mine was soon reported as far down as the Admiral's division, which was still on the 14,000 yard line, and at 4.5 the *Lord Nelson's* picket-boat thought she had destroyed one by gunfire. Immediately afterwards the *Inflexible*, which since 2.30 had resumed her station in Line A, struck a mine which took her on the starboard bow by the fore submerged flat, every man in it was killed, it flooded immediately and the ship began to list and settle by the head. She at once made for Tenedos, but it was doubtful whether she could reach it. The water continued to increase on her, her bulkheads were straining badly, and so critical was her condition that the wounded were got into the cutter.

Those on the spot had little doubt what had been the business of the vessels seen at work in the Narrows when the attack began, for in the opinion of the Admiral the time of the mines' appearance pointed to their having been released from Chanak after the ships entered the Straits. Shortly afterwards came another shock. About 4.15 the *Irresistible*, which, in opening out the range, had reached the 11,000 yards line, was drifting with engines stopped, when she was struck. At first her Captain was uncertain whether or not it was a torpedo, but he soon realised that it was a mine, and that it was moored. The results were disastrous.

---

[1] The Turks state that the periodical silence of the forts was mainly due to the need of cleaning the mechanism of their guns, which became choked with dust thrown up by shells exploding in front on the emplacements. Those which burst behind the guns did no harm.

[2] The Léon mine is one that is unmoored and oscillates between certain set depths below the surface.

It took her under the bilge of the starboard engine-room, very near the centre line of the ship, and the engine-room flooded so quickly that only three of the men who were in it were able to escape. Then under the pressure of the water the midship bulkhead buckled, the port engine-room flooded in its turn and the engines were completely disabled.

With a list of 7 degrees to starboard and down by the stern, her condition was easily visible to the enemy, and their fire on her redoubled as the destroyer *Wear* and a picket boat hurried to her assistance. The Admiral, who was then ignorant of the extent of the damage or of its cause, ordered the *Ocean* to stand by and tow her out of action if necessary. The remaining vessels did all they could to keep down the new outburst of fire from the forts and batteries. By the time the *Wear* came up, Captain Dent, seeing it was impossible to save his ship, decided to abandon her. It was no easy matter; shells were raining on her deck, causing many casualties, but by a fine display of seamanship Captain Christopher Metcalfe of the *Wear* managed to take off 28 officers and 582 men. Only ten volunteers were left on board to get out a wire to the *Ocean*.

It was not till 4.50 that the *Wear* got back to the flagship with the rescued crew, and only then did Admiral de Robeck learn that it was a mine that had caused the trouble. He at once signalled the advanced line to fall back. At 5.10 the *Irresistible*'s crew were disembarked from the *Wear*, which was then ordered to close on the *Ocean* and instruct her to withdraw if the *Irresistible* could not be towed. The *Ocean* had by this time approached the mined ship, and Captain Dent went on board to confer with Captain Hayes-Sadler, but the *Irresistible*'s list had increased so much, and she lay so awkwardly bows on to the Asiatic shore, that it soon became obvious this was impossible, and as the *Ocean* was under a considerable cross fire, it was decided to remove the remainder of the crew and carry out the Admiral's orders. At 5.50 the ship was abandoned 10,000 yards from Rumili, the intention being to make an attempt to save her after dark with destroyers and minesweepers. As soon as he saw that the *Irresistible* had been abandoned the Admiral hoisted the "General Recall" and began to return to Tenedos for the night. It was clear, in view of the unexpected danger and the losses sustained, that battleships could not be left inside the Straits after dark to cover the minesweepers, so that all idea of clearing the Kephez minefield that night had to be abandoned.

How real the danger was was quickly demonstrated. The *Ocean* began to withdraw under a heavy fire from Dardanos and Suandere. At about five minutes past six she was a mile from the *Irresistible*, when a heavy explosion on her starboard side announced that she also had struck a mine.[1] The adjacent coal bunkers and fore and aft passages flooded and the helm jammed hard a-port. Almost at the same moment a shell got home on the same side aft and so flooded the tiller-room and starboard steering engine-room that they could not be reached and repairs were impossible. In spite of a prompt flooding of the port wing compartments the ship rapidly took a list of 15°. So critical was the situation that Captain Hayes-Sadler signalled the destroyers, *Colne, Jed* and *Chelmer*, which were passing at the time, to close. With great skill and pluck, under a cross fire from Dardanos and the barrage batteries on both sides, they removed the whole crew, and the *Ocean*, being well out in the channel, was abandoned to drift out of danger if she continued to float. Till dark Captain Hayes-Sadler lay off a mile away in the *Jed*, and then returned to the ship and was able to remove four men who had been left by accident on board. It was obvious, however, that nothing more could be done, and she was then finally abandoned about 7.30 p.m.

After reporting to the Admiral at Tenedos Captains Hayes-Sadler and Dent went back to join the destroyers, which, with six minesweepers, had been ordered to go in and endeavour to tow the *Irresistible* into the current and prevent the *Ocean* drifting out of it. But though they searched till nearly midnight not a trace of either ship could be found. Their end was unseen. In the silence of the night they settled down quietly somewhere in deep water and no man knew their resting-place.[2]

No other ship was lost. In spite of the *Inflexible's* perilous condition, thanks to the devotion of the engine-room, who had to work almost in the dark and with the ventilation fans stopped, Captain Phillimore succeeded in getting her to Tenedos, and an hour and a half after she was struck he anchored her safely on the north side of the island. But

[1] Her exact position at the time could not be determined, as the standard compass and upper bridge had been completely destroyed (Captain's report March 24).

[2] On Turkish information it was stated that the *Ocean* drifted into Morto Bay and sank there about 10.30 p.m. The *Irresistible*, they said, was caught in a cross current and carried back within range of the Narrows forts. After being fired on by them and by Dardanos she was believed to have sunk about 7.30.

that was all that could be done. It was soon evident she
would have to stay where she was till a coffer dam had been
constructed to enable her to proceed to Malta. It was also
found that both the *Suffren* and *Gaulois* would have to be
docked before they were fit for further service. The *Suffren*
had a bad leak forward caused by a shell, and the *Gaulois*,
when she left the Straits, was in so serious a condition that
for some time it was doubtful whether she could be saved,
but eventually she was beached successfully on Drapano
Island, in the south of the Rabbit group.

Not till long after was the real cause of the disasters
ascertained. The truth was, that on the previous night, or
a few nights earlier, the Turks, unknown to us, had laid a
line of twenty moored mines in Eren Keui Bay parallel to
the shore, and our sweeping craft had missed them. They
had been deliberately placed in our usual manœuvring ground,
and, in spite of all our precautions, they had achieved a
staggering success.[1]

The great attempt to force the Narrows with the fleet had
ended in what could only be regarded as a severe defeat. Out
of the sixteen capital ships engaged three had gone down and
three more, including the only battle cruiser, had been put out
of action for an indefinite period. Of the whole Allied battle
fleet, therefore, one-third was spent in the one day's operation.
At such a rate of loss, with results apparently so meagre, it
looked extremely doubtful whether the navy unaided could
ever force a passage. Long afterwards reports that were
received from Constantinople went to show that the day's
work had had as serious an effect on the Turks as on the Allies.
So terrible was said to have been the havoc of the heavy
ship guns, and so far spent the *moral* and ammunition of
the garrisons, that further resistance seemed hopeless. The
impression prevailed that, had the attack been renewed,
nothing would have induced the men to stand to their guns,
and all the forts must have been abandoned. Such reports
are not unusual under similar conditions, and later inquiries
made in quieter circumstances tended to show they were
at least exaggerated. The Turkish official returns admit that
the fabric of all the main forts had been seriously damaged.
In Hamidieh II the barracks were destroyed and both its
guns knocked out, but Rumili, they say, had only one gun
put temporarily out of action. Namazieh lost one gun, and
its barracks were burnt. The barracks at Hamidieh I were
also burnt, but it only lost one heavy gun. In Chemenlik a

[1] See footnote, p. 225, *post*.

magazine was exploded. They insist, however, that the damage did little to destroy the general confidence. So little had the defences of the minefield been touched that the General Staff were confident it could not be cleared, and felt sure that, if the attempt to pass the Straits was repeated, the forts and the Turkish fleet could deal with any ships that might scrape through.

Their confidence was probably justified. It is now known that, before the ships could reach Sari Sighlar Bay, they would have to run the gauntlet of five lines of mines besides the new Eren Keui line. Once in Sari Sighlar Bay, the surviving ships would have been within 3,000 to 4,000 yards of the Narrows forts, whose ammunition, though much of it was of inferior quality, was by no means exhausted. Enough at least appears to have been available for continuing the resistance.[1] Further, it must be borne in mind that only one of the fort guns had been permanently damaged. Some that had been put out of action were repaired during the night, and the volume of fire would have been as great as ever had the struggle been renewed. On the other hand, our own ships at so decisive a range would have had a fair chance of knocking out the fort guns without too much delay, although the barrage fire would probably have been little less difficult to deal with than before. Assuming, however, they could have avoided serious trouble from the guns by continuing the rush, there were still five more lines of mines to pass before they reached Nagara, where the Narrows and their defences end. It is true the Nagara group of forts was obsolete and practically negligible, but the chances against getting so far through the unswept minefields, which in all contained nearly 350 mines, are calculated to have been 15 to 1—that is, out of sixteen ships only one could have hoped to reach the Sea of Marmara. Though the mines themselves were of inferior type, they had proved themselves capable of sinking the old type battleships

[1] An impression seems to have prevailed in Constantinople that the ammunition was practically exhausted on March 18 (see Morgenthau, *Secrets of the Bosporus*, pp. 147, *et seq.*). The official statement of the Turkish War Office, however, says "modern ammunition for heavy guns was very short, but there was a plentiful supply of older ammunition. Ammunition for medium and light guns was so plentiful that many attacks could have been repulsed." Possibly this was a sanguine view, but a further statement was furnished which purports to give the actual number of rounds per gun remaining after the action was over. This shows an average for the heavy guns of about seventy rounds; for 6-inch, 130 rounds; and for the smaller mine defence guns 150 rounds—a proportion which in view of our own shortage of ammunition was far from negligible. For the howitzers and barrage guns there is no return.

of which the fleet was mainly composed and of disabling a vessel so modern as the *Inflexible*.[1]

The whole of these facts could not be known at the time, but enough had been seen to indicate that an immediate renewal of the attack was scarcely to be thought of. It was fully believed that the main mischief had been done by floating mines, and until some means had been found for dealing with them, another attempt to force the minefield in open daylight could scarcely be regarded as a fair risk of war. It seemed clear that if disaster were to be avoided, different methods must be tried, and even before the results of the day were known a radical change in the plan of operations was in contemplation.

On the eve of the attack General Sir Ian Hamilton reached Tenedos. On the same day the last group of the French division arrived, under General d'Amade, who had been selected for the command as being an officer experienced in oversea expeditions. During the South African war he had been Military Attaché at the British headquarters, he had won a high reputation for his campaign in Morocco, and in the early days of the war he had had committed to him the difficult task of holding the line between Dunkirk and the British army with a group of Territorial divisions known as " L'Armée d'Amade." The British General's first conversation with the Admiral and a personal reconnaissance on March 18 impressed him with the difficulty which the mobile guns presented to the success of the fleet, and the impossibility of dealing with them without landing troops in strength. Success, therefore, could not be looked for unless the force was reorganised for the operation. The French contingent was no better prepared for a contested landing than his own, and, after a conference with Admiral Wemyss, General d'Amade and other senior officers, he had come to the conclusion that the best and quickest way of reorganising was to send all the troops to Alexandria, since Mudros had no facilities for dealing with so large a force. This difficulty had been foreseen and reported by General Maxwell a week earlier. It had been referred to Admiral Wemyss, and, two days before the attack, he had pronounced in favour of the proposed change

---

[1] Information furnished by the Turks after the Armistice leaves practically no doubt that the damage was done by the newly-laid mines in Eren Keui Bay and not by the floating mines. These were not of the Léon type, but " Ramis " mines attached to floats. Some forty of this type had been manufactured at Constantinople. and about a dozen of them had been let go from time to time during the afternoon operations, with no effect. On March 18 the steamer *Bulair* was ready below Nagara with twenty of them, but the Turks state that they were not dropped.

of base, but a final decision by the Government at home had been postponed till General Hamilton could see for himself.

When, therefore, the day after the attack on the Narrows, the War Council met, they had before them a momentous decision. That the base must be changed, in spite of the delay it would entail, was certain. It was further indisputable that if the troops were to be employed in forcing the passage of the Straits, instead of proceeding direct to their original objective in the wake of the fleet, the enterprise meant a much more serious commitment than had hitherto been contemplated. Naturally, therefore, there was a pronounced tendency to cling to the idea of forcing the passage with the fleet alone, and the main question was whether or not Admiral de Robeck should be instructed to make another attempt. As yet there was nothing from him beyond an announcement of the defeat and loss he had sustained, but General Hamilton, in telegraphing his decision that the base must be changed, had stated that, while the Admiral did not minimise the difficulties of the task, he was clearly determined to exhaust every effort before calling for military assistance on a large scale. This was before the attack took place, and now, in view of the military appreciations on the spot—to say nothing of all previous experience —it was more than doubtful if a renewal of the naval operations could do any good. On the other hand, our information was that the Turks were short of ammunition and mines, and, until we knew better what damage had been done to the forts, it was impossible to say that another attempt would not be decisive. Furthermore the political reasons for carrying on were very strong. To wait for the reorganisation of the army would involve probably a month's delay, and at the moment it was of crying importance not to admit even a check by suspending operations. In Italy especially the effect was likely to be very bad. It was only a fortnight since she had made her first overtures towards joining the Entente Powers, delicate negotiations were in progress, and Italian opinion seemed about equally divided on the desirability of breaking her neutrality. No less serious was the probable reaction on the Mohammedan world. In that quarter it seemed essential not to disturb the impression which had been produced by the defeat of the attempt on Egypt and our successes in Mesopotamia. Still, in view of the meagreness of the ascertained facts of the situation at the Dardanelles, it was impossible to send the Admiral a direct order to carry on. The man on the spot alone could judge, and the final resolution was that he should be authorised to continue the operations if he thought fit.

In order to give him at least a chance of doing this and at the same time create an impression that we did not mean to accept the rebuff, the Admiralty at once decided to make good his losses. The *Queen* and *Implacable* were already within a day's steaming of Malta, and an hour or two after the meeting, the last two ships of the 5th Battle Squadron, the *Prince of Wales* and *London*, were ordered to follow them. Thus the Channel Fleet finally disappeared. As Admiral Bethell was senior to Admiral de Robeck, they were sent out under Admiral Stuart Nicholson, who had been commanding the 6th Battle Squadron at Sheerness, and Admiral Bethell took his place. At the same time the French were asked, if only for the moral effect, to announce that they intended to replace the *Bouvet* and *Gaulois*, and their reply was to order the *Henri IV*, from the Suez Canal, to join Admiral Guépratte's flag.

In informing Admiral de Robeck of the resolution that had been come to and of the reinforcement he was to expect, the Admiralty impressed upon him the importance of not giving the enemy time to repair the forts or encouraging them by any apparent suspension of operations. It was entirely the Admiral's own view. What he wanted to do was to resume the bombardment over the land with the *Queen Elizabeth*. If she could be provided with proper air reconnaissance, he still believed he could dominate the forts sufficiently to allow of the minefield being swept. For this reason he was opposed to the change of base. Although he concurred that for military reasons it might be necessary, yet he believed that if the troops were used at once to make feints at various points, they would attract so much of the noxious mobile artillery that his sweepers would be able to work in spite of it. So eager indeed was the Admiral to carry on that had the heavens been propitious, this expedient might have been tried, but again the weather had the last word. Day after day it blew strong north-easterly gales, with a visibility so low that firing was out of the question. On the night of the 21st, torpedo-boat *064* was wrecked on the east side of Lemnos, and still the gale blew relentlessly. Nothing could be done, and, before the weather abated, the Admiral had reason to modify his views.

General Hamilton had come out with a perfectly open mind as to the best use to make of his troops. Admiral de Robeck's view was that, after the Straits had been forced by the ships, a landing should be effected at Bulair, in order

to cut off the Turkish army on the peninsula; but the
General's first conference (March 17) with the Admiral
had raised doubts in his mind as to the wisdom of the plan.
It admittedly depended for its success on the fleet being
able to force its way into the Sea of Marmara, and when the
Admiral explained the unexpected difficulties of the mobile
guns the General began to realise the practical impossibility
of dealing with them, except by a landing in force on the
peninsula.   Clearly a landing at Bulair would not help.
It would not lead to the occupation of the forts when they
were dominated, nor would the seizure of the neck alone
force an evacuation of the peninsula, since the main line of
supply was by sea.   From a military point of view, a landing
at Bulair was no less objectionable, since any force disembarked there would be in the precarious position of having
to face two fronts—one towards the Bulair lines and one in
the opposite direction against an attack from the mainland.
As for a direct attack on the lines from the sea, it was obvious
that precautions had been taken to render such an attempt
extremely hazardous.   Convinced,   therefore,   as   General
Hamilton was, that the fleet could not succeed by the help
of mere demolition parties, he turned to the possibilities of
landing all his force in the peninsula, and, whilst the great
attack on the Narrows was in progress, made a close reconnaissance of the whole coast in the *Phaeton* accompanied by
his French colleague.   From Bulair to Suvla he found that
the precipitous fall of the hills left no practicable beaches
except at a few narrow gullies where deployment after
landing was impossible.   Beyond Suvla as far as Tekke
Burnu, at the end of the peninsula, there were several
serviceable landing-places, but all of them appeared to be
heavily entrenched and wired.   Only at the southern end
of the peninsula, between Tekke Burnu and Morto Bay, did
a disembarkation in force seem practicable.[1] As for a landing
inside the Straits, the reception he met with when the *Phaeton*
entered them put that out of the question, and if any doubt
remained in his mind as to how he would have to employ
his force, it was removed by what he saw of the results of
the great attack.
    His view of the situation was not immediately conveyed
to the Admiral.   In the flagship it was still taken for granted
that the main landing would be near Bulair, and feeling, as
he and his staff did, how hopeless was such an operation if
the German-Turkish fleet was left in command of the Sea
of Marmara, they saw only a fresh necessity for repeating

[1] See Plan No. 4.

their effort to break through at all costs. There was a belief that it could still be done when the reinforcing ships arrived and the destroyers were equipped for sweeping, if only the General would make feints of landing to occupy some of the attention of the mobile guns, and for this purpose would postpone for a few days his change of base. It was a matter not to be settled in a moment, and it was arranged that a decision should be taken at a conference of the principal flag and general officers, to be held on March 22.

Meanwhile, as we have seen, the Admiral had informed the Admiralty that he intended to persevere with the fleet alone. But by the time the conference met, the few days that had elapsed since the attack on the Narrows had brought home the full significance of what had happened, and Admiral de Robeck now agreed with the General's view that the whole military force would have to be employed. Reluctant as he had been—in accordance with his instructions—to call for military assistance in force, he had felt from the first, like every one else, that the right way of doing the work was by combined operations. He now knew not only that the General was ready to employ his whole force in assisting the fleet to get through, but, after hearing the military views, he was convinced that the object of the campaign could only be attained by the continuous co-operation of the two services, the main reason being that even if the fleet got through, transports and supply ships could never follow it unless the Gallipoli peninsula was held. By this means alone could the mobile guns on the Asiatic side be held in check and the channel kept clear of mines.

The delay involved was greatly to be regretted, but the Admiral understood it would not extend beyond April 14, and to this he was reconciled by the bad weather; for it was now only too plain that it would be extremely hazardous to land any large body of troops before the spring was further advanced. Nor need it involve the fleet being idle. The ships could be well employed in searching out concealed batteries and sweeping the area in which they would have to manœuvre. The aeroplanes had just arrived, a practicable aerodrome had been prepared at Tenedos, and as soon as the weather moderated he intended to begin. The *Queen Elizabeth* was also to resume her bombardment of the Narrows over the land. The French squadron would operate in the Gulf of Xeros and endeavour to attack Gallipoli and the Bulair camps with their aircraft, while his own seaplanes would, if possible, attack the Turkish depots at Maidos and some vessels, reported to be full of mines, which were lying above the Narrows. In this way he felt he could keep the enemy occupied till the middle of April, when the General expected the troops to be ready.

At home some disappointment was felt at the Admiral's change of attitude. The Admiralty pointed out how the delay might mean the appearance of enemy submarines on the scene, and expressed their unwillingness to call on the army for operations which must necessarily be costly. But, as the Admiral explained, the conditions of the case had now entirely changed. The General on the spot had confirmed his own view that troops were necessary to enable him to get through. Until March 18 experience had not conclusively revealed how inadequate were high-velocity guns for the destruction of forts at long range. Their own failure and recent reports from Tsingtau showed that the operation was far more difficult than had been thought. Not that he accepted the check of March 18 as decisive —he had been quite ready to try again. But when he found that General Hamilton regarded a landing in force as a sound operation, and that he was ready to co-operate in forcing the Narrows, there could no longer be any question of making another attempt with the fleet alone. Nor was this all. For, as he pointed out in his appreciation, it was now clear that even if the fleet could force the passage into the Sea of Marmara, it could not maintain itself there unless its communications were secured by the occupation of the Gallipoli peninsula. It was only, therefore, by a combined operation that the ultimate object of the campaign could be attained. This being so, his obvious course was to husband his ships for the combined effort. His intention, therefore, till the troops were ready, was to confine himself to the preparatory work. To renew the attack on the Narrows single-handed could hardly lead to any decisive result, while it would certainly cripple his power of co-operating with the army and jeopardise the execution of the sounder and larger scheme.

So it was decided. All the troops, except the 3rd Australian Brigade and the Marines, began at once to leave for Egypt, the General sailed on March 24, and with the departure of army headquarters, the first stage of the ill-fated enterprise came to an end.

THE DARDANELLES.
THE ATTACK ON THE NARROWS.

March 18th, 1915.

Ships of Line A ....
Ships of Line B ....
Ships in support ....
Actual minefields ....
Supposed minefields ....
Approximate positions of mined vessels ....

NOTE. The arcs denote the ranges from Fort N°5; the numerals against ships names indicate the run for which they were detailed.

SCALE.

(1) GAULOIS
(2) CHARLEMAGNE
(1) INFLEXIBLE
(1) IRRESISTIBLE
(2) OCEAN
(1) SUFFREN
(1) BOUVET
(2) ALBION

N°5, 47 Mines
N°5, 39 Mines
N°5, 30 Mines
N°7, 50 Mines
N°8, 53 Mines
N°9, 46 Mines
N°9, 29 Mines

Prepared in the Historical Section of the Committee of Imperial Defence.

Malby & Sons, Ltd.

TRUE

CHAPTER XIV

PROGRESS OF THE OVERSEA EXPEDITIONS AND COMMERCE
DEFENCE IN THE OUTER SEAS DURING THE FIRST QUARTER
OF 1915

To appreciate justly all that was involved in the decision
to change the plan of the Dardanelles campaign, the conflicting anxieties which led up to it must be seen in the
light of the general naval situation. In the outer seas, as
will appear directly, it had been cleared of its original embarrassments, but, although the battle of the Falklands had
broken the back of the enemy's cruiser efforts against our
commerce, the trouble had not been finally eradicated without
prolonged operations and the occupation of a considerable
proportion of our cruiser force. The difficulty had been
increased by the needs of our combined expeditions against
the German oversea possessions. Nowhere, except in the
Pacific, had they attained their end. In Africa we had still
three in hand—the Cameroons, German "South-West"
and German "East"; all of them were causing a drain
upon the navy, and in none had progress been as rapid as
had been hoped.

In the Cameroons, since the beginning of December,
when we had captured Baré and the railhead of the northern
railway, no substantial advantage had been obtained. At
the end of December General Dobell had pushed two columns
forward from this point, and with the assistance of a naval
gun party they had destroyed the German fort at Dschang,
thirty miles north of Baré early in the new year, but owing
to the difficulty of the communications, they were then
ordered to fall back and establish themselves at Baré and
the railhead. To the westward of this point the forces in
Southern Nigeria were in contact with the enemy, but could
not advance, and in the north the troops acting with the
French from Lake Chad could do no more than watch
Garua and Lere.[1] The French were occupying the midland
railway as far east as Edea, at the crossing of the Sanaga
River, and in the south and south-east General Aymerich,
assisted by Belgians, by continuous activity was preventing
the enemy concentrating for operations in the main theatre.
But the failure of the French to clear the coastal area south

---

[1] See Map No. 16, Vol. I.

of Edea put a heavy strain on Captain C. T. M. Fuller and his slender blockading force, which consisted at this time of the light cruiser *Challenger*, the gunboat *Dwarf*, a picket boat and a steam pinnace which the *Cumberland* had left with him, and about a dozen vessels of the Nigerian Marine.[1]

Seventy miles south of Edea the French were holding the little port of Kribi. It was frequently attacked, and to assist in its defence the *Ivy* or *Dwarf* was constantly there, and Captain Chéron's cruiser, the *Pothuau*, as well. Towards the end of January, as the French required more troops at Edea, part of the garrison was transferred there, and was replaced by four companies of our West African Regiment and a detachment of our Marines, that had been stationed at Kampo, in the extreme south, in order to control the passage of supplies to the enemy through the Spanish enclave. Between Kribi and the Jabassi River the coast was open, and incessant activity was necessary to prevent supplies being thrown in from the Spanish island of Fernando Po. Posts had to be established at various points from which the flotilla patrols could work, nor was the work confined to the sea. The enemy were constantly appearing in small bodies on the coast, and whenever they did so landing-parties had to be organised to drive them off and prevent them establishing themselves. In this work the *Dwarf* (Commander F. E. K. Strong, R.N.) was especially active, and more than justified her existence.[2]

The whole position was very unsatisfactory and promised no visible conclusion. Although the Allies greatly outnumbered the Germans, the vast distances and the number of troops that were absorbed in maintaining necessary posts and defending the long lines of communication, made concerted

---

[1]

		Guns.
Ivy, Government steamboat	.	1–12 pdr., 1–7 pdr. M.L., 2–6 pdrs., Q.F.
Alligator, Motor launch .	.	1 Maxim.
Crocodile, Motor launch .	.	1 Maxim.
Manatee, Motor launch .	.	1–3 pdr., 1 Maxim.
Remus, Paddle tug .	.	3–12 pdrs., & W/T.
Porpoise, Paddle tug .	.	2–12 pdrs., 1–3 pdr.
Vigilant, Steam launch .	.	1–3 pdr., 1 Maxim.
Moseley, Steam lifeboat .	.	1 Maxim.
Walrus, Steam tug (German prize)		1 Maxim.
Balbus, Steam tug .	.	3–37 mm.
Mole, Dredger . .	.	1–6″ B.L. & W/T.
Lighter (300 tons) .	.	1–6″ B.L.

Also about half a dozen German ships, tugs and motor boats.

[2] She was completed in 1899 under the Naval Defence Act programme of 1889, 710 tons, 2–4″, 4–12-pdrs., 6 Maxims.

movements, such as a general offensive required, extremely difficult to arrange. In the middle of January the French Government proposed a conference for establishing a closer co-operation between the Allied forces, and by the end of the month this was agreed to, but as the commanders concerned were separated by the whole length of the Cameroons, it could not take place before March. Something, however, was done on our side. Colonel Cunliffe, commanding the forces in Nigeria, came down to Duala at the end of January to confer with General Dobell, and it was then decided to push on the northern operation against Garua in concert with the French and to send up another naval gun party to batter the place. Both the French and the British Generals received reinforcements early in February from West Africa, but nothing serious could be done till after the March conference.

During the period of inactivity ashore the work of the navy became more exacting than ever. It was of the utmost importance to intercept traffic from Fernando Po, where the Germans had succeeded in landing supplies, and owing to the Spanish Governor's lax interpretation of his responsibilities as a neutral they were practically establishing a base. When, therefore, on February 21 an intimation came that the Admiralty wanted to replace the *Challenger* by the *Astraea* from the Cape, General Dobell protested, as he had done before when the *Cumberland* was withdrawn.[1] The *Challenger* had, in fact, just been instrumental in preventing a land attack on Duala. Rumour was about that enemy ships were off the coast, and the Germans seem to have believed that a naval force had reoccupied the estuary of the Cameroon River and that Duala would be an easy prey. Their intention to attack was detected. On February 17 Captain Fuller sent ashore half a company of small-arm men with a 12-pounder and field-gun party, and at dark turned his searchlights on the approaches to the town. It was all that was necessary. The enemy quickly dispersed, and the attack never developed. There were, however, further causes of anxiety. In addition to the constant threats to our patrol bases, parties of Germans with native troops had begun to appear on the coast, evidently on the look-out for supplies. In these circumstances General Dobell urged that the naval operations were more important than ever, and begged that Captain Fuller and his ship should remain till his own active operations were concluded. Reports were still being received of intercepted German

[1] Vol. I., p. 370.

wireless signals which seemed to be passing between the
Karlsruhe, Kronprinz Wilhelm and *Dresden.* Fernando Po
was very strictly watched by our patrol vessel, and Captain
Chéron, in the *Pothuau,* was cruising on its northern approaches. Though Captain Fuller discredited the reports,
Captain Chéron thought it prudent to pick up a party of
his marines whom he had landed at Kribi, and he left his
patrol to proceed there. The result was that the moment his
back was turned a German supply ship came up and slipped
into Fernando Po with a quantity of provisions and ammunition. The stoppage of this kind of work was obviously of
the last importance, but the Admiralty did not alter their
decision about the *Challenger,* though there was no suggestion
of withdrawing Captain Fuller. It was even decided to
increase his force in order to justify the declaration of a
regular blockade. For this purpose the old light cruiser
Sirius, and the sloop *Rinaldo,* which since their work on the
Belgian coast had been serving as guardships on our Eastern
coast, were ordered to be prepared for foreign service (March
21), and the *Astraea* came up from the Cape and relieved the
Challenger at the end of April.

There the operations against German South-West Africa
had opened as early as September 1914 by the occupation
of Luderitz Bay and the landing of the southern force at
Port Nolloth in Namaqualand; but Walfisch Bay, which we
had evacuated in September, had not been re-occupied, and
the northern force had not commenced operations. Further
development had been arrested, first by the rebellion, and
secondly by the need of keeping Vice-Admiral H. G. King-
Hall's squadron concentrated till Admiral von Spee was dealt
with, and the consequent inability of our squadron to protect
two bases so far apart as Walfisch Bay and Luderitz Bay.[1]
It was possible, however, to begin preliminary operations at
once, and as soon as the squadron was concentrated it left
Table Bay for Luderitz Bay, escorting three transports with
Union troops. They sailed while the battle at the Falklands
was being fought, and landed on December 10 as the news
of the victory reached them. There was now no reason
for not re-occupying Walfisch Bay; and a new plan was

---

[1] The ships which Admiral King-Hall had with him were the cruisers
Minotaur (flag) and *Defence,* the light cruisers *Astraea, Hyacinth* and *Wey-
mouth,* and the battleship *Albion.* The armed merchant cruiser *Armadale
Castle* remained at Simon's Bay.

After the battle of the Falklands the *Minotaur* and *Defence* were ordered
home to join the Grand Fleet, the Admiral transferring his flag to the
Hyacinth; the *Weymouth* after refitting was to relieve the *Chatham* for the
operations against the *Königsberg* in the Rufiji River.

devised, the main idea of which was that the troops should operate in overwhelming force in four columns. The northern force, which was the main one, was intended to operate from Walfisch Bay and seize Swakopmund, the port from which started the northern railway and that to Windhuk. A central force was to operate from Luderitz Bay on the line of the southern railway. A southern force of mounted troops was to cross the frontier and seize Warmbad, while a small eastern force was to strike in from Rietsfontein in Bechuanaland and seize Keetmanshoop, the railhead of the Luderitz Bay line. Accordingly Admiral King-Hall ordered the *Albion* to Walfisch Bay as guardship and returned himself to Table Bay, with the *Hyacinth*, *Astraea* and *Weymouth*, to fetch the advanced troops of the northern force, and on Christmas day 5,000 of them were landed at Walfisch Bay without opposition. The *Albion*, after docking at Simonstown, sailed to join the squadron that was being formed for the attack on the Dardanelles, while the troops advanced on Swakopmund, which they occupied on January 14. It was found to have been abandoned, but the wells had been poisoned and everything of use in the port and the railway terminus had been destroyed. We ourselves had destroyed the pier in the earlier days of the war, and as the place was consequently useless as a base, a railway had to be begun to connect it with Walfisch Bay. All had now to stand fast till the northern force was complete, and during the next three weeks, while the last embers of the rebellion were being stamped out, troops were continually pushed up. Before the end of the first week in February all was ready, and on the 6th General Botha left Cape Town to take command. He was brought up by Admiral King-Hall in the *Armadale Castle*, and after arranging on the spot what was required of the navy, the Admiral returned to Simon's Bay. Now that all was in order for the operations to begin in earnest, the Admiralty considered his presence was more requisite at the other end of his station, where the *Königsberg* was still in being in spite of all attempts to destroy her. Accordingly, waiting only till the *Goliath*, which had arrived from Mombasa to refit, was ready for sea, he sailed in her on February 25 for German East Africa, whither the *Hyacinth* had preceded him; and Rear-Admiral O. F. Gillett, commanding the *Armadale Castle*, was left in charge at the Cape.[1]

[1] Admiral Gillett's force was the *Astraea*, and the two armed merchant cruisers *Armadale Castle* and *Laconia*. The *Laconia* was a new Cunarder of 18,000 tons, and 16 knots speed, and armed with 8-6″ quick-firing guns. *Armadale Castle* was 13,000 tons—17 knots—8-4·7″ guns.

Of all the oversea attacks that had been planned, that
against German East Africa had proved the most unsatisfactory. Since the ill-judged attempt on Tanga in November
had met with so sharp a reverse, land operations had been
at a standstill and the control of military operations had
been transferred from the India Office to the War Office. It
was obvious that the strength and preparedness of the enemy
had been entirely miscalculated, and General Wapshare, who
took over the command in December, was instructed to
confine himself to a defensive attitude, with liberty to undertake such minor offensive operations as he might find
practicable pending the provision of further force. Certain
operations of this character were undertaken, and a post in
German territory across the lower Umba—the frontier river
—was occupied. The post had to be abandoned next month,
and finally, at the end of January, we had retired to the line
of the Umba itself.

Naval operations showed little better progress. The
most active work was at Dar-es-Salaam. Towards the end
of November there was reason to believe that the floating
dock which had been sunk in the harbour no longer closed
the exit, and there was danger that the ships inside might
slip out and block our harbours at Mombasa and Kilindini.
It was therefore decided to destroy them, and remove all
coal lighters and small craft that could be used to supply
the *Königsberg*. The idea was to do the work with a couple
of small armed craft under threat of bombardment by the
Fox and *Goliath*. On November 28, when they appeared off the
port, the white flag was flying on the flagstaff, and the acting
Governor came off to the *Fox*. What was intended was
explained to him. He returned without giving a definite
reply, saying he must consult the military authorities.
After waiting an hour and seeing the white flag had not been
hauled down, Captain F. W. Caulfeild of the *Fox*, who was in
command, ordered the boats to proceed. Three vessels and
some harbour craft were disabled and their crews taken
off without opposition, but as the boats were coming out
they were fired on, though the white flag was still flying on
the harbour flagstaff. The resulting casualties were one
man killed, three officers and eleven men wounded and four
officers and eight men missing. In reply to the treacherous
attack the *Fox* and *Goliath* opened fire, and before dark
the Governor's residence was burned to the ground and many
other buildings demolished. Still in view of what had
occurred further punishment seemed necessary. Having
landed the wounded at Zanzibar the two ships returned on

November 30, and, after waiting all the morning flying a flag of truce without any reply, they began a systematic bombardment which so far as could be ascertained was of doubtful efficacy.

After the bombardment the *Fox* and the armed tugs *Adjutant* and *Helmuth* joined the *Chatham* in the blockade of the *Königsberg*, and the squadron was joined on December 3 by the *Kinfauns Castle* with another seaplane. Since there seemed no present possibility of getting at the *Königsberg* to destroy her, Captain S. Drury-Lowe's immediate object was to ascertain whether she was securely blocked in. For this a reconnaissance was necessary with his small craft or a seaplane. Our armed tugs were sent into the river, but were received with such heavy fire from hidden quick-firing and machine guns on the banks that they could not proceed. As for the seaplane, being unable to carry an observer, her work gave no very definite results, and finally, on December 10, she came down out of control in the estuary. Her pilot was taken prisoner, and though the machine was gallantly towed out under fire it was no longer serviceable. Enough, however, had been done to make it certain that besides the channel in which the *Newbridge* had been sunk there were two others by which the *Königsberg* could reach the sea. There was nothing for it, therefore, but to maintain the cruiser watch, and as the Admiralty wished to recall the *Chatham* for urgent service nearer home, they had to order the *Weymouth* up from the Cape to relieve her.

Nor was the *Königsberg* the only consideration. The deadlock ashore threw further burdens on the sea service. Thorny as was the situation, there was no thought of letting go when we had once taken hold. If assault was for the present out of the question, we could still fall back on investment. There was at least a hope that by establishing an effective blockade the 4,000 Germans in the colony could be starved into submission. This task the Admiralty agreed to undertake in the middle of December, but it was long before they could collect the necessary force. The coast to be watched extended for over 400 miles from our own East African territory to the Portuguese colony of Mozambique. The work of blockade, however, was facilitated by our possession of the islands of Pemba and Zanzibar, off the northern section of the coast. Half-way down was another large island, Mafia, which was a German possession. As it lay off the mouth of the Rufiji it formed a convenient base for operations against the *Königsberg*, and as a first step Captain Drury-Lowe had suggested its occupation by a small combined expedition.

This was approved. General Wapshare furnished six companies of native troops,[1] and on January 10 they sailed from Mombasa in the *Kinfauns Castle*, escorted by the *Fox*. As the German garrison consisted of no more than six Europeans and forty native police, there was little opposition, and two days later the island surrendered.

For the present, however, no blockade could be declared, as the ships available were too few in number to make it effective. By the middle of January, when Captain W. D. Church of the *Weymouth* took over the duties of Senior Naval Officer, the *Chatham*, *Kinfauns Castle* and *Fox* had left for Bombay to refit, and there was nothing but the *Weymouth* watching the Rufiji, with the two armed tugs, *Duplex* and *Adjutant*, and the *Pyramus* of the old New Zealand squadron, which had arrived to relieve the *Fox*. At the end of the month, however, the *Hyacinth* joined from the Cape in time to take over the watch on the Rufiji from the *Weymouth*, who was wanted elsewhere. So unhealthy had the posts on the Umba proved to be that in the first week in February it was decided to evacuate them, and the assistance of the *Weymouth* was required for withdrawing the troops. By February 10 the work was successfully carried out, and she was able to return to the Rufiji. In her absence the tugs had attempted another reconnaissance, during which the *Adjutant* had been lost. Coming under a severe fire which cut her steampipe she had to surrender, and her crew were made prisoners.[2] It was clear nothing more could be done till the seaplanes arrived, which the *Kinfauns Castle* was to bring on her return. In their impatience to get rid of the burden of the obnoxious cruiser the Admiralty had offered to provide 2,000 Marines if the General thought with their assistance she could be cut out by means of a combined operation. But the General regarded the plan as impracticable, and the Marines went to the Dardanelles instead, to provide Admiral de Robeck with a demolition force.

It was the middle of February when this idea was abandoned, and by that time the blockading force was nearly complete. The Australian light cruiser *Pioneer* had arrived, and also four steam whalers which had been taken up at the Cape and armed.[3] The *Kinfauns Castle* arrived shortly

---

[1] One half-battalion King's African Rifles, and a quarter-battalion of the 101st Indian Grenadiers.

[2] She was salved by the Germans and taken to Lake Tanganyika.

[3] *Pioneer* was a " P " class cruiser, like the *Pyramus*. The whalers were two German prizes detained at the outbreak of war—*Seeadler* and *Stürmvogel* and two British vessels—*Barrowby* and *Norvegia*—they had been renamed

afterwards with the seaplanes, and the blockade was formally declared to begin on March 1.

Before it had been in operation a week it had to be modified.   On March 7 Admiral King-Hall arrived at Mafia in the *Goliath* to find signs of so much activity in the Rufiji region as to indicate a probable attempt by the *Königsberg* to break out on the equinoctial tides.   He therefore thought it prudent to proceed there himself, and to keep both the *Weymouth* and *Hyacinth,* as well as two of the whalers, off the river, and leave the rest of the ships to do the best they could with the blockade.   His own hope was to have destroyed the hidden cruiser with the help of aerial reconnaissance or bombing, but the seaplanes proved unfit for the work, and the idea had to be abandoned.   Both by sea and land, except for a short bombardment of Lindi by the *Goliath,* the operations remained at a standstill, and the Germans could enjoy the spectacle of their impotent ship holding up a battleship and two light cruisers.   On March 25, however, orders came for the Admiral to shift his flag to the *Hyacinth,* and a week later the *Goliath* sailed for the Dardanelles.

Far more serious than the drain caused by the oversea expeditions during the first quarter of the year had been that caused by the German raiders still at large.   Their existence, indeed, had been the chief cause why the cruisers engaged in protecting the South African and Cameroons expeditions could not be reduced in number.   Fortunately, however, by the time it had become apparent that the Dardanelles enterprise must be conducted as a combined operation, sufficient progress had been made in clearing the outer seas to set free most of the ships originally devoted to the work for service elsewhere.

It will be recalled that after the Battle of the Falklands three enemy cruisers were at large : the *Dresden* had escaped from the action, the *Prinz Eitel Friedrich* had been left behind in the Pacific, and the *Kronprinz Wilhelm,* another armed merchant cruiser, was beginning to make herself felt in the Pernambuco area, in which the *Karlsruhe* had done so much mischief.   For practical purposes the *Karlsruhe* herself was still in existence.   Her loss was still unknown; both by ourselves and the German cruisers she was believed to be somewhere in the North Atlantic.   She had, indeed, become another " Flying Dutchman," being continually reported in various directions, and we have seen how the return of the

---

respectively *Pickle, Fly, Echo* and *Childers,* and were each armed with two 3-pounders from the *Goliath.*   They were from 160 to 180 tons.

Princess Royal to the Grand Fleet was consequently delayed by several weeks.[1]   Phantom as she was she could not be ignored, and directly after the battle the Admiralty set about providing a special squadron for dealing with her.   The idea was to separate the West Indies Station from North America, and reconcentrate at Jamaica the original Australian squadron (that is, the *Australia, Melbourne* and *Sydney*) under Vice-Admiral Sir George Patey.[2]   On its being represented to the Commonwealth Government that it was in the Atlantic the ships could be most effectively employed for the common good, they agreed with their usual readiness.

Admiral Patey, it will be recalled, had been on the west coast of America with the *Newcastle* and the Japanese ships on the look-out for Admiral von Spee; and he was now directed to leave the station under the command of Admiral Moriyama and proceed to Jamaica in the *Australia* by way of the Panama Canal.   The instructions for the Japanese Admiral—now that Admiral von Spee was disposed of—were to sweep south in search of the *Prinz Eitel Friedrich* and the German supply ships which were known to be on the coast.   But it was soon found that this arrangement could not be carried out.   The *Australia* was too long to pass through the canal locks, and she was consequently ordered to make for the Atlantic by way of the Strait of Magellan. On her way, in concert with the *Newcastle*, she would do the sweep south as far as Valparaiso, where the *Kent* and *Orama* from Admiral Sturdee's squadron would meet her sweeping north.   Admiral Moriyama was to remain north to watch the coast of Equador and the Galapagos Islands, and maintain wireless touch with Jamaica.   From Valparaiso Admiral Patey would make direct for his new station, but, until he arrived, the rearrangement of the North Atlantic area was not to take effect, and Rear-Admiral R. S. Phipps Hornby would continue to command the whole of it.

This was on December 12, and next day the news came from our Consul at Punta Arenas that the *Dresden* had put in there on the 11th, three days after the battle.   Admiral Sturdee's

---

[1] Within a week of her loss, on November 4, there had been a report in the Canaries that she had sunk, but it was not credited, and can only have been a rumour.   After the arrival of her survivors in Norway, at the end of November, it was whispered in Germany that she too had reached a home port.   These reports continued throughout January, but on February 17 Admiral von Koester announced that she was "continuing her activities in American waters, with success."   It was not till about March 19 that our Admiralty had definite evidence that she had been sunk for over four months.

[2] The *Melbourne* and *Sydney* had already been ordered to the Atlantic. See Vol. I., p. 401.

squadron was still at the Falklands, and the *Bristol*, which was the only ship ready for sea, was sent off at once. She arrived on the 14th, only to find the bird had flown.[1] As the *Dresden* was reported to have gone south from Punta Arenas, the *Bristol* carried on to the western entrance of the Straits, and with the *Glasgow*, who caught her up on the 15th, went up through Smyth's Channel and held on north to the Gulf of Peñas. There on the 17th they met Captain Phillimore in the *Inflexible*, who had swept round the Horn. Having been placed in charge of the search, he intended to send the *Kent* and *Orama* to work up the coast while he himself made a cast out to the Juan Fernandez Islands, which the Germans had been using so freely as a rendezvous. But this same day the Admiralty sent out the peremptory recall of both battle cruisers, and Admiral Sturdee ordered Captain Phillimore to return to Port Stanley. He himself had started for home on the previous day.

The station was now left in the hands of Admiral Stoddart. By Admiral Sturdee's orders he had been searching the Patagonian coast in company with the *Cornwall*. On taking over the command he sent his consort to examine Staten Island in the extreme south, and went himself into the Straits. Besides his flagship, *Carnarvon*, he had at his disposal for the Magellan area only the *Glasgow* and *Bristol*. The *Kent* and *Orama* were definitely engaged upon the Chilean coast, while the *Newcastle*, after her sweep down to Valparaiso with the *Australia*, went north again on the lookout for the *Prinz Eitel Friedrich*, and the *Cornwall*, after her search of the Staten Island, was allotted, with the *Otranto*, to watch the Falkland Islands.

In the maze of half-charted channels and inlets that made Tierra del Fuego and its confusion of desolate islands an ideal hiding-place, his means were slender enough for finding a cunning enemy, and in default of any intelligence it was difficult to know how to dispose his ships. He began himself, while the *Glasgow* and *Bristol* were completing their examination of the Chilean islands outside the Straits, by making a thorough search of Admiralty Sound, the great fjord which opens from the Strait south-east of Punta Arenas. Thence he turned back and entered the next inlet to the westward. This was Magdalen Sound, whence the Cockburn Channel leads out into the Pacific. Some ten miles within the Sound was a small bight known as Sholl Bay. It was a well-known charted anchorage, and here on the night of December 10 the *Dresden* had anchored, for it was by

---

[1] See Plan No. 5.

the Cockburn Channel she had made for Punta Arenas after rounding the Horn. On reaching Punta Arenas it is said the German Consul tried to persuade her commander, Captain Lüdecke, to suffer internment, but to his high credit, though he had already learned he was the sole survivor of the squadron, he refused, and resolved to carry on. Unknown to the Government at Santiago, he was permitted by the local authorities, against all law, to take in a large supply of coal, and to remain over thirty hours in order to complete his arrangements for a regular flow of supplies. He then, after dark on the 13th, disappeared to the southward, and, as we have seen, the *Glasgow* and *Bristol* followed in his wake in the afternoon of the 14th. But he was not making for the Pacific, as they assumed, for instead of following the westward turn of the Straits he continued south, either by Magdalen Sound or the less-frequented Barbara Channel, the next passage to the westward which separates Santa Ines and Clarence Islands. In any case the hiding-place he chose was Hewett Bay, close to the southern end of this little-known passage. There he anchored on December 14, and began cleaning his ship and repairing his engines as best he could.

He was thus occupied when, a week later, the *Carnarvon* reached Sholl Bay on the 22nd. Admiral Stoddart, however, did not carry his search further south, but went out again into the Straits, and after making a cast to the eastern entrance he turned back to meet his two cruisers at the Pacific end. The movement brought him on the direct tracks of what he sought. In the afternoon of the 26th, as he was proceeding westward, he found in Snug Bay the *Sierra Cordoba*, which was known to be a German supply ship, for it was she who, a month earlier, had brought the crew of the *Kronprinz Wilhelm's* prize, *La Correntina*, into Montevideo. She was now actually engaged as tender to the *Dresden*, but he could not touch her. She was in a neutral anchorage, and as the Admiral found a Chilean destroyer was watching his proceedings, it was to be presumed that the *Sierra Cordoba* was equally under observation to prevent unneutral service. After boarding her, he therefore went on to Fortescue Bay, opposite the northern entrance of Barbara Channel, and anchored there for the night. At the same time, whether by accident or design, the *Dresden*, at the southern end, slipped out of Hewett Bay, and proceeded to a still more secluded anchorage to the westward, on the south shore of Santa Ines Island. It lay behind the little Pleiades group in Stokes Bay, in waters which, as far as we knew, were uncharted, and was known as Port Loberu.

There it would seem the *Sierra Cordoba* proceeded to join her, when Admiral Stoddart's back was turned.

This she could do with impunity, for he now went on to the western end of the Straits. After meeting his two light cruisers he turned back, and, leaving the *Bristol* to examine Xaultegua Gulf, went on with the *Glasgow* to search Otway Water, the great inlet which opens out of the middle of the Straits to the northward. Finding nothing there he returned to Sholl Bay, and spent next day in a thorough search of the Cockburn Channel, in company with the *Glasgow*. Once more the scent was hot, for his search took him within fifty miles of the *Dresden's* new hiding-place, and within thirty of her old one. But again he turned back to Sholl Bay, and there the *Bristol* joined.

It was now the last day of the year, and his fortnight's search had led to nothing. Having thoroughly examined the Straits and all its main outlets, he decided to send away his light cruisers to the southward to work out the Beagle Channel and the coasts of Tierra del Fuego. He himself went on to Possession Bay, to guard the eastern outlet of the Straits, and on his way spoke Admiral Patey, who was then passing through the Straits in the *Australia* to take up his new station. After coaling at the Falklands he carried on north, keeping a sharp look-out for the *Eleanore Woermann*, a ship notorious for her activities in supplying German cruisers, which was known to have left Buenos Aires on December 1 renamed the *Anna*. On January 6, the first day out, Admiral Patey had the luck to fall in with her, and as the evidences of her guilt were plain, and he could neither spare a prize crew nor drag her along with him without great delay, she was sunk. The *Australia* then passed on her way, and on reaching the Abrolhos rocks to coal found orders to proceed to Gibraltar to dock.

Meanwhile the *Glasgow* and *Bristol* had rejoined Admiral Stoddart at Possession Bay on January 5 without having found a trace of the enemy to the southward, and leaving the *Glasgow* to patrol the eastern entrance, and sending the *Bristol* to the western end, he went to the Falklands to coal.

He was entirely baffled. The *Dresden* had covered her tracks apparently with complete success, but there was one man who had found her out. This was our Consul at Punta Arenas, Mr. Milward. After following the sea in his youth, he had been carrying on business there for seventeen years in partnership with a German. There was little he did not know of the region or of German ways, and his knowledge had enabled him to find out the locality to which the *Dresden* supplies were going.   On January 2 a French hunter came into Punta Arenas and reported that on December 2 he had seen her, with a tender alongside, in a bay south of Santa Ines Island and north of the Pleiades, that is, in the inner recesses of Stokes Bay, while a second tender was in a bay fifteen miles away.   There could be no doubt about her identity, for the Germans had boarded his boat.   This information the Consul telegraphed to the Admiralty on January 4, and he also communicated it to the Admiral, but unfortunately it was discredited.[1]   The region was uncharted, and moreover, being exposed, as the whole chain of the Patagonian Islands is, to incessant westerly gales and continuous storms of snow and sleet, no part of the world had a more forbidding reputation.   Consequently the Consul's report was regarded as more than suspicious.   It looked so much like the outcome of a German scheme to entice our ships into the dangers of remote and unknown waters in order to give the *Dresden* a chance of escaping, that the Admiral thought it unwise to act upon it, and, as we have seen, he went on to the Falklands without altering his dispositions.

A month had now elapsed since the battle had been fought, without any trace having been found either of the *Dresden* or the *Prinz Eitel Friedrich*.   The latter ship had, indeed, quitted the area.   As soon as she heard of Admiral von Spee's fate she realised it was impossible for her to keep the station, and decided to clear away from the coast before the British cruisers appeared.   Her point of refuge was the remote and lonely Easter Island, and on the way she captured another British ship and also a French sailing vessel with 3,500 tons of Welsh coal.   It was a godsend : after sinking the British ship, she towed her new prize to Easter Island, and there proceeded to establish herself in defiance of the Chilean authorities.   She even went so far as to keep an armed look-out party ashore, apparently expecting supply ships to reach her there.   But, exasperated by the German contempt for their neutrality, the Peruvian and Chilean authorities had interned every one of Admiral von Spee's tenders that had put into port, and were keeping so strict a watch on all German ships that their game was completely stopped. Accordingly, after spending about a fortnight at Easter Island, the *Prinz Eitel Friedrich* decided to attempt to reach a German port.   It was on January 6 she put to sea, meaning to make a wide sweep round the Horn into the Atlantic. This was also the day that Admiral Stoddart left Possession

[1] The telegram was not received by the Admiralty at the time.

Bay for the Falklands.   As he put out he overhauled, in the mouth of the Straits, a Dutch collier, and finding her papers suspicious, he detained her, and took her on to his base.   At the same time the *Australia* was capturing the *Eleanore Woermann*, thus, it would seem, dealing the last blow to the German coaling arrangements in the south.

The *Prinz Eitel Friedrich* was now as completely lost as the *Dresden*, and before the Admiral could renew the search for the hidden cruiser a fresh complication was introduced. When, on January 9, Admiral Stoddart reached the Falklands, he found that another raider had become active.   On January 3 a Hamburg-Amerika liner, called the *Otavi*, had put into Las Palmas with the crews of two ships, which the *Kronprinz Wilhelm* had captured a month previously in the region of St. Paul Rocks.   Ever since the *Bristol* and *Macedonia* had been called away from those waters to join Admiral Sturdee's squadron the whole of the Pernambuco focal area had been unguarded.   Notwithstanding its importance, it had been decided, in order to secure a full concentration against Admiral von Spee, to leave it to take its chance, as Admiral Cradock had originally suggested, and after the battle the home-going ships were so constantly passing through or near the area that it had seemed hardly necessary to detail special cruisers to watch it.   Now, however, it was obvious that further steps must be taken.

Admiral de Robeck, who at that time was still in command of the Canaries Station, was up at the Salvages, but returned to Las Palmas the day after the *Otavi* appeared. He quickly secured her internment, and as soon as he had ascertained the facts of the case, the *Highflyer*, with her two merchant cruiser consorts, *Marmora* and *Empress of Britain*, were sent from the Cape Verde Station to sweep the infected area.   The *Dartmouth* [1] also, which had been searching for the *Karlsruhe* on the Spanish Main, and was under orders for the Dardanelles, was to cross the area on the way to St. Vincent (Cape Verde).   But this area was not the only one threatened by the *Kronprinz Wilhelm's* reappearance. Until the *Otavi* appeared the last that had been heard of her was when the *Sierra Cordoba*, on November 22, had put into Montevideo with the crews of the prizes she had taken during October, both of which had been captured off the River Plate.   As Argentine maize and wool were now moving in vast quantities, and the no less important New Zealand meat trade was streaming through the area,

---

[1] This light cruiser, after the defeat of Admiral von Spee, had been moved from St. Helena to the West Indies.

it could not be left unwatched. Admiral Stoddart's squadron had to be drawn upon, and he had little enough as it was. The *Cornwall*, which had been watching the Falklands, had just been sent away to St. Helena, where the opening of the operations against German South-West Africa called for an increase of force, and there was nothing for it but to use the *Glasgow*. When therefore, on January 15, Admiral Stoddart was able to get back to the Straits, he sent her away up to Montevideo, with orders to search the anchorages along the Patagonian coast as she went.

It was likely enough the *Dresden* might be lurking in one of them, with the intention of striking the River Plate area or joining her consorts to the northward. But the Admiral, on his return to Punta Arenas, found the Consul more certain than ever that he knew where the chase was hiding. It appears that she had recently shifted her berth, and he had reason to believe she was at Kempe Island, the outermost of the group, that lies where the Cockburn and Barbara Channels meet. On this information the Admiral decided to act, and, after hiring a tug to search the more dangerous waters, he proceeded, on January 24, to Sholl Bay, in company with the *Bristol*, which had joined him from the western entrance of the Straits. On January 27 Kempe Island was reached, but nothing was found there. The Consul had mentioned several other anchorages in the vicinity which she might be using, but, unwilling to venture further into those wild and uncharted waters, the Admiral turned back, as much at a loss as ever. Yet he had been very close. She was actually only a dozen miles from Kempe Island, in the southern end of the Gonzales Channel, an unsurveyed passage that led from the Barbara Channel to Stokes Bay. Had the tug been permitted to search for another day in the vicinity the chase might well have been located, but, unfortunately, the Admiral sent her south to examine the Beagle Channel once more, while he, with the *Bristol*, spent the last days of the month in making another cast round Admiralty Sound. Nothing was seen, but in the early hours he actually passed a small steamer which was taking provisions to the *Sierra Cordoba*. He was then on his way from Sholl Bay to Punta Arenas, and on January 31 he sailed again with both ships for the Falklands.

The effect of his second failure was to convince him that the local information was either tainted or worthless, though in point of fact it was neither one nor the other. Admiral Stoddart was now strongly of opinion that the *Dresden* had left the inhospitable labyrinth of crags and glaciers and intended to work in the Atlantic. He therefore decided to give up the search of the Magellan area, and after cruising up the Patagonian coast as far as Montevideo, with the *Bristol* in company, to go north to Abrolhos Rocks. There he ordered the *Otranto* to escort his colliers, and the southern guard was left to Captain Luce, in the *Glasgow*, who had just returned from Montevideo.

The Consul, knowing provisions were still being sent to the *Dresden*, was sure she had not moved far away, but Captain John Luce did not feel justified in searching the locality again. The situation was undoubtedly difficult, and was made all the more so by the fact that the Germans, in order to get our ships out of the way, were secretly spreading rumours that the lost ship was hiding in one of the deep culs-de-sac which open out of the Straits to the northward. About February 10 one of these reports reached the Admiralty. It stated that the *Dresden* was in Last Hope Inlet; this is the remotest recess of the maze of intricate and almost inaccessible fjords which spread north-eastward from Smyth's Channel, and nowhere would our ships be so completely out of the way. Unlikely as it was that the *Dresden* would venture into waters whence there was no escape, the rumour was believed, and orders were sent from the Admiralty for the *Glasgow* to proceed there and for the *Kent* or *Orama* to get charts from Valparaiso and search it if it proved to be navigable. Two days later they telegraphed that the *Dresden* was actually at Port Consuelo, a little trading station in Last Hope, and ordered the *Bristol*, which was at Montevideo, to return and assist in the search. In vain the Consul protested that it was a transparent ruse to get our ships out of the way. The Germans had succeeded in getting him suspected, and the false scent was followed, as ordered, by the *Glasgow*, *Bristol* and *Kent*. The only result was that the *Bristol* seriously damaged her rudder on an uncharted shoal, and that Captain Luce made up his mind the Consul was right, and that the Admiralty were being deceived.

At Punta Arenas there was fresh news that, on February 14, the *Dresden* had been at the south end of the Barbara Channel, and on the strength of it, by March 3, Captain Luce was back at Sholl Bay, with the *Kent* and a small steamer called the *Galileo*, which the Consul had chartered. Proceeding to the south end of the Barbara Channel, the two cruisers worked up it, while the *Galileo* was ordered to make a cast round Santa Ines Island and rejoin them at the top of Barbara Channel. But it was too late. On February 4, that is, a week after Kempe Island had been searched

by Admiral Stoddart, she had put to sea. According to a
German account, she had been found in the Gonzales Channel
by a Chilean destroyer, and had been ordered to leave within
twenty-four hours.[1] Consequently, she moved westward to
the Grafton Islands, and, after lingering there for ten days
in the Wakefield Passage to coal from the *Sierra Cordoba*,
made off into the Pacific. It may be that the rumours
which the Germans had spread were to facilitate her escape,
but, in fact, they hampered her. Her intention, it seems,
was to run up to Talcahuano, the port of La Concepcion in
Northern Chile, there to intern herself, as her boilers were
almost burnt out. But hearing the wireless of our cruisers
that were coming down to search Last Hope, she changed
her destination to Juan Fernandez.

In spite of the fact that the search had discovered nothing,
the Admiralty still clung to the idea that she was in the
northern cul-de-sac, and, when, late on March 4, Captain
Luce reached the head of Barbara Channel, he was surprised
by an Admiralty order directing him to search Last Hope
again. That they should be twice so easily deceived affords
a striking instance of the danger of taking such operations
out of the hands of the men on the spot, who have the best
means of sifting local intelligence. But there was nothing
to do but obey, and, leaving the *Bristol* behind, as she could
now only steer with her engines, he went off to make the
search with the *Orama*.

But already, before the order reached him, the Admiralty
had other intelligence. It was that a collier called the *Gotha*
was under orders to meet the *Dresden* on March 5 at a rendezvous 300 miles west of Coronel, and, without changing
Captain Luce's orders, they told the *Kent* to go and capture her. The position indicated was actually one of the
rendezvous which the *Dresden* had fixed for her colliers
since the *Sierra Cordoba* was empty and had been dismissed;
and on February 27, while hovering about it, she had captured
and sunk the British sailing vessel, *Conway Castle*, transferring
the crew later on to a Peruvian ship. It was not, however,
till a week afterwards—that is, March 7—that the *Kent*
reached the spot. There was nothing there. Still she waited in
the hope she was not too late. Next morning was too foggy
to see anything, but in the afternoon the weather cleared,
and she found not the *Gotha*, but the *Dresden* herself, about
a dozen miles to the westward. Away she went in chase,
working up to 21½ knots, but, for all she could do, she could
not get within eight miles before nightfall, and then the

[1] *Weser Zeitung* (Bremen), July 13, 1915.

Dresden disappeared.   To continue the chase was impossible. The *Kent* had only 300 tons of coal left in her bunkers, and Captain J. D. Allen could do nothing but return to the rendezvous and send out a signal to report his encounter.

When Captain Luce got the message he was deep in the maze of the northern fjords, and it was impossible to pass through the narrow outlet till daylight.   But on the 9th he hurried off to join the *Kent,* and sent the *Orama* away to Possession Bay to order the colliers to the rendezvous at Vallenar.   The *Bristol* was, of course, useless till she had been docked.   The *Kent,* however, had gone to Coronel to coal, and Captain Luce waited on the *Dresden's* rendezvous till the morning of the 13th, where the *Orama* joined up. His intention was to seek the chase at Mas a Fuera, the outermost of the little Juan Fernandez group, which he knew the Germans had used.   It was a shrewd guess, and before he was ready to proceed he learned how nearly right it was.   In the nick of time it was ascertained that a collier was to meet the *Dresden* at Mas a Tierra, the main island of the group. The *Kent,* which, after a smart spell of coaling, had just left Coronel, was at once directed to the same destination, and a combined raid was arranged for the following day.

To ensure that the enemy should not escape, the *Glasgow* and *Orama* were to approach from the westward and the *Kent* from the eastward, and at daylight on March 14, precisely to time, all three ships were in position.   Whether the chase was actually there or not was still uncertain, but, as the *Glasgow* closed in from seaward, she was gratified to see the long dance was at its end.   There in Cumberland Bay, silhouetted against the precipitous cliffs, lay the *Dresden* at anchor, with her colours flying.   She was clearly not interned, and smoke in increasing volume was coming from her funnels, as though she meant to make a run for it.   Obviously there was no time to be lost.   The port was neutral, but the Chileans had been quite unable to assert the neutrality of their remote possession; the lonely group had been used by Germans, with notorious contempt for the Government; there was no one to enforce internment but the " Maritime Governor," and he was no more than the lighthouse-keeper.   Captain Luce could not hesitate, and, waiting only till he brought the houses of the little settlement out of the line of fire, he gave her a salvo at 8,400 yards.   It got home well on board her; the second struck all along her side.   She replied at once as the *Kent* joined in with her 6″ battery.   The punish ment was too severe to last, and in about three minutes she hauled down her colours and flew what appeared to be a white flag.[1]

Our ships then ceased fire and closed in. The enemy cruiser could be seen to be on fire, her crew were taking to the water and she was making a signal to communicate. In reply, a boat was sent off from the *Glasgow* with the Commander and Staff-Surgeon, but before they reached the burning ship the *Dresden's* steamboat was seen coming out under a flag of truce. On reaching the *Glasgow* the officer in charge stated he came from the captain to state that the ship was interned. This was certainly untrue, for she had refused to sail within twenty-four hours or to be interned. Captain Luce's answer was—as the tradition of the service required—that he could treat on no basis but that of unconditional surrender. As the boat returned another came out, bearing the lighthouse-keeper in his capacity as Maritime Governor. He was naturally agitated over our breach of neutrality, particularly as he had put out to meet our ships when they first appeared, and, having forgotten his flag, had narrowly escaped being sunk by our fire. Though he protested against the action that had been taken, he had to confess he had no power of controlling the German ship, and that she had been there ever since the *Kent* first chased her. All he had done, by his own account, was to send a boat to Valparaiso asking for a ship of war, and he expected her that night or next morning. Captain Luce offered full and immediate compensation for all actual damage done, and at the request of the Maritime Governor was arranging measures for disabling the enemy's machinery when the *Dresden* was seen to blow up.

On the return of her flag of truce with Captain Luce's reply, Captain Lüdecke had decided to put in action the preparations he had made for exploding her fore magazine. As the smoke of the explosion cleared she was seen to be slowly settling. In about an hour she was nearly gone, and, as she disappeared, her people lined up on shore and, led by the Captain, gave her dolefully " Deutschland über alles " for a dirge. Twenty of them had been killed or drowned in leaving the ship, and on shore were a number of wounded. To assist them all the medical staff of the squadron were sent in, and, as there was no means of treating them on the spot, they were taken off to the *Orama*. Till the next morning Captain Luce waited for the Chilean warship to appear, but there was no sign of one, and, after settling the

[1] Captain Lüdecke in his declaration said his colours were shot away and re-hoisted.

Governor's claims for damage in full, he sailed away, leaving the islands to the age-long loneliness from which they had been so rudely awakened by the limitless spread of the war.

Chile, of course, lost no time in protesting against the whole proceeding, not only to our Government, but to that of Germany as well. They were glad enough to be rid of the obnoxious cruiser, but their honour was touched. So far as we were concerned there was little difficulty in meeting the complaint. For months the *Dresden* had been violating Chilean neutrality. She had coaled at Punta Arenas, and stayed there over twenty-four hours. From there she had been supplied by tugs owned by the German Consul; in Chilean waters she had prepared herself for a new cruise, and when she was ready had sunk another British ship. A week before her destruction we had formally asked for her internment, and given friendly notice that, if she sought to escape our cruisers by taking refuge on a part of the Chilean coast where the Government had no means of detaining her, then, on the accepted principle of " hot chase," our captains would have to sink her where she was. On our Minister communicating this at Santiago, he was given to understand that our doctrine was accepted. On these lines, then, our reply was drawn, with a full expression of regret that in the circumstances there was no course for Captain Luce except to act as he did. The prompt apology was accepted as frank and courteous, and was in sharp contrast with the attitude of the Germans, who for at least six months did not even deign to reply. So far, then, from the incident having any evil effect, it rather increased the sympathy of the Chileans for the Allied cause as against that of the Central Powers.

In all our Staff studies of the question of commerce protection the moral effect of overriding the accepted principles of international law had always been regarded as a by no means negligible factor, and the surest guarantee that they would not be too flagrantly violated was that the failure to give them decent respect had always tended to raise up fresh enemies for the offending belligerent. We ourselves had learnt the lesson by bitter experience, and so had France, but Germany had not. It was not that she regarded neutral sentiment as amongst the *imponderabilia* that do not count. Indeed no more costly and elaborate efforts were ever spent than those she was lavishing on land to secure the goodwill of the American Republics. But she was too blind to see that they weighed little in the balance against what she was doing at sea.

In Brazil, which she had always regarded as specially subject to her influence, and where the ground had been most carefully prepared before the war, the same process was going on. Off the coast the *Kronprinz Wilhelm* was still active, and had been relying on supply ships from Brazilian ports. From Pernambuco had come the *Otavi*, which was now interned at Las Palmas. In another month a ship called the *Holger* was to follow. She had been detected in reporting departures of vessels to a German cruiser by wireless, and, finding herself under suspicion, had slipped out to sea on January 1 without clearance. The double violation of Brazilian regulations so irritated the Government that they resolved to refuse clearance to all the ships of any company that had once offended. They dismissed the captains of the port and guardship of Pernambuco, closed the Fernando Noronha wireless station and instituted an active search for secret and illicit installations ashore, and their neutrality became more warmly benevolent to the Allies than before.

The *Holger*, though narrowly escaping the *Inflexible* on her way homewards, succeeded in joining her cruiser. By that time the *Kronprinz Wilhelm* had captured another British vessel, the *Hemisphere*, 300 miles south of St. Paul Rocks, and well to the eastward of the usual tracks. She was a collier of 3,500 tons, a happy windfall, and from her the *Kronprinz Wilhelm* proceeded to coal. Where the *Holger* joined her is uncertain, but it was not at the rendezvous we had anticipated, for all that area was being thoroughly searched by the *Highflyer* and her two merchant consorts from Admiral de Robeck's squadron, without result. All we know is that she shifted her ground further north, and on January 10 captured the Royal Mail steamer *Potaro* of 4,400 tons, outward bound in ballast, and on the 14th the *Highland Brae*, a Nelson liner of 7,600 tons, with a general cargo and passengers for Buenos Aires. Both were carefully observing the latest Admiralty instructions about deviations of course. The same day she also captured and destroyed by ramming a small Nova Scotian schooner, the *Wilfred M.* The other two ships were retained. Being equipped with wireless, they were valuable auxiliaries, and with them she joined the *Holger*, apparently some eighty miles from where the *Highflyer* was searching.

This was on January 16, and the next fortnight was spent in gutting the *Highland Brae* and in disguising the *Potaro* and equipping her as an auxiliary. She was kept, but the Nelson liner was scuttled. During this period the raiders were in no little danger. British ships were all round them.

The last two captures were actually made within the area which the *Highflyer* was covering. On the 17th the *Australia*, on her homeward passage, passed close to the westward of them, and the *Dartmouth* did the same two days later. Still narrower was the escape from the *Canopus*, which, like the other battleships detached for support of cruiser squadrons, was on her way to the Dardanelles. As she proceeded she took in a signal from a merchantman saying that the *Kronprinz Wilhelm* and her consorts were off St. Paul Rocks. She therefore went out of her course to search the vicinity, but though she came across the waterlogged remains of the *Wilfred M.*, no other trace of the raiders was found. So she passed on, and as she neared St. Vincent, the *Highflyer* and her two consorts started for another sweep through the infected area. The *Kronprinz Wilhelm* was still working in it, and on February 3 had a narrow escape from the British cruisers close to the spot where she took the *Highland Brae*, and where she was scuttling the Norwegian barque *Semantha*, with wheat from Astoria (Oregon) to England.

By this time the *Prinz Eitel Friedrich*, after suffering terribly in the stormy seas south of the Horn, had reached the Atlantic, but, having no further hope of assistance, and being several knots slower than any British cruiser or armed liner, she did not dare to approach the fertile waters off the coast. She had to be content to cruise up the sailing track wide of the Plate, and here on the last days of January she had the luck to capture four ships. One was Russian, two were French and the fourth, the *William P. Frye*, a four-masted barque from Seattle to Queenstown, with wheat, was American. The first three were sunk out of hand. As the fourth was neutral, an attempt was made to jettison the cargo, but the work proved too difficult, and she too against all law was scuttled.[1] A fortnight later, on February 12, she captured another British wheat ship from Oregon, the *Invercoe*, but by that time it was clear her coal would not suffer her to cruise any longer. She therefore determined to run for internment to a North American port, doing what harm she could on the way. And she was not without success. On February 18 she approached the main steamer track to Pernambuco, and on that and the two succeeding days sank three more ships.[2] None of them was a collier,

---

[1] After a warm controversy over this ship with the United States Government, the Germans were forced to pay a large sum in compensation.

[2] *Mary Ada Short*, with 5,000 tons of maize, from the Plate to England; *Floride*, of the Cie. Générale Transatlantique; *Willerby*, outward bound from Havre to the Plate.

so she ran on across the track, passing between Fernando Noronha and St. Paul Rocks.

It was a hazardous movement, and it brought her within an ace of her end. On February 14 there had been a report that a German supply ship was proceeding to Lavandeira Reef, which lies at the east end of the north coast of Brazil. It was thought she was to meet there the *Kronprinz Wilhelm* and the *Karlsruhe*, which was still believed to be alive, and a combination was rapidly arranged for dealing with them. The *Sydney*, which had been watching German ships in Port San Juan, Porto Rico, and had just been relieved by the *Condé*, was directed to the spot. The *Edinburgh Castle*, which was bringing down two colliers fitted with wireless from St. Vincent (Cape Verde), was directed to meet her there, and Admiral Stoddart was ordered to come up from Montevideo and take charge of the operations. The result was that, on February 21, the *Edinburgh Castle*, making for the reef, and the *Prinz Eitel Friedrich*, going north, crossed each other's track quite close, about 150 miles north-north-west of St. Paul Rocks, but neither saw the other. The *Sydney* and *Edinburgh Castle* duly met at the suspected rendezvous on February 26, but the Admiral did not appear. On February 22 he had duly left Abrolhos Rocks for the north, but half an hour after weighing the *Carnarvon* struck an uncharted shoal and tore a rent 95 feet long in her bottom. She had to be beached, and was, of course, completely out of action. So there was nothing for it but for the Admiral to shift his flag to the *Vindictive*, which, since the *Canopus* had left for the Dardanelles, was guardship at the Abrolhos base. He was able, however, to patch up the *Carnarvon* sufficiently to send her into Rio, where, as she had suffered peril of the sea, the Brazilian authorities readily permitted her to dock. The accident was the more annoying, for next day the Admiralty had information that the *Karlsruhe, Dresden, Kronprinz Wilhelm* and a supply ship were going to meet at some unknown rendezvous. Some anxiety was felt lest it might portend an effort to deal a blow for the relief of the Cameroons, where the Germans were then making their effort to regain some of the positions they had lost on the coast, and the *Amphitrite* and *Laurentic* were ordered with all speed to St. Vincent (Cape Verde). In the Pernambuco area active steps were at once taken, and the *Sydney* and *Edinburgh Castle* made a cast to Rocas Island and Fernando Noronha. Nothing, however, was seen, and they carried on to join the Admiral at Abrolhos.

The *Kronprinz Wilhelm* was actually working at this

time well off the track, about 300 miles south-east of Fernando Noronha. Like the *Prinz Eitel Friedrich*, she, too, was almost at the end of her tether, owing to the rigorous hold the Brazilian Government was keeping on suspicious ships. But on February 22 she captured two prizes that were keeping wide of the track. One was the *Guadaloupe*, of the Compagnie Générale Transatlantique, with clothing for the French army and 150 passengers, and the other the *Chasehill*, with nearly 3,000 tons of British coal for the Plate. By this stroke of luck her life was prolonged, and for the next fortnight she lay drifting while she cleared her prizes. It was not till March 9 that the work was complete. She then sank the *Guadaloupe*, and sent the *Chasehill* into Pernambuco with the prisoners, while she herself held away north, but only just in time to save her skin. For next day the merchant cruiser *Macedonia*, which, after being re-armed with 6″ guns, was coming out to join Admiral Stoddart, ran over the spot where she had been gutting her prizes.

The general situation was now clearing. On the 9th the *Prinz Eitel Friedrich* had put into Newport News, and on the 12th the *Chasehill* arrived to reveal what the *Kronprinz Wilhelm* had been doing. Some difficulty was experienced in arranging further action against her. The West Indian squadron was fully engaged in watching German ships at Havana and Porto Rico, and the *Prinz Eitel Friedrich* had to be watched by the North American squadron, for the whole month passed away before the United States Government were satisfied that our demand for her internment was justified. As this squadron had also to keep its ceaseless guard off New York, there was nothing to do the work but the reduced squadron of Admiral Stoddart. Having shifted his flag to the *Sydney*, he proceeded to sweep the area indicated with the *Edinburgh Castle* and two colliers, but at the same time suggested that the *Liverpool* and *Gloucester*, which had been detached from the Grand Fleet at the end of February to sweep down the African coast in quest of the *Kronprinz Wilhelm*, should now come direct to Rocas Island to meet him. They were under Captain Edward Reeves of the *Liverpool*, who at the moment was at Sierra Leone coaling. On March 19, in response to an order from the Admiralty, he put to sea in company with two colliers which, as was now the usual practice, were fitted with wireless, so that they could act as scouts.

His original orders were to sweep the two zones in the vicinity of St. Paul Rocks and Fernando Noronha, where the *Kronprinz Wilhelm* was known to have been operating, but before he started it was possible to give him a more precise indication of where to find her. She was reported to be expecting two colliers. One of these was the *Odenwald*, which the *Melbourne* was now securely holding at Porto Rico. The other was the Hamburg-Amerika liner *Macedonia*. In the early days of the war she had run out of New Orleans to meet the *Kaiser Wilhelm der Grosse*, but she was still far away when that ship was sunk by the *Highflyer* on the Morocco coast. For months the *Macedonia* hung about in the Canaries, where, for fear of hurting Spanish susceptibilities, our cruisers were not permitted to watch her closely, and she was comparatively free, until at Admiral de Robeck's instance, she was finally interned at Las Palmas. Her machinery was partly disabled by the Port authorities, but in the course of time she managed secretly to repair it, and on March 15 quietly slipped her anchor and made off to find the *Kronprinz Wilhelm* at a certain rendezvous. It became known that it lay approximately on the equator, north of Fernando Noronha, and for this point Captain Reeves was ordered to make.

The *Kronprinz Wilhelm* was still in the same area cruising to the southward of St. Paul Rocks, and there, on March 24, five days after Captain Reeves started, she captured the Royal Mail steamer *Tamar*, with a rich cargo of 4,000 tons of coffee. Three days later, having moved about 100 miles to the north-westward—that is, towards the *Macedonia's* rendezvous—she fell in with the *Coleby*, homeward bound with 5,500 tons of wheat. Not only was the ship of no use to her, but it brought her one of her moments of acutest danger. For, as she was sinking her prize, Captain Reeves' ships, sweeping on a wide front to the westward, passed to the northward, and without sighting her, carried on to the rendezvous which had been given him.

He had missed her by barely sixty miles, but he had hardly taken up his assigned position when he was able to put an end to her career. While the *Gloucester* (Captain Howard Kelly) was patrolling there on March 28, in company with the *Liverpool*, she chased and captured a suspicious ship, which, on being boarded, was found to be none other than the runaway *Macedonia*. This ship, which was indispensable to the *Kronprinz Wilhelm's* continued activity, was made a prize and fitted with a spare set of wireless, and with this addition to his squadron Captain Reeves continued to patrol the vicinity of the rendezvous, keeping rigid wireless silence and expecting any hour to have sight of the cruiser he sought. But nothing appeared, and, in fact, all danger was now over.

A week earlier the Admiralty had been able to announce that the *Karlsruhe* was believed to have been lost in the West Indies at the beginning of November, and that the survivors of her crew had reached Germany in one of her tenders. This fact Captain Kelly also ascertained from the *Macedonia*. As for the *Kronprinz Wilhelm*, she never appeared at the rendezvous. By this time she badly needed docking. She had been seriously damaged in ramming the *Wilfred M.* and by coaling at sea, and sickness was rife on board. Moreover, she had little coal or provisions left, and despaired of meeting the supply ships she was expecting. From such wireless messages as she could hear, she believed herself to be surrounded by at least eight cruisers, and, according to her commander, on March 27 he decided to give up the struggle and run for a United States port. Even so she had another miraculous escape, for next day, as she went northward, she actually saw the *Gloucester* chasing the *Macedonia*, but she herself managed to get away before she was sighted. A few days later she intercepted a message saying that the *Prinz Eitel Friedrich* was in Newport News, and, as she had encountered no ship from which she could relieve her necessities, she eventually decided to join her there. By running in during the night without lights she avoided our watching cruiser and came to anchor safely on April 11.[1] Two days later orders were given for the squadron to disperse.

So ended the first phase of the German attack upon our seaborne trade. Never in the long history of our wars had the seas been so quickly and so effectually cleared of commerce destroyers, and in comparison with what had been anticipated, the whole campaign had been singularly ineffective. During the first eight months of the war the loss to British commerce in all seas was estimated at £6,691,000, and in that period the value of imports and exports to and from the United Kingdom alone amounted to £776,500,000. If we add to this the value of the tonnage employed we get a total actually risked at sea of not far short of a thousand million, so that the percentage of damage done was no more than two-thirds of one per cent. In so far as it could affect the issue of the war, so small an impression on the vast bulk of our seaborne trade was negligible, but already there had begun the new form of attack—the results of which were destined to surpass all previous experience, and to reach a total so formidable, that by comparison the losses of the first period, grave as they seemed at the time, and great

---

[1] Account given by her commander, Kapitänleutnant Thierfelder, *Weser Zeitung*, May 8, 1915.

as was the naval energy and thought that their suppression exacted, are now only remembered as a pin-prick.

By the time the original attack had been mastered and no raider was left upon the High Seas the new one had been already launched in Home waters. The submarine as a commerce destroyer was threatening to become one of the most formidable factors in the war at sea, and what it might achieve if brought to bear upon a large combined expedition, such as the Dardanelles venture was becoming, could only be regarded with grave concern.

CHAPTER XV

FEBRUARY 18, the day before the attack on the Dardanelles opened, was the day on which, in accordance with a notice issued by the Germans a fortnight earlier, their new departure in commerce warfare was to begin. The decision to adopt it had not been reached without misgiving. Admiral von Tirpitz, the Minister of Marine, though he looked forward eventually to a rigorous submarine attack on our seaborne trade, regarded the declaration of a war zone round the British Isles as an impolitic extension of legitimate naval warfare, mainly because it was premature. At the moment Germany had not enough submarines to blockade the whole of the British coasts effectively, and unless a blockade was effective under the terms of the Declaration of Paris it was not lawful, and neutrals would be placed in a position to resent it. His view was that the submarine blockade should be for the present confined to the Thames. It could then be defended as a legitimate extension of naval practice to meet the new conditions on all fours with our own extension of the doctrines of blockade and continuous voyage which neutrals seemed inclined to condone. Admiral von Pohl, however, who was now Commander-in-Chief, High Seas Fleet, took the opposite view. It was he who had fathered the policy for which the country was clamouring more and more loudly, and it was he who had the ear of the highest quarters. The result of the Dogger Bank action had completed in the Kaiser's mind the impression which Heligoland had begun. He was resolved more than ever to keep in being the fleet he had created, and his impatience to see his submarines at work increased with his stiffening determination to deny the fleet all offensive action.[1]

The precise step which the new departure marked in the degradation of German policy at sea must be clearly apprehended. Hitherto, apart from sowing mines in the open sea, they had fairly well observed the accepted limitations of naval warfare. On the high seas, beyond the fact that in

[1] Von Tirpitz, *My Memoirs*, Chap. XIX., *et passim*, Eng. Ed.

one or two cases they had availed themselves too freely of the
right to sink neutral prizes in case of necessity, there had
been little to be ashamed of. In Home waters, as we have
seen, there had recently been some inexcusable cases of
destruction of merchant ships without warning, and with no
attempt to save life, and one shameless attack on a hospital
ship, but their offences had been sporadic—explainable
possibly by the perverted zeal of individual officers who had
lost their heads.[1] Until all their cruisers had been swept
from the sea, and our command according to accepted standards was fully established, there had been no indication of
deliberate and organised lawlessness. Now, however, when
they saw their trade completely paralysed and our own
enjoying full freedom of movement, they threw off all disguise.
Following the semi-official warnings to neutrals—already
referred to—the German Admiralty, on February 4, issued
their declaration forbidding all traffic in British waters.
Though lacking in definiteness, its intention was not in doubt,
and at last our eyes were opened to the fact that Germany
did not mean to shrink from extending to the sea the lawlessness of which she had from the first been guilty on land.
The text of the official notice was as follows :—

" All the waters surrounding Great Britain and Ireland,
including the whole of the English Channel, are hereby
declared to be a war zone. From February 18 onwards every
enemy merchant vessel found within this war zone will be
destroyed without its being always possible to avoid danger
to the crews and passengers.

" Neutral ships will also be exposed to danger in the war
zone, as, in view of the misuse of neutral flags ordered on
January 31 by the British Government, and owing to unforeseen incidents to which naval warfare is liable, it is impossible

---

[1] Up to February 18 the following losses by German mines and submarines
had occurred :—

Sunk by submarines • • •	{	11 British merchant vessels.
		1 Allied merchant vessel.
Sunk by mines • • •	{	15 British merchant vessels.
		18 British fishing craft.
		4 Allied merchant vessels.
		38 neutral merchant vessels.
Damaged by submarine • • •		1 Allied merchant vessel.
Damaged by mines • • •	{	6 British merchant vessels.
		3 neutral merchant vessels.

(*N.B.*—Of the British ships sunk by submarines four were torpedoed
without warning, as was the Allied ship damaged. Of six British ships which
escaped two appear to have been attacked without warning. One of these
was the hospital ship *Asturias.*)

to avoid attacks being made on neutral ships in mistake for those of the enemy.

" Navigation to the north of the Shetlands, in the eastern parts of the North Sea and through a zone at least thirty nautical miles wide along the Dutch coast is not exposed to danger."[1]

This notice was accompanied by a long memorandum justifying the action of the German Government on the ground that we had been carrying on war against their commerce in defiance of all the principles of international law.   In particular, it alleged that we had added to the list of contraband various articles not useful for military purposes, and in applying the doctrine of ultimate destination had actually abolished the distinction between conditional and absolute contraband.   Not content with overriding the rules of the Declaration of London, which they themselves, so they claimed, had strictly observed, we had violated the Declaration of Paris by seizing in neutral vessels German property which was not contraband.   They further charged that " in violation of our own decrees concerning the Declaration of London," we had also removed from neutral ships German subjects liable to military service and made them prisoners of war.[2]   Their final point was that we had declared the whole North Sea a military area, and thereby set up a blockade of neutral coasts.   By thus seeking to paralyse legitimate neutral trade, our obvious object was not only to strike at German military strength, but also at their economic life, and ultimately by starvation to doom the population to destruction.

Were it not that the world had become used to the effrontery of similar German declarations, it was scarcely to be believed such a defence was put forward seriously.   So far from strictly observing the Declaration of London, Germany had consistently ignored it in her treatment of neutral prizes. As a mere matter of convenience, her cruisers had made a practice of sinking them even in cases where the ship was not liable to condemnation in a Prize Court, and where it was impossible to pretend that sparing the ship would involve danger to the safety of the cruiser and to the success of her operations.   The Declaration provided expressly that to

---

[1] Translated from the *Reichsanzeiger*, February 4, 1915.
[2] The allusion is presumably to the Order in Council of August 20, 1914, adopting the Declaration with certain modifications.   The article referred to is No. 47, which provides that " any individual embodied in the armed forces of the enemy who is found on board a neutral merchant vessel may be made a prisoner of war."   This article was not amongst those modified by the Order in Council.

justify occasional departures from the rule the captor must show that he had acted " in the face of an exceptional necessity," and the report explained that " danger " meant a danger that existed " at the actual moment of the capture." In seven carefully guarded articles, the Declaration had made all this clear, yet in spite of them, the German cruisers had consistently made the exception the rule.[1]

Moreover, it was untrue that we had put on our list of contraband articles not useful in war. The accusation was presumably made to cover their own irregularity in the matter. On November 17 they had declared all ordinary wood and lumber unworked or only roughly worked to be contraband, as being capable of being used as fuel within the meaning of the 24th Article of the Declaration of London. Mining timber and paper wood were expressly included, and under this order they proceeded to detain in the Baltic neutral vessels laden with pit-props and similar cargo. By a supplementary notice of November 23, they had declared that the order extended to all woods hewn, sawn, planed or grooved, so that all timber except certain hard foreign woods like mahogany were constituted contraband as being fit for fuel. In no case had our orders so perversely strained the doctrine of contraband.

Their contention that we had gone far to abolish the distinction between absolute and conditional contraband had more justification, but they had also done the same, as in the case of the *Maria*.[2] This, however, was a minor point. The speciousness of the German case is not fully revealed till we come to the accusation that we had made prisoners of men not embodied, but only liable to military service, found in neutral ships. We had certainly done so, and had thereby violated the letter of one article in the Declaration of London which we had not repudiated. But to our declared reasons for doing so, the German memorandum did not venture to

---

[1] There were three known cases of German cruisers capturing neutrals bound to belligerent ports with contraband, and they had sunk them all. The *Maria* (Dutch), sunk by the *Karlsruhe*, September 21, 1914; the *William P. Frye* (American), sunk by the *Prinz Eitel Friedrich* on January 28; and the *Semantha* (Norwegian), sunk by the *Kronprinz Wilhelm*, February 3. In none of these cases was there exceptional danger to the ship, nor could releasing the prizes have endangered the success of the operations, which were to harass enemy trade.

[2] The Dutch ship *Maria*, which the *Karlsruhe* had sunk, was bound for Belfast and Dublin with wheat, and although at that time, September 21, 1914, Dublin at least was not a naval port, the action of the cruiser was upheld by the German Prize Court on the plea that although the cargo was consigned to civilians it might be requisitioned by the Government.

refer. Those reasons were her flagrant breaches not only of the letter, but also of the spirit of the Hague Conventions. On these conventions she was silent. Yet the Hague Conventions were solemnly ratified acts that had passed into the written Law of Nations, and the Declaration of London was unratified and bound nobody. From the outset, they had trodden the conventions underfoot as it pleased them. They had begun by sowing mines of illicit type broadcast in the open sea, and not content with seizing British ships in their ports at the outbreak of war without conceding the usual Days of Grace, they had imprisoned the crew of one that was sunk by a mine in the Elbe before war was declared.[1] On land their violations had been still more flagrant and numerous. The special offence in point was that in France and Belgium they had made prisoners of war of all male inhabitants who were of military age. It was in retaliation for this, that we had declared our intention of extending to all men of military age our right to arrest from neutral ships men embodied in the enemy forces. Though the German memorandum was guiltily silent on the point, the evidence was considered conclusive at the time, and the Prime Minister had announced it in Parliament on November 17, 1914. Compared with the magnitude of the provocation, the retaliation fell far short of an equal adjustment of account, and could by no means warrant further steps by the enemy.

As to their accusation that in breach of the Declaration of Paris we had confiscated enemy goods in neutral ships, it was not true; and if it had been, it did not lie in their mouth to make it. For though by the Declaration innocent neutral goods were free under an enemy flag, they claimed the right to sink enemy merchant ships without paying indemnity for neutral cargo they carried.[2]

The real German grievance was, as the memorandum clearly suggests, that we were endeavouring to paralyse the economic life of the nation. We certainly were, and with perfect justice, for this is the ultimate object of all war, and it is to give a belligerent the power of exerting such pressure that he seeks to destroy the enemy's armed forces.[3]

[1] *San Wilfrido*, a tank steamer returning empty from Hamburg.

[2] The claim by Norwegian owners for compensation in the case of the British ship *Glitra* (Grangemouth to Stavanger), the first ship sunk by a submarine, was dismissed on appeal, apparently on the ground that if indemnity had to be paid for neutral cargoes enemy ships would often have to be released.

[3] This view in regard to foodstuffs had been officially recognised thirty years previously by the Germans themselves. In 1885, at the time when His Majesty's Government were discussing with the French Government this

Otherwise their destruction would bring the hope of peace no nearer. We had already acquired the power by having established a domination over the enemy's naval forces, such as they could not venture to dispute by any means that had hitherto been regarded as legitimate. Equally untenable was the excuse of our having abused neutral flags. It was not even true that the alleged order had been given. But on January 31, after the publication by an American journalist of an interview with Admiral von Tirpitz, in which a submarine war on commerce was adumbrated, and after three British merchant ships had been torpedoed without warning, the Admiralty did issue a confidential instruction advising merchantmen to keep a sharp look-out for submarines, and when near the British Isles to show either neutral colours or none at all. It was a well-established ruse of war, which all nations had practised as a matter of course. By no means could it justify a revolution in the code of civilised warfare, and in any case it was issued after the new German policy had been sanctioned.[1]

On the other hand, the firm conviction which we then held that they themselves had been abusing the neutral flag in a wholly unprecedented manner, was regarded as the main justification of our own war zone.

It will be remembered that on November 2, 1914, just

---

question of the right to declare foodstuffs not intended for the military forces to be contraband, and when public attention had been drawn to the matter, the Kiel Chamber of Commerce applied to the German Government for an official statement of their views on the subject. Prince Bismarck's answer was as follows :—

" In answer to their representation of the 1st instant, I reply to the Chamber of Commerce that any disadvantage our commercial and carrying interests may suffer by the treatment of rice as contraband of war does not justify our opposing a measure which it has been thought fit to take in carrying on a foreign war. Every war is a calamity, which entails evil consequences not only on the combatants, but also on neutrals. These evils may easily be increased by the interference of a neutral Power with the way in which a third carries on the war, to the disadvantage of the subjects of the interfering Power, and by this means German commerce might be weighted with far heavier losses than a transitory prohibition of the rice trade in Chinese waters. The measure in question has for its object the shortening of the war by increasing the difficulties of the enemy, and is a justifiable step in war if impartially enforced against all neutral ships."—*Correspondence Relating to the Rights of Belligerents*, Cd. 7816 (1915), p. 15.

[1] It seems clear that our alleged abuse of the neutral flag was not regarded by the Germans themselves as a serious point in their case. The clause was added at the last moment at the instigation of Admiral von Tirpitz, after the policy had been decided in spite of his opposition and behind his back. His fear was that the new departure would alienate neutrals, and his proposal was probably no more than a last effort to avert the worst of their resentment. (See Von Tirpitz, *My Memoirs*, Vol. II., p. 398.)

after the *Audacious* and the *Manchester Commerce* had been
lost on the minefield which the *Berlin* had laid, as was then
believed, under neutral colours, we had issued a notice that
as secret minelaying in the open sea under a neutral flag had
become the common practice of the Germans, counter-
measures had become necessary which would render the North
Sea unsafe for navigation, and that all ships passing between
Iceland and the Hebrides would do so at their peril.   Traders
to and from Scandinavia, the Baltic or Holland, were therefore advised to proceed by the Channel, between which and
their destination a safe route would be given them.

Clearly, then, the measure did not amount to a blockade
of neutral ports, and though an extension of former practice,
it was not without precedent.   During the Russo-Japanese
war, the right to declare an area of active operation a prohibited zone had been exercised without question, and it could
not be pretended that the narrow waters of the North Sea,
lying as they did between the coasts of the opposed belligerents, was not an area of active operation.   The waters we
closed were actually those which lay between our own and the
High Seas Fleet.   But granted that the German extension
of the precedent was legitimate, it was not this which we
reprobated, so much as their claim to destroy at sight, without
visit or identification, without thought of innocent life, every
ship that entered the vaguely defined area.[1]

The threat to neutrals was undisguised, but it is possible
that to the German Government the atmosphere seemed
favourable, and that this was why they would not listen to
Admiral von Tirpitz's warning.   The only neutral they had
to fear was America, and at the moment the relations between
the United States Government and our own appeared to be
strained.   In the cotton districts of the South, where lay
the President's chief political support, the shrinkage of available tonnage for exporting the crops was being severely felt,

---

[1] Admiral von Tirpitz seems to have taken a similar view.   When the
plan of the war zone was submitted to him by Admiral von Pohl he wrote
in his reply (December 16): " The reference to the measures taken by the
English, in proclaiming navigation in the North Sea dangerous, does not seem
to me apt.   The English have not declared these waters to be dangerous simply
as a result of their own action, but on the ground of their allegation (false,
I agree) that we had laid minefields there and that neutral ships were exposed to the danger of being mistaken for German minelayers and treated
as such."   From this and other passages in his book it is noteworthy that
he does not seem to have known that German minelayers had laid mines
in the open sea.   Presumably he believed they had carried out the declared
intention of laying them in the entrances of our ports (*My Memoirs*, Vol. II.,
p. 394).

and to relieve it the President was pressing a bill authorising the purchase by the State of German ships held up in American ports.   The admissibility of such a transfer of flag in war-time was more than doubtful, even if the purchase was made by a neutral Government, but the situation had been intensified just before the new year by the announcement that the German ship *Dacia* had been sold to a New York firm, and had been given an American register to enable her to take a cargo of cotton from Texas to Germany.   We at once intimated that we must reserve our rights as to recognition of the transfer.[1]   It was clearly a test case, for options had been secured on a number of other German vessels.   Negotiations followed during January, but as each side fully sympathised with the other's embarrassments, they were of a very friendly character.   The outcome was, that as there was no question of principle between us, but only the question of *bona fides*, the ship, if captured, would have to go into the Prize Court; but we agreed, in order that the shippers should suffer no loss, that we would pre-empt the cargo at the price the Germans had agreed to pay.   On this understanding, so far as we were concerned, things were left to take their course, but our arrangement could not bind France, whose view of the law was severer than our own.   For her there could be no doubt, and, in fact, on January 24, while the matter was still under consideration in London, the Ministry of Marine informed us that orders had been given to the Admiral of their Western Patrol to capture the *Dacia* if she was sighted by one of his ships.   This decision did much to ease the situation, for as at this time the Western Patrol consisted of six French cruisers and only three of ours, the probability was that the *Dacia* would fall into French hands.   In the end this was what happened.   On February 27 a French ship captured her. As between ourselves and the American Government, the main result of the affair was further to impress them with our earnest desire to make things as easy for neutrals as possible, and if the incident did anything to affect the American attitude to the German war zone, it was certainly not what the Germans wished or appeared to expect.

As was only natural, a protest from Washington against the German declaration was neither slow in coming nor wanting in precision.   In a note of February 12 the United States Government reminded Berlin that the sole right of belligerents in

---

[1] Such transfers had been disallowed by the Declaration of London and the German Prize Manual.   Previous to the Declaration France and Russia had held them to be illegal in any circumstances, while Great Britain and the United States of America held them illegal unless made *bona fide*.

dealing with neutral vessels on the high seas was limited to visit and search, unless blockade was not only proclaimed, but effectively maintained.   To declare or exercise the right to attack and destroy any vessel entering a prescribed area of the high seas without first establishing her belligerent nationality or the contraband nature of her cargo, would be an act so unprecedented that they were reluctant to believe that Germany really contemplated putting the declaration in force.   Should such acts be committed, they added, the American Government could only regard them as an indefensible violation of neutral rights, which would be very hard to reconcile with a continuation of friendly relations between the two countries.

In their reply, which was dated February 17—the day before the war zone was to be put in operation—the Germans avoided meeting the American case in so far as it rested on established law.   To confuse the issue they made play with their afterthought as to the abuse of neutral flags, and introduced the question of our arming of merchantmen, which, as they contended, made visit and search impracticable—that is, impracticable for submarines, the only means they had left.   Their real defence was implicitly based on two contentions, both of which were new.   One was that neutral traffic in contraband was not legitimate trade, and the other that an attempt to starve an enemy into submission was not legitimate warfare.   So long therefore as neutrals submitted to our interference with their import of foodstuffs, they intended to stop contraband trade by all means in their power, fair or foul.

The chief flaw in the German case, as thus presented, was that we were not treating foodstuffs as contraband.   It is true that on August 20, when it was reported that the German Government had assumed control of foodstuffs, orders had been issued to the fleet that such cargoes were to be detained.[1]   That order had not been cancelled, but as it was ascertained that the report was erroneous, foodstuffs, except when consigned to an enemy's naval port, had never been put in the Prize Court; they were dealt with by pre-emption or agreement by a special committee set up for the purpose.   The trade was simply diverted to our own ports, so that while it failed to reach the enemy, neutrals suffered little or no loss, and gained a nearer and more convenient market.   It was a method not without precedent, for we had used it freely with

---

[1] This order was issued to the fleet with the Order in Council of the same date by which we adopted the Declaration of London with certain modifications.   The chief of them was that conditional contraband was subject to the doctrine of continuous voyage.

America during the war of the French Revolution. At that time the settlement of the vexed question of whether food could be made contraband or not was thus avoided by a compromise, and as between ourselves and America the plan had worked with full contentment. France, of course, had not been appeased, indeed she had protested so vehemently, and the United States had so warmly resented dictation as to where they were to sell their goods, that the two countries came to the brink of war, just as Germany and America seemed to be approaching it now. From all points of view, therefore, the system on which we had been acting promised well, and particularly as our power of inducing the compromise in the present war was much greater than before; for, owing to our control of the Marine Insurance market, it was very difficult for neutrals to obtain war risk policies for voyages across the mine-infested North Sea.

So securely, indeed, had the Germans blockaded themselves by minefields that direct voyages of neutrals, except within the Baltic, were so few as hardly to come into the question.[1] The trouble arose almost entirely over goods consigned to Dutch ports, and these imports were becoming so far above normal as to raise by their very volume a presumption of enemy destination. However, on October 1 we had so far relaxed the strict orders to the fleet as to exempt from detention all cargoes of foodstuffs not exceeding a hundred tons, and in November, in concert with our Allies, we offered to let all pass if the Dutch Government would constitute themselves sole consignees of foodstuffs, as they had already done with copper and petroleum, with a guarantee that they would not reach the enemy. To this compromise the Dutch Government agreed early in December.

American trade was no less seriously affected, and at the end of the month the United States Government presented a note protesting against our proceedings in treating foodstuffs consigned to neutral ports as contraband on mere suspicion that they might reach the enemy. But Sir E. Grey was able to reply that we had not, in fact, done so. Fully admitting the principle on which the United States of America insisted, he pointed out that we had never detained and put into the Prize Court foodstuffs in the absence of presumption that they were intended for an enemy Government, and to this rule it was still our intention to adhere, but no unconditional undertaking could be given in view of the enemy's

---

[1] No ship is recorded in *Lloyd's List* as having reached a United States port from Germany since the war began. The first arrival listed is that of the Swedish s.s. *Ran* on February 19, 1915, from Lübeck to Boston.

progressive violation of the hitherto accepted rules of civilised warfare.

So matters stood, till on January 25 the German Government announced its intention of taking over the control of all foodstuffs as from February 1. This measure, on the doctrine of their own Prize Court, entitled us to treat such cargoes as contraband, and the United States' ship *Wilhelmina* with wheat consigned to an American firm in Hamburg was seized at Falmouth and put into the Prize Court. The American Government objected on the ground that the cargo was intended for the civil population, and that the ship had sailed before the recent German food order. To this we replied that if Scarborough was a fortified place, as the Germans contended, Hamburg was certainly in the same category. Eventually the case was settled out of court. But by this time Germany had issued her declaration of the war zone, and in replying to the American protest Sir E. Grey, in accordance with his previous intimation, had indicated that the time seemed now to have come when we should be forced to treat all foodstuffs as contraband in retaliation for Germany's persistent breaches of International Law.

Till the eleventh hour we, no less than the Americans, were " reluctant to believe " that she would put her threat in force. During February there had been very few attacks. On the 15th the *Dulwich* was torpedoed without warning off Havre, and the French steamer *Ville de Lille* was sunk off Cape Barfleur by *U 16*. The most notable attack was that on the *Laertes*, a Holt liner bound from Liverpool to Amsterdam on her way to Java. About 4.0 in the afternoon of February 10, some twelve miles from the Schouwen bank light-vessel, off the estuary of the Schelde, her commander, Captain Propert, sighted a submarine about three miles on his starboard bow. As he altered a little to avoid her she summoned him to heave to, but instead of complying he ordered the engines to be opened out to the full and made all ready for abandoning ship. Seeing his intention to escape, the submarine, *U 2*, made straight for him at top speed, while he manœuvred to bring her right astern. The submarine quickly closed, and at about three-quarters of a mile opened fire with machine-guns and rifles. The *Laertes* was unarmed and could do little more than 11 knots at best, so as the chase went on the enemy gained, firing briskly all the time. Still, though a good deal of damage was done to the bridge, boats and upper works, no one was hit. By 5.15, that is, after an hour's chase, the submarine was within a quarter of a mile and there seemed little chance of escape. Then suddenly she slowed down, but the danger was not yet over, for now she fired a torpedo. Its track was seen, and by a smart change of helm avoided by a few yards. The submarine, which seemed to be in difficulty, then gave up the chase, and Captain Propert was able to bring his riddled ship safely into Ymuiden without a single casualty. For this fine performance he was given a commission as Lieutenant R.N.R. and the D.S.C., while all his officers and crew received suitable recognition.

The resource and spirit displayed by all concerned was very timely. For as an example it gave hope that even if the Germans did proceed to extremities the worst they could do would have no appreciable effect on our trade, so long as it kept moving. This important consideration was put clearly forward by the First Lord in introducing the Naval Estimates on February 16. Without disguising the fact that losses must be expected, the Admiralty believed that no vital impression could be made if traders put to sea regularly with proper precaution and acted in the spirit of the *Laertes*. The response of the shipowners and the Mercantile Marine was all that could be desired. During the first week after the war zone had come into force, although owners had been warned that the enemy would probably begin with a supreme effort in order to make a paralysing impression, there was no diminution of sailings or arrivals that could be traced to the threat. The little fall that occurred was almost entirely in coasting vessels, and this was due to the ports being specially congested at the time.

But for all the confidence of the shipowners, the prospect of the coming attack could only weigh heavily on those who were responsible for meeting it. The German declaration had been made at a moment when our still incomplete patrol system was in a state of disturbance, owing to the appearance of the submarines off Liverpool bar in the last days of January. At the same time information had been received from our Legation at Copenhagen that in a week's time the Germans intended to begin an organised submarine attack on the cross-channel communications of the army. The announcement was all the more serious, since in the second week of the month the Canadian division was due to sail for France, and in order to deal with submarines in the Irish Sea a whole flotilla of destroyers had been detached to that area. If the enemy's operations off Liverpool were intended to confuse our control of the Channel and its approaches, they could scarcely have been more cleverly designed, but from the first alarm the Admiralty had been taking energetic and comprehensive measures to counter the German move.

As a first step, it was finally decided to withdraw the slow old cruisers of our Western Patrol and to assign Portland as a coaling base for the faster French merchant cruisers which had been acting with them, leaving on the station no ships of our own beyond a few boarding steamers. Our own share of the work was, in fact, to be done by the Devonport Patrol, whose area (No. XIV) covered the home side of the Western Patrol area, and measures were taken to increase its force, as well as that of other areas, by ordering no less than a hundred more trawlers to be armed with guns. At the other and more important end of the Channel a plan for blocking the eastern entrance to the Straits of Dover with a new minefield south-west of our existing one had been settled. At the end of January it was communicated to the French, and with a slight modification approved by them. The work was commenced at once and completed by February 16. By this means, and the new device of indicator nets, it was hoped to render the passage of the Dover Straits at least highly dangerous for submarines.[1]

Experiments with these nets had been in active operation for some time, and gear had been devised by which they could be run out with great rapidity. They were to be operated by special flotillas of net drifters, which, being unarmed, were to be attended by patrol yachts or other vessels furnished with guns and explosive sweeps. By February 13 seventeen miles of these nets had been laid across the Dover Straits; other flotillas were ready for St. George's and the North Channels, and next day an order was issued establishing net bases all round the coasts.[2]

As a further precaution, it was now decided to extend the principle of defensive armament to vessels engaged in Home waters. Fifty were to be armed at once and two marines allotted to each to work the guns; half of these ships were to be Admiralty colliers or storeships working to France, and half west coast and Channel traders not going north of the Clyde or the Thames.

All these measures, extensive as they were, could be taken without any disturbance of the general strategic distribution of the fleet, but they were not enough. There

---

[1] See foot-note (1), p. 18.

[2] The first instituted were as follows: for Scotland—Scapa, Cromarty, Peterhead, Firth of Forth; for the East Coast—Yarmouth, Harwich, the Nore and Dover; for the Channel—Portsmouth, Poole, Portland, Devonport and Falmouth; others for the Irish Sea and West Coast were to be established as soon as possible at Larne, Milford Haven, Queenstown, the Clyde and Liverpool. Nets were being supplied as fast as possible, and on February 24 a number were sent out to the Dardanelles.

still remained the question of escort for important navy
ships and liners entering or leaving dockyard or commercial
ports, as well as for transports and special munition ships.
For this a radical redistribution of destroyers was found
necessary. The eight destroyers originally assigned to the
defence of Scapa were ordered south, to join the Dover Patrol,
and to escort transports sailing from Plymouth and Avonmouth. A flotilla of twelve coastal destroyers (now classed
as torpedo-boats) which had been under the Admiral of Patrols
on the east coast, were also assigned for Channel escort,
and the area for which he was responsible was reduced, so
that Area **X**, south of Winterton Ness, came under Harwich.
Provision for Channel escort was completed by abandoning
the idea of absorbing the eight " Beagles " at Portsmouth
into a new 10th Flotilla. They were to remain under Admiral
Meux, and the 10th Flotilla was confined to the *Aurora* and
" M " class destroyers.

Finally, on the day the war zone came into force, the
Western Auxiliary Patrol areas were reorganised in accordance
with their increased importance by making them flag officers'
commands. The Larne, or North Channel area, was given
to Admiral Barlow; the Kingstown, or Irish Channel area,
to Rear-Admiral E. R. Le Marchant; and the Milford area,
which included the St. George's and Bristol Channels, to
Vice-Admiral C. H. Dare. Liverpool, at the same time, was
constituted a separate area, like the Clyde, and entrusted to
Rear-Admiral H. H. Stileman, who was established there in
charge of the 10th Cruiser Squadron base. An independent
squadron of six armed yachts was also established at Belfast
for service wherever it was needed.

Before these arrangements were complete the Canadian
division had crossed, but not by the usual route to Havre.
Though its base depots and other advance units had gone
to Channel ports, the division proceeded from Avonmouth
to St. Nazaire, thus keeping clear of the Channel altogether.
They sailed in groups between February 9 and 12, escorted
by the two divisions of destroyers which had been working in
the Irish Sea under the orders of the *Undaunted* since the
enemy's submarines had appeared there, and which now went
back to Harwich. The whole movement was completed
without interference, but the German submarine blockade
had not then begun. After it had been in operation a week,
another division was due to cross. This was the North
Midland Territorials. They were to go by the regular route
from Southampton to Havre, and it was a much more serious
undertaking, for it was already clear that the measures taken

to bar the Straits of Dover to submarines were not entirely effective.

On February 18 the war zone was inaugurated by the torpedoing of a ship off Dieppe; on the 20th, a submarine, which had passed through the minefield, was caught in the nets to the south of it near the Varne, but though two of the watching destroyers followed the buoys and exploded charges the submarine seems to have torn through and escaped. Keen disappointment was felt at the failure, but the nets were still incomplete. No satisfactory detachable clip for joining them had yet been supplied, and better success could be hoped for in the future. On the other hand, new difficulties were making themselves felt. That ancient highway, through which the traffic of the seas had thronged for ages, was strewn with wrecks, and in their forgotten resting-places they were obstructing the fight against the new peril which they had never known. Owing to them and the bad weather that prevailed, nearly ninety nets had already been lost, but the Admiralty only ordered more—enough to cover the whole twenty-five miles of the Straits—and gave directions that they should be shot by night as well as by day.

On February 22, two days after the disappointment off the Varne, the North Midland Division began to cross. That night two troopers and one storeship left, each escorted by a destroyer. Next night eight troopers left, similarly escorted, although, in spite of the Dover nets, two ships had been lost off Beachy Head. Next day three more were lost in the same waters, and neither the patrol nor specially detached destroyers could find trace of an enemy. Four transports were to sail that night, but as they were slow ships and there was a bright moon the Admiralty ordered that none of them was to leave without three destroyers for escort, and Admiral Meux had to detain two of them. No less than eleven transports were now waiting to start, three of 19 knots and the rest of 13 or under, and there were only eight destroyers for escort. To Admiral Meux's request for instruction the Admiralty replied that the fast ships could sail without escort, and slow ones, for which no escort was available, must be detained. As the fast ships were paddle steamers the system, as Admiral Meux pointed out, was not without hazard, for the beat of the paddles could be heard at a long distance. But it was the best that could be done, and in this way the whole division, as well as the usual drafts and stores, was got across during the week without loss. What it meant for the overworked destroyers must never be forgotten. The *Beagle* had had her fires alight for no less than twenty-six days in

February. But the system had to be continued. On March 8 instructions were given to Admiral Meux that slow ships carrying vehicles, horses, or a small number of men, should be escorted by two destroyers. Fast transports carrying troops must also have one when the moon was bright. Some risks, it was pointed out, must be taken to get troops across in sufficient numbers, and to relieve the pressure on his destroyers the four Newhaven torpedo-boats, which were good for fair weather, were placed at his disposal.

On this system the work of keeping up the flow of men and stores for the army—from which the navy, with all its other preoccupations, was never free for a day—went on uninterruptedly, and not without hope of success. The experience of the first week was distinctly encouraging. How many submarines were out it was impossible to say, but out of 1,381 arrivals and departures only eleven British ships were attacked, and of these four escaped. Five were sunk in the eastern part of the Channel and two in the Irish Sea. A French vessel was also damaged, but was able to make Dieppe. The most sinister feature of the week's work was that a Norwegian steamer, the *Belridge*, was torpedoed without warning in the approach to the Dover Straits. Though she succeeded in getting into Thameshaven, the case, which was the first of its kind, was peculiarly flagrant, for she was bound from America with oil for the Dutch Government.[1]

So far the rate of damage was less than what had been caused by the cruisers, and the next week only increased the ineffective impression of the attack. Only three ships were molested and all of them escaped. One was the *St. Andrew*, another hospital ship, which was attacked off Boulogne. Another was the *Thordis*, whose escape was entirely due to the spirit and readiness with which her master, Captain John W. Bell, acted on the instructions of the Admiralty. They had been issued confidentially on February 10, and were designed to instruct masters as to the best means of eluding submarine attack. There was no suggestion that they should attempt to destroy an assailant —nothing, indeed, which could be used by the enemy to prejudice their status of non-combatants. If a submarine was sighted at a distance they were advised to turn their stern towards her, as Captain Propert had done, and make off at full speed, if possible, into shoal water. If, however, a

[1] According to the German Official History only two boats, *U 8* and *U 30*, were out at this time. On February 25 three more started, *U 6* to relieve *U 8*, *U 20* for the Irish Sea, north of the Isle of Man, and *U 27* by way of the Channel for the Irish Sea, south of the Isle of Man. (See *Der Krieg zur See*. Nordsee, Vol. IV., p. 19.)

submarine came up close ahead, so that a turn would only expose them to effective attack, they should steer direct for her so as to force her to dive. By carrying on and passing over her they would thus be able to bring her astern and make off as before. It was the latter situation with which Captain Bell had to deal. On February 28, as he was passing down Channel, he saw off Beachy Head a periscope on his starboard bow. The submarine was crossing athwart his course, and when she was only thirty to forty yards off on his port beam she fired a torpedo without warning. It apparently passed under the ship, and Captain Bell, when he saw its wake to starboard, immediately put his helm hard over and ran at his assailant. As he passed over the periscope a jar and a crash told that he had hit her, and oil was seen on the water, but nothing more of the submarine. It is now known that she was *U 6*, and that she was damaged, but returned to port. When the *Thordis* was docked for examination it was found that her keel plate was torn and dented and that she had lost a blade of her propeller. Clearly, then, the submarine must have been badly damaged, and a reward was granted in recognition of his skilful conduct in saving his ship. The activity the enemy was displaying against our cross-Channel communications brought no relief in the North Sea, and here we fared badly. Owing to the heavy call for destroyers elsewhere the floating defences of the east coast were seriously reduced in strength. Though submarines were being reported almost daily, and though many ships were attacked and several lost, only one success, due to an accident, was claimed. On February 23, a hundred miles east-north-east of the Farn Islands, a fishing trawler, the *Alex Hastie*, reported she had capsized and destroyed another submarine by getting her foul of her trawl hawsers, and the claim was allowed, though it was ascertained later that the submarine reached port.

In the Channel zone March opened well with news from the Devonport area. Start Bay, by Dartmouth, was suspected of being a resting-place for the submarines which were operating in the Channel, and a net was shot across it. On March 1 part of the nets were seen to sink and begin to move to the inner part of the bay. They were found to be foul, violent pulls and vibrations were seen and the lead gave only 6 fathoms when the chart showed 9½. Next day an explosive sweep was obtained and exploded over the spot, with the result that such quantities of oil came to the surface as to leave little doubt the submarine had been destroyed. On March 4 there was another success about which there could be no doubt.   This time it was the turn of the Dover nets and destroyers.   At 1.15 p.m. the destroyer *Viking* signalled a submarine near the Varne buoy and followed the track, paying out her explosive sweep.   On receipt of the signal the rest of the division, under Captain C. D. Johnson, was ordered to close.   A little after 2.0 an indicator buoy, moving fast to the eastward, gave the chase's position away, and presently her periscope came to the surface again as though she was in trouble with the nets.   The *Viking* ran up to the spot and exploded her sweep.   There was no result, except that for a moment the periscope reappeared.   An hour later it was seen again by the *Maori* further to the westward.   The submarine was clearly moving down Channel, and Captain Johnson directed the *Ghurka* to work her sweep across the track.   At 5.0 it was exploded and with complete success.   The submarine shot up to the surface nearly vertically and stern first.   A few shots at her conning-tower finished her.   Her crew of four officers and twenty-five men surrendered, and ten minutes later she sank.

She proved to be *U 8*, the first boat that had started from Heligoland to enforce the war zone.   After a week's cruise in the Channel she had returned to Zeebrugge for repairs and was now about to resume her work of destruction. To the hard-worked Dover Patrol the success was a great encouragement after their disappointments, but to the enemy it was no deterrent.   In hope of making it so the Admiralty ordered that the crew were to be segregated in detention barracks and treated not as prisoners of war, but as pirates awaiting trial.   But it was an attitude that could not be maintained.   The Germans replied with reprisals on military officers, and the order was soon after rescinded.   Still we could congratulate ourselves on having found one means of dealing with the pest, and as a result of these two incidents an order was issued, at Admiral Hood's suggestion, that one drifter in every four should be furnished with an explosive sweep.   Other means were also being prepared; chief among them were decoy ships with concealed guns; the hydrophone for locating submarines by sound, and depth or lance bombs for destroying them when located beneath the surface, but the latter two were still in an experimental stage.

The weak point of our defence was the inadequate number of destroyers.   A large number had been ordered, but they would not be coming forward till the summer, and during March the considerable movements of troops which had to take place made the shortage a special cause for anxiety.   In the first week of the month the Royal Naval Division began to sail for the Dardanelles. Their port of departure was Avonmouth, and they had to be escorted clear of the danger zone. On March 1, 3,400 men of the Marine brigade were to leave in three transports, but as the weather was too bad for even the " L " class destroyers to keep up with them they were sent away without escort. Three days later three ships, under escort of the *Essex*, arrived at Queenstown with reinforcements for the Canadian division, and had to be brought over to Avonmouth by destroyers. In the following week a London Territorial division was to cross to Havre, and on March 9, the day the movement began, a collier was sunk by a U-boat off Dungeness and a French trawler twenty miles west-south-west of Beachy Head. Other submarines were reported in the Channel, and before the transport of the division was complete they were busy again in the Bristol and North Channels. On the 9th, in spite of the eighty drifters and two patrol units which Admiral Barlow now had at Larne, a ship was torpedoed off Liverpool Bar, and on the 11th one of the 10th Cruiser Squadron, H.M.S. *Bayano*, on her way to coal at Liverpool, met the same fate in the North Channel. She had slowed down so as not to pass the net line before daylight and was an easy prey. The same afternoon another ship of the squadron, H.M.S. *Ambrose*, also coming in to coal, was attacked three times as she approached the Channel, but keeping up her speed, she escaped, and at the third attack was able to get in some shots at her enemy, which, whether damaged or not, did not reappear. Another submarine attacked two ships off Liverpool and was driven off by the *Dee*, one of the two destroyers attached to the port. Later in the evening another steamer, the *Florazan*, was sunk off the entrance to the Bristol Channel.[1]

In view of the force that was being devoted to the area these results were very disappointing, but, as Admiral Barlow explained, the strength of the tides made it impossible to keep the nets athwart the Channel, and none of his armed patrol vessels were fast enough to deal with submarines that were sighted. Apart from actual losses it was a serious interference with the working of the Northern Cruiser Patrol on which our blockade mainly depended. Four other ships of the squadron had to be detained in the Clyde, till, at Admiral Jellicoe's suggestion, he was authorised to detach half of one of his flotillas to patrol the approach to the North

---

[1] According to Gayer, all this work was done by *U 20* and *U 27*. Vol. II., p. 14. (See also *Der Krieg zur See*, Nordsee, Vol. IV., p. 21.)

Channel. For this purpose he placed the *Faulknor* and six other destroyers at Admiral Barlow's disposal, mainly for the protection of the ships of the 10th Cruiser Squadron, but, as will appear directly, so widespread and determined was the effort the Germans were now making that they had to be recalled in four days.

Following the bad day in the North Channel two other areas became infected. On March 12 *U 29* was attacking ships off the Scillies.[1] The local patrol, though on the spot, proved too slow or too inexpert to interfere with her, and during the morning she torpedoed three steamers. Next day another was lost off the Irish Coast opposite the Isle of Man, and it was specially disconcerting that on the same day (the 13th) H.M.S. *Partridge*, attached to the West Coast of Ireland squadron, which was still patrolling, found and engaged, without success, a submarine off the Fastnet (south-west point of Ireland). This was the first time that one had appeared in that quarter, and the indication it gave of the intensification and reach of the submarine campaign was the more serious, for the time had come for the XXIXth Division to leave for the Dardanelles. All the week before it was due to sail, the submarines had been specially active all round our coasts. On March 16, when the first group of four transports left, one was operating in the mouth of the Bristol Channel, but she was so persistently harried by an unarmed drifter that she was forced to dive. Each ship was escorted by two destroyers, and sailing daily in small groups, as escort was available, the transports and storeships were all away by the eighth day and not one was attacked. The submarine activity had, indeed, subsided everywhere except in the North Sea and the eastern end of the Channel, where more ships were lost off Beachy Head, in spite of an increase in the patrol.[2] But in these areas the enemy had not had things all their own way.

About sunset on March 6 a submarine, which proved to be *U 12*, the boat which claimed to have sunk the *Niger* off Deal in November, was sighted twenty-five miles south-east of Aberdeen by the *Duster*, a trawler of the local patrol (Area V). The submarine was steering west-north-west, as though just arriving from the Bight. The *Duster* gave chase, but only to lose her as she dived, nor was it till next morning

---

[1] She was commanded by Lieut.-Commander Otto Weddigen, the hero of the "Cressys" episode. It was he also who had sunk the *Hawke*.

[2] There appear to have been three more submarines operating in the Channel during March 1915, *U 34*, *U 35* and *U 37*, the last of which never returned. (*Der Krieg zur See.* Nordsee, Vol. IV., pp. 20, 22.)

when she fell in with the yacht *Portia*, that she was able to pass the news to the Rosyth naval centre.   Then ensued a hunt which affords a fine example of how our then existing anti-submarine system worked, as organised by Rear-Admiral Sir R. S. Lowry for the coast of Scotland.   The Peterhead Admiral at once got to sea every available unit of his patrol, but it was not till next morning that the enemy was sighted again.   She was then seen off Cruden Bay, south of Buchan Ness, by a minesweeping trawler.   She must then have moved south, for in the evening a trawler picked her up seventeen miles east by north of Girdle Ness, that is, Aberdeen, but lost her again.   Next morning, the 9th, however, she was found again by the trawler *Martin* and was chased down to Stonehaven, when she dived and got away.   All day the hunt went on, and at 3.0 p.m. she was seen by the trawler *Chester* between Montrose and Red Head, but again she escaped by diving.   Meanwhile another submarine had appeared off Aberdeen, and all these reports were being rapidly passed to the naval centres and war signal stations by the patrol yachts, and Admiral Sir Robert Lowry at noon had ordered out Captain W. F. Blunt in the *Fearless*, with thirteen destroyers of the 4th Flotilla from Rosyth, to sweep northward.   *U 12* was now in great danger.   She must have been actually making for the estuary of the Forth, for at 5.30 she was near the Bell Rock, which the *Leviathan* was about to pass, having just been ordered to Rosyth, on the suppression of the 6th Cruiser Squadron, to hoist Admiral Patey's flag for the North American Station.[1]   Apparently before the *Leviathan* saw her she fired a torpedo, but as the cruiser was zigzagging it missed.   The submarine was preparing another attack when a trawler came up, opened fire and forced her to dive.   The inference from this was that the flotilla must have passed over her and they were at once recalled to sweep south.

The following morning (the 10th) from various trawlers Captain Blunt ascertained positions off the Forth where a submarine had been seen, and distributed his force accordingly. One of these positions, reported by the fishing trawler *May Island*, was twenty-five miles east of Fife Ness, and thither he despatched Commander B. M. Money with the *Acheron*,

---

[1] In the course of the cruiser re-distribution that was going on, the North American and West Indies Station was being strengthened by newer and more powerful ships.   Admiral Patey, who had been commanding the 2nd and 3rd Squadrons of the Battle Cruiser Fleet, had been appointed to command it, with Admiral Phipps Hornby, who was then in charge of it, as his Second in Command.   Admiral Pakenham from the 3rd Cruiser Squadron succeeded Admiral Patey in the Battle Cruiser Fleet, and Rear-Admiral W. L. Grant took the 3rd Cruiser Squadron.

Attack and *Ariel*. Making for the spot in line abreast at one mile intervals, they sighted her at 10.10 a.m. about a mile and a half ahead. Putting on full speed they all converged upon her, a most delicate manœuvre, that required the coolest and most skilful steering to avoid collision. The *Attack* (Lieutenant-Commander Cyril Callaghan), which was nearest and had seen her first, opened fire. The submarine dived and the *Attack* rushed over the boil of water without feeling anything. For a minute or two the enemy was lost, but then the *Ariel* saw her periscope about 200 yards four points on her starboard bow. With both engines at full speed and helm hard over, Lieutenant-Commander J. V. Creagh dashed for her conning-tower, which was just coming awash, and rammed her fair amidships. She then came to the surface and the destroyers opened fire. One of the first shots hurled her gun overboard, and then the crew were seen scrambling on deck holding up their hands. The destroyers ceased fire, but before the boats could get to her she was sinking, and only ten survivors of her crew could be rescued. So ended a hunt which had lasted nearly four days and had covered at least 120 miles. Every one concerned in the operation was highly commended by the Admiralty, for success was due not only to the organisation, but to the smart way every man did his part, from the signal stations to the fishing trawlers.[1]

Elsewhere there were similar indications of the enemy's activity. On the same day the Dover destroyers and drifters came upon another submarine, again near the Varne. After a three hours' hunt the *Ghurka* got her sweep home and exploded it with the result that a " probable loss " was allowed, though we now know the submarine escaped. The following evening the second submarine, which had been sighted during the hunt for *U 12*, attempted to attack the *Indomitable* off Montrose. She was on her way from Scapa to Rosyth, when, in the last of the light, she sighted a submarine getting into position to fire, but turning promptly towards it she forced it to dive under her and it was seen no more.

From this and other incidents it seemed evident that an organised attack was being made on the Grand Fleet as well as upon our commerce. No such attack was in fact contemplated, though from March 15 submarines were constantly reported in the Firth of Forth area. All sailings from Rosyth were stopped, and though neither indicator

[1] Five hundred pounds was allotted to the fishing trawler *May Island*, and lesser money rewards to the other fishing trawlers, the armed yacht *Portia* and to the patrol trawlers *Duster, Coote, Chester* and *Martin*.

nets nor the Patrol destroyers could catch one of the intruders, the defence was active enough to prevent any ship being attacked during the four days the alarm lasted. It was not till the 18th, when the weather was too bad for submarines to lie on the bottom, that the indications ceased and the port could be opened again.

It was on this day the *Faulknor* and her six destroyers, which had been detached from Scapa to the Larne area, were recalled. Simultaneously there was another attempt on the Grand Fleet. Admiral Jellicoe had taken out the battle squadrons for a few days' tactical exercises with his cruisers east of Scapa, but owing to the numerous reports of submarines in the area, he had cut the programme short, and on the morning of March 18 the fleet was zigzagging west-north-west for the Pentland Firth with the divisions in line ahead disposed abeam—northernmost were the two divisions of the 4th Squadron and southernmost those of the 1st Squadron, with his flagship and the 2nd Squadron in the centre. By noon they were within fifty miles of the Firth, and signal was made to Admiral Sturdee to turn the 4th Battle Squadron to the southward and proceed to Cromarty, passing under the stern of the other two squadrons. He was just doing so when, at 12.15, the *Marlborough*, flagship of the 1st and southernmost squadron, signalled there was a submarine ahead. A torpedo had just been seen to pass astern of the *Neptune*, the *Marlborough's* second astern, and the enemy was clearly bent on another shot. But as Admiral Sturdee had just started to swing to starboard upon his new course he could not turn away, as laid down in the standing orders. The *Dreadnought* was outermost ship to port, the submarine's periscope was on her port bow, and increasing to full speed Captain W. J. S. Alderson made directly for it; the *Temeraire*, which was next in the line, did the same. In vain the submarine doubled this way and that; the *Dreadnought*, handled as she was by Commander H. W. C. Hughes, the navigating officer, was too nimble for her, and after a breathless ten minutes the famous battleship crashed over her. For a minute her bows reared out of the water astern of the *Dreadnought*, there was just time to read her number " 29," and then she slowly settled by the stern and that was her end. Nothing but oil and a little wreckage came to the surface; every man went down with her, including Captain Weddigen, her commander, and thus was avenged the loss of the three " Cressy's " and the *Hawke*.

We now know that the incident was not part of an organised attack on the Grand Fleet, and that Captain

Weddigen was returning north-about after his recent depredations off the Scillies. It was from one of his victims in that area we learnt who the commander was. Possibly he had reserved his last torpedoes to use on the way home. In any case, the end of this intrepid commander marked the completion of the first month of the new campaign, and some idea could be formed of what it meant. During the period we had lost one armed merchant cruiser, and twenty merchant vessels. On the other hand, twenty-two merchant vessels had been attacked and escaped, and we had destroyed at least three submarines. Though our losses were disquieting, the navy could be congratulated on having kept open the communications of the army, as well as the vital home terminals of our trade routes. Since the beginning of the war there had been conveyed to France alone about 600,000 men and 150,000 horses, with all their stores and munitions, and the merchantship sailings and arrivals showed no diminution.

But our efforts did not stop at prevention. In view of the lawless course the enemy was taking, more drastic retaliatory measures were deemed justifiable, even at the cost of a further stretch of belligerent rights. In effect, Germany, in setting up her war zone, had declared a blockade of the British Isles, which her opening had shown she was unable to make effective according to time-honoured standards. Moreover a blockade must not only be effective, it must be maintained, but owing to the limited sea endurance of the submarine, and the insufficient number Germany possessed, she had periodically to withdraw the blockading force. Under the Declaration of Paris such a blockade was illegal, and on this ground alone we claimed the right to enforce measures of retaliation. To declare a blockade of German ports without also closing those of adjacent neutral countries was clearly useless, and, as the Declaration of London had reasserted, the blockade of neutral ports was inadmissible. What was done, therefore, as the method which would involve least loss of legitimate trade to neutrals, was to declare that no ship bound to or from a German port would be allowed to proceed on her voyage. Her cargo would have to be discharged at a British port, and so far as the goods consigned to a German port were not contraband or were not requisitioned by the Government, they would be restored to the owners on such terms as the Prize Court deemed just. Goods coming from a German port would all be seized subject to neutral claims of ownership. As to voyages to or from adjacent neutral ports, goods with an enemy destination, or which were enemy owned, might be similarly treated. The Declaration was issued on March 11 by Order in Council, and was to apply to all ships that had sailed after March 1. In so far as it amounted to a blockade of neutral ports it was irregular, but in that neither ships nor innocent cargoes were to be confiscated it was much less severe than a blockade, and seeing that it did not involve the destruction of life or property, it fell far short of the ruthless system that had provoked it.

That system continued to be pressed so far as German means allowed, and although it was falling far short of producing the interruption of our supplies which the Germans had so confidently promised, it remained a heavy weight on the Admiralty, and one which they did not doubt would increase. With the measures that were being taken to prevent the submarines reaching the army's line of communications they could not be content. It was clear that our Dover minefield was not stopping the submarines, for two at least were known to have got through. Many explosions were heard in the barrage minefield, but it was probable they were due to the defects of the mines themselves. The pattern then in use was proving very unsatisfactory and they were constantly breaking adrift.

Nor were the indicator nets yet giving the results that had been hoped for—owing to defective clips, floats and buoys and the insuperable trouble of tides and wrecks. It was even found impossible to keep them out at night, and the Admiralty had to rescind the order to that effect. Seeing therefore that the time was nearing when the new armies would be passing to France in ever-increasing numbers and offering a more enticing objective to the enemy's submarines, more drastic measures had to be taken. They were already on foot. Towards the end of February it had been decided to attempt the herculean task of throwing a boom right across the Straits of Dover. The plan was to run an anti-submarine steel net, suspended from buoys, from a point just east of Folkestone, across the Varne Shoal to Cape Gris Nez, with a " gate " at either end. Such devices were already in use to protect our chief fleet anchorages, but as yet they had not been used for the open sea. The difficulties in the way of the new scheme were, of course, enormous, especially in a locality where tides were so strong and complicated as in the Dover Straits. From the first it was doubtful whether such a boom would stand the inevitable strains, but the attempt seemed worth while, and the work of design and collecting material was tackled at once with promptitude and energy. In view of all the other calls that were pressing on our power of production it was a stupendous task. The distance to be covered was twenty nautical miles, and as a result of the change of plan at the Dardanelles much of the gear that was first collected had to be diverted to the Mediterranean for the defence of the new base at Mudros, so that the work of laying the boom could not begin till April.

Still, in the last two weeks of March only ten British, one French and three neutral ships were sunk, while masters were growing so skilful in acting on the Admiralty instructions that no less than sixteen British ships foiled attempts to attack them. Nor had the enemy any success against military objectives. In the last days of the month another division of the new army (the South Midland Territorials) was transported by way of Boulogne and Havre without loss. The main trouble was in the Bristol Channel, where *U 28* was now active. Taking up a position where the tracks to the Bristol and the St. George's Channel diverge, she destroyed on March 27 three steamers, and next day chased three more and sunk a fourth. In two cases of the ships destroyed the behaviour of the submarine commander, Lieut.-Commander Freiherr von Förstner, was characterised by wanton brutality. One of them was the *Falaba*, and her destruction became specially notorious, for she was full of passengers. Not only was this the first instance of such a ship being sunk, but the German captain, after ordering her to be abandoned, fired a torpedo while the boats were being got out, and before passengers or crew could leave the ship, with the result that over a hundred lives were lost. The *Aquila* was treated with like savagery, and the bitterness which the incident engendered was increased by reports from signal stations that S.O.S. calls were being used to lure ships to destruction.

If such conduct, of which Captain von Förstner set the example, was not dictated by mere wanton cruelty, it may have been part of a deliberate design to deter mariners from going to sea. If this was so it had no effect. The Mercantile Marine was not so easily intimidated. Both in owners and mariners the old spirit burnt as steadily as ever, and in sturdy defiance of the new terrors arrivals and departures went on as though nothing unusual were happening. The confidence of courage proved well founded, for the percentage even of ships attacked was very small. During the four weeks ending March 31 the total movement of British shipping in and out amounted to over 6,000 vessels, while the losses numbered only twenty-one, and the tonnage destroyed was less than 65,000.   During the same period twenty-nine other ships were molested, of which only five were damaged and the rest escaped.

But the Germans were now well started on the downward road of intimidation, and how far they were ready to go in ignoring the established customs of the sea by which the hardships of commerce warfare had been mitigated, further appeared this month in attacks by aircraft on merchant vessels.   Eight British ships were attacked in this way off the estuary of the Thames, but in all cases without result. On the other hand, losses from mines almost ceased during March.   The increasing number and efficiency of our patrols had doubtless much to do with the immunity, but it would also seem that the Germans at the same time temporarily restricted their minelaying in the open sea, so as not to hamper unduly the action of their submarines.

The offensive work of our own submarines, though equally persistent and daring, was necessarily more restricted. Targets were few and difficult to reach.   Only in the Bight and the Baltic were they to be found, and in those perilous waters was the main scene of operations.   Inside Heligoland and off the mouths of German rivers the Harwich submarines of the "diving patrol" kept the enemy continually on the alert.   In the whole area of their guard the enemy swarmed about them, under the water, upon it and in the air.   In every direction were lines of patrol trawlers to be dived under, all kinds of aircraft to be avoided and groups of well-handled destroyers hunting like hounds.   Conflicts were frequent, but with small material gain.   But it was not in material gain that much was to be hoped for.   The significance of the diving patrol submarines was more subtle.   They were, in fact, the tentacles of the Grand Fleet.   Though apparently inert in its lair, its reach was long, and at the mouths of the enemy's ports it was feeling — always feeling — for its opportunity.

Nor was it only in the North Sea that the enemy was smarting under its stings.   E 1 and E 9 were still in the Baltic, under Lieutenant-Commanders N. F. Laurence and M. K. Horton.   At the end of October 1914, after their first raids, we have seen how they came definitely under the orders of Admiral von Essen.   All through the winter, with short intervals in port, he kept them busy, mostly in the approaches to the Sound which the Chief of the German Naval Staff had not permitted to be mined.   It was watched by a force under Rear-Admiral Jasper, consisting of four old light cruisers and some destroyers operating from Kiel, and it was one of these light cruisers, the *Victoria Luise*, which Lieutenant-Commander Laurence had attacked on October 18, and not the *Fürst Bismarck*, as he had conjectured.[1] To the eastward, keeping observation on the Russian fleet, was another force under Rear-Admiral Behring, consisting of the cruiser *Friedrich Carl* (flag), a few light cruisers and about half a flotilla of destroyers. It was based at Neufahrwasser, where Lieutenant-Commander Laurence had seen the cruisers when he looked into the Gulf of Dantzig. As soon as it was known that the British submarines had gone to the eastward, Admiral Behring, reinforced by Admiral Jasper's light cruisers, was ordered to attack Libau to prevent its being used as a base by the unwelcome intruders. It seems that the Germans were unaware of the extent to which the Russians had dismantled the port, and his orders were to close the entrances with blockships and to destroy the place by bombardment. Owing to adverse weather it was not till November 25 that the expedition was able to leave Dantzig, and in the small hours of the 26th, as the *Friedrich Carl* was proceeding to her covering position, she was twice struck by a mine about thirty miles off Memel, and later on another ship was blown up nearer the coast. Clearly it was Russian work, and about ten days previously several mysterious ships had been sighted in this vicinity by a German light cruiser, who neglected to attack them. By a fine effort the flagship was kept afloat, and, further north, the operations against Libau went on in a heavy snowstorm. Though the entrances were found to have been already partially obstructed, the blockships were sunk to complete the work, while the *Augsburg*, which had been supporting two submarines in the Gulf of Finland, came hurrying down to the rescue of the *Friedrich Carl*, and by 6.30 a.m. the crew of the flagship had been taken off and she was left to sink.

This was the price the Germans paid for an operation which was quite unnecessary, since, as we know, our submarines had long given up the idea of using Libau. To add to the disturbance they were creating, it was felt that Dantzig was now no longer a fit base for Admiral Behring's detached squadron, and it was withdrawn to Swinemünde, with the heavy cruiser *Prinz Adalbert* for flagship in place of the lost *Friedrich Carl*. How deep was the impression made by our appearance in the Baltic is seen in a General Instruction issued by Prince Henry to the German submarines of the

[1] See Vol. I., p. 237.

Gulf of Finland patrol when it was known where our submarines were based. In warning them against wasting effort on the local surface patrol, he said, "I consider the destruction of a Russian submarine will be a great success, but I regard the destruction of a British submarine as being at least as valuable as that of a Russian armoured cruiser." [1]

During the winter the German Baltic forces were mainly employed in efforts to control the flood of contraband from Sweden to Russia across the Gulf of Bothnia and in an expedition to the Åland Islands, where they suspected an advance base was being formed for operations in the southern Baltic. Nothing was found, and again the price paid was severe. In the course of the various operations the *Augsburg* struck a mine east of Bornholm, and the *Prinz Adalbert* ran aground off Steinort, near Libau, where *E 9* proceeded in order to destroy her, but found her gone. Both ships were out of action for about three months, and besides these mishaps, the *Gazelle*, one of the old light cruisers of the Sound Patrol, was also mined and injured past repair.

During this period our submarines had been operating with the Russian fleet between Bornholm and Gothland. Several attacks on the patrols were made till they had to go into dock for a refit. Towards the end of January they were again active, and on the 29th Lieutenant-Commander Horton reported having torpedoed a destroyer off Möen on the Danish coast, and believed he had sunk her. The work was beyond measure strenuous, and demanded endurance almost past bearing. When on the surface the spray froze on the bridge and hands had to be continually employed keeping the conning-tower hatch free from ice; even so it sometimes became immovable, and return to port was necessary. Periscopes when put out of water were almost immediately cased in ice, bow and stern caps became fixed in like manner, and a more or less prolonged dive into the warmer depths was needed to put them in action again. Still they carried on, to the complete satisfaction of the Russian Commander-in-Chief. He himself, though as eager for action as he had always shown himself during the Russo-Japanese war, had been kept quiet by higher authority. Since the unfortunate loss of the *Pallada*, sunk by a German submarine off Hango on October 11, he had not even been permitted to maintain his cruiser patrol between Gotland and the Gulf of Finland. Nothing else was to be expected. Russia had adopted the specious principle of a single com-

---

[1] The above account of the German operations is from the Official History *Der Krieg zur See* Baltic Sea, Vol. I.), pp. 205–52.

mand. Both army and navy were under the Grand Duke Nikolai Nikolaevich as supreme commander by land and sea, with the result that the Baltic Fleet was regarded as part of the defence force of the capital and an extension of the right wing of the Sixth Army. Admiral von Essen was actually placed under the immediate orders of the General commanding that army, who was responsible for Finland and the coast provinces south of the gulf, and he was allowed no such freedom as was enjoyed by Admiral Ebergard in the Black Sea. Seeing how inferior the Russian fleet was to the German, for the two new Dreadnoughts that were completed had not yet finished their trials, the policy was probably correct in principle, though it hardly justified complete inaction. On the other hand, it must be said that minor operations with the existing force must have been precarious for lack of destroyers. Those which Admiral von Essen had were too slow, and though many more were on the slips, most of their machinery had been ordered in Germany, and there was consequently no hope of the bulk of them being completed for a long time to come. Their new submarines were similarly crippled, and thus it was that *E 1* and *E 9* had to bear the whole weight of active operations in the Baltic.

While we in these ways were employing our oversea submarines against strictly naval objectives, it became clearer every week that those of the Germans were devoting their main energy to the development of their commercial " blockade." All our intelligence indicated that in the near future it would increase in intensity as it was increasing in barbarity, while, on the other hand, there was a growing doubt whether the means we were adopting for destroying submarines at sea and barring their access to vital waters would ever prove adequate to meet the situation. It was not by such means we had been wont in former days to meet attempts to undermine our command of the Narrow Seas. The sound old tradition had been to prevent the enemy ever getting to sea, and if this could not be done by blockade, to destroy or capture the bases from which he was acting. It was natural, then, seeing how difficult it was to close the submarine ports by mine and active blockade, that the idea of attacking them gained new strength. As we have seen, a plan of campaign to this end was in preparation, and in naval opinion there was a growing belief that nothing less would serve to parry the insidious attack. Yet it was at this juncture that the Government found itself entangled, owing to an incorrect beginning, in a distant operation which promised to absorb so much naval force that the elaborately-laid plans for the North Sea offensive might prove impracticable. On the other hand, it was also a moment when the great lines of the war seemed to be taking a new direction, which raised doubts whether the North Sea plan was that best adapted to meet the threatening development.

CHAPTER XVI

IN all wars it is a familiar feature that the spring of the year tends to exhibit new developments in their course, and never perhaps has the tendency been more conspicuous than in the spring of 1915. On each side the traditional opening had been pushed to its utmost capacity, and showed no clear prospect of a quick decision. The vast and sudden effort which the Central Powers had so long prepared had exhausted itself without having even secured on either front a defensive position from which there was any prospect of decisive operations in view. The opening of the Maritime Powers had been, on the whole, more successful, for they had secured, according to old standards, a complete control of the sea, but unless they could use it to strike in a new direction the prospect of a decision was as remote for them as for their enemy.

Both sides were therefore bent on breaking fresh ground. At sea Germany, in order to tilt the balance in her favour, was seeking to sap our control by a wholly new departure in naval warfare, and at the same time was gathering what force she could to strike towards the Balkans on the line where lay her ultimate goal. At the same time we had persuaded our French Ally to join us in an attempt to wrest the initiative from the land Powers in our traditional manner, by giving the Continental war a new direction that was best suited to the position and resources of Maritime Powers. Whatever effect the new departure of the Germans was destined to have upon our control of the sea, it was clear that for some time at least it could not affect it sufficiently to prevent our developing the advantages which the command we had already established afforded us. Those advantages were the power of freely combining naval and military force against the point where the system of the Central Powers was weakest, while standing securely on the defensive in the main theatre, where its strength was greatest.

In the main theatre such operations have never been found possible, unless indeed we except the Walcheren expedition, which for the importance of the forces engaged

290

and in its strategical conception most nearly approached that which we were about to attempt. But that expedition had failed by a spell of bad weather, and whether the success that was so nearly attained would have been decisive, must remain a matter of speculation. But there were at least three instances in which it had been shown that, when a war is sufficiently maritime in character for the sea to become an essential factor, secondary theatres may be decisive. It was in the Peninsula we had made our chief contribution to the overthrow of Napoleon; in the Crimea the Russian war had been won, and by the conquest of Havana we had brought the Seven Years' war to its sudden and triumphant conclusion. In all three examples the result was due to the concentration of naval and military force where the enemy was weakest.

The difficulty of such combinations is that they necessarily require elaborate preparation, so as to secure perfect harmony of action between the two forces, and in recent times this drawback had tended to increase. For while the time required for such preparation had not sensibly diminished, railway transport had greatly accelerated the enemy's power of taking effective counter-measures. The drawback is specially strong where the expedition has to be prepared in the actual theatre of operation and cannot conceal its objective. So it was in the present case. Since the army had been sent out merely to make good what the navy had won, and to push on thence to ulterior operations, it was unfit to undertake a wholly different operation, and, as we have seen, it had to concentrate in Egypt for reorganisation. But it was not only for the army that this process was necessary; the fleet also had much to do. An essential feature of the naval operations was minesweeping, and, since the civilian-manned trawlers had proved unfit for the work under fire, the whole flotilla had to be reorganised and naval ratings distributed through it. Moreover beach-gear for a disembarkation in force had to be improvised, a landing flotilla had to be collected, and the transport anchorages thoroughly protected, work which could not be done in less time than the army would require for its own preparations.

It would, of course, have been possible to have made the attempt at once, trusting to surprise as the lesser risk, but the risk would have been very great, especially at a season when the weather was not yet settled. By the men on the spot a postponement was regarded as inevitable, nor was it without good precedent. In the analogous case of Lord Keith's and Sir Ralph Abercrombie's expedition against Alexandria in

1801, they had chosen to remain nearly six weeks in Marmarice Bay, in order to perfect their force before attempting to land at Aboukir. The decision to sacrifice surprise for the sake of training and organisation proved justified, but in that instance surprise was not so important, since it was quite impossible for the French in Egypt to receive material reinforcement. In the present operation, though the road from Berlin to Constantinople was not yet open, it was possible for the Germans to furnish the Turks with supplies, and, above all, with officers to direct the defences of Gallipoli and to expedite and organise a concentration of force to man them. Air reconnaissances confirmed that the damage done to the forts in the Narrows was slight, and proved that new works were being constructed, especially to cover the vital point of the Kephez minefields. No time was therefore to be lost in pushing on the reorganisation of the army; but it must be done thoroughly, for it was only too clear that if success were now to be attained every available unit would have to be thrown into the scale at the first onset. And this was no less true for the naval than for the military forces. When the time came, therefore, Admiral Peirse, at Port Said, was to transfer his flag to a small cruiser and send the *Goliath*, *Euryalus* and anything else he could spare to the Dardanelles, subject always to the situation in the canal permitting the withdrawal of his ships for the time required.

This was on March 28, by which time indications were not lacking that the Germans were forcing a demonstration against the canal to compel us to keep troops in Egypt. It is even possible that they regarded the return of the army from Mudros as a result of their effort, for it was just when the decision was taken to withdraw the base to Alexandria that enemy patrols began to reappear in the vicinity of the canal. On March 22 an Indian patrol from El Kubri came in contact with a party of Turks, numbering about 400, who were only dispersed when the havildar in charge had enticed them within range of the guns of his post. Measures had promptly to be taken to reconstitute the floating defence of the canal. It was no easy matter. Admiral Peirse had parted with all his torpedo-boats and most of his aircraft, and the French had ordered the *Henri IV* to the Dardanelles to replace the lost *Bouvet*. Small craft patrols, however, were got to work, the *Philomel* and *Requin* took up stations in the canal, the *Bacchante* steamed up from Suez to a supporting position, and next morning a composite force moved out to round up the intruders. They were found, and after the exchange of a few shots they made off, leaving behind them a quantity of kit and ammunition, but owing to heavy sand the cavalry was unable to cut off their retreat.

For a few days there was little further activity on the part of the enemy, but by the end of the month there were signs of another serious movement against the canal. The Intelligence reports indicated troops moving in considerable numbers on both the central and northern lines of approach, and an advanced post was located at Katia. At El Arish there seemed to be 14,000 men, with 10,000 more on their way to join them from Ramleh. At El Sirr, twenty miles to the southward, were 12,000 men with fifty guns, and at Nekhl 4,000 with twenty guns, besides reinforcements that had come by the Hejaz Railway to Maan. A heavy fall of rain in Sinai facilitated an attack. By the 30th enemy patrols and scouts were close to the canal, and Arab reports timed the coming attack for April 3. To meet the menace the *Montcalm* and *Philomel* had taken their stations at Ismailia and the Bitter Lakes, and on April 1 the Royal Naval Division, which had arrived at Port Said on March 27 *en route* to the Dardanelles, sent four half battalions to take over the defences about Kantara.[1] But with nearly the whole Mediterranean Expeditionary Force in Egypt it was no time for the enemy to deliver an attack. April 3 passed without any further sign of an offensive movement, and next day the Royal Naval Division detachment returned to Port Said. For some days cavalry patrols hovered near the canal, but the training of the Dardanelles force was not interrupted again, and Admiral Peirse reported that the *Bacchante* and *Euryalus* would leave for Tenedos on the 10th if there were no further developments. Nothing further occurred in the canal area, and on the 12th the re-embarkation began. On the same day orders were sent for the *Goliath*, which was on her way to Suez from East Africa to proceed direct to the Ægean.

In the meantime considerable preparatory progress had been made at the Dardanelles. The only new development was a sudden activity of the German aircraft. On March 28 one of their machines made a bombing attack on the *Ark Royal*, but it was unsuccessful, and the following day all the British aeroplanes were landed and established in the new aerodrome in Tenedos. It was now completed and defended by the anti-aircraft guns, and from this time the British air service was able to assert a full ascendancy over that of the enemy. During the week, while the minesweepers, covered by battleships, worked inside under fire, the aircraft made continual reconnaissances, combined with bombing attacks on the enemy's positions, apparently with good effects. On

[1] See Plan p. 118.

April 9 Admiral de Robeck was able to report that he had eighteen aeroplanes, and, as the French had an equal number, he had all he required for the present; but as he had had to send away several of his seaplanes, at the urgent call of Admiral Peirse, for the defence of the canal, he would require others, at least when it came to operating in the Sea of Marmara. For spotting purposes, however, he had now the Kite Balloon section, which had that day arrived.

The plan of these further operations, which were to follow the forcing of the Straits, had now been worked out. They depended, it will be remembered, on the co-operation of a large Russian force, and a scheme for concerted action was in course of development. The future status of Constantinople had been settled to the satisfaction of the Tsar's Government, and they were ready to provide an army corps when the time came, and meanwhile to place their Black Sea squadron at Admiral de Robeck's disposal. On March 29 our Admiralty was informed that the Grand Duke Nicholas had ordered Admiral Ebergard to get in touch with the British Admiral and to be guided by his wishes.

They had, in fact, been in communication for some time through the *Askold*, which had been attached to the Allied squadron by the Russian Admiralty as linking ship, and Admiral de Robeck had been kept informed of his colleague's operations. On March 28, the day before the Russian Ambassador communicated the new arrangement, Admiral Ebergard had delivered an attack against the entrance of the Bosporus. Forts Elmas and Riva, to the eastward of the entrance, were shelled, fires were seen, and a large steamer, believed to be an armed transport, was driven ashore and burnt. Later in the day, while one of his planes attacked a destroyer in the strait, he bombarded the group of forts at Cape Rumili, on the European side, and was rewarded by getting two heavy explosions.[1] The forts made no reply, as the range was too great, nor did any of the enemy's ships show themselves, although it was known that the *Goeben* was out of dockyard hands. On the following morning (the 29th) he closed the Bosporus to within seven miles, and at noon his aircraft reported the Turkish fleet, including the *Goeben* and *Breslau,* coming down the Straits; but though he maintained his position all day they did not venture out, and on the 30th he moved away and once more bombarded the quays and establishments at Zungaldak, Erekli and Koslu, along the Anatolian coast.

[1] *Morskoi Sbornik,* May 1915. The Turks state that the only damage was a few houses destroyed and a few persons wounded.

It was after learning of these operations that Admiral de Robeck took the first step towards co-ordinating the work of the fleets by suggesting to Admiral Ebergard that his next attack on the Bosporus should synchronise with ours on the Dardanelles, advising at the same time that all important communications should be sent by way of London, to avoid the risk of wireless messages being intercepted.   On April 5 he was informed of the Russian military arrangements so far as they had gone.   Owing to the fatal limitation of the Russian fleet's coal capacity the blockade of the Bosporus could not be maintained, and Admiral Souchon decided to make use of his advantage by raiding coastal trade, which was now starting on the seasonal opening of navigation, and by striking a blow at the transports assembling off Odessa. In the early morning of April 3 Admiral Ebergard's squadron was getting under way, when heavy smoke clouds were sighted to the south-westward, and an aeroplane reported that the *Goeben* and *Breslau* were approaching the harbour.   Almost simultaneously the Russian Admiral was informed that another force had been sighted off Odessa.   This latter actually consisted of the cruisers *Medjidieh* and *Hamidieh* with some light forces attached to them, for Admiral Souchon appears to have decided on making his attack in two divisions, and intended the vessels under his immediate command as a covering force for the lighter squadron to the westward.

Hastening to sea Admiral Ebergard did his utmost to bring the *Goeben* to action, and although for a time it was hoped that she would give battle, she persistently declined. For five hours he pressed the chase, till, in spite of the enemy's efforts to keep away from him, he got within extreme range, a few rounds were exchanged, and then, presumably as the Russians had been drawn far enough away from the Odessa force, the Germans made off.   The Russian destroyers followed, and at nightfall delivered a torpedo attack.   They were detected and fired on; all the torpedoes missed, and before they could get into position for another attempt the moon rose.   Nothing further was possible, but on his return journey the Russian Admiral learnt that the *Medjidieh* had sunk in the minefield off Odessa.

The two German cruisers escaped, but the failure of the attempt against the Odessa transports appears to have deepened the anxiety which the Russian threat was already causing in Constantinople.   The impossibility of ignoring the menace of troops brought down to the sea, with transports gathering to them, has been recognised by all great commanders from Napoleon downwards.   As a method of disturbing the equilibrium of the enemy or diverting his attention it was frequently used by our most capable masters of war, but seldom perhaps had it been used with more grave and immediate effect than in this campaign. During March precautions had begun to be taken, in view of the menace materialising when our own troops began to move on Gallipoli, and from now onwards to the end of June the effect was practically to detain no less than three Turkish divisions on the Bosporus —one on the Asiatic side and two on the European. When it is considered that it also entailed the allocation of twenty-eight 6″ guns brought from the Chatalja lines—that is, the advanced defences of the capital—for the protection of the Bosporus entrance, it is clear that it meant a very serious diminution of force available to resist a combined attack on the Dardanelles.

On our side the recent occurrences in the Black Sea had the opposite effect. It was a week before Admiral de Robeck heard of them, and in his eyes, showing as they did that the *Goeben* was still active, they materially modified the prospect of Russian co-operation; for so long as the enemy had a battle cruiser free to move in the Black Sea it would mean high risk to pass an army corps across it. This difficulty was, in fact, pointed out by Admiral Ebergard on April 11, when he informed Admiral de Robeck of his recent operation, adding that he had found the *Goeben* could still steam 25 knots. The transportation of troops, he said, would therefore be a more complicated operation than had been anticipated. In reply Admiral de Robeck agreed he had better not embark the troops, but informed him that a naval demonstration off the Bosporus, to coincide with the coming attack on the Dardanelles, would be of great assistance.

The three weeks originally fixed for the reorganisation of the force had gone by and it was not nearly ready. When on April 10 General Ian Hamilton returned to Mudros from Alexandria the bulk of the Australian Division was there, but only the first transports of the XXIXth. It was still uncertain when the French would arrive—it would not be for ten days at least—and as their part in the plan was subordinate to the two main landings on which it was based, the General was minded to begin without them. The Admiral, whom he at once consulted, fully concurred in his plan of operation, but urged that, in addition to the main landings, a demonstration should be made at the Bulair lines. This was approved, and the Royal Naval Division was ordered to embark on the 12th and come on to Skyros, seventy miles south of Lemnos. Trebuki, its port, was also to be the point of assembly for the

French, since the political objections to using the well-placed
and far more convenient island of Mityleni, as they at first
intended, had proved insuperable. Admiral de Robeck also
pressed for two days' practice in landings under naval super-
vision, and the enforced delay was thus utilised with excellent
results.[1]

Of Russian military assistance there was no longer any
hope for months, for on April 13 it appears to have been
decided that their transport to the Bosporus was out of the
question till the *Imperatritza Mariya*, one of the new Dreadnoughts completing at Sevastopol, was ready for sea, and that
was not likely to be before June. At the moment, it is true,
there existed in some quarters a feeling that a way out of the
difficulty might be found much sooner. There were indications
that certain sections of opinion in Bulgaria were being turned
by the display of Allied force away from the Central Powers.
Should they decide to throw in their lot quickly with the
Entente, friendly ports would be open to which the Russian
troops might safely be transported. Our ships which had
been sent to Dedeagatch, to prevent contraband reaching
Turkey that way, had met with so friendly a reception that
it was even suggested that it might be well to give Bulgaria
time to decide before commencing operations. But the
eventual attitude of King Ferdinand was far too shifty a
factor to reckon with, and the proposal was at once rejected.
Still the idea that Bulgarian ports might be open when the
crisis came was sufficiently in the air to make play with, and
what the Admiral did, when he realised that the Russians
would not be able to move their troops, was to request that
they should be embarked in the transports to deter reinforcements being sent from Constantinople to the Dardanelles.
Whether this suggestion was ever acted on is doubtful, but,
as we have seen, it was unnecessary; their mere presence was
a sufficient threat.

To prevent reinforcement of the Gallipoli peninsula was
one of the Admiral's chief cares till the troops were ready.
Continual reconnaissances of the shore in the upper part
of the Gulf of Xeros were maintained; Bulair was shelled;
the landing facilities at Enos were thoroughly examined
by the picket boats of the *Swiftsure* and *Majestic*, and the
troops that came down to oppose them were driven off by
ship fire. But the Admiral's main idea was to use his submarines for the actual interruptions of the enemy's communications. Their instructions were to enter the Straits singly,
at intervals of twenty-four hours, two or three days before
the operations began, and try to get up to Gallipoli to cut

[1] See Plan p. 382.

the enemy's sea line of supply. Until the moment came the Turks were kept busy by picket boats with explosive sweeps making night attacks on the Kephez minefield. By day the troops on the peninsula were continually harassed by fire from the sea, and as the air service improved, the patrolling battleships had some success in hitting concealed gun positions. An explosion was also caused by the *Lord Nelson* in their main magazine at Taifar Keui, a village which lay abreast of Gallipoli on the road to Maidos, about a mile and a half inland from the north coast. Still little could be done to stop the night activity of the Turkish working parties that swarmed over the broken ground of the peninsula. Every morning fresh work could be seen. Amongst other additions a new battery was located in the Gulf of Xeros, and was engaged by the *Majestic* on the 14th. The next day the *Triumph,* with military officers on board, entered the Straits to carry out experimental firing on the trenches and wire entanglements which could now be seen line after line on the confused slopes culminating in Achi Baba, but the results were not satisfactory, and the fact had to be faced that our supply of ammunition was quite insufficient for producing any serious impression on the formidable obstacles which had been growing up under our eyes.

Ever since a few days after the attack on the Narrows, when General Liman von Sanders had accepted the command of the Dardanelles area, work on the defences had been pushed on with energy and skill. Every possible landing-place was entrenched, and battalions of Armenian and Greek Christians were kept at work making a network of roads to connect them to the main points of concentration.[1] The chief difficulty of planning the defence was that the theatre of operations was so well adapted for bringing out all the advantages of amphibious attack. It was impossible to tell where the Allies would land, or even what their main line of operation would be, and it was on a thorough appreciation of these conditions that our plan was based. When, therefore, on March 25, General Liman von Sanders took over the Gallipoli command, he began at once to reorganise the whole system of defence, basing it on a few well-placed concentrations, whence, by improving the mule-tracks, the troops could be rapidly moved to any point on the coast. Two divisions, under Weber Pasha, were left on the Asiatic side, and were concentrated about Chiplak Keui, close to the site of Troy, which thus once more asserted its strategical importance.

---

[1] *Gallipoli, der Kampf um den Orient.* By an officer on the General's Staff. See *Journal of the Royal United Service Institution,* May 1917, p. 342.

In the peninsula were four divisions, under Essad Pasha, the hero of Janina, with his headquarters at Gallipoli. Owing to the amount of reconnaissance work which the ships had been carrying out in the Gulf of Xeros, Bulair was a special source of anxiety, and it was hard by, at Gallipoli, that the General also established his headquarters. To meet the special dangers new fortifications had been built where the Kavak River flows into the head of the Gulf, and the position of some of the Bulair guns was altered to cover it. Cohesion between the northern and southern sections of the Gallipoli forces was obtained by arranging for water transport in the Straits, and similarly at Chanak and Nagara, on the Asiatic side, embarkation facilities were provided so that the troops could be passed rapidly across to the peninsula and vice versa.[1]

So far as was in the enemy's power, his preparations also took the more active form of attempts to interfere with our own concentration. During the week that followed General Hamilton's arrival at Mudros there had been a continual stream of transports coming up from Egypt. The last British troops had embarked by the 16th, and on that day the first group of the French were sailing from Alexandria. The British transports, which proceeded in small groups or singly, were unescorted, for the dangerous part of the route seemed sufficiently well covered. The only visible possibility of attack was from two or three torpedo-boats that had been reported by aircraft in the Gulf of Smyrna, which, ever since Admiral Peirse's departure, had been strictly blockaded.[2] It was now being watched by two destroyers, *Wear* and *Welland*, with the *Minerva* in support. On the route itself at Port Trebuki, in Skyros, under the command of Captain Heathcoat Grant of the *Canopus*, there was also a group of ships in

[1] Major E. R. Prigge, *Der Kampf um die Dardanellen*, pp. 28–30 and 34. According to information supplied subsequently by the Turks the detail of the distribution was as follows : The force under General Liman von Sanders was the Fifth Army, consisting of the 3rd and 15th Army Corps, with the Vth Division and an independent Cavalry Brigade.

3rd Corps—(Essad Pasha)—(VIIth, IXth and XIXth Divisions) on the European side. Headquarters at Gallipoli, with the Vth Division in reserve near Yeni Keui and the Cavalry brigade near Keshan, on the north coast of the Gulf of Xeros. Approximate strength : 40,000 infantry and 100 guns.

15th Corps—(Weber Pasha)—(IIIrd and XIth Divisions) on the Asiatic side. The IIIrd Division had one regiment in the vicinity of Yeni Shehr, on the west coast, and two regiments at Chiplak, near Troy. The XIth Division was in reserve between Kalafatli Keui and Chiplak. Approximate strength : 20,000 infantry and 50 guns, of which two batteries of 4·7″ guns could be moved across to the peninsula.

[2] According to an official statement by the Turkish Admiralty there was no ship of war at Smyrna until the arrival of the *Demir Hissar*.

which were the *Dartmouth, Doris,* the destroyers *Jed* and *Kennet,* and a number of transports.

This was the position when, early on April 16, the *Manitou,* one of the last of the XXIXth Division transports, which had just passed Skyros, sighted a torpedo-boat ahead making for her. Thinking that she was a British boat that wanted to communicate, the transport stopped. She was, in fact, the adventurous little *Demir Hissar,* still under the same German officer who had torpedoed the seaplane carrier *Anne Rickmers* a month previously, when Admiral Peirse was arranging his truce with the Vali of Smyrna. After a month's delay, during which time she had been thoroughly overhauled and had had her torpedo armament replenished, the *Demir Hissar,* on the night of April 15–16, became active again and, by hugging the northern shore of the Gulf, managed to steal out past our blockading destroyers. She had then made straight for the transport route, and, on sighting the *Manitou,* came close up and ordered the ship to be abandoned in three minutes. There was no possibility of resistance, for, though the transport carried troops and guns, there was no ammunition available even for rifles, and at that time no instructions had been issued for unescorted transports defending themselves.[1] As she had only boats enough for a third of the men on board, the captain protested against the shortness of the time allowed, and the German commander extended it for ten minutes. Meanwhile the men, who were actually starting boat drill at the time, began lowering the boats without orders. There was consequently some confusion. Boats were overloaded, one so heavily that the davits broke and she capsized. Many men who could find no place took to the water, and in the midst of the confusion the enemy fired two torpedoes. Both missed, and the torpedo-boat held off after the unarmed despatch-boat *Osiris,* which was just coming up with mails for Mudros. She, however, easily got away, and the enemy went back to the *Manitou* and fired her last torpedo, which, like her other shots, also missed. She then made away at her utmost speed, and it was high time.

It happened that when the attack took place Captain Heathcoat Grant was holding a conference with General Paris and his staff of the Royal Naval Division on board the Headquarters transport, *Franconia,* at Port Trebuki. Orders could, therefore, be given promptly the moment the S.O.S. was heard. The *Kennet* was away at once, and the *Jed*

---

[1] She carried the 147th Brigade, R.F.A., a transport unit and an infantry working party, in all 20 officers, 626 men and 615 horses.

quickly after her, while the *Dartmouth* and *Doris* went to the assistance of the transport. Captain Warleigh of the *Minerva*, who was then coaling at Port Sigri, in the west of Mityleni, also ordered the *Wear* to the scene of action and made in the same direction himself. Hearing, however, that the chase had swerved for Cape Mastiko, the south end of Khios, he quickly altered to the southward and signalled to the Skyros destroyers that both he and the *Wear* were coming down the channel between Khios and the main-land. Meanwhile the *Kennet* and *Jed*, having sighted the enemy's smoke, had been fast overhauling her. About 3.0 p.m. the chase had reached Cape Mastiko, with the *Kennet* now hard on her heels, so close indeed that a few minutes after she had rounded the point, to pass up the Khios Channel, the *Kennet* was able to open fire. The chase at this time was making to double the next point ahead, which forms the northern arm of Kalamuti Bay, but suddenly she swung to port, for ahead of her the *Wear* was rounding the point for which she was making. So she was fairly trapped, and, seeing no escape, she beached herself in the bay, a complete wreck. The crew, after attempting to blow her up, escaped ashore and were interned by the Greek commandant of the island.[1]

The attempt of the *Demir Hissar* was undoubtedly an act of extreme daring, and perhaps deserved a larger measure of success. As it was, owing to the hurry in lowering the *Manitou's* boats and so many of the men taking prematurely to the water, fifty-one lives were lost by drowning and ex-haustion. The episode, however, did little to delay the completion of the concentration. With the assistance of the French Admiral, arrangements were rapidly made for escort-ing the rest of the transports, and the last of them left Egypt three days later.

Our own attempts on the Turkish communications were even more disappointing. Towards the middle of April the Admiralty became persuaded that quantities of oil intended for submarines were being accumulated at the little town of Budrum, which lies at the western entrance to the Gulf of Kos, in the south-eastern portion of the Ægean. Admiral de Robeck was too deeply engaged in perfecting his final plans for the landing to be burdened with further duties, and Admiral Peirse was directed to move up from Alexandria and

---

[1] As an example of German diplomatic methods it may be mentioned that the release of the crew was demanded of the Greek Government on the plea that the crew of our submarine *E 13* had been released by Denmark, whereas the fact was that they were kept strictly interned.

raid Budrum with a small force detached for the purpose from the Dardanelles. In order to ensure complete surprise and secrecy Admiral Peirse ordered the ships detailed to join his flag at sea, after which they were to proceed together for the objective. Further investigation showed that the reports were false, and that no expedition was necessary. On the 20th the plan was countermanded.

The submarine operations up the Straits began the day after the attack on the *Manitou*. The first trip was assigned to *E 15*, Lieutenant-Commander Theodore S. Brodie, and in her went Mr. Palmer, the former Vice-Consul at Chanak—now a Lieutenant, R.N.V.R., whose services Admiral Carden had found so invaluable in the early days that he had got him attached to his staff for intelligence duties. The general idea was for the submarine to be submerged off the Soghanli Dere at daybreak, and then proceed, keeping the centre of the channel, while a succession of aeroplanes watched the passage and created a diversion by dropping bombs. The attempt was made as arranged, but about 6 a.m. heavy firing was heard in the neighbourhood of the minefield, and soon afterwards the first of the aeroplanes returned, to report that the submarine was aground south of Kephez light, and only a few hundred yards from Fort Dardanos. Caught by a strong current, it would seem she had been swept into shoal water and was apparently uninjured. A Turkish destroyer was endeavouring to haul her off, but this attempt the aeroplanes frustrated by bombing. Still it was only too certain that the enemy would continue their efforts to salve her, and it was of the utmost importance to prevent her falling into their hands intact. Whether the crew had managed to disable her was quite uncertain. In fact they had not. Before the Turks realised she was aground they had opened fire on her and killed the commander in the conning-tower. Another shell burst in the ammonia tank, and the fumes asphyxiated six of the crew. The rest took to the water and were rescued by the Turks. The dead were buried on the beach.[1]

Though these facts were not known till long afterwards, Admiral de Robeck assumed she was still intact, and decided to destroy her—no easy task, seeing how close she lay under the guns of Fort Dardanos. One of our small submarines (*B 6*) was at once ordered in to try to torpedo her. She failed to get a hit owing to the heavy fire with which she was greeted. Nevertheless she got back safely. At nightfall two destroyers, *Scorpion* and *Grampus*, tried their hands. They were quickly

[1] Einstein, *Inside Constantinople*, p. 2.

picked up by the beams of the searchlight and heavily fired upon, and so well were the lights handled to screen the wreck that, though the *Scorpion* got within 1,000 yards, she could not locate it. Next morning (the 18th) another small submarine, *B 11*, went in, but, owing to a fog, she was equally unable to find the wreck. In the afternoon the weather cleared, and another plan was tried. The *Triumph* and *Majestic* were ordered in to see what they could do with their guns. But so soon as they were inside they were received with such a shower of shell that it was impossible to get within 12,000 yards of their target, and as at that distance firing was mere waste of ammunition, they returned and asked for further orders.

They were not long in coming. In spite of successive failures, the Admiral was determined to persevere. There was still a chance. It was possible that picket-boats might steal in without attracting the attention of the sentries ashore. This was the plan he meant to try. It was hazardous in the extreme, for more guns had been placed in position to cover the enemy's salvage operations, and nothing could get near the spot without coming under their fire at close range, but it was worth trying. To the *Triumph* and *Majestic* fell the honour of providing the two boats. They were fitted with dropping gear for 14″ torpedoes, manned by volunteers, and placed under the command of Lieutenant-Commander Robinson of the *Vengeance*, the same officer who had displayed so much nerve and resource in his single-handed destruction of the guns at Achilles' Tomb on February 26. It was a pitch black night as they went in, and in silence, with all darkened, they stole up under the Gallipoli shore till they reached the point for their last dash. Nothing could be seen, and steering could only be done by the faint glimmers on the compass; yet all went well till, by sheer ill-luck, just as they reached the bend before the Narrows, two beams shot out of the darkness and lit up both boats. In a moment the sea about them was in a boil with shrapnel and bursting shell, and in the glare of the searchlights the void before them was blacker than ever. It seemed hopeless now to find what they sought. Still Lieutenant-Commander Robinson led on, and he had his reward. By a miracle neither boat had yet been touched, when suddenly, by careless handling of searchlight, the edge of a beam caught the wreck. It was only for a moment, but time enough for Lieutenant Claud H. Godwin, who commanded the *Majestic's* boat, to fire his torpedo. What happened could not be seen. There was a loud explosion, a blinding flash inshore, and almost at the same moment a shell burst in the boat's sternsheets, and she began to sink rapidly. But the *Triumph's* boat, having fired her shot, rushed up to the rescue, and, in spite of the hail of shell, was able to take off the last man just as the sinking boat went under. They had done their work, and their luck stood by them. Somehow the doubly-laden boat managed to get back without being hit, only one man had been lost, and in the morning the airmen were able to report that *E 15* was nothing but a heap of scrap-iron. It was a gallant feat, finely executed, and one which it is pleasant to know extorted the highest admiration from the enemy. An official of the American Embassy has recorded the impression it made upon German officers in Constantinople, and how one of them said, in discussing it, " I take off my hat to the British Navy." [1] He also recorded that, when Djevad Pasha heard that the dead from *E 15* had been buried on the beach, he ordered them to be re-interred in the British cemetery and a service read over them. By the destruction of the lost submarine one source of anxiety was removed. With that the Admiral rested content, and no further attempt at this time was made to get submarines past the minefields.

Every energy was now devoted to the final preparations for opening the combined attack. It was centuries since the slumbers of the Ægean had been disturbed by anything comparable with that vast array. Not even the fleet of the Holy League, when it gathered to stem the tide of Turkish expansion at Lepanto, could have equalled it in numbers or in force. The spacious shelter of Mudros would not alone contain the host. Besides the warships and the crowd of auxiliaries which a modern fleet requires, there were some fifty transports of the XXIXth Division and the Anzac Corps. The Royal Naval Division and its attendant squadron had to lie at Trebuki. At Trebuki, too, was the first echelon of the French, but they were to move up to Mudros before the operations began. From these two starting-points the elaborate plan of attack had to be developed, and what that meant for Admiral Wemyss and his slender staff can only be conceived when it is remembered that six weeks before Mudros was just a slumbering Ægean port, disturbed by little except the sparse and drowsy local trade.

It was a plan no less complex than that of its nearest prototype, Walcheren, but by this time it had been worked out to its last ramification. The general idea, it will be remembered, was that the army was in the first instance to devote itself to assisting the fleet in forcing the Straits,

---

[1] Einstein, *Inside Constantinople*, p. 3.

and, with this object, to endeavour to take in reverse the European group of the Narrows forts and secure a vantage ground from which it could dominate those on the opposite shore. Its main objective, therefore, was the position which covered the European group of defences. The chief feature of this position was the Kilid Bahr plateau, which extended in a semicircle two-thirds of the way across the peninsula between Maidos and the Soghanli Dere.[1] The plateau, being of great natural strength and well entrenched, presented a very formidable obstacle by itself, but, in fact, the position had been extended by elaborate works both to the north and south, so that the lines actually began well to the north of the Narrows where the Kakma Dagh ridge touches the Straits. The position thus not only included a sea base at Maidos, but also commanded the Kilia plain, one of the most important tactical features of the theatre of operations. Between the Straits north of the ridge and the sea at Gaba Tepe, the land contracts to a width of five miles. The neck so formed is occupied by the Kilia plain, and its importance was that it cut off from the main portion of the peninsula all we wished to occupy, while the Kilid Bahr position afforded an ideal front for holding it.

From their Maidos termination the lines of the principal Turkish defences followed the Kakma Dagh ridge to its western extremity, nearly half-way across the neck, and thence, crossing to Ayerli Tepe, they touched the north-western point of the Kilid Bahr plateau, and ran along its western edge towards the village of Maghram; but instead of turning here to the sea again, the lines had been prolonged over the Soghanli Dere, so as to include the Achi Baba group of heights, and finally came down to the Straits over the Tener Chift knoll, just east of Chomak Dere. In addition to this main system of defence, it was thought that the enemy might have organised a complete line of entrenchments along the Achi Baba ridge.

A *coup de main* at Achi Baba was, therefore, no longer possible, but it had been hoped that nothing serious would be encountered between that hill and Sedd el Bahr, since by such maps as were available the whole end of the peninsula seemed exposed to a cross-fire from the sea. Further reconnaissances, however, had shown that this was not so. Owing to the cup-like formation of the area, the bulk of it was not open to direct ship fire. It was also found that during the absence of the Expeditionary Force in Egypt trenches had been constructed from the mouth of the Gully ravine to the

[1] See Plan No. 4.

mouth of Kereves Dere; while a strong defence line had been organised, commanding the narrow landing-places at the toe of the peninsula, which previously had been undefended.

The situation was obviously a thorny one to tackle, nor was there any admissible way of getting round it. General d'Amade's idea was to avoid it altogether by landing on the Asiatic side at Adramyti, in the Gulf of Mityleni, and marching by way of Balikesier and Brusa to Skutari, but such a move would involve us in continental operations of unlimited extent, and would prevent any co-operation from the fleet. For these reasons operations on the Asiatic side had been ruled out by Lord Kitchener. Similar objections barred a direct advance on Constantinople on the European side from the head of the Gulf of Xeros beyond Bulair. As for the method of turning the whole system by the seizure of the Bulair neck itself, which at first sight had seemed the obvious way, we have seen already why it would not bear examination.

The nearest alternative was Suvla Bay, and this was the most tempting of all. A splendid, well-sheltered beach beyond the main system of coast defence and easy to debouch from, it seemed to offer all that was desired, but, after full consideration, it had to be rejected. It was at the widest part of the peninsula, and therefore furthest from the objective. It was also too far from the Gaba Tepe–Maidos neck, which would have to be held in order to secure our foothold in the tail of the peninsula. But the main objection to a landing at this point was that the salt lake at this season of the year was full of water and impassable, and the only available map showed the road south from Suvla as a defile between the Sari Bair ridge and the sea. The route running to the eastward involved a detour through difficult country, believed to be strongly held, and where no assistance could be derived from the guns of the fleet.[1]

Further down to the south of the Gaba Tepe–Maidos neck was another excellent beach. Here was the landing-place which had been selected by the Greek General Staff during the Balkan war, and there can be little doubt the selection was known to the enemy. The whole coast, from a place called " Fishermen's Huts," north of Ari Burnu, as far as the cliffs that run north-east from Tekke Burnu, had been heavily wired and entrenched, and it was moreover so closely commanded by the Kilid Bahr guns and other specially placed batteries as to be practically impregnable.

The result, then, of the first reconnaissance was that a

[1] Aspinall-Oglander, *Gallipoli*, Vol. I.

landing should be made as near as possible to Achi Baba, and at a point whence we might turn the formidable entrenchments which ran across the extremity of the peninsula from the Old Castle above Sedd el Bahr and formed the outworks of the hill. Morto Bay, just within the Straits, was the obvious place, but it had the serious drawback that it could probably be reached by the heavier guns on the Asiatic side about Eren Keui and the Achilleum, and also by concealed howitzers behind Achi Baba. This being so, the troops landed there would require all the assistance it was possible to give them. Other landings were to be made on the two beaches at the toe of the peninsula between Sedd el Bahr and Tekke Burnu. Another possible plan was to effect a landing at a point some two miles north of Tekke Burnu, where a ravine ran down to the sea, and which was known to us as Gully Beach. Owing to the difficulties involved it was not, however, seriously considered. Nowhere else in this region was there anything better than a strip of foreshore, but it was hoped both to the north and south of Gully Beach small bodies of men might be able to get a footing and scramble up the cliffs, and so materially assist in turning the Turkish advanced line.

All this work, which constituted the main operations, was to be committed to the XXIXth Division and the Marine Brigade of the Royal Naval Division, under General Hunter-Weston. Subsequently, however, the scheme had to be modified. The Naval Staff pronounced Morto Bay to be so much encumbered with reefs as to be unfit for landing any considerable force. There was, in fact, no practicable landing-place except a small beach at its eastern arm under De Tott's old battery, and here there was room for no more than one battalion. This landing, then, as well as those at the foot of the cliffs on the other side, came to be regarded primarily as subordinate operations to protect the flanks of the main attack and distract the attention of the enemy. In accordance with this modification, the landings on the west coast had been reduced to two—one at X Beach, about a mile north of Tekke Burnu, and the other at Y Beach, a mile and a quarter north of Gully Beach where abreast of Krithia a scrub-covered gully broke the cliffs and made it possible for active infantry to crawl up—a place not unlike that by which Wolfe's men reached the Heights of Abraham. Subject to this alteration the general idea remained the same—that is, to throw ashore a force sufficient to rush the Krithia–Achi Baba position and develop from it the attack on Kilid Bahr.

The rest of the troops were to be employed in feints to distract the enemy and threaten his communications. The most important of these—in that it was hoped it might be converted into a real attack—was committed to the Anzac Corps, under General Birdwood.[1]   The point selected was a beach north of Gaba Tepe, at the northern end of the coastal entrenchments, where a tenable covering position had been marked out on the foothills of the Sari Bair ridge—extending from Fishermen's Huts to Gaba Tepe.   If this position could be seized, there would be at least a possibility of developing from it a further penetration through Koja Dere as far as the height known as Mal Tepe, which completely commanded the road from Gallipoli to Maidos, but in any case it would serve to hold troops away from the toe of the peninsula.

Scarcely less important was the task committed to the French.   A part of General d'Amade's force was to be thrown ashore at Kum Kale and to advance as far as it could towards Yeni Shehr, with a view to attracting and keeping down the fire of the Asiatic mobile batteries, while at the same time the French squadron with the rest of the troops made a demonstration of landing in Bashika Bay.   The intelligence reports pointed to no considerable number of troops as likely to be met with, but for the success of the British landing in Morto Bay it was essential to prevent the enemy placing field guns in the Kum Kale section to harass the transports in the bay.   Otherwise, the French landing was to be regarded as purely diversionary, and the operations were not to be extended beyond what was necessary to clear the area between the sea and the Mendere River from Kum Kale as far as Yeni Shehr. The British Staff considered that for this work a regiment and one battery of 75's would suffice, and General d'Amade was informed that a large force was to be deprecated, because as soon as a footing had been secured on the European side his men were to be re-embarked and landed at Cape Helles in readiness for the general advance.   Finally, as Admiral de Robeck had suggested, the Royal Naval Division, acting as an independent force, was to make, with its attendant ships, a similar demonstration off Bulair, so as to prevent any relief coming from the Gallipoli–Bulair area.   The whole elaborate scheme was to be completed, as we have seen, by Admiral Ebergard's demonstration off the Bosporus, and the promised concentration of a Russian army corps at Odessa, as a means of holding down the Turkish troops in the Adrianople and Constantinople areas.

In concert with Admiral de Robeck the general lines of the plan had been settled by April 13, three days after

[1] The Australian Division (three Infantry brigades), and the New Zealand and Australian Division (two Infantry brigades).

General Hamilton had rejoined him from Egypt. Its admitted defects were that it broke up the landing force into fragments, but owing to the restricted accommodation on the available beaches this was unavoidable if a force adequate for establishing itself was to be flung ashore at the first onset. The separation of the Anzac Corps from the XXIXth Division was not so serious as that of the units of the latter from each other; as Wolfe had shown at Quebec, an army based upon a fleet can be freely divided without prejudice to its real cohesion. Given command of the sea, the ease and elasticity of the communications will keep the detachments almost as firmly knit for mutual support, and as free to retire as though they were all physically in touch one with the other. At the same time, the multiplicity of the constituent parts rendered the detailed staff work exceptionally heavy. Every beach had to be provided with its separate organisation, each required its covering force and its main force, and each its supporting squadron and landing flotilla. But, complex as the work was, it was expected to be complete in ten days, and eventually, at a meeting of the principal officers held on April 19, Admiral Wemyss was able to announce that everything was ready, and the attack was fixed for the 23rd, if weather permitted.[1]

It was a week later than had been hoped, but, in fact, no time had been lost, for had all been ready earlier the abnormal condition of the weather must have kept the force idle. As a succession of calm days was essential the weather was all-important. It was also the most disturbing factor. It was still far from settled, and it was of the last importance that the enemy should not be allowed further time to perfect his defences or increase his force. So far as we had been able to ascertain up to this time the total force of the enemy in the peninsula was three first line divisions (Nizams) and one second line (Redifs), in all about 34,000, and the main concentrations were reported to be about Bulair, Kilid Bahr and between Achi Baba and the front of attack.[2] A similar force was believed to be on the Asiatic side. Our own strength, with the French division and the 29th Indian Brigade in reserve in Egypt, was now all told rather over 75,000 officers and men, with 140 guns.[3] But the main artillery

[1] The above account of the plan is from (1) General Hamilton's private letters to Lord Kitchener, (2) the omitted portion of his first despatch, (3) his evidence before the Commission.

[2] Force Order No. 1, Headquarters, Mediterranean Expeditionary Force, April 13.

[3] Headquarters Diary, April 14, 2,250 officers, 58,459 men approximately. The consolidated Field Returns give the " Effective Strength "

strength lay, of course, in the ships. The losses of the fleet had been to a great extent made good by fresh arrivals,[1] and although the *Inflexible, Suffren and Gaulois* were still out of action, it numbered, without auxiliaries and minesweeping craft, fifty-nine pennants—that is, eighteen battleships, twelve cruisers and about twenty-four British and five French destroyers. There were also eight British submarines, including the Australian *AE 2* and four French. In order to enable it to carry out its functions in regard to the various operations, it had been organised in seven squadrons, as follows :—

Fleet Flagship : *Queen Elizabeth.*
Vice-Admiral (Act.) John M. de Robeck,
Commodore Roger J. B. Keyes, Chief of Staff.
Captain G. P. W. Hope.

FIRST SQUADRON

Rear-Admiral Rosslyn E. Wemyss.
Rear-Admiral Stuart Nicholson.

BATTLESHIPS.

Swiftsure (2nd flag) . . .	Captain C. Maxwell-Lefroy.
Albion	A. W. Heneage (Captain " S "), Acting Captain, Commander H. L. Watts-Jones.
Lord Nelson . . .	Captain J. W. L. McClintock.
Implacable . . .	Captain H. C. Lockyer.
Vengeance . . .	Captain B. H. Smith.
Prince George[2] . . .	Captain A. V. Campbell.
Goliath	Captain T. L. Shelford.
Cornwallis . . .	Captain A. P. Davidson.

CRUISERS

Minerva	Captain P. H. Warleigh.
Euryalus (flag) . .	Captain R. M. Burmester.
Talbot	Captain Fawcet Wray.
Dublin	Captain J. D. Kelly.

Six fleet-sweepers.

for April 25 as 2,840 officers and 72,646 men, which was 45 officers and about 4,000 men short of establishment. The French had one infantry division, consisting of the "Metropolitan" brigade (the 175th Regiment of the Line and a composite African regiment—two battalions of Zouaves and one of the Foreign Legion) and one " Colonial " brigade of two regiments each composed of one battalion of Colonial Infantry and two of Senegalese. With them were two groups of Field Artillery, *i. e.,* six batteries of 75's (four guns each) and one Mountain group, *i. e.,* three batteries of 65's (six guns each).

[1] At the end of March the battleship *Jauréguiberry* had arrived to replace the *Suffren* as Admiral Guépratte's flagship, and also the coast defence ship *Henri IV,* while two armoured cruisers, *Latouche-Tréville* and *Jeanne d'Arc,* which had been serving in the Western Channel Patrol, came on with the troops.

[2] Attached to Rear-Admiral Guépratte's squadron for the landing operations of April 25.

SECOND SQUADRON

Rear-Admiral Cecil F. Thursby.

BATTLESHIPS

Queen (flag)	Captain H. A. Adam.
London	Captain J. G. Armstrong.
Prince of Wales . . .	Captain R. N. Bax.
Triumph	Captain M. S. FitzMaurice.
Majestic	Captain H. F. G. Talbot.

Cruiser, *Bacchante*, Captain The Hon. A. D. E. H. Boyle.

Adamant, submarine depot ship, Commander F. A. Sommerville.
Ark Royal, seaplane carrier, Commander R. H. Clark-Hall.
Manica, balloon ship, Lieut. D. H. Metcalfe.

Eight destroyers, Captain C. P. R. Coode (Captain " D ").
Four trawlers.

THIRD SQUADRON

Captain Heathcoat S. Grant.

Battleship, *Canopus*, Captain Heathcoat S. Grant.
Cruisers, *Dartmouth*, Captain Judge d'Arcy.
         Doris, Captain F. Larken.
Two destroyers.
Two trawlers.

FOURTH SQUADRON

(Attached to First Squadron)

CRUISERS

Sapphire	Commander P. W. E. Hill.
Amethyst	Commander G. J. Todd.

Twelve trawlers.

FIFTH SQUADRON

Captains H. A. S. Fyler and A. W. Heneage (Captain " S ").

Battleship, *Agamemnon*, Captain H. A. S. Fyler.
Ten destroyers.
Three French minesweepers.
Two trawlers for net-laying.

SIXTH SQUADRON

Rear-Admiral P. F. A. H. Guépratte.

BATTLESHIPS

Jauréguiberry (flag) . .	Captain A. R. Beaussant.
Henri IV . . .	Captain G. F. C. Varney.
Charlemagne[1] . . .	Captain J. A. E. Salaun.

---

[1] Did not take part in operations of April 25.

CRUISERS

Latouche-Tréville [1]	.	.	.	Captain C. H. Dumesnil.
Jeanne D'Arc .	.	.	.	Captain M. F. A. Grasset.
Askold .	.	.	.	Captain S. Ivanov.
Savoie .	.	.	.	Captain Tourrette.

Seven destroyers.
Five torpedo boats.

SEVENTH SQUADRON
Captain C. P. Metcalfe.

Four destroyers.
Triad, armed yacht, Commander A. L. Ashby.
(Smyrna blockade.)

The general idea of the organisation was to provide each zone of operations with a separate squadron, which in its turn was divided into " covering ships " and " Attendant ships." The function of the " covering ships " was to prepare for the landing with their fire, and subsequently to cover it by searching the enemy's trenches and batteries inland. The function of the " attendant ships " was to carry the advance echelons of the covering troops, who were to seize the beaches and advance to a position in which they could cover the completion of the landing. These ships could also take part in the artillery preparation and support, but this duty was secondary to their special purpose.[2] In delivering an attack from the sea against a position which some of the highest military skill in the world had had ample time to prepare for troops renowned for their stubbornness in defence, the first consideration had been how to reduce the time during which the troops would be exposed in boats during the final approach. General Hamilton had been in favour of a night operation, even though it would entail dispensing with the preliminary bombardment. The naval objections, however, had been found insuperable. The difficulty of transferring heavily equipped troops into the boats in the dark, the difficulty of finding the narrow beaches, which it was not permissible to mark beforehand, and finally the danger of

---

[1] Did not take part in operations of April 25.

[2] The terminology is a little confusing here owing to the difference between naval and military usage. " Covering troops " are those intended to seize a " covering " position ashore. " Covering ships," as the expression was used in the operation orders, were those which " covered the landing " with their guns, but they would more correctly be called " supporting ships." According to traditional phraseology these ships were not the " covering squadron," for the function of a covering squadron is to prevent the enemy interrupting from the sea. Admiral de Robeck's covering squadron was, strictly speaking, the seventh, which was watching Smyrna. The true covering squadron was the French fleet blockading the Adriatic.

uncharted rocks, rendered a night landing, at least on the southern or main front, altogether too precarious. The gravest objection to an attack after dawn was that the transports could not lie within range of the enemy's heavy guns without danger of being sunk. The navy ships were less tender, and as an alternative the Admiral had offered to take the advance troops close in before transferring them to the landing flotilla as soon as possible after dawn. It was a method which would considerably reduce the exposure, and at the same time permit a preparatory bombardment. This plan was therefore adopted for the main landing. Landing ships were also to be employed for the subsidiary attempts on the west coast, but in these cases the pilotage difficulties were smaller, and, as being primarily intended as diversions they should logically precede the main attack, the disembarkations were timed to take place before dawn.

For one of the main beaches these precautions were not deemed sufficient. This was the beach between Sedd el Bahr and Cape Helles, known as " V," which promised to be the most difficult of all. The foreshore, which was wired down to and even under the sea, was like the stage of a well-entrenched amphitheatre, and was commanded from one flank by the village and half-ruined works of Sedd el Bahr, and from the other by precipitous cliffs.[1] Such a death-trap was not to be dealt with by ordinary means, and a device almost mediæval in character was hit upon to nullify its worst dangers. Here, as at all places, the advance party was to land in boats, but the bulk of the covering force was to be run ashore at the Sedd el Bahr end of the beach in a collier. For this purpose the *River Clyde*, a vessel capable of taking over 2,000 men, was told off, and the work of preparing her and arranging the whole scheme was entrusted to Commander Edward Unwin of the *Hussar*. His idea was to let her advance as far as possible till she took the ground, and to arrange for the immediate formation of a floating pier to connect her with the beach, the means of forming it being taken in with her. From a spar guyed out to port she was to tow a steam hopper, which, as soon as the *River Clyde* grounded, was to push on under her own steam till she was brought up by the beach, when she would shove out over her bows a specially constructed gangway to reach the shore. To complete the pier, the *River Clyde* would tow alongside four lighters, two on either bow, which the troops could enter from large ports cut in her sides, and two to fill the gap between her and the hopper. In order to cover the troops in the actual process of

[1] See Plan pp. 328–9.

landing, she had also machine-guns mounted on her forecastle behind steel plates, and to complete the work she carried in her all the material for constructing a permanent pier. Indeed, every detail of the novel expedient was worked out by Commander Unwin with the utmost foresight and skill.

To the main landings at the toe of the peninsula the First Squadron was devoted, under Admiral Wemyss, in the *Euryalus*. His reward for the labour of organising the base and working out the complex details of the approach was that he was given the whole direction of the landing operations. To him were also attached the two light cruisers of the Fourth Squadron, which were told off to Y Beach. The covering squadron, which was placed under the command of Admiral Nicholson, included, besides these two ships, six battleships, *Swiftsure* (flag), *Lord Nelson*, *Albion*, *Vengeance*, *Prince George* and *Goliath*, and the three cruisers of the First Squadron, *Minerva*, *Talbot* and *Dublin*. The Second Squadron, under Admiral Thursby, was assigned to the Anzac landing at Gaba Tepe, with the *Triumph*, *Majestic* and *Bacchante* forming its covering division, and as this zone of operations was out of convenient reach of the aeroplanes, he was to have the seaplane carrier *Ark Royal*, and the balloon ship *Manica*, to direct the ship fire. The small Third Squadron, under Captain Heathcoat Grant, in the *Canopus*, was to attend to the feint on Bulair. Captain Fyler, in the *Agamemnon*, had charge of the Fifth Squadron, which, with its flotilla under Captain Heneage, was to look after the minesweeping and net-laying inside the Straits. Admiral Guépratte's force, which formed the Sixth Squadron, was devoted to the landing and demonstration on the Asiatic side, while the *Triad* with four destroyers which formed the Seventh Squadron watched Smyrna to guard against torpedo attack from that direction.

Complex as this arrangement was with all its incidental details, the organisation was complete by April 19. By that time, in spite of the unfavourable conditions, nearly all the troops which were detailed as the covering forces for the various landings had been exercised in landing at least once, and all other preparations made so far as the not too adequate material allowed. The work had been onerous and exacting in the extreme. Though Admiral Wemyss's staff had been increased by both naval and civil officers, it was still inadequate, even if it had been a question of landing a homogeneous British force, but in this case to the strain of working harmoniously with an Allied army and fleet, there was added the labour of conducting the civil administration of Lemnos, which belonged to a neutral Power. The place became thronged with all the rascality of the Levant, upon whom the most watchful eye had to be kept. Order and sanitation had to be carried on and undesirables removed, and all without offending Greek susceptibilities. As Acting Governor and Senior Naval Officer, moreover, Admiral Wemyss had to adjust the inevitable questions of accommodation which arose between British and French officers ashore. The readiness of the French, both on sea and land, to fall in with his suggestions did much to smooth the difficulties, and the devotion of his small and overworked staff did the rest. As he afterwards wrote, it was only through the happy spirit of co-operation between the two services, and the determination of all ranks that nothing should be left undone to ensure success, that the endless obstacles and deficiencies were overcome.

But all the goodwill in the world could not control the weather. It was still so far from settled that some doubt was felt in fixing the attack for April 23. For the success of the landing a promise of at least four days' fine weather was essential, since, in order to have the lighters and the less mobile and seaworthy units in place to time, it was necessary to begin the approach two days ahead. Accordingly they were to start from the base on the 20th, but it could not be. During the afternoon of the 19th—a few hours after the decision had been taken—the glass began to fall again, and so threatening was the outlook that Admiral de Robeck had to postpone everything for twenty-four hours. Next day brought no improvement, and another postponement of twenty-four hours had to be signalled. So, in spite of the desperate exertions that had been made to expedite the attack, the enemy was afforded another two days to complete his already too formidable dispositions to meet it. He had already had a month, and that had proved barely sufficient. " If the enemy," wrote a German officer on the staff, " had only attacked a little earlier, Heaven knows how the matter would have ended. But by this time all companies were in well-entrenched positions at the various important military points along the coast, and behind them the reserves, who were to hold the assailant till the big divisions could come up." [1]

---

[1] "Gallipoli, der Kampf um den Orient," *Journal of the Royal United Service Institution*, Vol. LXII., p. 343.

CHAPTER XVII

THE DARDANELLES—LANDING OF THE EXPEDITIONARY FORCE, APRIL 25

It was not till midday on April 23—a full five weeks since the attack on the Narrows—that the weather began to give promise of the fine spell that was essential for the combined operation. Admiral de Robeck, therefore, gave the word for the preliminary movements to begin as arranged about sundown, and during the afternoon five aeroplanes were able to get away from Tenedos to bombard the enemy's base at Maidos. No dumps were exploded, but buildings were seen to collapse, and all five machines returned safely.[1] Seaplanes also went up and brought back further reports of the condition of the enemy's defences and gun positions.

The first movement was to get the twelve lighters for the two southern beaches away to the anchorage north of Tenedos. About sunset they started, towed by three transports, in which were the two advanced battalions of the covering force for W and V Beaches and the battalion which was to land in Morto Bay. They were followed by Admiral Wemyss, in the *Euryalus*, with the other two attendant ships, *Implacable* and *Cornwallis* ; and to the same rendezvous the *River Clyde* proceeded, and the tugs, towing floating piers. During the following day the rest of the transports moved out in successive groups. The main rendezvous for the XXIXth Division was off the mouth of the Straits, that for the Anzac attack off Cape Kephalo, in Imbros, and that for the Royal Naval Division west of Xeros Island, at the head of the gulf. The work of getting each section of the force into its station, without mutual interference in those confined waters, was probably more arduous than anything of the kind which the navy had undertaken. Numbers can give but a faint impression of what it meant. The British transports alone numbered over sixty, trawlers and sweeping craft over

---

[1] Maidos was also the headquarters of the IXth Division, which was responsible for the defence of the tail of the peninsula from the Kilia plain to Helles. According to Turkish official information twenty soldiers were killed and some fires started. As a result two battalions of the 27th Regiment which were then in reserve for the Gaba Tepe (Anzac) area had to be moved out into the open on the Kilia plain, about five miles from Anzac Cove, or about one and a half miles nearer to it than they had been at Maidos.

thirty, besides tugs and other auxiliary craft. So that, as the ships of war and torpedo flotilla numbered well over ninety, the whole operation must have involved the movement of at least 200 vessels.

On the 24th General Ian Hamilton transferred his headquarters from the *Arcadian* to the *Queen Elizabeth.* The first group to move on that day was the Royal Naval Division and its attendant ships from Skyros.[1] They had the farthest to go, for, in order to keep clear of the Mudros groups, they were to proceed by an indirect course. At the first gleam of dawn therefore they left Trebuki harbour and made for their distant rendezvous by a course which took them outside Lemnos, Imbros and Samothraki. The first group of the French, with the troops intended for Kum Kale, had already moved up to Mudros three days previously. There the movement began at 10.0, with the *Sapphire* and *Amethyst* and two transports carrying the King's Own Scottish Borderers and the Plymouth Marines, who were to rendezvous off Tekke Burnu for Y Beach. Then followed a group of munition ships making for a position twenty miles south of Mudros, whence after nightfall they were to proceed to the main rendezvous off the Straits. Shortly before 2 p.m., when they were well clear, Admiral Thursby took out his squadron, with the leading battalions of the Anzac covering force embarked in his three attendant ships and their supports in four transports. He was to make for a rendezvous five miles west of Gaba Tepe, leaving the rest of the Anzac Corps to assemble off Cape Kephalo, in Imbros. At 3.30 six transports followed with the battalions of the XXIXth Division, which were to land when the covering force was ashore and were to make for the main rendezvous. The remaining transports of the XXIXth Division were not to leave till next day. The French, in order to clear the harbour, had anchored outside. They had had no practice in landing, and at the eleventh hour, at Admiral Guépratte's suggestion, the opportunity was seized for conducting a rehearsal. The result was to show how much both troops and ships, except the *Askold*, had to learn. There was, however, no time to repeat the exercise, and at 9 p.m. they sailed for their rendezvous at Tenedos, where the rest of the French were also proceeding.

At nightfall all the British sections had reached, or were nearing their rendezvous, but it was still doubtful whether another postponement would not be necessary. The glass had begun to fall again, and during the afternoon the wind

[1] See Plan p. 382.

had got up, with a choppy sea that was by no means favourable for towing the lighters. The moon, too, rose with a wet, windy halo, but the presage of bad weather soon passed. At sunset the wind had begun to die down, till shortly after midnight it fell away to nothing, with a perfectly smooth sea. So the last anxiety passed, and as the transports, with their attendant ships and destroyers, stole quietly to their positions, Admiral Wemyss, in profound silence and without a light showing, was transferring the three leading battalions of the main landing from their transports to the *Euryalus*, *Implacable* and *Cornwallis*. The evolution had been frequently practised, and in the now brilliant moonlight and perfect calm it was carried out quickly and without a hitch; and, well to time, the three ships were able to move away for their final positions off their respective beaches.

By 4.30 a.m. on the 25th Captain Grant with the Royal Naval Division was off Xeros Island and ready to make his demonstration. Anchoring his convoy there out of range from the shore, he ordered the *Dartmouth* and *Doris* to go in and bombard the Bulair lines, while under cover of their fire the trawlers attached to the squadron swept Bakla Bay as though a landing was intended north of the lines. There was no reply, nor could the *Canopus* when she too stood in see any trace of the enemy. Not even when the *Kennet* with military officers on board made a close reconnaissance of the whole of Xeros Bay were any troops seen. Only once did she draw the fire of a small gun, and the seaplane which went up from the *Doris* reported the lines apparently deserted. At the time, therefore, it seemed that the feint had little or no effect in relieving pressure at the real landing-places, but we now know that it did all that Admiral de Robeck hoped from it.

Its effect on General Liman von Sanders' dispositions was immediate. It will be recalled that four divisions of Essad Pasha's 3rd Corps to which was assigned the defence of the peninsula had been divided into two groups, one for the north or Bulair area, and one for the south below the Kilia plain. The corps headquarters were at Gallipoli, where the General had also established himself. In this area were the VIIth and the Vth Divisions, the VIIth being at Gallipoli itself, less one regiment, which was distributed for the defence of the coast from Ejelmer Bay to the head of the gulf, and the Vth held in reserve at Yeni Keui, a village north-west of Gallipoli, about three miles from the north coast and twelve miles west of the Bulair lines. The southern area beyond the Kilia plain was occupied by the IXth Division, with its headquarters at Maidos. Here, too, had been two of its battalions until they had been bombed out on April 23 by our aircraft. Four other battalions were distributed along the coast from Suvla round to Morto May, with the remaining regiment in support at a central position on the Kilid Bahr plateau. Between the two areas was the XIXth Division, a newly-formed unit, incomplete in its artillery. It was held in reserve at Boghali, about four miles north of Maidos, with one battalion completing the coast cordon from Ejelmer Bay down to Suvla. From this disposition it would appear that the General regarded the Bulair area as the most likely, or at least the most dangerous point of attack, and possibly this view gave special weight to the demonstration. At any rate we are told that as soon as the Royal Naval Division transports were signalled off the coast he moved up the VIIth Division from Gallipoli to a road centre to the north-east—that is, towards Bulair, and ordering Essad Pasha to go down to Maidos and take command of the Southern Force, he himself hurried to the threatened front, and for over twenty-four hours had his post of command on a height near the central fort of the Bulair lines.[1]

The result of these arrangements was that at Gaba Tepe—some thirty miles south of Bulair—when the Anzacs were landing, there was nothing to oppose them except a single battalion of the IXth Division, that is, the division which was charged with the defence of the whole of the area of the real attack.[2] At Gaba Tepe affairs were already well advanced. This landing, it will be recalled, was to be the first to develop, and the only one to be attempted before dawn. Its details had been left entirely to Admiral Thursby and General Birdwood, commanding the Anzac Corps, and they had taken special precautions to prevent things going wrong in the dark. The *Triumph* had been sent on overnight, with orders to anchor quietly on the exact rendezvous five miles west of Gaba Tepe, and to show a dim light if called for. There at midnight Admiral Thursby arrived with 1,500 men of the 3rd Australian Brigade, which formed

[1] Liman von Sanders, *Fünf Jahre Türkei*, pp. 83 *et seq.*, and Prigge, pp. 42 and 44. General Liman von Sanders became convinced on the 26th that Captain Grant's squadron was only demonstrating, and during that and the next day practically cleared the Bulair lines of troops, so as to reinforce the southern end of the peninsula. See also *post*, p. 348.

[2] Prigge, pp. 43–4. The Turks state that it was the 2nd Battalion of the 27th Regiment, and that it had attached to it three batteries—one field artillery, one mountain and one of 6″ short guns—besides some Nordenfeldts.

the advanced guard of the covering force in his three attendant ships, *Queen, London* and *Prince of Wales.* The rest of the brigade, numbering about 2,500, had been transferred to six of his eight destroyers at the Imbros rendezvous two hours earlier, and joined him at 1.30 a.m. under Captain Coode (Captain D.). The transports with the bulk of the corps were anchored to seaward till the covering force was ashore. As the laden destroyers joined the Admiral the advanced guard were being silently put on board the boats in which they were to land. As a surprise was aimed at, absolute quiet was essential. The beauty of the night, without breath or ripple, helped all to go smoothly, and yet it could not promise a complete surprise. For behind the squadron the moon was setting, and the silhouettes of the ships were clear for the watchers ashore to see. But by 3.0 a.m. it was dark, and word was given to carry on. Stealthily, at five knots, the attendant ships crept in over the motionless sea, each with her train of sixteen boats disposed abreast in four tows, and astern of them followed the destroyers with the second echelon.

The point settled for the landing was just north of Gaba Tepe, where the general character of the coast was so rugged and difficult that in the General's opinion the Turks would hardly expect it to be chosen for a descent. Close to the cape, however, it looked less formidable. There was a fair piece of beach, and tracks could be seen leading towards the Sari Bair ridge, which was the first objective. Though the beach would be closely commanded by whatever troops might be found on Gaba Tepe itself, it was decided to risk a landing here, rather than involve the force in the almost impossible ground further north. The right wing, of which the flagship had charge, was to make for a point 800 yards north of the cape; the centre, in charge of the *Prince of Wales*, was to try 800 yards further north; and the *London* with the left, the same distance beyond it. Each section had its covering ship, which, after leaving her boats with the attendant ships, moved to her assigned position—the *Triumph* 2,600 yards west of Gaba Tepe for the right, the *Bacchante* about a mile from the centre landing-place, and the *Majestic* to the northward, a mile off Fishermen's Huts, to prevent the approach of reinforcements. For there she could command a point at which the road from Biyuk Anafarta joined the coast road from the Huts to Suvla Bay and the hills immediately on the Anzac's left.

Shortly before 3.30, when the attendant ships were within two or three miles from the coast, they stopped, and the picket boats crept on with their tows. All went well half-way to land, when traces of the shore became faintly visible. But a current had been setting them too far to the north and the guiding officer commanding the starboard wing of the tows, mistaking some half-seen feature on his port bow for Gaba Tepe, inclined across the centre, crowding it upon the port wing. Here was Commander Dix, the senior officer, who quickly realised the error. If he conformed, the boats would reach the shore much too far to the northward and after dawn. With prompt decision he therefore led on astern of the crossing tows, trusting they would follow his motions. It meant that the right wing of the troops would find themselves on the left, but time and direction were everything and he judged it the lesser evil. The rest of the tows happily altered to his course, and so in the silence of the fast-coming dawn all made direct for the land.

Ashore there was no sign of life, and every breathless minute gave increasing hope that a complete surprise was in store. All was still quiet when, a few minutes after 4.0, the first glimmer of dawn began to detach the outline of the forbidding hills. In another ten minutes the tows found themselves within 100 yards or so of the beach, and in the waxing light word was quietly passed for the boats to cast off and row in. Still no sound broke the quiet of the serene dawn except the murmur of the muffled oars. Then in a moment all was changed. Progress in the stealthy approach had been too slow, and the light had made sufficiently for the watchers ashore to give the alarm. A single shot rang out, and before the leading boats had grounded they came under scattered rifle fire from Ari Burnu. But nothing daunted, as boat after boat touched the ground, the men sprang into the water waist deep and made for the beach, stumbling and falling on the smooth, water-worn stone which formed the bottom. Still without pause they staggered on, but only to find in front of them ground entirely different from what they had expected.

The point at which they had actually reached the shore was about a mile and a half north of the selected place, on a narrow strip of sand about 1,000 yards in length, between Ari Burnu and Fishermen's Huts, where the forbidding coast was at its worst. All they could make out in the dim light was that they were on a cramped ribbon of beach, from which, instead of the sloping ground and goat tracks they expected, sandy cliffs rose abruptly before them to a height of two or three hundred feet. To make matters worse, it was also apparent that during the blind approach units had become mixed. But even this was not allowed to check them. For two minutes only they lay down to fix bayonets and throw off their packs. Then at the first word of command, all unformed as they were, they sprang to their feet and with a wild cheer made for the precipitous bluffs. Heavy as was the fire while they scrambled up, nothing could stop that first fine rush, and in a few minutes they were on the top, with the enemy flying in front of them. For a raw force, assured till the last moment of an unopposed landing and confused by the mixing of battalions and a landing on unstudied ground, it was a notable feat that gave good augury of a great success.

The whole operation had been watched by the Admiral and General Hamilton in the *Queen Elizabeth*, which had come up during the dark hours from her night anchorage off Avlaka point, in the south of Imbros, and so successful did the first attempt appear that they steamed off for Cape Helles. As yet, however, the Anzac's hold was precarious, but help was at hand. When Admiral Thursby heard the first burst of firing there was just light enough to see that the boats had reached the shore, and he at once ordered the destroyers with the second echelon of the covering force to push on through the squadron and land their troops. They had therefore been coming on close astern of the tows. As they approached the shore they came under a fairly hot fire of shrapnel, as well as rifles and machine-guns, but by 5.30 the whole of the covering force was ashore and the destroyers were starting back to fetch the main body from the transports, which were just beginning to close the shore.

It was clear, however, that the enemy was now fully on the alert, and had no mind to let the covering force be supported too easily. As soon as the transports drew within range of the Turkish field guns they met with so warm a reception that the Admiral had to order them to stop and lie outside the battleships. One of them, however, the *Galeka*, with the 7th Australian Battalion on board, had already pushed so far in that, finding no naval boats coming to her she began to land her men in her own boats. One company put off in six boats, but came under a heavy fire when close to the shore. It suffered heavy losses, but the survivors were able to seize a trench which enfiladed the narrow beach from behind Fishermen's Huts, and so quench the worst of the fire that had galled the landing of the covering force. The rest of the transports had stopped as directed, but notwithstanding the delay this inevitably caused, 4,000 more men were ashore by 7.20, making 8,000 in all, and as no reorganisation was yet possible they were pushed up into the line as they landed, wherever was the greatest need.

In spite of the confusion which the original mistake had caused, it to some extent proved a blessing in disguise, for though by edging too far to the north they had hit on an ugly part of the coast, they had just missed the formidable system of trenches by which the selected beach was defended. But from that side the fire was very severe. Shrapnel from Gaba Tepe was specially deadly, and to subdue it the Admiral ordered the *Bacchante* to close in and try what she could do. Captain Boyle responded in the old naval spirit of close action. The fire seemed to be coming from a depression behind the bluff of the cape, and in order to get at the guns, he determined to steam right inshore till the depression was open to his broadside. With his lead going continually he moved slowly in dead on to the beach, and kept on till his stem actually touched the ground. Though the guns were still invisible, he could now locate their position, and with his broadside he so swept the place that the guns were effectively kept under, and, indeed, seem subsequently to have been removed altogether. It was a fine feat of seamanship and measurement of risk that was deservedly applauded.

With this assistance and what the covering ships could give, by 8.30 the troops had penetrated about a mile inland, and there they proceeded to entrench till the main body could land. It was none too soon. For at the first alarm the two Turkish reserve battalions which had been bombed out of Maidos had been ordered to march. Thanks to the shortness of the distance from the fresh position they had had to take up, they had already reached the central ridge and were creeping down to attack.[1] Afloat too there was another delay, for just when the main body of the troops were beginning to take to the boats a sudden burst of fire fell amongst the transports, not only from heavy howitzers, but also from the *Turgud Reis*, which the airmen spotted above the Narrows off Maidos.[2] As the transports were being straddled, there was nothing for it but to order them to retire out of range. The battleships also moved, but only to take up new billets a little further north and more directly off the landing-place. Here the transports closed in again, for the *Triumph*, firing over the land, had soon shifted the Turkish battleship up the Straits. She with the other

[1] Prigge, p. 43.

[2] *Turgud Reis*, formerly *Weissenberg*, 9,900 tons, 6–11″ guns, completed 1893, purchased from Germany.

covering ships had also checked the howitzer fire, and by 9.30 the disembarkation was once more in full swing.

So well indeed did it proceed that the three brigades of the Australian Division (12,000 men) and two batteries of Indian Mountain Artillery were ashore by 2.0 p.m. All this time Turkish reinforcements were creeping into the fight, and the Anzac covering force and its supports struggled desperately to maintain the position they had so brilliantly seized, while shrapnel never ceased to rain on the beach for all the ships could do. But through it all the crews of the destroyers and boats, exposed and helpless as they were, toiled on without flinching to enable their comrades ashore to win the undying fame they did. Theirs was the inglorious part, but no one better than the hard-pressed troops knew what it meant to them, and their recognition of it was unstinted. " I can never speak sufficiently highly of them," General Birdwood wrote, " from admirals down to able seamen. The whole Anzac Corps would do anything for the navy. . . . Our men were devoted to those ships and their crews, and will always remember the British Navy with admiration and devotion."

While this happy brotherhood was thus performing its famous feat, the other subsidiary landing, ten miles to the southward, had developed at Y Beach. About 2.30 a.m., at a rendezvous four miles west of the landing-place, two companies of the King's Own Scottish Borderers, which formed the advanced guard of the covering force, were transferred to the four trawlers which were attached to the squadron. The rest of it, consisting of the remainder of the battalion and one company of the South Wales Borderers, remained in the *Sapphire* and *Amethyst*, while the Plymouth Marine battalion stood fast in their transport.[1] At 4.0, while it was still dark, the trawlers shoved off, and with the *Sapphire* and *Amethyst* on either flank began to make for the shore in line abreast, each towing six boats. At 2,000 yards from the beach the two light cruisers took up stations to support the flanks, while the *Goliath* got into position between 4,000 and 5,000 yards off the shore. At this landing a surprise was confidently expected, and though the dawn was fast breaking, no sign of life could be detected as the trawlers pushed in. Not a sound broke the stillness, till about 5.0, when they were close to the shore, the guns of

[1] By the instructions issued on April 17 the Marines were to land first, but by the order of the 21st the privilege was accorded to the King's Own Scottish Borderers, the reason being that the Marines were mainly recruits as yet too imperfectly trained to be used as a covering force.

all the ships disposed around the end of the peninsula suddenly proclaimed that the great attack had begun. Far inland and along the coast the burst of the first shells was telling the enemy what was at hand when the trawlers touched the ground. Their orders had been to push on till they felt the bottom. The troops were already in the boats; the oars were out in a moment and a dash began for the beach. Still not a sign of opposition. Undisturbed, the troops reached the shore in perfect order. The ground on which they quickly formed was a mere strip of sand at the foot of a steep, crumbling cliff some 200 feet high and covered with scrub. A number of small gullies, however, made an ascent possible. Scouts were soon at the top, reporting no enemy in sight. It was clear the surprise was complete. Apparently the landing had been expected by the Turks to take place a mile and a half to the southward. This was Gully Beach, where the Zighin Dere, or " Gully Ravine," as it was known to us, runs out to the sea nearly parallel to the coast. There elaborate defences had been constructed, but at Y there was nothing. The Marines' transport was at once ordered in, the trawlers quickly returned for the rest of the covering force, and shortly afterwards the whole of it was on the top of the cliff without a single casualty or trace of opposition. The trawlers by this time were well on their way to fetch the Marines, and by 6.0 they too had landed. As soon as the force was complete Colonel Matthews of the Marines, who was in command, signalled for the ships to cease fire on the lower part of Gully Ravine, since his intention was to advance along the ridge between it and the sea, in order to hold out a hand to the force landing at X Beach as soon as that force appeared to the southward. To facilitate the movement part of the troops were pushed forward across the upper part of the ravine to occupy a ridge about 1,000 yards inland which overlooked the road from Krithia to Sedd el Bahr. From this point scouts were thrown towards the south and as far as Krithia, but up till now nothing was seen either of enemy or friends.

At X, though there was no sign of an advance to join hands with the Y force, the landing had gone no less satisfactorily.[1] Here, as the operation was part of the main disembarkation, the force was larger, comprising three battalions, one each from the Royal Fusiliers, the Royal Inniskilling Fusiliers and the Border Regiment, with a working party of fifty men from the Anson battalion of the Royal Naval Division. The Royal Fusiliers, who were told off as the

[1] See Plan pp. 328–9.

covering force, were brought up from the general rendezvous off the mouth of the Straits in the *Implacable*, and the rest, when the time came, were to come in from their transports in the fleet-sweepers attached to the squadron. At four o'clock, simultaneously with the Y Beach force, the *Implacable* stood in with the leading companies in two tows and the other half of the battalion in two of the fleet-sweepers. Since there was here no chance of surprise, everything depended in the first instance on the *Implacable's* preparatory fire, and Captain Lockyer was ready to run all legitimate risk in making it as crushing as possible. It was soon evident that his utmost effort would be required, for as he stood in at five knots with the tows a heavy fire was opened on them from the cliffs on both sides of the beach. He therefore held on till close on the five-fathom line, and then anchored with only a shackle and a half out (18¾ fathoms), and there, with very little to spare under his keel, he brought his broadside to bear no more then 450 yards from the shore. From this close range he developed over the tows as they advanced an intense fire from his four 12″ and six of his 6″ guns on the cliffs and beach, and with eight of his 12-pounders on a ridge to starboard whence rifle fire was reaching the ship. In this work, he was supported by the *Dublin*, who also came under rifle fire, and till the boats were nearly touching the ground they kept it up. But for this support the losses might have been very great, for the beach was no more than a ribbon of sand 200 yards long and not ten yards broad, with a low cliff rising from it. As it was, the fire at the decisive range to which Captain Lockyer had pushed in was so overwhelming that the troops were able to leap ashore and form up with nothing but distant rifle fire to annoy them, and the whole battalion was quickly landed without a single casualty.[1]

As the troops landed Captain Lockyer lifted his fire to set up a barrage, and this he kept up till seven o'clock, when, on receiving a signal from the *Euryalus*, in which Admiral Wemyss' flag was flying, that his " overs " were falling close ahead of the men landing on the southern beaches, he ceased fire. Then, in accordance with his instructions, he moved out to his assigned bombarding position about 3,000 yards to seaward, and there he anchored while the fleet-sweepers took in the main force from the transports. At no point was the disembarkation carried out with so much precision and success as here. Admiral de Robeck, who had left Gaba

---

[1] The *Implacable* drew nearly 28 feet full draught and had 4–12″, 12–6″ and 16–12-pounders. While covering the landing she fired twenty rounds of 12″, 368 of 6″ and 308 of 12-pounders.

Tepe as soon as the Anzac covering force was well ashore, to bring the General down to the southern beaches, was passing as the *Implacable* was taking up her new station, and could give him the good news. He pronounced it a model landing, not only for the work of the ship, but also for the way the troops profited by the combined drill they had had at Mudros. The army's appreciation of what the navy had contributed was no less high, and thenceforth the place became known as " Implacable Beach." And justly so, for the Turks have testified that nowhere was the ship fire so terrible and effective as there.

The operations on the southern beaches which had stopped the *Implacable's* fire had been of a very different character from the rest. It was here the main attack had evidently been expected, and the enemy's organisation for defence was most complete. The configuration of the land was ideal for opposing a landing. The toe of the peninsula was marked by three hills, 114, 138 and 141,[1] corresponding to the three capes in which the peninsula terminates, Tekke Burnu, Helles and Sedd el Bahr. Between Tekke Burnu and Cape Helles the valley between the hills ran down through a break in the cliffs to a foreshore of deep powdery sand. This beach, which was known as " W," began close under Tekke Burnu, and with a breadth of fifteen to forty yards extended for about 350 yards to where the cliffs rose again precipitously at Cape Helles. Thus on each flank it was commanded by high and inaccessible ground, while along the centre the sandhills sloped gently upward, affording admirable ground for trenches with a perfect field of fire. General Hamilton, indeed, described it as a mere death-trap. Its natural capabilities had been increased by every device of German skill. The whole length of the foreshore was deeply wired at the water edge, another line of wire was concealed under the sea, and, in addition to this, both land and sea mines had been laid. The high ground moreover was seamed with trenches, machine guns enfilading on the wire were cunningly hidden in holes in the cliffs, and the crest, if ever it could be reached, was commanded by redoubts on the hills in rear which must be captured before a lodgment could be made. That on the slopes above Cape Helles, in the centre, was particularly formidable, for besides being protected by an entanglement twenty feet broad, it had a natural bare glacis, and was cut off from the next beach by wire extending to the shattered ruins of the Helles lighthouse.

This beach, known as V, where the main effort was to be made, was even more formidable. About the same

[1] These heights are given in feet.

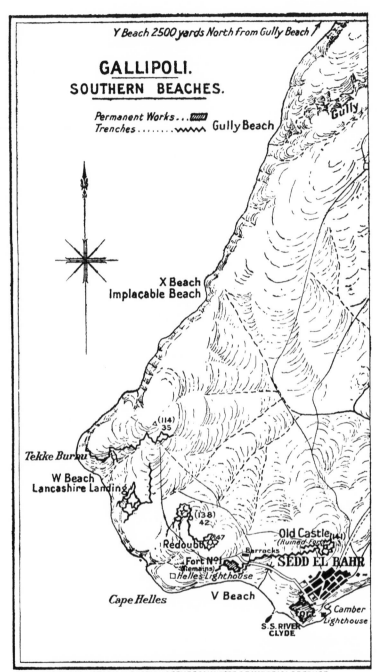

Y Beach 2500 yards North from Gully Beach

GALLIPOLI.
SOUTHERN BEACHES.

Permanent Works...
Trenches........

Gully Beach

Gully

X Beach
Implaçable Beach

△(114)
35

Tekke Burnu

W Beach
Lancashire Landing

(138)
42

△47

Redoubt

Old Castle
(Ruined Fort)

Barracks

Fort Nº1
(Remains)

SEDD EL BAHR

□Helles Lighthouse

Cape Helles

V Beach

Fort

Camber
Lighthouse

S.S. RIVER
CLYDE

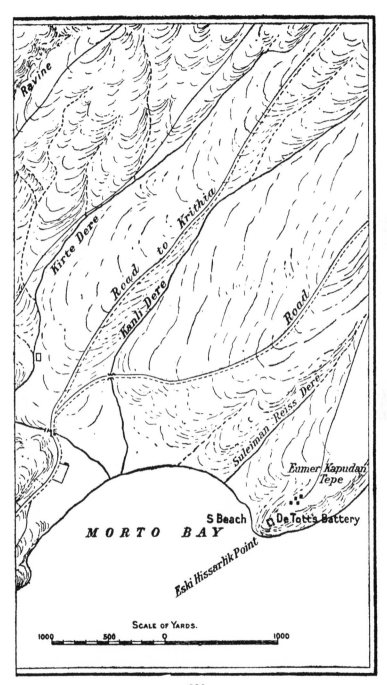

Ravine

Kirte Dere

Road to Krithia

Kanli Dere

Road

Suleiman Reiss Dere

Eumer Kapudan Tepe

S Beach

De Tott's Battery

MORTO BAY

Eski Hissarlik Point

SCALE OF YARDS.

1000   500   0   1000

length as that at W, but narrower, it formed as it were the stage of an amphitheatre, bounded on the east by the bluff on which stood Sedd el Bahr village and on the west by the slopes of Hill 138, near which stood the half-demolished but still tenable works of Fort No. 1. From a height of 100 feet above the shore grassy terraces sloped down in a natural glacis to a low stretch of sand dunes about four feet high, which formed an escarpment at the inner edge of the curving beach. Here was the only dead ground where a force could form, and before it could be reached there was another maze of wire and mines to be passed.

To storm such positions from the sea was by all experience an almost impossible enterprise without a severe preparatory bombardment, and it was this consideration that had gone far to reconcile the General to abandoning his idea of a night attack in deference to the technical naval objections. Still the experiments which had been made of the effect of ship fire on wire had not been encouraging, and when the hour came the weather conditions gave little hope that previous results would be improved upon. The beauty of that Sunday morning brought with it a soft haze which veiled the shore, so that nothing could be seen distinctly. To make matters worse, when at dawn the signal was given to open fire the glare of the approaching sunrise directly behind the hills threw the shore into shadow, so that picking out a target or accurate spotting was impossible, but by 5.0 a.m. all the bombarding ships were hard at it.

A mile to seaward off W Beach was Admiral Nicholson, commanding the main covering squadron in the *Swiftsure*, while the *Albion* was nearly the same distance off V Beach. For the best part of an hour with all calibres they searched the hills, the valley between the hills dominating Tekke Burnu and Cape Helles and every point that commanded the beaches. But it was blind work. By 5.30, the hour for which the landing was timed, the smother of smoke and mist ashore was so thick that the *Albion* had to cease fire, but as the tows were not yet approaching she began again. The troops were, in fact, behind time. At 4.0 the *Euryalus* had transferred to the boats her three companies of the 1st Lancashire Fusiliers, and a platoon (50 men) of the Anson battalion of the Royal Naval Division; the fourth, which completed the covering force for W Beach, was to come from the *Implacable*. The start was punctual enough, but owing to the unexpected strength of the current and the weakness of some of the towing steam-boats progress was slow. It was not till 5.50 that the *Euryalus* steamed in with her tows past the *Swiftsure*, who then made her final effort, and kept it in full blast till the boats were close in. At 1,500 yards from the shore Admiral Wemyss stopped, and the *Euryalus*, taking station north of the *Swiftsure*, joined in the bombardment while the tows went on.

The effect of the ship fire was to hold the enemy in his dugouts and support trenches, and he was kept completely silent till the boats were so close to the beach that the bombardment had to cease. Then in a moment, as the steamboats slipped the tows, the fire trenches were manned and a murderous fire of rifles, machine guns and pom-poms broke out from every point. Before the boats grounded numbers of men were killed and wounded, and in front of them they saw the maze of wire barely touched by the ship fire. Nothing daunted they hurled themselves ashore. Beneath their feet buried torpedo-heads exploded, and the fire increased. Still they pushed on, and under the converging storm of bullets and shell began hacking at the wire. Many fell, more took their places, and still success seemed impossible. But relief was at hand. At the west end of the beach, right under Tekke Burnu, were rocks on which it was believed a landing was possible. The tows of the left company made for it, and thus avoiding the worst of the cross fire they were able, by consummate handling of the boats, to get ashore with little loss. Pushing forward at once they surprised the enemy in a position which enfiladed the beach, captured some well-concealed pom-poms, and so turned the worst of the defences. At the same time the ships closed, and thanks to their help and the flanking fire of the left company the remaining three companies, or what was left of them, broke through the wire and past the exploding mines and began rapidly to reform to storm the higher ground.

To the sister service, breathlessly waiting for the result, the feat appeared no less than miraculous. "From the forebridge of the *Euryalus*," wrote Admiral Wemyss, "it seemed as though the impossible had been performed, for before many minutes had passed it became apparent that the beach was gained. I cannot conceive that it has ever been the lot of anybody to witness a finer exhibition of heroism." [1] In the glory of those crowded minutes the sailors shared and suffered their full portion, sitting at their oars with no means of retaliation. Yet, defenceless as they were, their spirit was as high as their losses; not a single boat failed to return for its second load, though in some of them there were not more than two men to pull an oar. While encumbered with dead and

---

[1] This beach was subsequently known as "Lancashire Landing."

wounded, they painfully made their way back, the survivors
of the gallant Lancashire Fusiliers, covered by the naval guns,
were already pushing up the slope. At 9.30 more troops were
being put ashore in order to press the advantage gained by
the successful landing at Implacable Beach; everything was
favourable to an early junction between the forces on either
side of Tekke Burnu. But of their comrades from V Beach
there was no sign.

There the daring had been no less, but success had proved
beyond human endeavour. It had been fully realised that
this would be the most hazardous landing of them all, and it
was for this reason it was to be made in larger force than the
rest and in a different manner. As at W Beach, the first
echelon of the covering force—three companies of the Dublin
Fusiliers with fifty men of the Anson battalion—was to be
taken in from the fleet-sweepers in six tows, each tow consisting of three or four service boats, manned by a mid-
shipman and six seamen, but simultaneously the rest of
it was to be run ashore in the *River Clyde*, close under
Sedd el Bahr. In her were the rest of the Dublins, the
Munster Fusiliers and half of the 2nd Hampshires, with the
West Riding Field Company, Royal Engineers, and a further
fifty men of the Anson battalion. It was hoped that by the
means which Commander Edward Unwin had devised for
expediting the landing, all these troops, numbering about
2,500, could be very quickly thrown ashore without undue
exposure.

The operation had been timed for 6.0 a.m., at which hour
the *River Clyde* was to be off the *Albion* and go straight in.
But here also the boats had been delayed. Commander
Unwin, who was in charge of the *River Clyde*, signalled to
know if he should go in. He was told to do so as soon as the
tows got up in line and to run ashore as they landed. It was
over half an hour before they arrived and the final push in
could begin. In deference to the wish of the Brigadier on
board, the *River Clyde* still held back a little for the boats
to land first, according to plan, but by 6.44 the tows were so
close in that the *Albion* had to cease fire on the beach and
lift to the hills above. As she did so the boats cast off and the
starboard tow, carrying a half-company of the Dublin Fusiliers,
made for the camber at Sedd el Bahr, where a landing was
also to be effected. As yet the beach was silent, and the tows
held on, the next two for the shore between Sedd el Bahr
and the *River Clyde* and the other three to the west of her.
For about five minutes they were undisturbed. Then, as
the steamboats cast off the boats, and the oars were got out,

the same murderous fire broke out as at W. And here, owing to the configuration of the ground and the impossibility of turning the flank, it was far worse. In a few minutes nearly every man was killed or wounded and the boats were seen drifting about helplessly, some broadside on with men taking cover behind them. In several not a man was untouched, in one of them only two hands were left alive, and another entirely disappeared. The attack was simply wiped out, and it was no more than a few stragglers that were able to struggle through the unbroken wire to the shelter of the low escarpment of the sandhills.

Nothing could now save the situation but the success of the experiment with the *River Clyde*. She was coming on, with her hopper and big lighters in tow alongside, under a hail of shell from the Asiatic batteries. But heavy as it was, added to the local fire, it did nothing to unnerve the hand of her commander. With precise accuracy he ran his ship ashore in exact position at the eastern end of the beach and all seemed well. Had the shore been what was believed, there would have been no hitch. But unhappily it proved to shelve so much more gently than had been expected that the hopper took the ground before she was high enough for her flying gangway to reach the shore. The foremost lighter, moreover, instead of being carried on by its own way to make the connection, swung away to port in the wind. Thus a gap was made, and as nearly all the men in the lighter and the hopper were quickly shot down, the accident could not be immediately rectified.

So the well-considered plan had failed, but failure was a thing that neither service was ready to admit. Commander Unwin promptly left the *River Clyde* and, standing up to his waist in water in the galling fire, directed operations for putting things right.[1] In about five minutes, " thanks," as the Brigade Diary records, " to the extraordinary gallantry displayed by the naval party, the barges were got into some sort of position." One was close on the starboard bow, and Captain E. L. H. Henderson of the Munsters at once led his company out into it through the deadly fire. Many were shot down on the gangways and lighters as they ran from one to the

---

[1] The names specially mentioned by Admiral Wemyss for the " extraordinarily gallant conduct " were, besides Commander Unwin, Lieutenant John A. V. Morse (*Cornwallis*), Midshipmen G. L. Drewry, R.N.R. (*Hussar*), and W. St. A. Malleson, R.N. (*Cornwallis*), Petty Officers J. H. Russell and Rummings (R.N.A.S.) and Able Seamen W. C. Williams, R.F.R., and G. McK. Samson, R.N.R. (both of *Hussar*). Commander Unwin, both the midshipmen and Samson were awarded the Victoria Cross, and Lieutenant Morse the D.S.O.

other; those that reached the hopper began leaping into the water, but not more than a platoon reached the beach. Nothing dismayed, Captain G. W. Geddes immediately followed with his company. He, too, reached the hopper, but only to find that a flaw of wind off the shore had drifted it out into deep water. Even that did not stop them. He himself gave a lead by jumping overboard, and though he succeeded in reaching the shore, those that followed him were nearly all drowned by the weight of their ammunition and equipment. Such an effort was far too costly to continue, and the remnant could do nothing but stay where they were.

Yet there was no word of defeat. Commander Unwin and his party were still at work. For an hour, in spite of all the enemy's fire could do, they toiled on. He seemed to bear a charmed life, but even so, he and his gallant band could not have survived for five minutes but for the well-served machine-guns in the bows of the *River Clyde*. It had been Commander Unwin's idea to take in with the troops a ready-made fort, and it now well served his turn. The detachment of the armed motor-car contingent of the Royal Naval Division who manned the machine guns on board could at least make sure of their target, and so hot and accurate was their fire that the Turks kept quiet in the trenches, and their fire was almost confined to snipers. In this way the machine-gunners were able not only to keep the naval men going in the water, but also to prevent a complete massacre of the troops who were sheltering in the lighters.

The result was that by 8.0 the floating bridge was connected up again. Then, covered by the *River Clyde's* machine-guns, Major C. H. B. Jarrett led out another company of the Munsters to complete what their comrades had begun. Their heroism and their fate were the same. The spit of sand and half-submerged ledge of rock over which they had to pass were at once the focus of a tornado of fire. Few passed alive, and when Major Jarrett saw how behind him the gangways and lighters were choked with dead and wounded he passed the word that no more should leave the ship. There at least they were safe from rifle and machine-gun fire, and there they waited while the few survivors ashore sought what shelter they could find at the foot of the cliffs by digging themselves into the sandy escarpment. Until the ships could do something more to subdue the enemy's fire it was madness to proceed in daylight.

At present there was only the *Albion*, and she could do little; for about half an hour earlier a signal had come from the *Lord Nelson* inside the Straits to say that our men were in Sedd el Bahr village, and she had to cease firing on it and devote her attention to the centre hill, against which the Lancashire Fusiliers were preparing to advance from W Beach. Half a company of the Dublin Fusiliers from the starboard tow had, in fact, landed at the Camber. It was dead ground, and their landing had been unopposed, but when they attempted to advance up the steep and narrow approach which led to the village they were met with a blast of rifle and machine-gun fire that was quite impassable. Again and again, with the greatest gallantry, they strove to close the loopholed ruins of the fort, and so far did they push on that from the sea it looked as if they had actually reached the village. But it was, in fact, beyond human effort, and at last—reduced to a bare skeleton of the party that had come ashore—they had to be re-embarked, and leave the well-organised Turkish position to do its worst against V Beach.

Another ship, the *Cornwallis*, had been told off to support the *River Clyde* landing, but for the moment she had other work to do and was long in arriving. Her first task was to act as landing ship for Morto Bay. Although it had been found necessary, owing to the confined nature of the approaches, to reduce the force below what was originally intended, this landing had a special importance. The idea of using it in combination with that at Y Beach to envelop the enemy's advanced force had naturally become less hopeful since its strength was reduced, but as a security for the right flank of the main attack it was still a vital link in the chain. Since Morto Bay had been rejected as too badly exposed to be used for the main landing, the venture had all the character of a forlorn hope. Three companies of the 2nd South Wales Borderers had been detailed for the attempt. It was one of the best battalions in the division, but there had been no opportunity for exercising the men in boat work. Success depended on ship fire, and the night before the attack Captain Davidson of the *Cornwallis* had received a signal from Admiral Wemyss that after taking in the troops he was not to come out to his bombarding station immediately, but to stay and support them till they were landed. This he took as a further expression of the anxiety that was felt about this landing, owing to its exposure to shell fire from the Asiatic batteries. Two covering battleships had already been told off to it, the *Lord Nelson* at Morto Bay and the *Vengeance* a mile or so above it, off the Kereves Dere. The *Prince George* was also in the entrance, with orders to attend to the Asiatic batteries, and the *Agamemnon* was well inside, covering Captain Heneage's minesweeping and net-laying flotilla. Besides these five ships there were also three of the French squadron supporting their own landing. The cover provided by the original plan was therefore very strong, and for this reason Captain Davidson interpreted the new order in a sense beyond what appears to have been intended. His view of its meaning was emphasised by a further difficulty about the particular landing. It was that no destroyers and no steamboats or naval boats of any kind were available for the operation. Four trawlers, each towing six boats, were to take them in, and as it was impossible for fully equipped soldiers to row them against the current the trawlers were to carry on till they ran ashore. Even so the distance the untrained troops would have to cover by their own efforts might be considerable, and two seamen for each boat were all that could be spared. The first company was to land just inside Eski Hissarlik Point, the precipitous headland which marks the eastern end of the bay, and to endeavour to seize the old De Tott's battery which crowns it. Further in the bay a well-wooded slope falls gently from a lower ridge to a good beach. It was known to be entrenched, but here the other two companies were to disembark and rush the defences. Thus, while the right flank of the troops would be well protected by the sea, their left would be in the air. Captain Davidson therefore arranged with Colonel H. G. Casson, who commanded the South Wales Borderers, that besides providing a coxswain and bowman for each boat he would send in his marines in his own boats to form a flanking party, and twenty-five seamen as a beach party to help drag in the transports' boats and disembark the ammunition quickly.

During the night at a rendezvous outside the Straits the troops had been transferred from the *Cornwallis* to the trawlers, and about daybreak, when well inside, they were quietly moved from the trawlers to the boats, and as the trawlers laboured on against the strong current for the two or three miles that remained to do, the *Cornwallis* kept station to conceal them from the European side, and fired on the beach and adjacent hills as she proceeded. As soon, however, as the light made, the Asiatic batteries detected them, and were soon showering shrapnel, but though some boats were hit, there were no casualties before the trawlers went forward to enter the bay. Captain Heneage, who had been proceeding ahead of them with his ten destroyers and five minesweepers, covered by the *Agamemnon*, had already swept the bay, and at the last moment, at Admiral Wemyss's orders, had detached two of his destroyers, *Basilisk* and *Grasshopper*, to support the landing. The special covering ships, *Lord Nelson* and *Vengeance*, had taken up their station at 5.0 a.m., and ever since had been assiduously searching their assigned fire areas, and especially the hill, above De Tott's battery. Owing to the number of our own ships and those of the French entering at the same time and to the strength of the current it was not till 7.30 that the trawlers with their tows passed the *Lord Nelson*, and as they went in both she and the *Cornwallis*, as well as the two destroyers, swept the whole shore with their guns.

In a few minutes the trawlers had taken the ground 400 yards from the shore. They were still under distant howitzer fire, but here again, either owing to the ship fire or a general order, not a shot came from the shore, nor could any enemy be seen as the boats, in excellent order, rowed in. As an eye-witness says, it was as though they were landing on a desert island. But as the first company on the right took to the water up to their waists a heavy rifle fire opened on them. Still, without a moment's hesitation, while the other two companies were wading in, they formed and made for the cliff. By 7.30 nearly all were ashore. The other two companies quickly rushed with the bayonet a trench they found right in front of them, and by the time the *Cornwallis's* landing party reached the shore the first company were half-way up to De Tott's. With the naval party was Captain Davidson himself. In order the better to carry out his orders to support the landing he had decided to anchor his ship and come ashore with his men. With him was Colonel Casson, the intention being to land at the same time as the troops, but through having to keep clear of the *Agamemnon* they were late in reaching the beach. Once ashore they were quickly at work. While the bluejackets ran to draw in the boats and help the troops clear them, the marines were in time to assist in taking the second trench. When the bluejackets' work was done they, too, begged leave to join the fighting line, and being unencumbered with equipment were in time to take a hand with the third trench. Everything indeed had gone with such speed that by 8.0 De Tott's battery and the ridge above the slope were won, and the position secured with comparatively little loss. The unexpected facility with which the forlorn hope accomplished its task was undoubtedly due to ship fire. A special field battery had been placed north-east of the bay to command it, another was sent down from Krithia, where the 25th Regiment was in reserve, but the Turks say that owing to the severity of the naval bombardment neither was able to fire, while a howitzer battery north of Morto could only get in a shot occasionally. As for the infantry defending the place, of whom prisoners state there was a whole battalion,[1] their first experience of heavy shell from the sea had a demoralising effect for the time being.

That the fire from the Asiatic side had also proved less troublesome than had been anticipated was, no doubt, owing to the *Prince George* and the French ships keeping the guns busy on that side. Though the French covering force did not begin to disembark till nearly ten o'clock, the ships had opened their bombardment about a quarter to six, more than an hour before our troops began to land in Morto Bay. Admiral Guépratte, in the *Jauréguiberry*, was well inside, some 3,000 yards east-north-east of Kum Kale, and the *Henri IV* north of it, both concentrating on the fort, barracks and village. Outside was the *Askold*, keeping up her reputation for smartness and exciting every one's admiration by the neatness and accuracy of her salvoes. With her was the *Jeanne d'Arc*, distributing her fire between Kum Kale, Yeni Shehr and Orkanie, but shortly before 8.0, when our troops were all ashore, she was ordered off at high speed to join the demonstration in Bashika Bay, where the French auxiliary cruiser *Lorraine*, with five transports and a destroyer, had been left to operate. The effect of this feint was scarcely less successful than that of the Royal Naval Division in the Gulf of Xeros, for Weber Pasha was forced to move there and deploy one of the two divisions which he had concentrated near Troy.[2]

The French Staff, who had detailed a complete regiment for the Kum Kale landing, intended to put them ashore at the pier, where our own marines had previously met with so hot a reception. On this experience the Royal Marine officer attached to General d'Amade persuaded him to substitute the beach just outside, where, under shelter of the ruined fort, was fairly dead ground. At 6.20 the Admiral made the signal to land, but, as was only to be expected from the previous day's trial, there were serious delays in carrying it out. It had been bad enough when rehearsing in the still waters of Skyros, but at the entrance of the Straits the old-type steamboats of the French ships were unequal to the strong current, and torpedo boats had to be called up to take their place. Owing to this difficulty and others arising

---

[1] The Turkish official statement is that this day there was only one company.

[2] Prigge, p. 37.

from want of practice it was nearly three hours before the
Askold's steamboat got the first tow clear of the foremost
transport.   At 10.0 the boats were cast off, but too near the
pier, and they came under fire from guns on In Tepe and also
from machine-guns which had been concealed in a windmill
at the mouth of the Mendere River.   One boat was sunk
and the other six were swept back by the current.   The
obnoxious redoubt which had done the damage was, however, quickly silenced by the ships and the mill blown to
pieces, and the other tows, making more directly for the
selected beach, covered by the destroyers, were able to
land their men almost unopposed.[1]   The covering force which
thus got ashore was the 6th Colonial Regiment, and by
10.30 it could be seen that their leading company of Senegalese was right through the village.   So without difficulty
the regiment was able to establish itself in the fort and village
and along the shore to the south of it, and there they waited
for the other battalions before making a push for the cemetery and Yeni Shehr, where a battalion of Weber Pasha's
other division (IIIrd) was now deploying, while its reserves
were being hurried up from Chiplak Keui, six miles away.

By this time also the covering forces of the Allied army
had everywhere got a firm hold on the first positions they
were intended to seize—everywhere, that is, except at the
fatal Sedd el Bahr (V) Beach.   But there another attempt
was about to be made.   At 8.15, just as the second effort
failed, Admiral de Robeck and General Hamilton had come
up near the *Albion* in the *Queen Elizabeth*, and having
ascertained that the report of troops being in Sedd el
Bahr was false, ordered the flagship to open fire on the
village with her 15″ guns.   The *Albion*, who had just heard
of the failure of the lighter bridge, seized the opportunity
to ask leave to send in two of her boats to make good the
gap.   It was granted, and shortly before 10.0 her launch
and pinnace, with casks lashed under the thwarts and manned
by volunteer crews, were towed in, but so heavy was the fire
they met that work was almost impossible.

Still the new attempt was not abandoned.   General
Napier, commanding the 88th Brigade, approached the beach
in a fleet sweeper.   With him were the Brigade Staff and
detachments of the Worcestershire and Hampshire Regiments.   When some distance from the shore, he awaited

---

[1] Vedel, *Nos Marins à la Guerre*, p. 135.   Prigge says there was only one
company in Kum Kale, and that it had lost heavily under the shrapnel fire
of the ships, pp. 36–7.

the return of the tows which were to land his troops. Soon after 9.0 some of the boats remaining after the disaster to the Dublin Fusiliers came alongside. They were quickly emptied of the dead and wounded, and in a few minutes General Napier and his Staff, with the Worcestershire detachment and a small party of the Hampshire, were heading for the beach. The Brigadier and his Staff reached the hopper, but their gallant attempt to land was foiled by a renewed burst of Turkish fire, and in a quarter of an hour General Napier and his Brigade-Major were killed.

Unless the Turkish positions could be destroyed by further bombardment it was clearly useless to persevere. But although at 8.0 the *Lord Nelson* had signalled from Morto Bay that the South Wales Borderers were already on the top of Eski Hissarlik, above De Tott's battery, the *Cornwallis* had not come away. At 8.45 she herself reported them in possession of the hill and ridge from the bay to the Straits, and the *Queen Elizabeth* signalled for her to take her new station. Still Captain Davidson was too busy getting off the wounded, to obey at once. Again and again the signal was repeated with increasing emphasis, but it was not till 10.0, when the Asiatic guns had ceased to be troublesome and the troops seemed firmly established, that he began to withdraw his landing party. By the time his ship was in position off Sedd el Bahr it had been decided to abandon any further attempt to land from the *River Clyde* till nightfall, and the remainder of the troops allotted to this point, consisting mainly of the Worcestershire Regiment, had been diverted to W Beach.

There, too, after the ridge had been seized in the first rush the advance had been held up. The Lancashire Fusiliers had pushed far enough on the right, however, to establish a signal station in the ruins of the Helles lighthouse, and could now communicate more easily with the ships. About eight o'clock it looked as if the ship fire on the centre hill (138) had done its work. The redoubt seemed evacuated, but when the Fusiliers tried to advance they found it still too well occupied to enable them to pass the unbroken wire which covered its glacis.[1] On the left the movement which had begun against the hill above Tekke Burnu (114) was also held up. The attempt which the first two companies of the Royal Fusiliers had been making to take it in reverse from Implacable Beach had been checked, but, reinforced by a third company, they pushed on again, and by 11.0 had a good hold on the hill and

---

[1] The Turks state that the troops fighting in this area—Tekke Burnu to Sedd el Bahr—were four companies of infantry and one of engineers.

over forty prisoners. Meanwhile, however, their left, which had advanced too far forward, were being thrust back to the edge of the cliff with heavy loss, and for a time the position was precarious. From Y Beach came no help, for though, as we have seen, the King's Own Scottish Borderers and Marines had been reaching out from their advanced position since 10.0, they had not been able to get touch, and finding themselves in the air and without support, they had just decided to retire back across the gully and establish themselves behind it closer to the landing-place.

Here, then, began the second hitch in the combined plan. It was the more regrettable since the landing itself had been so complete a success, and since the failure at Sedd el Bahr Beach it had gained increased value as a turning movement. So much importance indeed did General Hamilton attach to its development that, about 9.0, when he was aware how completely the attack at Sedd el Bahr was held up, he had it in mind to divert the troops intended to support that landing to reinforce Y Beach. Admiral de Robeck had trawlers available, and shortly before 9.30 General Hunter-Weston was asked if he would like to see it done. No reply was made, and when at 10.0 it was clear that the Worcestershire Regiment must be diverted from Sedd el Bahr Beach he asked again. But after consulting Admiral Wemyss and the principal transport officer, General Hunter-Weston declined the offer, on the ground that his naval colleagues thought that such an interference with the existing arrangements would too greatly delay the general disembarkation.

From Y therefore nothing further could be done, but at Implacable Beach they were quickly able to secure the position with the force assigned to it. The two supporting battalions, 1st Border Regiment and 1st Inniskilling Fusiliers, had been all ashore for half an hour. It had been intended to keep them there in reserve till the advance from the southern beaches began to reach them, but now reinforcements for them were sent up the cliff, when an immediate bayonet charge drove the Turks back for 1,000 yards. By this smart piece of work they obtained elbow room to establish a tenable position and about noon make a firm connection with W Beach, where by this time the left wing of the Lancashires had hold of the other side of the hill above Tekke Burnu.

Owing to the havoc that had been made with the boats the main body of the force had been seriously delayed. It was not till nearly 9.30 that the Essex Regiment began to land at W Beach. They were later followed by the

Worcestershire Regiment who had been diverted from Sedd el Bahr, and both battalions were at once thrown into the gap between the two wings of the Lancashires for an attack on the crest of Hill 138. But in face of the fire from this hill and with no sign of support from Sedd el Bahr progress was impossible. Thus as the forenoon wore to an end we were everywhere just clinging to the ground which the covering forces had won, and the prospect was black for the intended advance on Achi Baba.

To the Turks the outlook was no less dark. General von Sanders' dispositions had been based on a firm belief in the impregnability of the southern beaches. No more than one regiment of the IXth Division, it would seem, had been devoted to their defence; the other two were in reserve and still far away. One of them had reached Krithia, but had had to turn its attention to X and Y Beaches. The third regiment had not yet arrived. It was noon before Essad reached Maidos, and then he found that part of the reserves of his XIXth Division had been already sent to Gaba Tepe. Hurrying to the top of the Kilid Bahr ridge, he was so impressed by the gravity of the Anzac threat to his communications that he ordered the third regiment to follow the other two. Thus all his main reserve was absorbed, and hearing a new outburst of fire from the fleet he went on to Krithia.[1]

We had still, in fact, a good chance of extending the footing gained, and the Essex and Worcestershire battalions advanced to the assault of the centre hill under cover of the unceasing bombardment from the sea. The demoralising effect on the Turkish infantry was all that could be desired. By 1.30 the Worcestershire had reached its south-east slopes, but there they were brought up by a maze of wire. It had been too close to our own troops for the ships to destroy it, but officers and men got to work with wire-cutters, while from the sea the shells screamed over their heads to keep down the fire from the summit. For two hours the terrible struggle went on. They had now fresh troops in front of them, for by this time a regiment of the IXth Turkish Division had come up and been thrown into the fight. But in spite of the numbers against them our men persevered, and as they crept on the ships never ceased to fire close beyond. The effect seems to have been to crush almost entirely the fresh forces of the enemy. In the end, out of the whole regiment, only two officers are said to have been left fit for duty.[2] The accuracy

[1] Prigge, pp. 44–5.   [2] Ibid., p. 49.

of the *Swiftsure's* fire elicited special admiration, and under cover of the storm of shell lanes were gradually opened in the wire. The price in gallant lives was heavy enough to shake the stoutest troops, but these men were not shaken. By 4.0 they had captured not only the hill, but also the redoubt in which its almost impregnable defences culminated.

Still they were not content. Severely as the heights commanding Sedd el Bahr Beach had been punished, no advance on that side was yet possible. Trenches close to the Helles lighthouse still denied any attempt to leave the *River Clyde* or to move the men, who, all day long, parched and scorched by the sun, had been crouching under the low escarpment of the sand-dunes. To release them the Worcestershire began to push to their right to take the lighthouse trenches in reverse. But again they were checked by wire. The entanglement which stretched between the two beaches barred the way, and it was swept by machine-guns established in the ruins of Fort No. 1 above Sedd el Bahr beach, but again the wire-cutters were got to work, while on board the ships men watched and wondered. " Through glasses," wrote General Hamilton, " they could be seen quietly snipping away under a hellish fire as if they were pruning a vineyard." But all was in vain. In spite of the utmost the ships could do in the failing light the enemy's fire grew hotter and hotter, and exhausted at last with a long day's fighting under a hot sun after a sleepless night, the undaunted remnants of those immortal regiments had to desist.

At sea there could be no rest. All day long, while afloat and ashore the fighting rose and fell, streams of boats passed incessantly between ships and shore, taking off the wounded as best they could and bringing in gear and stores, nourishing the thinning ranks, and hour by hour tightening the grip the troops had seized. The hold was still far from secure, and progress was far short of what had been hoped. Since the first landings, the covering ships, whenever no more urgent target offered, had been bombarding Achi Baba in anticipation of an assault, but the key of the situation was still beyond our reach when the sun was low. In the struggle with the unbroken wire and in the costly failure at Sedd el Bahr the power to advance was spent.

Still much had been done. By 4.0 the line was continuous from Implacable Beach to Helles. At headquarters in the *Euryalus* it was even believed that it reached unbroken to Y, but this was far from the truth. There from 3.0 p.m. till 5.0 the troops had been digging themselves in on the sea side of the gully, when, just before sundown, it was discovered that a heavy attack upon their left was developing from Krithia. Half the Turkish reinforcements which had reached that place about noon were being launched against them. Essad had not ventured to attack earlier, so deadly was the fire from the sea in daylight. Even now he was too soon. The evening glow was still enough for the ships to see the Turks making their way from the northward along the cliff. The *Goliath, Dublin, Sapphire*, and *Amethyst* were on them at once, and before the sun set the attack was swept away.

On the Asiatic side the French operations had equally failed to develop as intended. About noon the second landing began, and by 2.30 the whole of the infantry was ashore and an advance could be begun against the cemetery. But though they captured some prisoners, the moment they debouched from the village they were met with such heavy fire that further progress was impossible without artillery. The battery of 75's was just approaching the beach, but almost as soon as the guns were in position they were found by the enemy's howitzers, and by 5.0, when the whole force was ashore, it was realised that the chance of a quick success was passed. An aeroplane had just reported that strong reinforcements were coming up to Yeni Shehr, and seeing that the operation was only intended as a diversion, to storm the position was not worth the sacrifice it would entail. They therefore stood fast where they were, while every attempt of the Turks to counter-attack from Yeni Shehr was easily crushed by the ships deployed along the shore. Those within the Straits equally prevented any reinforcements crossing the Mendere River. Thus on the Asiatic side, though less had been accomplished than had been intended, there was little doubt the diversion served its purpose in reducing the distant fire on Morto Bay and Sedd el Bahr beach. So slight indeed was the interference of the Asiatic guns at Morto Bay, where they had been most feared, that General Hamilton afterwards regretted that the whole of the troops assigned to Sedd el Bahr had not been sent there instead.

Up at the extreme left of the operations the Australians and New Zealanders had had a very different experience from the French on the extreme right. There the counter-attacks had been almost incessant and always in superior force. Prisoners said that besides the troops they first met, a whole division had concentrated at Boghali. As we have seen, all three regiments of the main reserve, that is, the XIXth Division, had been thrown in against them. Seldom have untried troops received so severe a baptism of fire—never have they borne it with more fortitude. There had been no time to reorganise. Every company as it landed had to be pushed up into the firing line wherever it was most needed. They had no artillery, and were galled by shrapnel, which the ships, being as yet without direct communication with the observation officers ashore, could not entirely subdue. The advanced position, which had been seized after the first rush, was lost, and under every kind of difficulty an attempt was made to establish themselves on the ridge above the landing-place. So they clung on, looking anxiously for the delayed reinforcements. About 3.0 p.m. the transports with the New Zealand and Australian Division (two brigades) began to arrive, and in half an hour the first echelon was making for the shore. At the moment our left was being dangerously pressed back, but with a seaplane to direct her fire the *Majestic* was able to give assistance, and as the fresh troops could be pushed in to the rescue, the position was saved. From then till midnight the exhausted seamen toiled on to get men and stores ashore, and at the same time to evacuate the wounded, of whom at one time there were 1,500 on the beach. So busy indeed were the boats in getting them off, that at sunset the Turkish divisional commander reported that the force was re-embarking.[1] The night was wet and dark; the attacks and shelling continued, even the last comers had suffered severely, and the spirit of the force was well-nigh spent. They had endured beyond all that could be expected of young troops, but what would happen if they were heavily attacked in the morning? If they stayed where they were it might mean the massacre of the whole corps, and as darkness fell it began to be a question whether the only course left was not to re-embark while there was yet time.

As night closed in upon that day of sacrifice, Morto Bay and Y Beach were also causes of anxiety. Owing to the failure of the intended advance from the southern beaches, both these forces were still in the air, and there was every prospect that during the night the enemy would have time to bring up fresh strength to drive them into the sea. No troops were available to reinforce them. All that could be done was to increase the ship support. The Admiral therefore ordered the *Lord Nelson* and *Agamemnon*, who had seen the sweeping completed within the Straits, to come outside and lie off Y Beach for the night, while the *Prince George* was directed to join the *Vengeance* off Morto Bay.

[1] Prigge, p. 55.

Meanwhile Captain Heathcoat Grant and General Paris had been carrying out their demonstration with the Royal Naval Division at the head of the Gulf of Xeros in accordance with the original plan. After a prolonged bombardment a feint of landing began just before dark. Some 1,200 men were put into the transports' boats and towed in by trawlers. Till 9.30 they remained off the shore without drawing a shot or causing any perceptible movement. They were then withdrawn. It had been intended that a naval party should now land and light flares on the beaches in hopes of attracting the enemy's attention, but at the suggestion of Lieutenant-Commander B. C. Freiberg, he was allowed to swim ashore alone. He lit the flares and even penetrated some distance inland without finding a trace of Turkish troops. So entirely deserted seemed both the coast and the Bulair lines that Captain Grant had some hope of getting orders to carry out a real landing next day, and in view of this possibility he ordered his trawlers to sweep an approach to the landing-place just east of Bulair. But shortly after midnight, when Freiberg returned with his report, Captain Grant was surprised by orders of a very different character.

After making his dispositions for the night in the southern area Admiral de Robeck, about 11.0 p.m., started up to see how things were going at Gaba Tepe. General Hamilton had seized the opportunity of snatching a few hours sleep, but his rest was short. Just about midnight he was aroused to deal with a question which he alone could decide. The flagship was now off the Anzac beach, and Admiral Thursby and two of General Birdwood's brigadiers had come on board with a staggering report of the position ashore. They bore a letter from General Birdwood in which he expressed the gravest doubts whether his crippled and exhausted force could hold on in the face of another such experience as they had had during the past day. In the condition the troops were a few hours more shelling or a heavy attack would probably lead to a disaster, and if they were to re-embark the work must begin at once. What was to be done? Opinion ashore was clearly unanimous that retreat was the only course. Yet even if such a lamentable end to so brilliant a beginning had to be admitted, was a re-embarkation possible without the practical annihilation of that splendid force? In Admiral Thursby's eyes alone could the General discern a ray of hope, and to him he turned in desperation. How long would the re-embarkation take? The best part of three days. And where were the Turks? Right on the top of them. Then what was to be done? The Admiral, having seen what

he had seen, did not hesitate in his reply. If the men who
had forced that landing were told they must hold on, hold
on they would. General Hamilton knew the men, too, and
he agreed; so that was the answer he had the courage to
send. Since it would take at least two days to get them off,
they must dig in and hold their ground, and to lighten the
gloomy order he told them that the Australian submarine
had just sent word that she had made her way past the
Narrows and had torpedoed a gunboat off Chanak. In the
course of the night the rest of the Anzac Corps were
disembarked.

It was this decision which interrupted Captain Grant's
proceedings at Bulair. Admiral de Robeck was doing everything possible to make good the desperate resolution that
had been taken, as well as to prepare for the worst. Captain
Grant's orders were to collect every boat he could and have
them towed down to Gaba Tepe, while he himself was to leave
his transports in charge of the *Dartmouth* and come down at
once to support the *Majestic* on the left of the Anzacs. The
Doris was to join the *Triumph*, while the Admiral remained
with the *Queen Elizabeth* on the right, just south of Gaba
Tepe. Every ship was given the particular battery for which
she was to be responsible, and the Admiral signalled that
he relied on the squadron to relieve the pressure on the
Anzacs at daylight. Every available lighter and trawler had
also been called up from Mudros, and long before dawn the
Bulair trawlers, with thirty-six boats, were on their way
to Gaba Tepe.

So that strenuous period of twenty-four hours came to an
end in gravest doubt and anxiety, but with an unparalleled
feat to its credit—a feat accomplished in the face of every
difficulty that delay, inadequate means and a well-prepared
enemy could place in the way of success. Still for all that
had been done it was far short of the aim, and much remained
to do. As yet the force had barely got its claws in. The
cost had been heavy beyond all expectation, and even the
stoutest hearts could not look forward to the morrow without
misgiving.

And yet the anxiety was not confined to our own side.
To the anxious enemy it seemed that in effecting a landing
on the southern beaches the British had achieved the impossible; from Gaba Tepe the Anzacs were threatening to cut the
Turkish army in two, and General Liman von Sanders' system
of defence had been upset by General Hamilton's plan of
attack. In announcing the success of the landing, the officer
commanding at the southern beaches stoutly proclaimed

that at nightfall he was going to attack with his whole force and drive the enemy into the sea.   But to von Sanders the situation appeared so critical that he felt he must take the risk of moving his two divisions away from Bulair.   The ships and transports were still hovering in the offing, but as no attempt had been made to land it might only mean a feint. So with a disturbing sense of the hazard he was running he decided to send both divisions by water to Maidos, leaving nothing but his cavalry brigade to watch the head of the gulf.[1]

[1] Liman von Sanders, p. 89.

CHAPTER XVIII

THE DARDANELLES—THE INITIAL ADVANCE APRIL 26-28, AND THE FIRST BATTLE OF KRITHIA

DURING the night the rain ceased and the dawn came again in perfect serenity, promising another day that left nothing to be desired for the work there was to do. And up at Anzac with the dawn came a new spirit as calm and promising. The troops had been left in comparative quiet, and it soon became evident that the confidence which had been placed in them had bred fresh confidence in themselves. They had been able to dig themselves in snugly; guns had been landed, hauled up to the crest and dug in too, and to seaward, as the day broke gloriously, it lit up an imposing array of battleships and cruisers taking station to back their efforts.

The original squadron under Admiral Thursby had been reinforced by the *Queen Elizabeth*, whilst the bulk of the force that had demonstrated off Bulair was hurrying south to the threatened position, and as soon as day had set in Admiral de Robeck signalled the new arrivals to take station on either flank, whence support could be most efficaciously given. Boats were still streaming between the shore and the transports. During the night ample supplies of water and ammunition had been landed. A reserve of men was accumulating on the beach as the last units of the 4th Australian Brigade were being brought in, and nothing had been left undone to meet a decisive attack.

With the first light of day the ships opened on their assigned targets, but they were still difficult to locate, and the rain of shrapnel continued both on the position and the beach. For two or three hours the situation remained critical. Heavy fighting took place in parts of the line, and here and there ground had to be given, but the fire from the sea—which prisoners afterwards described as appalling—made it almost impossible to get the shuddering Turks from the shelter of the broken ground and prevented anything like an organised assault from developing. By 9.0 a.m. the *Queen Elizabeth* had succeeded in knocking out the most annoying of the batteries and the Turkish attack died away exhausted. It was now possible to organise and improve the line, and so enheartening were the messages from the shore that General Hamilton could feel confident that the position was no longer in acute danger, and that he had not counted on the spirit of the Australians and New Zealanders in vain.

Still until the crisis was clearly past the flagship stood by them, much as she was needed elsewhere. As there was no news of any progress at the southern beaches General Hamilton about 7.0 had offered General Hunter-Weston the French brigade, which was in reserve in its transports at Tenedos. Though he was as yet unaware of it, some slight progress had, in fact, been made in the southern zone. Under cover of the first hours of darkness the devoted naval party in the *River Clyde* had succeeded in re-establishing connection with the beach, and the troops that were still in her had stolen ashore. So rapidly was it done that about an hour after midnight they had succeeded in advancing a little way up the slope, and though after about two hours they were forced to retire to the beach again, they had succeeded in getting touch with the Worcestershire on their left. It was little enough. In reply to the Commander-in-Chief's message General Hunter-Weston could only say that his reports assured him the XXIXth Division was not strong enough without further assistance to take Hill 141, which dominated Sedd el Bahr beach. He would therefore like the French brigade as soon as possible, and suggested that one regiment should land at W Beach and work with the British right to make good Sedd el Bahr—the rest of the brigade could then land there. General Hamilton therefore sent a message to General d'Amade requesting him to bring up everything he had at Tenedos and to meet him off Sedd el Bahr. There, now that the Anzacs were safe, he had asked the Admiral to take him; for quite apart from the need of meeting the French General, there was now another cause for anxiety. The flagship's wireless room had just taken in a disturbing message from Colonel Matthews to the ships off Y Beach. It was to say that he was holding the ridge till the wounded had been embarked. Seeing that this had been the easiest landing of all, the signal was difficult to understand. The disquieting inference was that the beach which had been so cleverly seized and was so vital to the development of the General's plan was being abandoned. Its evacuation would mean the failure of the hoped-for envelopment. It was a situation that needed immediate clearing up, and shortly after 9.0 the flagship started for the spot.

The truth was that at daybreak Colonel Matthews had signalled that "without fresh ammunition and reinforcements he could not hold on," but it would seem that the message had not got through to General Hunter-Weston. There had been no reply, and his position seemed critical. His force, which had been unmolested during the greater part of the first day, had been more heavily pressed than any other in the night. After the ships had crushed the attempt on his left the enemy, who had been reinforced from Krithia, seem to have worked their way down the gully, and shortly after dark a new and more formidable attack developed all along the line and most heavily against his centre. All night long it continued with headlong rushes that sometimes reached our trenches. In the darkness the ships could do nothing to help except by bringing up ammunition from the transports. Still the line held. It was a fine defence against superior numbers, but by dawn the men were exhausted and ammunition was very short. Fortunately as the growing light revealed the miserable plight of the force there came a respite. In the desperate fighting the Turks had been so roughly handled that they were no less exhausted than our own men. To seaward they could see the *Goliath* and her four cruisers, *Dublin*, *Talbot*, *Sapphire* and *Amethyst*, closing in to repeat the punishment of the previous day, and as soon as their guns began to speak the Turks broke off and retired apparently into the gully.

The respite was seized to call for ships' boats to take off the wounded, and the result appears to have been a serious misunderstanding. The right, it seems, believed that an order to re-embark had been given. They began to leave the trenches and make down the cliff. The centre followed, and the Turks began to come on again, but before the break went further it was stopped, a counter-attack was quickly organised and the enemy driven back. By this time the boats were at work on the beach, and again there was a mistaken retirement. It would seem—but the whole episode is very obscure—that an order was given to move to the right down the coast and make another effort to get contact with the Fusiliers at Implacable Beach. This, too, by some error was taken on the left for an order to retire, and they in their turn began to make for the beach. Again the Turks came on, but again our men rallied and with another counter-attack drove the Turks right back.

Well as the troops had responded, it was only too clear that most of the comparatively raw men of the Royal Naval Division had been shaken by their hard night's work, and were in no condition to meet another attack in force, and now it was (8.30 a.m.) that Colonel Matthews had sent out the signal which had reached the flagship. He followed it with another to General Hunter-Weston saying that unless he received reinforcements he could not maintain his hold on the ridge, and that he would have to retire to the beach under cover of the ships' guns. This, he says, was approved, but whether the idea was to re-embark at once or merely to take cover and wait for reinforcement is not clear. What he did was to organise from the King's Own Scottish Borderers and the South Wales Borderers, who were still perfectly steady, a rear guard to cover the withdrawal, while at his request the ships stood by to open fire on the crest the moment he gave the signal that his men were off it.

Such was the situation when, a little after 9.30, the flagship arrived. All was quiet ashore save for a shot now and then from a sniper. The wounded were being passed to the *Goliath* and her cruisers, a trickle of troops could be seen coming down the cliff to the clusters of men and boats on the beach, but no precise information could be got of what it all meant. On board the supporting ships there was no doubt that evacuation was in hand, and that their pressing duty was to carry it out with all speed and do their best to cover it. A request, originating no one knew how, actually came from the *Sapphire* for the *Queen Elizabeth* to fire on the ridge to cover the re-embarkation. This she did for a quarter of an hour, while she tried vainly to get a signal through to General Hunter-Weston. Then, under the belief that the evacuation must have been ordered from the divisional headquarters, she passed on towards Helles to ascertain what the situation really was.

At Implacable Beach there was no sign of movement. The three battalions landed there had maintained their position without disturbance, but it was necessary to inform them of the changed situation. The officer commanding was therefore warned of the danger to which his left flank was exposed now that Y was being abandoned, and was informed of the intended advance from the south, which was to be attempted as soon as the French troops were landed.

At 10.30 the flagship was in touch with the *Euryalus* off W Beach, and then, to his surprise, General Hamilton learnt that at divisional headquarters nothing was known of the evacuation of Y. An urgent signal was immediately made to the *Goliath* asking who had given the order, and the reply was that the shore had asked for boats. For half an hour the flagship was off Helles, but it would seem that nothing could be arranged to prevent the unfortunate evacuation. No troops, at any rate, were immediately available to clench the hold.   The deadlock in the southern zone appeared at this time so complete that presumably the whole of the disposable French troops were considered necessary to break it.   General Hunter-Weston had, in fact, just given orders to Colonel Doughty-Wylie, who was in command at Sedd el Bahr Beach, that he was to reorganise and consolidate, as no advance would be attempted till the French arrived. Except this French brigade there was no reserve which could be thrown in to turn the scale at Y, and things had to be left to take their course, while with a heavy heart the Commander-in-Chief carried on to meet General d'Amade off Sedd el Bahr.

Shortly before noon he came on board the flagship.   The pressing question was what was to be done with the troops that had occupied Kum Kale.   General d'Amade was anxious to re-embark his men.   Though they were for the present well established after some hard fighting, and had taken between 400 and 500 prisoners, the position could not be maintained without capturing Yeni Shehr, and the Turks were so well entrenched there that it would mean a major operation and the landing of more troops.   This, of course, was beyond the scope of the plan, and even if it had not been in direct opposition to Lord Kitchener's instructions, General Hamilton felt his hold on the peninsula was still far too precarious to permit of his getting entangled on the Asiatic side before he had seized Achi Baba.   He was therefore forced to share his colleague's view that the only thing to do was to get the troops away as soon as possible, and with these instructions General d'Amade at once left.

The moment he was gone General Hamilton asked the Admiral to take him back with all speed to Gaba Tepe to see how the Anzacs were faring, and to assist them if the great attack which was so much feared had developed.   By half-past twelve the *Queen Elizabeth* was again passing Y Beach.   By that time the evacuation was in full swing, and the General—to his deep mortification—saw the bold and well-planned surprise on which he had most hopefully counted for outwitting the enemy being dropped out of his plan. To make matters worse there seemed no need for it.   The re-embarkation was not being molested.   The enemy were evidently either entirely cowed by the fierce resistance to the night attack or else after the previous day's experience could no longer be brought to face exposure to the ships' guns on the high ground in daylight. We know now that at all points, though the ships' fire had produced less material effect than had been hoped, its moral effect was being underestimated. Dissatisfied as our naval officers were with what they had been able to do, the enemy took quite a different view. To them the fire of the ships was so systematic as to preclude movements either of guns or troops except at night, and so far from its tactical value being negligible, there is no longer any doubt that it was the determining factor which saved our men from heavy counter-attacks in the early stages.[1] Even to our own people it was clear that it could prevent any serious pressure upon the Y Force, for about noon the *Implacable* completely dispersed a concentration that was gathering at Krithia, the point from which any attack must come.

At the southern beaches also the improving fire of the ships had already produced an effect which, had it been known, might still have caused a reconsideration of the unhappy abandonment of the Y landing. Just before Colonel Doughty-Wylie got General Hunter-Weston's order to stand fast he had found it possible to advance. Since daybreak his men on the left, who were in touch with the force landed at W, had been snugly entrenched close to No. 1 fort. On his right the men from the *River Clyde* were still stealing ashore singly, and there also the remnants of the first landing had crept out of the dugouts they had made in the sandhills, and were concentrating with the newcomers under the shattered earthworks of Sedd el Bahr fort, which appeared to have been made untenable by the ships' fire and to be deserted. At dawn, however, when an attempt to get round it into the village was made, a machine-gun hidden in the ruins of the south-west tower forced the men to take cover again; but not for long. At a signal from the *River Clyde* the *Albion* quickly knocked out the obnoxious gun and by request continued her fire till the tower was battered to pieces. Then, when more men had come ashore, a push was made for the village under cover of an intense bom-

---

[1] Prigge, p. 56 *et passim*. See also Liman von Sanders, who speaks of the devastating fire of the ships and its crushing effect during the first days. "Seeing that the Dardanelles campaign is the only great contest in the World War in which a land army has been compelled to fight continuously against an enemy on land and sea, it is worthy of note that the effect of the ships' guns was to give a support to their land forces which was quite out of the ordinary. On land no heavy artillery can shift its position so easily, or bring its fire to bear so effectively on the rear and flanks of an opponent as can be done by fire from ships." *Fünf Jahre Türkei*, p. 94. Turkish official statements after the Armistice have fully confirmed this view.

bardment from the sea.   Stealing along below the ruined walls of Sedd el Bahr they were soon in the north end of the village, and began to work their way into it.   There was some very hard fighting amongst the ruins and no little loss, but under Colonel Doughty-Wylie's fine leadership the Dublins, Munsters and Hampshires were not to be stopped; by 11.30 they were through the village and the Colonel was calling for artillery support to enable him to storm Old Castle and the adjacent Hill 141.   During his advance through the village and up the slopes the bombardment had been checked.   Now all the ships reopened, for since cable communication had been established with the shore the response was quick and targets could be taken up more accurately.   From Morto Bay the *Lord Nelson*, too, could give invaluable help.   Above the village she had located trenches full of troops which she could enfilade.   They were quickly emptied, and by 1.0 p.m. she was shelling strong bodies of Turks in full retreat through the woods at Morto Bay.   The result was that about an hour later, before the French transports had appeared Old Castle was in Colonel Doughty-Wylie's hands, and he was only waiting for a concentrated bombardment of Hill 141 to assault the last position which dominated his beach.   The French had not been required.   This remarkable success had been won with the help of the ships alone by a force scarcely less precariously situated or sorely tried than that which had let go of Y.

Up at Gaba Tepe there was a similar story to tell.   In the forenoon the great attack, for which so much anxiety was felt, had begun.   The *Queen Elizabeth* had arrived just in time to see the opening and to add the weight of her 15″ guns to the terrific bombardment that greeted it.   Here, too, cable communication had been established with the shore; fire control was much improved, and moreover, before reaching the Anzac lines the Turks had to cross open country in full view of the ships.   It was more than troops new to high explosives and heavy shrapnel could face.   The attack was beaten back; but the Anzac force was still galled by artillery fire from the distant heights of Koja Chemen Tepe and its spur, the Chunuk Bair.   Till the Anzac artillery could be got ashore no more could be done.   Its landing had been delayed by the fact that from time to time ships appeared above the Narrows and by firing over the hills compelled the transports to keep out to sea.   Though the ascent of the balloon and a few rounds from the ships were usually enough to hurry them up the Straits again, the interference was serious.   Meanwhile the Anzac guns already in position and those of the

Queen Elizabeth and the rest of the ships sufficed in a short time to dominate the fire from the hills sufficiently to prevent adequate preparation for a renewal of the Turkish attack. By 4.0 the efforts of the enemy had completely died away; and the moment was seized for a general advance to improve the position and make good the line originally selected. In half an hour more the situation was so satisfactory that the General, with a quiet mind, could return to the south.

There by the time he arrived he was astonished to find a striking change for the better. The French transports had arrived, but the troops had not been landed, nor had Colonel Doughty-Wylie waited for them. Without their aid, under cover of the ship fire, which the Turkish supports could not face, he had brilliantly captured Hill 141 as well as its redoubt.[1] The Turks, thoroughly routed, had fallen back half-way to Krithia, the British line had been established from Tekke Burnu to Sedd el Bahr, and the deadly beach was at last practicable for landing. It was a brilliant and wholly unexpected exploit, but Colonel Doughty-Wylie, to whose daring and sagacious leading the success was mainly due, lay dead, shot down in the last stage of his priceless success. For troops who had gone through what those men had suffered it was a feat hard to rival. On board the *Albion*, where they had had to watch it all at close quarters—almost helpless to assist, as it seemed to them—it was a day never to be forgotten. " I cannot refrain," wrote the captain in his report, " from expressing the admiration felt by all officers and men of the *Albion* for the splendid attack made by the troops on Hill 141. We witnessed first their tribulation and then their triumph."

So ended the second day of the great adventure. Much had been done—more, as some of the leaders confessed, than they had really believed to be possible—but it was far short of what was needed. In the southern zone the plan had looked to being in possession of the Achi Baba–Krithia ridge. In the north the Anzacs should have been on the backbone of the peninsula dominating the main roads to the Kilid Bahr position. But nowhere had anything more than the preliminary covering positions been made good. The hope of enveloping the enemy's advanced force had entirely gone. The Morto Bay force was still isolated, and when, during the morning, the leading battalion of the Turkish VIIth Division arrived from the north, the South Wales Borderers had been forced to give up their hold on the ground above Eski Hissarlik Point and fall back to De

[1] Prigge, p. 58.

Tott's battery. On the other side of the peninsula the complementary force at Y had lost its hold and was afloat again. To make matters worse, no immediate advance was possible. Even the footing that had been so heroically gained had cost very heavily. Some battalions had lost half of their strength, and all were much exhausted with the prolonged effort. Nor had the General any fresh blood to infuse new life into his force. Contrary to all practice it had been sent out without the usual ten per cent. of strength to replace casualties. The needs of the army in Flanders had been deemed to be paramount, and the normal result was that even so fine a division as the XXIXth were incapable of following up their first blow. Reluctantly, therefore, it had to be admitted that they must have a day's rest before a fresh call was made upon them.

The arrest of the offensive necessarily raised new anxieties about the Asiatic guns, particularly since the Morto Bay force must remain in the air for a considerable time longer. This was a point on which Admiral de Robeck felt very strongly. Just after General d'Amade had left the *Queen Elizabeth* to re-embark his troops, he and his staff had come to General Hamilton to urge upon him the vital importance for the French retaining their hold on Kum Kale for another twenty-four hours. It was then too late for this view to be pressed upon General d'Amade, but about 7.0 p.m. Admiral Guépratte arrived to report how well things had gone at Kum Kale. To him the position seemed excellent. The fire of the ships on the exposed Turkish trenches and concentrations and the admirably served 75's which the French had established ashore had inflicted losses so severe that, although no advance on Yeni Shehr was deemed possible, the Turks showed little disposition to renew their attacks. In any case the French Admiral agreed that the small risk there was in remaining was well worth running for the sake of keeping down the howitzer fire and preventing enemy troops being diverted to the European side till the attack on the Achi Baba position could be delivered. He accordingly left to see if anything could be done to hold on, as his British colleague desired. But unfortunately it was too late, and at 2.0 a.m. he sent word to the *Queen Elizabeth* that the General had given the order to re-embark; the operation had already begun, and it was out of his power to stop it.

It was unfortunate, but there were brighter sides to the picture. The Australian submarine was reporting herself, all well, off Gallipoli, and though her attempts to attack the enemy's battleships that had been disturbing the Anzac zone had been frustrated by the extreme calmness of the weather, she could give assurance that no large transports had ventured to approach the port during the day. General Cox's Indian brigade was also signalled as nearing Lemnos. It was the only reserve behind the Expeditionary Force, but until General Peyton's mounted division arrived at Alexandria it had had to be held back on the canal. Had it come on with the rest of the force Y Beach could certainly have been held, and how great a change that might well have meant in the fortunes of the whole enterprise was soon to become apparent.

The French brigade from Tenedos moreover was landing smoothly at V Beach. Thanks to the untiring efforts of the *River Clyde* party, the shot-torn collier with the hopper and lighters had been turned into a convenient landing-stage, and though one of the French transports had broken down, the bulk of the brigade was ashore by the morning. Of the enemy there was no sign on the British front, and accordingly General Hunter-Weston decided to make a forward movement to join hands with the Morto Bay force as soon as the French were ready, which was expected to be about noon (27th), and the ships were directed to take positions to support it. The Kum Kalé force could now be looked on as an effective reserve, for the evacuation had been very successfully accomplished, thanks to the barrage which the ships were able to put down between Yeni Shehr and Achilles' Tomb. The withdrawal had begun shortly after 10.0 the previous night, and as soon as the Turks were aware of it they opened a heavy fire from In Tepe. But this, as usual, the ships were quickly able to silence and prevent its recurrence to any serious extent. By 2.0 a.m. nothing but a rear-guard was left, and by 5.0 the whole force was on board again on its way to the Tenedos anchorage.

At Gaba Tepe, when the *Queen Elizabeth* went up there early in the morning, she found the enemy no more inclined to activity. The night had passed with little disturbance, and at 8.0 a.m. General Birdwood began to push forward his left. It was met by a counter-attack which was repulsed, but until the position was more fully restored and the force reorganised it was evident that no serious advance could be undertaken. The work too was hampered by a continuous shelling of the beach and the tows as they left or approached it. As the morning wore on the fire became heavier, the worst of it evidently coming from ships above the Narrows. It would seem, indeed, that the Anzac threat to the Turkish communications was formidable enough to have brought down the *Goeben* from the Bosporus. At dawn the kite balloon from the *Manica* had reported her in the Straits, and at 9.0 the *Doris's* seaplanes signalled that both she and the *Turgud Reis* were firing. The *Queen Elizabeth* at once prepared to engage the German battle cruiser. For all concerned there was something peculiarly dramatic in the idea of a single combat between the two champions. The *Goeben* was the Hector of the new Iliad. It was from her too had sprung the trouble which had forced us to undertake the great adventure, and excitement was high with hope from the Homeric contest. But the hope was not fulfilled. As soon as the balloon was up the *Queen Elizabeth* fired. The shot fell quite close, so close indeed that the *Goeben* thought well not to await another round, and moved up out of sight under the shelter of the cliffs.

It was well she did, as the sequel was to show. In about an hour's time the *Manica* reported a squadron of transports near the same place. They had come, it seems, from Constantinople to bring over troops from the Asiatic side, and having reached Nagara were making for Kilia Liman and Maidos. The *Queen Elizabeth* was on them at once with the balloon spotting for her. Selecting the largest ship, she straddled her with the first two rounds, and in the strained silence that followed the third came the welcome signal " O.K."—a direct hit. One was enough. The transport was seen to be sinking fast, and in a few minutes nothing but her forecastle was showing above water. Seeing that the range was about seven miles it was a feat of gunnery on which both gunlayer and spotter could be heartily complimented. The effect was excellent. The ferry which General von Sanders had arranged was no longer practicable. The transports had to make for Ak Bashi Liman, five miles above Maidos, where, though they were covered by the surrounding hills, there were no wharves or other conveniences for landing.[1]

The *Queen Elizabeth's* exploit was therefore no mere display of what she could do with her 15″ guns. For it gave assurance that, quite apart from our submarines, the reinforcement of the peninsula by sea would be no simple matter for the enemy. And reinforcement was what was most to be feared if the Anzacs were to be able to carry out their part of the plan, or even to hold their own. It happened that their threat to the Turkish communications was General von Sanders' immediate anxiety. He himself had come down to Maidos in time to witness the disturbance of his

---

[1] Prigge, p. 60. He says the vessel destroyed was a British ship which had been detained on the outbreak of war.

transports, and the bulk of the troops which were slowly landing at Ak Bashi Liman were ordered to push across to Gaba Tepe.[1] General Hamilton on his part had already taken steps to reinforce the Anzacs, as well as to prevent further pressure; word had been sent to Mudros that the Indian brigade was to be met and sent on direct to Gaba Tepe, and the *Dartmouth* was ordered to make another demonstration next morning at the head of the Gulf, with the *Amethyst*, the Royal Naval Division transports and one of the Australian Artillery ships.

Having made their dispositions the two Commanders-in-Chief, shortly after midday, went back to the south to support the afternoon advance. They found the Turks had just been attempting to forestall it by an attack from Krithia. But the ships on both sides of the peninsula, which all the morning had been intermittently firing on such batteries and bodies of troops as they were able to locate, prevented it developing beyond what the troops could easily repulse. In preparation for the advance their effective searching continued. Krithia itself was cleared of troops, and several attempts to debouch from its vicinity or from behind Achi Baba were caught by heavy shrapnel and high explosive while the troops were in close formation.

By this time two French battalions that had landed during the morning were in line on the right of the XXIXth Division, and though the third one in the disabled transport had not arrived, other French troops were landing rapidly at the River Clyde pier. No enemy movement was discernible on the front, and in order to give the men as much time for rest as possible the advance was postponed till 4.0. Then, covered by an increased fire from the ships and by the field batteries that were now in position, it began all along the line. So effective had been the preparation that no opposition was encountered except desultory shelling from the Asiatic side, which our ships and the French could not entirely subdue. As our line progressed the advanced Turkish posts retired, and some of these troops were caught by the *Lord Nelson* in Morto Bay. There about 3.0 the South Wales Borderers had already got touch with a French patrol from Sedd el Bahr, and before dark the intended line was reached. From Eumer Kapudan Tepe above De Tott's battery it extended astride the Krithia road as far as Gully Beach, close to which the left of the force was already entrenched. The line had in effect swung into a new position about two miles from the end of the peninsula and half-way

---

[1] Prigge, p. 60.

to Krithia. There had been no opposition to the advance.
The destruction which the ships' guns had wrought in the
comparatively open country had put an end to all talk of
driving us into the sea, and Essad Pasha had ordered the
whole Southern force to fall back on the lines that had been
prepared in front of Krithia, in order, so we are told, to save
it from being annihilated by the fire of the fleet. There
the three gullies of the Zighin, Kirte and Kereves Dere
afforded some protection from the sea and made it possible to
bring up reinforcements and supplies without undue exposure.[1]
On this position the attack was to be delivered on the morrow,
and in their new alignment the Allied troops were permitted
to complete their rest for the critical day before them, while
on either flank the battleships mounted guard with their
searchlights to prevent a surprise.

The night, both here and at Anzac, passed quietly, and
at dawn on the 28th the *Dartmouth* and *Amethyst*, with the
Royal Naval Division, carried out the demonstration as
directed. This time the feint of landing was made further
to the westward, before the little port of Ibriji, but again
no troops were seen, and after the ships had destroyed the
sheerlegs and some lighters that were seen in the harbour,
they withdrew, and General Paris came down to Helles to
report to the Commander-in-Chief.[2]

The attack on Krithia was already developing when he
arrived, but as General d'Amade had also come off to report,
the flagship had not yet moved up to her supporting position
on the left. Five French battalions were now in line on the
right and had taken over the Morto Bay flank from the
South Wales Borderers, who during the night had marched
across country to Implacable Beach to form a reserve for their
own brigade (87th) on the extreme left. Here too the Drake
battalion had been moved up towards Gully ravine as a
reserve, as the fourth battalion of the brigade, the King's
Own Scottish Borderers, from Y Beach, had only just been
landed at W Beach. Beyond them, between the two ravines
which ran down from Krithia, were the county regiments
of the 88th Brigade, with the remains of the gallant
Fusilier brigade (86th) in reserve behind them. From their
right to De Tott's battery the line was held by the French.
Since they took over from the South Wales Borderers they
had not been disturbed. Their orders were now to advance
on Krithia, with their left up the Eastern ravine, while their
right pushed forward as far as the Kereves ravine, which
came down from Achi Baba. Here in immediate support

[1] Prigge, p. 59.   [2] See Plan p. 123.

were stationed the *Lord Nelson, Vengeance, Cornwallis* and *Albion,* while the *Prince George* still helped the French ships with the Asiatic batteries. On the opposite flank was the *Implacable* in her old station, and north of her were the *Goliath, Dublin* and *Sapphire,* and there too the *Queen Elizabeth* proceeded shortly after 10.0.

Since an early hour the ships had never ceased doing their best to prepare the attack, but it was little enough, for a mist shrouded the shore and targets were very difficult to take up. Still at first the advance along the whole line up to about a mile from Krithia had been very promising. On the extreme left, when the flagship stopped off Y Beach, the Border Regiment, advancing rapidly between the gully and the sea, had nearly reached it. Almost at once she had a fresh experience of the difficulty of supporting troops from the sea. Down a hollow in the ground were seen a mass of men moving at the double from the direction of the enemy. Some thought they were Turks—some that it was our men retiring. They were a splendid target and the *Queen Elizabeth* had two of her 15″ guns loaded with shrapnel. As each shell could throw 13,000 bullets, a fair burst would be the practical annihilation of the moving mass and go far to decide the day. But were they friends or foes? It was for the General to decide. The temptation was great, but the appalling results of a mistake were not to be easily faced. There was scarcely a doubt they were enemy, but while there was a grain of doubt he could not give the word, and before he was certain the mass was out of sight. The question was soon settled. It was a mass of enemy that had so narrowly escaped destruction. Two companies of the Borderers were now actually in the deserted Y Beach trenches, and when the Turks came into sight again they were deployed and advancing in bold rushes to turn them out. One company was clearly in view, working in perfect style along the edge of the cliff with bayonets glittering in the sun. The Borderers were suffering severely from their fire. Another rush brought the enemy's line to a point where the flagship exactly enfiladed it. Then a 15″ gun spoke—the shell burst fifty yards from the enemy's right and when the smoke cleared there was not a man to be seen.

The counter-attack was stopped, bodies of the enemy were retiring over the ridge exposed to the fire both of ships and troops, and the advance of the Borderers could be continued. But it was only to be brought up quickly before well-concealed trenches at close range which were hard to locate from the sea. Everything the ships could do to break the deadlock they did. They were all firing hard. The *Goliath* had been ordered to move in and use her 12-pounders at the closest possible range. Still for two hours our left was held up. The unhappy abandonment of Y Beach was telling its tale with fatal effect. By about noon the centre, after desperate fighting, had worked up to within a mile of Krithia, but with the left of the line held fast they could not push the frontal attack further. In the firing line, where the whole 88th Brigade was by this time engaged, ammunition was failing, and the 86th had to be sent forward to give the attack new impetus. On the right the French were equally feeling the want of ammunition and were also checked. If only the right of the Turks could be turned all might yet be well, and if as our left advanced against it they had found a friendly force securely entrenched above Y Beach with a new base of supply it might have been done, exposed as the enemy's flank was to the fire of the *Queen Elizabeth* and her consorts. But the keystone of the General's plan had fallen out and the battalions which should have been there were still on W Beach or afloat. For a final effort first the Anson men and then the Drake battalion were pushed up into the firing line, but just as the attack was to be renewed an unhappy contretemps occurred incidental to the inherent difficulties of all operations based upon open beaches.

The weakness of the supply units, which as yet it had been possible to land, and the congested state of the beaches, which there was no means of clearing quickly enough, made it impossible to get ammunition forward as fast as it was expended. The only chance was more hands on the beach, and at the critical moment a call came for the Anson men to return to their fatigue duty at Implacable Beach. Sailor fashion they responded at the double over the cliff in order to get back along the shore. By the troops near them this rapid movement was taken for a retirement, and a number of men who had lost all their officers were carried away with it. They were soon rallied, and by getting the Drake battalion forward and some troops from the other side of the main gully a really strong firing line was formed. It was enough to deal with a counter-attack, but a further advance against the Turkish trenches was still beyond their strength. Seeing no further movement, General Hamilton, still bent on making full use of the flexibility which the sea gave him, signalled to General Hunter-Weston that if he wanted to reinforce his left or develop a flank attack troops could come along under the cliffs at Y and climb up under cover of the *Queen Elizabeth's* guns. But there was no reply.

At that time General Hunter-Weston had no reason to believe that the left was held up. But in truth the men were too much exhausted for a further effort against the powerful forces in front of them; and it was the same all along the line. Lack of ammunition both for infantry and artillery made it impossible to prevent the enemy counter-attacking. On the right the French, whose left had reached within a mile of Krithia, had been unable to hold their own and already were retiring. In conformity their right fell back from the Kereves ravine on De Tott's. They too were rallied, but the centre of the Allied line had been left in the air. In such a position a fresh attack by the enemy would be fatal, and after holding on till nearly 5.0 they were ordered to fall back. Fortunately the Turks had been too much shaken to attempt another counter-attack, or perhaps were unwilling even in the failing light to expose themselves in the open to the devastating fire of the ships' heavy guns. So by sunset the whole Allied force was digging itself in undisturbed, but on a line far short of what it had been intended to reach. The right was still no further than the hill above De Tott's, and thence the front ran to Y Beach, but with an awkward re-entering angle in the centre whose apex almost touched the line they had started from. From the nearest troops Krithia was still more than a mile away and Achi Baba more than twice as far.

What was to be done? It was clear that after all they had gone through in the past four days the troops were too few to renew the attack with much hope of success until they had had further time to recover and until more guns could be landed and the rear services more fully organised. Yet to wait and abandon the basic idea of a *coup de main* was to give the Turks time to reinforce and strengthen their position. But where were our reinforcements to come from? The reserves on the spot were far from adequate, the Indian brigade had not yet appeared, and there was nothing else but the still raw Royal Naval Division, part of which had been already absorbed for working parties and reserves. At an early hour in the day General Paris had been directed to place one brigade at General Birdwood's disposal till the belated brigade from Egypt arrived. The rest were to make another demonstration at the head of the gulf. It was made in the afternoon, but once more no movement of troops was seen. At Gaba Tepe things were so quiet that General Birdwood did not call on the brigade that had been offered him, and no part of this reserve was used by him. With the unemployed bulk of the Royal Naval Division and the other French and British troops which had taken no part in the day's operations there was little enough to promise success after the first day's failure. But in fact since the morning the problem with which the General had to deal had assumed quite a new aspect.

CHAPTER XIX

WHEN the news reached home of how great the first
effort had been, how much it had cost, and how far short
it had fallen of executing the *coup de main* that had been
planned against Achi Baba, it became clear that the enterprise could not be carried on without greater military force.
Lord Kitchener had promised that if need arose the army
would see the navy through, and the need had arisen. Still,
in view of the condition of affairs on the Western Front, it
was considered that nothing could be moved either from
France or Home—Egypt was the only source. The 29th Indian
Brigade had left Egypt for Lemnos on April 26.[1] There in
garrison was the fine East Lancashire Territorial Division,
and General Peyton's Mounted Division arrived by the end
of the month. Some, at least, of the troops remaining in
Egypt could be spared. True, the Turks were showing
renewed activity on the frontier. The new railway from
the north had almost reached Ludd, and large camps both
there and at Ramleh had been located by the French aeroplanes with the Syrian Squadron. Reports also came in
of some 8,000 troops at Nekhl, about twice as many at Gaza,
and a brigade with twenty guns at El Arish. Just as the
operations against Gallipoli were opening, a force was reported to have left Nekhl, threatening an attack on some
of the Gulf of Suez ports or Suez itself, and the *Desaix*
had to be kept there with 500 men on board ready to move
at a moment's notice.[2] From the west also danger was
beginning to be feared, for it was found that the Turks
were intriguing with the Senussi. But it was so generally
admitted that the best defence for Egypt was an attack
on Constantinople, that these symptoms could be dismissed
as efforts at diversion or attempts to mine the canal or its
approaches. So long as the Expeditionary Force was in
action at the Dardanelles no attack upon the Canal in force
was likely to develop.

[1] The 29th Indian Brigade consisted of the 14th Sikhs, 69th and 89th
Punjabis, 1/6th Gurkhas.
[2] See Plan p. 382.

On April 27, therefore, Lord Kitchener had sent General Hamilton word that if he wanted more troops the transports that had brought out Peyton's division were available, and that General Maxwell would send him anything he asked for. Early next morning, before the message came to hand, General Hamilton telegraphed home to know if he could have the East Lancashire division if he wanted it. Meanwhile Lord Kitchener had heard through the French Admiralty that reinforcements would be required, and he at once instructed General Maxwell to have all his troops ready to embark, and suggested he should send the East Lancashire division if it was called for. No sooner had this telegram gone off than General Hamilton's arrived asking for a call on this division. The Admiralty had already instructed Admiral Robinson, the Port Admiral in Egypt, to be ready to embark it, and Lord Kitchener replied to General Hamilton that he had better inform Egypt at once that he wanted it.

A further important reinforcement was by this time in sight. General D'Amade knew that the French Government were holding another division in reserve for the Dardanelles, and when early on Wednesday (the 28th) he visited the flagship, he informed General Hamilton he would like to have it, and suggested that he, as Commander-in-Chief, should ask for it.

About the immediate despatch of the Egyptian reinforcement there was some difficulty. It was objected that the cavalry transports would want altering before infantry could use them. This objection was overruled : they were to be used as they were, and the embarkation of the East Lancashire division as well as over 3,000 Anzac reinforcements commenced on May 1.[1] But another objection was not so easily disposed of. In the evening of April 28 the Bikanir Camel Corps had engaged Turkish patrols eighteen miles west of Hod el Bada, and the threat of an attempt to mine or obstruct the canal became more insistent. The departure of the troops for Gallipoli left only three reliable Indian brigades for the canal defences, both Cairo and Alexandria were stripped of infantry, and but little artillery was available for the canal. Though General Peyton's division, which had been assigned to the Egyptian garrison, could supply the

---

[1] The East Lancashire (XLIInd) Division was composed of the Lancashire Fusiliers Brigade (5th, 6th, 7th and 8th Battalions, Lancashire Fusiliers), the Manchester Brigade (5th, 6th, 7th and 8th Battalions, Manchester, Regiment) and the East Lancashire Brigade (4th and 5th Battalions, East Lancashire Regiment, and 9th and 10th Battalions, Manchester Regiment).

place of infantry, the lack of artillery was a serious matter, and only from the ships could the need be made good.

But ships were hard to find. Since the bulk of Admiral Peirse's squadron had been diverted to the Dardanelles, the only ship of force in the canal was the *St. Louis*. The *Philomel* had been detached for special duty. A few days before she had been sent down to Aden with two gunboats for the Persian Gulf. Both of them had foundered on the way, and now she was under orders to co-operate with a military force that was proceeding to Somaliland, for even that forlorn outpost seemed to feel the repercussion of the all-embracing war. This left only one British ship, the light cruiser *Proserpine*, for the canal, though the *Himalaya* was coming up the Red Sea after a refit at Bombay. There were, however, three other French ships—the *Desaix*, which, as we have seen, was also detailed for special service; the worn-out cruiser *Montcalm*, stationed at Ismailia; and the old coast defence ship *Requin*. It meant but little strength in heavy guns, on which the army so much depended, and without further naval force the position could not be considered secure.

Further advance parties of the enemy were appearing close to the canal in several places, and there was every indication of a serious attack being imminent. To deal with it a strong force of Imperial Service cavalry was moved out on the 29th. The Turks retired in front of it, but owing to the exhaustion of the horses our men were unable to effect anything. While the operation was in progress, Admiral Peirse informed the Admiralty of the dangerous state of affairs, and asked to have the *Euryalus* and *Bacchante* returned to him at once. Orders were accordingly given to Admiral de Robeck to send them or two equivalent ships. Compliance with the order could not fail to be a serious disturbance to the Dardanelles operations, which presumably was just what the enemy was aiming at by their threat to the canal, and to avoid playing into their hands the French Admiralty were informed that we should be very grateful if they could send their Syrian squadron to Port Said, as all our ships were fully occupied at the Dardanelles.

At the moment the strain there was even greater than the Admiralty knew. The *Albion* was out of action. During the morning of the 28th she had been supporting the right of the French off Kereves Dere, and shortly after midday, just as the *Lord Nelson* was relieving her, she was so badly hit that she had to retire to Mudros with a leak that would take three days to make good. To spare either the *Euryalus* or *Bacchante* was out of the question, and with one battle-ship short all Admiral de Robeck could do was to detach the *Goliath*. To withdraw another ship, he submitted, would dangerously imperil the situation, not merely by the loss of the ship itself, but also because of the officers and men who could not be spared from communication and beach work. The strain put upon the personnel of the fleet by the multitudinous requirements of an army thrown ashore from the sea was already almost beyond endurance. It had always been a recognised feature of combined expeditions that the officers and men of the supporting squadron were as important as its guns, and in the hey-day of our ripe experience in the old French wars the number of hands required for the amphibious work was a recognised factor in determining the strength of the naval part of the force.

Thanks, however, to the readiness of the French to help, no call had to be made. In reply to our request Admiral Dartige du Fournet was ordered to send at once to Port Said the *Jeanne d'Arc, D'Estrees* and *D'Entrecasteaux* for the defence of the canal, and Admiral de Robeck was told he could recall the *Goliath* and keep his other ships. On April 30 the first of the French cruisers arrived in the canal, but all was then quiet. The attack, if indeed an attack had ever been intended, had not developed. The enemy had disappeared from the vicinity of the canal and no trace of them was left, except indications of an attempt to lay a minefield in the Bitter Lakes.

At the Dardanelles also the fighting had died down. The two days after the abortive attack on the Achi Baba-Krithia position had been devoted to reorganisation. In the southern area the line which, as we have seen, ran from in front of the hill above De Tott's to Y Beach, had been strengthened, and the bulk of the artillery had been landed. At Gaba Tepe the Royal Marine brigade had relieved some of the most hard-worked Australians, and save for two strong attacks on them as soon as they got into the line things had been fairly quiet. Even the artillery fire was so much reduced that it looked as if the enemy had withdrawn the bulk of his northern force to deal with the main attack. So much, indeed, was the pressure reduced, that General Birdwood was contemplating an advance for May 1. The ships were still as busy as the need of husbanding ammunition permitted, and since an improved method of observation had been established they were able to give the enemy considerable annoyance, and even to dislodge them from their trenches south of Krithia. But do what they would they could not master the fire from the Asiatic guns, which continued to worry the southern beaches. During the last three days of the month our attempts to silence the shore batteries by ship fire, and to continue our sweeping operations, were met by a resistance that seemed to increase in vigour. The destroyer *Wolverine*, Commander O. J. Prentis, was hit on the bridge, and her commander killed; the *Agamemnon* was struck twice; the *Henri IV* eight times, and every other ship engaged met with similar difficulties.

Besides the usual inner squadron, we had now two submarines about the Narrows; a French one had also gone up to harass the Turkish communications, and in order to disturb their organisation as much as possible the *Lord Nelson*, on April 30, was sent up to Gaba Tepe with the balloon-carrier *Manica* to try what she could do against the enemy's headquarters at Chanak Kale. She found the *Goeben* again bent on punishing the Anzac transports, and at once engaged her. But she was no more inclined to accept the challenge than she had been the *Queen Elizabeth's*, and the *Lord Nelson* could only get off five rounds before the German flagship hid herself behind the cliffs. The *Lord Nelson* then turned her attention to Chanak, and after fifteen rounds had the town in flames. Her orders were then to attack Fort No. 13, in the Kilid Bahr group, but the balloon was again wanted inside the Straits, and she could do no more, but Chanak continued to burn fiercely till nightfall.

In this way something at last was done to hamper the flow of Turkish reinforcements, which in view of the forced arrest of our offensive was the immediate cause of anxiety. Of how the submarines had fared nothing was known since the Australian boat reported having sunk a gunboat. Both had been signalling off Gallipoli, but then there was silence. The French boat had come out again with no success to report, and the *Minerva* was up at Xeros, trying to get into wireless touch with the other two.

Whether to forestall the enemy by hurrying on another attack or to wait for the coming reinforcements, was a difficult question to decide. The whole French Expeditionary Force was now ashore and comparatively fresh, but the XXIXth Division, after its prolonged struggle, was thoroughly exhausted, and with no fresh blood in the form of drafts its heavy losses were severely felt. The remains of the Dublins and Munsters had actually to be re-formed into one battalion, the 1st Lancashire Fusiliers had also lost over half their numbers, and the effective strength of the 86th Brigade was reduced to less than 2,000, while the total drafts required to replace casualties in the division amounted to over 5,000. Large numbers of men, instead of resting, had still to be employed in getting up stores and ammunition and doing heavy fatigue work in improving the piers. On May 1, however, the tension was somewhat relaxed by the arrival of the Indian brigade from Egypt. The idea of using it at Gaba Tepe had been abandoned. It was too much needed in the southern area, and there it was landed during the day. Better late than never was the universal feeling, but no one could fail to think how different the position might have been had they come in a week earlier.

As it was, they were just in time to meet a new crisis. The comparative apathy of the Turkish troops during the past three days had seemed to promise us the initiative in our own time, but in fact the Turks were quietly, but with energy, preparing to deliver a crushing attack. The whole of their XIth Division, which had previously been held at Bashika Bay by the French demonstration, had been brought over from the Asiatic side, apparently by night, and part of the IIIrd Division from the Kum Kale area followed them. The battalions as they arrived were pushed up wherever they were most needed, regardless of their proper formations, and often with great difficulty by mule tracks which had not yet been improved into roads. Owing to their experience of the deadly effect of the ship-fire during daylight the attack was to be made by night, and Colonel von Sodenstern, who had been commanding the Vth Division up at Bulair, was placed in command of the southern area to conduct it.[1]

By the evening of May 1 everything was ready, but outwardly all was still so quiet that in the fleet the impression of the apathy of the enemy was deepened. The night fell very dark and preternaturally still. Not even a gun was firing anywhere, when suddenly, a little after 10.0, the whole of the Turkish batteries burst out. In a moment a raging din had replaced the death-like silence: from the Asiatic side and from Achi Baba, shells were raining down on our front trenches, and in a few seconds the uproar was redoubled by our counter-battery. For half an hour the artillery duel continued with the utmost fury, and then the anxious watchers in the ships could hear the rattle of machine-guns and rifles all along the line. Not a word came from shore. It was impossible to tell what was happening, till presently the distant roar of " Allah-Din ! " told that the Turks were charging, and answering hurrahs that the charge was being met. But soon it could be seen that the Turkish guns had lifted, and the fall

[1] Prigge, pp. 61–2.

of the shell seemed to tell that our line was falling back. In the dark the ships could do little to help. On the left the *Agamemnon* was firing as directed from the signal station above Y Beach, and so was the *Implacable*, guided by star shells. But on the right the *Vengeance*, which was on guard, could do next to nothing for the French, and from this quarter the reports were specially alarming. The Senegalese were being overpowered, and some support became imperative to prevent a rout. General Hamilton was keeping under his own hand a reserve composed of two battalions of the Royal Naval Division and the Indian brigade, whose arrival released the 88th Brigade for the trenches, and at 2.0 a.m. so serious was the position on the extreme right that he sent off one of the naval battalions to General D'Amade. In another hour, during which the struggle raged in the dark with undiminished intensity, rumour told that the British line was broken and falling back on the beaches. It was but half the truth, for at 4.0 came word from General Hunter-Weston that it had been pierced at one or two points, but elsewhere the thrusts had been repulsed with heavy loss. For the General, who was anxiously waiting for news in the *Arcadian*,[1] it was the moment to react, and the order was given for a general counter-attack. Exhausted as the troops were, the response was magnificent. The whole line swept forward, the Turks fell back before it, at dawn the whole area in our front was covered with men in full retreat, and as the light made, the ships could join the field guns in taking heavy toll. Ground was rapidly gained, till our line, as it pushed resolutely forward, began to be enfiladed by machine-guns cleverly hidden in the broken ground. The far-spent energy of the weary troops was exhausted by the check; to find and rush the deadly emplacements was beyond their strength, and in the end there was nothing for it but to fall back to the trenches they had so splendidly defended in the midnight attack. Hundreds of prisoners had been taken, and the ground over which the retirement was made was covered with Turkish dead, but our ranks, too, were sadly thinned, and we were back at the point from which we had started, still no more than half-way to Krithia and Achi Baba.

Encouraged by his successful defence Colonel von Sodenstern ordered another general night attack for the night of May 2. On this occasion the weight of the blow fell on the

---

[1] General Hamilton had shifted his headquarters to that vessel on April 30; he visited General Hunter-Weston at his headquarters on shore on April 29, 30 and May 1, and had taken the opportunity, on the last two occasions, of visiting French headquarters.

French, who drove off the Turks with heavy losses. A further attack on the following night was equally unprofitable and General von Sanders prohibited any further offensive operations, and directed that the troops were to be devoted to strengthening the Krithia–Achi Baba position.[1]

The enemy's altered tactics were soon detected, and in spite of all our men had gone through, and serious as was the shortage of ammunition, General Hamilton felt it was impossible to leave the situation as it was. The Turks could be seen hard at work with spade and wire, and it was clear that if they were left alone till our reinforcements arrived they would soon have a continuous line of formidable defences between our front and Achi Baba. It was also evident that since the French had withdrawn from Kum Kale the enemy was passing troops across from the Asiatic side. Some of them had even taken part in the previous night's attack. Still more disquieting was intelligence that troops were moving from the Adrianople district to Constantinople, and there was now little hope that a Russian demonstration could be counted on to hold them there.

On April 28 the Admiralty had been informed from Petrograd that the Caucasian Army Corps, which we had been given to understand had been embarked at Sevastopol, had been landed. It was stated that they could be re-embarked in ten hours, but in view of the great effort which the Germans were known to be on the eve of making in Galicia, it was not likely that the force would be available, and whatever deterrent effect it may ever have had on German plans in Constantinople it would now be negligible for a considerable time. The only help could come from the Black Sea fleet, and Admiral de Robeck lost no time in begging Admiral Ebergard to exert the utmost pressure he could upon the Bosporus to check the flow of reinforcements to Gallipoli. Already, simultaneously with our landing on April 25, he had carried out a bombardment off the Bosporus with fourteen pennants. To the new request he responded by repeating the demonstration on May 2, this time with seventeen ships, and firing for two hours on the entrance forts, as well as those at the Kava Narrows. The following day he dealt with the right flank of the Chatalja lines and the adjacent coast forts. On the 4th sweeping operations and a reconnaissance were carried out further north in Inada Bay, a well-known landing-place within the Turkish frontier. The intention was to return next day to the Bosporus for a renewal of the bombardment, but a break in the weather

[1] Liman von Sanders, p. 94.

rendered further operations impossible. It was all the Russians could do, and we could scarcely hope that such operations would have much more effect upon the situation at Gallipoli. Current doctrine taught that, without a potent military force behind it, a mere naval menace could be ignored, and of such potent forces there was little prospect. On May 1 the great Austro-German counter-thrust in Galicia had begun, and it was developing with such crushing force that the Caucasian Corps at Sevastopol had to be hurriedly absorbed into the resistance. In spite of this bar to Russian combined action we now know, from official statements, that the Turks regarded the menace as too serious to be ignored. The unreal demonstration worked as it had so often done before in past wars, and for two months longer the three divisions and the heavy guns which had been assigned to the defence of the Bosporus area were kept where they were.

From our own effort to cut the Turkish communications, there was at present no sure promise of affecting the situation. So far as the land route was concerned, the unremitted naval observation of the Bulair neck was enough to prevent the road being used. But the sea route down the Marmara, in spite of all the skill and daring our submarines had been displaying, was still open. Much had been hoped from them, but the difficulties were too great. The French submarines had not sufficient range of action to reach the Marmara, and the *Bernoulli*, in trying to operate above the Narrows, was caught in the current and swept out again. The second French boat that went in was the *Joule*, commanded by a worthy scion of the famous naval family of du Petit-Thouars, but she unhappily got foul of a mine, and was destroyed with all hands. This was on May 1 and became known two days later; at the same time there were reports which could not be doubted that the Australian boat (*AE 2*) had fallen to a destroyer in the Marmara and that her crew were prisoners. She had, in fact, been caught on April 30 near the Island of Marmara by a torpedo boat—the *Sultan Hissar*—and after a gallant fight lasting two hours was sunk, but all her crew were saved by the enemy.

Lieutenant-Commander E. C. Boyle in *E 14* was now alone. He had begun well. At dawn on April 27, after negotiating the minefields, he ran past Chanak on the surface, with all the forts firing on him. About the Narrows a number of steamboats were seen to be patrolling, and amongst them a torpedo gunboat. This ship he selected for attack. The result was a large column of water flung up as high as her mast. It could only mean a hit, but he could not wait to see more, for he was aware of men in a small boat trying to seize hold of his periscope—an unusual method of attack, which he had to avoid by diving. After mastering the dangerous swirls of the current round Nagara Point, he proceeded to cruise in the eastern opening of the Straits, but here he was so industriously hunted by destroyers, torpedo boats and patrolling steamers that he had to keep constantly submerged, and was scarcely allowed to be on the surface long enough to charge his batteries. As it was, he had one of his periscopes smashed by gun-fire, and for the rest of his cruise he had to make shift with the other. Not till the afternoon of the third day (April 29) did he have another chance. Three destroyers were seen coming from the eastward escorting two troopships. It was glassy calm, so that the destroyers could not fail to see his periscope. Yet he attacked, but had to dive before seeing the result. An explosion was felt, and when half an hour later he ventured to come to the surface, there was only one transport with the destroyers. The other was making for the shore at Sari Keui, with dense clouds of yellow smoke pouring from her. That evening he met the Australian boat. She had a tale of bad luck to tell and had only one torpedo left. They arranged to meet next morning, but the patrols prevented their communicating and they never came together again.

As for *E 14* she still could do nothing, so active was the hunt for her. On May 1 she determined to attack one of her pursuers. A small gunboat fitted apparently as a minelayer was the victim. She was fairly hit and sank in less than a minute. A larger gunboat was then attacked, but the torpedo did not run straight and she tried to ram. The effort was parried and another torpedo fired, but the glassy sea revealed its track too clearly, and by using her helm smartly she was able in her turn to avoid it. After that the patrols were less bold, but still the sea was too calm and the look-out posts ashore too vigilant for the boat to do any positive mischief. She did, no doubt, act as a disturbing influence, though she could not entirely stop the flow of reinforcements even in the Sea of Marmara, and the line across the Straits was entirely open.[1]

This was the more to be regretted, for it was of the utmost importance that the enemy should not be allowed to develop further force before our next attack was delivered. Every day's delay must increase his strength in the Achi Baba position, and reluctantly the General felt he must call on the

---

[1] Lieutenant-Commander Boyle was awarded the V.C. on his return.

shattered brigades for one more effort.   After a week's almost incessant fighting by night and day and under peculiarly trying conditions they could not be expected to do it without help, and help they were to have.

Up at Gaba Tepe at dawn on May 2, the *Colne* and *Usk*, with a party of New Zealanders on board, had made a raid on Suvla Bay, and surprising an observation post on Nibrunesi Point, had destroyed it and returned with most of the occupants prisoners.   In the evening, under cover of a heavy and effective fire from the ships, an attack was made in force on the Turkish trenches, and though it did not achieve all that was hoped, the effect was to advance and strengthen the Anzacs' position.   So good, indeed, was their situation, that General Hamilton felt he could without undue risk make use of his advantage of the sea to give him what was wanted in the southern area.   General Birdwood was therefore called upon to provide two brigades.   The plan was to shift them secretly and in the dead of night on board destroyers and minesweepers, and land them at W Beach in time for the attack.   The original idea was that the transfer should be carried out on the night of the 4th, but the operation was postponed to allow of five batteries being shifted first.   Moreover, for the night of the 4th Admiral Thursby had planned a raid similar to the last to destroy another observation station which evidently existed on Gaba Tepe.   A small force of about 100 infantry had been placed at his disposal, and he detailed for their inshore support four destroyers, *Colne*, *Chelmer*, *Usk* and *Ribble*, and the steam pinnaces of the *Triumph* and *Dartmouth*, with the *Bacchante* and *Dartmouth* as attending ships.   While it was still dark the tows were taken close to the north shore of the cape, and at the first glimmer of dawn the boats rowed in.   But this time the surprise failed. As they neared the beach they were received with so heavy a fire that on landing they could only take cover under the high bank.   It was then found that the place was so strongly occupied and heavily wired that the slender force was quite unequal to doing anything more.   At 6.30, under cover of the destroyers' fire, the men were taken off again with very little loss, and Gaba Tepe continued to be a thorn in the side of General Birdwood's force.

May 5, the day fixed for the embarkation of the two brigades for Helles, was the day the weather broke, and, as we have seen, prevented Admiral Ebergard from resuming his demonstration off the Bosporus.   The night came on dark and stormy.   The Admiral had ordered that the eight destroyers and six fleet-sweepers which were to effect the operation should arrive in daylight, in order that final arrangements for the delicate task could be made. So high, however, were wind and sea that they were delayed till after dark, but Captain Coode, who as Captain (D) had charge of the arrangements, sent their commanders forward in the *Amethyst*. The Admiral was thus able to give them their orders in time, but it was not till 11.30, when the moon was already up, that the embarkation could begin. Thanks, however, to the unremitting and harmonious toil of the beach and fatigue parties of the two services, there were now seven piers and a good beach available from which nearly 3,000 men could be embarked at each trip of the boats, and so well had the whole evolution been organised that by 2.0 a.m., in spite of the adverse conditions, the destroyers were away with the New Zealand brigade. The violent weather caused some delay in getting hold of the fleet-sweepers which were to convey the 2nd Australian Brigade, and it was not till 4.30, when day was breaking, that they started. On arrival, they were formed with a mixed naval brigade, composed of the Plymouth and Drake battalions, into a new division, which General Hamilton retained as his General Reserve. In addition to this increase of force, the Lancashire Fusiliers brigade of the East Lancashire Division had landed the previous afternoon, and the next brigade was close at hand.

It was this day, May 6, that the attack was to begin, and in the meantime the ships available to support had been sensibly reduced in number. In the evening of May 2, the *Albion*, who had only just come back from repairing the damage received on April 28, and was operating on the French right, had been hit from the Asiatic side so badly that she had to retire again to Mudros to make good defects. Next day the *Prince George* met a similar mishap. The Asiatic batteries, which had all along been her special care, had become very active, and during the morning she was holed by a 6″ shell abaft her armour. She, too, had to retire to Mudros, and there the damage was found so serious as to oblige her to go on to Malta to be docked. The *Agamemnon* had therefore to be used to help the French keep down the Asiatic batteries, and as the *Goliath* was due to coal and the *Latouche-Tréville* had exhausted her ammunition, Admiral Guépratte in the *Jauréguiberry* came in to help the *Lord Nelson* and *Vengeance* on the right flank. The *Swiftsure* and *Euryalus* were on their old stations at Tekke and Helles, while the *Queen Elizabeth* joined the *Implacable* and *Sapphire* on the left flank.

The attack was timed to begin at 11.0 a.m., for General Hunter-Weston felt unable to adopt the Commander-in-

Chief's suggestion of an advance before dawn. He preferred to rely on a preparative bombardment by sea and land; for his loss in regimental officers had been too great to permit of attempting to operate over such confused ground in the dark. Moreover, during the past three days the troops had had but little rest. They had been constantly disturbed by night attacks and by the fire of the flanking ships trying to check them. But, on the other hand, it was probable that the continual night attacks must have left the Turks even more exhausted for want of sleep than our own men. On the whole therefore the best chances of success were to be looked for in a daylight operation.

The general idea was to attack Krithia from the west and south-west, that is, to turn the Turkish right by pivoting the line on the French. After half an hour's bombardment, which was all that the supply of ammunition would permit, the advance began punctually, and the troops were quickly involved in heavy fighting. The resistance was very strong, and the number and disposition of the enemy's machine-guns made progress very slow. Still, some progress was made all along the line, except, unhappily, where it was most essential. The left was being held up by a formidable redoubt or cluster of trenches close to Y Beach, and the fatal abandonment of that landing again declared itself. It was apparently somewhere behind the top of the precipitous cliff just north of the beach—afterwards known for good reason as " Gurkha Bluff "—but its exact position had been cleverly concealed. The weather was still too stormy for aircraft to work, and without their help neither the artillery nor the *Sapphire* could find it. In the end, an advance of from 200 to 300 yards was all that could be made, when about 4.30 the troops had orders to dig in in preparation for a renewal of the attack next day. The only real advantage was on the right, where the French, after hard fighting and with the assistance of the ships on that side, had made good a position on the Kereves ridge which would serve as an excellent pivot for the further development of the tactical plan.

It was clear, however, that unless the redoubt at Y Beach could be overcome the scheme must break down, and the military called on the Admiral to help. The attack was to be renewed at 10.30 next morning (May 7), and Admiral de Robeck at once ordered the *Manica* to meet him an hour earlier near Y Beach. The *Talbot* was also there, and Admiral Nicholson was summoned with the *Swiftsure* to assist. But neither from the kite balloon nor from the shore could any information be obtained as to the locality of the redoubt, and they had to devote their fire mainly to the guns on Yazy Tepe—the height about 2,000 yards north of Krithia from which a gully ran down to the sea near Gurkha Bluff—this hill being the objective of the left that day.   Then the *Swiftsure* closed in to see what she could do by searching the whole ground behind Gurkha Bluff with her 14-pounders. No ship had done better in co-operating with the military. She was one of the ships who had had an artillery officer allotted to assist in directing fire, and the results had been excellent.   Now, since the army advanced, these officers had been withdrawn ashore, and their loss was severely felt.   All her efforts proved unavailing : owing to the height of the cliffs the ground immediately behind them could not be searched effectively, and in spite of all the ships could do the Lancashire Fusilier brigade, to whom the task of rushing the redoubt had been entrusted, found it impossible to get on.   Elsewhere there had been substantial gain of ground.   The French, who had lost the pivot position on the ridge over Kereves Dere in the night, had regained it by 3.0 in the afternoon, thanks, so the Turks state, to the ships having entirely destroyed the front trenches in this area.   General Hamilton now ordered an intensive bombardment for a quarter of an hour, to be followed by a general advance.   The response of the weary troops was magnificent.   In the centre and on the right, where the ship fire had also been very effective, trench after trench was rushed with the bayonet, nor did the men stop until the enemy had been pressed back nearly as far as Krithia, but till the extreme left got forward it was impossible to take advantage of it by a swing to the right; and towards Gurkha Bluff, though fresh troops had been poured into the sector between Zighin Dere and the sea, scarcely any progress had been made.   More troops were brought up, but the redoubt remained intact, and the night closed in with the sea flank still held up, and the rest of the troops digging in on the ground their splendid work had won.

But what they had won was still far from enough.   To pause now was to admit failure, and to call on the troops for yet another day's effort was no light thing, but there was no help for it, and the orders went out.   The Lancashires on the left were relieved by the New Zealanders, and the General went in person to the critical point to direct the final effort.   Another appeal went to the Admiral, and once more the *Queen Elizabeth* tried to find the redoubt, but again the kite balloon could not see it.   At 10.30 a.m. the New Zealanders advanced to the attack, but met with strenuous opposition and made but little progress.   It was now evident on this side that all that valour could do had been done; it was hopeless to break the enemy's hold on the bluff, and in desperation the General called up the Australians from the General Reserve and ordered an advance of the whole line. Again it was to be prepared with a quarter of an hour's bombardment with all that the ships and artillery could throw in. The storm of shell began at 5.15, but at half-past it ceased, and then in a moment the whole plain was alive with bayonets glittering in the low sun. With loud cries the men rushed forward as keenly as though the fight had just begun, and quickly from shore to shore the opposing lines closed in a tumultuous *mêlée* beyond all that had yet been seen. Back and forward the wild struggle swayed in undiminished intensity till darkness fell. Then in sheer exhaustion it died away, and the ugly truth had to be faced. After a fortnight's effort, in which soldiers had done all that soldiers could do, the great combined attack on Achi Baba had culminated and we had failed.

Still something had been gained. The Allied line had been advanced some 600 yards on the right and 400 on the left and centre, and where space was so confined every little increase of elbow room had its value. Determined counter-attacks during the succeeding nights testified how sensible the Turks were of what they had lost. Their efforts were as unavailing as costly, and the new line was held and entrenched, and even in some sections improved. Against the new French position the enemy's reaction had been specially violent. For two successive nights their struggle to dislodge our Allies had been incessant, but with the assistance of the Royal Naval Division and the support of the ships enfilading the Kereves Dere, the new ground overlooking it had been held and organised. The line now ran for about a mile up the western side of the Kereves Dere, and thence fairly straight across the peninsula to the Zighin Dere, opposite Y Beach, but there it was still bent back where the redoubt at Gurkha Bluff had held up our extreme left. Though the General now felt for the first time that he had a secure grip on the peninsula, he could not be satisfied till this defect in the position was made good.

Force having failed, he was resolved to try stratagem. His idea was, in effect, a variation of the *coup de main* which had originally been so successful. The coast section was now held by the Indian brigade, with the 6th Gurkhas on the sea flank, and to them was committed an operation which was after their own heart. While it was being prepared General Birdwood up at Anzac endeavoured to exert fresh pressure on the troops in front of him, and so perform his function of holding as much force as possible away from the Achi Baba front. On the 9th a smart local attack enabled him to seize new ground, but next day a violent counter-attack in superior strength compelled him to give it up.

While this was going on at Gaba Tepe a reconnaissance of Y Beach and its vicinity was carried out in the *Sapphire* by the military officers concerned with the coming attempt. It proved the bluff to be so difficult of access as to give good hope of a surprise, and no naval co-operation was asked for. The left of the Gurkhas was on the cliffs a little to the south of Y Beach. Just beyond the north end of it the bluff rose precipitously, with nothing to give a foothold except where the weather had scored its bare face with little runnels. The plan was for the men to climb down the cliff after dark, steal along the beach and then scale the steep face of the bluff. It was work exactly suited to Gurkha methods, and creeping through the broken ground under the cliffs till the beach was passed, they began on hands and knees to crawl up the face of the bluff undetected. But the moment they reached the top they were met with so hot a fire that they had to return back whence they came. The surprise had failed, but the failure was not accepted. As a reconnaissance it was very valuable, for it revealed the unsuspected fact that a gully which formed a depression covered with scrub below the crown of the bluff was thick with well-concealed snipers and machine-gun posts enfilading the whole length of Y Beach. To deal with them naval co-operation was needed, and Admiral Nicholson was instructed to organise it, while the General arranged for a diversion ashore. For he was resolved to try again, this time with two ships in support.

The 11th was devoted to a joint reconnaissance, and this time, in order to get as close a view as possible, it was made in a destroyer. Every detail could thus be settled, and at 6.30 on the 12th, as night fell, the Gurkhas once more began to steal down the cliff. As they did so the Manchester brigade, which was inshore of the Indians, made a demonstration of attacking with heavy artillery support. In half an hour the double-company of the Gurkhas, which was to lead the attempt, was massed at the foot of the cliff, and when the moment came for them to leave their shelter to pass the beach the *Dublin* and *Talbot* began smothering the gully with salvoes at 1,600 yards. The effect was overwhelming; and in three-quarters of an hour the Gurkhas were able to reach the dead ground under the bluff without a casualty. Then, as the men began the almost impossible ascent, the salvoes ceased, and in another quarter of an hour they were on the top unperceived. The military demonstration appears to have entirely distracted the enemy's attention. During the night the triumphant Gurkhas were able to entrench along the top of the cliff, while further companies were sent out to join them. By the morning they were so well established that they were able to occupy ground which gave us Y Beach once more and the bluff itself, and the whole left of the line was able to move up in conformity. So the desired position was made good. The whole affair had been brilliantly planned and executed, and once again it proved the truth of Wolfe's maxim that successful surprise need not always be looked for at the first coming on. Its happy result was that the whole position across the peninsula had been so far secured that it was possible to await in comparative security the solution of the new problems with which the Expeditionary Force was now faced.

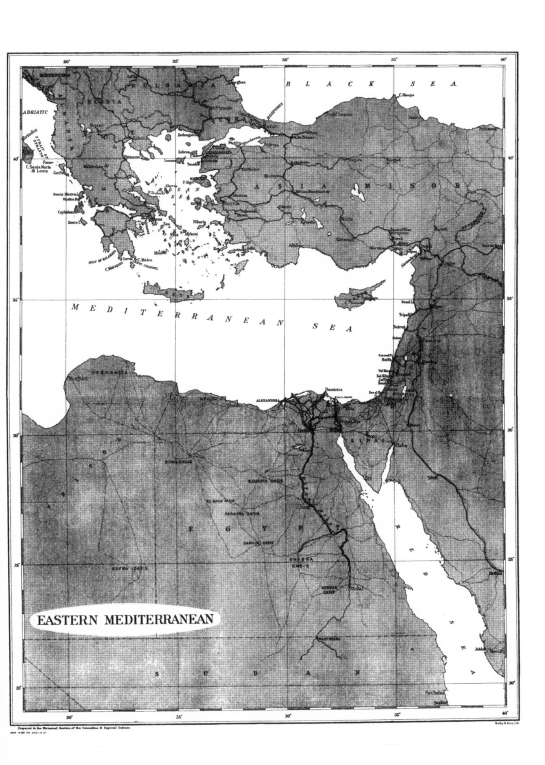

EASTERN MEDITERRANEAN

CHAPTER XX

PROGRESS OF THE SUBMARINE CAMPAIGN AND LOSS OF THE
LUSITANIA—THE ITALIAN CONVENTION—RESIGNATION OF
LORD FISHER AND MR. CHURCHILL, AND FORMATION OF
A COALITION GOVERNMENT

THE breakdown of the second attempt to force the Turkish defences in Gallipoli constitutes a definite landmark in the progress of the war. The hope of rapidly completing the investment of the Central Powers and opening up our direct communications with Russia was at an end. Further progress by combined operations was out of the question without many more troops, and we were faced with the fact that to carry through the enterprise would mean a drain upon both our naval and our military resources beyond anything that had been originally contemplated. Standing alone it was a disturbing prospect, but it did not stand alone. By a dramatic coincidence there had occurred simultaneously one of the outstanding tragedies of the submarine war against commerce which, for the time, overshadowed the really more vital check at the Dardanelles, and in its reactions intensified the difficulties of the problem. For it made suddenly patent how imperfect was the control of the sea which we had already won, and how exacting must be the struggle to perfect it. There could be no certainty that our maritime resources would be equal to the increased strain which a serious prolongation of the Dardanelles operations must entail, and it was clear they must be prolonged. The arrest of our offensive would permit the Turks to complete their defences, and future operations could only take the form of a regular siege like that of Port Arthur. That alone would mean a greatly increased weight upon our means of transport and supply, without the active interference of the enemy, to the menace of which we were at the moment so tragically awakened.

As yet neither at home nor at the Dardanelles had the possibilities of the submarine as a means of disputing the command of the sea made themselves felt except as an annoying irritation. In the Ægean constant rumours of coming submarine interference had kept men alive to the profound difference it would make. We have seen how carefully Budrum, in the Gulf of Kos, was being watched on suspicion of its being prepared as a submarine base, but up to the middle of April all the reports proved false. After that, however, they began to increase in number and coherence, and there could be no doubt that the Germans were developing a systematic plan for getting submarines into the Eastern Mediterranean. In Spain, near Vigo, a German subject was reported to be establishing a depot for their supply; before the end of the month intelligence from various quarters told of their presence in the Mediterranean, and of others coming down the coast of Portugal. On May 2 one was reported off Taormina, coming out of the Strait of Messina. It was doubtless a false alarm, but on May 6 torpedo-boat *92*, of our Gibraltar Patrol, which on Admiralty orders had been sent to watch Alboran, fell in with one steering east forty miles west of the island.[1] The submarine fired a torpedo, which missed, and the torpedo-boat was able to run over her twice, but had not draught enough to do her serious damage and she escaped. Next day this same boat, apparently, chased a British steamer south of Cartagena, which looked as though she were making for the Balearic Islands, where at Palma the *Pelorus* for six weeks past had been watching a suspicious German steamship equipped with wireless.[2]

To complete the impression of coming danger, the Austrian submarines had become so active in the Adriatic that they had forced a relaxation of the French blockade. Since the attack on the *Jean Bart* the blockade had been maintained by an advanced squadron of seven cruisers and a flotilla of destroyers. The system appeared to work well till the night of April 26–27, when the *Gambetta*, flying the flag of Admiral Sénès, was on patrol with two other cruisers. It was a brilliant moonlight night; and being then off the coast of Italy—so

---

[1] The Gibraltar Patrol at this time consisted of three armed boarding steamers and ten torpedo-boats. The *Pelorus*, which also belonged to it, had been detached on special duty. The submarine must have been *U 21*, the first to attempt to reach the Mediterranean. She left the Ems on April 25 under Lieut.-Commander Hersing, proceeding north-about to meet an oil ship "about half way," hence probably the suspected depôt near Vigo. The oil proved unsuitable, but having just enough to reach Cattaro with luck, Lieut.-Commander Hersing went on and reached that port on May 13 with his fuel all but spent. Ten of the smaller "UB" class were also being sent by rail to Pola in sections. Three had already arrived—*UB 3, 7* and *8*— and were being assembled by German constructors. Gayer, Vol. II., p. 24.

[2] She was the Bremen s.s. *Fangturm*, 5,000 tons. She had been in Palma, Majorca, since the early days of the war, and continual protests to the Spanish Government had failed to get her wireless dismantled.

near that she was periodically in the beam of a lighthouse—
she had slowed down and sent off a boat to examine a sailing
vessel. Before it returned a torpedo from an unseen submarine struck her with terrible effect. So quickly did she
sink that every one of her officers perished at his post, and
out of a complement of 714 only 136 were saved. As another
ship of the squadron, the *Waldeck-Rousseau,* had narrowly
missed the same fate not long before, it was now decided to
leave the blockade patrol to the destroyers and to withdraw the cruisers to a supporting position. The comparative
weakness of the arrangement quickly declared itself. Austrian
submarines, emboldened by success, began to appear off Corfu,
and on May 6—the day our torpedo-boat *92* had her encounter
near Alboran—one of the newest Austrian light cruisers was
sighted outside the Adriatic in the open sea between Cepha-
lonia and the Calabrian coast. She was chased by the French
cruiser *Jules Ferry* and the destroyer *Bisson,* but neither
was fast enough to overhaul her, and she got away to the
northward. Seeing how many of our transports were passing
through the Mediterranean, this was a new source of anxiety,
and it was destined to have a marked effect on the distribution
of our Mediterranean Squadron. Representations were made
to the French Admiralty as to the importance of preventing
such movements, and Admiral Peirse as well as Admiral
Limpus at Malta were warned to take precautions against
submarine attack on the transports, but this they were
already doing so far as their resources permitted. They
were slender enough, but in view of what was threatening
at home it was difficult to increase them.

There, after a period of comparative quiescence, the
expected increase of the enemy's submarine effort was
declaring itself. April began like March, with a week of
considerable activity, during which five British and three
Allied ships were sunk, and a new development in inhumanity,
which the Germans seemed to have abandoned since the first
month of the war, recurred. Early in April five British
fishing craft, a class of vessel which the French and ourselves,
even in our bitterest days, had always held immune, were
destroyed by submarines. After that the activity died
down for a time. In the second week only three British and
two Allied ships were sunk, but one of the British losses was
a particularly bad case, for she was the *Harpalyce,* a Belgian
relief ship, sunk off the North Hinder light-vessel, with the
loss of fifteen lives. A Dutch vessel, the *Katwijk,* was also
sunk without warning in the same vicinity, although it was
within the zone which the German warning had declared free

from danger.[1] Besides the above, very few attacks were reported, but one from the locality in which it occurred was of exceptional boldness. It was off St. Catherine's, in the Isle of Wight, upon the tug *Homer*, with a French barque in tow. To an order from the submarine to cast her off the tug replied with a spirited attempt to ram, and though she was subjected to a hot fire, both she and the barque escaped.

For the rest of the month the attack slackened. A few more fishing craft were destroyed, but after two more unsuccessful attempts by aircraft that form of attack also appeared to have ceased. Still, though the losses during April were small compared with what the Germans seem to have expected, they were serious enough to cause anxiety for the future, since it was probable the respite was due to the submarines having returned to prepare for further operations. During the month eleven British merchant ships had been lost, measuring 22,000 tons. Of these there were sunk without warning four ships, with the loss of thirty-eight lives, besides two fishing craft, with the loss of eighteen, and in one of these cases, the *Vanilla*, the submarine actually prevented the crew from being rescued by another trawler. The Allied ships sunk numbered six and the neutrals the same, one of them being a Greek vessel torpedoed without warning in the declared " free zone " near the North Hinder.

In the Channel, after the middle of the month, there were no sinkings at all, and we now know that the Germans considered there was no longer a single place in the Straits of Dover where submarines could penetrate without incurring serious danger. *U 28* and *U 33* had reported our new barrages, and the loss of *U 37* was attributed to them. On April 10 the Dover route was absolutely prohibited by the German Admiralty. Their decision was confirmed when *U 32* reported that early in the month she had fouled a net, and though she had broken through she dared not return by the way she came. The larger boats were ordered to go north-about, and operations in the south were to be confined to a new class of small submarine known as " UB," of which a " Flanders Flotilla " was being formed at Ostend and Zeebrugge. Three of these " UB " boats were at work in the first half of the month with some success, but their construction proved so faulty that they had to be withdrawn for overhauling.[2] Unaware of the success his measures had gained Admiral Hood was far from content. The indicator nets were giving constant trouble. On April 7

---

[1] For the *Katwijk* the German Government afterwards tendered an apology.
[2] Gayer, Vol. II., pp. 20–22. Nordsee, Vol. IV., pp. 101, 102.

he reported that almost every day some of them were carried away by submarines without the buoys indicating. But glass balls were now coming forward for floats, and an improved indicator buoy had been found. The great Folkestone–Gris Nez boom, in spite of every kind of difficulty, was progressing, and other measures more offensive in character were being taken. On April 8 two new cross-Channel steamers, the *Prince Edward* and *Queen Victoria*, which had been fitted for laying wire nets at high speed, made their first venture off Ostend, under escort of two destroyers. It proved a complete success. At break of day they ran out about one and three-quarter miles of nets in twelve minutes within range of the batteries, but so smartly was the work done that it was completed before the guns opened fire, and both net-layers got away untouched. With this operation Admiral Hood's connection with the Dover Patrol ceased. The following day he was appointed to the Irish squadron, and on the 13th Admiral Bacon took his place.

The apparent success of the recent measures was the more welcome, for in the last half of the month three more divisions of the Territorial force (the West Riding, the Northumbrian and the Highland) were crossing to France, and with the lengthening days the transports could not make the whole passage in the dark hours. The West Riding Division began to move on April 13 and the Northumbrian on the 17th, partly from Southampton and partly from Folkestone; the Highland Division followed in the last week of the month, and all crossed without interference.[1]

During May the pressure on these routes was to continue. For besides the usual drafts and stores, three New Army divisions (the IXth Scottish, the XIVth and the XIIth), which were now ready for service, were to go over to France. Before they sailed a new form of protection had begun to be tried. It took the form of deep mine-fields in the usual lurking places of the enemy's submarines. One of these was laid off Beachy Head on April 24, and one off Dartmouth on May 2. But, as we now know, no enemy submarines were permitted to enter the Channel at this time; and again the troops, mainly in small fast steamers and by night, were put across, to the number of about 100,000 men, without accident.

In the other area which had caused so much anxiety— that is, Area XVII, in which lay the North Channel and the approaches to Glasgow, Liverpool and Belfast—success seemed no less assured. Here on April 2 Rear-Admiral

---

[1] Some battalions of these divisions had already crossed.

The Hon. R. F. Boyle had succeeded Admiral Barlow. He had then at his disposal about 80 drifters, a number which was raised to about 130 by the end of the month. Although the North Channel between the Mull of Cantyre and the Antrim coast is barely eleven miles across—little more than half the width of the Straits of Dover—it required twice the length of net. The reason was, that while in the Straits the accumulation of wrecks and the comparatively shoal water made it difficult for submarines to get through by diving under the nets, in the North Channel the depth averages about seventy fathoms, and diving under a single line of nets was a simple matter. The problem had therefore to be tackled on a different principle. It was dealt with by a system designed not so much to entangle the submarines, as to force them to keep beneath the surface for so long that their batteries would be exhausted. To this end a netted area was arranged. It was a parallelogram twenty miles long by twelve miles wide, touching Rathlin Island with its north-west angle, and extending ten miles each way from the narrowest part of the Channel. In this area with the large number of drifters available it was possible, weather permitting, to keep four or five lines of nets athwart the fairway, and as it was also patrolled, it was practically impossible for a submarine to come to the surface for at least twenty miles. The arrangement was completed by the patrol areas which extended five miles beyond either end of the netted area. The idea was that the patrol vessels would force the submarines to dive at least five miles before reaching the netted area and to remain submerged till they were five miles clear of it. In this manner a submerged run of thirty miles would be forced upon them, which would leave them so far exhausted that on rising they would have little chance of escaping the patrol vessels. For the trade a passage was left between Rathlin Island and the mainland and so down the Antrim coast. It was only three miles wide, and could therefore be easily patrolled, but for the present the area was left undisturbed, and the merits of the system were not put to the proof.[1]

[1] Admiral Boyle organised his drifters into nine sections, with at first nine and afterwards twelve drifters in each, six sections working, and three resting. Each drifter could hold half a mile of net, so that it was eventually possible to keep thirty-six miles of nets in action. The northern end was patrolled by the Belfast armed yacht squadron, the southern by three armed trawler units, the netted area by two destroyers and the armed boarding steamer *Tara*. To maintain this patrol service he had four destroyers of the 8th Flotilla and three Auxiliary Patrol units. These were over and above the Clyde and Liverpool patrols.

It was apparent, in fact, that the Germans were turning their attention to another quarter. Though submarines were constantly reported in St. George's Channel and the western approaches to the English Channel, there were never more than three in the area, which was calling for special attention as being the starting-point of our communications to the Dardanelles. When on April 8 General Peyton's Mounted division began to leave Avonmouth for Egypt, a large submarine had been moving in the entrance to the Bristol Channel and near Scilly. Others were reported off the south-east of Ireland.[1] The provision of escort had been difficult, and even though the transports sailed by twos and threes, it had been found impossible to give them destroyer protection further than forty miles west of Lundy Island. The result was that one of them, as she was passing Scilly, was torpedoed. She succeeded in getting into Queenstown, and there her troops were transferred to another ship. Four days previous to this it had been decided that no more troops should leave Avonmouth. Plymouth was to be substituted as the port of embarkation for long-distance voyages, so that not only would the transports have the protection of the patrols in Area XIV, but the destroyers would have less distance to cover in convoying them to a safe distance and escort would therefore be a simpler matter.

Hitherto the area, though well furnished with six patrol units and thirty-six drifters, had not been giving satisfaction. Ships had been harassed and even sunk, especially off Scilly, with impunity, and as the result of a report which Lord Fisher called for, it was reorganised in the middle of the month. On April 15 the Commander-in-Chief at Devonport was informed that the whole area was to be under Captain Valentine Phillimore, who, with his office at Falmouth, would work it in four sections, with sub-bases at Penzance, Falmouth, Plymouth and St. Mary's, Scilly. The Scilly section was to have a yacht and two and a half patrol units, and the other three sections a yacht and one and a half units, and a wireless station was to be set up at St. Mary's.

By the end of April, then, the Auxiliary Patrol had made considerable progress both in numbers and organisation, but its efficiency was still hampered by the difficulty of finding sufficient wireless operators and guns. Besides the regular flotillas there were now in Home waters about sixty armed yachts and over five hundred trawlers and drifters, and twenty more yachts and a hundred more trawlers and drifters were being fitted out. These figures did not include the

---

[1] The three submarines out at the time were *U 32*, *U 24* and *U 33*.

minesweepers, boom defence vessels, or motor-boats, so that with the fifty trawlers at the Dardanelles the total number of auxiliary small craft in commission was already well over 1,500.

Two-thirds of the patrol vessels and minesweepers were employed in North Scottish waters and the North Sea, but nearly all the net drifters were assigned to the Straits of Dover, the Western Channel and the Irish Sea, in order to protect our ocean trade and the communications of the army, against which the enemy had seemed to be concentrating his main effort. But it soon became clear that he was extending his sphere of action. The increased size of his new submarines enabled him to turn the well-defended Straits of Dover by going north-about. They had already appeared near St. Kilda, and by the end of the month there could be no doubt that a number of these vessels were passing that way into the Atlantic. The menace to the all-important 10th Cruiser Squadron, on which our whole policy of blockade depended, could not be disguised. Admiral de Chair's hard-worked ships were still based on Liverpool and the Clyde, and the long passage to and from their exhausting vigil was no longer safe. One of them, the *Oropesa*, had already encountered and driven off a submarine near Skerryvore, and it had become necessary for Admiral de Chair to seek some place further north where a coaling station could be established.

Nor could Admiral Jellicoe be less anxious about his own communications. His supply ships were passing up by the west coast of Ireland; on April 28 one of them, the collier *Mobile*, was torpedoed off the Butt of Lewis, and next day another, the *Cherbury*, sunk near Eagle Island, the usual landfall on the coast of Mayo. Owing to pressing preoccupations elsewhere the Hebrides Patrol (Area I) had not yet received the full number of craft assigned to it, and he had to ask for it to be reinforced by twelve trawlers. But it was soon clear that the danger extended further. On the 30th the Russian s.s. *Svorono* was reported sunk off the Blaskets, in the south-west of Ireland, and close by, apparently the same submarine, destroyed another collier transport, the *Fulgent*. Further down there was even greater activity, and by May 1 three more ships had been caught in the vicinity of Scilly, one of which had an importance far beyond its local effect. It was a large oil-tanker, the *Gulflight*, and was the first American ship to fall a victim to the U-boats. Though she was successfully towed into Scilly her master lost his life. For a while opinion in the United States smarted under the outrage, and though no immediate action ensued, the seed was sown from which great things were destined to grow.

With us the extension of activity meant a reconsideration of our system of protection. The Grand Fleet supply ships were now directed to proceed by the Irish Channel and the Minch, but they would still be exposed as they left the English Channel and its approaches. The weak point in these western waters was Area XXI, which took in the south coast of Ireland from the Blaskets to Carnsore Point, at the entrance of St. George's Channel. Though it covered the landfall of the main route from New York, the calls of other areas had been more pressing, and as yet it had been given only four weak units, each consisting of an armed yacht and four trawlers. Three of the units were based at Queenstown and one at Berehaven. Hitherto the liners frequenting the route had relied for safety mainly on their speed and the general Admiralty instructions, the chief of which were to keep a mid-channel course, to avoid approaching headlands, to make their port if possible at dawn, and when in infested waters to adopt the expedient of zigzagging.

So far these precautions had sufficed. But when, in the first week of May, it became obvious that there were submarines in the area, one of these ships, the largest and fastest of them all, became a source of special anxiety. She was the *Lusitania*, due off Queenstown on May 7. Since in the early days of the war she had been returned to the Cunard Company as unsuitable for an auxiliary cruiser, she had been running as a passenger ship, and though her boiler power had been reduced enough to make the venture cover expenses, she still remained the fastest ship on the Atlantic. In this way she had already made five round trips with impunity, but this time, on the eve of her leaving New York, a general warning to all passengers travelling through the danger zone in British or Allied vessels was issued from the German Embassy in Washington. She carried over 1,250 passengers, of whom 159 were Americans, and there was no indication that the threat was especially intended for her; therefore no extra precautions were taken beyond giving her special warning as she approached the danger area.

The enemy's activity in it became every day more evident. On May 4 a ship reported being attacked off the Fastnet, but the torpedo missed. It was not known till next day, and then the *Lusitania* was informed that submarines were active off the south coast of Ireland, and the Berehaven section of the Queenstown Patrol was ordered to search the

Fastnet area. The same evening a sailing vessel was lost off the Old Head of Kinsale. Shortly before noon on the 6th, another ship, the *Candidate*, was sunk south of the Coningbeg lightship, off Waterford, that is, at the east end of the Queenstown area, and a couple of hours later another, the *Centurion*, was caught near the same spot.[1] In the course of the day submarines were also reported close off Queenstown, and off Castletownsend to the westward. All ships were now warned, the *Lusitania* amongst them, and again cautioned to avoid headlands and steer a mid-channel course. At the moment only ten vessels of the units based on Queenstown were available. Three trawlers were working in the Fastnet section, four where the Coningbeg sinkings had occurred, and three were patrolling the coast between the two groups, with a motor boat off the Old Head of Kinsale. Of the Berehaven unit one boat was patrolling south of Mizen Head, and another guarding the cables off Valencia. From the Milford area there were also two units working north and south from the Coningbeg lightship.

During the morning of the 7th numerous reports came in from look-out stations of submarines sighted at various points along the coast from Waterford to Cape Clear. At 11.25 the *Lusitania* was again warned. She was just then entering the danger zone, keeping approximately her ordinary course, except that, having received warning the previous day that submarines were off the Fastnet, her usual landfall, she was steering to give it a wide berth. At 8 a.m. she had reduced speed from 21 knots to 18, so as to reach the Liverpool bar at early dawn, when the tide would serve for crossing it. A few minutes later she ran into fog and the captain reduced 3 knots more, and began blowing his siren. Shortly before noon she ran into clear weather again, and increased to 18 knots. As the horizon cleared, Brow Head came into view abaft the port beam, but since the captain did not feel quite certain as to its identity, at 12.40 he altered course to port to close the land, in order to fix his position accurately. This was essential. His last warning was that other submarines were off Coningbeg. When last seen they were twenty miles to seaward of it, and he had therefore decided to pass it close inshore. As he was altering course another message was passed to him through Valencia saying that submarines had been seen that morning south of Cape Clear, which was now thirty miles astern. Accordingly, feeling himself well clear of that danger, he held on till, at 1.40, the Old Head

[1] All these vessels appear to have been sunk by *U 20*, which left Borkum on April 30.

of Kinsale came in sight to port. He then returned to his original course, which would take him past the headland at a distance of about ten miles. The weather was now quite clear and the sea calm. Nothing was in sight but the motor-boat patrol off Kinsale, when at 2.15, as the passengers were coming on deck after luncheon, the track of a torpedo was seen to starboard. It took the great liner amidships and exploded with deafening violence; a second explosion followed almost immediately, and she began at once to take a heavy list. Some on board, including a look-out who said he saw its wash in the wake of the first, declared that the second explosion was due to another torpedo. An American passenger, on the other hand, was convinced that the second explosion was not due to a torpedo, and this is supported by other evidence. In twenty minutes the huge vessel plunged down head foremost and was gone.[1]

The suddenness of her end, combined with the heavy list, which interfered with the lowering of the boats, made the work of life-saving lamentably difficult. Vessels of all kinds flocked to the spot at her first cry for help—among them Admiral Hood, the new commander of the Irish Coast Station, in the *Juno*, which had just put into Queenstown—but when it was known how quickly the lost ship had sunk he was recalled. The rest held on, but in spite of all they could do the loss of life was appalling. Her crew and passengers numbered within two score of 2,000 souls, and of these there perished of men, women and children no less than 1,198. Never had there been such a war loss on the sea; never one which so violently outraged the laws of war and dictates of humanity. The Germans justified their act on the plea that she carried some 5,000 cases of small arm ammunition and shrapnel. This was true. But even so by every accepted canon it would not warrant the destruction of a ship whose chief freight was non-combatant

[1] She was sunk by *U 20*, Lt.-Com. Schwieger, who went down in *U 88* in September, 1917. The following account is from his diary:—

"An unusual detonation followed which gave off a very large smoke cloud, rising far above the foremost funnel. The super-structure over the point of impact and the bridge are torn asunder, fire breaks out and smoke envelops the upper bridge. The vessel stops at once and heels over rapidly to starboard, at the same time sinking further by the head. Everything seems to indicate that she will capsize shortly. Great confusion arises on board. The boats are cleared away and some are lowered into the water. Many people appear to have lost their head, as a number of fully manned boats almost fall from the davit heads and strike the water bow or stern first, only to be swamped immediately. I could not have fired a second torpedo into this crowd of people trying to save themselves." (Nordsee, Vol. IV., p. 112.)

passengers, and least of all her destruction without warning. In further defence of the indefensible the Germans asserted she was armed as a cruiser. This was not true. She was not even armed defensively.

As the news spread it was received throughout the world with a shudder. In America the loss of so many of her citizens brought her to the brink of war, but for that the time was not yet ripe. At home its moral effect was a keener sense of the deepening intensity of the struggle, a heightened faith in the justice of our cause, and a passionate determination to greater effort, which displayed itself in a suddenly increased flow of recruits both for land and sea. In Germany there was loud exultation over the lesson they had given us, but what we learnt from it was not what they sought to teach, and in the national sentiment the *Lusitania* took her place beside Belgium as a symbol of faith in the crusade on which we had embarked.

For those on whose shoulders rested the conduct of the war it could only bring a heavier sense of responsibility, and it was while the shock of the outrage was tingling that the news of the failure at Gallipoli came in. The first suggestion for breaking the deadlock came from the navy. Experience had shown that the fleet could do little to help the army against trenches and machine-guns, but amongst the Naval Staff on the spot there was a strong opinion that it could help in another way. Their belief was, now that they had reorganised the sweeping flotilla and brought it to a high state of efficiency, they could rush the Straits without reducing the batteries, and establish a powerful force in the Sea of Marmara. They were eager to try, but in the eyes of Admiral de Robeck the chance of overcoming the difficulty in this way did not justify the risk. Seeing what the spirit of the Turkish resistance had proved to be, and how it must now be heightened by success, he did not believe that the presence of a more or less maimed fleet in the Sea of Marmara could produce any decisive effect. The Straits would certainly be closed behind it, and an enforced return when supplies were exhausted might well mean a disaster, which would place the whole expedition in jeopardy.

On these lines he submitted an appreciation to the Admiralty for decision (May 10). There the idea of another naval attack could not be entertained, for quite apart from the Admiral's doubts there were other considerations which forbade it. The chief of these was the adhesion of Italy to the Entente; instead of relieving our burden in the Mediterranean, as might have been expected the effect was to increase it materially. After prolonged negotiations, which turned mainly on the ultimate allocation of the Dalmatian coast and its fringe of islands, it was left to the British Government to suggest a compromise. On April 14 their proposals were accepted, and an agreement had been come to on April 26 by which Italy undertook to declare war on Austria within a month. Of help in the Dardanelles it gave no hope. Russia was opposed to seeing Italy operating against Turkish territory, and Italy herself was naturally bent on concentrating her efforts upon her special objects in the Trentino and the Adriatic. The agreement provided for a naval convention between France, Italy and Great Britain, the terms of which were delegated to a naval conference to be held in Paris, and Sir Henry Jackson, with the Assistant Director of Operations, went over to attend it. His instructions were based on a memorandum which had been drawn up by the First Lord the day the Dalmatian compromise was accepted—that is, a fortnight earlier, when the Dardanelles expedition was reconcentrating in the Ægean for the combined attack. The memorandum provided for an Adriatic fleet, to be commanded by the Duke of the Abruzzi. It was to be mainly Italian, but was to be reinforced by four French battleships and a flotilla, and also by four British battleships and four light cruisers as soon as the Dardanelles and Bosporus were open. But from the first certain difficulties arose which rendered an arrangement on this basis impossible. The plan which the Italians presented was based entirely on the Allied fleet being used to give direct support to the Italian army as it advanced at the head of the Adriatic. For this they wished to have the Allied fleet divided into two squadrons, one to go up the Adriatic to act on the right of the army, the other to cover the base at Brindisi. But when it came to the question of who should command, there was a deadlock. For moral and political reasons both the French and the Italians found it impossible to give way. In neither country would national sentiment endure to see their ships commanded by a foreign Admiral, and it was left to the British representatives to find a way out.

The strategical objections which they found in the Italian plan indicated a line of compromise. They had already pointed out that to attempt to operate with a fleet at the head of the Adriatic, in the immediate vicinity of the enemy's chief naval bases, was little short of suicide. To prevent interference from the enemy's fleet in those narrow waters they could well trust to their flotillas and submarines. The

British proposal, then, was to form for the support of the flotillas an advanced squadron mainly composed of Italian heavy and light cruisers,[1] which would operate in the Adriatic under the Duke of the Abruzzi, while the French Admiral remained in command of the battle fleet to support him, and to blockade the Straits of Otranto. But this arrangement, although it gave the most active functions to the Italians, did not satisfy them. Their alternative proposal was to form two fleets, separately commanded, their own to act north of the Straits of Otranto, the French to the south, and if the two had occasion to act together the supreme command would be determined by the area in which the combined fleet was operating.

Besides the obvious objections to such a scheme of alternating command, there was the difficulty that without the assistance of their Allies the Italians could not form a fleet capable of assisting their army and protecting their coasts and trade. The French, however, while ready to lend a destroyer flotilla, were still unable to see their way to placing ships of force under the Italian flag. Little hope as there was of the Italian Government accepting such a solution, a draft convention on these lines was submitted to them, but they felt compelled to reject it. The deadlock was now complete, and the British alone could unloose it. There was only one way. It would mean a serious dislocation of our plans, but, heavy as our responsibilities were in the Mediterranean, it had to be done for the common cause. As the sole means of saving the situation we offered to reinforce the Duke of the Abruzzi's fleet at once with a division of four battleships, and also with a squadron of four light cruisers from the Dardanelles, as soon as the French replaced them with an equal number of cruisers. This the French had undertaken to do, and also to increase the number of their battleships at the Dardanelles as soon as possible to six. The French further agreed to place at the Duke of the Abruzzi's disposal twelve destroyers and as many torpedo boats, submarines and mine-sweepers as their Commander-in-Chief could spare, and, if possible, a seaplane carrier with a squadron of seaplanes. The Convention thus provided for two fleets, independently commanded, but with co-ordinated functions, and in this form it was signed on May 10, the same day that Admiral de Robeck's submission deprecating

[1] The Italians had no battle cruisers of British type, but the *San Marco* and *San Giorgio* carried 2-10″ and 8-7·5″; the *Amalfi* and *Pisa* had 4-10″ and 8-7·5″; three others were armed with 1-10″, 2-8″ and 14-6″ —the first four were designed for 23 knots, the last three for 20 knots.

another naval attempt to force the Dardanelles reached the Admiralty.

The actual situation in the Mediterranean which Ministers had before them when it came to hand was that the difficulty of reconciling the divergent views of our Allies had involved a lamentable waste of strength. Of active ships of force, the Austrians had only three or possibly four Dreadnoughts, six other battleships, two cruisers and six light cruisers, only four of which were up to date. Against this the Italians would have an active fleet of four or five Dreadnoughts, five other battleships, seven cruisers, of which five carried 10" guns, and five light cruisers, with two more nearly ready, while the French, except in light cruisers, would be still more powerful.

From a purely strategical and tactical point of view, therefore, this dispersion of our force was probably unnecessary, but the needs of the new situation in the Adriatic were by no means the only exigency which the British Government had to consider in coming to a decision about the Dardanelles. The naval outlook at this juncture was disturbed by military reactions. The battle of Ypres, which had followed the German gas attack, was just dying out, the casualties had been very heavy, and we had lost a large part of the famous salient to the retention of which so much had been sacrificed. Further down the line, moreover, we were committed to a new and extensive operation. The French, with the idea of relieving the pressure on the Russians, had opened a strong offensive in Artois, and we had undertaken a complementary attack towards Lille. The resistance of the Germans was proving very strong, and it was only too clear that the sanguine expectation that they were becoming exhausted by the gigantic efforts they had made must be abandoned.

The opening attack of May 9 on Aubers Ridge had proved that since Neuve Chapelle the Germans had had time to develop a new and highly effective system of defence upon which we could make little impression, and simultaneously with the news of our check in Gallipoli it was known that our offensive in Flanders had completely failed. All hope of breaking through had to be given up, and the subsequent operations took the less ambitious form of pressure in support of the French attack. This was proving a little more successful, but was far from promising a break in the enemy's line. The military authorities at home had therefore come to the conclusion that there was nothing to be done in the main theatre for some time to come except stand on the defensive.

By all experience, therefore, it was the moment to press

a minor offensive within the capacity of our surplus force at some other point vital to the enemy. But in the opinion of the military authorities there was little or no surplus force. Our losses in the recent fighting had been very heavy, and, moreover, it was not only of the security of our line in France they were thinking, but also of the security of our own shores. The spectre of invasion had again arisen, as it always had done when our arms were unsuccessful abroad, and the elaborate efforts to lay it, to which so much thought had been devoted before the war, proved of no effect. The first line Territorial force was nearly all abroad, one of the few remaining divisions, the "Lowland," was already under orders for Gallipoli, and the second line had been so heavily depleted to furnish drafts, that as a defence force it was considered to be impotent. True the first of the new armies had completed its training, and the second would be fully equipped in a month or two, but these troops it was considered necessary to regard as general reserve in case the Germans, content with their success in the Eastern Front, should elect to return in force to the west. So deep, indeed, was the apprehension in military circles, that they began to express discontent with the naval dispositions in the North Sea, and to press the Admiralty to take further precautions.

It was an attitude which the Admiralty was even less able to understand than ever it had been in the days when St. Vincent was First Lord. There had been great changes in the mechanism of naval war since sailing days, but after repeated consideration they were convinced that all those changes told in favour of the defence. Experience during the war had deepened conviction. The two cruiser raids on our coast had shown that the disposition in the North Sea could ensure that even the most mobile force attempting to pass across it would be brought to action if it remained on our shores more than an hour or two. And since that time our hold had materially strengthened. There were now based on the Forth the ten battleships of the Third Battle Squadron, and, under Admiral Beatty, whose flag was again flying in the *Lion*, eight battle cruisers (soon to be nine), the 3rd Cruiser Squadron and three squadrons of light cruisers with the 1st Destroyer Flotilla. At Scapa were the other three battle squadrons, the 1st, 2nd and 7th Cruiser Squadrons and the 2nd and 4th Destroyer Flotillas, which were constantly engaged in patrol for submarines. And there, too, was the *Warspite* of the "Queen Elizabeth" class, doing her gunnery before definitely taking her place in the fleet. On the other hand, it was felt in certain naval quarters that owing to recent developments the old confidence of the sea service in its ability to intercept any formidable raiding force could scarcely be maintained in full integrity. It could not be disguised that the scouting movements of cruisers were now to some extent restricted by the menace of submarines, and contact with an enemy's force was therefore more difficult to obtain. It appears to have been mainly for this reason that it was considered necessary to maintain the large reserve of troops which, instead of being reckoned as a disposable surplus, were concentrated about Cambridge as the central force of the Home Defence army.

To some military authorities, at least, it appeared that the precaution was beyond what the reasonable risks of war demanded. If to the British navy the enemy's submarines were a bar to free cruiser action, to the German General Staff, unused to risking troops in transports at sea, the submarine factor would be likely to act ten times more strongly as a deterrent. Our own experience of the hasty withdrawal of transports which followed the appearance of the enemy's submarines in the Dardanelles was adduced as a complete confirmation of this view. To soldiers who had witnessed it, it seemed to put out of court the possibility of any landing in force on our own coast being attempted. It appears, however, to have had no effect, and at home the anxiety continued unabated.

Since the winter the possibility of such an attempt on the part of the Germans had never ceased to affect the distribution of the fleet. After the battle of the Dogger Bank and the supersession of Admiral von Ingenohl by Admiral von Pohl, the apprehension was aggravated by indications of a revival of activity in the High Seas Fleet. As the spring advanced these indications became so strong that we were forced to infer that the change in the German command meant the inauguration of a new policy at sea.

Admiral von Pohl, the original Chief of the Staff, has himself informed us that from the first the German plan had been not to risk the fleet in any large offensive operations. Even an attempt to interrupt the flow of our troops to France was not to be permitted. The policy was simply to keep the fleet in being with two objects—the one defensive, to deter us from undertaking any large combined enterprise against German territory; the other in a sense offensive, that is, it was thought, by denying the Grand Fleet the opportunity of a battle, its inactivity would eventually exasperate public opinion to such a degree that it would be forced to operate in German prepared waters where it could be engaged with advantage and was certain to suffer serious damage.[1]   As we have seen, this policy had been modified to the extent of allowing certain latitude to the cruiser force till the Dogger Bank action gave cause for reconsideration.

On assuming the chief command afloat Admiral von Pohl's intention was to adhere to his original policy, and the movements of the High Seas Fleet were to be confined to occasional cruises in the Bight, in hope of forcing the Admiralty's hand and enticing the British fleet into the snare which, in his inexperienced eyes, seemed so cunningly set.   The fowler was young but the bird was old.

Only two such sorties are said to have been made in February and March.   April and May were regarded as more favourable months.   This was equally obvious to ourselves, and the Commander-in-Chief had orders to carry out his practice cruises in the North Sea.   As a supplementary measure it was also decided to lay an intercepting minefield north-west of Heligoland.   This was begun on the night of May 8–9 by the newly fitted liners *Princess Margaret* and *Princess Irene,* under escort of the *Aurora* and two divisions of destroyers from Harwich, and was completed two nights later by the minelayer *Orvieto* with the *Broke* and six destroyers from Scapa.[2]   During this and the preceding month we made four sorties in which the various squadrons were combined on prearranged plans.   They were never the same, but, generally speaking, it may be said that they were based on getting out the 3rd Battle Squadron and the battle cruiser squadrons on a line between their base in the Forth and the Skagerrak, where they patrolled while the rest of the Grand Fleet was coming down to concentrate upon them. At the same time Commodore Tyrwhitt's force was brought up to a patrol station between the Broad Fourteens and Terschelling, ready to join an action if it took place, or to stop a raid, which, it was imagined, the Germans might attempt under a demonstration of offering battle further north.

When the concentration was complete the battle fleet advanced as far towards the Bight as, in Admiral Jellicoe's opinion, could be done without playing into the German hands.   The movements lasted, as a rule, from three to four

---

[1] *Minutes and Letters,* by Admiral von Pohl, August 8, 1914.

[2] The *Princess Margaret* and *Princess Irene* were two new vessels of 6,000 tons, built for the Canadian Pacific Railway, which were taken up as minelayers by the Admiralty early in 1915.   The *Princess Irene* was destroyed by an internal explosion at Sheerness on May 27 the same year.

days, but nothing was ever seen of the enemy, for it appears that he never advanced further than 120 miles from Heligoland, that is, only just beyond the arc which, for the Germans, marked the limits of the Bight.

The German policy of inaction with the main fleet naturally gave all the greater importance to the minor offensive. Continual teasing by subsidiary methods was indeed a supplementary means of forcing our hand. In any case, the enemy's narrow escapes off Scarborough and the Dogger Bank taught the wisdom of confining offensive operations to the flotilla and subsidiary craft.

At the end of April a new development on these lines was on foot. The operation appears to have been designed for a new type of torpedo-boats which had been constructed at Hamburg and sent to Antwerp overland in sections.[1] The idea was that an integral part of the "Flanders Flotilla," which we have seen was being formed out of the new small submarines and torpedo-boats, using Zeebrugge as a base, should operate against our armed trawlers that patrolled the approaches to the Channel on the look-out for submarines. As a first step two torpedo-boats, *A 2* and *A 6*, on May-day morning were sent out to ascertain whether any of our destroyers were about. At the same time four of our Yarmouth trawlers (*Columbia, Barbados, Miura* and *Chirsit*) had been sent to the North Hinder to search for a submarine that had been reported in the vicinity the previous day. Simultaneously two old destroyers of the Nore defence flotilla (*Recruit* and *Brazen*) were patrolling at the Galloper, the outermost of the Thames Estuary shoals, about thirty miles south-west of the North Hinder light-vessel. Here at 11.20 a.m. the *Recruit* was cut in two by a torpedo from an unseen submarine. She sank immediately. Four officers and twenty-two of her men were rescued by a passing Dutch steam vessel, but the submarine, for it was actually one of the new "UB" class that had fired the shot, escaped the *Brazen* and a Harwich trawler who gave chase.[2] In the same hour a torpedo was fired, probably by another of the small submarines, at the *Columbia*, which at this time was off the mouth of the Scheldt. It missed, and the trawlers continued their search without success till 3.0 p.m. when, being then back at the North Hinder, they were sighted by *A 2* and *A 6*. The

---

[1] This was the "A" class, of which there were apparently eight of about 100 tons burden and 20 knots speed. Their armament was believed to be one 4-pdr. gun and two 18″ tubes—completed in 1915.

[2] Gayer states that the *Recruit* was sunk by *UB 6*, Lieutenant Häcker. Vol. II., p. 27.

torpedo-boats were steaming west-south-west, and at once attacked. Four torpedoes were fired, only one hit and that sank the *Columbia*. Then for twenty minutes they all fell to with their guns, but no harm had been done when the two German boats suddenly made off towards their base. The reason for their flight was that as soon as the loss of the *Recruit* was known a division of the Harwich destroyers (*Laforey, Lawford, Leonidas, Lark*) had been hurried out to look for her supposed assailant. In the course of the search they had run up against the action with the trawlers, and the German reconnoitring boats quickly learnt what was to be expected from Commodore Tyrwhitt's alertness. In vain the enemy tried to escape into Dutch waters or their own mine-fields. Long as was the range, our destroyers began to hit at once, and in about an hour both the German boats sank with colours flying. It seems that as soon as our guns had fairly got the range the German crews had abandoned ship and taken to the water, and most of them were rescued.

A few days later the Germans had something to set off against this reverse. Further operations were being called for on the Belgian coast, partly from Headquarters in France and partly from Dunkirk, where guns from somewhere were dropping shell into the harbour. The *Venerable* was warned to be ready for a return to her old work, and destroyers of the Dover Patrol were told off to reconnoitre the coast and settle marks to guide her fire. On May 7 the *Maori* and *Crusader* were thus engaged when the *Maori* was sunk by a mine, and though the crew got away in the boats, the fire from the shore was too hot for the *Crusader* to rescue them. Three days later the *Venerable*, off Westende, was trying to find the guns that were worrying Dunkirk, but so severe was the enemy's counter-battery that she could not anchor, and she seems to have done little or nothing effective before she was ordered off to the Dardanelles (May 15).

With all this activity of the enemy in the southern part of the North Sea it was at the time particularly difficult to deal. The extension of the German submarine attack had involved a serious weakening of the Harwich Force by the withdrawal of a number of destroyers for escort duty in the western approaches to the Channel. Ever since the dead set at the *Lusitania* this area was infested with the enemy's submarines; they were being continually seen even in the Bristol Channel, and constant attacks were reported. During May this area demanded ever-increasing attention. Not only did the loss of the *Lusitania* emphasise its importance for trade defence, but with our deepening commitments at the Dardanelles

its security was more than ever vital from the point of view
of our Mediterranean communications. Between hunting
reported submarines and escorting munition ships and transports, as they were ready for sea, the work of the destroyers
was incessant. In the latter half of the month it became
strenuous almost past endurance. On May 18 three transports, with 250 officers and 4,400 men of the Royal Naval
Division and drafts, sailed for the Mediterranean, and two
of the six destroyers that escorted them beyond the danger
point had to wait out and meet a home-coming Canadian
transport. Three days later the 52nd Lowland Division was
to sail from Liverpool and Devonport, but the movement
had to be stopped while destroyers scoured the sea for submarines that had appeared in the transport route and another
Canadian transport was met. So the work went on night
and day for the rest of the month; the destroyers were run
off their legs, and no praise can be too high for the men who
endured the strain or for those who built the no-less-sorely-
tried hulls and engines. Still the flow went on with scarcely
a break, and no outgoing ship or incoming Canadian transport
was lost—not to mention the Grand Fleet ships that had
to pass in and out of dock, and all demanded destroyer escort.
It is a marvel how the work was done in the face of so intrepid
and tenacious an enemy. Naturally we fix our attention on
the great operations of the war, but what they meant can
never be understood unless we keep in mind the unceasing
undercurrent of exhausting labour in small craft that made
them possible.

Nor was it only the destroyers that felt the weight of
what our increasing military commitments demanded. The
Auxiliary Patrol was also called on to take a hand in the
work, and in consequence the enemy had freer scope for his
minor operations in the North Sea. Indications of new
minefields were being detected in the waters between the
Humber and Terschelling, and these operations the enemy
supplemented by raids on our fishing-boats. In the air they
were scarcely less persistent than beneath the water, and
from Harwich both the light cruisers and the remaining
destroyers were continually at sea on the watch for Zeppelins,
till a special squadron could be formed in the Humber to help
with the guard.[1]

[1] This was the 6th Light Cruiser Squadron, formed of five of the " Senti-
nels "—the old type of flotilla cruiser, *Sentinel, Skirmisher, Adventure, Forward,
Foresight.* It was soon dispersed for other duties. A new type of destroyer,
termed " flotilla leader," was coming forward. Four of them (*Kempenfelt,
Nimrod, Lightfoot, Marksman*) were completed between August and November
1915. By July the same year eight more had been ordered.

So much is all that can be said of the stir and strain in Home waters. It never ceased, nor were the efforts to deal with the problem of minor attack ever relaxed. Owing to the drain upon our resources to the westward much energy had to be expended in making good in the North Sea. All down our East coast the patrols were being materially increased. In the middle of May over and above the vessels in the six Auxiliary Patrol areas between the Forth and the Nore, we had thirty submarines, two defence and two patrol destroyer flotillas (about fifty in all), and, besides this defence force, there were the destroyers and submarines at Harwich and the three Grand Fleet flotillas based at Cromarty and Rosyth. It was all too few. During the summer and autumn the twenty " M " class destroyers ordered in September 1914 would be coming forward for service, and behind them were thirty-two more, ordered by Lord Fisher in November for his grand design. But as yet the whole system was not adequate to deal with the enemy's submarines and minelayers, and the problem of getting certain contact with a raiding force was still with us.

To some extent, however, the difficulty was less serious than it seemed on the surface. The North Sea was now so widely sown with mines that only certain known lines of approach were open.[1] It was, indeed, practically certain that if a hostile force could get round these difficulties and succeed in effecting a landing it could only be small and lightly equipped. By no means could it have time to land guns and ammunition on a scale that the war had proved to be necessary for effective action, and its sea communications must be immediately and permanently cut. In these circumstances, seeing how much the Germans had on their hands, how hazardous was the enterprise, and how disastrous would be its failure, nothing seemed to the Admiralty less likely than an attempt to land at the existing juncture, and Ministers shared their view.

Military opinion was not entirely convinced, and the highest authority was still pressing for further precautions in the North Sea. They were already in hand. The new destroyers and sub-

---

[1] According to Gayer the sorties of the High Seas Fleet at this period were for the purpose of laying minefields in the open sea, apparently to catch the Grand Fleet. But it was found that these minefields were so quickly detected and reported by our fishermen, and that they so hampered the movements of the German submarines that the policy was abandoned at the end of the year. He also states that the Germans, on their part, discovered that a great part of the areas which we had declared dangerous was free from mines. Vol. II., p. 30.

marines were being pushed on, and measures had been taken
to reinforce the Grand Fleet.   The whole situation rested
ultimately on the power of this fleet to deal decisively with
the High Seas Fleet if it ventured to sea.   That it would do
so before long was regarded as quite likely.   There was reason
to believe that the Germans would soon have some new and
very powerful units ready to join it, and for this reason the
Admiralty had decided to recall the *Queen Elizabeth*.   She
was required to head the line with her sister, the *Warspite*.
An order was consequently sent to Admiral de Robeck on
May 12, instructing him that she was to sail for home at once
with all despatch and secrecy, and it was to replace her that the
Venerable was being taken.   With her was to go the *Exmouth*,
and at the end of the month they would be followed by the
first two of new monitors, *Abercrombie* and *Roberts*, each
of which was armed with a pair of 14″ guns and provided
with bulges against mines and torpedoes.   At the same time,
he was informed of the Italian Convention and ordered to
detach Admiral Thursby with the *Queen, Implacable, London*
and *Prince of Wales*, and four of his light cruisers as soon as
French ships arrived to replace them, but independently
of these ships they had ordered to his flag two other cruisers.
They were the *Cornwall* and *Chatham* from the East Coast of
Africa, where they had been operating against the *Königsberg*
in the Rufiji River.

The means chosen for strengthening our position in the
North Sea was one which the highest military opinion was
unable to approve.   The recall of the *Queen Elizabeth*, though it
was the one thing necessary to allay their legitimate anxiety,
they resented a little bitterly.   They themselves had just
decided to reinforce General Hamilton with the Lowland
Territorial division and 1,000 drafts for the XXIXth; and
the withdrawal of the most powerful unit of the squadron
looked to them like desertion.   They pleaded the serious
moral effect it would have, not only on the troops, but on
the whole Mussulman world.   They further urged that what
had most weighed with them in assenting to a combined
expedition, was the knowledge that the *Queen Elizabeth* was
to form part of it, and the Admiralty representations as to
the power of her guns.   The Admiralty's view was that she
had been sent out when little more than a naval attack was
contemplated, and now that the operations were to be mainly
military, the ships of lesser force and the monitors were all
that were required, and that in any case her presence in the
Grand Fleet was vital to the home situation.

Regrettable as was the conflict of opinion, it will be clear on a general view of the way the war as a whole had been developing, why the Admiralty felt they could not sanction any idea of an attempt to rush the Straits. Even on the spot there was a sharp difference of opinion as to whether it was practicable. In their own judgment it could do little even if successful to assist the further progress of the army, and as a naval operation the danger was out of all proportion to the prospect of tangible result. Day by day the menace of the submarine was closing in. Three U-boats had been definitely located making for the Eastern Mediterranean. One had passed Malta, and on the 11th had been unsuccessfully attacked by French destroyers off the south-east point of Sicily. Another was reported off Bizerta, and instructions had been sent to Admiral de Robeck to take measures to meet them. This he had already done. An anti-submarine defence was in position at Mudros, and all transports were to remain there, leaving the troops to be taken on in fleet-sweepers and destroyers. An elaborate system of patrol had also been organised. The *Doris*, with two destroyers, was to search the coast south of the Gulf of Smyrna for likely anchorages, while a submarine watched Smyrna itself. An Allied patrol of four fleet-sweepers and four submarines watched the channels east and west of Mykoni which gave access to the inner Ægean. A French patrol was established at Cape Matapan, and four of their destroyers were told off to search the vicinity for oil depots that had been reported.

But there was another danger nearer still which had not been expected. It declared itself the night after the Gurkhas had secured the left of our line. On the right, the French were still holding the position they had gained at the Kereves Dere, but the Turks seemed so determined to wrest it from them that the French General had made a special request for ship support. Every evening two battleships were sent in, and on the night of May 12–13 the ships detailed for the duty were the *Goliath* and *Cornwallis*. The *Goliath* anchored off Morto Bay and the *Cornwallis* astern of her. Above De Tott's battery was a protecting patrol of two destroyers, *Beagle* and *Bulldog*, while the other subdivision, *Wolverine* and *Scorpion*, were on guard on the opposite side in Eren Keui Bay, and in mid-channel was the *Pincher*. The night was very still and dark, there was no moon, and about midnight to increase the obscurity a fog began to roll down the Asiatic shore and spread across the Straits. It was an ideal opportunity for a torpedo attack, and it was noticed that except far up in the Narrows the enemy's searchlights were not working as usual. Orders were therefore issued for special vigilance, and they were not superfluous. That day Lieutenant-Commander Firle, a German officer, had begged leave to make an attempt to check the flanking fire of the British ships which each night was proving so disturbing to the Turks at Kereves Dere. Permission for the hazardous adventure was given, and after sunset he started down the Straits in the Turkish destroyer *Muavanet-i-Miliet*.[1] Keeping as close under the cliffs of the European shore as the depth of water would allow, and going dead slow, he was able towards 1.0 a.m. to steal past the *Bulldog* and *Beagle* without being detected, and a little later the two battleships could be made out at anchor.[2] But for all his care, as he crept on under the steep Eski Hissarlik Point, at 1.15 he was detected from the bridge of the *Goliath*. The night challenge was made to him, he flashed some kind of a reply, the challenge was repeated and then he could be seen to dash ahead. The order to fire was given, but before three rounds could be got off a torpedo hit the old battleship abreast of the fore turret. Almost immediately another got home abreast the foremost funnel. By that time she was already listing badly to port, and the list rapidly increased till she was nearly on her beam ends, when a third torpedo struck her near the after turret.[3]

The attack had been carried out as skilfully as it had been daringly conceived. No ship could survive such punishment, and so rapidly had the blows followed one upon the other that before most of those below could reach the deck she turned turtle, and after floating so a couple of minutes she plunged under, bows foremost. Of her assailant nothing could be seen. She had sped away into the darkness, but as craft of all kind hurried to the spot, and tried to rescue the survivors her exultant wireless signals could be heard up the Straits, " Three torpedo hits ! Sunk, sunk." " An English battleship sunk." This was about three o'clock, and the *Wolverine*, realising that an attack had been made, went off with the *Scorpion* towards Kephez Point to cut off the invisible enemy's retreat; but though the increasing strength of the signals told them they were very close, and though in spite of heavy fire they maintained their position near

[1] She was one of a group of four destroyers of 600 tons, and 33 knots, with three torpedo tubes, built in 1909.

[2] From the account sent by the Constantinople correspondent of the Berlin *Lokalanzeiger*, reproduced in the *Weser Zeitung*, June 3, 1915.

[3] So the officer of the watch reported officially in the afternoon. The account he seems to have given on board the *Cornwallis* when he was first rescued differed, but in no material point except that it made the first hit on the port side and the other two on the starboard. See Stewart and Pashell, *The Immortal Gamble*, p. 168,

Kephez, nothing more was seen of the Turkish destroyer. Meanwhile the work of rescue was proceeding. In the intense darkness and the swift current it proved very difficult. In the end, of the *Goliath's* complement of 750, nearly 570 were lost, and amongst them her commander, Captain Shelford.

Such was the latest news when the War Council had to decide what was to be done with an enterprise which, if pushed to a decisive conclusion, must obviously involve them in much heavier liabilities than had been originally contemplated. There had been no formal meeting since March 19, when, after the failure of the naval attack on the Narrows, it had been decided to continue the enterprise as a regular combined operation with the troops that had been ordered out. In this they followed precedent. During the wars of the eighteenth century, when the Cabinet system became established, it was the practice for the Cabinet, after deciding that a campaign was to be undertaken, to leave its conduct to the Chief Minister and the heads of the two service departments, and not to intervene unless some large question of policy developed from it which involved a new departure in our relations with Allies. Such a juncture had now arisen, and on May 14 the War Council met.[1]

The difference of opinion between the naval and the military authorities proved as strong as ever. The Admiralty had informed Admiral de Robeck that all idea of the fleet breaking through must be given up. They had always regarded the plan as a measure of necessity, and had they known that in three months an army of 100,000 men would have been available, they would never have undertaken a purely naval attack. In view of the new factors—the submarines, the Italian Convention and the needs of the Grand Fleet—a revival of the idea was out of the question. The campaign had become, and must continue to be, mainly military. In other words, instead of a military force to assist the fleet, it was now a question of a naval force to assist the army, and for this purpose the naval force they were now organising was in their estimation as good as, and even better than the original one. This the military authorities doubted, and maintained that their promise to see the fleet through was based on the power of the *Queen Elizabeth's* guns. Nor could they hold out hope of success for a mainly military campaign. They were ready to maintain General Hamilton's force up to strength, as well as the reinforcements that had been promised him, but in view of the military situation on the Continent, and the needs of home defence, they could do

[1] *Dardanelles Commission Report*, II., p. 23.

no more, and in their opinion this force would not be equal to breaking through the Kilid Bahr position.

On these appreciations three courses seemed to be open—to withdraw at once, to push on for a quick decision, or to settle down to a siege. Immediate withdrawal could scarcely be contemplated, a rapid decision was equally out of the question, and as to the third alternative, it was agreed that no conclusion could be come to until it was known what force would be required to ensure success. After hearing all that both the Admiralty and the War Office had to say of the danger of a German attempt on our shores, Ministers were not convinced that more troops could not be spared from home defence. About the security of the Allied line in France they were less easy, and the final decision was to ascertain from General Hamilton what force he considered necessary.[1]

But the matter could not end here, for unhappily it was not only the Admiralty and War Office who could not see eye to eye. The course things had taken at the War Council brought to a head a difference of opinion within the Admiralty itself which had long been increasing in force, and it was one that struck deep into the roots of our war plans. When Lord Fisher first supported the idea of perfecting the unity of the Allied line by opening the Dardanelles and the Bosporus, he contemplated making the attempt with a strong combined force which was to strike suddenly and quickly. In this way it seemed possible to do what was needed and get it over before his own plans for the North Sea and Baltic were ripe for execution. It was only with reluctance he had assented to the Dardanelles enterprise as it was actually undertaken, and so soon as it became clear that the political situation in the Balkans and the available military force gave no prospect of success by a *coup de main* he became frankly opposed to it. His apprehension was, that if undertaken with inadequate or unsuitable force the work would be long and costly, and when the time came, we should find ourselves saddled with liabilities which would put it out of our power to carry on the offensive campaign in northern waters, which he believed to be the only way of bringing the war to a quick and successful conclusion. Ever since his accession to office he had been devoting all his well-known energy almost entirely to its preparation. His plans involved a large building programme of specially designed ships and other material. Under the influence of his inspiration, every one concerned had thrown himself into the work with almost

[1] *Dardanelles Commission Report*, II., p. 24.

unprecedented enthusiasm, and the programme was rapidly approaching completion. As it progressed the slow development at the Dardanelles more and more justified his fears and hardened his opposition. Now that the meeting of the War Council had made it clear the attempt could not be abandoned, and must be continued as a military operation which could only be of a prolonged nature, he saw his war plan doomed. The same evening his apprehensions were confirmed. In order to meet the military objection and remove the ill effects of the withdrawal of the *Queen Elizabeth*, the First Lord drafted orders for an increase of the naval part of the expedition. They involved the absorption of the whole of the new monitors which had been designed as an essential element in the North Sea plans. Without them the offensive could not be pushed into German waters, and in view of the determination of the Government and the War Office to proceed with the Dardanelles operation it was equally impossible to oppose their diversion. Other special units were also involved. The plan which, as Lord Fisher believed, could alone give decisive results within measurable time was obviously to be postponed indefinitely, and feeling unable any longer to be responsible for the conduct of the war at sea, he next morning resigned.[1]

The loss at such a crisis of a man who bulked so large in popular opinion could only add to the general depression. To the country at large he was the embodiment of the old fighting energy of the navy—the man to whom we owed the organisation and strategical disposition which rendered the German fleet impotent when the long-expected struggle began, and the all-embracing combination against Admiral von Spee which had given us our only decisive success at sea. But his loss proved to be only the first step in a far-reaching process of disintegration. In a few days Mr. Churchill, whose untiring energy had perfected Lord Fisher's design in the last days of peace, also left the Admiralty, and so it was destined that the progression of events which had begun with the failure to intercept the *Goeben* brought about the loss of the two men to whom the navy chiefly owed its readiness for war. The tragedy which had had its origin in what seemed at the time so small a thing had gathered force

---

[1] Lord Fisher's plan was to occupy the Baltic in sufficient strength to enable an army to land in Pomerania. He had instituted a vast building programme of 612 ships, including battle cruisers, light cruisers, destroyers, submarines, monitors and smaller vessels, a large number of which were specially designed for service in the Baltic. The new Board did not proceed further with the plan.

from point to point, till it precipitated a situation which neither of them could survive.

Nor was this the end. The general uneasiness about the conduct of the war, which had been vaguely displaying itself for some time past, received a deeper and more restless impetus. The confidence in the Government, which had been inspired by their grasp and handling of the initial problems of the war, had gradually been sapped, as it always had been, by lack of telling successes at the outset, which in past times the public had ever expected and never seen realised. The break at the Admiralty gave the final shock, and within five days of Lord Fisher's departure the leaders of the great parties in the State were sitting in council to form a Coalition Government.

APPENDIX A

ORGANISATION OF THE GRAND FLEET. JANUARY 24, 1915

(Ships in parentheses in dockyard hands)

SCAPA

Commander-in-Chief : Admiral SIR JOHN R. JELLICOE.
Fleet Flagship : *Iron Duke.*
Attached ships $\begin{cases}\text{Light Cruiser : } Sappho. \\ \text{Destroyer : } Oak.\end{cases}$

FIRST BATTLE SQUADRON

Vice-Admiral SIR CECIL BURNEY.
Rear-Admiral H. EVAN-THOMAS.

Marlborough (flag of V.A.).
St. Vincent (flag of R.A.).
Collingwood.
Colossus.

Hercules.
Neptune.
Vanguard.
(Superb).

Light Cruiser : *Bellona.*

SECOND BATTLE SQUADRON

Vice-Admiral Sir George J. S. WARRENDER, BT.
Rear-Admiral ARTHUR C. LEVESON.

King George V. (flag of V.A.).
Orion (flag of R.A.).
Ajax.

Centurion.
Monarch.
Thunderer.
(Conqueror).

Light Cruiser : *Boadicea.*

FOURTH BATTLE SQUADRON

Vice-Admiral SIR DOUGLAS A. GAMBLE.
Rear-Admiral ALEXANDER L. DUFF.

Benbow (flag of V.A.).
Emperor of India (flag of R.A.).
Agincourt.
Bellerophon.

Dreadnought.
Erin.
Temeraire.

Light Cruiser : *Blonde.*

FIRST CRUISER SQUADRON
Rear-Admiral SIR ROBERT K. ARBUTHNOT, BT.

Duke of Edinburgh (flag, temp.).   *Warrior.*
Black Prince.

SIXTH CRUISER SQUADRON
Rear-Admiral WILLIAM L. GRANT.

Drake (flag).   *Leviathan.*
Donegal.

SEVENTH CRUISER SQUADRON [1]
Rear-Admiral ARTHUR W. WAYMOUTH.

Minotaur (flag).   *Hampshire.*
Cumberland.

SECOND LIGHT CRUISER SQUADRON
Rear-Admiral TREVELYAN D. W. NAPIER.

Falmouth (flag).   *Yarmouth.*
Gloucester.   *(Liverpool.)*

SECOND DESTROYER FLOTILLA

Galatea, Broke, and 20 destroyers.

ROSYTH

THIRD BATTLE SQUADRON
Vice-Admiral EDWARD E. BRADFORD.
Rear-Admiral MONTAGUE E. BROWNING.

Dominion (flag, temp., of V.A.).   *Hindustan.*
Hibernia (flag of R.A.).   *Zealandia.*
Africa.   *(King Edward VII.)*
Britannia.   *(Commonwealth)*

Light Cruiser : *Blanche.*

THIRD CRUISER SQUADRON
Rear-Admiral WILLIAM C. PAKENHAM.

Antrim (flag).   *Devonshire.*
Argyll.   *(Roxburgh.)*

FIRST BATTLE CRUISER SQUADRON
Vice-Admiral SIR DAVID BEATTY.

Lion (flag).   *Tiger.*
Princess Royal.   *(Queen Mary.)*

SECOND BATTLE CRUISER SQUADRON
Rear-Admiral SIR ARCHIBALD G. H. W. MOORE.

New Zealand (flag).   *Indomitable.*

---

[1] This squadron, which was proceeding to Scapa west-about, was ordered to join the battle fleet, but did not arrive till after January 24.

FIRST LIGHT CRUISER SQUADRON

Commodore WILLIAM E. GOODENOUGH.

Southampton (broad pendant).   *Lowestoft.*
Birmingham.   *Nottingham.*

CROMARTY

SECOND CRUISER SQUADRON

Rear-Admiral THE HON. SOMERSET A. GOUGH-CALTHORPE.

Shannon (flag).   *Natal.*
Achilles.   (*Cochrane.*)

FOURTH DESTROYER FLOTILLA

Caroline, Faulknor, and 20 destroyers.

HARWICH

DESTROYER FLOTILLAS

Commodore REGINALD Y. TYRWHITT.

Arethusa (broad pendant).   *Aurora.*

FIRST FLOTILLA

(*Fearless*) *Meteor,* and 20 destroyers.

THIRD FLOTILLA

Undaunted, Miranda, and 20 destroyers.

(Attached to this Flotilla were also 8 "M" class destroyers, which were shortly to be formed into the Tenth Flotilla.)

OVERSEA SUBMARINE FLOTILLA

Commodore ROGER J. B. KEYES.

Firedrake, Lurcher, and 21 submarines.

APPENDIX B

BRITISH WAR VESSELS IN THE MEDITERRANEAN, EGYPTIAN AND EAST INDIAN WATERS. FEBRUARY 19, 1915

EASTERN MEDITERRANEAN

Commander-in-Chief : Vice-Admiral SACKVILLE H. CARDEN.
Chief of Staff : Commodore ROGER J. B. KEYES.
Second in Command : Rear-Admiral JOHN M. DE ROBECK.
S.N.O., Mudros : Rear-Admiral ROSSLYN E. WEMYSS.

BATTLESHIPS

Agamemnon	Captain H. A. S. Fyler.
Albion	Captain A. W. Heneage.
Canopus	Captain H. S. Grant.
Cornwallis	Captain A. P. Davidson.
Irresistible	Captain D. L. Dent.
Lord Nelson	Captain J. W. L. McClintock.
Majestic	Captain H. F. G. Talbot.
Prince George . . .	Captain A. V. Campbell.
Queen Elizabeth . . .	Captain G. P. W. Hope.
Triumph	Captain M. S. FitzMaurice.
Vengeance (flag of R.A.) . .	Captain B. H. Smith.

BATTLE CRUISER

Inflexible (flag of V.A.) . .	Captain R. F. Phillimore.

LIGHT CRUISERS

Amethyst	Commander G. J. Todd.
Dartmouth	Captain Judge D'Arcy.
Dublin	Captain J. D. Kelly.
Sapphire	Captain P. W. E. Hill.

AIRCRAFT-CARRIER

Ark Royal	Commander (act.) R. H. Clark-Hall.

GUNBOAT

Hussar	Commander (ret.) E. Unwin.

DEPOT SHIP FOR T. B. Ds.

Blenheim	Captain C. P. R. Coode. (Captain, D.)

16 T. B. Ds., 6 submarines, and 21 minesweepers.

EGYPT AND EAST INDIES
Vice-Admiral Sir RICHARD H. PEIRSE.

BATTLESHIPS

Swiftsure (flag) . . .	Captain C. Maxwell-Lefroy.
Ocean	Captain A. Hayes-Sadler.

CRUISERS

Bacchante	Captain The Hon. A. D. E. H. Boyle.
Euryalus	Captain R. M. Burmester.

LIGHT CRUISERS

Chatham [1] .	.	Captain S. R. Drury-Lowe.
Doris	Captain F. Larken.
Fox [1]	Captain F. W. Caulfeild.
Minerva	Captain P. H. Warleigh.
Philomel	Captain P. H. Hall Thompson.
Proserpine	Commander G. C. Hardy.

---

[1] Refitting.

ARMED MERCHANT CRUISERS

Empress of Asia	.	.	.	Captain P. H. Colomb.
Empress of Japan	.	.	.	Commander M. B. Baillie-Hamilton.
Empress of Russia	.	.	.	Commander A. Cochrane.
Himalaya .	.	.	.	Commander (act.) A. Dixon.

SLOOPS

Clio .	.	.	.	.	Commander C. MacKenzie.
Espiegle	.	.	.	.	Captain W. Nunn (Persian Gulf).
Odin	.	.	.	.	Commander C. R. Wason (Persian Gulf).

VESSELS OF THE ROYAL INDIAN MARINE

Dalhousie .	.	.	.	Commander (act.) E. M. Palmer (Persian Gulf).
Dufferin	.	.	.	Commander A. W. Lowis.
Hardinge .	.	.	.	Commander (act.) T. J. Linberry.
Lawrence .	.	.	.	Commander (act.) R. N. Suter (Persian Gulf).
Minto	.	.	.	Lieut.-Comm. C. E. V. Crauford.
Northbrook	.	.	.	Commander A. E. Wood.

6 T. Bs. for duty in Suez Canal.
4 armed tugs in the Persian Gulf.

APPENDIX C

GRAND FLEET, CHANNEL FLEET, AND OVERSEA SQUADRONS EXCEPT THOSE SHOWN IN APPENDIX B. FEBRUARY 22, 1915

GRAND FLEET

Commander-in-Chief : Admiral SIR JOHN R. JELLICOE.
Chief of Staff : Rear-Admiral C. E. Madden.
Fleet Flagship : *Iron Duke*, Captain R. N. Lawson.
Attached ships { Light Cruiser : *Sappho*, Commander G. V. C. Knox.
{ Destroyer : *Oak*, Lieut.-Comm. D. Faviell.

FIRST BATTLE SQUADRON

Vice-Admiral SIR CECIL BURNEY.
Rear-Admiral H. Evan-Thomas.

Marlborough (flag of V.A.) .	.	Captain E. P. F. G. Grant.
St. Vincent (flag of R.A.) .	.	Captain W. W. Fisher.
Collingwood	.	.	.	Captain J. C. Ley.
Colossus	.	.	.	Captain The Hon. E. S. Fitzherbert.
Hercules .	.	.	.	Captain H. H. Bruce.
Neptune .	.	.	.	Captain T. D. L. Sheppard.
Superb [1] .	.	.	.	Captain E. Hyde Parker.
Vanguard .	.	.	.	Captain C. S. Hickley.

Light Cruiser : *Bellona*, Captain P. M. R. Royds.

---

[1] In dockyard hands.

SECOND BATTLE SQUADRON

Vice-Admiral SIR GEORGE J. S. WARRENDER, BT.
Rear-Admiral ARTHUR C. LEVESON.

King George V (flag of V.A.) .	Captain G. H. Baird.
Orion (flag of R.A.) . . .	Captain F. C. Dreyer.
Ajax	Captain Sir A. J. Henniker-Hughan, Bt.
Centurion [1]	Captain M. Culme-Seymour.
Conqueror [1]	Captain H. H. D. Tothill.
Monarch	Captain E. H. Smith.
Thunderer	Captain C. L. Vaughan-Lee.

Light Cruiser : *Boadicea*, Captain L. C. S. Woollcombe.

THIRD BATTLE SQUADRON

Vice-Admiral EDWARD E. BRADFORD.
Rear-Admiral MONTAGUE E. BROWNING.

King Edward VII. (flag of V.A.) .	Captain Crawford Maclachlan.
Hibernia (flag of R.A.) . .	Captain A. Lowndes.
Africa	Captain H. J. O. Millar.
Britannia [1]	Captain H. G. G. Sandeman.
Commonwealth	Captain M. Woollcombe.
Dominion	Captain H. L. Mawbey.
Hindustan	Captain J. Nicholas.
Zealandia	Captain R. M. Harbord.

Light Cruiser : *Blanche*, Captain R. Hyde.

FOURTH BATTLE SQUADRON

Vice-Admiral SIR F. C. DOVETON STURDEE.
Rear-Admiral ALEXANDER L. DUFF.

Benbow (flag of V.A.) . . .	Captain J. A. Fergusson.
Emperor of India (flag of R.A.) .	Captain W. C. M. Nicholson.
Agincourt	Captain D. R. L. Nicholson.
Bellerophon	Captain E. F. Bruen.
Dreadnought	Captain W. J. S. Alderson.
Erin	Captain The Hon. V. A. Stanley.
Temeraire	Captain A. T. Hunt.

Light Cruiser : *Blonde*, Captain A. C. Scott.

BATTLE CRUISER FLEET

Vice-Admiral Commanding : Vice-Admiral SIR DAVID BEATTY.
Fleet Flagship : *Lion*,[2] Captain A. E. M. Chatfield.

FIRST BATTLE CRUISER SQUADRON

Commodore OSMOND DE B. BROCK.

Princess Royal (broad pendant) .	Captain W. H. Cowan.
Queen Mary	Captain C. I. Prowse.
Tiger	Captain H. B. Pelly.

---

[1] In dockyard hands.
[2] In Tyne, repairing damages received in Dogger Bank action.

Attached.—FIRST LIGHT CRUISER SQUADRON.

Commodore E. S. ALEXANDER-SINCLAIR.

Galatea (broad pendant) . .	Commander F. A. Marten.
Caroline	Captain H. Ralph Crooke.
Cordelia	Captain A. V. Vyvyan.
Inconstant . . .	Captain B. S. Thesiger.

SECOND BATTLE CRUISER SQUADRON

Vice-Admiral SIR GEORGE E. PATEY.[1]

Australia (flag) . . .	Captain S. H. Radcliffe.
Indefatigable . . .	Captain C. F. Sowerby.
New Zealand . . .	Captain L. Halsey.

Attached.—SECOND LIGHT CRUISER SQUADRON.

Commodore WILLIAM E. GOODENOUGH.

Southampton (broad pendant) .	Commander E. A. Rushton.
Birmingham . . .	Captain A. A. M. Duff.
Lowestoft	Captain T. W. B. Kennedy.
Nottingham . . .	Captain C. B. Miller.

THIRD BATTLE CRUISER SQUADRON

Indomitable [2] . . .	Captain F. W. Kennedy.
Inflexible [3] . . .	Captain R. F. Phillimore.
Invincible [4] . . .	Captain A. L. Cay.

Attached.—THIRD LIGHT CRUISER SQUADRON.

Rear-Admiral TREVELYAN D. W. NAPIER.

Falmouth (flag) . . .	Captain J. D. Edwards.
Gloucester	Captain W. A. H. Kelly.
Liverpool	Captain E. Reeves.
Yarmouth	Captain T. D. Pratt.

FIRST CRUISER SQUADRON

Rear-Admiral SIR ROBERT K. ARBUTHNOT, BT.

Defence (flag) . . .	Captain E. La T. Leatham.
Black Prince . . .	Captain J. D. Dick.
Duke of Edinburgh . .	Captain H. Blackett.
Warrior	Captain G. H. Borrett.

SECOND CRUISER SQUADRON

Rear-Admiral The Hon. SOMERSET A. GOUGH-CALTHORPE.

Shannon (flag) . . .	Captain J. S. Dumaresq.
Achilles	Captain F. M. Leake.
Cochrane	Captain W. G. E. Ruck-Keene.
Natal	Captain J. F. E. Green.

---

[1] Relieved by Rear-Admiral W. C. Pakenham, March 8, 1915.
[2] In dockyard hands.
[3] At Dardanelles. To join later.   [4] To be flagship.

Third Cruiser Squadron.
Rear-Admiral William C. Pakenham.

Antrim (flag)	.	.	.	Captain V. B. Molteno.
Argyll	.	.	.	Captain J. C. Tancred.
Devonshire [1]	.	.	.	Captain E. V. Underhill.
Roxburgh .	.	.	.	Captain B. M. Chambers.

Sixth Cruiser Squadron
Rear-Admiral William L. Grant.

Drake (flag)	.	.	.	Captain A. C. H. Smith.
Cumberland	.	.	.	Captain C. P. Beaty-Pownall.
Leviathan .	.	.	.	Captain M. R. Hill.

Seventh Cruiser Squadron
Rear-Admiral Arthur W. Waymouth.

Minotaur (flag)	.	.	.	Captain E. B. Kiddle.
Donegal	.	.	.	Captain C. D. Carpendale.
Hampshire	.	.	.	Captain H. W. Grant.
Lancaster [1]	.	.	.	Captain W. H. D'Oyly.

8 armed boarding steamers (attached to Commander-in-Chief).

GRAND FLEET DESTROYER FLOTILLAS
Second Flotilla

Active . . . . Captain J. R. P. Hawksley.
(Light Cruiser)   (Captain D.)
Broke . . . . Commander C. D. Roper.
(Flotilla Leader)   (2nd in Command.)

20 destroyers.

Fourth Flotilla

Swift . . . . Captain C. J. Wintour.
(Flotilla Leader)   (Captain D.)
Faulknor . . . . Commander A. J. B. Stirling.
(Flotilla Leader)   (2nd in Command.)

20 destroyers.

HARWICH DESTROYER FLOTILLAS
Commodore Reginald Y. Tyrwhitt.
(Commodore T.)

Arethusa (broad pendant) . . Commander (ret.) E. K. Arbuthnot.
(Light Cruiser)
Penelope . . . . Captain H. Lynes.
(Light Cruiser)

First Flotilla

Fearless . . . . Captain W. F. Blunt.
(Light Cruiser)   (Captain D.)
Meteor . . . . Commander A. B. S. Dutton.
(Destroyer)   (2nd in Command.)

20 destroyers.

---

[1] In dockyard hands.

THIRD FLOTILLA

Undaunted . . .	Captain F. G. St. John.
(Light Cruiser)	(Captain D.)
Miranda . . .	Commander B. E. Domvile.
(Destroyer)	(2nd in Command.)

20 destroyers.

TENTH FLOTILLA

Aurora	Captain W. S. Nicholson.
(Light Cruiser)	(Captain D.)

10 destroyers.

HARWICH SUBMARINE FLOTILLA

EIGHTH (OVERSEA) FLOTILLA

Commodore SYDNEY S. HALL.
(Commodore S.)
Captain A. K. WAISTELL.
(Captain S.)

Firedrake	Commander A. T. Tillard.
(Destroyer)	
Lurcher . . .	Commander W. Tomkinson.
(Destroyer)	

20 submarines.

CRUISER FORCE "B"

TENTH CRUISER SQUADRON
(Armed Merchant Cruisers)

Rear-Admiral DUDLEY R. S. DE CHAIR.

Alsatian (flag) . . .	Captain G. Trewby.
Ambrose . . .	Commander C. W. Bruton.
Bayano . . .	Commander H. C. Carr.
Calyx . . .	Commander T. E. Wardle.
Caribbean . . .	Commander F. H. Walter.
Cedric . . .	Captain R. E. R. Benson.
Changuinola . .	Commander H. C. R. Brocklebank.
Columbella . .	Captain H. L. P. Heard.
Digby . . .	Commander R. F. H. H. Mahon.
Eskimo . . .	Commander C. W. Trousdale.
Hilary . . .	Commander R. H. Bather.
Hildebrand . .	Captain H. Edwards.
Mantua . . .	Captain C. Tibbits.
Motagua . .	Captain J. A. Webster.
Oropesa . . .	Commander N. L. Stanley.
Orotava . . .	Commander G. E. Corbett.
Otway . . .	Captain E. L. Booty.
Patia . . .	Captain G. W. Vivian.
Patuca . . .	Lieut.-Comm. J. H. Neild.
Teutonic . . .	Captain G. C. Ross.
Virginian . . .	Captain H. N. Garnett.

CHANNEL FLEET

FIFTH BATTLE SQUADRON

Vice-Admiral The Hon. SIR ALEXANDER E. BETHELL.
Rear-Admiral CECIL F. THURSBY.

Prince of Wales (flag of V.A.)	Captain R. N. Bax.
Queen (flag of R.A.)	Captain H. A. Adam.
Implacable	Captain H. C. Lockyer.
London	Captain J. G. Armstrong.
Venerable	Captain V. H. G. Bernard.

Light Cruisers { *Diamond*, Commander L. L. Dundas.
{ *Topaze*, Commander W. J. B. Law.

SIXTH BATTLE SQUADRON

Rear-Admiral STUART NICHOLSON.

Russell (flag)	Captain W. Bowden Smith.
Albemarle	Captain A. W. Craig.
Exmouth	Captain H. R. Veale.

Detached on Special Service.

Jupiter	Captain D. St. A. Wake.
Revenge	Captain C. H. Hughes-Onslow.

WESTERN CHANNEL PATROL

TWELFTH CRUISER SQUADRON

Diana (S.N.O.)	Captain G. B. Hutton.
Eclipse	Captain F. H. Mitchell.
Talbot	Captain F. Wray.

4 armed boarding steamers.

IRISH COAST PATROL

ELEVENTH CRUISER SQUADRON

Rear-Admiral HENRY L. TOTTENHAM.

Juno (flag)	Captain A. K. Macrorie.
Isis	Captain J. T. Bush.
Sutlej	Captain H. M. Doughty.
Venus	Captain R. G. D. Dewar.

4 armed boarding steamers.

MID-ATLANTIC

NINTH CRUISER SQUADRON

Rear-Admiral SIR ARCHIBALD G. H. W. MOORE.

Europa (flag)	Captain H. G. C. Somerville.
Amphitrite	Captain H. Grant-Dalton.
Argonaut	Captain R. A. Nugent.
Calgarian	Captain T. W. Kemp.
Carmania	Captain N. Grant.
Edinburgh Castle	Captain W. R. Napier.
Ophir [1]	Commander J. M. D. E. Warren.
Victorian	Captain H. B. T. Somerville.

---

[1] In dockyard hands.

CRUISER FORCE "D"

Highflyer (S.N.O.) . . .	Captain H. T. Buller.
Empress of Britain . . .	Commander G. B. W. Young.
Marmora	Captain R. W. Glennie.

NORTH AMERICA AND WEST INDIES SQUADRON
Rear-Admiral ROBERT S. PHIPPS-HORNBY.

Glory (flag)	Captain C. F. Corbett.
Berwick	Captain L. Clinton-Baker.
Caronia	Captain F. S. Litchfield.
Essex	Captain H. D. R. Watson.
Melbourne	Captain M. L'E. Silver.
Niobe	Captain R. G. Corbett.
Suffolk [1]	Captain B. J. D. Yelverton.
Sydney	Captain J. C. T. Glossop.

SOUTH-EAST COAST OF AMERICA SQUADRON
Rear-Admiral ARCHIBALD P. STODDART.

Carnarvon (flag) . . .	Captain H. L. D'E. Skipwith.
Bristol	Captain B. H. Fanshawe.
Celtic	Captain O. McD. English.
Glasgow	Captain J. Luce.
Kent	Captain J. D. Allen.
Macedonia	Captain B. S. Evans.
Orama	Captain J. R. Segrave.
Otranto	Captain H. M. Edwards.
Vindictive	Captain C. R. Payne.

CAPE OF GOOD HOPE SQUADRON
Rear-Admiral HERBERT G. KING-HALL.

Goliath (flag) [1] . .	Captain T. L. Shelford.
Armadale Castle . . .	Captain O. F. Gillett.
Astræa	Captain A. C. Sykes.
Laconia	Captain C. S. Wills.

WEST COAST OF AFRICA

Challenger	Captain C. T. M. Fuller.
Dwarf	Commander F. E. K. Strong.
Laurentic	Captain V. G. Gurner.

EAST COAST OF AFRICA

Weymouth (S.N.O.) . . .	Captain W. D. Church.
Hyacinth	Captain D. M. Anderson.
Kinfauns Castle . . .	Captain D. B. Crampton.
Pioneer	Lieut.-Comm. (R.A.N.) T. W. Biddlecombe.
Pyramus	Commander Viscount Kilburn.

4 armed whalers.

---

[1] In dockyard hands.

PACIFIC

Newcastle (S.N.O.)	.	.	.	Captain F. A. Powlett.
Rainbow	.	.	.	. Commander W. Hose.
Shearwater	.	.	.	. Lieut.-Commr. A. St. V. Keyes.

CHINA

Vice-Admiral Sir Thomas H. Jerram.

(Flag flown on shore at Singapore.)

Cadmus	.	.	.	. Commander H. D. Marryat.
Rosario	.	.	.	. Lieut.-Commr. F. A. N. Cromie.

4 destroyers.

AUSTRALIA

Encounter .	.	.	.	. Captain C. La P. Lewin.

3 destroyers; 2 armed vessels.

INDEX

Chatfield, Capt. A. E. M. (*Lion*), 86

Chatham, Brit. Cr. (Capt. S. R. Drury-Lowe), blockades *Königsberg*, 234 *n.*, 235, 237; in the Dardanelles, 405

Chelmer, Brit. T.B.D. (Lt.-Commr. H. T. England), 222

Cherbourg, Fr. T.B.D.'s at, 14

Cherbury, Brit. S.S., sunk, 390

Chéron, Capt., Fr. Navy (*Pothuau*), 232, 234

Chester, Brit. A.P. Trawler, 279, 280 *n.*

Chile, protests against British breach of neutrality, 251

Chirsit, Brit. A.P. Trawler, 401–2

Church, Capt. W. D. (*Weymouth*), 238

Churchill, Rt. Hon. Winston S., First Lord of the Admiralty, his views on proposed naval attack on the Dardanelles, 104, 106–9, 152; his statement on German blockade of British trade, 270; his memorandum on the Italian Convention, 395; his resignation, 410

Clacton, Brit. Fleet Sweeper, 17 *n.*

Clark-Hall, Commr. R. H. (*Ark Royal*), 311

Clio, Brit. sloop (Commr. Colin Mackenzie), in the Suez Canal, 112, 113

Clyde, River, Patrol area at, 18 *n.*; 10th Cr. Sq. based on, 277, 390

Coalition Government, 411

Coleby, Brit. S.S., sunk, 256

Colne, Brit. T.B.D. (Commr. C. Seymour), in the Dardanelles, 222, 376

Columbia, Brit. A.P. Trawler, sunk, 401–2

Commander-in-Chief, Grand Fleet. *See* Jellicoe, Ad. Sir John.

Commerce, international law and protection of, 251; end of first phase of German attack on, 257, 258; new form of attack on, 259–69

—— Raiders, German, in S. Atlantic and S. Pacific, 239–58. *See Dresden; Karlsruhe; Prinz Eitel Friedrich; Kronprinz Wilhelm;* Submarines, German; Blockade, German S/M.

Communications, Military, lines of, across the Channel, 3, 5, 56, 60, 130, 133, 134; S/M attacks on, 13, 132; precautions for guarding, 14, 133, 134; S/M menace to, 270, 271–4, 277, 278; kept open, 282–4, 389. *See* Convoys; Blockade

Condé, Fr. Cr., relieves *Sydney*, 254

Conqueror, Brit. B. (Capt. N. C. Palmer, relieved by Capt. H. H. D. Tothill), in 2nd B. Sq., 25; collides with the *Monarch*, 53, 64, 82, 141

Constantinople, proposals to force the Straits and enter, 64, 65, 69, 73, 77, 104–5, 126, 154, 185–6, 203–4; effect

of reports from Dardanelles in, 223, 304; plans for advance on, 306, 308; German supplies for defence of, 292; attack on, considered best defence for Egypt, 366. *See* Turkey; Dardanelles.

Contraband Trade, watch against in Ægean, 71, 312; Orders in Council for extending list of, 133; German attitude towards, 262, 263 *n.*, 264 *n.*, 267–9; American position towards, 265–8; general position of neutrals towards, 267–9. *See* Blockade; Cotton; Cruiser Squadrons, British, 10th; Patrol, Northern; Patrol, Western.

Convention, Naval, between Great Britain, France and Italy, 394–6

Convoys and Transports, British, to France, 7, 8, 13, 14, 56, 134, 272–4, 277, 282–4, 387; from India, 8; to Egypt, 113–14, 389; to the Dardanelles, 278, 299, 300–2, 304, 316–8, 322, 346–7, 349, 358, 360, 367, 370, 385–7, 389, 403, 406

—— ——, French, to the Dardanelles, 195, 308, 355–6, 358

—— ——, Russian, in the Bosporus, 295, 297

—— ——, Turkish, in Black Sea, 70; in the Dardanelles, 358–60

Conway Castle, Brit. S.V., sunk, 248

Coode, Capt. C. P. R. (*Blenheim*) (Capt. D.), 72, 311, 320, 377

Cook, Corporal, R.M.L.I., 180 *n.*

Coote, Brit. A.P. Trawler, 280 *n.*

Corfu, anchorage to be prepared at, 60; Austrian S/Ms off, 385

Cormoran, Ger. A.M.C., interned, 1 *n.*

Cornwall, Brit. Cr. (Capt. W. M. Ellerton), searches for the *Dresden*, 241; in German S.W. Africa, 246; in the Dardanelles, 405

Cornwallis, Brit. B. (Capt. A. P. Davidson), in the Dardanelles, 142, 144–6, 148, 157, 159, 163, 170 *n.*, 171, 178–81, 194, 205–6, 213 *n.*, 310, 316, 318, 335–7, 340, 362, 406, 407 *n.*

Coronel, the lesson of, 49

Cotton, export of, from America, 265

Cox, Major-Gen. H. V., 358

Crabbe, Lt.-Commr. L. G. E. (*Hardy*), 26, 27

Cradock, R.-Ad. Sir Christopher, 245

Creagh, Lt.-Commr. J. V. (*Ariel*), 280

Crimea, *Goeben* and *Breslau* off the, 70

Crocodile, Nigerian Marine, 232 *n.*

Cromarty, considered as base for Grand Fleet, 9; boom defence at, 51; B. Cr. Sq. at, 21, 50; 2nd Cr. Sq. at, 82; Grand Fleet Flotillas at, 404

Cruiser Squadrons, British: 1st Cr. Sq. (R.-Ad. Sir A. G. H.W. Moore to Jan. 1915, R.-Ad. Sir R. K. Arbuthnot, Jan. 1915), replaces B. Crs., 9; completed, 16; with Grand Fleet, 17, 131; at Scapa, 82; at Dogger Bank, 85, 88

——, 2nd (R.-Ad. The Hon. S. A. Gough-Calthorpe), at Cromarty, 82; at Dogger Bank, 85, 88; with Grand Fleet 131; at Scapa, 398

——, 3rd (R.-Ad. W. C. Pakenham to March 1915, R.-Ad. W. L. Grant from March 1915), at Rosyth, 10, 50, 82, 398; in the Yorkshire Raid, 25, 29, 30, 38, 40; at Dogger Bank, 85, 88; with Grand Fleet, 131; change of command, 279 n.

——, 6th (R.-Ad. W. L. Grant), completed, 9, 16; at Scapa, 82; suppressed, 131 n., 279, 279 n.

——, 7th (R.-Ad. A. W. Waymouth to April 1915, R.-Ad. H. L. Tottenham from April 1915), at Scapa, 398

——, 10th (R.-Ad. D. R. S. de Chair), "Edgar" class, paid off, and replaced by A. M. Crs., 8, 17, 50–1, 135. See Patrol, Northern.

——, Light, 1st (Cmdre. W. E. Goodenough to Feb. 1915, Cmdre. E. S. Alexander-Sinclair from Feb. 1915), at Scapa, 21, 82; at Dogger Bank, 85, 85 n., 86, 88, 89

——, ——, 2nd (R.-Ad. T. D. W. Napier to Feb. 1915, Cmdre. W. E. Goodenough from Feb. 1915), with the C.-in-C., 50, 50 n.; at Scapa, 82; at Dogger Bank, 84, 88, 100

——, ——, 6th, Special Squadron for defence against Zeppelins, 403, 403 n.

Crusader, Brit. T.B.D. (Lt.-Commr. T. K. Maxwell), 402

Cugnot, Fr. S/M, 60

Cumberland, Brit. Cr. (Capt. C. P. Beaty Pownall), 9, 232–3

Cunliffe, Col. F. H. G., in command of forces in Nigeria, 233

Curie, Fr. S/M, 60

Cuxhaven, raid on Zeppelin sheds at, 11, 51

D

D 6, Brit. S/M (Lt.-Commr. R. C. Halahan), 52

Dacia, Ger. S.S., transfer of flag in wartime, 266, 266 n.

D'Amade, General, French Army, in command of French Division in the Dardanelles, 225, 306, 308, 338, 339, 350, 353, 357, 361, 367, 372.

Danube, River, Monitors built for, 108, 185

D'Arcy, Capt. J. (*Dartmouth*), 311

Dardanelles, initiation of operations against, 64–9, 103–9, 128–9; Ad. Carden's plan of attack, 69, 103, 143–5, 155, 205, 208; Lord Fisher's views on forcing the Straits, 105, 107; Lord Kitchener's views on operations, 64, 66, 68, 79, 107

——, Allied forces for Naval bombardment, 140–4; organisation of Allied Fleet, 71, 141–4, 170 n., 213 n., 310–15

——, Allied military forces detailed for combined expedition, 154–6, 195, 201–3, 296, 304, 308–9, 316–7, 366, 367, 371; concentration of troops for combined expedition, 296; plan of the combined attack, 304–9

——, Allied S/Ms in the Straits, 71–3, 140, 143, 297, 302–4, 310, 347, 357–8, 370, 374–5. *See B 6; B 9; B 10; B 11; E 11; E 14; E 15; AE 2; Saphir; Bernoulli; Joule.*

——, First Battle of Krithia, 360–5; Second Battle of Krithia, 376–82

——, forcing the entrance (Feb. 19–March 4), 145–9, 157–75; demolition landings: European side (Sedd el Bahr and Morto Bay), 163, 165–6, 172, 178, 181–3; Asiatic side (Kum Kale), 163–5, 177 n., 178–81

——, French and Russian opinion on operations, 121–2, 128–9

——, German views on possibility of the Straits being forced, 125–6

——, importance of Achi Baba, 174–8, 305

——, initiation of combined expedition, 149–56, 201–5, 208, 212, 225–30, 290–315; shift of military base from Mudros to Alexandria, 212, 225–30; change of naval command, 211–12;

——, minesweeping in the Straits, 160, 169, 172, 206–9, 220–2, 275, 291, 293, 314, 317, 324–5, 346

——, naval attack on the Narrows: March 5–8, 186–95; March 18–24, 213–25; cost and result of attack, 223; Turkish reports on effect of bombardment, 194 n., 223–5

——, Russian co-operation in Allied operations, 184, 202–3, 294, 297, 308, 373–4

——, strategical considerations, 64, 66–9, 103–7, 184–5, 201–4, 231, 290–2, 383, 394–7, 405, 408–10; reactions of the operations in other theatres, 63–4, 66, 123–4, 149–56, 292, 366–7, 371, 373, 397, 405; political effects

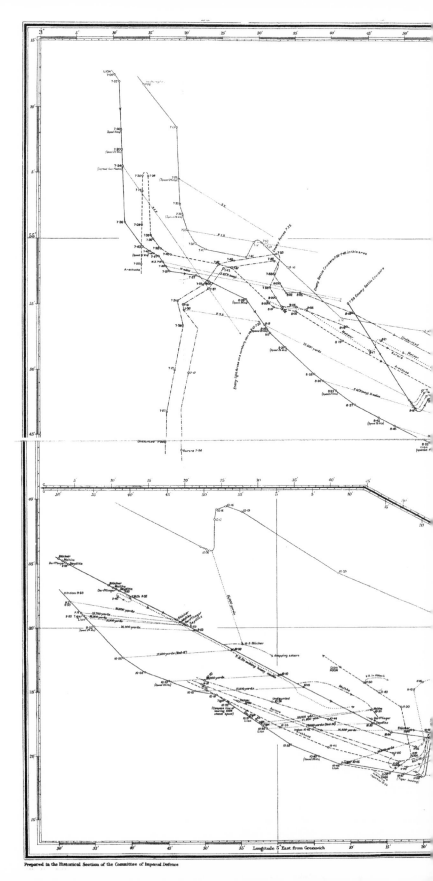

BATTLE of DOGGER BANK

JANUARY 24TH 1915.

TRACKS OF

LION & 1ST & IIND BATTLE CRUISER SQUADRONS	1ST & 3RD FLOTILLAS
LEADING SHIP	ARETHUSA
LION	AURORA
TIGER	UNDAUNTED
PRINCESS ROYAL	INDIVIDUAL DESTROYERS
NEW ZEALAND	
INDOMITABLE	

1ST LIGHT CRUISER SQUADRON

SOUTHAMPTON	ENEMY MAIN FORCE
BIRMINGHAM	" LIGHT CRUISERS
NOTTINGHAM	" DESTROYERS
LOWESTOFT	

BEARINGS
LINES OF FIRE

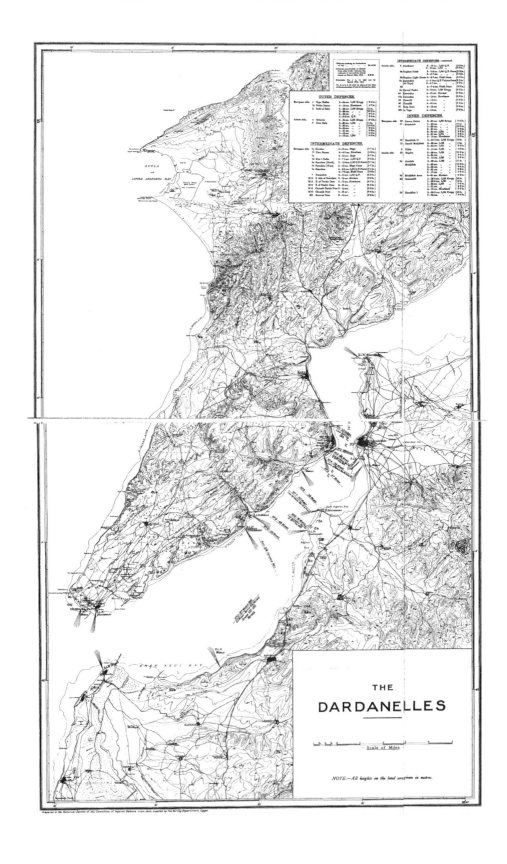

THE
DARDANELLES

Scale of Miles

NOTE.—All heights on the land are given in metres.

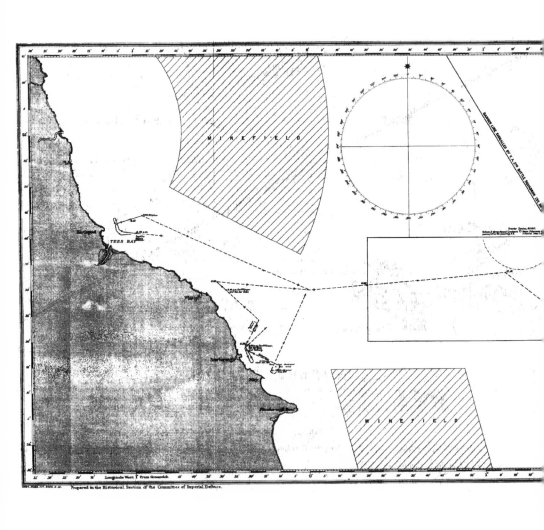

MINEFIELD

MINEFIELD

TEES BAY

MINEFIELD

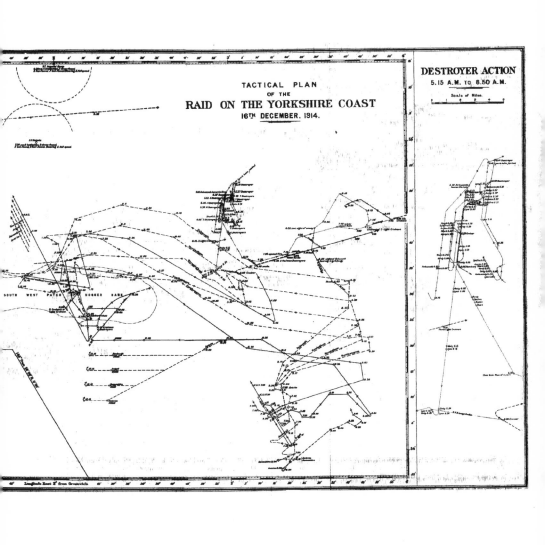

TACTICAL PLAN
OF THE
RAID ON THE YORKSHIRE COAST
16TH DECEMBER. 1914.

DESTROYER ACTION
5.15 A.M. TO 6.50 A.M.

Scale of Miles.

Made in the USA
Middletown, DE
28 July 2022

70136090R00295